THE CHANGING CONSTITUTION

Sixth Edition

EDITED BY

JEFFREY JOWELL

AND

DAWN OLIVER

OXFORD
UNIVERSITY PRESS

Great Clarendon Street, Oxford OX2 6DP

Oxford University Press is a department of the University of Oxford.
It furthers the University's objective of excellence in research, scholarship,
and education by publishing worldwide in

Oxford New York

Auckland Cape Town Dar es Salaam Hong Kong Karachi
Kuala Lumpur Madrid Melbourne Mexico City Nairobi
New Delhi Shanghai Taipei Toronto

With offices in

Argentina Austria Brazil Chile Czech Republic France Greece
Guatemala Hungary Italy Japan Poland Portugal Singapore
South Korea Switzerland Thailand Turkey Ukraine Vietnam

Oxford is a registered trade mark of Oxford University Press
in the UK and in certain other countries

Published in the United States
by Oxford University Press Inc., New York

First edition 1985
Second edition 1989
Third edition 1994
Fourth edition 2000
Fifth edition 2004
Sixth edition 2007

British Library Cataloguing in Publication Data
Data available

Library of Congress Cataloging in Publication Data
Data available

Typeset by Newgen Imaging Systems (P) Ltd, Chennai, India
Printed in Great Britain
on acid-free paper by
Ashford Colour Press Ltd

ISBN 978–0–19–920511–0

1 3 5 7 9 10 8 6 4 2

PREFACE TO THE SIXTH EDITION

The first edition of this book was published in 1985, one hundred years after the publication of A. V. Dicey's *The Law of the Constitution*. We wrote in the preface that Dicey's shadow then still dominated British constitutional law and political theory. His notion of the Rule of Law still featured strongly in our political debates, and his insistence upon the virtues of an unwritten constitution, and upon the sovereignty or supremacy of the UK Parliament, still influenced opposition to entrenched protection of our civil liberties. Dicey's word almost served as a surrogate written constitution. In 2007, as this sixth edition goes to press, each of those notions has come under pressure as constitutional arrangements in the UK respond to changing political, economic, social and international circumstances and to changing conceptions of the values and institutions which should support a modern constitutional democracy.

It is often assumed that, because the UK has no written constitution, it has no constitution at all. Over the past decade our judges have been at pains to make clear that we do have constitutional principles and even constitutional rights, which are implied from the fact that the UK is a democracy – a constitutional democracy. Many of the chapters in this book articulate these principles and examine them in a range of areas of governance. Over the six editions of *The Changing Constitution* chapters have been added so as to engage changing constitutional concerns and new developments. Yet other chapters have been removed, as the issues they dealt with have become obsolete, of less concern or have been reformed. The changing chapters of this book thus provide an insight into evolutionary constitutional developments in the UK over the course of the 22 years that straddle the twentieth and twenty-first centuries.

One of the innovative characteristics of the first edition was the inclusion of a number of chapters by political scientists. At that time lawyers and political scientists spoke different languages and referred to different literatures. We felt that the disciplines needed to meet one another. These days, there is more congruence of approach between public law and the disciplines of the social science and political and moral philosophy, much to the benefit of our constitutional discourse.

Three particularly fundamental changes can be highlighted since 1985. First is the fact that the UK constitution is no longer a purely domestic affair. In the third edition we noted how the constitution was then firmly placed in the context of British membership of the European Union, and recognized to be so. In the fifth edition we included an important chapter on international influences on UK public law. The incorporation of the European Convention on Human Rights into domestic law in 1998 brought with it a requirement that our courts take into account the case-law of the European Court of Human Rights in interpreting the Convention. More generally, the interpretation of democratic practices by courts in the Commonwealth and elsewhere is increasingly being considered by our highest courts. An international conversation is taking place on the fundamental requirements of democratic constitutionalism, in which the UK is an important participant.

The second fundamental change has been decentralization, both in the form of devolution of central governmental powers to Scotland, Wales and Northern Ireland, and in respect of the privatization of industries formerly in public ownership. This change has, however, not been entirely coherent. Local government lost power during the Thatcher administration, and other areas were centralized, such as the Health Service and the police. Yet a great deal of government activity had been 'hived off' to semi-independent executive agencies or trusts, or 'contracted out' to the private sector. Political accountability for some tasks has therefore been relaxed, while at the same time a host of regulatory bodies which previously had had no place in our governmental structure were introduced to control market inefficiencies, promote competition and impose some basic standards in the public interest upon the privatized industries and elsewhere. The question then arises as to the accountability of those bodies.

Thirdly, and perhaps most significantly, Parliamentary sovereignty as our prime constitutional principle has been radically reconsidered. It may now be that the rule of law has supplanted Parliamentary sovereignty as our prime constitutional principle. The very concept of democracy and the commonly held assumption that majoritarian representative democracy is the appropriate form for the UK is being questioned as pressure builds up for more deliberative, participatory opportunities in the political process. Senior judges have referred to a 'new constitutional hypothesis' under which the rule of law and other democratic fundamentals may override Parliament's will.

Other changes reflected in the newer chapters in this book show that even an established democracy needs constantly to be reviewed and renewed. The separation of powers has not really been considered fundamental to British democracy, but recent reforms have endorsed that principle by removing the Lord Chancellor from any judicial role and establishing a judicial appointments commission. These reforms have encouraged others which will advance the independence of the system of tribunals. In the near future a Supreme Court will be established, outside of the House of Lords. In May 2007 a Ministry of Justice was created. Standards in public life have moved on to the constitutional agenda, as has access to governmental information, as the Freedom of Information Act 2000 comes into effect. Parliament has taken modest steps to reform itself so as better to scrutinize government's work. Yet other reforms, signalled in previous editions, disappear from the active agenda, examples being elected regional assemblies for England and the introduction of proportional representation for the House of Commons.

CONSTITUTIONAL REFORM: UNDERLYING ISSUES

The book begins with a consideration of the Rule of Law and the sovereignty of Parliament and the relationship between them. The Rule of Law is seen to have been the driving principle behind a number of values, such as legality, certainty, formal equality, accountability, due process, and access to justice. It has provided a critical focus for public debate, and it has practical significance in establishing both formal and substantive standards that are considered to be necessary elements of democratic constitutionalism. The classic legal doctrine of parliamentary sovereignty, that an Act of the UK Parliament is the highest form of law and that a later Act impliedly repeals incompatible provisions of an earlier Act, is under pressure from various quarters. The issue of sovereignty has been considered in a number of the chapters of this book, so central is it to our constitutional arrangements.[1] It concentrates the exercise of legislative and governmental power in and through Parliament, and thus through

[1] Notably Chapters 1–4, and 7–10.

the main political parties. Thus it serves to marginalize the influence of those who do not participate in party political activity, particularly in the activity of the two main parties.

The legal doctrine of sovereignty has been modified by British membership of the European Union and the concomitant importation into the UK hierarchy of norms of the doctrines of primacy and direct effect of Community law that have been developed by the European Court of Justice.[2] Here clearly the influence of Parliament and of political parties in the UK is reduced. On the face of it, much European legislation, though it forms part of the law of the UK, is 'foreign' to the UK and imposed externally. The UK judiciary has shown considerable political adeptness in dealing with this development. This is well illustrated in three cases that are discussed in Chapters 1, 2 and 3: first, in the dicta of Lord Bridge in the *Factortame* case[3] in which the disapplication of a UK Act was justified on the assertion that Parliament knew full well when it passed the European Communities Act 1972 that this would mean that the British courts would have to disapply incompatible legislation. In other words, this was part of the deal done by the UK and the EC and surrender of sovereignty was conscious and voluntary and not imposed unilaterally by the EC.[4] Secondly, in the approach of Laws LJ in the *Thoburn* case,[5] in which he rejected the argument advanced by counsel for the respondent local authority that the court should give primacy to EU law *because this was what the European Court of Justice's case law required*. Laws LJ preferred to base the court's application of European legislation on the common law and what he identified as a newly developing doctrine, that there is a distinction between constitutional statutes (of which the European Communities Act 1972 was one) and ordinary statutes, the former category not being subject to the doctrine of implied repeal. It is probably less unpalatable to those who object to the primacy of European law and are concerned about the democratic deficit in Europe and a loss of parliamentary sovereignty, that changes in the doctrine of parliamentary sovereignty should be home grown, rather than imposed from outside. Thirdly, in *Jackson* v. *Attorney-General*[6] some members of the Appellate Committee of the House of Lords indicated, *obiter*, that they might revisit the doctrine of legislative supremacy: if Parliament were to pass an Act that was contrary to principles of constitutionalism or the rule of law the courts might not give effect to the measure.

Politically, too, the doctrine of parliamentary sovereignty is under pressure. The assumption that the electorate of the day, represented by its Members of Parliament, is rightly entitled to secure legislation on any matter by simple majority of those present and voting in the Parliament is coming under challenge on a number of counts. First, it is not the case that the party with a majority in Parliament will have won the majority of the votes cast in a general election. Under the first past the post electoral system the person elected as MP is the candidate who received more votes than any other candidate, and commonly this will be a person who won fewer than half of the votes cast in his or her constituency. And the overall result of an election commonly is that a party with a majority in the House of Commons won fewer than half of the votes cast in the election.[7] Majoritarian theory, in other words, is based on dubious assumptions about the facts.

[2] See discussion in Chapter 3.

[3] [1991] 1 AC 603; see discussion of this case in Chapters 2 and 3.

[4] But see the discussion of this issue by D. Nicol in *EC Membership and the Judicialisation of British Politics* (2001), in which he shows how less well informed British MPs were about the implications of membership than Irish MPs, who had to approve constitutional amendments to facilitate Irish membership of the EC.

[5] [2002] 3 WLR 247.

[6] [2006] 1 AC 262.

[7] See *Report of the Independent Commission on the Voting System* (The Jenkins Report), Cm 4090 (1998); D. Oliver, *Constitutional Reform in the UK* (2003) ch. 7.

Parliamentary sovereignty is also being weakened as a result of measures for the devolution of legislative power to the Scottish Parliament and the Northern Ireland Assembly, and the Human Rights Act (HRA).[8] While all of this legislation preserves the formal legal supremacy of the UK Parliament, the political realities are that the Westminster Parliament is inhibited in various respects from legislating on matters devolved to the Scottish Parliament without their consent, and from passing laws that are incompatible with Convention rights. While some of the inhibitions in relation to human rights are based in the Human Rights Act itself (for instance, in the duty of ministers to make statements of compatibility when introducing bills into Parliament),[9] the political sources of these inhibitions are not statutory. They are partly cultural, reflecting a commitment to these new arrangements on the part of the government and the legislature. They find expression, for instance, in the Sewel convention relating to legislation on matters devolved to the Scottish Parliament;[10] and in the institutional and procedural arrangements in Parliament for the scrutiny of legislation for compatibility with Convention rights and constitutional implications by the Joint Committee on Human Rights and the Constitution Committee of the House of Lords.[11] They are also responses to the new political and legal arrangements in devolved areas, whose elected bodies would object to unilateral encroachments on their areas of responsibility from the UK level.

It is worth reminding ourselves at this point that the doctrine of parliamentary sovereignty is peculiarly English. It entered the system when, under the Bill of Rights 1689, most of the powers of the sovereign were transferred to the Parliament. Justification had been sought for the sovereign's once absolute powers in the doctrine of Divine Right of Kings. The King or Queen was God's representative in the Kingdom and was presumed to be perfect – and thus immune from suit in the courts.

This was not a democratic justification for the monarch's sovereignty, and no more was the transfer of sovereignty to Parliament based upon democratic theory: in 1689 democracy, in the sense that the legislature ought to be elected by universal adult suffrage, was widely regarded as a dangerous and subversive doctrine. The transfer of sovereignty to Parliament was based instead on a more passive concept of government by consent of the Lords and the Commons.

Before the Unions of the Parliaments of England and Scotland in 1706, the Parliament of Scotland did not enjoy sovereignty in the same way as the English Parliament did, and a theory of limited government prevailed in Scotland.[12] When the Parliaments were united, the Scottish doctrine was displaced by the English doctrine of sovereignty. There was, then, no *democratic* foundation for the doctrine of parliamentary supremacy in 1689, nor under the English and Scottish Acts of Union 1706. It was essentially a doctrine designed to limit the powers of the monarch. Given that the majoritarian justification noted above will not necessarily be accepted as legitimating the doctrine any longer, either some other convincing justification for parliamentary sovereignty needs to be identified in the present conditions, or a different theory of democracy will take its place. Here a glance overseas may cast light on the possibilities.

[8] See for instance M. Elliott, 'Parliamentary sovereignty and the new constitutional order: Legislative freedom, political reality and convention' (2002) 22 *Legal Studies* 340.

[9] See HRA, s. 19.

[10] See *Memorandum of Understanding*, Cm 5240 (2001), para. 13; and see discussion in Chapter 7, and D. Oliver, *Constitutional Reform in the UK* (2003) 251–2.

[11] See Chapters 4 and 7.

[12] See *MacCormick* v. *Lord Advocate* 1953 SC 396.

Theories of limited government and rights-based democracy have come to gain primacy over majoritarian theory in many countries. Most written constitutions place obstacles in the way of a government using its parliamentary majority to alter the constitution or to interfere with certain fundamental principles. On this view – which emerged during the French revolution and American War of Independence and gained further credence in the light of experience of Nazism and fascism in the Second World War – principles of majoritarianism are subject to exceptions in order to guarantee respect for minorities, for human rights, and for principles such as the independence of the judiciary, division of powers, respect for federalism, and the like.

In the UK, a shift to a rights-based theory of democracy and limited government is implicit in the judicial development of concepts of fundamental common law rights and constitutional statutes and in the judicial review jurisdiction, discussed in Chapter 1. Scotland, Wales, and Northern Ireland, when devolution is operative there, all operate under limited, rights-based constitutions. UK membership of the European Union gives further support to the shift to a rights-based approach to democracy and government.

Feldman shows in Chapter 5 how international instruments have affected the ways in which government in the UK is conducted. Most notably the Human Rights Act gives domestic effect to important articles in the European Convention on Human Rights. The British courts have not however been willing to give as much weight to international instruments as they do to the jurisprudence of the courts of other common law jurisdictions. The legitimacy of judicial importation of ideas and standards from other countries or from international instruments may be challenged, since not all such imports will fit well with the domestic legal system. However, it seems likely for the time being that some borrowing between legal systems will continue, this being yet another potential source of constitutional change.

The democratic theories that underlie the changing UK constitution are developing in other ways than those produced by the tension between majoritarianism and limited or rights-based government. Many of the constitutional reform measures that have been introduced in recent years have been fashioned to support the broadly liberal concepts of representative democracy that these theories represent. These function well in a polity where trust and consensus are embedded in the culture, and the electorate is accustomed to and accepts a pragmatic, non-ideological approach to constitutional matters and government. But, as McCrudden suggests in Chapter 8, the tradition has not worked well in Northern Ireland, where trust and consensus have had to be cultivated so that that part of the island of Ireland can enjoy devolved or self-government. Hence attempts have had to be made in Northern Ireland to establish a power-sharing, communitarian, ideological system.

The liberal representative system focuses democratic procedures on elected institutions, which are dominated by the parties. It is hard for 'voices' to be heard and responded to except through the parties on this model. Increasingly, however, policy is in practice delivered, even developed, by bodies outside this magic circle of formal state bodies and political parties. As Morison and Drewry note in Chapters 6 and 11, a system of 'governance'[13] in contrast to 'government' is evolving, often operating alongside the formal representative system. This is characterized by the use of partnerships between state and private bodies to deliver policy, and by consultative arrangements of various kinds. Morison suggests in

[13] See J. Newman, *Modernising Governance. New Labour, Policy and Society* (2001).

Chapter 6 that democracy need not only be a *framework* for decision making – which is what representative institutions produce – and it could be, or also be, a *process* for preference building from which decisions may emerge – deliberative democracy. The influence of this theory is seen in much administrative law, for instance in requirements of procedural propriety in decision making – consultation, the giving of reasons, openness. It is also reflected in some novel constitutional arrangements or proposals for constitutional reform: the proposals of the Royal Commission on Reform of the House of Lords for appointment to the Second Chamber of members who are independent of party, who would act as 'voices' for sections of society not heard through the political parties[14] would, if implemented, be an example of the constitutionalization of preference-building processes and deliberative democracy. An obstacle in the way of the development of such a role is that the parties and the party system itself are challenged by it and resist it.[15]

PRESSURE POINTS: TOWARDS MORE CONSTITUTIONAL REFORM?

Reforms tend to give rise to pressure for further reforms or adjustments. This is especially the case in the UK, where there is no blueprint or grand plan for reform, and reforms have been incremental and often explicitly provisional. Let us consider some of these pressure points.

PARLIAMENT AND GOVERNMENT

Since 1997 the House of Commons has had to struggle against its own conservatism and the vested interests of the parties and the government to achieve some relatively modest modernizing reforms to its legislative procedures and committee system.[16] However, the House of Commons is becoming increasingly aware of its own limitations in relation to the scrutiny of government policy and administration, and of legislation. Its limitations have been highlighted by the relative success of public inquiries in eliciting information from government, for instance over the Arms to Iraq affair in the 1990s and the background to the invasion of Iraq in 2004. The Government has drifted into a desire to save time and effort by marginalizing Parliament in the legislative process altogether, as the original terms of the Legislation and Regulatory Reform Bill of 2006 (which sought to facilitate executive amendment of statutes) showed. The domination of party, especially the party of government, serves to suppress any sense of a *corporate* House of Commons function or identity in holding government to account as opposed to sustaining it in power.[17] Whether the introduction of proportional representation for elections to the House would make for a more consensual style of politics is for debate and speculation only, since such a reform is at this time nowhere near the top of any realistic political agenda.

The Government has had difficulties in achieving reform of the House of Lords since New Labour was elected in 1997, apart from the removal of all but 92 hereditary peers in

[14] Cm 4534 (Jan. 2000), ch. 13. [15] See Chapter 7. [16] See Chapter 7.

[17] See B. Winetrobe, 'The Autonomy of Parliament', in D. Oliver and G. Drewry (eds), *The Law and Parliament* (1998).

1999. The Royal Commission on the Reform of the House of Lords which reported in 2000 recommended an elected element of no more than a third. This did not find favour in the House of Commons or in the press, where the pressure has been for a substantially elected House. The problem in moving to the next step in reform has been largely because the government and many commentators lack any clear view of the proper role of the House and what kind of composition would enable it to perform its role, and because of the conflicting interests at stake. Most of the world is unable to conceive of a democracy including among its institutions a body known as a chamber of Parliament that is not elected. And yet the relatively non-political character of the second chamber is valued by many. If the House were to become more politicized, for instance through a substantially elected membership, it may be impossible for the House of Lords to continue to perform the relatively non-partisan functions of scrutiny and constitutional checking that need to be performed in any democracy subscribing to constitutionalism, and which it does rather well. The parties are also uncomfortable with the idea, implicit in the Royal Commission's proposals, that the second chamber should be a forum not dominated by party politics, in which a deliberative style of debate and preference building would take place: to adopt Morison's analysis in Chapter 6, their assumptions are very much towards Parliament as a framework for decision making rather than part of a process for preference building leading to decisions. We have here a strong example of the difficulties of fit between different democratic models and theories.

The executive sits uncomfortably between representative government and 'governance' models of the constitution.[18] Its presence in and domination of the House of Commons, and in particular the dominance of the Prime Minister, imply a top-down style of government. On the other hand, the development of sectoral policy networks and policy communities breaks down the separations between government and the governed, and between a traditional hierarchical style and the more collaborative or market-oriented styles of the private sector which are influential in contemporary governance structures. The breakdown of public-private divides and categories may be seen particularly in local government, where local authorities have been given a role in encouraging partnerships and community involvement in the delivery of local services and acting as community leaders.[19] These techniques serve to remove much service delivery from party politics – to depoliticize it – an experience by which parties and institutions of representative democracy may feel threatened. By contrast the civil service, at the heart of the formal government, has become increasingly politicized, and this has given rise to pressure for a Civil Service Act and clarification of the relationships between ministers and civil servants, and ministers and special advisers.[20] Thus in some areas clarification and separation of functions and interests are perceived to be necessary, whereas in others the breaking down of separations and boundaries is regarded as a positive development.

DEVOLUTION

The devolution arrangements in the UK are highly asymmetrical. Northern Ireland is a special case to which we shall return. But the degree of devolution granted to Scotland – in

[18] See R. A. W. Rhodes, *Understanding Governance. Policy Networks, Governance, Reflexivity and Accountability* (1997); see also Drewry, Chapter 8.

[19] See Chapter 12; I. Leigh, *Law, Politics and Local Democracy* (2000); Oliver (2003), n. 9 above, ch. 16.

[20] See discussion in Chapter 8; Oliver (2003), n. 10 above, ch. 12.

response to widely debated and well-formulated demands from civil society in Scotland, and influenced by the fact that Scotland retained many national legal and political institutions after the Union with England – was much greater than that granted to Wales in 1998.[21] This resulted in some pressure from Wales for further devolution and amendment to their settlement to bring them closer to the Scottish position.[22] Some of these pressures were accommodated in the Government of Wales Act 2006, discussed in Chapter 11. In Scotland too there is scope for adjustments to be made to the devolution arrangements, for instance by grant of independent revenue-raising powers and the transfer of further powers to the Parliament and government.

The place of England in the devolution settlement is different again – in fact so far there is no devolution of power to elected bodies at regional level in England, save in relation to Greater London. Proposals for such arrangements were rejected in a referendum in the North East of England in 2004, and the issue is currently dormant. But even if regional assemblies were put in place in the future, it is not envisaged that they should have any legislative power, whether primary, as the Scottish Parliament and Northern Ireland Assembly have, or secondary, as the Welsh Assembly has.[23] The asymmetry is not necessarily a negative aspect of the devolution arrangements, but it does generate sensitivities about unequal treatment in parts of the UK and it has a potentially ratcheting effect, as activists in one part of the UK press to be brought into line with the country on the next step up the devolution ladder – pressure from Wales to be treated more like Scotland, from England for its own Parliament, and so on. Asymmetry may also generate ill feeling in the House of Commons on the part of English MPs, as Scottish MPs exercise their rights to vote, decisively, on measures that will have no application to Scotland. Irritation at this will be the greater as different parties are in power in different parts of the UK, bringing greater partisanship and competitiveness to the relationships. This may lead in turn to the need to develop new conventions in the House of Commons about such matters, so that Scottish MPs refrain from using their votes to push through measures for which there is no majority in England or in England and Wales.

Devolution has not only spawned pressures for the transfer of greater powers to elected national bodies. It has also given rise to different styles of politics in different parts of the UK. These in turn may generate pressure for further change at Westminster, the least changed level of government. An obvious point of comparison is that systems of proportional representation are used for elections to the Scottish Parliament, the Northern Ireland Assembly and the Assembly for Wales, and this can lead to the formation of coalitions or pacts between parties and a more consensual style in the elected bodies and in government than operates at the centre. As Winetrobe has noted in Chapter 9, there were hopes in Scotland that a form of 'new politics' would come with devolution, helped in part by the fact of proportional representation and the formation of coalitions.

These devolution arrangements do not involve the devolved bodies having taxing powers, save for the as yet unused power at Edinburgh for the Parliament to vary the rate of income tax. The devolved bodies therefore rely almost entirely on grants from the centre for their revenue. The allocation of money to the different levels is extraordinarily unregulated by

[21] See Chapters 9–11.

[22] The Richard Commission on the powers and electoral arrangements for a National Assembly for Wales was appointed by the Welsh Assembly in July 2002 and produced its final report in March 2004: see Chapter 11.

[23] See government White Paper, *Your Regions, Your Choice Revitalising the English Regions*, Cm 5511 (2002), and Chapters 11 and 12.

statute, being based on the so-called 'Barnett formula'.[24] Currently this is not causing much controversy, probably because the UK has been going through a period of increasing public expenditure. If this trend were to reverse there would doubtless be pressure from the various constituent parts of the UK for the formula to be breached and for each to be treated as a special case because of its own hardship. It would be politically very hard to replace the Barnett formula in a period of financial retrenchment, for every change produces losers as well as winners.

There would be a particular problem over the treatment of England if the Barnett formula were to be breached, or replaced. England and its regions have no voice of their own in the devolution arrangements. Decisions about England are made by the government of the UK, whose primary obligation is to be even-handed in promoting the interests of the whole of the UK, not prioritizing England or its regions. In the absence of a voice of its own, England could find its interests subordinated to those of the other parts of the UK that do have voices of their own and whose main concern is their own interests, not those of other parts of the UK or even of the UK as a whole.[25]

Thus the working of devolution and its stability depend in large part upon the state of relations between the various levels in the UK. These are not provided for by law to any great extent, but by concordats and memorandums of understanding and by a culture of mutual self-restraint and respect.[26] This culture may not survive a change of political control at one of the levels of government.

Northern Ireland's devolution arrangements were reinstated in March 2007, having been suspended in 2000. As McCrudden shows in Chapter 8, they are based on a consensus- and trust-*building* model in which values are made explicit and politics is governed to a greater degree than is the case in Great Britain by law. The lack of trust between the two communities in Northern Ireland makes the traditional pragmatic approach unworkable, and reminds us of the cultural basis on which the UK's constitutional arrangements operate in Great Britain. It is however clear that a consensus- and trust-building approach cannot on its own create or substitute for actual trust and actual trustworthiness, both of which again are cultural, and are valuable social capital where they exist. But, as Northern Ireland has demonstrated, they are hard to create and, once lost, hard to rebuild.

CONSTITUTIONALISM, REGULATION AND ACCOUNTABILITY

Although the British constitution remains in some respects a 'political constitution'[27] it is becoming increasingly formalized. For example, the separation of powers, which is a key constitutional principle in many democracies, has never been wholeheartedly embraced in the UK. The ancient office of the Lord Chancellor in particular combined the roles of judge, cabinet minister, legislator and appointer of the higher judiciary. The reforms to the judiciary and the office of Lord Chancellor in the Constitutional Reform Act 2004 introduce a clear separation between the judiciary on the one hand and Parliament and the executive on

24 See D. Bell and A. Christie, 'Finance–The Barnett Formula: Nobody's Child?', in A. Trench (ed.), *The State of the Nation 2001* (2001) 136–9; Oliver (2003), n. 10 above, 253–5.

25 See for instance B. Hadfield, 'Towards an English Constitution' in (2002) 55 *Current Legal Problems*, 151; and Chapters 7–9.

26 See R. Rawlings, 'Concordats of the Constitution' (2000) 116 *LQR* 257; Oliver (2003), n. 10 above, chs 1 and 13.

27 See J. A. G. Griffith, 'The Political Constitution' (1979) 42 *MLR* 1.

the other and seek to advance the independence of the judiciary. The Lord Chancellor may no longer sit as a judge, and the appointment of the judiciary has been placed in the hands of an independent Commission. As is shown in Chapter 13, this is part of a trend towards constitutionalism, where individuals are considered holders of enforceable rights and entitlements, with access to independent and impartial judges. At present this trend is continuing through the reform of the tribunal system in order to achieve its greater independence (although at the same time challenges by individuals to official decisions may be achieved by less formal methods of dispute-resolution). However a contrary trend is also taking place, for informal dispute resolution and informal administrative justice. In his chapter Le Sueur argues that administrative justice is itself a constitutional principle and care should be taken not to undermine it through an emphasis on informal processes of alternative dispute resolution.

The Freedom of Information Act 2000 is another example of the provision of opportunity to the citizen to challenge official decisions. It requires all public bodies to be transparent in their dealings with the public and enhances public accountability. The privatization of much of the economy since the 1980s has been accompanied by the establishment of independent regulators in order to seek public accountability of even ostensibly private entities.[28]

Regulation does not always take the form of legislation. Much of it is in the form of 'soft law'. We have already noted the Barnett formula for the making of grants to the devolved bodies, the Sewel convention, and concordats and memorandums of understanding regulating devolution relationships. The resolutions of the two Houses of Parliament on ministerial responsibility passed just before the 1997 general election (noted in Chapter 10) are further examples, as is internal 'self-regulation'. For instance, control over public spending is largely exercised by the Treasury over government departments, through soft law documents such as *Government Accounting*.[29] Standards of conduct in public bodies are also largely regulated by non-statutory codes and procedures, most notably in the two Houses of Parliament.[30] This is a relatively new issue in the constitution and is considered by Leopold in Chapter 17. But here, as in other areas of the constitution, there are anomalies that give rise to pressures for further reform, often in the form of statutory provisions. For instance, certain breaches of standards of conduct in the devolved bodies, including taking bribes and failure to register interests, are criminal, whereas such conduct is not criminal if done by members of the House of Commons or the House of Lords. The Houses of Parliament are exempt from the Human Rights Act, but there is doubt whether their arrangements for dealing with breaches of their codes and other standards of conduct by their members or by outsiders meet the requirements of the European Convention on Human Rights, Article 6, for access to an independent and impartial tribunal.

So the British constitution, like most constitutions, will continue to change, and the pace of change has quickened in recent years with the programme of constitutional reform adopted by the Labour Government since 1997. Some of the most fundamental principles of the constitution, notably the conception of democracy, the sovereignty of Parliament, and the Rule of Law, are being recast by a combination of legislation, judicial decisions, and incremental informal reform of governmental practice. Pressures from the European Union

[28] See Chapter 14. [29] See discussion in Chapter 16.

[30] Discussed in Chapter 17; and see P. Leopold and O. Gay (eds), *Conduct Unbecoming* (2004).

and its member states, and from international developments, are increasingly influential in constitutional matters, here as in other countries. Overall in the UK the move from a primarily political constitution to a law-based one is likely to continue, with important implications in the reduced scope of party politics and an increased role for the courts.

We thank our contributors, both old and new, for the enthusiasm with which they have participated in this fresh edition. We are grateful to colleagues at OUP for continuing to have faith in the changing editions of this book.

Finally the chapters in this book are up to date to the end of January 2007. Some subsequent developments up to May 2007 have been noted.

Jeffrey Jowell
Dawn Oliver
UCL
May 2007

CONTENTS

TABLE OF CASES

TABLE OF LEGISLATION

UK AND SCOTTISH ACTS

EUROPEAN UNION LEGISLATION

FOREIGN LEGISLATION

INTERNATIONAL TREATIES AND CONVENTIONS

SECONDARY LEGISLATION

LIST OF ABBREVIATIONS

ACE	Agency Chief Executive
AME	Actually Managed Expenditure
BIIC	British-Irish Intergovernmental Conference
C & AG	Comptroller and Auditor General
CAA	Civil Aviation Authority
CFI	Court of First Instance
CJEC	Court of Justice of the European Communities
CPR	Civil Procedure Rules
CSG	Consultative Steering Group
CSPL	Committee on Standards in Public Life
CSR	Comprehensive Spending Review
DCA	Department for Constitutional Affairs
DEFRA	Department of the Environment, Food and Rural Affairs
DEL	Departmental Expenditure Limit
DETR	Department of the Environment, Transport and the Regions
DoE	Department of the Environment
DSS	Department of Social Security
DTI	Department of Trade and Industry
DUP	Democratic Unionist Party
EC	European Community
ECA	European Communities Act
ECHR	European Convention on Human Rights
ECJ	European Court of Justice
ECSC	European Coal and Steel Community
ECtHR	European Court of Human Rights
EDC	European Defence Community
EEC	European Economic Community
EIR	Environmental Information Regulations
EMU	Economic and Monetary Union
EOC	Equal Opportunities Commission
EP	European Parliament
EPC	European Political Community
EU	European Union
FoI	Freedom of Information
GCHQ	Government Communications Headquarters
GFAP	General Framework Agreement for Peace
GIAM	Government Internal Audit Manual
GNP	Gross National Product (or national income)
GRECO	Council of Europe's Group of States against Corruption
HLAC	House of Lords Appointments Commission
HMSO	Her Majesty's Stationery Office
ICO	Information Commissioner's Office

HRA	Human Rights Act 1998
ICT	Information and Communication Technology
IDEA	Institute for Democracy and Electoral Assistance
IGC	Inter-governmental Conference
IICD	Independent International Commission on Decommissioning
IMF	International Monetary Fund
IRA	Irish Republican Army
MSP	Member of the Scottish Parliament
NAO	National Audit Office
NATO	North Atlantic Treaty Organization
NEDO	National Economic Development Office
NHS	National Health Service
NIHRC	Northern Ireland Human Rights Commission
NPM	New Public Management
OECD	Organisation for Economic Co-operation and Development
Offer	Office of Electricity Regulation
Ofgas	Office of Gas Supply
Ofgem	Office of Gas and Electricity Markets
Oftel	Office of Telecommunications
Ofwat	Office of Water Services
ORR	Office of the Rail Regulator
OSCE	Organisation for Security and Co-operation in Europe
PAC	Public Accounts Committee
PASC	Public Administration Select Committee
PCA	Parliamentary Commissioner for Administration
PCS	Parliamentary Commissioner for Standards
PES	Public Expenditure Survey
PFI	Private Finance Initiative
PHSC	Political Honours Scrutiny Committee
Postcomm	Postal Services Commission
RPI	Retail Price Index
RUC	Royal Ulster Constabulary
SAS	Special Air Service
SBS	Special Boat Service
SDLP	Social Democratic and Labour Party
SNP	Scottish National Party
TLRC	Tax Law Review Committee
TME	Total Managed Expenditure
UUP	Ulster Unionist Party
VFM	Value for Money

LIST OF CONTRIBUTORS

JEFFREY JOWELL, QC Professor of Law, University College London

DAWN OLIVER Professor of Constitutional Law, University College London

RODNEY AUSTIN Senior Lecturer in Law at University College London

KATE BEATTIE Parliamentary Legal Officer, The Odysseus Trust

ANTHONY BRADLEY of the Inner Temple, Barrister, Emeritus Professor of Constitutional Law, Edinburgh

PAUL CRAIG Professor of English Law, St John's College, Oxford

GAVIN DREWRY Professor of Public Administration, Royal Holloway, University of London

DAVID FELDMAN Rouse Ball Professor of English Law, Cambridge

BRIGID HADFIELD Professor of Law, University of Essex.

IAN LEIGH Professor of Law, Durham University

PATRICIA LEOPOLD Professor of Law at Reading University

LORD LESTER OF HERNE HILL, QC Visiting Professor in the Faculty of Laws, University College London

ANDREW LE SUEUR Professor of Public Law, Queen Mary, University of London

CHRISTOPHER MCCRUDDEN Professor of Human Rights Law, University of Oxford

JOHN MCELDOWNEY Professor of Law, University of Warwick

JOHN MORISON Professor of Jurisprudence, Queen's University, Belfast

TONY PROSSER Professor of Public Law, University of Bristol

BARRY K. WINETROBE Reader in Law, Napier University

PART I

THE CONSTITUTIONAL FRAMEWORK

Editorial note

This book is divided into three parts. The chapters in this first part are concerned with fundamental principles and theories that underpin the UK constitution. What Dicey in his *Introduction to the Law of the Constitution* referred to as the 'twin pillars' of the constitution are the Rule of Law and the sovereignty of the UK Parliament. These two principles form the focus of the first five chapters. To them may be added, since the Human Rights Act 1998 came into force in 2000, respect for the fundamental civil and political rights contained in the European Convention of Human Rights, which are incorporated into UK law by that Act. This is the subject of Chapter 3. The Human Rights Act supplements the Rule of Law. Although it does not authorise the courts to strike down an Act of Parliament, it erects a number of political and procedural obstacles in the way of legislation that might interfere with Convention rights protected by the Act.

The fact that the UK is a member of the European Union affects many aspects of government in the UK. These are discussed in Chapter 4. The structure of the European Union is outlined there. The Union wields very great power over member states, and this raises issues about accountability arrangements and democracy within the Union. The approach of the courts in the UK to European legislation differs from that of the European Court of Justice, and the two approaches are discussed in Chapter 4. British membership has altered the common law doctrine of parliamentary sovereignty in ways that are discussed in Chapters 1, 2 and 4. Chapter 5 follows on from Chapter 4 by focusing on further international influences on the UK constitution. It shows how concepts from other legal systems influence domestic constitutional developments, and it discusses the filters and defences in our arrangements which protect the legal system from some unwelcome outside influences.

Many of the constitutional reform measures introduced in the UK since 1997 have been based on liberal democratic principles of representative democracy. These are strongly reflected in, for instance, devolution to Scotland and Wales, and the Human Rights Act. Alongside this set of theories, another concept of democracy is being developed, a more participatory, deliberative concept than representative democracy offers. This has come about partly because of the increase in the use of partnerships between government and non-governmental bodies to deliver policy – a shift from 'government' to 'governance' – and partly in response to pressure from citizens for their voices to be heard directly in decision making and not only through elections and parties. Information technology and the internet – with blogs and other forms of communication between citizens – facilitate this development. A more participative, deliberative approach is also reflected in arrangements for devolution in Northern Ireland, discussed in Part II of the book. This trend towards participatory democracy forms the subject of Chapter 6.

1

THE RULE OF LAW AND ITS UNDERLYING VALUES

Jeffrey Jowell

SUMMARY

Dicey believed that discretionary power offended the Rule of Law as it would inevitably lead to arbitrary decisions. His critics pointed out that in the modern state discretion is necessary to carry out a variety of welfare and regulatory tasks. Nevertheless, the Rule of Law contains a number of important values, including legality, certainty, accountability, efficiency, due process and access to justice. These are not only formal values but also substantive. The Rule of Law is not a theory of law but a principle of institutional morality inherent in any constitutional democracy. In a country without a written constitution it constrains the way power is exercised. It is enforced and elaborated through judicial review but also serves as a critical focus for public debate. Although the Rule of Law is not the only requirement of a constitutional democracy, it is of great practical significance in promoting fair decisions and restraining the abuse of power.

INTRODUCTION

Professor Albert Venn Dicey told us, in 1885, that the two principles of our unwritten constitution were the sovereignty of Parliament and the Rule of Law.[1] Although he regarded Parliamentary sovereignty as the primary principle – one that could override the Rule of Law – he recognized that, ideally, Parliament and all public officials should respect the Rule of Law as a quality that distinguished a democratic from a despotic constitution.

What is meant by the Rule of Law and what is its value? Is it any more than a statement that individuals or officials should obey the law as it is? Or does it require positive legal authority for the acts of all public officials? Is it a guide to the justice of public decision-making – a framework that constrains the abuse of power? Or is it an assertion that law itself

[1] A.V. Dicey, *The Law of the Constitution* (1885) referred to here in its 10th edn, edited by E.C.S. Wade (reprinted 1960). For an account of Dicey's conception see the articles on 'Dicey and the Constitution' in [1985] *Public Law* 583–724; I. Harden and N. Lewis, *The Noble Lie* (1986), ch. 2; P. Craig, *Public Law and Democracy in the United Kingdom and the United States of America* (1990) ch. 2; M. Loughlin, *Public Law and Political Theory* (1992); T.R.S. Allan, *Constitutional Justice: A Liberal Theory of the Rule of Law* (2001); A. Hutchinson and P. Monahan (eds.) *The Rule of Law: Ideal or Ideology?* (1987). See also, Lord Bingham or Cornhill, 'Dicey Revisited' [2002] *PL* 39. See also D. Dyzenhaus, *The Constitution of Law* (2006).

contains inherent moral qualities? Is its proper place not in the realm of constitutional legality but in the rhetoric of liberal–democratic values? Is it, as a distinguished legal historian has written, an 'unqualified human good'[2] or, as alleged by another, a device that 'enables the shrewd, the calculating, and the wealthy to manipulate its form to their own advantage'?[3]

Despite the uncertainty attached to the precise definition of the Rule of Law it is, in the UK, accepted as never before as one of the fundamental principles of our unwritten democratic constitution. It is frequently invoked by the courts as a standard by which to judge whether power has been abused. It is engaged as a yardstick by which to assess the democratic validity of government proposals. Senior judges have very recently devoted extra-judicial speeches to elaborating the content of the Rule of Law.[4] It has even received statutory recognition in the Constitutional Reform Act 2005,[5] the first section of which states that that Act does not adversely affect 'the existing constitutional principle of the rule of law'. Most significantly, some of our judges have recently suggested that Dicey's hierarchy of principle, with the Rule of Law playing second-fiddle to the sovereignty of Parliament, might be changing, and that 'the rule of law enforced by the courts is the ultimate controlling factor on which our constitution is based'.[6]

DICEY'S RULE OF LAW: ITS CRITICS AND SUPPORTERS

Because its connotations have been developed so much by historical interpretation it is necessary, even today, to start with Dicey's interpretation of the Rule of Law, because of the immense authority he exercised for so long over the perception of our constitutional arrangements.[7]

For Dicey, the Rule of Law distinguished the British (or 'English', as he preferred to call it) from all other constitutions. He described how foreign observers of English manners (Voltaire and de Tocqueville in particular) visited England and were struck by the fact that here was a country distinguished above all by the fact of being under the Rule of Law:

> When Voltaire came to England – and Voltaire represented the feeling of his age – his predominant sentiment clearly was that he had passed out of the realm of despotism to a land where the laws might be harsh, but where men were ruled by law and not by caprice.[8]

That passage encapsulates Dicey's approach to the Rule of Law. By allowing for 'harsh' laws to coexist with the Rule of Law it is clear that he does not equate the Rule of Law with the

2 E. P. Thompson, *Whigs and Hunters: The Origin of the Black Act* (1975) 266.

3 M. Horwitz, book review (1977) 86 *Yale LJ* 561 at 566.

4 Lord Bingham, 'The Rule of Law', Sir David Williams Lecture, Cambridge, December 2006; Sir John Laws, 'The Rule of Law: Form or Substance' London School of Economics, November 2006.

5 The Act seeks to further the principle of the separation of powers and independence of the judiciary. In particular, it removes the power of appointment of judges from the Lord Chancellor and places it in the hands of an independent Judicial Appointments Commission. It also precludes the Lord Chancellor from any judicial role and establishes a Supreme Court outside of the House of Lords.

6 Lord Hope, obiter, in *Jackson* v. *Her Majesty's Attorney General* [2005] UKHL 56 at [107].

7 The conception of the Rule of Law has an older provenance than Dicey. For an account of its origins in the ancient world see M. Loughlin, *Swords and Scales* (2000), ch. 5; B. Tamanaha, *On the Rule of Law: History, Politics and Theory* (2004), ch. 1.

8 Dicey, *Law of the Constitution*, 189.

notion of 'good' law. Nor does he contend that in order to qualify as 'law' a particular rule has to be fair, or reasonable, or just. So what did he mean by the Rule of Law?

According to Dicey, the Rule of Law has at least three meanings. The first is that individuals ought not to be subjected to the power of officials wielding wide discretionary powers. He wrote that no one 'is punishable or can be lawfully made to suffer in body or goods except for a distinct breach of law established before the ordinary courts of the land'. Fundamental to the Rule of Law, therefore, is the notion that all power needs to be authorized. But he took that notion further by contrasting the Rule of Law with a 'system of government based on the exercise by persons in authority of wide, arbitrary or discretionary powers of constraint'.[9] Here Dicey contends that to confer wide discretion upon officials is equivalent to granting them scope to exercise arbitrary powers, to which no one should be forced to submit. He writes that 'wherever there is a discretion there is room for arbitrariness'[10] and so would exclude discretionary powers from what he later calls 'regular law'.

Dicey's second meaning engages a notion of equality – what he calls the 'equal subjection' – of all classes to one law administered by the ordinary courts. He contrasts here what he saw as special exemptions for officials in continental countries such as France, where he considered that the French *droit administratif* operated a separate form of justice that treated ordinary citizens differently from the way it treated its public officials. 'With us', he wrote, 'every official, from the Prime Minister down to a constable or a collector of taxes, is under the same responsibility for every act done without legal justification as any other citizen.'[11]

Thirdly, Dicey saw the Rule of Law as expressing the fact that there is here no separate written constitutional code, and that the constitutional law is 'the result of the judicial decisions determining the rights of private persons in particular cases brought before the courts'.[12] Like Bentham before him, he was against a basic document setting out a catalogue of human rights and saw our law and liberties as arising from decisions in the courts – from the common law.

One of the first attacks on Dicey's meanings of the Rule of Law came in 1928 when William Robson wrote his celebrated book *Justice and Administrative Law*, in which he roundly criticized Dicey for his misinterpretation of both the English and French systems on the question of whether officials were treated differently from others. He pointed out that there were, in England 'colossal distinctions'[13] between the rights and duties of private individuals and those of the administrative organs of government even in Dicey's time. Public authorities possessed special rights and special exemptions and immunities, to the extent that the citizen was deprived of a remedy against the state 'in many cases where he most requires it'.[14] Robson also convincingly showed how Dicey had misinterpreted French law, where the *droit administratif* was not intended to exempt public officials from the rigour of private law, but to allow experts in public administration to work out the extent of official liability. Robson also noted the extent of Dicey's misrepresentation that disputes between officials and private individuals in Britain were dealt with by the ordinary courts. He pointed to the growth of special tribunals and inquiries that had grown up to decide these disputes outside the courts, and was in no doubt that a 'vast body of administrative law' existed in England.[15]

[9] Ibid., 188. [10] Ibid. [11] Ibid., 193. [12] Ibid., 195.

[13] W. A. Robson, *Justice and Administrative Law* (1928; 2nd edn, 1947) 343. [14] Ibid., 345.

[15] Ibid. Robson approved of, and wished to develop, administrative law, but through a separate system outside of the 'ordinary courts'. See his 'Justice and Administrative Law reconsidered' (1979) *Current Legal Problems*

The attack on Dicey continued a few years later with W. Ivor Jennings's *The Law and the Constitution*, which appeared in 1933. Repeating many of Robson's criticisms of Dicey's second and third meanings of the Rule of Law, Jennings also delivered a withering, and almost fatal, attack upon Dicey's first meaning – his claim that wide discretionary power had no place under the Rule of Law. It should be remembered here that Dicey was a trenchant critic of notions of 'collectivism'. An unreconstructed Whig, he had, throughout his life, believed in a *laissez-faire* economic system and had resisted the increasing regulatory role of the state.[16] He was supported by other constitutional theorists of his time,[17] and had an ally in the 1920s in Lord Hewart, who expressed similar views in his book *The New Despotism*.[18] Robson and Jennings were committed to the expansion of the state's role in providing welfare and other social services. Robson, George Bernard Shaw, Leonard Woolf, John Maynard Keynes, Harold Laski, and others worked together in the 1930s to promote these ideas.[19]

Jennings felt that the Rule of Law implicitly promoted Dicey's political views. He equated Dicey's opposition to state regulation with that of the 'manufacturers who formed the backbone of the Whig Party', who

> wanted nothing which interfered with profits, even if profits involved child labour, wholesale factory accidents, the pollution of rivers, of the air, and of the water supply, jerry-built houses, low wages, and other incidents of nineteenth-century industrialism.[20]

Jennings then turned his attention directly to Dicey, who

> was more concerned with constitutional relations between Great Britain and Ireland than with relations between poverty and disease on the one hand, and the new industrial system on the other.[21]

Jennings concluded that if the Rule of Law

> means that the state exercises only the functions of carrying out external relations and maintaining order, it is not true. If it means that the state ought to exercise these functions only, it is a rule of policy for Whigs (if there are any left).[22]

There were not too many Whigs or unreconstructed Diceyists left by the 1930s, when further legitimacy for the growth of official power was provided by the Donoughmore Committee, inquiring in 1933 into the question whether the growth of subordinate legislation (promulgated at the discretion of the executive) violated the Rule of Law.[23] Donoughmore found that it was inevitable, in an increasingly complex society, that Parliament delegate powers to ministers to act in the public interest. The Second World War then provided further compelling reasons to centralize power, an opportunity built upon by the Labour Government of 1945. As Robson wrote in the second edition of his book in 1947, increasingly Parliament had given powers to resolve disputes between the citizen and the state not to the courts – to

107. For an excellent critique and historic corrective of Dicey see H. W. Arthurs, 'Rethinking Administrative Law: A Slightly Dicey Business' (1979) 17 *Osgoode Hall LJ*, Part I; and *Without the Law* (1985).

16 See R. A. Cosgrove, *The Rule of Law: Albert Venn Dicey, Victorian Jurist* (1980), and the review by D. Sugarman (1983) *MLR* 102.

17 Such as Maine and Bryce.

18 Published in 1929.

19 See, for example, Keynes's lecture published by Leonard and Virginia Woolf at The Hogarth Press in 1926, entitled *The End of Laissez-Faire*. See Victoria Glendinning, *Leonard Woolf* (2006).

20 Sir W. Ivor Jennings, *The Law and the Constitution* (1933) 309–10.

21 Ibid., 311.

22 Ibid.

23 Report of the Committee on Ministers' Powers (1932) Cmd 4060.

Dicey's 'ordinary law' – but to specialized organs of adjudication such as administrative tribunals and inquiries. This was not 'due to a fit of absentmindedness' but because these bodies would be speedier and cheaper, and would possess greater technical knowledge and have 'fewer prejudices against government' than the courts.[24] Here he may have been echoing the words of Aneurin Bevan, Minister of Health in the 1945 Labour Government and architect of the National Health Service, who caused a stir in the House of Commons by establishing tribunals in the Health Service, divorced from 'ordinary courts', because he greatly feared 'judicial sabotage' of socialist legislation.[25]

Despite this onslaught on Dicey's version of the Rule of Law, its epitaph refused to be written. Two particularly strong supporters wrote in its favour in the 1940s. F. A. Hayek's *The Road to Serfdom* in 1943 graphically described that road as being paved with governmental regulation. C. K. Allen, with less ideological fervour, pleaded for the legal control of executive action.[26] Not much heed was paid to these pleas until the late 1950s when the Franks Committee[27] revived interest in Diceyan notions by proposing judicial protections over the multiplying tribunals and inquiries of the growing state. It was in the 1960s, however, that disparate groups once again started arguing in favour of legal values. Some of these groups were themselves committed to a strong governmental role in providing social welfare, but objected to the manner in which public services were carried out. Recipients of supplementary benefit, for example, objected to the fact that benefits were administered by officials in accordance with a secret code (known as the 'A Code') and asked instead for publication of a set of welfare 'rights'.[28] They also objected to the wide discretion allowed their case-workers to determine the level of their benefits. The heirs of Jennings and his followers, such as Professor Richard Titmus, opposed this challenge to the free exercise of official discretion and objected strongly to a 'pathology of legalism' developing in this area.[29]

Another plea for the Rule of Law came at about the same time from individuals who were being displaced from their homes by programmes of urban redevelopment. While not asking for a catalogue of 'rights', their claim was for participation in decisions by which they were affected.[30] Their plea did not primarily concern the substance of the law. Just as the welfare recipients were not simply arguing for higher benefits, but for pre-determined rules and fair procedures to determine the benefits, citizens' groups directed their demands for the Rule of Law less at the content of the decisions ultimately taken than at the procedures by which they were reached. They were by no means adopting the undiluted Diceyan view that all discretionary power is bad. Nevertheless, they asked not to be condemned (in those cases, evicted from their communities) unheard

THE VALUES UNDERLYING THE RULE OF LAW

Dicey's Rule of Law has been criticized, as we have seen, for the fact that it tendentiously seeks to promote an individualistic political theory and because of its inaccurate descriptions of

24 Robson, *Justice and Administrative Law* 347. 25 HC Rep., 23 July 1946, col. 1983.

26 See C. K. Allen, *Law and Orders* (1945). See also F. A. Hayek's *The Constitution of Liberty* (1960), and *Law, legislation and liberty* (2 vols, 1976).

27 Report of the Committee on Administrative Tribunals and Inquiries (1957) Cmnd 218.

28 See e.g. T. Lynes, *Welfare Rights* (1969); and in the USA: C. Reich, 'The New Property' (1964) 73 *Yale CJ* 733.

29 R. Titmus, 'Law and Discretion' (1971) 42 *Polit Q* 113.

30 N. A. Roberts, *The Reform of Planning Law* (1976); Patrick McAuslan, *The Ideologies of Planning Law* (1980) esp. chs 1 and 2.

the then-existing systems of governance – both in France and England. Yet it remains a compelling idea, although variously interpreted.[31] Some see the Rule of Law as embodying formal qualities in law (such as clarity, prospectivity, stability, openness and access to an impartial judiciary).[32] Others criticize that view. Ronald Dworkin has called it the 'rule-book conception' of the Rule of Law and prefers the 'rights conception', under which legal rules contain inherent moral content.[33] Dworkin's view must be seen in the context of his and others' opposition to the view of the positivist thinkers who contend that even extremely harsh and unjust laws, such as the discriminatory laws of Nazi Germany, must be regarded as law, despite their moral repugnance.[34] Dicey and Dworkin are aiming at different targets. Dworkin is seeking a general theory of law, and Dicey is seeking a general principle of how power should be deployed by government in a democracy. But is it true that Dicey's Rule of Law is wholly formalistic and lacks any substantive content? To answer this question we must consider the different values underlying Dicey's Rule of Law.

Legality

At its most fundamental, Dicey's Rule of Law requires obedience to law, or legality, which contains two features. First, the law must be followed. This requirement of the Rule of Law is often asserted by those who call for 'law and order' in the face of lax enforcement of the law. It speaks both to the public (who are expected to obey the law) and to law-enforcement officials (who are expected to implement the law).

Secondly, in so far as legality addresses the actions of public officials, it requires also that they act within the powers that have been conferred upon them. All decisions and acts of public officials must therefore be legally authorized. Taken together with Dicey's view that discretionary power is insufficiently accessible to fulfil the Rule of Law's requirements, legality thus avoids the arbitrary or capricious decision – the improvised justice of despots.

Certainty

The essence of Dicey's Rule of Law is that law should be certain and predictable. Both he, and his followers, Hewart and Hayek, mistrusted the grant of virtually any official discretion, and extolled the virtue of defined rules to govern the exercise of public power. We have seen that Dicey was less concerned that laws were 'harsh' than that they be known. Certainty, rather than substantive fairness, was the key value. Maitland wrote that 'Known general laws, however bad, interfere less with freedom than decisions based on no previously known rule.'[35] Hayek said:

> [I]t does not matter whether we all drive on the left or the right-hand side of the roads so long as we all do the same. The important thing is that the rule enables us to predict other people's

[31] See P. Craig, 'Formal and Substantive Conceptions of the Rule of Law: An Analytical Framework' [1997] *Public Law* 467; N. Barber, 'Must Legalistic Conceptions of the Rule of Law Have a Social Dimension?' (2004) *Ratio Juris* 474.

[32] J. Raz, 'The Rule of Law and its Virtue' (1977) 93 *LQR* 195; *The Authority of Law* (1979). Compare Lon Fuller's requirements of 'legality': generality, clarity, public promulgation, stability, consistency, fidelity to purpose and prohibition of the impossible. L. Fuller, *The Morality of Law* (1964) p.153. See also R. Summers, 'The Principles of the Rule of Law' (1999) *Notre Dame LR* 1691; J. Waldron, 'Is the Rule of Law an Essentially Contested Concept?'(2002) *Law and Philosophy* 137.

[33] R. Dworkin, *A Matter of Principle* (1985), ch.1, p. 11 ff.

[34] See generally, H.L.A. Hart, *The Concept of Law* (1961).

[35] *Collected Papers*, Vol. i (1911) 81. Maitland equated arbitrary power with power that was 'uncertain' or 'incalculable': ibid., 80.

behaviour correctly, and this requires that it should apply in all cases – even if in a particular instance we feel it to be unjust.[36]

An official possessed of discretion frequently has a choice about how it should be operated: whether to keep it open-textured, maintaining the option of a variety of responses to a given situation, or to confine it by a rule or standard – a process of legalization. For example, a local authority that provides grants for students could allocate them on a case-by-case basis, deciding each case on its merits. Or it could promulgate some rules, excluding grants for certain university courses etc. Similarly, laws against pollution could be enforced by a variable standard whereby the official must be satisfied that the polluter is achieving the 'best practicable means' of abatement. Alternatively, levels of pollution could be specified in advance, based on the colour of smoke emission, or the precise quantities of sulphur dioxide. A policy of promoting safe driving could, similarly, be legalized by a rule specifying speeds of no more than 30 miles per hour on given streets.

Dicey and his followers prefer rules to discretion largely because rules allow affected persons to know what they are required to do – or not do – in advance of any sanction for breach of the rule. Certainty in that sense has an instrumental value in that it allows decisions to be planned in advance and people to know clearly where they stand. However, the value of legal certainty is also based in *substantive fairness*. It is unfair to penalize someone for an action that was lawful when it was carried out and it is unfair to punish someone for the breach of a law which they were not able to discover.

Consistency

Related to the value of certainty is that of consistency, or formal equality. The application of policy through rules promotes even-handed application of standards. Like cases can then be treated alike. In contrast, discretionary powers may be applied selectively. There is also an aspect of substantive equality in this aspect of the Rule of Law; as Dicey says, the highest official will be treated similarly to everyone else. The extent to which substantive equality, as well as formal equality, is contained within the Rule of Law will be considered further below.

Accountability

A third value of the Rule of Law is accountability. First, rules provide a published standard against which to measure the legality of official action. They thus allow individual redress against those officials who are not acting within the scope of their conferred powers. An announced level of resources to qualify for welfare assistance should allow a person who qualifies but is refused assistance to mount a legal challenge to the refusal. Secondly, the actual process of *making* rules and their publication generates public assessment of the fidelity of the rule to legislative purpose. Many statutes confer on the decision-maker broad discretionary powers to further the policy of the Act. The power may be to allocate housing, or to provide for the needs of children, or to diminish unacceptable pollution of the air or water. The process of devising a points system for housing allocation, benefit levels for the needy, and acceptable emission levels of pollution thus forces the official into producing a formal operational definition of purpose.

[36] Hayek, *The Road to Serfdom* 60.

The legalization of policy does not simply allow officials to 'congratulate themselves – and await obedience'.[37] The process of making rules, as well as the rules themselves, may generate scrutiny and appraisal that make officials subject to assessment on the basis of fidelity to the purpose of the governing scheme.

Efficiency

Although not considered in any detail by Dicey, rule-based action also provides the benefit of efficiency. Rules announce or clarify official policies to people who will be affected by them. The process of clarification thus facilitates the implementation of the rules. A zoning system in planning or a list of features of 'substandard' housing, a list of required grades for university admission all allow people to comply themselves with the appropriate standard. Fruitless applications will be avoided. From the perspective of the decision-maker, rules allow decisions to be taken more quickly than a general standard that requires constant reappraisal of each case on its merits. Required grades for university admission can be routinely applied. Rules therefore reduce the anxiety and conserve the energy needed to reach decisions on a case-by-case basis. The portrayal by the sociologist Max Weber of his ideal-type bureaucrat applying rules '*sine ira et studio* – without hatred or passion, and hence without affection or enthusiasm'[38] – alludes to the neutral and non-affective approach to a legalized framework and the possibility of insulating the decision-maker from the pressure of constant reconsideration.

Due process and access to justice

Another of Dicey's features of the Rule of Law is that no person should be condemned unheard – that there should be no punishment without a trial. The requirement of 'due process' or 'natural justice' (these days called 'procedural fairness') is associated with his notion of legality, as it assumes that the person will be able to challenge both the announced rule or the implementation of the rule by the official. In order to do this, the claimant will need access to the courts. So access to justice is another feature of the Rule of Law.

Once the claimant reaches the court, another aspect of Rule of Law is engaged, namely the requirement that the decision-maker be unbiased, that is both independent (in the sense of free of external pressure) and impartial (not apparently interested in the outcome of the case in favour of any one of the participants). Even if perfect impartiality on the part of the adjudicator is an unattainable goal (because we all have unconscious predilections and biases), the process of justification involved in adjudication does not easily permit predetermined or arbitrary decisions. Adjudication encourages 'purposive decisions',[39] by inviting the decision to be justified by reference to a general rule, standard, or principle. Due process is therefore also associated with Dicey's faith in legal certainty and prospectivity. The purpose of the trial is to judge whether the accused is guilty by existing legal standards. Due process also encourages decisions that are consistent, since like cases should be treated alike. In addition, due process is in itself a technique of accountability, especially when reasons are required, which then invite public scrutiny of those decisions.

Viewed in that light, due process is not a merely formal virtue. Its substantive dimension emerges when we consider that it endorses the notion that every person is entitled to be

[37] P. Selznick, *Law, Society and Industrial Justice* (1969) 29.

[38] M. Weber, *The Theory of Social and Economic Organisation*, trans. A. Henderson and T. Parsons (1947) 340.

[39] P. Nonet, 'The Legitimation of Purposive Decisions' (1980) *Calif L Rev* 263.

treated with due regard to the proper merits of their cause. Failure to provide that treatment diminishes a person's sense of individual worth and impairs their dignity.[40] The right to due process goes further than forbidding actual punishment without a trial. It extends to concern that individuals should not have decisions made about their vital interests without an opportunity to influence the outcome of those decisions. And it requires restrictions on rights, liberties and interests to be properly *justified*. The culture of justification, rather than the culture of authority,[41] is another mark of the difference between democracy and despotism. Due process therefore provides 'formal and institutional expression to the influence of reasoned argument in human affairs'.[42] Overt reference to irrational or particularistic factors (such as the defendant's race or political views) will therefore be difficult to sustain. Because procedural fairness promotes full and fair consideration of the issues and evidence, as Lord Steyn has said, it plays 'an instrumental role in promoting just decisions'.[43]

Although Dicey favoured adjudication through the regular courts of law, adjudicative mechanisms of different kinds provide procedural checks on discretion in order to comply with the Rule of Law. Some are provided through appeals – for example, in planning, from local to central government by means of written representations or a public inquiry; or in immigration and asylum matters, from an adjudicator to an appeal tribunal. Special tribunals exist to permit appeals from the decisions of a variety of officials upon issues as diverse as the registration of a new variety of rose to compensation for the acquisition of land.

Some decisions decide not only rights between the individual and the public organization, but also questions of policy, such as whether a motorway should be built over a stretch of land. In those situations the decision may be structured by means of an inquiry or tribunal hearing, or may simply be made by an official within a government department. There has been a demand for public participation in those decisions. Even though those seeking participation have mere interests (rather than vested rights) in the decision's outcome, they ask for the right to participate in the process of making that decision. Neighbours want to be consulted about an application for planning permission on a local site, and people want to be consulted about the closure of hospitals, local railway lines or coal pits.[44] If the Rule of Law is concerned to protect individuals from being deprived of their rights without an opportunity to defend themselves, the concern is only narrowly stretched to protect group interests from being overridden without the opportunity to express views on the matter to be decided.[45]

THE LIMITS OF THE RULE OF LAW'S VALUES

The Rule of Law contains, as we have seen, the values of legality, certainty, consistency, accountability, efficiency, due process and access to justice. These values in themselves promote both

40 For a full account of the variety of justifications of procedural protections see D. J. Galligan, *Due Process and Fair Procedures* (1996), and see G. Richardson, 'The Legal Regulation of Process', in G. Richardson and H. Genn (eds), *Administrative Law and Government Actions* (1994). The aspect of natural justice that requires the decision-maker to be unbiased also incorporates an aspect of the principle of separation of powers into the Rule of Law.

41 Mureinik, 'A Bridge to Where? Introducing the Bill of Rights' (1994) 10 *SAJHR* 31.

42 L. Fuller, 'Collective Bargaining and the Arbitrator' (1963) *Wisconsin L Rev* 1 at 3. See also Rawls's view of natural justice as an element of the Rule of Law, in his *A Theory of Justice* (1972) 241–2.

43 *Raji* v. *General Medical Council* [2003] UKPC 24.

44 *R.* v. *British Coal Corpn and Secretary of State for Trade and Industry ex parte Vardy and others* [1993] ICR 720 (CA).

45 For an account of 'the ideology of public participation', see Patrick McAuslan, *The Ideologies of Planning Law* (1980); Nonet, n. 44 above; J. Habermas, *Towards a Rational Society* (1971).

formal and substantive qualities. However, they are not unqualified. Flip over the coin of the Rule of Law and we see some of the defects of rule and adjudication as techniques of governance.

The benefits of rules – their objective, even-handed features – are opposed to other administrative benefits, especially those of individual treatment, and responsiveness. The virtue of rules to the administrator (routine treatment and efficiency) may be a defect to the claimant with a special case (such as the brilliant applicant for a university place who failed to obtain the required grades because of a family upset or illness just before the examination). The administrator's shield may be seen as an unjustified protection from the claimant's sword. Officials themselves may consider that a task requires flexibility, or genuinely want to help a particular client, but feel unable to do so. Hence the classic bureaucratic response: 'I'd like to help you – but this is the rule.'

Our administrative law itself recognizes the limits of rule-governed conduct through the principle against the 'fettering' of discretion. Where an official has wide discretion – for example, to provide grants to industry or to students or to regulate safety standards for taxi drivers – a rule will often be introduced both to assist in the articulation of the standard and its even-handed application, and also to announce the standard to affected persons. The safety rules, for example, may require seat belts, and regular vehicle maintenance inspections. The courts do not object to the use of a rule in itself, but they do object to its rigid application without giving a person with something new or special to say about his case the opportunity to put his argument to the decision-maker. The principle against the fettering of discretion acknowledges how the rigid application of rules can militate against good and fair public administration.[46]

This balance of rule and discretion can be found etched into particular areas of public administration. In town and country planning, for example, permission is needed for development of land. By what criteria is that permission granted or refused? Some countries have adopted a system of zoning, by which the local map clearly marks out what can be done in each area. A would-be developer knows from the colour coding whether he can build a factory or change a shop to an office on a given site. In Britain this approach, whereby the zoning map in effect creates a series of rules about what can be done on the land, is greatly softened. Officials will take into account the formal plan for the area, but account may also be taken of 'other material considerations'.[47] So rule and discretion are mixed together, in an attempt to gain the benefits of each. Thus, an applicant for a craft centre in an area zoned as residential on the plan may nevertheless be granted permission because the centre fits in with the area, does not adversely affect its amenity, and generates local employment. These 'other material considerations' provide the flexibility to mitigate the rigours of a rule-bound plan.

We must note too that the existence of a rule does not automatically ensure its implementation. Nor is it always desirable that rules be enforced. Sometimes the prosecuting official will lack the resources to prosecute the law. This happened when the police withdrew full enforcement of the law against unlawful protesters against the shipping of live animals across the channel. The House of Lords accepted that the action was justified because it was stretching the chief constable's resources to the detriment of policing elsewhere in the

46 See D. Galligan, 'The Nature and Function of Policies within Discretionary Power' (1976) *Public Law* 332 and *Discretionary Powers* (1986); C.Hilson, 'Judicial Review, Politics and the Fettering of Discretion' [2002] *Public Law* 111.

47 Town and Country Planning Act 1990, s. 54A.

county.[48] Full enforcement may also distort the purpose of the rule and require, for example, the prosecution of a doctor who narrowly exceeded the speed limit on a deserted street late at night while rushing to the scene of an accident. That prosecution makes no sense in furthering the goal of preventing unsafe driving.

Sometimes an invitation to bargain may be built into a regulatory scheme. For example, our system of regulating planning, under which permission to develop is required, is supplemented by a different procedure, under which an applicant for permission to develop land may engage in a system of bargaining. Instead of being granted or refused planning permission in accordance with known rules and standards (however flexible) an applicant might offer, in exchange for planning permission, a benefit (sometimes known as 'planning gain') that was not part of the original application. For example, an applicant for permission to build offices may be granted that permission, perhaps at a density higher than would normally be acceptable, under the terms of an agreement where the developer would in turn dedicate part of the site to be used as a public right of way, a community centre, or housing for use by the local authority.[49]

Other schemes institutionalize the bargaining process in land of special amenity value in the countryside. Although relatively few planning controls are imposed on agricultural activities, the relevant authority is empowered, when notified that such activity may take place in sensitive environmental areas, to enter into 'management agreements' with owners under which the authority agrees to pay compensation for the net loss of profit occasioned by not undertaking the activity. For example, when a farmer seeks to plough up and grass over special moorland, or to drain unique wetlands, the authority may agree to pay the farmer to refrain from such development, and may also insert additional terms in the agreement, relating to public access to the owner's land, maximum stocking rates, etc.[50]

There is no doubt therefore that some of the twentieth century critics of Dicey's Rule of Law were right that discretionary power is often desirable and, in a complex modern state, is inevitable. Many statutes these days therefore are simply 'framework Acts' conferring wide discretionary powers to officials to tax, spend, lend, grant, subsidize, borrow, levy, license, issue, purchase, and raise tariffs – as well as to impose financial controls – over prices, incomes, dividends, rents, credits, interest rates, investment, exports and imports, and capital movements.[51] 'Government by contract' has become an acceptable technique of modern public regulation, although there are concerns that it may evade the values of legal certainty and accountability inherent in the Rule of Law.[52]

As with rules, adjudication is not appropriate in all situations. In the nineteenth century, writers such as Bentham[53] and his disciple Chadwick voiced strong opposition to the judicialization of administration. They agreed that to introduce such procedures would lead to mindless disputes upon 'such simple questions as to whether a cask of biscuits was good or bad'.[54]

48 *R* v. *Chief Constable of Sussex ex parte International Traders' Ferry Ltd.* [1999] 2 AC 418. But see also *R.* v. *Coventry City Council ex parte Phoenix Aviation* [1995] 3 All ER 37, where it was held that substantial non-enforcement of the law was in breach of the Rule of Law.

49 See Town and Country Planning Act 1990, s. 106; See *R* v. *Westminster City Council ex parte Monahan* [1990] 1 QB 87 (gain in the form of refurbishment of the Royal Opera House in Covent Garden offset by lifting of planning restrictions on office building).

50 See Wildlife and Countryside Act 1981, as amended.

51 See generally, J. T. Winkler, 'The Political Economy of Administrative Discretion' in M. Alder and S. Asquith (eds), *Discretion and Welfare* (1981); and 'Law, State and Economy' (1975) *Brit J Law and Society* 103.

52 See I. Harden, *The Contracting State* (1992).

53 L. J. Hume, *Bentham and Bureaucracy* (1981) 82.

54 H. Parris, *Constitutional Bureaucracy* (1969) 82.

Due process may impede speed and despatch. Could we really allow a hearing as to whether the firefighters should douse a burning house with water? Or a pavement hearing before a police officer is able to tow away an illegally parked car? Should there be an appeal from a university lecturer's examination grade? Or from a decision to reject admission to a university? Sometimes parties who have to live with each other after the dispute prefer techniques of mediation to negotiate an acceptable solution.[55] These forms of resolving disputes differ from adjudication where the final decision is taken by the independent 'judge' and is imposed rather than agreed.

MODERN CONCEPTIONS OF THE RULE OF LAW

The notion of the Rule of Law has greatly occupied the attention of legal historians. Writing about American law from 1780 to 1860, Morton Horwitz describes the growth of legal power to bring about economic redistribution in favour of powerful groups who carefully disguised under a neutral façade the class bias inherent in the law.[56] Robert Unger distinguishes the Rule of Law, which exists in societies governed by formal rules and procedures, from one in which communal bonds and shared values leave no need for this formal legality.[57] In his book *Whigs and Hunters*[58] on the origins of the Black Act of 1723, which led to a 'flood-tide of eighteenth-century retributive justice',[59] E. P. Thompson, the Marxist historian, concludes that 'the Rule of Law itself, the imposing of effective inhibitions upon power and the defence of the citizen from power's all-intrusive claims, seems to me to be an unqualified human good'.[60] In a critical review, Horwitz disagreed:

> I do not see how a man of the left can describe the Rule of Law as an 'unqualified human good'! It undoubtedly restrains power, but it also prevents power's benevolent exercise. It creates formal equality – a not inconsiderable virtue – but it *promotes* substantive inequality by creating a consciousness that radically separates law from politics, means from ends, processes from outcomes. By promoting procedural justice it enables the shrewd, the calculating, the wealthy to manipulate its forms to their own advantage. And it ratifies and legitimates an adversarial, competitive, and atomistic conception of human relations.[61]

Horwitz's view of the Rule of Law is misleading. Law can, of course, be oppressive, and respect for legality by both the 'dominant' and 'subservient' class can legitimate the enforcement of oppressive laws. But we must be careful about equating the Rule of Law with the substance of particular rules or with the substantive quality of the legal system. To claim that unjust laws and their rigorous enforcement demonstrate that the Rule of Law is an instrument of oppression is as misleading as the claim (often made in totalitarian countries) that the world described in Kafka's *The Trial*, with its maze of legal procedures, consistently yet heartlessly enforced, represents a state of perfect legality. Legality must be distinguished from legalism; rule *by* law is different from the Rule of Law.[62]

[55] See V. Aubert, 'Competition and Dissensus: Two Types of Conflict and Conflict Resolution' (1963) *J Conflict Res* 26.

[56] M. Horwitz, *The Transformation of American Law 1780–1860* (1977).

[57] R. Unger, *Law in Modern Society* (1976).

[58] *Whigs and Hunters: The Origin of the Black Act* (1975).

[59] Ibid., 23.

[60] Ibid., 266.

[61] Horwitz, n. 3 above. Like Horwitz, Unger (above, n. 57) sees general rules as crystallizing and legitimizing the power of the ruling class, yet giving a false appearance of neutrality.

[62] This has been the Chinese government's understanding of the Rule of Law. See further, B. Tamanaha, *On the Rule of Law: History, Politics, Theory* (2004), p. 92.

Surely Thompson is right that the Rule of Law does impose 'effective inhibitions upon power' and the defence of the citizen from power's 'all-intrusive claims'. The Rule of Law is not a principle of moral law, yet it is not a mere injunction to bare legality that requires only that the exercise of power requires a lawful source. The Rule of Law is a principle of institutional morality. As such it guides all forms both of law enforcement and of law making. In particular, it suggests that legal certainty and procedural protections are, if not 'unqualified human goods' as suggested by Thompson, then at least fundamental requirements of democratic constitutionalism. Nor are all its virtues simply formal. It encourages accountability, efficiency, fairness and respect for human dignity.

In a country like the UK that does not have a written constitution, the Rule of Law serves as a principle that constrains governmental power. We return now to Dicey's contention that the Rule of Law stands together with parliamentary sovereignty as a constitutional principle. Although many of Dicey's notions may have delayed the development in this country of a coherent public law, his genius was to recognize that our constitution does contain unwritten implied principles. The principle of Parliamentary sovereignty, together with what he called conventions, *enables* powers to be exercised by government and specifies how it is to exercised. The Rule of Law however *disables* government from abusing its power.

In countries with written constitutions the text itself provides the enabling features (such as who may vote and the composition of the executive and legislature). It also normally provides the disabling features through a Bill of Rights that constrains government, even elected parliaments, from interfering with certain fundamental rights and freedoms (such as freedom of expression and association) which are considered necessary and integral to democracy. In Britain, the Rule of Law as an unwritten principle performs a similar disabling function, but only in the area where its values apply. It is by no means the only principle constraining the 'all-intrusive claims' of a sovereign Parliament

THE PRACTICAL IMPLEMENTATION OF THE RULE OF LAW

How does the Rule of Law operate in practice in the UK? Let us first note that our courts have not yet, outside of directly effective European Community law, felt themselves able to disapply primary legislation that offends the Rule of Law.[63] However, since 1998 the Human Rights Act incorporates into domestic law most of the provisions of the European Convention on Human Rights, some of which contain values that inhere in the Rule of Law (such as the prohibition against retroactive laws, and the requirement of a fair trial). All decisions of public officials, including the courts, must now conform with Convention rights. Parliament's statutes may be reviewed by the courts for compatibility with Convention rights, but the courts may not, under the Act, strike down statutes that offend the Convention; it may only declare them incompatible with Convention rights.

However, the absence of judicial authority to disapply primary legislation that is contrary to the Rule of Law does not mean that the Rule of Law has no influence on the content of legislation. As a constitutional principle, the Rule of Law serves as a basis for the evaluation of all laws and provides a critical focus for public debate. There have been a number of occasions in recent years where proposals to evade the Rule of Law (for example, by prohibiting judicial review of decisions about asylum or immigration) were abandoned, in the face of

63 But see the account of *Jackson*, below, p. 23.

strong opposition on the ground that the proposals offended the Rule of Law's moral strictures.[64]

Even before the Human Rights Act came into force, the courts would seek to reconcile the principles of Parliamentary sovereignty and the Rule of Law where possible. For example, in the case of *Pierson*,[65] it was held that, despite the fact that the Home Secretary had very broad discretionary power to set a prisoner's tariff (the minimum sentence prior to parole), the decision to increase the tariff retrospectively – contrary to an earlier indication that the lesser sentence would be imposed – offended the Rule of Law in its substantive sense. Lord Steyn in that case said:

> Parliament does not legislate in a vacuum. Parliament legislates for a European liberal democracy based upon the traditions of the common law . . . and . . . unless there is the clearest provision to the contrary, Parliament must be presumed not to legislate contrary to the Rule of Law.[66]

This presumption in favour of the Rule of Law (and other fundamental constitutional principles, such as freedom of expression) was later called the 'principle of legality', described by Lord Hoffmann as follows:

> Parliamentary sovereignty means that Parliament can, if it chooses, legislate contrary to fundamental principles of human rights. . . . But the principle of legality means that Parliament must squarely confront what it is doing and accept the political cost. Fundamental rights cannot be overridden by general or ambiguous words. This is because there is too great a risk that the full implications of their unqualified meaning may have passed unnoticed in the democratic process. In the absence of express language or necessary implication to the contrary, the courts therefore presume that even the most general words were intended to be subject to the basic rights of the individual. In this way the courts of the United Kingdom, though acknowledging the sovereignty of Parliament, apply principles of constitutionality little different from those which exist in countries where the power of the legislature is expressly limited by a constitutional document.[67]

The practical implementation of the Rule of Law has taken place primarily through judicial review of the actions of public officials. During the first half of the twentieth century, a time of reaction to Dicey's Rule of Law, the courts rarely interfered with the exercise of discretionary powers.[68] From that time on, however, they began to require that power be exercised in accordance with three 'grounds' of judicial review, each of them resting in large part on the Rule of Law.

The first ground, 'legality', requires officials to act within the scope of their lawful powers. The courts ensure that the official decisions do not stray beyond the 'four corners' of a statute by failing to take into account 'relevant' considerations (that is, considerations that the law requires), or by taking into account 'irrelevant' considerations (that is, considerations

64 See the account by R. Rawlings, 'Review. Revenge and Retreat' [2005] *MLR* 378; and A. le Sueur, 'Three Strikes and You're Out? The UK Government's Strategy to Oust Judicial Review from Immigration and Asylum' [2004] *Public Law 225*. In December 2006 the Attorney-General suspended an investigation of corruption in relation to a foreign arms contract. He announced that in this case the Rule of Law had to be sacrificed to national security as the government concerned was threatening to withdraw co-operation in the surveillance of terrorist operations. Whether the Rule of Law should be sacrificed in such situations is the subject of a lively debate at the time of this book going to press and the decision is apparently being challenged by way of judicial review.

65 *R. v. Secretary of State for the Home Departmen ex parte Pierson* [1998] AC 539.

66 Ibid., 575.

67 *R. v. Secretary of State for the Home Department ex parte Simms* [2003] 2 AC 115 at 131.

68 For an account of this history see J. Jowell, 'Administrative Law', and R. Stevens, 'Government and the Judiciary' in V. Bognador (ed.), *The British Constitution in the Twentieth Century* (2003).

outside the object and purpose that Parliament intended the statute to pursue).[69] This exercise is a clear instance of the implementation of the Rule of Law, whereby the courts act as guardians of Parliament's intent and purpose. The definition of the purpose of a given statute is no mere mechanical exercise, and is often complicated by the fact that the statute confers very wide discretionary powers on the decision-maker, for example to act 'as he sees fit'. For example, where a statute conferred broad powers upon a local authority to sell its own dwellings to their inhabitants, and where some local councillors decided to sell those dwellings for the cynical purpose of securing electoral advantage for their party, the courts had to grapple with the question whether the councillors were entitled, as elected politicians, to assist their party to win the next election. The House of Lords held that statutory powers are conferred on trust, and not absolutely, and that the motive of the councillors – party gain – was extraneous to the purpose for which the powers were conferred.[70]

Although there are a number of administrative tasks that cannot be pre-determined by any rule, the courts have reconciled Dicey's fear of any discretion with a view that no discretion is wholly unfettered. As was said in a leading case on the issue of 'legality', even if a discretion were expressly defined as 'unfettered',

> The use of that adjective, . . . can do nothing to unfetter the control which the judiciary have over the executive, namely that in exercising their powers the latter must act lawfully and that is a matter to be determined by looking at the Act and its scope and object in conferring a discretion upon the Minister rather than by the use of adjectives.[71]

The second ground of review, that of 'procedural propriety', requires decision-makers to be unbiased and to grant a fair hearing to claimants before depriving them of a right or significant interest (such as an interest in livelihood or reputation). We have seen that the right of due process – the right not to be condemned unheard – is a central value of the Rule of Law, which the courts presume Parliament to respect. The courts have affirmed the principle of procedural fairness, even where the statute conferring the power to decide was silent on the matter. In the nineteenth century the courts were not slow to allow the 'justice of the common law' to supplement the legislature's omission, looking back to the Garden of Eden as an example of a fair hearing being granted before Adam and Eve were deported from their green and pleasant land.[72] In the first half of the twentieth century the courts were more reluctant to grant hearings, restricting them to matters where rights were in issue (rather than privileges). The case of *Ridge* v. *Baldwin*[73] then extended the hearing to the protections of more important interests, such as reputation or livelihood.

This kind of procedural protection, whether established by statute or the common law, is a concrete expression of the Rule of Law. Its content is variable, depending on the issue. However, as was recently said:

> The Rule of Law rightly requires that certain decisions, of which the paradigm examples are findings of breaches of the criminal law and adjudication as to private rights, should be entrusted to the judicial branch of government.[74]

69 E.g. *Padfield* v. *Minister of Agriculture, Fisheries and Food* [1968] AC 997.

70 *Magill* v. *Porter* [2001] UKHL 67.

71 Per Lord Upjohn in *Padfield v Minister of Agriculture, Fisheries and Food* [1968] AC 997.

72 *Cooper* v. *Wandsworth Board of Works* (1863) 14 CB (NS) 180.

73 [1964] AC 40.

74 *Alconbury Developments Ltd.* v. *Secretary of State for the Environment, Transport and the Regions* [2001] UKHL 23, at [42], per Lord Hoffmann. See also *Runa Begum* v. *Tower Hamlets LBC* [2003] UKHL 5 at [4].

Over the past few years, the courts have extended the requirement of a fair hearing even where the claimant does not possess a threatened criminal or private right or even an important interest. A hearing will be required where a 'legitimate expectation' has been induced by the decision-maker.[75] In such a case the claimant has, expressly or impliedly, been promised either a hearing or the continuation of a benefit. The courts will not sanction the disappointment of such an expectation unless the claimant is permitted to make representations on the matter. The notion of the legitimate expectation is itself rooted in that aspect of the Rule of Law which requires legal certainty.

The third ground of judicial review, 'irrationality' or 'unreasonableness', also applies aspects of the Rule of Law. Suppose the police charge only bearded drivers, or drivers of a particular race, with traffic offences? Suppose an education authority chose to dismiss all teachers with red hair? Suppose a prison officer refused to permit a prisoner to communicate with his lawyer? Suppose a minister raised the minimum sentence of a prisoner, having earlier told him that the sentence would be set at a lower level? Would these decisions offend the Rule of Law? If so, the Rule of Law becomes a substantive doctrine and not merely formal or procedural. Our courts, through judicial review, tread warily in this area, interfering only if, on the authority of the *Wednesbury* case,[76] the decision was beyond the range of reasonable responses. However, where the Rule of Law or other constitutional principles are in issue, the courts scrutinize the decision with greater care[77] and also adopt the 'principle of legality' that we have seen above, which presumes that Parliament intends the Rule of Law to prevail.

In practice, many of the decisions held unreasonable are so held because they offend the values of the Rule of Law discussed above. The concept of 'unreasonableness', or 'irrationality', in itself imputes the arbitrariness that Dicey considered was the antithesis of the Rule of Law. Decisions based upon insufficient evidentiary basis,[78] or which are inconsistent,[79] fall foul of the Rule of Law's values. Where byelaws are not sufficiently clear they have been held unlawful for 'uncertainty'.[80] Dicey's abhorrence of arbitrary decisions is also endorsed when a decision is struck down because it is simply unresonably harsh or oppressive.[81]

The practical implementation of the Rule of Law over the years makes it clear that its substantive aims underlie and endorse the striking down of a number of decisions, albeit often without mentioning its name. A local authority which withdrew the licence of a rugby club whose members had visited South Africa during the apartheid regime fell foul of the Rule of Law on the ground that there should be no punishment where there was no law (since sporting contacts with South Africa were not then prohibited).[82] A minister's rules allowing a prison governor to prevent a prisoner corresponding with his lawyer, even when no litigation was contemplated, was held to violate the prisoner's 'constitutional right' of access to

75 Endorsed in the House of Lords in *Council of Civil Service Unions* v. *Minister of the Civil Service* [1985] AC 374.

76 *Associated Provincial Picture Houses* v. *Wednesbury Corpn* [1948] 1 KB 223.

77 Under the Human Rights Act, applying the European Convention on Human Rights, the courts will adopt the even stricter scrutiny under the test of 'proportionality'. See Chapter 3 below.

78 *E* v. *Secretary of State for the Home Department* [2004] EWCA Civ 49.

79 See R. Clayton, 'Legitimate Expectations, Policy and the Principle of Consistency' [2003] *CLJ* 93. See *R (Rashid)* v. *Secretary of State for the Home Department* [2005] EWCA Civ 744.

80 *Percy* v. *Hall* [1997] QB 924. And see *R (L)* v. *Secretary of State for the Home Department* [2003] EWCA Civ 25 ('Legal certainty is an aspect of the rule of law' at [25]).

81 See eg. *Wheeler* v. *Leicester City Council* [1985] AC 1054 (HL).

82 Ibid.

justice.[83] Access to Justice as a value of the Rule of Law (and considered a 'prior order' right) was again held to have been violated by the Lord Chancellor's imposition of substantial court fees which an impecunious litigant was unable to afford.[84]

The legitimate expectation, which began by grounding a procedural right to a fair hearing,[85] has since been extended to a substantive doctrine, grounding a right not merely to a fair hearing but to the promised benefit itself. For example, a local authority that promised the claimants a 'home for life' in an institution for the chronically ill, was not permitted to disappoint the resultant legitimate expectation.[86]

The remarkable elasticity of the Rule of Law, and the richness of its underlying values, was demonstrated in a case that concerned the legal effect of a decision that had not been communicated to the person affected. The relevant legislation permitted asylum seekers' right to income support to be terminated once their application for asylum had been refused by a 'determination' of the Home Secretary. The refusal in this case was recorded only in an internal file note in the Home Office and communicated to the Benefits Agency, which promptly denied the appellant future income support. The determination was not, however, communicated to the appellant.[87]

The appellant in this case could not easily invoke the normal requirements of the Rule of Law in her favour. The decision did not take effect retrospectively; ignorance of the law does not normally excuse its application, and the doctrine of prior notice normally applies only to permit the appellant to make representations on the case to the primary decision-maker (here the Home Secretary). Nevertheless, the House of Lords, by majority, held that the decision violated 'the constitutional principle requiring the Rule of Law to be observed'.[88] Lord Steyn, with whom the majority of their Lordships concurred, based his argument both upon legal certainty ('surprise is the enemy of justice') and upon accountability: the individual must be informed of the outcome of her case so 'she can decide what to do' and 'be in a position to challenge the decision in the courts' (this being an aspect of the principle of the right of access to justice).[89] The House of Lords had no truck with the notion that the Home Secretary's determination had formally and strictly been made. This was 'legalism and conceptualism run riot', which is reminiscent of the state described by Kafka 'where the rights of an individual are overridden by hole in the corner decisions or knocks on the doors in the early hours'.[90]

The Rule of Law does, therefore, possess substantive content.[91] It always has. Its promotion of the core institutional values of legality, certainty, consistency, due process and access to justice do not merely, as Jennings would have it, further the aims of free trade and the market economy. They also promote respect for the dignity of the individual and enhance democratic accountability. The Rule of Law thus advances substantive as well as formal goals.[92]

[83] *R.* v. *Secretary of State for the Home Department ex parte Leech (No. 2)* [1994] QB 198.

[84] *R.* v. *Lord Chancellor ex parte Witham* [1997] 1 WLR 104. [85] See n. 75, above.

[86] *R.* v. *North and East Devon Health Authority ex parte Coughlan* [2001] QB 213.

[87] *R. (on the application of Anufrijeva)* v. *Secretary of State for the Home Department* [2003] 3 WLR 252.

[88] *Per* Lord Steyn at para. 28. [89] *Per* Lord Steyn at paras 26 and 31.

[90] *Per* Lord Steyn at paras 32 and 28. See also *FP (Iran) v Secretary of State for the Home Department*, where Arden LJ invoked the Rule of Law to safeguard access to a tribunal – a right which 'cannot be taken away before it has been communicated to the person entitled to it'. At para. 61.

[91] This passage was cited with approval by Lord Steyn in *R.* v. *Secretary of State for the Home Department ex parte Pierson* [1998] AC 539 (HL).

[92] See Rawls, *A Theory of Justice* 235–43 and cf. Joseph Raz's view of the Rule of Law as a negative value in 'The Rule of Law and its Virtue' (1977) *LQR* 195–211. See also J. Raz, *Ethics in the Public Domain* (1994) ch. 16. See also J. Finnis, *Natural Law and Natural Rights* (1980) 270–6.

As a principle rather than a specific rule, the Rule of Law is elaborated in the light of the practical reason of each generation and the developing imperatives of contemporary democracy.[93]

THE SCOPE AND STATUS OF THE RULE OF LAW

The scope of the Rule of Law is broad,[94] but not broad enough to serve as a principle upholding a number of other requirements of a democracy. It does not, for example, address the full range of freedoms protected by bills of rights in other countries or in international instruments of human rights, or those now protected by our recently enacted Human Rights Act 1998, as set out in the European Convention on Human Rights (such as the right not to suffer torture, or the right to freedom of expression or rights of privacy or sexual freedom).

THE RULE OF LAW AND EQUALITY

One lively question is the extent to which the Rule of Law contains the principle of equality. We have seen that Dicey considered that the Rule of Law required all officials, from the Prime Minister down to a constable or a collector of taxes, to be subject to the same responsibility for every act done without legal justification as any other citizen.[95] Dicey is here claiming for the Rule of Law what has been called formal equality, by which he meant that no person is exempt from the enforcement of the law; rich and poor, revenue official and individual taxpayer are all within the equal reach of the arm of law's implementation.

This type of equality, although sometimes derided,[96] is important. It is inherent in the very notion of law, and in the integrity of law's application that like cases be treated alike over time. Its reach however is limited because its primary concern is not with the content of the law but with its *enforcement* and *application* alone. So long as laws are applied equally, that is without irrational bias or distinction, then formal equality is complied with. Formal equality does not however prohibit *unequal laws*. It forbids, say, racially biased enforcement of the law, but does not forbid racially discriminatory laws from being enacted. For Dicey, the Rule of Law embraced only formal equality. This is because for him the role of equality in the Rule of Law was instrumental; to buttress the central value of certainty. It was not espoused as a virtue for its own sake. We have seen how Dicey's supporters freely acknowledged that it is more important that the law be certain than it be not 'harsh', 'bad', or 'unjust'.[97] Discriminatory or arbitrary enforcement of the law would violate legal certainty, but laws themselves that discriminated against certain groups or classes, but were uniformly enforced within the groups or class, would not violate legal certainty, or therefore the Rule of Law.

[93] See D. N. McCormick, 'Jurisprudence and the Constitution' (1983) *Current Legal Problems* 13. See also Allan, n. 1 above, and Craig, and Barber, n. 31 above.

[94] See e.g. Lord Steyn in *R.* v. *Home Secretary ex parte Venables* [1988] AC 407 at 526, who states that it would be 'an abdication of the Rule of Law' for the Home Secretary, in sentencing the children, to have regard to views expressed in a campaign by a popular newspaper.

[95] Dicey, op. cit., 193 n. 1 above.

[96] See Horwitz, n. 3 above.

[97] See Maitland and Hayek, nn. 35 and 36 above.

There are two opposing views as to whether substantive equality qualifies as a feature of the Rule of Law.[98] Those who believe that discriminatory laws are not 'law' would of course not permit them to qualify as fulfilling the Rule of Law.[99] On the other hand, as Lord Hoffmann has said equality is in itself 'one of the building blocks of democracy'.[100] It is therefore not necessary to subsume substantive equality within the Rule of Law in order to demonstrate that discriminatory laws violate one of the fundamental requirements of democratic constitutionalism.[101]

THE RULE OF LAW AND PARLIAMENTARY SOVEREIGNTY

What about the Rule of Law's status in relation to the sovereignty of Parliament? In the UK the principle of Parliamentary sovereignty has always been able to override the Rule of Law; not on the authority of any written constitution, but on the authority of commentators such as Dicey and repeated assertions by the courts over time. In the absence of any formal constitutional source, is it theoretically open to the Rule of Law to replace the sovereignty of Parliament as our primary constitutional principle? This issue was raised in a most unlikely case involving a challenge to the Hunting Act 2004, which banned the hunting of most wild mammals with dogs.[102] The central issue in the case was the validity of the Parliament Acts, which were invoked to ensure the passage of the Bill without the approval of the House of Lords. The Parliament Acts were upheld, as was the Hunting Act 2004, but three significant *obiter dicta* questioned the relation of Parliamentary sovereignty to the Rule of Law as had never been done before.

Lord Steyn said that:

> in exceptional circumstances involving an attempt to abolish judicial review or the authority of the courts, [the courts] may have to consider whether this is a constitutional fundamental which even a complaisant House of Commons cannot abolish.

Lady Hale said:

> The Courts will treat with particular suspicion (and might even reject) any attempt to subvert the rule of law by removing governmental action affecting the rights of the individual from all judicial powers.

And Lord Hope, even more forthrightly, said that 'it is no longer right to say that [Parliament's] freedom to legislate admits of no qualification' and that 'the rule of law enforced by the courts is the controlling principle upon which our constitution is based'.

It may take some time, provocative legislation and considerable judicial courage for the courts to assert the primacy of the Rule of Law over Parliamentary sovereignty, but it is no longer self-evident, or generally accepted, that a legislature in a modern democracy should be able with impunity to violate the strictures of the Rule of Law.[103]

98 Raz, n. 32 above, thinks not. Bingham, n. 4 above, thinks it does.

99 See Dworkin, n. 33 above.

100 *Matadeen* v. *Pointu and Minister of Education and Science* [1999] AC 98 (PC). See also *Ghaidan* v. *Godin Mendoza* [2004] 2 AC 557 (same-sex partner entitled to same inheritance rights as different sex partner): '[Unequal treatment] is the reverse of rational behaviour . . . Power must not be exercised arbitrarily' (per Lady Hale).

101 I have expanded on this point in 'Is Equality a Constitutional Principle?' (1994) 47 *Current Legal Problems* (Part 2) 1. See also R. Singh 'Equality: The Neglected Virtue' [2004] *EHRLR* 141. For a view that equality (both formal and substantive) is part of the Rule of Law see works by Allan, n. 1 above.

102 *Jackson* v. *Her Majesty's Attorney General* [2005] UKHL 56.

103 See J. Jowell, 'Parliamentary Sovereignty under the New Constitutional Hypothesis' [2006] *PL* 562.

CONCLUSION

In 1938, the American jurist Felix Frankfurter wrote that:

> the persistence of the misdirection that Dicey has given to the development of administrative law strikingly proves the elder Huxley's observation that many a theory survives long after its brains are knocked out.[104]

Dicey's Rule of Law has indeed been damaged over the years by those who attacked it for failing to recognize that official discretion is necessary to perform the welfare and regulatory functions of modern government. It has been less affected by the additional assaults of those who doubt either the efficacy of legal techniques, or the competence of judges, to inhibit the all-inclusive claims of a sovereign Parliament (or of officials on whom Parliament has conferred wide discretionary power). Despite the limits of Dicey's conception of the Rule of Law, it compels the view that all power, however legitimately gained, needs, in a democracy worthy of its name, to be exercised in a manner that is constrained by its underlying values.

Perhaps the most enduring contribution of our common law has been the elaboration of the content of the Rule of Law by means of judicial review. The Rule of Law thus rises, time and again, to defeat the designs of the executive and other officials who step outside their conferred powers or who act unreasonably or unfairly. Twentieth century tyrannies were marked by their failure to observe the Rule of Law. Many of them claimed legitimacy for their oppressive actions from the fact of majority support. Britain, like so many countries in this new century, is moving steadily to a model of democracy that limits governmental power in certain areas, even where the majority may prefer otherwise. The Rule of Law supplies the foundation of that new model. It is a principle that requires feasible limits on official power so as to constrain abuses which occur even in the most well-intentioned and compassionate of governments. It may not be sufficiently elastic to contain all the necessary requirements of a rights-based democracy; there is a range of coercive state action that it is unable to withstand without being buttressed by other constitutional principles. Nevertheless, it has displayed enduring qualities – both formal and substantive – that have over the years demonstrated that the Rule of Law is a fundamental and constituent feature of any true constitutional democracy, irrespective of whether its constitution is written or unwritten.

FURTHER READING

Allan, T. R. S. *Constitutional Justice: A Liberal Theory of the Rule of Law* (2001).

Craig, P. 'Formal and Substantive Conceptions of the Rule of Law: An Analytical Framework' [1997] *Public Law* 447.

Raz J. 'The Rule of Law and its Virtue' (1977) 93 *LQR* 195.

Dworkin, R. 'Political Judges and the Rule of Law', in his *A Matter of Principle* (1985), ch. 1.

Lord Bingham 'The Rule of Law' Sir David Williams Lecture (Cambridge, Dec. 2006).

104 F. Frankfurter, Foreword to 'Discussion of Current Developments in Administrative Law' (1938) 47 *Yale LJ* 515 at 517.

2

THE SOVEREIGNTY OF PARLIAMENT – FORM OR SUBSTANCE?

Anthony Bradley

SUMMARY

As the primary forum for political debate and because of its role as a legislature, the Westminster Parliament occupies a central place in both the legal and the political constitutions. It is regarded as a fundamental constitutional rule that there are no legal limits upon Westminster's legislative powers, and that the courts may not question or review the validity of legislation. The authority of Parliament includes the power to make constitutional changes by ordinary process of legislation, unlike the specific amendment procedures that apply to most written constitutions. But does this authority extend to the principles governing the relationship between the courts and Parliament that lie at the heart of the 'Rule of Law'? It has long been asserted that Parliament may not 'bind its successors' and thus may not create limitations on its own powers. However, so long as the UK remains a member of the European Union, Westminster's authority is limited by Community law and the courts must disapply UK legislation if it conflicts with Community law. Different questions are raised by the creation of the Scottish Parliament with its own law-making powers, which as a matter of political practice affects the authority of Westminster to legislate for Scotland. The Human Rights Act 1998 maintains legislative sovereignty as a matter of form, but it authorizes the superior courts to declare that legislation by Parliament is incompatible with the European Convention on Human Rights. Against this background of constitutional change, the extent of which largely depends on the response of the courts to the changes initiated by Parliament, it must be asked whether the reasons for stressing the 'sovereign' authority of Westminster go to matters of form rather than to the substance of legislative power. A further question is whether the democratic process in the UK works so perfectly as to justify the absence of any limit upon the authority of Parliament to legislate.

INTRODUCTION

Analysis of 'the British constitution' is bound to be influenced by the perspective of the analyst. Within a democracy, the worlds of government, law and politics necessarily coexist. A legal analysis will examine the extent to which rules of law penetrate government and politics and will emphasize the legal framework by which the state is organized. A political analysis will concentrate on the way in which political power is exercised, on how leaders emerge, on the organization of parties, on the conduct of elections, and on the way in which democracy determines the choice of a government and influences the way in which government exercises its powers.[1]

Both legal and political analyses must deal with the place of Parliament in the state. From a political perspective, Parliament is the forum where political leadership is given public exposure, the contest between the parties is fought out between general elections, public opinion is expressed, social and economic questions are debated, new laws approved, and the government called to account. From a legal perspective, Parliament underpins the entire legal system and machinery of justice (by authorizing and funding the existence of courts and tribunals, the judiciary, legal aid, and so on), and meets the need for legislation that exists in every contemporary legal system. Politicians are often interested in the process of legislation (for instance, in securing maximum advantage from supporting or opposing Bills as they go through Parliament), whereas lawyers must be concerned with the outcome of that process. What new laws are enacted is decided in a democracy by the political process, not by the inclinations of the judges.[2] In fact, the work of the courts influences the content of legislation; by deciding how the law applies in specific situations, the judges may demonstrate the need for legislative reform.

From both legal and political perspectives, Parliament has a central role amongst the institutions of the state, even if it often appears to have a merely instrumental role in giving effect to executive decisions taken outside Parliament. The phrase 'sovereignty of Parliament' is imprecise, but it does not mean the sovereignty of the House of Commons. From a political perspective, the House of Commons expresses the democratic ideal: only to that House do elected representatives come from every part of the UK; only does that House have the power, by withdrawing its confidence from the government, to require there to be a change in government or the holding of a general election. The personal authority of the Speaker of the Commons symbolizes the legitimacy inherent in the people's choice of their representatives. But, although the House of Commons is the dominant House in Parliament, the general rule is that legislation must be approved by both the Commons and the House of Lords. Even though the House of Lords continues

[1] In making this comparison, Neil MacCormick has said that 'politics is essentially concerned with the power of decision making in human communities on matters of communal interest or importance, with competition for that power, and with its exercise. As for law, the essence is not power but normative order. . . . Law is about institutional normative relations between normatively recognised persons of all sorts'. N. MacCormick, 'Beyond the Sovereign State' (1993) 56 *MLR* 1, 11.

[2] Until the new Supreme Court for the UK is created under the Constitutional Reform Act 2005, the 'Law Lords' (the Lords of Appeal in Ordinary) continue to sit in the House of Lords but play a very limited part in legislative work. See Report of the Royal Commission on the future of the House of Lords, *A House for the Future*, Cm 4534 (2000), ch. 9; and HL Debs, 22 June 2000, col. 419 (statement by Lord Bingham, the senior Lord of Appeal in Ordinary).

not to be democratically elected, the sovereignty of Parliament is better than the sovereignty of a hereditary monarch or of a modern state executive. Moreover, the authority of Parliament as the national legislature parallels the authority of the UK as a state in international law.[3]

This chapter examines the meaning that the doctrine of the sovereignty of Parliament has for the constitutional lawyer, but (it is hoped) without forgetting the political significance of the authority of Parliament.

THE LEGAL DOCTRINE OF LEGISLATIVE SOVEREIGNTY

From the perspective of law, the sovereignty or supremacy of Parliament forms one of the pillars vital to the structure of the entire legal system. As Lord Bridge said in 1991,

> In our society the Rule of Law rests upon twin foundations: the sovereignty of the Queen in Parliament in making the law and the sovereignty of the Queen's courts in interpreting and applying the law.[4]

As the twin foundations of the legal system, the two 'sovereignties' exercise related but distinct functions: on the one hand, law making; on the other, interpreting and applying the law. Plainly both courts and legislature must coexist, whatever the dividing line between their respective functions. Lord Cooke of Thorndon, when President of the New Zealand Court of Appeal, observed that the modern common law should be 'built on two complementary and lawfully unalterable principles: the operation of a democratic legislature and the operation of independent courts'.[5] Sir Stephen Sedley, a senior English judge, has written of 'a new and still emerging constitutional paradigm, . . . of a bi-polar sovereignty of the Crown in Parliament and the Crown in its courts, to each of which the Crown's ministers are answerable – politically to Parliament, legally to the courts'.[6] Such an approach inevitably raises questions as to the respective boundaries of the legislature and the courts, questions as to whether these two institutions neatly complement each other or whether there is scope for competition or rivalry between them – and, if there is a dispute or disagreement between them, which of the two should have the last word.

In the interests of legal certainty, most complex legal systems observe a 'hierarchy of norms', since not all laws have the same inherent authority and in case of conflict a law, or norm, that is superior in the hierarchy prevails over one with lesser authority. In UK law, the authority of the laws made by Parliament serves in one sense as the yardstick by which the validity of other laws are assessed. In general, a clear provision in an Act of Parliament prevails over rules contained in subordinate legislation, or over rules of the common law. When in 1968 Ungoed-Thomas J was asked to set aside a provision in income tax legislation on the

[3] There is a compelling argument that legal and political analysis alike must consider whether political organization, at least in the European Union, has moved beyond the notion of the 'sovereign state': see MacCormick, op. cit., and C. M. G. Himsworth, 'In a State no longer: the End of Constitutionalism' [1996] *Public Law* 639.

[4] *X* v. *Morgan-Grampian (Publishers) Ltd.* [1991] 1 AC 1, 48.

[5] 'Fundamentals' (1988) *NZLJ* 158, 164.

[6] S. Sedley, 'Human Rights: a Twenty-First Century Agenda' [1995] *Public Law* 386, 389.

ground that it was contrary to international law, he said:

What the statute itself enacts cannot be unlawful, because what the statute says and provides is itself the law, and *the highest form of law that is known to this country*. It is the law which prevails over every other form of law.[7]

In view of the date of this judgment, we may note that for several reasons a statement about the authority of statute law in precisely these words would be unlikely today. One reason is the overriding effect that the courts now ascribe to European Community law (as we shall see later). Another reason is the awareness of international human rights law that has developed since 1968.[8] Moreover, as regards the judge's statement that 'what the statute says and provides *is itself the law*', it is fundamental to the Rule of Law that the meaning of a statute and its application to particular circumstances are matters for the courts to determine. Although the courts today, when a statutory provision is ambiguous, are prepared to look in Hansard at ministerial statements made in Parliament about the intended meaning,[9] an authoritative ruling on the effect of a statute comes only from a judicial decision.

THE ESSENCE OF PARLIAMENTARY SOVEREIGNTY AS A LEGAL DOCTRINE

Nevertheless, not only since the publication in 1885 of A. V. Dicey's *The Law of the Constitution* but also long before this,[10] the sovereignty of Parliament has been accepted as one of the fundamental doctrines of constitutional law in the UK. In 1689, after the overthrow of James II but before the union of the English and Scottish Parliaments in 1707, the Earl of Shaftesbury wrote:

The Parliament of England is that supreme and absolute power, which gives life and motion to the English Government.[11]

The significance of Dicey's analysis is that, despite the extensive political and social changes that have occurred since 1885, and despite criticism which his work received from constitutional lawyers such as Sir Ivor Jennings,[12] his statement of the doctrine has retained a remarkable influence on both legal and political thinking about Parliament. Dicey summarized his views in this way:

The principle of Parliamentary sovereignty means neither more nor less than this, namely, that Parliament [defined as the Queen, the House of Lords, and the House of Commons, acting together] . . . has, under the English constitution, the right to make or unmake any law whatever; and, further, that no person or body is recognised by the law as having a right to override or set aside the legislation of Parliament.[13]

[7] *Cheney* v. *Conn* [1968] 1 All ER 779, 782 (emphasis supplied).

[8] See below and Chapters 5 and 6.

[9] *Pepper* v. *Hart* [1993] AC 593. See also *R.* v. *Secretary of State for the Environment, ex parte Spath Holme Ltd* [2001] 2 AC 349 and J. Steyn, 'Pepper v. Hart: a Re-examination' (2001) 21 *Ox J Legal Studies* 59.

[10] See J. Goldsworthy, *The Sovereignty of Parliament: History and Philosophy* (1999), arguing with much illustrative material that Dicey's analysis of the sovereignty of Parliament was in essence the restatement of a central theme in English legal history.

[11] *Some Observations Concerning the Regulating of Elections for Parliament* (1689), quoted ibid., 150.

[12] See I. Jennings, *The Law and the Constitution* (5th edn, 1959).

[13] Dicey, *Law of the Constitution* (10th edn, 1959, by E. C. S. Wade) 39–40.

The principle, 'looked at from its positive side', ensures that any new Act of Parliament will be obeyed by the courts. The same principle, 'looked at from its negative side', ensures that there is no person or body of persons who can make rules which override or derogate from an Act of Parliament or which, 'to express the same thing in other words',[14] will be enforced by the courts in contravention of an Act of Parliament.

A further implication drawn from the sovereignty of Parliament is that a sovereign Parliament is not bound by the Acts of its predecessors, and thus no Parliament can bind its successors. This facet of sovereignty has arisen in part because the courts, when faced with two conflicting statutes on the same subject, have applied the rule that the later Act of Parliament prevails. By the doctrine of implied repeal, the later Act repeals the earlier Act to the extent that the later Act is inconsistent with provisions in the earlier Act.[15] This doctrine has been pressed into service to sustain the proposition that the one rule of the common law that Parliament may not change is the rule that the courts must always apply the latest Act of Parliament on a subject.[16] But this view ought not to be taken as axiomatic and a contrary view is examined below.

THE SOURCE OF LEGISLATIVE SOVEREIGNTY

Discussion of the source of legislative sovereignty necessarily raises fundamental questions about the relationship between courts and Parliament and the source of that relationship.[17] It would be attractive if we could identify the legal source of the doctrine of sovereignty, but this is not an easy task. Could the source of the sovereignty of Parliament be found in an Act of Parliament itself? A well-known, but possibly over-simple, answer to this question was given by the jurist, Sir John Salmond:

> No statute can confer this power on Parliament for this would be to assume and act on the very power that is to be conferred.[18]

But Parliament might be entitled to make such an assumption if over many years it had enacted a wide variety of statutes without its authority to legislate being questioned. Indeed, this leads directly to the next question, whether the legal source of authority for the doctrine of sovereignty may be found in decisions of the courts. Decisions of the courts are authoritative in determining the common law. Thus the sovereignty of Parliament can be said to be based upon decisions of the courts in applying Acts of Parliament, since, if the courts apply Acts of Parliament and say that they must do so because they are bound by *all* such Acts, then the courts are declaring a fundamental rule, namely that effect must be given to Acts of Parliament, whatever their content.

A third and intermediate possibility, rather than attributing the source of legislative sovereignty to Parliament or to the courts acting separately, is to examine the past and present relationship between the courts, the legislature, and other holders of office in the

[14] Ibid.

[15] See *Ellen Street Estates Ltd* v. *Minister of Health* [1934] 1 KB 590; and the text at n. 73 below.

[16] H. W. R. Wade, 'The Basis of Legal Sovereignty' [1955] *Cambridge LJ* 172, 186–9.

[17] 'Traditionally, English lawyers have not worried about the problem of first causes; for them it is enough that authority can be found in Acts of Parliament *and* decisions of the courts': R. Q. Quentin-Baxter (1985) 15 *Victoria University of Wellington LR* 12, 13.

[18] Salmond, *Jurisprudence* (7th edn, 1924) 170; and see Wade, n. 16 above, at 187.

state, looking at what the courts and the legislature have done in relation to each other, and also at the stance of other key actors in the political system (such as ministers of the Crown).[19] Such an explanation looks at past institutional behaviour and assumes that this can be expected to continue. However, if the rule of legislative sovereignty came about from a historical process, rather than as a result of a 'big bang' creation of a fundamental rule, can we be certain that this area of constitutional evolution has come to a full stop? On this basis, changes in the relationship may occur over time. Indeed, such changes may happen more rapidly where the incentive to change is created by an event such as a radical initiative taken by the legislature. In this situation the courts might respond to such an initiative in a manner for which there was no direct precedent, and in a manner that the new legislation might not have expressly invited.

'THE CONSTITUTION' AS THE SOURCE OF LEGISLATIVE SOVEREIGNTY?

In the passage quoted above, Dicey said that the Queen in Parliament 'has *under the English constitution* the right to make or unmake any law whatever'.[20] Where a state has a written constitution, the constitution may be regarded as the formal source from which all organs of the state, including the legislature and the courts, derive their powers as a matter of constitutional law. The United States Constitution of 1787 allocated the legislative, executive, and judicial powers of the new federal state respectively to Congress, the President, and the Supreme Court and other federal courts. Plainly the framers intended the Constitution to be binding on these federal bodies, but their text did not state whether an Act of Congress that was inconsistent with the Constitution must be applied by the Supreme Court, or whether the Court could declare the Act to be unconstitutional and thus unlawful. In the leading case of *Marbury* v. *Madison*, Chief Justice Marshall said:

> The constitution is either a superior paramount law, unchallengeable by ordinary means, or it is on a level with ordinary legislative acts, and, like other acts, is alterable when the legislature shall be pleased to alter it. If the former part of the alternative is true, then a legislative act contrary to the constitution is not law; if the latter part be true, then written constitutions are absurd attempts, on the part of the people, to limit a power in its own nature illimitable.[21]

It was, Marshall continued, 'emphatically the province and duty of the judicial department to say what the law was'. *Marbury* v. *Madison* is one of the most influential constitutional decisions of English-speaking courts in the last 200 years.[22] Today, judicial review of legislation on constitutional grounds is practised in many countries. Where such review occurs, the legislature is not sovereign but is limited by constitutional rules that are enforced by a supreme or constitutional court.

By contrast, since the UK has no written constitution, for Dicey to refer to 'the constitution' as the source of Parliament's authority is but to create difficulty. What *is* the constitution, in the absence of a written text? One political historian has written that the

[19] See Goldsworthy, n. 10 above, ch. 11 and authorities there cited.

[20] Implications of the word 'English' in Dicey's usage are relevant to discussion of Scottish devolution below.

[21] Cranch 103, 177 (1803).

[22] Another is also a Supreme Court decision, *Brown* v. *Board of Education* 347 US 483 (1954).

constitution is a historical process, 'an integrated expression of historical experience conferring a unified meaning on political existence'.[23] A senior judge, Sir John Laws, has suggested that the absence of a written constitution 'means that the legal distribution of public power consists ultimately in a dynamic settlement, acceptable to the people, between the different arms of government'.[24] Emphasis on a dynamic historical experience is important, since the 'constitution' of the UK is today experiencing a period of change, some of it resulting from deliberate political initiative, some of it resulting from evolving relationships within the state. The substance of constitutional law reflects the evolutionary nature of the unwritten constitution. To quote Sir John Salmond again:

> The constitution as a matter of fact is logically prior to the constitution as a matter of law. In other words, constitutional practice is logically prior to constitutional law. . . . Constitutional law follows hard upon the heels of constitutional fact.[25]

Just as the UK's constitutional law after 1945 came to reflect the end of Empire, so more recently it has adjusted to events that have taken the UK into the European Union. Since 1998, the incorporation in national law of rights under the European Convention on Human Rights and the devolution of powers to Scotland and Wales are important political events to which the structure of constitutional law must also adjust.

DEMOCRATIC BASIS FOR PARLIAMENTARY SOVEREIGNTY

Dicey's belief in the legislative power of Parliament was directly related to his view of the representative character of the legislature in the 1880s.[26] Thus he wrote:

> as things now stand, the will of the electorate, and certainly of the electorate in combination with the Lords and the Crown, is sure ultimately to prevail on all subjects to be determined by the British government. . . . *The electors can in the long run always enforce their will.*[27]

Dicey considered that this expression of the democratic ideal was closely related to the sovereignty of the nation itself. However, there are many sovereign states in the world without sovereign Parliaments, and there is no necessary connection between national sovereignty and the authority of the national legislature. Nor does legislative sovereignty in itself imply any particular degree of democracy in the structure of Parliament.[28] However, if the nature of the political system in 1885 was a vital influence on Dicey's analysis of sovereignty, events since then may call for sovereignty to be reassessed in the light of the changed political process. The expansion of executive power since 1885, developments in the party system, changes in the electoral system, and the dominance of the government over the House of Commons mean today that the government can use the legislative process to carry out its policies, often without there being effective restraints or control. It would be complacent to assume that the electorate can always achieve its will, even supposing that it is possible to discover what the will of the electorate as an entity may be.

[23] M. Foley, *The Silence of Constitutions* (1989) 87.

[24] J. Laws, 'Law and Democracy' [1995] *Public Law* 72, 81.

[25] Salmond, n. 18 above, 154, 155.

[26] Dicey, *Law of the Constitution* 68.

[27] Dicey, *Law of the Constitution* 73, emphasis supplied. And cf. P. P. Craig, *Public Law and Democracy in the UK and the USA* (1990) ch. 2.

[28] Cf. Dicey, *Law of the Constitution* 70–85.

SOVEREIGNTY OF PARLIAMENT EXCLUDES JUDICIAL REVIEW

We have seen that under the sovereignty of Parliament, the courts may not review legislation with a view to deciding on its validity. As was crisply stated in 1967, 'All that a court of law can do with an Act of Parliament is to apply it'.[29] Lord Morris said in 1974,

> In the courts there may be argument as to the correct interpretation of the enactment: there must be none as to whether it should be on the statute book at all.[30]

This position is thus very different from that in those countries where the ordinary courts or a constitutional court may review the validity of legislation to see whether it conforms with the constitution. Is it possible that, in the continuing absence of a written constitution, the judges would of their own initiative begin to review legislation by Parliament, based (say) on the need to respect fundamental human rights? The practice of British judges has long been to deny that they have any such role.[31] As Willes J said in 1871,

> We sit here as servants of the Queen and the legislature. Are we to act as regents over what is done by Parliament with the consent of the Queen, lords and commons? I deny that any such authority exists.[32]

In 1872, the court said,

> There is no judicial body in the country by which the validity of an Act of Parliament can be questioned.[33]

Nevertheless, in the years before the enactment of the Human Rights Act 1998, a few judges began to warn that 'some common law rights . . . lie so deep that even Parliament could not override them'.[34] In 1995, Lord Woolf argued that both Parliament and the courts were ultimately subject to the Rule of Law and suggested that if Parliament were to embark on the unthinkable by enacting legislation that undermined in a fundamental way the Rule of Law on which the unwritten constitution depends, the courts would not necessarily be required to uphold such legislation.[35] But in decisions made shortly before the Human Rights Act 1998 came into effect, the courts emphasized the power of Parliament to infringe even fundamental rights if it makes a sufficiently clear statement of its intention to do so. Thus Laws J upheld what he described as a 'common law constitutional right' (namely the right of all persons to have access to a court) in striking down the validity of regulations made by the Lord Chancellor prescribing court fees that had to be paid by every litigant; the basis of the decision was that Parliament had neither expressly nor by necessary implication authorized the effect of the regulations.[36] Adopting a similar approach, the House of Lords observed that there is a constitutional principle of legality in the light of which all legislation must be interpreted. While accepting that Parliament 'can, if it chooses, legislate contrary to

29 D. L. Keir and F. H. Lawson, *Cases in Constitutional Law* (5th edn, 1967) 1.

30 *Pickin* v. *British Railways Board* [1974] AC 765, 789.

31 Goldsworthy, *The Sovereignty of Parliament* passim.

32 *Lee* v. *Bude and Torrington Railway Co.* (1871) LR 6 CP 577, 582.

33 *Ex parte Selwyn* (1872) 36 JP 54.

34 *Taylor* v. *New Zealand Poultry Board* [1984] 1 NZLR 394, 398 (Sir Robin Cooke).

35 Lord Woolf, 'Droit Public – English Style' [1995] *Public Law* 57, 67–9. See also Woolf (1998) *LQR* 579; J. Laws [1995] *Public Law* 72; and S. Sedley [1995] *Public Law* 386.

36 *R.* v. *Lord Chancellor, ex parte Witham* [1998] QB 575. Other public law decisions in which Laws LJ has taken part include *R. (Bancoult)* v. *Secretary of State for Foreign and Commonwealth Affairs* [2001] QB 1067 and *Thoburn* v. *Sunderland City Council* [2002] EWHC 195 (Admin); [2003] QB 151.

fundamental principles of human rights', Lord Hoffmann observed that the constraints on the exercise by Parliament of this power 'are ultimately political, not legal. But the principle of legality means that Parliament must squarely confront what it is doing and accept the political cost'.[37] In the same case, Lord Steyn described the general principle of legality as 'a presumption of general application operating as a constitutional principle'.[38]

We will examine below what the effect of the Human Rights Act 1998 has been on these basic propositions. For the moment, it is enough to note that the Act appears to have taken away the need that had been felt by some judges to speculate on what their response might be if Parliament were to enact 'unthinkable' legislation. The fundamental question (whether a judge must in all circumstances give effect to legislation that affects fundamental rights in a manner that is morally repugnant) may however need to be answered in the future should fears of 'unthinkable' legislation re-emerge despite the Human Rights Act.

ONLY ACTS OF PARLIAMENT ARE SUPREME

The immunity of Acts of Parliament from judicial review does not extend to other documents or instruments that lack the same status in law. Measures that are in principle subject to judicial review include declarations or decisions by the Crown under prerogative power,[39] acts of subordinate legislatures within the UK,[40] and subordinate instruments made by ministers of the Crown under delegated powers.[41] Nor is a resolution of the House of Commons effective to change the law.[42] Subject now only to the Parliament Acts 1911 and 1949,[43] for a Bill to become law it must have been approved by both Houses of Parliament, and must have received the Royal Assent.[44] To decide whether these conditions are satisfied, and to avoid interfering with the internal proceedings of Parliament,[45] the courts have a limited but important function. As Lord Campbell said as long ago as 1842:

> All that the Court of Justice can do is to look to the Parliament roll: if from that it should appear that a Bill has passed both Houses and received the Royal Assent, no Court of Justice can inquire into the mode in which it was introduced into Parliament, or into what was done previous to its introduction, or what passed in Parliament during its progress in its various stages through both Houses.[46]

[37] *R* v. *Secretary of State for the Home Department, ex parte Simms* [1999] 3 All ER 400, 412. See also *R.* v. *Secretary of State for the Home Department, ex parte Pierson* [1998] AC 539. Both common law principles and the Human Rights Act 1998 were applied in *R. (Daly)* v. *Secretary of State for the Home Department* [2001] UKHL 26; [2001] 2 AC 532.

[38] *Ex parte Simms*, 411.

[39] *CCSU* v. *Minister for the Civil Service* [1985] AC 374; *R.* v. *Secretary of State for Foreign Affairs, ex parte Rees-Mogg* [1994] QB 552.

[40] See e.g. *R. (Hume et al)* v. *Londonderry Justices* [1972] NILR 91 and, under the Scotland Act 1998, *Anderson et al.* v. *Scottish Ministers* [2001] UKPC D5; [2003] 2 AC 602.

[41] *Hoffmann-La Roche & Co.* v. *Secretary of State for Trade* [1975] AC 295, 365; *R.* v. *HM Treasury, ex parte Smedley* [1985] QB 657. See also *R. (Bancoult)* v. *Secretary of State for Foreign and Commonwealth Affairs* (above, n. 36).

[42] *Bowles* v. *Bank of England* [1913] 1 Ch 57.

[43] These are discussed below at p. 39.

[44] *The Prince's case* (1606) 8 Co. Rep. 1a.

[45] And thus risk breaching Art. 9 of the Bill of Rights 1689 (which protects 'proceedings in Parliament' from being impeached or questioned in any court or place out of Parliament). It does not breach Art. 9 for the courts to read Hansard for resolving an ambiguity in legislation (*Pepper* v. *Hart* [1993] AC 593). Recourse to Hansard to decide whether a restriction of a Convention right is justifiable was severely criticized in *Wilson* v. *First County Trust Ltd* [2003] UKHL 40; [2004] 1 AC 816.

[46] *Edinburgh and Dalkeith Railway* v. *Wauchope* (1842) 8 Cl. & F. 710, 725; and *Pickin* v. *British Railways Board* [1974] AC 765.

On this approach, the task of the courts is merely to apply the test that is known as the 'enrolled Act' rule.

THE QUESTION OF DEFINITION – WHAT IS AN ACT OF PARLIAMENT?

Disputes occasionally arose in the past as to whether a document before the court was an Act of Parliament.[47] It would be highly unusual today for an issue to arise as to whether a particular instrument is or is not an Act of Parliament.[48] Indeed, the reluctance of British courts to review the content of legislation extends to matters of process. Thus the courts decline to deal with questions of internal Parliamentary procedure, taking the view that these are a matter for Parliament itself.[49] In relation to Acts of the devolved Parliament of Scotland, section 28(5) of the Scotland Act 1998 prevents issues being raised in the courts as to whether the procedures of the Parliament have been properly observed before the measures were enacted. But for this provision, the courts could have been asked to declare that a failure to follow the procedure for legislation invalidated the outcome.[50] The position is different where a written constitution governs the process of legislation and the courts enforce the essentials of that process. To be valid, legislation must have been passed in the 'manner and form' required by the constitution.[51]

There is a strong argument to be made that the 'enrolled Act rule' (by which the courts identify an Act of Parliament) could be changed by Parliament, even though the rule was first declared by the courts and has not been laid down in an Act.[52] The rule stated in 1841 was in fact modified by the Parliament Acts 1911–49, which converted the House of Lords' power to veto legislation into a delaying power, and enabled Bills to receive the Royal Assent after a period of delay without the Lords' approval.[53] The rule would be changed again if (for example) the House of Lords were to be abolished or if a second chamber were to be created without the task of approving Bills. Doubtless the 'enrolled Act rule' could be modified to the extent necessary to reflect the change in the composition of Parliament. But what would be the position if Parliament at the same time introduced new procedural requirements into the legislative process (such as the need for a referendum, or for a special majority in the Commons) before certain Acts could be amended or repealed? Could means such as these protect (or 'entrench') certain laws from being changed by the ordinary course of legislation? Those who answer yes to this question consider that an attempt by a future Parliament

47 See Goldsworthy, n. 10 above, 144, quoting Sir Orlando Bridgeman in 1660: 'it is no derogation to parliaments, that what is a statute should be adjudged by the common laws. We have often brought it into question, whether such and such a thing was an Act of Parliament, or not'. Howell, *State Trials*, v, 1066.

48 But see *R. (Jackson)* v. *Attorney-General*, discussed at p. 39. Under the Human Rights Act 1998 problems may arise as to the distinction between primary and subordinate legislation drawn by the Act: below, n. 152.

49 *Pickin* v. *British Railways Board* (above). See also *Manuel* v. *Attorney-General* [1983] Ch 77 (Canada Act 1982 challenged unsuccessfully on the basis that, as Indian people in Canada had not consented to it, the consent and request of Canada itself had not been given).

50 And see *Whaley* v. *Lord Watson of Invergowrie* 2000 SC 125 (observation by Lord President Rodger that Scottish courts have no discretion not to enforce the law against the Scottish Parliament; and that Westminster, compared with many national legislatures, is unusual in its immunity from judicial review).

51 *A-G for New South Wales* v. *Trethowan* [1932] AC 526; *Bribery Commissioner* v. *Ramasinghe* [1965] AC 172. For the 'new view' of sovereignty based on 'manner and form' arguments, see R. F. V. Heuston, *Essays in Constitutional Law* (2nd edn, 1964) ch. 1; and G. Marshall, *Constitutional Theory* (1971) ch. 3.

52 See n. 46 above. 53 See p. 39 below.

to legislate on the 'entrenched' matters without observing the special procedures would be declared by the courts to be ineffective. Those who answer no insist that Parliament would remain sovereign and that the courts must apply the latest legislation by Parliament. It will be evident that the latter answer begs the question of whether Parliament has in the circumstances legislated on the subject in dispute.

Opinion is divided on this question. Should the need for an answer arise, the outcome would depend both on the nature of the new procedural requirements which had to be observed, and on the purposes that they were meant to serve.[54]

JUDICIAL INTERPRETATION AND APPLICATION OF LEGISLATION: A VITAL ASPECT OF THE RULE OF LAW

We have seen that the courts play a vital role in making authoritative decisions as to the meaning and effect of legislation. For Dicey, this role of the courts was an essential element in the 'Rule of Law':

> Powers [of the executive], however extraordinary, are never really unlimited, for they are confined by the words of the Act itself, and, what is more, by the interpretation put upon the statute by the judges. Parliament is supreme legislator, but from the moment Parliament has uttered its will as law giver, that will becomes subject to the interpretation put upon it by the judges. . .[55]

One instance of this, of particular importance in administrative law, is the proposition that the executive's statutory powers are never 'unfettered'; indeed, it is a basic rule of administrative law that even when a statutory discretion is phrased in absolute terms, the courts do not accept that the power is absolute or unlimited.[56] Statutory interpretation, and more broadly the judicial review of administrative action, are very far from being mechanical processes; the courts must be able both to respond to social change[57] and to protect constitutional values.[58] At the least, judicial interpretation of statute minimizes the risk of unintended constitutional changes being made through the use of general, and not express, words.[59] These presumptions include such matters as the presumption that property should not be taken without compensation, that those accused of criminal offences are to be presumed innocent until the contrary is proved,[60] that an individual's access to the courts should not be taken away,[61] and so on.

[54] The Human Rights Act 1998, s. 19 requires the minister in charge of a government Bill that is introduced in Parliament to state whether the Bill is compatible with the Convention rights. Enforcement of this rule is a matter for Parliament. A failure to make such a statement would not enable the courts to intervene in Parliament to prevent further consideration of the Bill. If the Bill were to become an Act without the omission having been remedied, it is unlikely that the courts would be willing to decide whether s. 19 of the 1998 Act had been duly observed. And see N. Bamforth [1998] *Public Law* 572, 575–82, citing *Mangawaro Enterprises* v. *Attorney-General* [1994] 2 NZLR 451.

[55] Dicey, *Law of the Constitution* 413. See also T. R. S. Allen, *Law, Liberty and Justice: the Legal Foundations of British Constitutionalism* (1993) 35–9 and ch. 4.

[56] *Padfield* v. *Minister of Agriculture* [1968] AC 997.

[57] *Fitzpatrick* v. *Sterling Housing Association Ltd* [2001] 1 AC 271 (House of Lords holding by 3–2 that the same-sex partner of a protected tenant is capable of being a member of the original tenant's family for the purpose of succeeding to a statutory tenancy under the Rent Act 1977).

[58] See D. Feldman (1990) 106 *LQR* 246 and cf. F. Bennion, *Statutory Interpretation* (4th edn, 2002), 887–912.

[59] See *Nairn* v. *University of St Andrews* [1909] AC 147.

[60] As to which see *R.* v. *Lambert* [2001] UKHL 37; [2002] 2 AC 69.

[61] See n. 36 above.

In the House of Lords, Lord Steyn has described such a presumption as 'a presumption of general application operating as a constitutional principle'.[62] Effect may be given to such presumptions either when a statutory provision is ambiguous, or, more importantly, where general powers are conferred and the issue is whether the powers extend to encroaching upon human rights. In these decisions, the judges have accepted that Parliament can if it chooses legislate contrary to fundamental principles of human rights. Thus the role of the courts in interpreting and applying Acts of Parliament is not enough in itself to guard against wide and far-reaching executive decisions. In dealing with the effect in national law of the European Convention on Human Rights at a time before the Human Rights Act 1998, the House of Lords held that where an Act granted a general power to a minister of the Crown to take action of a certain kind, the power was not ambiguous and its width could not be cut down by reference to the Convention.[63] The House of Lords subsequently stated its willingness to rely on a presumption in favour of the principle of legality even where there was no statutory ambiguity.[64]

Although these presumptions were judge made, and are now seen as instances of a general constitutional principle of legality, the approach of the courts to matters of statutory interpretation can be altered by Act of Parliament.[65] One striking feature of the Human Rights Act 1998 is, as we shall see, that it introduced a new rule of interpretation whereby all legislation must, 'so far as it is possible to do so', be interpreted so as to be consistent with the Convention rights protected by the Act. The existence of this duty is pivotal to the entire scheme of the Act.

PARLIAMENT MAY BY LEGISLATION MAKE CHANGES IN CONSTITUTIONAL LAW

In countries in which there is a written constitution that provides a procedure for its own amendment (for instance, by requiring that an amendment should be approved by referendum, or by a special majority in the legislature), the constitutional text can be lawfully amended only if that procedure is followed.[66] By contrast, Westminster has authority to make changes in constitutional law, and no special procedure is needed. Thus, Parliament authorized the abdication of Edward VIII, extended the life of Parliament during two world wars, and in 1975 authorized the holding of a referendum on Britain's continuing membership of the EEC. Since 1997, Parliament has authorized referenda in Scotland and Wales on proposals for devolution, has created elected assemblies in Scotland and Wales to exercise devolved powers, has enacted the Human Rights Act 1998, has introduced the registration of political parties, and has excluded most hereditary peers from the House of Lords. The authority of Parliament is demonstrated by the fact that the exclusion of hereditary peers took effect at the end of the 1998–99 session of Parliament, even though the peers excluded had in May 1997 received writs of summons from the Queen to attend at Westminster for the life of the Parliament.[67]

62 In *R.* v. *Secretary of State for the Home Department, ex parte Simms* (n. 37 above) at 411.

63 *R.* v. *Secretary of State for the Home Department, ex parte Brind* [1991] 1 AC 696.

64 Above, text at n. 38.

65 This is not to say that the role of statutory interpretation could be taken away from the courts or that the fundamentals of interpretation could be subverted. Such an attempt would infringe the principle of legality that is protected by the European Convention on Human Rights, especially by Art. 6(1).

66 See e.g. *Harris* v. *Minister of the Interior* 1952 (2) SA 428.

67 *Lord Mayhew of Twysden's Motion* [2002] 1 AC 109.

Plainly the sovereignty of Parliament provides a remarkably flexible and efficient instrument for achieving constitutional reform. As the Royal Commission on Reform of the House of Lords commented in 2000:

> There can be little question that the raft of constitutional legislation introduced by the current Government in its first two years of office . . . would have been impossible under the laborious systems required to amend the written constitutions of many other countries.[68]

The powers of Parliament extend to reforming the composition and powers of its two Houses. Thus the Parliament Acts 1911–49 in certain circumstances allow legislation to be enacted that has not been approved by the House of Lords. Although the Parliament Acts procedure has seldom been used to its full extent,[69] the availability of the procedure influences the relations between the two Houses. The Parliament Act 1911 was itself enacted by the sovereign Parliament, when the House of Lords gave way to democratic pressure in withdrawing its opposition to the Liberal insistence on ending the veto power of the Lords. But is an Act enacted by the 1911–49 Acts procedure itself the Act of a sovereign Parliament? It was nearly a hundred years before the judges were able to give an answer to this question. In 2005, a challenge to the validity of the Hunting Act 2004 was brought by those who passionately opposed the abolition of fox-hunting with dogs. The challenge to the Act failed,[70] but the reasons given by the judges for rejecting it raised some difficult questions that will be discussed below.

DOES PARLIAMENT'S POWER EXTEND TO LEGISLATING ON ALL FUNDAMENTAL CONSTITUTIONAL RULES?

Difficult questions arise about Parliament's power to legislate on certain constitutional matters. First, it is widely held that a sovereign Parliament is not bound by the Acts of its predecessors, and thus that no Parliament can 'bind its successors'; but if this is right, does this mean that a later Parliament may simply ignore an earlier Act? Second, on a related point, it is said that an Act of Parliament may change all rules of the common law except the rule whereby the courts recognize as law the Acts of Parliament.[71]

The rule that Parliament may not bind its successors has arisen in part because of the rule that when the courts are faced with two conflicting statutes on the same subject, they must apply the later Act of Parliament – the doctrine of implied repeal.[72] As Maugham LJ said in *Ellen Street Estates Ltd* v. *Minister of Health*,

> The legislature cannot, according to our constitution, bind itself as to the form of subsequent legislation, and it is impossible for Parliament to enact that in a subsequent statute dealing with the same subject-matter there can be no implied repeal.[73]

This proposition may be a means of resolving some conflicts that arise as between two Acts passed at different dates, but in its absolute terms it is vulnerable to changing judicial

68 *A House for the Future*, Cm 4534 (2000) para. 5.2.

69 Between 1911 and 2005, seven Acts were enacted under the Parliament Act procedure: Government of Ireland Act 1914, Welsh Church Act 1914, Parliament Act 1949, War Crimes Act 1991, European Parliamentary Elections Act 1999, Sexual Offences (Amendment) Act 2000, Hunting Act 2004 (and see p. 39 below).

70 *R. (Jackson)* v. *Attorney-General* [2005] UKHL 56, [2006] 1 AC 262; p. 39 below.

71 H. W. R. Wade, 'The Basis of Legal Sovereignty' (1955) *Cambridge LJ* 172 at 186–9.

72 See above (text at n. 15).

73 [1934] 1 KB 590, 597.

attitudes.[74] In any event, since Parliament may legislate on constitutional matters, such legislation may determine the composition of Parliament. Thus if in future the House of Commons were to be elected by proportional representation and the House of Lords were replaced by a Senate consisting of persons appointed to serve for periods of 15 years, the future Parliament would be a very different body from Parliament today. But that Parliament would have the sole authority to decide whether further changes in the composition of Parliament should be made. So too, as demonstrated by numerous statutes enacted at Westminster that have conferred independence on territories overseas, a sovereign Parliament may make an irreversible renunciation or transfer of legislative authority in respect of particular territory.[75] Parliament could legislate for such territory notwithstanding the renunciation of sovereignty, but such legislation would have no effect in the territory concerned unless the national courts were prepared to give effect to it (as they might if, effective government having collapsed or for other reasons, circumstances in the territory favoured the resumption of rule from London).

Closely related to the question of whether Parliament can bind its successors is the proposition that the only rule of the common law which Parliament may not change is the rule that courts recognize Acts of Parliament as law. We have seen that legal authority for the sovereignty of Parliament is not to be found in legislation. Sir William Wade, in a celebrated exposition of the legal basis of sovereignty, argued as follows: 'If no statute can establish the rule that the courts obey Acts of Parliament, similarly no statute can alter or abolish the rule'.[76] But the argument at this crucial point depends upon use of the word 'similarly' (consider the argument, 'No person can bring his or her own life into being; *similarly*, no person can bring his or her own life to an end') and it does not take account of the fact that Parliament's legislative power includes power to make constitutional changes, affecting even Parliament itself. If the sovereignty of Parliament is a fundamental rule that governs the relationship between the legislature and the courts and requires the courts to apply the latest Act of Parliament in the event of a conflict between two Acts, does it follow that the legislature is unable to modify the rule by giving the courts greater power of decision?[77] In particular, it appears that Parliament may modify the doctrine of implied repeal by endowing the courts with power in certain circumstances to apply an earlier Act rather than a later inconsistent Act.[78]

It is now time to move from generalities to considering the effects on parliamentary sovereignty of the Parliament Acts 19114–9, the European Communities Act 1972, the Scotland Act 1998, and the Human Rights Act 1998.

[74] See in particular *Thoburn* v. *Sunderland City Council* (above, n. 36) for the view that 'constitutional Acts' are not subject to implied repeal.

[75] See e.g. the Canada Act 1982 and the Australia Act 1986. There is no doubt that the Westminster Parliament could, if it wished to spend its time fruitlessly, purport to legislate for Canada and Australia; but any such attempt would be ignored by Canadian and Australian courts. Whether or not courts in the UK would give effect to such legislation is unlikely to be material.

[76] Wade, 'Basis of Legal Sovereignty', 187.

[77] Cf. T. R. S. Allan 'Parliamentary Sovereignty: Law, Politics and Revolution' (1997) 113 *LQR* 443, 445, 448.

[78] Support for this proposition is found in *Thoburn* (above), despite an insistence in the judgment that changes in the doctrine of implied repeal are solely the work of the courts. The 'constitutional Acts' which the judgment considers were, of course, the work of Parliament.

THE EFFECT OF THE PARLIAMENT ACTS 1911–49

We have seen that the effect of the 'enrolled Act' rule, taken with the refusal of the courts to investigate the internal workings of Parliament,[79] is that the courts rarely have to decide whether a document that appears to be an Act of Parliament is in law a valid Act of Parliament. The challenge in *R. (Jackson)* v. *Attorney-General*[80] to the Hunting Act 2004, which sought to abolish the ancient liberty of hunting wild animals with hounds, was indeed a rarity. The House of Lords had in two successive sessions of Parliament blocked the Hunting Bill, and the Hunting Act was then enacted under the Parliaments Acts 1911–49. In judicial review proceedings, the claimants asserted that the Hunting Act was not law because its validity depended on the Parliament Act 1949, and that Act was itself invalid.

At the forefront of the challenge was the fact that the 1949 Act (which reduced the delaying power of the House of Lords from two years, as in the Parliament Act 1911, to one year) had been passed under the 1911 Act, without the approval of the House of Lords. Did this fact affect its legal authority? It was argued by the claimants that the Act must be regarded as delegated legislation, and that the delegated authority conferred on Queen and Commons in 1911 to legislate without consent of the Lords could not be used to amend the 1911 Act by reducing the delaying power of the Lords to one year. The Law Lords, sitting as a court of nine judges, unanimously rejected this argument. Their speeches gave a variety of reasons for this conclusion.[81] One common theme was that in 1911 Parliament had intended to enable the Commons and monarch to legislate without the approval of the Lords. That procedure was an alternative to the usual process of legislation. A measure passed under the Parliament Act was primary legislation, not delegated legislation, and the principle behind the maxim *delegatus non potest delegare*[82] did not apply. The power to legislate under the 1911 Act was not subject to implied limitations, only to the express limitations set out in the 1911 Act. The most important of these express limitations was that the Act excluded from the procedure any power to prolong the life of Parliament beyond five years.

Although the Court of Appeal in *Jackson* had rejected the challenge to the Hunting Act, it did so on the basis of the following propositions: (a) the Parliament Act procedure was subject to the implied limitation that it could not be used to make fundamental constitutional changes (for instance, the abolition of the House of Lords); however, (b) the reduction of the delaying power from two years to one year in 1949 was not a 'major constitutional change' and had been validly enacted. This reasoning was supported by neither side on appeal to the Law Lords. One difficulty with it is that the vague test suggested as a limit on the Parliament Act procedure would have been exceptionally uncertain in practice.

[79] See *Pickin* v. *British Railways Board* (n. 49 above)

[80] N. 70 above.

[81] For a fuller analysis of the judgments, see the 7th report of the House of Lords' Committee on the Constitution, 'Constitutional aspects of the challenge to the Hunting Act 2004', HL Paper 141 (2005–06), App. 3 (AW Bradley). See also Lord Cooke of Thorndon, 'A Constitutional Retreat' (2006) 122 *LQR* 224 and M Plaxton, 'The Concept of Legislation: *Jackson v Attorney-General*' (2006) 69 *MLR* 249.

[82] This is the principle that 'someone with delegated power may not use it to sub-delegate that power'. By analogy, it was argued in *Jackson* that such a person could not use the delegated power to reduce limitations placed upon the exercise of that power. This argument was first propounded by the late Professor O Hood Phillips: see O. Hood Phillips and P. Jackson, *Constitutional and Administrative Law* (8th edn, 2001) 798–1. For discussion of the implications of *Jackson* in this respect see A. McHarg, 'What is delegated legislation?' [2006] *Public Law* 539.

Moreover, the contemporary record of the debates leading to enactment of the 1911 Act does not support the imposition of an implied limit of this kind.[83] Its effect would have been that a dispute between the two Houses over a controversial constitutional reform would be subject to deep uncertainty as to whether the House of Lords had a power to veto the proposal, or merely a delaying power.

In *Jackson* the Attorney-General, appearing for the government, accepted that the judges had jurisdiction to decide whether the Hunting Act was or was not a valid Act of Parliament. Accordingly the judges did not have to decide this question. That issue was rightly treated by the Law Lords as turning on a point of law (namely, the correct interpretation of the 1911 Act). Although the issue was an unusual one, it was a matter that the judges were competent to decide.

Three further comments on the case may be made.

(1) Although the end-product of the 1911 Act procedure was held to be an Act of Parliament, the judges did not hold that a law passed in that way is an Act of the sovereign Parliament. Since the majority of judges held that the Parliament Act process was subject to express limitations contained in the 1911 Act, it follows that Dicey's proposition that a sovereign Parliament has 'the right to make or unmake any law whatever' does not apply.[84] Indeed, a majority of judges were of the view that the 1911 Act could not be used to force through an extension in the life of Parliament beyond five years, even if the exercise were to be attempted in two stages – first, in an Act to remove the limitation on the power, and second, only then to extend the life of Parliament.[85]

(2) If the way is open for major constitutional changes to be made by use of the Parliament Act procedure, it could be used by the Government and the Commons to force through a radical reform of the House of Lords itself (possibly even extending to its abolition), against the wishes of that House.[86] This may seem to open an unduly wide door for constitutional reform based solely on the wishes of the majority in the Commons, and to provide inadequate safeguards against a mistaken reform. However, the historical evidence suggests that this wide door was opened in 1911 as an aspect of the constitutional settlement that was then imposed on the upper House. It may have been a desire to reinterpret the Parliament Act provisions (and to limit their width) that caused the Court of Appeal to attribute a constitutional role to the House of Lords that might be acceptable today (given the changed composition of the House since 1911); but such a role would not have been acceptable to the Commons at a time when the upper House had a permanent majority of Tory hereditary peers and claimed a power of veto over all legislation coming from the Commons.

(3) Several speeches in *Jackson* made observations on the sovereignty of Parliament that were not directly called for by issues in the case. These passages suggest that some judges

83 The speeches of Lord Bingham and Lady Hale in *Jackson* set out the historical background to the 1911 Act. See also 7th report of the House of Lords' Committee on the Constitution (n. 81 above), app. 1 (R. Brazier).

84 On the broad implications of *Jackson* for parliamentary sovereignty, see A. Young, 'Hunting Sovereignty: *Jackson v A-G*' [2006] *Public Law* 187.

85 See the speeches of Lords Nicholls, Steyn, Hope, Carswell and Lady Hale. Lords Rodger and Brown reserved their position. Lord Bingham said that a two-stage course of legislation would succeed.

86 For earlier discussion of whether the House of Lords could be abolished under the Parliament Acts, see P. Mirfield (1979) 95 *LQR* 36 and G. Winterton (1979) 95 *LQR* 386.

have deep reservations as to the power of the majority in the Commons to legislate in ways that adversely affect matters of constitutional principle (for example, by encroaching on functions of the courts that are considered to be fundamental to the legal system). Lord Steyn, dealing with an argument by the Attorney-General (Lord Goldsmith) based on the supremacy of Parliament, said: 'We do not have in the United Kingdom an uncontrolled constitution as the Attorney-General implausibly submits'. Further, Lord Steyn said that Dicey's account of 'the supremacy of Parliament, pure and absolute as it was, can now be seen to be out of place in the modern United Kingdom. While that supremacy 'is still the *general* principle of the constitution, [it] is a construct of the common law;' and it was not 'unthinkable that circumstances could arise where the courts may have to qualify a principle established *on a different hypothesis of constitutionalism*'[87]

Lord Hope began his speech in a robust way: 'Our constitution is dominated by the sovereignty of Parliament. But parliamentary sovereignty is no longer, if it ever was, absolute.'[88] And he cut down the traditional status of the doctrine by remarking that '[the] rule of law enforced by the courts is the ultimate controlling factor on which our constitution is based'. Instead of an absolute sovereignty divorced from a basis of popular assent, Lord Hope stressed that the ultimate rule by which people are prepared to recognise the existence of law 'depends upon the legislature maintaining the trust of the electorate'.[89] Lady Hale considered that, in addition to limitations on parliamentary sovereignty that have arisen from the European Communities Act 1972 and the Human Rights Act 1998, '[it] is possible that other qualifications may emerge in due course, In general, however, the constraints upon what Parliament can do are political and diplomatic rather than constitutional'.[90]

Statements of this kind are wholly consonant with the approach that this chapter takes in questioning the absolutist position associated with Dicey. It must not be assumed from these statements that today's judges are anxiously waiting to impose judicial supremacism upon the UK, but they indicate a willingness not merely to address the content of parliamentary sovereignty, but also to examine the link between that doctrine and the principles of democracy.

PARLIAMENTARY SOVEREIGNTY AND THE EUROPEAN UNION[91]

Doctrines of constitutional law cannot ignore the reality of Britain's international relations. By virtue of the Royal Prerogative in foreign affairs, the Crown has power to enter into treaties that bind the state in international law,[92] but not to alter the rights of individuals

87 Para. [102]. The first emphasis is Lord Steyn's – the second emphasis has been supplied. And see J. Jowell, 'Parliamentary Sovereignty under the New Constitutional Hypothesis' [2006] *Public Law* 562.

88 Para. [104]. 89 Para. [126].

90 Para. [159]. In this remark, 'constitutional' appears to have a legal content that it does not always have in British constitutional writing.

91 The literature includes L. Collins, *European Community Law in the United Kingdom* (5th edn, 1999); T. C. Hartley, *The Foundations of European Community Law* (5th edn, 2003); P. Craig and G. de Búrca, *EU Law: Text, Cases and Materials* (3rd edn, 2003); and S. Douglas-Scott, *Constitutional Law of the European Union* (2002). And see Chapter 4 below.

92 As demonstrated in *R.* v. *Secretary of State for Foreign Affairs, ex parte Rees-Mogg* [1994] QB 552.

within the UK. If such an alteration is required by a treaty, that can be done only by Act of Parliament. The UK would be in breach of its international obligations under such a treaty if Parliament failed to pass legislation that the treaty required.[93] In practice, a government backed by a majority in the House of Commons can ensure that the necessary legislation is passed.

The conduct of foreign affairs may thus lead to a situation in which Parliament legislates under the constraint that otherwise the UK will be in breach of its treaty obligations. The existence of such a constraint is not considered to infringe the sovereignty of Parliament. Parliament's authority to legislate is no more 'fettered' by the treaty than it is fettered by other political decisions that are taken by the Cabinet. Indeed, an Act of Parliament is enforceable by British courts even if it breaches Britain's treaty obligations. However, in interpreting statutes that are enacted to give effect to such obligations, the courts if possible interpret the statute so as to conform with the treaty.[94]

These established rules governing the division of functions between treaty making by the Crown and legislation by Parliament apply to the vast majority of treaties creating international organizations to which the UK is a party. But the European Union, of which the European Community forms part, is a unique grouping of states created in 1993 by the Maastricht Treaty. The European Economic Community (the precursor of the present Community) was created by the Treaty of Rome in 1957. The UK acceded to the EEC by the Treaty of Brussels 1972, which was implemented in the UK by the European Communities Act 1972. What is distinctive about the Community compared with other international organizations is that broad executive, legislative, and fiscal powers are vested in organs of the Community. The European Court of Justice at Luxembourg (together with the Court of First Instance) exercises judicial powers in applying and enforcing Community law. Regulations made by the Council of Ministers are directly applicable in all member states as soon as they have been promulgated by the Council.[95] Treaty provisions and other Community measures may have direct effect in member states, i.e. they may create rights that are directly enforceable by individuals in national courts, without needing to be implemented by national legislation.[96] As the Court of Justice said in 1963,

> the Community constitutes a new legal order of international law, *for the benefit of which the states have limited their sovereign rights*, albeit within limited fields, and the subjects of which comprise not only Members States but also their nationals.[97]

From the perspective of the Court of Justice, it is essential that the main rules of Community law should have direct effect in the legal systems of the member states:

> The binding force of the Treaty [of Rome] and of measures taken in application of it must not differ from one state to another as a result of internal measures, lest the functioning of the Community system should be impeded and the achievement of the aims of the Treaty placed in peril.[98]

93 *A-G for Canada* v. *A-G for Ontario* [1937] AC 326, 347–8.

94 *Salomon* v. *Commissioners of Customs & Excise* [1967] 2 QB 116; *Garland* v. *British Rail Engineering Ltd* [1983] 2 AC 75 (and below, text at note 111). And see F. G. Jacobs and S. Roberts (eds), *The Effect of Treaties in Domestic Law* (1987). And see Chapter 5 below.

95 EC Treaty, Art. 248 (old 189).

96 And see Chapter 4 below, pp. 99–106.

97 Case 26/62, *Van Gend en Loos* v. *Nederlandse Tarief Commissie* [1963] CMLR 105, 129 (emphasis supplied).

98 Case 14/68, *Walt Wilhelm* v. *Bundeskartellamt* [1969] ECR 1, para. 6.

Community law cannot be overridden by domestic legal provisions 'without being deprived of its character as Community law and without the legal basis of the Community being called into question'.[99] Community law thus creates obligations upon member states, and also individual rights enforceable in national courts.

The Community legal order is plainly inconsistent with the sovereignty of Parliament. Dicey asserted that 'no person or body is recognised by the law of England as having a right to override or set aside the legislation of Parliament'.[100] In fact, UK law now recognizes that Community organs have the right to make decisions and issue regulations which may override legislation by Parliament. The supremacy or primacy of Community law within the economic or social areas with which it deals was already a significant aspect of the Community system during the 1960s, but it does not stand comfortably beside structures of constitutional law based on national frontiers. While the problem takes a special form in the UK, other member states have experienced difficulties in adjusting their systems of constitutional law to take account of Community law.[101] The Court of Justice has repeatedly emphasized that the application of Community law may not be delayed by obstacles in national law, even where these arise from constitutional considerations, such as concern for the protection of fundamental rights.[102] As the Court said in 1978:

> A national court which is called on within the limits of its jurisdiction, to apply provisions of Community law is under a duty to give full effect to those provisions, if necessary refusing of its own motion to apply any conflicting provisions of national legislation, even if adopted subsequently, and it is not necessary for the court to request or await the prior setting aside of such provisions by legislative or other constitutional means.[103]

When Denmark, the Republic of Ireland, and the UK acceded to the European Community in 1973, each was required to take steps to accommodate Community law within its legal systems. In Denmark and Ireland, formal constitutional amendments were necessary. This course of action was not open to the UK, but it was essential that Parliament should authorize the reception of Community law. Legal effect had to be given not only to existing but also to future rules of Community law.

Given this necessity, the sovereignty of Parliament was 'at once an advantage and a source of difficulty'.[104] The advantage was that no constitutional amendment was necessary. It took only a few lines in an Act of Parliament to give effect to a massive body of Community law and to equip the British government with additional powers to handle Community affairs. The difficulty came so far as the future was concerned: could a guarantee be given or an undertaking entrenched that Parliament would in the future neither legislate to leave the

[99] Case 6/64, *Costa* v. *ENEL* [1964] CMLR 425, 455–6.

[100] Dicey, *Law of the Constitution* 40.

[101] See e.g. Craig and de Búrca, op. cit. ch. 7(3).

[102] These concerns, particularly from Germany and Italy, were influential in causing the Court of Justice to bring fundamental rights within the general principles of Community law: see e.g. the *Internationale Handelsgesellschaft* case 11/70, [1972] CMLR 255 and, for the German Constitutional Court's later position, the *Wünsche Handelsgesellchaft* case [1987] 3 CMLR 225.

[103] Case 106/77, *Amministrazione delle Finanze dello Stato* v. *Simmenthal SpA (No. 2)* [1978] 3 CMLR 263, 268. Hartley, citing decisions of the German Constitutional Court and the Danish Supreme Court, concludes that 'the supremacy of Community law in a country always depends, in the last analysis, on the constitution of that country': T. C. Hartley, 'The Constitutional Foundations of the European Union' (2001) 117 *LQR* 225, 243.

[104] J. P. Warner, 'The Relationship between European Community Law and the National Laws of Member States' (1977) 93 *LQR* 349, 364.

Community nor (whether by accident or design) legislate in a manner which conflicted with Community law?

The view of the Government in 1972 was that no absolute legislative undertaking by Parliament could be given, since a future Parliament could disregard such an undertaking. Instead, the European Communities Act 1972 went so far as was thought possible in instructing British courts how to apply Community law in the future.

Section 2(1) of the 1972 Act gave effect in the UK to all rules of Community law that have direct application or direct effect within member states. This applied both to existing and to future Community rules. By section 2(2), the Government acquired very wide powers of making regulations to implement the UK's Community obligations and to give effect to rights arising under Community law. These powers included power to amend Acts of Parliament.[105]

By section 2(4), it was provided that 'any enactment passed or to be passed, other than one contained in this part of the Act, shall be construed and shall have effect subject to the foregoing provisions of this section' – subject, in other words, to the comprehensive reception of existing and future Community law made by section 2(1). By section 3, questions of Community law were to be decided by the European Court of Justice or in accordance with the decisions of that Court, and all national courts were in future to take judicial notice of such decisions. It was, however, section 2(4) that was the subject of most discussion. In form a new rule of construction, it appeared to require all legislation, both existing and future, to have effect subject to the rules of Community law that operated in national law under section 2(1). Arguably, the rule went far beyond being a rule of construction by declaring that, within the post-accession 'hierarchy of norms', Community law would be superior to any Act of Parliament, whenever enacted.

When these provisions were debated in Parliament, it was widely agreed that they did not exclude the possibility that Parliament might one day wish to repeal the Act and thus prevent the continued operation of Community law within the UK. The ultimate sovereignty of Westminster was thus not affected, as ministers admitted, though they refused to allow a statement to this effect to be included in the Act.[106] But there was for many years uncertainty about a less extreme situation, namely what the position would be if an Act passed after 1972 contained a provision that was impossible to reconcile with a rule of Community law. In this situation, we have already seen that the European Court would insist that Community law must prevail. Should the British courts adopt the same position, as sections 2 and 3 of the 1972 Act might indicate was their duty, or does the later Act of Parliament override those sections of the 1972 Act, to the extent of requiring the later Act to prevail?

In 1972, since it was impossible to undertake that no such conflict would arise in future, the government accepted that a later Act might prevail over the European Communities Act 1972 to the extent of the conflict.[107]

The initial response of British judges to the questions posed by the 1972 Act showed a preference for resolving potential clashes and inconsistencies by interpretation, and they were reluctant to reach the sovereignty question. Thus in a much quoted dictum, Lord

105 In *Thoburn* v. *Sunderland City Council* [2002] EWHC 195 (Admin); [2003] QB 151, it was held that these 'Henry VIII' powers included power to amend future Acts of Parliament. For criticism of *Thoburn*, see D. Campbell and J. Younger, 'The metric martyrs and the entrenchment jurisprudence of Lord Justice Laws' [2002] *Public Law* 399.

106 HC Debs, 5 July 1972, cols 556–644.

107 For the advice of Lord Diplock on this point, see HL Debs, 8 Aug. 1972, col. 1029.

Denning MR said that the incoming tide of Community law could not be held back: 'Parliament has decreed that the Treaty is henceforward to be part of our law. It is equal in force to any statute'.[108] The crucial question, however, was not whether Community law has the same force as any statute, but whether it has greater force than a statute by prevailing over subsequent Acts which conflict with it. There occurred a succession of difficult cases in which UK law on sex discrimination and employment protection was called into question by the application of Community rules that required equal treatment of men and women as regards their conditions of employment and pay.[109]

We have seen that by section 2(4) of the European Communities Act 1972 any existing or future enactment 'shall be construed and shall have effect' subject to the directly effective provisions of Community law. Relying on section 2(4) as a rule of construction, the courts took the view that where possible national legislation must be interpreted and applied so that it did not conflict with Community law.[110] In *Garland* v. *British Rail Engineering Ltd*, Lord Diplock stressed that in relation to all international treaties,

> it is a principle of construction . . . now too well established to call for citation of authority, that the words of a statute passed after the treaty has been signed and dealing with the subject matter of the international obligation of the UK, are to be construed, if they are reasonably capable of bearing such a meaning, as intended to carry out the obligation and not to be inconsistent with it.[111]

That approach, said Lord Diplock, applied even more strongly to the Community treaties. As regards section 2(4), he left open the question of whether the courts would ever be justified in construing a future statute inconsistently with a Community obligation, except where the Act contained an express statement that the provision was intended to be made by Parliament in breach of a Community obligation.

The question of what the courts should do if Parliament legislated inconsistently with Community law eventually arose in *R.* v. *Secretary of State for Transport, ex parte Factortame Ltd*:[112] it was claimed by Spanish fishing-boat operators that provisions in the Merchant Shipping Act 1988 were in conflict with Community law. The background to this claim lay in the fact that foreign fishing interests had formed companies registered in the UK and transferred fishing boats to them, in order to benefit from the EC fishing quota allocated to the UK. In response to this, the 1988 Act introduced conditions relating to nationality, domicile, and residence in the UK which owners had to satisfy before their boats could be registered under the Act. If the Act came into force, the companies that could not satisfy these conditions would have to stop fishing; the loss that they would suffer while the matter was referred to the Luxembourg court would (it was believed) not be recoverable from the British government, even if the 1988 Act was eventually held to infringe their Community rights.

The initial issue was not whether the 1988 Act was contrary to Community law, as it was later held to be,[113] but the vital procedural point of whether the English courts could grant

[108] *H P Bulmer* v. *J Bollinger SA* [1974] Ch 410, 418. Cf. *Felixstowe Dock and Railway Co* v. *British Transport Docks Board* [1976] 2 Lloyd's Law Reports 656, 663.

[109] See e.g. Case 152/84, *Marshall* v. *Southampton and South West Hampshire Health Authority* [1986] ECR 723; [1986] QB 401 and Case 222/84, *Johnston* v. *Chief Constable, RUC* [1986] ECR 1651, [1987] QB 129.

[110] *Macarthys Ltd* v. *Smith* [1979] 3 All ER 325 and [1981] QB 180.

[111] [1983] 2 AC 751; and see T. R. S. Allan [1982] *Public Law* 562.

[112] [1990] 2 AC 85; and see N. Gravells [1989] *Public Law* 568; and Chapter 4 below, pp. 92–9.

[113] *R.* v. *Secretary of State for Transport, ex parte Factortame Ltd (No. 3)* [1991] 2 Lloyd's Rep 648.

interim relief to the fishing-boat owners against the British government, while the case was referred to the Court of Justice. In its first *Factortame* decision, the House of Lords held that it had no jurisdiction to grant relief against the 1988 Act, primarily for the reason that the Act must be presumed to be valid until the contrary had been shown. But the House referred to the Court of Justice the question of whether there was an 'overriding principle of Community law' that required national courts to secure effective interim protection for Community rights.

Answering this question affirmatively, the Court of Justice applied the principle that directly applicable rules of Community law 'must be fully and uniformly applied in all the member states from the date of their entry into force . . . in accordance with the principle of the precedence of Community law'.[114] This principle rendered 'automatically inapplicable' any conflicting provision of national law. Any legal rule or judicial practice that might withhold from the national court the power to ensure the full effect of Community rules was contrary to Community law.

When the case came back to the House of Lords, the House duly granted an interim injunction against the Secretary of State from removing the Spanish-owned ships from the register of British fishing vessels. On the constitutional question, Lord Bridge rejected the view that the decision of the Court of Justice was a novel and dangerous invasion upon the sovereignty of Parliament, saying:

> If the supremacy . . . of Community law over the national law of member states was not always inherent in the EEC Treaty it was certainly well established in the jurisprudence of the Court of Justice long before the UK joined the Community. Thus, whatever limitation of its sovereignty Parliament accepted when it enacted the European Communities Act was entirely voluntary. [There] is nothing in any way novel in according supremacy to rules of Community law in those areas to which they apply and to insist that, in the protection of rights under Community law, national courts must not be inhibited by rules of national law from granting interim relief in appropriate cases is no more than a logical recognition of that supremacy.[115]

Lord Bridge's judgment is the plainest possible statement that so long as the UK remains in the European Community, the laws made by the supreme Parliament must if necessary give way to the greater supremacy of Community law. *Factortame (No. 2)* may have been the landmark decision but it does not stand alone in evidencing the supremacy of Community law. Three examples may be given. First, the Court of Justice held that a limit on compensation for discrimination imposed by the Sex Discrimination Act 1975 was in breach of the Equal Treatment Directive to the extent that it prevented the victim of a discriminatory dismissal by a public authority from recovering adequate reparation for the loss and damage sustained.[116] Second, the House of Lords (without making a reference to the Court of Justice for a preliminary ruling) itself declared that conditions imposed by the Employment Protection (Consolidation) Act 1978 on the protection of part-time workers against unfair dismissal were discriminatory, since they were incompatible with the right of female workers under Community law to equal treatment with male workers, full-time workers being

114 *R.* v. *Secretary of State for Transport, ex parte Factortame Ltd (No. 2)* [1991] 1 AC 603, 643.

115 Ibid.; and see N. Gravells [1991] *Public Law* 180; P. P. Craig (1991) 11 *Yearbook of European Law* 221; H. W. R. Wade (1991) 107 *LQR* 1 and (1996) 112 *LQR* 568; and T. R. S. Allan (1997) 113 *LQR* 443, see n. 77 above.

116 Case C-271/91, *Marshall* v. *Southampton and South West Hampshire Health Authority (No. 2)* [1993] 3 CMLR 293, [1994] QB 126.

mainly male and part-time workers being mainly female.[117] Third, in a later phase of the *Factortame* litigation, in 1999 the House of Lords held that the British government was liable to compensate the fishing interests for the loss they suffered as a result of the Merchant Shipping Act 1988; liability arose in part because in 1988 the government had been advised by the European Commission in Brussels that the proposed Act infringed the right of establishment under Community law, but had chosen to ignore the advice.[118]

Thus in general British courts must not apply national legislation, whenever it was enacted, if to do so would conflict with Community law. The decision in *Factortame (No. 2)* has been described as constituting a 'constitutional revolution',[119] but an explanation in terms of legal and constitutional principle seems preferable.[120] Whatever the rationalization of the change, British membership of the European Union has caused a significant area of legislative power to pass to the European authorities. Today, the British courts must if necessary review Acts of Parliament to see if they are consistent with Community law, must decide whether an Act should be applied or disapplied, and may even award compensation for the improper exercise by Westminster of its legislative authority.

This profound change in the operation of parliamentary sovereignty is not necessarily permanent, because the duty of British courts to apply Community law would not exist as a matter of UK law but for the continued operation of the European Communities Act 1972. The constitutions of other member states have also had to adjust to the development of European integration and to the impact that this has had on ideas of national sovereignty.[121] If in the future European politics changed to a point at which the UK decided to leave the European Union, Westminster could exercise what might be called its ultimate sovereign authority to bring this about, a change that would involve repealing the 1972 Act. Short of such an extreme event, it is unlikely that Westminster would expressly mandate the courts to disregard a specific Community obligation. If it did so, it is impossible to predict the response of British courts so long as the UK remains in membership of the Union.

DEVOLUTION AND PARLIAMENTARY SOVEREIGNTY

In this section, we examine aspects of parliamentary sovereignty that arise in relation to the scheme of devolution in the Scotland Act 1998. We have seen above that parliamentary sovereignty facilitated the process by which the UK joined the EEC, only a short Act being needed to give legal effect within the UK to Community law. We also saw that no clear or binding undertaking was given that Parliament would in future always respect the primacy of Community law; there was, of course, no written constitution that could be amended to provide authoritatively for the place of Community law in national law. In the case of devolution to Scotland and Wales, the capacity of Westminster to devolve powers to elected bodies in those two countries was not in dispute.

117 *R. v. Secretary of State for Employment, ex parte Equal Opportunities Commission* [1995] 1 AC 1.

118 *R. v. Secretary of State for Transport, ex parte Factortame Ltd* [1999] 4 All ER 906.

119 H. W. R. Wade (1996) 112 *LQR* 568.

120 See Allan, op. cit., n. 115 above.

121 Cf. I. Pernice, 'Multilevel Constitutionalism in the European Union' (2002) 27 *Euro L Rev* 511; and N. MacCormick, *Questioning Sovereignty: Law, State, and Nation in the European Commonwealth* (1999).

For many reasons, the Government of Wales Act 1998 treated Wales differently from Scotland:[122] thus, Westminster has hitherto continued to be the legislature for the legal system of England and Wales. The powers conferred on the Assembly by the Government of Wales Act 1998 were in essence those powers for which the Secretary of State for Wales was formerly responsible, for example to make delegated legislation affecting Wales. Administrative devolution of this kind was unlikely to raise questions about the sovereignty of Parliament. In Scotland, by contrast, which has retained its own legal system since the Union with England in 1707, the Scotland Act gives wide law-making powers to the new Parliament and has a greater constitutional significance. In relation to both Wales and Scotland, what Westminster creates by legislation may in principle be varied or taken away by Westminster, particularly as there is no written constitution into which these schemes for devolution could be inserted. Thus no court has power to protect the new institutions from legislative override by the parent Parliament.

In the case of *MacCormick* v. *Lord Advocate*, which concerned the legality of the numeral in Queen Elizabeth's title, Lord Cooper, Lord President of the Court of Session, famously remarked: '[t]he principle of the unlimited sovereignty of Parliament is a distinctively English principle which has no counter part in Scottish constitutional law'.[123] Lord Cooper had in mind that the Treaty of Union of 1707, to which Acts of the Scottish and English Parliaments gave effect, contained guarantees for Scottish courts, Scots law, the Church of Scotland, and other institutions that were declared to be fundamental to the Union and that have at various time been argued to be binding on the Parliament at Westminster. In fact, the Scottish courts have not upheld such arguments.[124] Indeed, in expounding parliamentary sovereignty, Dicey referred to the Acts confirming the Treaties of Union with Scotland and Ireland to make the point that the history of subsequent legislation in respect of those Acts 'affords the strongest proof of the futility inherent in every attempt of one sovereign legislature to restrain the action of another equally sovereign body'.[125] Within Scotland, there was considerable resentment of this 'English' view of sovereignty and a fear that the existence of a Scottish Parliament (as a subordinate legislature) would always be subject to threats of legislation from Westminster, or might even be closed down by it, as the former Northern Ireland Parliament at Stormont had been in 1972.

In 1995, an influential report, *Scotland's Parliament. Scotland's Right*, calling for a Scottish Parliament, was drawn up by the Scottish Constitutional Convention, a non-governmental organization representing many bodies of opinion within Scotland, including the Labour and Liberal Democrat parties. Having outlined a scheme of how the new Parliament might operate, the framers of the report wished to ensure that it would not be at risk of legislative interference from Westminster.

122 See Chapters 7 and 9 below; V. Bogdanor, *Devolution in the United Kingdom* (1998); N. Burrows, *Devolution* (2000).

123 1953 SC 396, 411. The Government of Wales Act 2006 broadens the extent of legislative devolution to the Welsh Assembly, although a future Scottish-style power to make laws for Wales will be conditional upon the holding of a referendum.

124 *MacCormick* v. *Lord Advocate* 1953 SC 396; *Gibson* v. *Lord Advocate* 1975 SC 136; *Pringle, Petitioner* 1991 SLT 330. And see D. N. MacCormick, (1978) 29 *Northern Ireland LQ* 1; C. R. Munro, *Studies in Constitutional Law* (2nd edn, 1999), ch. 4; *Stair Memorial Encyclopedia, The Laws of Scotland* (1987) vol. 5, paras 338–60; M. Upton (1989) 105 *LQR* 79; and C. M. G. Himsworth and N. C. Walker (1991) *Juridical Review* 45.

125 Dicey, *Law of the Constitution*, op. cit., 65.

The Convention is adamant that the powers of Scotland's Parliament, once established, should not be altered without the consent of the Scottish Parliament representing the people of Scotland.[126]

The Convention had been advised by constitutional experts that 'in theory under Britain's unwritten constitution' an Act of the Westminster Parliament creating a Scottish Parliament 'can be repealed or amended without restriction'. The Convention however was firmly of the view that if there was 'widespread recognition of the Scottish Parliament's legitimate authority, both within Scotland and internationally', no Westminster government would be willing to pay the political price of 'neutralising or destroying' a Parliament supported by the people of Scotland.[127] The Convention urged further that the Westminster Parliament should make a solemn declaration of intent that the Act creating the Scottish Parliament 'should not be repealed, or amended in such a way as to threaten the existence of Scotland's Parliament, without the consent of the Scottish Parliament and of the people of Scotland, directly consulted through general election or referendum'.[128]

In July 1997, the Labour Government's white paper set out the advantages of creating a Scottish Parliament with lawmaking powers. The Government was plainly aware of the views of the Scottish Constitutional Convention and, on the other side, of fears from English critics that devolution might reopen debate on the desirability of the Union of 1707 itself. Trying to face both ways, the white paper explained that, while Westminster would be devolving wide legislative powers on the Scottish Parliament,

Scotland will of course remain an integral part of the UK. . . . The UK Parliament is and will remain *sovereign in all matters*: but as part of the Government's resolve to modernise the British constitution Westminster will be choosing to exercise that sovereignty by devolving legislative responsibilities to a Scottish Parliament *without in any way diminishing its own powers*. The Government recognise that no UK Parliament can bind its successors. The Government however believe that the popular support for the Scottish Parliament, once established, will make sure that its future in the UK constitution will be secure.[129]

Such popular support was expressed in September 1997, when in the Scottish referendum a clear majority of the electorate favoured the creation of a Parliament at Edinburgh.

The Scotland Act 1998 confers power on the Scottish Parliament to make laws on any matter except those matters that are declared by the Act to be outside its legislative competence.[130] Sched. 5 to the Act sets out a lengthy list of reserved matters: aspects of the constitution (including the Crown, the Union of England and Scotland and the Westminster Parliament), international relations, defence, the armed forces, and many detailed matters grouped under 11 subject heads (such as financial and economic matters, trade and industry, and social security). Two important restrictions are that the Parliament may not legislate incompatibly with Community law nor with rights secured by the European Convention on Human Rights. The power to make laws on all matters that are not reserved (such as education, local government, social services, criminal justice, the environment, and agriculture) necessarily includes power to amend or repeal existing Acts of the Westminster Parliament. The competence of the Scottish Executive created by the 1998 Act extends in general to matters that are within the legislative competence of the Scottish Parliament.

126 *Scotland's Parliament. Scotland's Right* (1995) 18. 127 Ibid. 128 Op. cit., 19.
129 *Scotland's Parliament*, Cm 3658 (1997) 12 (emphasis supplied).
130 Scotland Act 1998, ss. 28(1), 29(1).

Several procedures created by the Scotland Act seek to ensure prospectively that legislation being considered by the Scottish Parliament does not go outside its competence.[131] But should it be claimed that the Scottish Parliament has enacted an Act that exceeds its competence, the matter is likely to be raised in the courts as a 'devolution issue'.[132] Since the Scottish Parliament and Executive have no power to act incompatibly with rights under the European Convention on Human Rights, measures and decisions that it is claimed breach Convention rights also raise devolution issues. Under the Scotland Act, devolution issues are decided by the superior courts and may ultimately be decided by the Judicial Committee of the Privy Council, or, after 2009, by the new Supreme Court of the UK.[133]

Within this legal framework, or constitution, by which the domestic affairs of Scotland are now governed, Acts of the Scottish Parliament are not sovereign and may be set aside by the courts if they go outside the devolved powers. The Scottish Parliament may not enlarge its own competence, although this may be done at any time by the Westminster Parliament or in some cases by ministers of the Crown exercising delegated powers. Some guidance is given by the Act itself as to the way in which the courts should approach devolution issues. Thus, a provision of a Scottish Act which could be read in such a way as to be outside its competence, 'is to be read as narrowly as is required for it to be within competence, if such a reading is possible'.[134] However, no comparable interpretative duty applies to the Scotland Act 1998 nor to other Westminster Acts. Given the manner in which reserved matters are enumerated in the Act, it is left to the courts to determine the approach that they must take in determining the width of the powers conferred.[135]

How does this new constitution for Scotland affect the sovereignty of the Westminster Parliament? Section 28 of the 1998 Act, which provides that the Scottish Parliament may make laws for Scotland, includes a modestly phrased subsection: '(7) This section does not affect the power of the Parliament of the UK to make laws for Scotland'.[136] In one sense, this provision is legally unnecessary and exists only for the avoidance of doubt, to assist readers of the Act unfamiliar with Dicey's view of parliamentary sovereignty. Scottish MPs continue to sit at Westminster, but their opportunity to raise in the House questions about the domestic affairs of Scotland is now much reduced. Possibly this provision serves a symbolic purpose, or is meant to guard against any legislative intervention by Westminster in Scottish affairs being regarded as 'unconstitutional' or in breach of a convention to the contrary. When the Scotland Bill was passing through Parliament, many considered that it would be a rare event in future for Westminster to legislate on matters which were devolved to Edinburgh. In the event, this has been a frequent occurrence, mainly in the case of changes

131 See for the annotated text of the Act, C. M. G. Himsworth and C. R. Munro, *The Scotland Act 1998* (2nd edn, 2000). See also Chapter 9 below.

132 Scotland Act 1998, Sched. 6, Pt I. And see e.g. *Anderson et al* v. *Scottish Ministers* [2001] UKPC D5; [2003] 2 AC 602.

133 Scotland Act 1998, Sched. 6, Pts II–V. Under the Constitutional Reform Act 2005, s. 40(4) and Sched. 9, pt 2, jurisdiction over devolution issues will be transferred to the Supreme Court.

134 Scotland Act 1998, s. 101.

135 See P. Craig and M. Walters, 'The Courts, Devolution and Judicial Review' [1999] *Public Law* 274; and S. Tierney, 'Constitutionalising the Role of the Judge: Scotland and the New Order' (2001) 5 *Edin L Rev* 49.

136 Cf. the more flamboyant formula used in the Government of Ireland Act 1920, s. 75: 'the supreme authority of the Parliament of the UK shall remain unaffected and undiminished over all persons, matters and things in Ireland and every part thereof'. As to this and the equivalent provision in the Northern Ireland Act 1998, s. 5(6) see B. Hadfield [1998] *Public Law* 599.

in the law that relate to administrative schemes applying throughout Great Britain. However, both governments have observed a new convention (the 'Sewel convention') by which the Scottish Parliament by resolution grants its consent to the proposed legislation before it is enacted at Westminster.[137] While in law the Westminster Parliament could legislate on a devolved matter without the prior approval of the Scottish Parliament, such a breach of convention would be likely to give rise to much criticism in Scotland.

To summarize the effects of the Scotland Act on Westminster's sovereignty, the following propositions may be advanced: (a) as a matter of strict law, Westminster retains full capacity to amend or repeal the Scotland Act and may do so at any time, without any prior procedure such as a referendum of the Scottish electorate being necessary; (b) Westminster retains full capacity to legislate on any aspect of Scotland's affairs, whether or not they are within Edinburgh's legislative competence, but as a matter of political practice Westminster will legislate on devolved matters only with the approval of the Scottish Parliament; (c) within the limits of its devolved powers, the Scottish Parliament may amend or repeal existing Acts of the Westminster Parliament and also future Acts enacted at Westminster that deal with matters within Edinburgh's competence, unless those later Acts show a clear intention to take a particular matter outside that competence by amending the 1998 Act so as to achieve this.[138] What is likely to be more significant than the legal capacity of Westminster to legislate for Scotland on devolved matters is the strength of support that attaches to the Scottish Parliament in Scotland as a body that is more fully representative of the Scottish people than the Parliament at Westminster. Compared with the pre-1707 Scottish Parliament, the present Scottish Parliament has the marks of a subordinate legislature, but political opinion and national sentiment in Scotland will rate it more highly than this.

THE SOVEREIGNTY OF PARLIAMENT AND THE HUMAN RIGHTS ACT 1998

We have already seen in relation to certain forms of constitutional change that there are both advantages and disadvantages in the doctrine of parliamentary sovereignty. In relation to the protection of human rights and liberties, the disabling effect of the doctrine seems uppermost. The doctrine has often seemed to be a massive obstacle that prevents there being any significant increase in the level of formal protection given to human rights in our constitutional law. Where legislative sovereignty reigns, there are no individual rights or freedoms that may not be curtailed or suspended by Act of Parliament. In the past, legislative omnipotence may have been saved from becoming an intolerable tyranny by moral, social, and political restraints upon Parliament, and by the parliamentary process itself. Dicey's concept of the Rule of Law assumed that Parliament would not use its legislative power to

[137] For the terms of the 'Sewel convention' and its use in practice, see B.K. Winetrobe, 'Counter-Devolution? The Sewel Convention on Devolved Legislation at Westminster' (2001) 6 *Scottish Law & Practice Quarterly* 286; and A. Page and A. Batey, 'Scotland's Other Parliament: Westminster Legislation about Devolved Matters in Scotland since Devolution' [2002] *Public Law* 501. Between June 1999 and April 2002, 23 Sewel motions were adopted, covering 24 separate Bills: Page and Batey, pp. 502–5. See also J. Mitchell et al. in R. Hazell (ed.), *The State of the Nations 2003* (2003) ch. 5. See also Chapter 9.

[138] On the basis laid down in *Thoburn* v. *Sunderland City Council* (above, n. 36), the Scotland Act 1998 is a 'constitutional Act' and as such is not subject to implied repeal.

abrogate the liberties and freedoms which had emerged from the judge-made common law, and would not overturn such revered enactments as the Bill of Rights 1688 and the Habeas Corpus Acts (or, at least, not except in situations of acute and pressing emergency).

A strong argument for constitutional reform was put by Lord Scarman as long ago as 1974:

> It is the helplessness of the law in face of the legislative sovereignty of Parliament which makes it difficult for the legal system to accommodate the concept of fundamental and inviolable human rights. Means therefore have to be found whereby (1) there is incorporated into English law a declaration of such rights, (2) these rights are protected against all encroachments, including the power of the state, even when that power is exerted by a representative legislative institution such as Parliament.[139]

Britain's adherence to the European Convention on Human Rights from 1951 was an important step on the way towards meeting the need for greater protection for human rights.[140] The Convention provided machinery at Strasbourg for judicial investigation into claims brought by anyone within the jurisdiction of a member state against public authorities, and for deciding whether the treatment of that person had met the minimum standards prescribed by the Convention. The first decision of the European Court of Human Rights in a case against the UK was made in 1975;[141] the series of decisions that thereafter involved the UK[142] demonstrated the importance of the issues that arose and in time strengthened the argument for enabling such issues to be decided by judges in the UK.[143] Although the European Court held that a state that is party to the Convention may decide how the Convention rights should be protected within its jurisdiction,[144] the UK's unique position of having no formal means of protecting human rights while not having incorporated the European Convention in national law became exposed to criticism. During the 1980s and 1990s, continuing pressure was placed on British courts to find ways and means of giving effect to the Convention even in the absence of incorporation.[145]

The turning point came with the election in May 1997 of a Labour Government that was committed, with Liberal Democrat support, to the incorporation of the Convention. Before considering the implications for the sovereignty of Parliament of the Human Rights Act 1998, two preliminary points may be made. First, a distinction must be drawn between the process of interpreting statutory provisions and the process of judicial review of legislation by which the judge may strike down invalid legislation. The former but not the latter is accepted as being compatible with parliamentary sovereignty.[146] Second, a distinction may be drawn in providing constitutional protection between existing Acts of Parliament and future Acts. As we saw with regard to Community law, no sovereignty problems arise out of

139 L. Scarman, *English Law: The New Dimension* (1974) 15.

140 See Lord Lester and D. Pannick, *Human Rights Law and Practice* (1998) ch. 1; and Chapter 3 below.

141 *Golder* v. *United Kingdom* (1975) 1 EHRR 524.

142 See A. W. Bradley, in W. Finnie, C. M. G. Himsworth and N. Walker (eds), *Edinburgh Essays in Public Law* (1991) 185–214.

143 See Lord Browne-Wilkinson [1992] *Public Law* 397; Sir John Laws [1993] *Public Law* 59; and Lord Bingham (1993) 109 *LQR* 390.

144 *Swedish Engine-Drivers' Union* v. *Sweden* (1967) 1 EHRR 617, 631; *Republic of Ireland* v. *UK* (1978) 2 EHRR 25, 104.

145 See *R.* v. *Secretary of State for the Home Department, ex parte Brind* [1991] 1 AC 696; and M. Hunt, *Using Human Rights Law in English Courts* (1997).

146 The stronger the rule of interpretation, the greater the possibility that matters of interpretation may merge into matters of review: see T. R. S. Allan (1997) 113 *LQR* 443, 447, n. 77 above.

the former (since today's Parliament may modify the effect of all earlier Acts), but such problems do arise if today's Parliament attempts to regulate or limit legislation to be enacted in the future. Because of these distinctions, discussion of the legal form in which the European Convention on Human Rights might be incorporated envisaged three broad models from a sovereignty standpoint.[147]

Model 1: a new 'Interpretation Act', requiring the courts to take the Convention into account in applying all disputed legislation and, possibly, requiring the courts to give to that legislation a meaning consistent with the Convention, even if the disputed words are general and on their face are not ambiguous.[148] From a sovereignty standpoint, this model is uncontroversial since it does not affect the freedom of Parliament to legislate incompatibly with the Convention.

Model 2: the courts to be empowered to apply the Convention in respect of all earlier legislation, if necessary setting aside or quashing a statutory provision that is in conflict with a Convention right; in respect of all subsequent legislation, the courts to be required to apply the Convention in the form of an 'Interpretation Act' (in the sense used in Model 1). Again, from a sovereignty standpoint, this model is uncontroversial, although it goes significantly further than the first model.[149]

Model 3: the courts to be empowered to apply the Convention to override conflicting provisions in both existing and future Acts of Parliament (with a possible exception for future Acts in which Parliament had expressly indicated its intention to legislate inconsistently with particular Convention rights). From a sovereignty standpoint, there has been much controversy as to whether one Parliament may empower the courts to take such action in respect of future Acts of Parliament since, on the orthodox Diceyan argument, future Parliaments cannot be bound by the Acts of their predecessors. Thus, in 1978 a House of Lords Select Committee on a Bill of Rights concluded:

> There is no way a Bill of Rights could protect itself from encroachment, whether express or implied, by later Acts. The most that such a Bill could do would be to include an interpretation provision which insured that . . . so far as a later Act could be construed in a way that was compatible with a Bill of Rights, such a construction would be preferred to one that was not.[150]

In effect, the view of this committee was that any provision to protect human rights that went further than Model 2 would be nugatory in its effect on future legislation.

The scheme enacted by the Human Rights Act 1998 does not conform closely to any of these models. Its originality consists of the following key elements:

(1) A new strong interpretative duty is applied to all legislation, whether primary or subordinate legislation, regardless of the date of the legislation; this duty must be

[147] For fuller discussion of these models, and for parliamentary attempts to give effect to the Convention before 1997, see the third edition of this work, at 102–5.

[148] In effect, reversing *R.* v. *Secretary of State for the Home Department, ex parte Brind* (above). For an example of model 1, see the New Zealand Bill of Rights Act 1990.

[149] For such a Bill of Rights, see the Hong Kong Bill of Rights Ordinance 1991; and J. Allan [1991] *Public Law* 175.

[150] Report of the Select Committee on a Bill of Rights (1977–78) (24 May 1978, HL 176), 26. On the authority of *Thoburn* v. *Sunderland City Council* (above, n. 36) Parliament may pass a 'constitutional Act' that is protected against implied repeal.

observed by all persons who apply legislation, including courts and tribunals:

So far as it is possible to do so, primary legislation and subordinate legislation must be read and given effect in a way which is compatible with the Convention rights.[151]

(2) Where it is not possible to read and give effect to *subordinate* legislation in a way that is compatible with the Convention rights, such legislation may be quashed or disapplied, except where the parent Act under which it was made prevents removal of the incompatibility.[152]

(3) Where it is not possible to read and give effect to *primary* legislation in a way that is compatible with the Convention rights, such legislation continues in full force, but the High Court or other superior court may make a 'declaration of incompatibility'.[153] Such a declaration does not affect the validity or operation of the statutory provision in question, but one effect of a declaration is that it enables the government by means of 'fast-track' delegated legislation to take remedial action where there are 'compelling reasons' for doing so; a remedial order of this kind may make such amendments to the primary legislation as the minister considers necessary to remove the incompatibility.[154]

(4) All public authorities, defined broadly to include (*inter alia*) all courts and tribunals and also private persons exercising public functions, will be acting unlawfully if they act in a way which is incompatible with Convention rights.[155]

(5) All courts and tribunals must take into account relevant decisions of the Strasbourg Court and other Convention authorities.[156]

(6) A minister of the Crown in charge of a government Bill in Parliament must issue a statement to Parliament that either the Bill is compatible with the Convention or the government wishes the Bill to proceed even though he or she is not able to make a statement of compatibility.[157]

It will be evident from this summary that the scheme does not distinguish between existing and future Acts. In the case of primary legislation (whenever such legislation was enacted), the Act equips the courts with a dual function comprising: (i) the duty (applying to all courts and tribunals) to interpret legislation compatibly with Convention rights, 'so far as it is possible to do so' and (ii) where this is not possible, the power of superior courts to make a declaration of incompatibility. This approach prevents the courts having power to strike down or disapply Acts of Parliament. The reasons for denying the courts this power were set out in the government's white paper, *Rights Brought Home: the Human Rights Bill*:

The Government has reached the conclusion that courts should not have the power to set aside primary legislation, past or future, on the ground of incompatibility with the Convention. This

151 Human Rights Act (HRA) 1998, s. 3(1). For discussion of this duty, see G. Marshall [1998] *Public Law* 167, [1999] *Public Law* 377; F. Bennion [2000] *Public Law* 77; R. A. Edwards, 'Reading down legislation under the Human Rights Act' (2000) 20 *Legal Studies* 353; P. Craig, 'The Courts, the Human Rights Act and Judicial Review' (2001) 117 *LQR* 589; R. A. Edwards, 'Judicial Deference under the Human Rights Act' (2002) 65 *MLR* 859; and K. Starmer, 'Two Years of the Human Rights Act' [2003] *EHRLR* 14.

152 HRA, s. 3(2) (by implication). For the novel demarcation between primary and subordinate legislation for this purpose, see HRA s. 21(1). It is an unfortunate aspect of this demarcation line that the protection given to 'primary' legislation by the Act goes considerably wider than the measures of a sovereign Parliament: and see P. Billings and B. Pontin, 'Prerogative powers and the Human Rights Act' [2001] *Public Law* 21.

153 HRA, s. 4.

154 HRA, s. 10 and Sched. 2.

155 HRA, s. 6(1) and for the related remedies, see ss. 7–9.

156 HRA, s. 2.

157 HRA, s. 19.

conclusion arises from the importance which the government attaches to Parliamentary sovereignty. . . . In enacting legislation, Parliament is making decisions about important matters of public policy. The authority to make those decisions derives from a democratic mandate. . . . To make provision in the Bill for the courts to set aside Acts of Parliament would confer on the judiciary a general power over the decisions of Parliament which under our present constitutional arrangements they do not possess, and would be likely on occasions to draw the judiciary into serious conflict with Parliament. There is no evidence to suggest that they desire this power, nor that the public wish them to have it.[158]

It is possible to criticize this reasoning on the ground that the policy avoids making a sufficiently strong commitment to the protection of human rights and takes refuge in an outdated conception of the authority of Parliament; certainly the policy relies on one unpersuasive argument, namely that 'present constitutional arrangements' do not provide for judicial review of Acts of Parliament. But given that (a) all courts and tribunals must apply the new rule of interpretation where it is possible to do so, and (b) if that is not sufficient to achieve an outcome that is compatible with Convention rights, the superior courts may make a 'declaration of incompatibility', the Act goes a very long way to enabling there to be judicial review of legislation in all but name.

Indeed, under the Act, the judiciary acquired very extensive new functions in relation to legislation by Parliament.[159] Earlier in the chapter, the statement that 'All that a court of law may do with an Act of Parliament is to apply it' was cited.[160] This statement must now be rewritten to bring out the significance of the new interpretative duty and the power of superior courts to declare incompatibility. Although the Human Rights Act states that a declaration of incompatibility 'does not affect the validity, continuing operation or enforcement of the provision in respect of which it is given',[161] a court that makes such a statement will have scrutinized the legislation closely against the Convention jurisprudence, and will have stated the extent of the incompatibility and the reasons for its view. The court will in effect have found that someone's Convention rights have been infringed because of a statutory provision which the court has no power to set aside. It would be surprising if that person did not immediately consider having recourse to the European Court of Human Rights.[162] Even if the Human Rights Act states that the offending legislation continues fully in force, in practice it may become inoperative, for the reason that every time it is applied, further individuals may be prompted to have recourse to Strasbourg. As the Home Secretary stated in the House of Commons,

One of the questions that will always be before Government, in practice, will be, 'Is it sensible to wait for a further challenge to Strasbourg, when the British courts have declared the provision to be outwith the Convention?'[163]

While therefore the Act does not entrust to the courts the power to strike down an Act of Parliament, the courts are empowered to deliver a wound to Parliament's handiwork that

[158] Cm 3782 (1997) para. 2.14.

[159] See K. D. Ewing, 'The Human Rights Act and Parliamentary Democracy' (1999) 62 *MLR* 79, 92: 'As a matter of constitutional legality, Parliament may well be sovereign, but as a matter of constitutional practice it has transferred significant power to the judiciary'.

[160] Above, text at n. 29.

[161] HRA, s. 4(6)(a).

[162] That Court is not, of course, required to take the same view of the legislation as that taken by the British courts and thus could find that the applicant's Convention rights had not been breached.

[163] HC Debs, col. 773, 16 Feb. 1998.

will often prove mortal, even though life support for the legislation must be switched off by the government or by Parliament, not by the courts.

Against this background, it is not possible to accept without qualification the many statements that judges and ministers have made assuring the public at large that the sovereignty of Parliament is not affected.[164] The fact that such assurances can be given, even though they tell only part of the story, certainly facilitated the passage of the Act. Lord Steyn has declared, 'It is crystal clear that the carefully and subtly drafted Human Rights Act preserves the principle of parliamentary sovereignty'.[165] But in 'preserving the principle', the Act has made a significant alteration to the legal status of legislation that affects Convention rights. Indeed, Lord Steyn also stated that 'a new legal order' would come into existence when the Human Rights Act came into effect.[166] In this legal order, Parliamentary sovereignty has been reasserted and continues as a matter of form. But the substance of legislative power which the doctrine implies has been subjected to an important measure of judicial control.[167]

One narrower question that may briefly be mentioned is whether the Human Rights Act has modified the doctrine of implied repeal.[168] Certainly the Act does not rely upon the doctrine as a means by which it affects earlier legislation. Even if an earlier statute plainly infringes a Convention right, and cannot be given an interpretation consistent with the right, it remains in force but subject to a declaration of incompatibility. Conversely, later Acts that cannot be interpreted consistently with a Convention right do not themselves repeal by implication the effect of the Convention rights, since the Human Rights Act must be applied to the later Act. The operation of the later Act is not affected, save that either it can be interpreted in a manner consistently with Convention rights, or it is subject to a declaration of incompatibility. For a later Act to protect itself against the strong duty of interpretation in section 3 of the Human Rights Act and against the possibility of a declaration of incompatibility, it would seem necessary for the later Act to include a provision that expresses a plain intention to exclude operation of the Human Rights Act.[169] Whether or not the doctrine of implied repeal is an indispensable facet of Parliamentary sovereignty, and earlier arguments in this chapter have suggested that it is not, the Human Rights Act has found a way of ensuring that in relation to Convention rights, there will be little space in which the doctrine can be applied.

164 See e.g. *R.* v. *Lambert* [2001] UKHL 37, [2002] 2 AC 545, para. [79] (Lord Hope); *Re S (Minors) (Care Order: Implementation of Care Plan)* [2002] UKHL 10, [2002] 2 AC 291, para. [39] (Lord Nicholls); and *Wilson* v. *First County Trust Ltd* [2003] UKHL 40, [2004] 1 AC 816 para. [127] (Lord Hobhouse). Cf. 32nd Report of the Joint Committee on Human Rights, 2005–06 (HL Paper 278, HC 1716): *The Human Rights Act: the DCA and Home Office Reviews.*

165 *R.* v. *DPP, ex parte Kebilene* [2000] 2 AC 326, 367.

166 [1999] *Public Law* 51, 55.

167 In addition to articles cited in n. 151, above, the expanding literature includes M. Elliott, 'Parliamentary sovereignty and the new constitutional order' (2002) 22 *Legal Studies* 340; A. L. Young, 'Judicial Sovereignty and the Human Rights Act' (2002) 61 *Camb L J* 53; and D. Bonner, H. Fenwick, and S. Harris-Short, 'Judicial Approaches to the Human Rights Act' (2003) 52 *Int & Comp Law Quarterly* 549.

168 See above, text at n. 73. See also N. Bamforth [1998] *Public Law* 572 for discussion of the Act's effect on implied repeal.

169 Cf. D. Feldman, 'The Human Rights Act 1998 and constitutional principles' (1999) 12 *Legal Studies* 165, 178–80. Part 4 of the Anti-terrorism, Crime and Security Act 2001, which introduced indefinite powers of detention without trial of suspected international terrorists, authorized a derogation from Art. 5, ECHR but did not expressly disapply the Human Rights Act 1998. And see *A* v. *Secretary of State for the Home Department* [2004] UKHL 56, [2005] 2 AC 68.

CONCLUSIONS

Having reviewed these four instances of constitutional legislation, we can see that each has affected the sovereignty of Parliament in a different way. The Parliament Acts 1911–49 provide a clear illustration of constitutional legislation by Parliament that affects the political dynamic of the legislative process and raises questions for the courts to resolve that cannot simply be answered in the well-worn terms of Diceyan orthodoxy. The European Communities Act 1972 goes furthest in enabling the courts to decide whether an Act of Parliament complies with Community law and, if it does not, to disapply it. The Human Rights Act has created a new point of constitutional balance, located somewhere between the two opposing poles of parliamentary and judicial supremacy. In the Scotland Act, Parliament has devolved legislative powers to a subordinate assembly that has the potential over time to acquire a political authority that could rival that of Westminster in matters of Scottish law and government. These instances all illustrate the undoubted power of Parliament to legislate on constitutional matters, including its own relationship with the courts. The response of the courts to such legislation must be ascertained before we can be certain of the extent of the constitutional changes that Parliament has initiated.

Discussion of parliamentary sovereignty is liable to become enmeshed in legal technicalities, and to give too little attention to the political significance of the relationship between the courts and Parliament. There is a defence to be made of legislative sovereignty on democratic grounds. Professor Ewing has referred to parliamentary sovereignty as 'a constitutional principle acquired before the advent of democracy yet one which might be said to be the most democratic of all constitutional principles'. The reason is that 'in the democratic era, parliamentary sovereignty is the legal and constitutional device which best gives effect to the principle of popular sovereignty, whereby the people in a self-governing community are empowered – without restraint – to make the rules by which they are to be governed through the medium of elected, representative and accountable officials'.[170]

This makes an important point, but it must be doubted whether any political system today works in such a perfect way as to justify the removal of all restraint upon the making of laws by a popular assembly. How much restraint, of what kind, and what checks and balances there should be on electoral power, are issues that must be addressed in every democracy.[171] And it is essential to consider as a matter of social justice what the outcomes may be, in terms of gainers and losers, from new layers of government at supranational level (as in the European Union) or within the state (as with the Scottish Parliament), or from new forms of protection for the individual (as under the Human Rights Act).[172]

If there are serious concerns in a democracy about ways in which the political process, the conduct of government, and the law's contribution to social order can be improved, they deserve to be debated in a mature and rational manner. The quality of such a debate will be stunted if it proceeds from the starting point that 'Parliament is unable to bind its

[170] K. D. Ewing, '*Just Words* and Social Justice' (1999) 5 *Review of Constitutional Studies* 53, 55. And see his account of the Human Rights Act in (1999) 62 *MLR* 79. For earlier statements of democratic arguments against extending judicial review, see J. A. G. Griffith, 'The Political Constitution' (1979) 42 *MLR* 1 and Lord McCluskey, *Law, Justice and Democracy* (1987). See too Lord Hoffmann (1999) 62 *MLR* 159.

[171] See S. Kentridge, 'Parliamentary Supremacy: Some Lessons from the Commonwealth' [1997] *Public Law* 96.

[172] And see S. Sedley, 'Human Rights: A Twenty-First Century Agenda' [1995] *Public Law* 386.

successors' or that the nineteenth- or mid-twentieth-century relationship between Parliament and the courts was preordained by a beneficent power and is unalterable. For the UK, membership of the European Community has necessarily meant changes in the structure of constitutional law;[173] other changes have been brought about by the Human Rights Act, which has made necessary a reassessment of inherited rules and procedures.

The place of the doctrine of parliamentary sovereignty in the government of the UK has changed in recent years and the process of change will continue during the present century. It may be, as in the case of the Human Rights Act and the Scotland Act, that ways can be found of retaining the form (or appearance) of parliamentary sovereignty; an emphasis on form may be expedient in facilitating the changes in substance that in reality are being made. T. R. S. Allan has advocated open debate based on constitutional principles: 'When constitutional debate is opened up to ordinary legal reasoning, based on fundamental principles, we shall discover that the notion of unlimited parliamentary sovereignty no longer makes any legal or constitutional sense'.[174] What we can be certain about is that future constitutional developments will not be restricted by what may be no more than an outdated straitjacket, and that past decisions will not be determinative of all future issues.

FURTHER READING

Allan, T. R. S. 'Parliamentary Sovereignty: Law, Politics and Revolution' (1997) 113 *LQR* 443.

Foley, M. *The Silence of Constitutions* (1989).

Goldsworthy, J. *The Sovereignty of Parliament: History and Philosophy* (1999).

MacCormick, N. *Questioning Sovereignty: Law, State and Nation in the European Commonwealth* (1999).

Wade, H. W. R. 'The basis of legal sovereignty' [1955] *Camb L J 172.*

USEFUL WEB SITE

www.parliament.uk is a rich storehouse of information about the recent and current work of Parliament, and it includes judgments of the House of Lords. For material relating directly to issues discussed in this chapter, readers are referred to legal journals and to law reports.

173 See F. G. Jacobs, 'Public Law – the Impact of Europe' [1999] *Public Law* 232 ('While some textbook writers continued to maintain that Parliamentary sovereignty was unaffected by Community law, the English judiciary has accepted without question that the most fundamental rule of the Constitution has been modified', at 245).

174 T. R. S. Allan, 'Parliamentary Sovereignty: Law, Politics and Revolution' (1997) 113 *LQR* 443, 449.

3

HUMAN RIGHTS AND THE BRITISH CONSTITUTION

Anthony Lester QC and Kate Beattie

SUMMARY

The European Convention of Human Rights was drafted in the aftermath of the Second World War to confer enforceable rights upon individuals against sovereign states. It provided for an individual right of petition to the European Court of Human Rights. The United Kingdom ratified the Convention in 1951 and accepted the individual right of petition in 1966. Many significant cases have been taken successfully by individuals against the UK to the Court, resulting in Parliament making major alterations to UK law. The courts were not prepared to give full domestic effect to the Convention in the absence of legislation incorporating it into domestic law, but they developed the common law to protect civil and political rights. With the passage of the Human Rights Act 1998, which came into force for the UK as a whole in October 2000, the Convention can be relied upon directly in domestic courts.

The Act reconciles the sovereignty of Parliament with the effective protection of Convention rights by requiring the courts where possible to read and to give effect to legislation in a way compatible with the Convention rights and also by requiring public authorities, other than Parliament – including the courts – to respect and uphold these rights. The courts now develop both public and private law in line with the Convention. Where legislation cannot possibly be interpreted in a way compatible with the Convention rights, the courts are unable to grant an effective remedy, but may grant a declaration of incompatibility stating that the legislation in question violates the Convention rights. The Joint Select Committee on Human Rights scrutinizes government measures for their compatibility with Convention rights, and from October 2007 the Commission for Equality and Human Rights will have broad powers and duties in relation to the promotion and protection of human rights.

Overall the Human Rights Act 1998 has exercised a magnetic force over the entire political and legal system, and is an Act of fundamental constitutional importance.

PARLIAMENTARY SUPREMACY VERSUS FUNDAMENTAL RIGHTS

Since the Second World War the universality of human rights has been recognized by the United Nations as inherent in the very nature of human beings, an essential part of their common humanity. For religious thinkers, human rights are considered to be fundamental because they derive from divine revelation or natural law. Secular thinkers treat human rights as fundamental in the sense that they have a special claim to protection because they are rooted in democratic concepts of popular sovereignty and government by consent, combined with equal rights of the citizen and legal protection against the abuse of power and what John Stuart Mill termed 'the tyranny of the majority'.

There are important British intellectual sources of the concept of fundamental rights, in particular, the writings of Locke, Paine, and Mill. However, for most of the past two centuries, the prevailing British constitutional ideology, influenced by the works of constitutional writers as different as Blackstone, Burke, Bentham, Dicey, and Sir Ivor Jennings, treated British citizens as subjects of the Crown, without the benefit of fundamental constitutional rights giving legal protection to the individual against the state and its agents. According to those writers, what are known as the 'liberties of the subject' are residual and negative in their nature; the individual has the freedom to do what he or she likes, unless forbidden to do so by the common law or by statute. The notion of special constitutional protection of human rights, based upon a higher legal order than ordinary law, was regarded as incompatible with parliamentary supremacy.[1]

The earlier concepts of 'fundamental rights', and of a 'fundamental' constitutional law taking precedence over ordinary laws, became eclipsed at the end of the seventeenth century by the concept of absolute parliamentary sovereignty. In the early part of the century, the judges had struggled not only for independence from undue executive interference but also for the right to withhold effect from laws that they regarded as unconscionable or as contrary to a higher, fundamental natural law. The judges won the struggle for independence against the Crown's claim to rule by prerogative, but the price paid by the common lawyers for their alliance with Parliament against the divine right of kings was that the common law could be changed by Parliament as it pleased. The 'glorious bloodless' revolution of 1688 was won by Parliament, and although the Bill of Rights of 1688–9 and the Act of Settlement of 1700 recognized some important personal rights and liberties, the terms of the constitutional settlement were mainly concerned with the rights and liberties of Parliament. The alliance of Parliament and the common lawyers ensured that the supremacy of the law would mean the supremacy of Parliament; more realistically, it came to mean, between general elections, the supremacy of the government in Parliament. The doctrine of the supremacy of Parliament, described by Lord Hailsham of St Marylebone as operating in practice as an 'elected dictatorship', became the keystone of the British constitution.

According to the traditional English political and legal theory that prevailed until the late twentieth century, as Parliament is sovereign (acting in place of the monarch who could do no wrong) the subjects of the Crown could not possess fundamental rights as against Parliament (which can do no wrong), such as are guaranteed by the many foreign and

[1] See Chapters 1 by Jowell and 2 by Bradley.

Commonwealth constitutions containing fundamental and paramount law. There were no rights that were 'fundamental' in the sense that they enjoy special constitutional protection against interference by Parliament. All Acts of Parliament are equal; a constitutional measure, such as Magna Carta, or the Petition of Right, or the Act of Union with Scotland, has no greater legal importance than, say, a statute to regulate the practice of dentistry. According to this tradition, the liberties of the subject are derived from two principles. The first principle is that we may say or do what we please, provided we do not transgress the substantive law, or infringe the rights of others. The second principle is that public authorities (including the Crown) may do only what they are authorized to do by some rule (including the Royal Prerogative) or by statute.

Again according to traditional English theory, the role of the independent judiciary is essential to maintaining the common law principles of the rule of law, but the courts are subordinate to Parliament. The task of law making is the exclusive province of Parliament, and it would be undemocratic for the non-elected judiciary to act as lawmakers. The judges' constitutional task is faithfully and strictly to interpret the will of Parliament, expressed in detailed legislation, to be read according to its so-called 'plain meaning', and to declare the common law when it is incomplete or obscure. In accordance with this constitutional orthodoxy, if either the textual analysis of the words of a statute or the courts' interpretation of the common law has undesirable consequences, the matter must be corrected by the legislature and not by the courts.

The surest and most effective safeguards, in the opinion of thinkers such as Jennings, are not the rigid legalism and paper guarantees of written constitutions and Bills of Rights, but the benevolent exercise of administrative discretion by public officials, acting as Platonic guardians of the public interest, accountable through their political masters to the legislature and the people. Until recently, the effective safeguards against the misuse of public powers were regarded as being not legally enforceable safeguards but malleable constitutional conventions: the sense of fair play of ministers and the professional integrity of civil servants in using their broad delegated powers; the vigilance of the opposition and of individual members of Parliament in calling the government to account; the influence of a free and vigorous press and a well-informed and active citizenry; and the periodic opportunity to change the government through free and secret elections. It was this state of mind that underpinned the refusal by successive governments to introduce a constitutional Bill of Rights or to make the European Convention on Human Rights directly enforceable in British courts.

THE SPREAD OF FUNDAMENTAL CONSTITUTIONAL LAW AND RIGHTS

Although the ideology of fundamental rights was rejected by successive generations of British governments and constitutional thinkers on the political left and right, it has been a potent force across the world. American and French concepts of human rights and judicial review shaped systems of government subject to binding constitutional codes in Europe and beyond. The conquests of Napoleon's armies spread through the European continent not only the Code Civil but also the public philosophy and public law of the United States and France. These ideas and systems were also spread to other continents. Today, the many countries whose legal systems are based upon the civil law have legally binding constitutional guarantees of fundamental human rights derived from seventeenth-century England and the eighteenth-century enlightenment. In the common law world, as the colonies of the British Empire gained independence, Bills of Rights were introduced giving constitutional protection to human rights.

The human rights-based philosophy also became profoundly influential in creating a new international legal order in the wake of the horrors of the Second World War. In December 1948, the UN General Assembly adopted the Universal Declaration of Human Rights,[2] recognizing certain rights as basic human entitlements: free speech as much as freedom from torture. In 1966, two International Covenants were opened for signature, a Covenant on Civil and Political Rights, and a Covenant on Economic, Social and Cultural Rights. The two Covenants came into force in 1976, and are reinforced by several UN human rights conventions, for example, against torture, race and sex discrimination, and protecting the rights of the child.[3]

THE EUROPEAN CONVENTION ON HUMAN RIGHTS

Meanwhile, in Western Europe, a second terrible war in half a century and the barbarous atrocities of the Nazi Holocaust convinced European politicians and jurists of the need to forge a new Europe. The need to guard against the rise of new dictatorships, to avoid the risk of relapse into another disastrous European war, and to provide a beacon of hope for the peoples of Central and Eastern Europe living under Soviet totalitarian regimes, inspired the foundation, in 1949, of the Council of Europe. Members of the Council of Europe are obliged to accept the principles of the rule of law and the enjoyment by everyone within their jurisdiction of human rights and fundamental freedoms.

One of the Council of Europe's first tasks was to draft a human rights convention for Europe, conferring enforceable rights upon individuals against sovereign states. It was a revolutionary enterprise. The inventors of the Convention were determined never again to permit state sovereignty to shield from international liability the perpetrators of crimes against humanity, never again to allow governments to shelter behind the traditional argument that what a state does to its own citizens or to the stateless is within its exclusive jurisdiction and beyond the reach of the international community. So they resolved to create a binding international code of human rights with effective legal safeguards for all victims of violations by contracting states.

For the first time, individuals would be able to exercise personally enforceable rights under international law, before an independent and impartial tribunal – the European Court of Human Rights – against the public authorities of their own states. No matter whether the violation occurred because of an administrative decision by a minister or civil servant, or because of the judgment of a national supreme court, or because of legislation enacted by a national parliament; there would be no privilege or immunity enabling state

2 See Lord Steyn, 'Human Rights: The Legacy of Mrs Roosevelt' [2002] *Public Law* 473.

3 See generally, A. Lester and D. Pannick (eds), *Human Rights Law and Practice* (2nd edn, 2004) ch. 9.

authorities automatically to shield themselves against supranational European judicial scrutiny.

The birth pangs of the Convention were not easy. In the UK, the Attlee government was particularly keen to preserve strong ministerial powers from judicial review by an international court of unknown worth.[4] It decided only very reluctantly to ratify the Convention, and only on the basis that it would not accept the right of individual petition to the European Commission and Court of Human Rights. The UK was the first country to ratify, on 8 March 1951, and the Convention came into force on 3 September 1953.

The Convention guarantees basic civil and political rights to everyone within the jurisdiction of the Contracting States: the right to life (Article 2); the prohibition of torture and inhuman or degrading treatment or punishment (Article 3); the prohibition of slavery and forced labour (Article 4); the right to liberty (Article 5); the right to a fair trial (Article 6); no punishment without law (Article 7); respect for private and family life (Article 8); freedom of thought, conscience, and religion (Article 9); freedom of expression (Article 10); freedom of assembly and association (Article 11); the right to marry and found a family (Article 12); the right to an effective national remedy (Article 13); and non-discrimination in the enjoyment of Convention rights (Article 14).

The UK ratified the First Protocol to the Convention on 3 November 1952, which added the right to the protection of property (Article 1); the right to education (Article 2); and the right to free elections (Article 3). The UK ratified the Sixth Protocol to the Convention on 27 January 1999, abolishing the death penalty. On 1 February 2004 the UK ratified the Thirteenth Protocol to the Convention, which abolishes the death penalty completely, including in time of war or imminent threat of war.

In December 1965, the first Wilson Government decided to accept the right of individual petition and the jurisdiction of the European Court of Human Rights to rule on cases brought by individuals against the UK. It was to prove to be a momentous decision, for it meant that, in fact if not in a formal sense, political (if not legal) sovereignty was henceforth to be shared with the European institutions created by the Convention. In spite of the importance of the decision and its controversial implications in making Acts of Parliament subject to judicial review, the matter was not discussed in Cabinet or in a Cabinet Committee.[5] Unlike the decision to join the European Community and make Community law directly effective in our courts, Parliament was not asked to legislate to give effect to the consequences of acceptance of the right of petition; there was no public consultation by means of a green or white paper.[6]

In January 1966, when the right of individual petition was accepted for the UK, the Convention was a sleeping beauty (or slumbering beast, depending upon one's viewpoint). The European Court of Human Rights had by then decided only two cases. No one foresaw how the Court's jurisprudence would develop or what a powerful impact its case law would have upon the British constitutional and legal system. It is therefore not surprising that there was no Cabinet consideration or public consultation about the decision to accept the right of petition.

[4] Lester and Pannick, n. 3 above, ch. 18.

[5] A. Lester, 'Fundamental Rights: The UK Isolated?' [1984] *Public Law* 46, at 58–61 and 'UK Acceptance of the Strasbourg Jurisdiction: What Went on in Whitehall in 1965' [1998] *Public Law* 237.

[6] Cf. *The United Kingdom and the European Communities*, Cmnd 4715 (1971).

BRITISH CASES BEFORE THE EUROPEAN COURT OF HUMAN RIGHTS

Judgments of the European Court of Human Rights, which is based in Strasbourg, may involve findings that any of the three branches of government breached the Convention: not only the actions of the Executive, but also of the Legislature or courts. These judgments are binding in international law upon the state concerned, and if it flouts them it risks expulsion from the Council of Europe. To obey them may mean having to enact legislation to repeal an offending statute or to overrule a judgment of the country's highest court.

Acceptance of the right of petition gave British lawyers an important opportunity to obtain effective redress for their clients under the Convention, for want of effective remedies within the UK. In the *East African Asians' case*,[7] the Commission decided that Parliament had breached the Convention in enacting the Commonwealth Immigrants Act 1968, which subjected British Asian passport-holders to inherently degrading treatment by excluding them on racial grounds from their country of citizenship.

The first case in which the European Court found a breach by the UK was *Golder*, which held[8] that the Home Secretary had infringed a prisoner's right of access to the English courts and his right to respect for his correspondence. The first case in which the Court held that the House of Lords had breached the Convention was in relation to an injunction restraining *The Sunday Times* from publishing an article about the 'thalidomide' tragedy because it was prejudicial to pending civil proceedings. By a narrow majority, the Court held[9] the Law Lords' decision to have interfered unnecessarily with the right to free expression.

In all, there have been some 200 judgments of the European Court finding breaches by the UK, many of them controversial and far-reaching. They include: the inhuman treatment of suspected terrorists in Northern Ireland; inadequate safeguards against telephone tapping by the police; unfair discrimination against British wives of foreign husbands under immigration rules; unjust restrictions upon prisoners' correspondence and visits; corporal punishment in schools; corporal punishment by a stepfather; criminal sanctions against private homosexual conduct; the exclusion of homosexuals from the armed services; the lack of legal recognition of transsexuals; ineffective judicial protection for detained mental patients, or would-be immigrants, or individuals facing extradition to countries where they risk being exposed to torture or inhuman treatment, or homosexuals whose private life is infringed; the dismissal of workers because of the oppressive operation of the closed shop; interference with free speech by unnecessarily maintaining injunctions restraining breaches of confidence, or because of a jury's award of excessive damages for libel, or by punishing a journalist for refusing to disclose his confidential source; the right to have a detention order under the Mental Health Act reviewed; parental access to children; access to child care records; review of the continuing detention of those serving discretionary life sentences and mandatory life sentences; blanket restriction on the right of prisoners to vote; lack of effective remedy for violations of privacy; access to legal advice for fine and debt defaulters; unfair court martial procedures; lack of availability of legal aid in some criminal cases; and lack of access to civil justice.

7 Commission's admissibility decision of 14 Dec. 1973 (1981) 3 EHRR 76.

8 *Golder* v. *United Kingdom*, 1 EHRR 524 (1975).

9 *Sunday Times* v. *United Kingdom*, 2 EHRR 245 (1979).

USE OF THE CONVENTION IN BRITISH COURTS

The landmark judgments of the European Court of Human Rights against the UK, despite not being directly enforceable, had a profound impact upon senior British judges. The Strasbourg jurisprudence made them more sensitive to the fault-line in the British legal system that had resulted in repeated failures to give sufficient legal protection to individual rights. It caused our senior judges to take European Convention law more seriously than had been the case in the 1970s and 1980s; and, eventually, to support moves to make Convention rights directly enforceable in British courts.

The Convention was frequently invoked in proceedings before English courts, even before it was fully incorporated.[10] The courts became willing to have regard to the unincorporated Convention and its case law as sources of principles or standards of public policy. They did so when common law or statutory law was ambiguous, or where the common law was undeveloped or uncertain, or in determining the manner in which judicial (as distinct from administrative) discretion should be exercised. In *Brind*,[11] however, the Law Lords decided that they would be usurping the functions of Parliament by incorporating Convention rights through the back door, if they were to interpret broad statutory powers as being limited by or subject to the Convention.

Nevertheless, the European Court's judgments influenced British courts in declaring, as a matter of common law, that there are fundamental constitutional rights, notably, the right to free expression,[12] the right of access to the courts and lawyers,[13] and the right to equal treatment without unfair discrimination.[14] Recently the courts have begun to recognize the right to personal privacy, founded on the existing legal doctrine of breach of confidence.[15] Although *Brind* was a narrowly restrictive decision, the Law Lords recognized that stricter scrutiny of administrative decisions was called for where fundamental human rights were at stake. The Court of Appeal also decided[16] that the more substantial the interference with human rights, the more the court would require by way of justification before it was satisfied that the decision was reasonable. However, the European Court of Human Rights held

[10] M. Hunt, *Using International Human Rights Law in English Courts* (1997) Appendix 1, contains a chronological table of English cases in which judicial reference has been made to unincorporated international human rights law.

[11] *R.* v. *Secretary of State for the Home Department, ex parte Brind* [1991] 1 AC 696 (HL).

[12] See e.g. *Reynolds* v. *Times Newspapers* [1999] 3 WLR 1010 (HL), at 1029, *per* Lord Steyn, and at 1023, *per* Lord Nicholls of Birkenhead; *Derbyshire County Council* v. *Times Newspapers* [1992] 1 QB 770 (CA); [1993] AC 534 (HL).

[13] See e.g. *R.* v. *Secretary of State for the Home Department, ex parte Leech* [1994] QB 198 (CA), at 210A, *per* Steyn LJ; *R.* v. *Lord Chancellor, ex parte Witham* [1998] QB 575 (CA), at 585G–586G, *per* Laws LJ.

[14] *Arthur J S Hall & Co.* v. *Melvyn Keith Simons; Barratt* v. *Ansell & Others; Harris* v. *Schofield Roberts & Hill* [2000] 3 WLR 543 *per* Lord Hoffmann.

[15] *Douglas, Zeta-Jones, Northern Shell plc* v. *Hello! Ltd* [2001] 2 WLR 992, *A* v. *B and C* [2002] EWCA Civ. 337, *Campbell* v. *MGN* [2004] 2 AC 457, *Ash* v. *McKennit* [2006] EWCA Civ 1714, *His Royal Highness the Prince of Wales* v. *Associated Newspapers Ltd* [2006] EWCA Civ 1776. But for limits to the right in English law see *Re S (A child)* [2005] 1 AC 593. See also J. Morgan, 'Privacy in the House of Lords, again' (2004) 120 *LQR* 563; Rachael Mulheron, 'A potential framework for privacy? A reply to Hello!' (2006) *MLR* 679; David Mead, 'It's a funny old game – privacy, football and the public interest' [2006] *EHRLR* 541; Rabinder Singh, QC and James Strachan, 'The Right to Privacy in English Law' [2002] *EHRLR* 129.

[16] *R.* v. *Ministry of Defence, ex parte Smith* [1996] QB 517 (CA), at 554E–G, *per* Sir Thomas Bingham MR for the Court of Appeal.

that this approach was insufficient to satisfy the requirement for an effective domestic remedy under Article 13 of the Convention.

Brind revealed a serious gap in the effective legal protection of human rights in the UK. English courts, influenced by the development of a modern system of public law and by the requirement to give effect to the supremacy of European Community law, did their best to give effect to Convention rights, without statutory incorporation, but it was deference to parliamentary sovereignty which made the Law Lords draw back from complete judicial incorporation. The gap could only be filled by legislation to make Convention rights directly enforceable in British courts.

THE CAMPAIGN FOR INCORPORATION[17]

The first public call for the incorporation of Convention rights by statute was made in 1968.[18] In 1974, Lord Scarman gave his great authority to the campaign to make the Convention directly enforceable, in his radical Hamlyn lectures.[19] In 1976, the Home Secretary, Roy Jenkins, published a little-noticed discussion paper on the subject,[20] and gave his personal support for incorporation. In 1977, the Northern Ireland Standing Advisory Committee on Human Rights published a report unanimously recommending incorporation.[21] In 1978, a Lords Select Committee also recommended incorporation.[22] However, the only political force in favour of incorporation was the Liberal Party.

During the 1980s, especially after the emergence of Charter 88 as an influential political movement, support for incorporation became more widespread, not least among senior judges. The Conservative and Labour Parties remained opposed to incorporation.[23]

On 1 March 1993, the then Leader of the Labour Party, John Smith, QC, gave a lecture under the auspices of Charter 88, entitled 'A Citizen's Democracy'. It represented a turning point in Labour Party policy on human rights in the UK, calling for statutory incorporation of the Convention, and a Human Rights Commission to advise on and bring human rights cases. The 1993 Labour Party Conference adopted a policy document[24] supporting a two-stage process on human rights in the UK: first, the incorporation of the Convention and, secondly, the establishment of an all-party commission to consider and draft a home-grown Bill of Rights.

In 1994, Lord Lester of Herne Hill introduced in the House of Lords the first of two Private Member's Bills to incorporate the Convention into UK law.[25] The first Bill adopted a

17 Robert Blackburn, *Towards a Constitutional Bill of Rights for the United Kingdom* (1999).

18 A. Lester, *Democracy and Individual Rights*, Fabian Tract No. 390, Nov. 1968.

19 Lord Scarman, *English Law – The New Dimension* (1974).

20 *Legislation on Human Rights with Particular Reference to the European Convention on Human Rights* (June 1976), Home Office.

21 *The Protection of Human Rights in Northern Ireland*, Cmnd 7009 (1977).

22 Report of the Select Committee on a Bill of Rights (HL 176 (1978)). There was a bare majority in favour caused by Baroness Gaitskell's refusal to adopt the negative Labour Party line.

23 The Fundamental Freedoms and Human Rights Bill, introduced by Lord Broxbourne in 1985, was passed by the Lords and later introduced in the Commons by Sir Edward Gardner, QC, MP. The Bill received broad cross-party support from the Liberal Democrat front bench and the Conservative and Labour back benches, but it was opposed by the Government and Labour front benches and failed to obtain a sufficient majority to be given a Second Reading (109 HC Official Report, cols 1223–89, 6 Feb. 1987).

24 Labour Party, *A New Agenda for Democracy: Labour's Proposals for Constitutional Reform* (1993).

25 Human Rights Bill, Second Reading Debate, 560 HL Official Report, col. 144 (25 Jan. 1995).

strong form of incorporation; it sought to give the Convention a similar status in UK law as is given to directly effective European Community law under the European Communities Act 1972, empowering the courts to disapply inconsistent existing and future Acts of Parliament, and creating effective remedies for breaches of Convention rights. The Bill had a turbulent passage through the Lords, and was mutilated by wrecking amendments supported by Conservative ministers.

By then, the most senior judges, including the Lord Chief Justice, Lord Taylor of Gosforth, Lord Browne-Wilkinson, and Lord Woolf of Barnes supported the Bill, but, given a political climate of concern about threats to parliamentary sovereignty perceived to come from the supremacy of European Community law, they suggested that it would be prudent to adopt a model that did not give the courts an express power to disapply or strike down inconsistent legislation. Their advice was heeded.

Lord Lester's second Bill, introduced in 1996,[26] was a strengthened version of the New Zealand Bill of Rights Act 1990.[27] It was to be influential in shaping what became the Human Rights Act 1998. Like the New Zealand Bill, it provided that whenever legislation could be interpreted in a manner consistent with Convention rights, then that interpretation would be preferred over any other. Unlike the New Zealand Bill,[28] it did not contain any limitation on the courts' powers to interpret statutes compatibly with Convention rights. Borrowing from the New Zealand model, it provided that, when a government Bill is introduced, it must be accompanied by a ministerial statement of compatibility with Convention rights. The Bill gave flexible powers to the courts to grant appropriate remedies, but did not give the courts the power to disapply or strike down inconsistent legislation. Its success depended upon the willingness of the judiciary to treat it not as ordinary legislation but as a unique constitutional measure, underpinned by international human rights law, to be interpreted and applied purposively.

In December 1996 Jack Straw MP, the then Shadow Home Secretary, and Paul Boateng MP, produced a consultation paper, *Bringing Rights Home*,[29] which set out the Labour Party's proposals for incorporation. In March 1997, the Labour and Liberal Democrat Joint Consultative Committee on Constitutional Reform, co-chaired by Robin Cook MP and Robert Maclennan MP, published its report. The joint report closely reflected the model of

[26] Human Rights Bill, Second Reading Debate, 568 HL Official Report, cols 1725–30 (5 Feb. 1997).

[27] The Bill was drafted with the benefit of advice from Sir Kenneth Keith, former chairman of the New Zealand Law Reform Commission and now a member of the Court of Appeal of New Zealand. He was adviser to Sir Geoffrey Palmer's administration, which had introduced a stronger Bill of Rights which was weakened by opponents during its passage: see Sir Geoffrey Palmer and M. Palmer, *Unbridled Power* (3rd edn, 1997) ch. 15.

[28] S. 4 of the New Zealand Bill of Rights Act 1990, which was introduced during the Bill's passage to satisfy MPs' concerns about parliamentary sovereignty, provides that 'No court shall, in relation to any enactment (whether passed before or after the commencement of the Bill of Rights), –

(a) Hold any provision of the enactment to be impliedly repealed or revoked, or to be in any way invalid or ineffective; or

(b) Decline to apply any provision of the enactment by reason only that the provision is inconsistent with any provision of this Bill of Rights.'

S. 6 provides that 'Whenever an enactment can be given a meaning that is consistent with the rights and freedoms contained in this Bill of Rights, that meaning shall be preferred to any other meaning'. S. 4 was intended to fetter the courts' interpretative powers under s. 6.

[29] Jack Straw MP and Paul Boateng MP, *Bringing Rights Home: Labour's Plans to Incorporate the European Convention on Human Rights into UK Law*, 18 Dec. 1996; the text of which was published in [1997] *EHRLR* 71.

incorporation adopted in Lester's second Private Member's Bill. It also envisaged that there would be a human rights commissioner or commission, or similar public body, to advise and assist those seeking protection of their Convention rights, and able to bring proceedings in its own name; as well as modification of the normal costs rules to promote effective access to justice.

On 1 May 1997, Tony Blair's New Labour Party was returned to office. In October 1997 the Government published a White Paper, *Rights Brought Home: The Human Rights Bill*,[30] together with the Bill itself. The Human Rights Act 1998 received the Royal Assent on 9 November 1998. It was brought fully into force on 2 October 2000.

THE HUMAN RIGHTS ACT 1998

INTRODUCTION

The Human Rights Act[31] reconciles formal adherence to the doctrine of parliamentary sovereignty[32] with the need to enable the courts to provide effective legal remedies for breaches of Convention rights. It is a constitutionally holistic measure, in the sense that each branch of government – the legislature and executive, as well as the judiciary – is called upon to use its public powers compatibly with Convention rights. Apart from Parliament itself,[33] the Act creates a duty upon all public authorities, including the Crown and the courts, to do so.

So far as Parliament is concerned, the Joint Select Committee on Human Rights enables systematic parliamentary scrutiny of government measures for their compatibility with Convention rights and the other human rights conventions to which the UK is party. Parliament, like every public authority, is bound in international law (subject to *Brind*) to comply with international human rights law. It is essential for each House to have the necessary information and expertise to be able to understand the implications for the protection of human rights of the enactment of primary and delegated legislation.[34] Parliament needs to be well informed where the government takes remedial action[35] to amend a statutory

[30] Cm 3782 (1997). [31] 1998 Cap 42. See generally, Lester and Pannick, n. 3 above, ch. 2.

[32] See *R. v. Secretary of State for the Home Department, ex parte Simms* [2000] 2 AC 131; *R. v. Special Commissioner and Another, ex parte Morgan Grenfell & Co. Ltd* [2002] 2 WLR 1299. See further Lord Irvine of Lairg, QC, 'The Impact of the Human Rights Act: Parliament, the Courts and the Executive' [2003] *Public Law* 308; N. Bamforth, 'Parliamentary Sovereignty and the Human Rights Act 1998' [1998] *Public Law* 572.

[33] The broad definition of 'public authority' in s. 6 does not include either House of Parliament or a person exercising functions in connection with proceedings in Parliament: see s. 6(3). However, it includes the House of Lords in its judicial capacity: see s. 6(4).

[34] In addition to the scrutiny work of the Joint Select Committee, other parliamentary select committees perform important scrutiny functions. In the House of Lords, the Constitution Committee examines the constitutional implications of all public Bills coming before the House and keeps under review the operation of the constitution. The House of Lords Select Committee on Delegated Powers and Regulatory Reform is required to report whether the provisions of any Bill inappropriately delegate legislative power, or whether they subject the exercise of legislative power to an inappropriate degree of parliamentary scrutiny; that Committee also scrutinizes Regulatory Reform Orders introduced under the Regulatory Reform Act 2001. The Select Committee on the European Union scrutinizes EU measures for their compatibility with human rights. The Joint Committee on Statutory Instruments has regard to the human rights implications of delegated legislation although the remit is limited to an assessment of whether the legislation is *vires* the enabling legislation. See also David Feldman, 'Parliamentary Scrutiny of Legislation and Human Rights' [2002] *Public Law* 323.

[35] Under s. 10 and Sched. 2.

provision declared by a UK court[36] to be incompatible with Convention rights. The Joint Select Committee on Human Rights also plays a key role in scrutinizing Government action in response to declarations of incompatibility[37] and to findings by the European Court of Human Rights that the UK has violated the Convention.[38]

THE CONVENTION RIGHTS

The Convention rights are civil and political rights and, as such, are regarded as appropriate to be interpreted and applied by the independent judiciary.

The Act does not empower the judiciary to strike down legislation that cannot possibly be read in a way compatible with Convention rights. To that extent, the Act gives a weaker legal status to Convention law than is given to directly effective Community law under section 2 of the European Communities Act 1972. The Act is also weaker than the written constitutions of other Commonwealth countries under which the courts are empowered and required to strike down unconstitutional legislation.[39] However, it endows the UK judiciary with strong interpretative powers which are intended to be used robustly.

DUTY TO AVOID INCOMPATIBILITY BETWEEN DOMESTIC LEGISLATION AND THE CONVENTION

Section 3 of the Act is pivotal. It imposes a duty on courts and tribunals to strive to avoid incompatibility between domestic legislation and the Convention. Existing and future legislation must, so far as is possible, be read and given effect in a way which is compatible with Convention rights.[40] The crucial words in relation to this interpretative obligation are 'possible' and 'must'. As Lord Steyn has pointed out, Parliament specifically rejected the legislative model of requiring a 'reasonable' interpretation, which is to be found in the New Zealand Bill of Rights Act.[41] As the White Paper explained:[42]

> This goes beyond the present rule which enables the courts to take the Convention into account in resolving any ambiguity in a legislative provision. The courts will be required to interpret legislation

36 Under s. 4.

37 Twenty-third Report of Session 2005–6, 'The Committee's Future Working Practices', Joint Committee on Human Rights, HL Paper 239, HC 1575, published 4 Aug. 2006; Nineteenth Report of Session 2004–5, 'The Work of the Committee in the 2001–2005 Parliament', Joint Committee on Human Rights, HL Paper 112, HC 552, published 26 May 2005. See also Janet L. Hiebert, 'Parliament and the Human Rights Act: Can the JCHR help facilitate a culture of rights?' [2006] *International Journal of Constitutional Law* 1.

38 Thirteenth Report of Session 2005–6, 'Implementation of Strasbourg Judgments: First Progress Report', Joint Committee on Human Rights, HL Paper 133, HC 954, published 8 Mar. 2006, and Report of the Council of Europe Parliamentary Assembly Committee of Legal Affairs and Human Rights, 'Implementation of judgments of the European Court of Human Rights', Doc. 11020, 18 Sept. 2006.

39 Apart from New Zealand. In Australia the courts are empowered to strike down unconstitutional legislation, but the Federal Constitution does not contain a full Bill of Rights.

40 'Convention rights' are defined in s. 1(1) of the Act. They are the rights guaranteed under Arts 2 to 12, and 14 of the Convention, Arts 1 to 3 of the First Protocol to the Convention, and Art. 1 of the Thirteenth Protocol to the Convention. Art. 13 – which provides that everyone whose rights and freedoms are violated shall have 'an effective remedy before a national authority' – is not included. That is because the Human Rights Act itself gives effect to Art. 13 by establishing a scheme under which Convention rights can be raised before our domestic courts: *K* v. *Camden and Islington Health Authority* [2002] QB 198 (CA), at 233G–H, *per* Sedley LJ.

41 *Ghaidan* v. *Godin-Mendoza* [2004] 2 AC 557 at 574F–G, *per* Lord Steyn.

42 *Rights Brought Home*, Cm 3782 (1997), para. 2.7.

so as to uphold the Convention rights unless the legislation itself is so clearly incompatible with the Convention that it is impossible to do so.

This duty applies to primary and secondary legislation. It requires courts and tribunals, using techniques developed by Commonwealth and United States courts to construe constitutional Bills of Rights, to 'read down' (that is, to interpret delegated public powers to be exercised only subject to Convention rights), and to read into legislation necessary procedural safeguards of Convention rights.[43] In the words of the Lord Chancellor, 'in 99% of the cases that will arise, there will be no need for judicial declarations of incompatibility'.[44] However, as the Lord Chancellor also observed,[45] the Act:

> does not allow the courts to set aside or ignore Acts of Parliament. [Section] 3 preserves the effect of primary legislation which is incompatible with the Convention. It does the same for secondary legislation where it is inevitably incompatible because of the terms of the parent statute.

Case law on section 3 has established certain fundamental principles to be applied when construing legislation to make it compatible with Convention rights. In the House of Lords in *Re S (Care Order: Implementation of Care Plan)*,[46] Lord Nicholls of Birkenhead stated that section 3 is 'a powerful tool whose use is obligatory. It is not an optional canon of construction. Nor is its use dependent on the existence of ambiguity.' Lord Bingham of Cornhill approved *Re S* in *R. (Anderson)* v. *Secretary of State for the Home Department*[47] but warned that section 3 allowed for judicial interpretation but not 'judicial vandalism' so as to give the statutory provision 'an effect quite different from that which Parliament intended'. Lord Steyn examined the interpretative obligation of section 3 in the rape shield case, *R.* v. *A (No. 2)*,[48] and concluded that,

> in accordance with the will of Parliament as reflected in section 3 it will sometimes be necessary to adopt an interpretation which linguistically may appear strained. The techniques to be used will not only involve the reading down of express language in a statute but also the implication of provisions. A declaration of incompatibility is a measure of last resort. It must be avoided unless it is plainly impossible to do so. If a *clear* limitation on Convention rights is stated *in terms*, such an impossibility will arise.[49]

In *Ghaidan* v. *Godin-Mendoza*[50] Lord Nicholls of Birkenhead observed that section 3 'is one of the primary means by which Convention rights are brought into the law of this country'. He stated that

> Parliament, however, cannot have intended that in the discharge of this extended interpretative function the courts should adopt a meaning inconsistent with a fundamental feature of legislation. That would be to cross the constitutional boundary section 3 seeks to demarcate and preserve. Parliament has retained the right to enact legislation in terms which are not Convention-compliant.[51]

43 See Lord Lester of Herne Hill, QC, 'The Art of the Possible: Interpreting Statutes under the Human Rights Act' [1998] *EHRLR* 665.

44 Lord Irvine of Lairg, 585 HL Official Report, col. 840 (5 Feb. 1998).

45 Lord Irvine of Lairg, 583 HL Official Report, cols 1230–1 (3 Nov. 1997).

46 [2002] 2 AC 291.

47 [2003] 1 AC 837 (HL) at 882G–883D.

48 [2002] 1 AC 45 at 68.

49 See *R.* v. *Secretary of State for the Home Department, ex parte Simms* [2000] 2 AC 115, 132A–B *per* Lord Hoffmann; *R.* v. *Lambert* [2001] 3 WLR 42 *per* Lord Hope of Craighead.

50 *Ghaidan* v. *Godin-Mendoza* [2004] 2 AC 557 (HL).

51 Ibid, at 572B *per* Lord Nicholls of Birkenhead.

Section 19 requires a minister in charge of a Bill to issue a statement that it is compatible with Convention rights. The compatibility statement is published on the face of the Bill. The Joint Select Committee on Human Rights has sought fuller explanations for Government views on the compatibility of Bills with the Act, with limited success.[52] Where the minister has expressed the official view that a Bill's provisions are compatible with Convention rights, the courts will readily conclude that nothing in the Bill was intended to override such rights. However, section 19 statements do not bind the court to conclude that the relevant legislation is compatible with Convention rights, nor do they have persuasive authority.[53]

IMPLIED REPEAL

The deliberate omission from the Act of the equivalent of section 4 of the New Zealand Bill of Rights Act 1990[54] is significant. Such a provision would have required the courts to apply the doctrine of implied repeal to the interpretation of the Act,[55] with the result that a future Parliament would have been deemed to have intended, by implication, to depart from Convention rights in a later statute. Such an approach would have seriously weakened the effectiveness of the Act in securing compatibility between future legislation and Convention rights. The significance of the deliberate omission of the doctrine of implied repeal is that the courts will require *express* provision in a later statute before deciding that a Convention right has been abridged.[56] As Lord Steyn has explained:

> What is the significance of classifying a right as constitutional? It is meaningful. It is a powerful indication that added value is attached to the protection of the right. It strengthens the normative force of such rights. It virtually rules out arguments that such rights can be impliedly repealed by subsequent legislation. Generally only an express repeal will suffice.[57]

The first question the courts must answer is whether the legislation interferes with a Convention right. At that stage, the purpose or intent of the legislation will play a secondary

[52] 'The Work of the Committee in the 2001–2005 Parliament', n. 37 above, paras 75–9; Thirty-second Report of Session 2005–6, 'The Human Rights Act: the DCA and Home Office Reviews', Joint Committee on Human Rights, HL Paper 278, HC 1716, published 14 Nov. 2006, paras 60–6.

[53] *R.* v. *A (No. 2)* [2002] 1 AC 45 (HL) at 75E, *per* Lord Hope of Craighead.

[54] See n. 28 above.

[55] According to the doctrine of implied repeal, if a later Act makes contrary provision to an earlier Act, Parliament (though it has not expressly said so) is taken to intend the earlier Act to be repealed. The same applies where a statutory provision is contrary to a common law rule: see e.g. F. A. R. Bennion, *Statutory Interpretation* (4th edn, 2002), s. 87.

[56] In *R.* v. *Lord Chancellor, ex parte Witham* [1998] QB 575 (DC) at 585G Laws J stated that the common law had given special weight to the citizen's constitutional right of access to the courts which could not be abrogated except by express statutory words. This proposition has been doubted: see *Pierson* v. *Secretary of State for the Home Department* [1998] AC 539 (HL) at 575, *per* Lord Browne-Wilkinson. However, it is submitted that such a proposition must inform the interpretation of future legislation under s. 3 of the Act, especially since the implied repeal doctrine has been deliberately rejected by government and Parliament. Sovereignty belongs to the Parliament of the day, but it must use express words before it will be taken to have decided to use its legislative powers in a way which is incompatible with Convention rights: *pace* Sir William Wade, 'Sovereignty: Revolution or Evolution?' (1996) 112 *LQR* 568 (in relation to the decision of the House of Lords in *R.* v. *Secretary of State for Transport, ex parte Factortame (No. 1)* [1990] 2 AC 85, at 240, *per* Lord Bridge of Harwich, interpreting s. 2(4) of the European Communities Act 1972.

[57] The Rt Hon Lord Steyn, 'The Intractable Problem of the Interpretation of Legal Texts' (2003) 25(1) *Sydney Law Review*. See also *Thoburn and Others* v. *Sunderland City Council and Others* [2002] 3 WLR 247.

role, for it will be seldom, if ever, that Parliament will have intended to legislate in breach of Convention rights. It is at the second stage, when the government is seeking to justify the interference with a Convention right, under one of the exception clauses, that legislative purpose or intent becomes relevant. It is at that stage that the principle of proportionality will be applied.

PROPORTIONALITY

In applying the principle of proportionality, the court needs to ask itself[58] whether (i) the legislative objective is sufficiently important to justify limiting a Convention right; (ii) the means used to impair the Convention right are rationally connected to it; and (iii) the means used to impair the Convention right are no more than is necessary to accomplish that objective.[59]

British courts already had the task of deciding, in areas where Community law governs, whether a statutory rule is necessary and proportionate to the legislative aim. This involved the judicial review of Acts of Parliament against European legal standards, requiring the courts to evaluate the measure's impact in the light of its aims, having regard to evidence about its policy and the social and economic context in which it operates.[60] That is also what is required in interpreting legislation to be compatible with Convention rights.[61]

Although the courts have adopted new interpretive techniques, they cannot usurp the legislative powers of Parliament by adopting a construction which it could not be supposed that Parliament had intended by enacting the Human Rights Act and by previously or subsequently enacting the impugned statutory provision. Where only a fanciful or perverse construction is possible to make the statute compatible with Convention rights, or where the problem created by the apparent mismatch between the statute and Convention rights requires extensive redrafting and choice among different legislative options, the courts can make a declaration of incompatibility. By doing so, they will be marking the boundary between the powers of the judiciary, the Legislature, and the Executive in deciding how the constitutional principles contained in the Act are to be applied. As Lord Steyn has commented, the Act has strengthened the rule of law and separation of powers in the UK, and has made Britain (in effect) a 'constitutional state'.[62]

58 See *de Freitas* v. *Permanent Secretary of Ministry of Agriculture, Fisheries, Lands and Housing* [1999] 1 AC 69 (PC) *per* Lord Clyde at 80C–H approved by Lord Steyn in *R.* v. *Secretary of State for the Home Department, ex parte Daly* [2001] 2 AC 532 (HL) at 547A–548B.

59 See *R. (Farrakhan)* v. *Secretary of State for the Home Department* [2002] 1 QB 1391 at 1418H (CA): a factor of considerable relevance to the test of proportionality is the extent to which the right (there the right to freedom of expression) is restricted.

60 See e.g. *R.* v. *Employment Secretary, ex parte Equal Opportunities Commission* [1995] 1 AC 1 (HL).

61 Although the principle of proportionality 'does not mean that there has been a shift to merits review': *R.* v. *Secretary of State for the Home Department, ex parte Daly* [2001] 2 AC 532 (HL) *per* Lord Steyn at 548B–C. But, as Lord Steyn there stated, 'the differences in approach between the traditional grounds of review and the proportionality approach may therefore sometimes yield different results'. In particular, 'the doctrine of proportionality may require the reviewing court to assess the balance which the decisionmaker has struck, not merely whether it is within the range of rational or reasonable decisions'. Also proportionality 'may require attention to be directed to the relative weight accorded to interests and considerations'. See also *Alconbury Limited* v. *Secretary of State for the Environment, Transport and the Regions* [2001] 2 WLR 1389 (HL).

62 Lord Steyn, 'Democracy, the Rule of Law and the Role of Judges' [2006] *EHRLR* 243 at 250.

In *R. (Anderson)* v. *Secretary of State for the Home Department*,[63] Lord Hutton stated that Parliament has made it clear that:

> it remains supreme and that if a statute cannot be read so as to be compatible with the Convention, a court has no power to override or set aside the statute. All that the court may do, pursuant to s 4 of the 1998 Act, is to declare that the statute is incompatible with the Convention. It will then be for Parliament itself to decide whether it will amend the statute so that it will be compatible with the Convention. Therefore if a court declares that an Act is incompatible with the Convention, there is no question of the court being in conflict with Parliament or of seeking or purporting to override the will of Parliament. The court is doing what Parliament has instructed it to do in s 4 of the 1998 Act.

JUDICIAL INTERPRETATION AND DECLARATIONS OF INCOMPATIBILITY

In deciding to what extent to defer to the opinion of the Legislature, and the area of discretion given to the Executive or other relevant public authority, the courts will take account of the nature of the Convention right involved.[64] Some rights are absolute, for example, the prohibition of torture and inhuman or degrading treatment or punishment.[65] Many Convention rights require a fair balance to be struck between competing rights and interests.[66] There are cases in the social, economic, and political spheres where the Legislature must reconcile competing interests in choosing one policy among several which might be acceptable.

The extent to which the decisionmaker has expertise is also a relevant factor. As Lord Bingham of Cornhill observed in *R.* v. *Secretary of State for the Environment, Transport and the Regions, ex parte Spath Holme Ltd*, 'the allocation of public resources is a matter for ministers, not courts'.[67]

The courts will also take into account the extent to which they have special expertise, for example in relation to what constitutes a fair civil or criminal trial.[68] Where the rights claimed are of particular importance, 'a high degree of constitutional protection' will be appropriate.[69] The European Court of Human Rights has recognized as being of especial importance the rights to freedom of expression, to access to the courts, and to the protection of intimate aspects of private life. In such contexts, judicial deference is far less appropriate, and the courts will carry out particularly strict scrutiny.

In view of the constitutional importance of a declaration of incompatibility, only specified higher courts may make such a declaration,[70] and the Crown must be notified where a

63 [2003] 1 AC 837 (HL) at 895G–H.

64 In *R.* v. *Secretary of State for the Home Department, ex parte Daly* [2001] 2 AC 532 (HL) Lord Steyn commented at 548C that Laws LJ was correct in *Mahmood* v. *Secretary of State for the Home Department* [2001] 1 WLR 840 to point out that 'the intensity of review in a public law case will depend on the subject matter in hand'. Lord Steyn added: 'That is so even in cases involving Convention rights. In law context is everything.'

65 Art. 3.

66 E.g. Arts 8–11, and Arts 1, 2, and 3 of the First Protocol.

67 [2001] 2 AC 349 (HL) at 395. See also *Secretary of State for the Home Department* v. *Rehman* [2003] 1 AC 153 at 187 and 195 (in relation to national security); *R. (Farrakhan)* v. *Secretary of State for the Home Department* [2002] QB 1391 (CA) at 1418B–D (in relation to public order and immigration matters).

68 *R.* v. *DPP, ex parte Kebeline* [2000] 2 AC 326 (HL) at 381.

69 *Libman* v. *A-G of Quebec* (1996) 3 BHRC 269 at 289–90; also *R.* v. *DPP, ex parte Kebeline* [2000] 2 AC 326 (HL) at 381.

70 S. 4(5) – the House of Lords; the Judicial Committee of the Privy Council; the Courts-Martial Appeal Court; in Scotland, the High Court of Justiciary sitting otherwise than as a trial court, or the Court of Session; and in England and Wales or Northern Ireland, the High Court or the Court of Appeal.

court is considering making such a declaration.[71] The declaration of incompatibility is expressed as a discretionary power, but the courts will usually exercise the power if it is impossible to interpret legislation compatibly with Convention rights, unless the government indicates its willingness to resolve the issue without the need for a remedial legislative order. A declaration is not binding on the parties involved, so as to leave open the possibility for the government to argue before the European Court of Human Rights that the measure concerned is compatible with Convention rights.

The declaration of incompatibility is essential in bringing the problem to the attention of the executive and the legislature, and acting as trigger for amending legislation by means of a remedial order. Despite its incompatibility with Convention rights, the offending legislation will remain valid and effective, unless and until legislative amendments are made.[72] Parliamentary sovereignty is maintained and Parliament's legislative powers remain intact in deciding whether to remove the incompatibility. However, failure to make such amendment to remedy the domestic court's declaration of incompatibility could lead to a complaint to the European Court of Human Rights in Strasbourg, with a high probability that the European Court will come to a similar conclusion. This will be a powerful incentive to the government to introduce, and for Parliament to approve, the necessary remedial order.

A number of declarations of incompatibility have been made, but not all of them have survived appeal to the House of Lords.[73] In each case the incompatibility has been remedied by primary or secondary legislation, or is under review with a view to being remedied. The Human Rights Act contains a specific mechanism for making swift remedial orders to remedy incompatibility.[74] One example of this procedure is *R. (H)* v. *MHRT (North and East London Region)*,[75] where the Court of Appeal found that provisions of the Mental Health Act 1983 concerning requirements for discharge from hospital were incompatible with Article 5 of the Convention. As a result the Mental Health Act (Remedial) Order 2001[76] was made, changing the burden of proof in discharge cases. In *International Transport Roth GmbH* v. *Secretary of State for the Home Department*,[77] the Court of Appeal held that the scheme under the Immigration and Asylum Act 1999 which imposed automatic penalties on those responsible for bringing clandestine entrants into the UK, even if they had done so without their knowledge, was incompatible with Article 6(2). In response to this finding, a clause was inserted into the Nationality, Immigration and Asylum Act 2002. In *A.* v. *Secretary of State for the Home Department*,[78] the House of Lords held that the indefinite detention of terrorist suspects under Part IV of the Anti-Terrorism, Crime and Security Act[79] was incompatible with Articles 5 and 14 of the Convention. In response the Government repealed the relevant provisions and created a system of control orders in the Prevention of Terrorism Act,[80] which has also been challenged as incompatible with the Human Rights Act.[81]

[71] S. 5. [72] S. 4(6); s. 10 provides for remedial action to amend the relevant provision.

[73] For a list of declarations of incompatibility, see the Appendix to judgment of Lord Steyn in *Ghaidan* v. *Godin-Mendoza* [2004] 2 AC 557 at 578–82; Appendix 8 to 'The Work of the Committee in the 2001–2005 Parliament', n. 37 above.

[74] S.10. See further Seventh Report of Session 2001–2, 'The Making of Remedial Orders', HL Paper 58, HC 473, published 17 Dec. 2001; Annex 5 to 'The Work of the Committee in the 2001–2005 Parliament', n. 37 above.

[75] [2001] 3 WLR 512. [76] SI 2001/ 3712. [77] [2003] QB 728. [78] [2005] 2 AC 68.

[79] 2001 Cap 24. [80] 2005 Cap 2.

[81] *Secretary of State for the Home Department* v. *MB* (2006) HRLR 37; *Secretary of State for the Home Department* v. *JJ* (2006) HRLR 38.

EFFECT ON POWERS AND DUTIES OF PUBLIC AUTHORITIES

The Human Rights Act radically affects the scope of the powers conferred and duties imposed upon public authorities. Section 6 creates a new constitutional or public law tort, committed whenever a public authority acts in a way which is incompatible with Convention rights, with a potential liability to pay damages for breach of the new statutory duty. A person who claims that a public authority has acted or proposes to act in a way made unlawful by section 6(1) of the Act is able, if he or she is a victim, to bring proceedings against the authority,[82] or rely on the Convention right or rights concerned in any legal proceedings.[83] In relation to any act (or proposed act) of a public authority, which the court finds is (or would be) unlawful, it is able to grant such relief or remedy, or make such order, within its powers as it considers just and appropriate.[84]

A public authority is expansively defined to include courts and tribunals and 'any person certain of whose functions are functions of a public nature'.[85] This is intended to ensure that a private body must act compatibly with Convention rights where, for example, it administers a prison, or runs a railway, or deals as a regulatory body with complaints against the press. In *Aston Cantlow Parochial Church Council* v. *Wallbank*,[86] Lord Nicholls of Birkenhead explained the purpose of section 6:

> those bodies for whose acts the state is answerable before the European Court of Human Rights shall in future be subject to a domestic law obligation not to act incompatibly with Convention rights. If they act in breach of this legal obligation victims may henceforth obtain redress from the courts of this country. In future victims should not need to travel to Strasbourg.

But the range of public authorities covered by the Act has proved a difficult issue. The courts have adopted a restrictive and narrow interpretation of the meaning of public authority, and are at risk of failing to give effect to the intention of Parliament in passing the Act.[87] The Joint Select Committee on Human Rights published a thorough, critical report on the subject[88] and sustained pressure on the Government, including during the passage of the Equality Act 2006 through Parliament, led to an assurance that the Government would intervene in a suitable test case to clarify the scope of 'public authority' in the Act.[89] It is vital

[82] S. 7(1)(a). [83] S. 7(1)(b).

[84] S. 8(1). No award of damages may be made unless, taking into account all of the circumstances of the case, including any other relief or remedy granted in relation to the act in question, and the consequences of any decision in respect of that act, the court is satisfied that an award is necessary to afford just satisfaction to the person in whose favour it is made: see s. 8(3). The award of damages is therefore a discretionary matter, not an entitlement: see *R. (KB)* v. *Mental Health Review Tribunal* [2003] 3 WLR 185 at 197G–199B (Stanley Burnton J) and *R. (N)* v. *Secretary of State for the Home Department* [2003] HRLR 583, 640–1, para. 196 (Silber J).

[85] S. 6(3). [86] [2004] 1 AC 546 at 553H–554A.

[87] See *R. (on the application of Heather)* v. *Leonard Cheshire Foundation* [2002] 2 All ER 936. The House of Lords gave a more expansive interpretation in *Aston Cantlow* but did not refer to the *Leonard Cheshire* or *Poplar Housing* decisions, leaving the law in an uncertain state.

[88] Seventh Report of Session 2003–04, *The Meaning of Public Authority under the Human Rights Act*, HL Paper 39, HC 3, published 3 Mar. 2004.

[89] Equality Bill, Second Reading Debate, 672 HL Official Report, col. 1303 (15 June 2005). The Government intervened in the case *R. (on the application of Johnson and others)* v. *London Borough of Havering* [2007] EWCA CIV 26, but the Court of Appeal upheld the narrow approach in *R. (on the application of Heather) v. Leonard Cheshire Foundation* [2002] 2 All ER 936. The case is on appeal to the House of Lords. The Lord Chancellor has indicated that the Government will seek out another suitable test case if necessary: 'The Human Rights Act: the DCA and Home Office Reviews', n. 54 above, Ev 8, 30 Oct. 2006.

that this issue is resolved, so that the UK is not at risk of breaching its international obligations to protect the rights of all those within its jurisdiction and to provide mechanisms for redress where those rights are breached. It may be that primary legislation is needed to clarify this area of uncertainty in the scope of the Act.[90]

The fact that courts and tribunals have a duty to act compatibly with the Convention is significant because of the Act's potential 'horizontal effect'.[91] The courts have a duty to act compatibly with the Convention, not only in cases involving other public authorities, but also in developing the common law when deciding cases between private persons. This is especially the case where the Convention imposes positive obligations on the state to protect individuals against breaches of their rights.[92] In *X.* v. *Y.*,[93] the Court of Appeal held that employment tribunals had, so far as it was possible, to read and give effect to employment legislation in a way that was compatible with the Convention, albeit the Human Rights Act did not give an applicant any cause of action against a respondent that was not a public authority.

RELATIONSHIP WITH THE COMMON LAW

The Act weaves Convention rights into the warp and woof of the common law and statute law. Convention rights have effect not as free-standing rights; they are given effect through and not around UK statute law and common law, by interpreting, declaring, and giving effect to written and unwritten law compatibly with Convention rights.[94] The courts must, so far as possible, declare the common law in a way compatible with Convention rights, just as they must, so far as is possible, interpret and give effect to legislation in that way.[95] Before the coming into force of the Act, the courts had already redrawn the contours of defamation law[96] and of the law protecting confidential information[97] to give greater weight to the right to free speech. A right of personal privacy is now being developed out of existing principles of law and equity.[98]

Wisely, the Act does not require the courts to interpret and apply Convention rights by treating the Strasbourg case law as binding precedent. They must have regard to the

[90] See 'The Human Rights Act: the DCA and Home Office Reviews', n. 52 above, paras 86–92.

[91] See further M. Hunt, 'The "Horizontal Effect" of the Human Rights Act' [1998] *Public Law* 423; A. Lester and D. Pannick, 'The Impact of the Human Rights Act on Private Law: The Knight's Move' (2000) 116 *LQR* 380; Ivan Hare, 'Vertically challenged: Private Parties, Privacy and the Human Rights Act' [2001] 5 *EHRLR* 526. See also the cases on privacy listed in n. 15 above.

[92] In *Costello-Roberts* v. *United Kingdom* (1993) 19 EHRR 112, at 132, paras 26–7 the ECtHR recalled that it has 'consistently held that the responsibility of a state is engaged if a violation of one of the rights and freedoms defined in the Convention is the result of non-observance by that state of its obligation under art. 1 to secure those rights and freedoms in its domestic law to everyone within its jurisdiction. . . . [T]he state cannot absolve itself from responsibility by delegating its obligation to private bodies or individuals.'

[93] (2004) ICR 1634.

[94] See s. 11: a person's reliance on a Convention right does not restrict any other right or freedom conferred on him or her by or under any law having effect in any part of the UK, or his or her right to make any claim or bring any proceedings which he or she could make or bring apart from ss. 7 to 9.

[95] For an example of judicial consideration of whether a common law offence is compatible with Convention rights, see *R.* v. *Rimmington* [2006] 1 AC 459.

[96] See e.g., *Reynolds* v. *Times Newspapers* [1999] 3 WLR 1010 (HL); and *Derbyshire County Council* v. *Times Newspapers* [1992] 1 QB 770 (CA), [1993] AC 534 (HL); *AG* v. *Guardian and Times Newspapers* [1990] 1 AC 109 (HL).

[97] See e.g. A. Lester, 'English Judges as Law Makers' [1993] *Public Law* 269 at 284–6.

[98] See n. 15 above and A. Lester, 'English Judges as Law Makers' [1993] *Public Law* 269 at 284–6. See also Dawn Oliver, *Common Values and the Public/Private Divide* (1999).

Strasbourg jurisprudence,[99] but are not bound to follow it. The European Court has recognized[100] that 'By reason of their direct and continuous contact with the vital forces of their countries, the national authorities are in principle better placed than an international court to evaluate local needs and conditions'. In *Kay* v. *Lambeth London Borough Council*,[101] the Law Lords held that although domestic courts were not strictly required to follow the rulings of the European Court of Human Rights, they were obliged to give practical recognition to the principles it laid down. However, UK judges must follow binding domestic precedent rather than a subsequent, inconsistent Strasbourg authority in the interests of adhering to the rules of precedent, even in the Convention context.[102]

The elastic and elusive Strasbourg doctrine of the 'margin of appreciation' is applied by the European Court on the basis of ad hoc pragmatic judgments, sometimes lacking in clear and consistent principles. There has been some hesitation about whether domestic courts should use the Convention as a floor or a ceiling in relation to interpreting the rights protected under the Human Rights Act. In *R. (Ullah)* v. *Special Adjudicator* Lord Bingham commented,[103]

> It is of course open to member states to provide for rights more generous than those guaranteed by the Convention, but such provision should not be the product of interpretation of the Convention by national courts, since the meaning of the Convention should be uniform throughout the states party to it. The duty of national courts is to keep pace with the Strasbourg jurisprudence as it evolves over time: *no more, but certainly no less.*

Lord Steyn has also observed that the purpose of the Human Rights Act 'was not to enlarge the rights or remedies of those in the UK whose Convention rights have been violated but to enable those rights and remedies to be asserted and enforced by the domestic courts of this country and not only by recourse to Strasbourg'.[104] While this was certainly an object of the Human Rights Act, it is to be hoped that our judges do not regard the Convention jurisprudence as a cage or limit on human rights protection in the UK.[105] If our judges continue to do so, it will strengthen the case for a British Bill of Rights.

In the previous version of this chapter it was remarked that the developing principles contained in the constitutional case law of courts in other common law countries – such as the Constitutional Court of South Africa, the Supreme Courts of the United States, Canada, and India, the High Court of Australia, and the Court of Appeal of New Zealand – were likely to be at least as persuasive as the Strasbourg case law. There have been several

[99] S. 2. Domestic courts should normally follow the decisions of the ECtHR: *R. (Alconbury Developments Ltd)* v. *Secretary of State for the Environment, Transport and the Regions* [2003] 2 AC 295 at 313C, *per* Lord Slynn of Hadley; and *R. (Anderson)* v. *Secretary of State for the Home Department* [2003] 1 AC 837 (HL) at 879H–80C (Lord Bingham of Cornhill for the HL). But it may be appropriate for the domestic court to depart from a decision of the ECtHR if the reasoning is unpersuasive. See *R.* v. *Spear and others* [2003] 1 AC 734 (HL) at 750D–751B (Lord Bingham of Cornhill) and at 774G–775F (Lord Rodger of Earlsferry). See also *R.* v. *Lyons and others* [2003] 1 AC 976 (HL) at 996H–997F (Lord Hoffmann).

[100] *Buckley* v. *United Kingdom* (1996) 23 EHRR 101 at 129.

[101] *Kay* v. *Lambeth London Borough Council* [2006] 2 AC 465 (HL).

[102] In *Kay* the allegedly inconsistent decisions were the House of Lords decision in *Harrow London Borough Council* v *Qazi* [2004] 1 AC 983 (HL) and the subsequent European Court of Human Rights decision in *Connors v UK* [2004] 40 EHRR 189.

[103] [2004] 2 AC 323 at 350C, emphasis added.

[104] *R. (SB)* v. *Denbigh High School* [2006] 2 WLR 719 at 730F *per* Lord Steyn.

[105] See Roger Masterman, 'Taking the Strasbourg jurisprudence into account: Developing a 'municipal law of human rights' under the Human Rights Act' [2005] ICLQ 907.

references to international and comparative jurisprudence in cases under the Human Rights Act,[106] but also some reservation expressed about its use. In *R. (Gillan)* v. *Commissioner of Police of Metropolis* Lord Bingham remarked that,[107]

> The Strasbourg jurisprudence is closely focused on the facts of particular cases, and this makes it perilous to transpose the outcome of one case to another where the facts are different. Still more perilous is it, in my opinion, to seek to transpose the outcome of Canadian cases decided under a significantly different legislative regime.

Courts have also continued to decide cases involving important principles of human rights on the basis of the common law, in addition to the Convention. For example, in *A.* v. *Secretary of State for the Home Department*,[108] which concerned the use of evidence obtained by torture, the House of Lords relied on principles of the common law, together with the Convention and the UN Convention Against Torture, to hold that evidence obtained by torture should be excluded as unreliable, unfair, offensive to ordinary standards of humanity and decency and incompatible with the principles on which courts should administer justice.

REMEDIES FOR BREACH

Where a court finds a breach of Convention rights, it may grant such remedy as is just and appropriate, provided that the remedy is within its powers.[109]

When all effective domestic remedies have been exhausted, applicants may apply to the European Court of Human Rights. Since the incorporation of Convention rights via the Human Rights Act, there have been over 100 judgments of the European Court finding violations of the Convention by the UK. Several Human Rights Act cases have been considered by the Strasbourg Court, and the Court has continued to find violations of the Convention despite the protection offered by the Human Rights Act.[110]

In two respects, Treasury concern about public expenditure persuaded the Government to require the courts to have regard to Convention law where domestic law provides well-developed and more appropriate standards.[111] The Act adopts[112] the Convention 'victim'

106 See for example *R. (Ullah)* v. *Special Adjudicator* [2004] 2 AC 323 at 351B–352A *per* Lord Bingham of Cornhill; *R.* v. *A (No 2)* [2002] 1 AC 45 at paras 100–2 *per* Lord Hope of Craighead; *R.* v. *Lambert* [2002] 2 AC 545 at paras 34–5 *per* Lord Steyn.

107 [2006] 2 AC 307 (HL) at 342E. See also *Brown* v. *Stott* [2003] 1 AC 681 at 724 *per* Lord Hope of Craighead.

108 [2006] 2 AC 221 (HL).

109 S. 8. The Act is intended to give effect to Art. 13 of the Convention by creating effective domestic remedies for breaches of Convention rights. Under s. 1(1), Art. 13 is not included in the list of Convention rights directly secured by the Act, because the Act gives effect to Art. 13 by establishing a scheme under which Convention rights can be raised before our domestic courts: see *K* v. *Camden and Islington Health Authority* [2002] QB 198 (CA) at 233G–H *per* Sedley LJ; *In Re S (Minors)* [2002] 2 AC 291 (HL) at 318E *per* Lord Nicholls of Birkenhead. See also *R.* v. *Secretary of State for the Home Department, ex parte Brind* [1991] 1 AC 696 (HL); *Rantzen* v. *Mirror Group Newspapers* [1994] QB 670 (CA); *R.* v. *Khan* [1997] AC 558 (HL).

110 See, for example, *Wainwright* v. *UK* (App. No. 12350/04), judgment of 26 Sept. 2006, and *Hirst* v. *UK* (2006) 42 EHRR 41, where the Strasbourg court found a violation of the Convention where domestic courts had not. By contrast, in *Pretty* v. *UK* (2002) 35 EHRR 1 and *Evans* v. *UK* (App. No.6339/05), judgment of 7 Mar. 2006, the Strasbourg court confirmed domestic decisions that there was no breach of Convention rights.

111 A similar concern probably explains the inclusion of s. 7(1)(a) which requires proceedings against a public authority by a victim of an unlawful act to be brought within one year from the date on which the act complained of took place, or such longer period as the court considers equitable. The framers of Commonwealth constitutional guarantees of human rights have not found it necessary to include such a limitation.

112 S. 7(3), (4), and (7).

test[113] as the requirement for standing to bring a direct action against public authorities for breaches of Convention rights; and, in an attempt to restrict liability in damages, the courts must have regard[114] to the European Court's case law[115] on what constitutes 'just satisfaction', when awarding damages for such breaches.

After some early indications that UK courts would apply domestic scales of damages, along the lines of tortious awards, and that awards of damages should not be on the low side as compared with tortious awards,[116] the House of Lords has indicated that our courts should not aim to be significantly more or less generous than the European Court, though they are not inflexibly bound by awards given in Strasbourg.[117] In *R. (Greenfield)* v. *Home Secretary*, Lord Bingham emphasized that a finding of violation will be an important part of the remedy and an important vindication of the right asserted, and further that damages need not ordinarily be awarded to encourage high standards of compliance by member states.[118] Our courts' restraint is in part attributable to the lack of clarity in Strasbourg case law about the principles of just satisfaction, which has frequently been remarked upon by UK courts. But UK judges have also displayed a more general reluctance to award damages in human rights cases, which cannot be attributed solely to the limited utility of Strasbourg jurisprudence.[119]

Whether the approach of UK courts to remedies under the Human Rights will stand up to scrutiny in Strasbourg remains to be seen. In *Wainwright v UK*,[120] the European Court of Human Rights found a violation Article 13 of the Convention (the right to an effective remedy) where the applicants had been subjected to a negligent strip search in violation of Article 8. One of the applicants had been awarded damages for battery, but the House of Lords held that they could not secure redress for the alleged breach of Article 8. While the European Court did not comment specifically on whether section 8 of the Human Rights Act could afford an effective remedy for the purposes of the Convention, it may be that the restrictive approach of our domestic courts will be revised in future.[121]

EXTRA-TERRITORIAL AND RETROSPECTIVE EFFECT

The territorial reach of the Human Rights Act has been tested in a number of cases, with some issues still to be resolved by the House of Lords. The approach of the UK courts has been to hold that the territorial ambit of the Act is coextensive with that of Article 1 of the Convention, thereby importing the Convention case-law on the ambit of Article 1.[122]

113 Under Art. 34 of the Convention, dealing with the standing to bring individual applications.

114 S. 8(4). 115 Under Art. 41 of the Convention.

116 *R. (Bernard) v. Enfield London Borough Council* [2003] HRLR 111; *R. (KB) v. South London and South and West Region Mental Health Review Tribunal* [2004] QB 936. See also *Anufrijeva v. Southwark London Borough Council* [2004] QB 1124 at 1160, where the Court of Appeal stated that the suggestion that damages should be on the low side in comparison to those awarded for torts 'should in future be ignored'.

117 *R. (Greenfield) v. Home Secretary* [2006] 1 WLR 673 (HL).

118 Ibid. at 684B–C, *per* Lord Bingham of Cornhill.

119 See, however, *Van Colle v Chief Constable of Hertfordshire* [2006] 3 All ER 963, where a total award of £50,000 was granted for violations of Arts 2 and 8 of the Convention.

120 *Wainwright* v. *UK* (App. No. 00012350/04), judgment of 26 Sept. 2006.

121 See R. Clayton, 'Damage limitation: the courts and Human Rights Act damages' [2005] *Public Law* 429; R. Clayton, 'HRA Damages after *Greenfield*: Where Are We Now?' [2006] *JR* 213.

122 See *R. (Skeini)* v. *Secretary of State for Defence* [2006] 3 WLR 508 (HL) (this case is on appeal to the House of Lords, to be heard in 2007); *R. (Quark Fishing Ltd)* v. *Secretary of State for Foreign and Commonwealth Affairs*

Several cases have established that the Human Rights Act offers no protection for acts committed prior to 2 October 2000, when the Act came into force, even though the UK was bound by the Convention before that date.[123] In the case of *R. (Hurst)* v. *Commissioner of Police of the Metropolis*,[124] the House of Lords rejected the prospect of a limited retrospective application for section 3 of the Act, on the basis that courts were not obliged to give effect to the UK's international obligations to respect the Convention rights which predated the coming into force of the Human Rights Act.

COMMISSION FOR EQUALITY AND HUMAN RIGHTS

In October 2007, Britain will at long last have a statutory body charged with the promotion and protection of human rights, as well as a unified approach to enforcing equality legislation across all strands. It was not until October 2003, three years after the Human Rights Act came into force, that the Government announced plans to create the Commission for Equality and Human Rights, despite many calls to do so at the time of incorporating the Convention.[125]

The Commission will play a vital role in improving public understanding and awareness of the Human Rights Act. Research suggests that most Britons are unaware of their human rights,[126] and there is limited evidence to suggest that the Human Rights Act has had a beneficial impact on public authorities and improved standards in public services.[127]

The Commission will be under a general duty to exercise its functions with a view to encouraging and supporting the development of a society in which individual human rights, equality and the dignity and worth of each individual are respected.[128] The Commission's work may extend beyond those rights guaranteed by the Human Rights Act to encompass human rights guaranteed by other international human rights treaties, including economic, social and cultural rights. The Commission will have a range of powers including monitoring the law and advising government about the effectiveness of equality

[2006] 1 AC 529 (HL); *R. (B. and others)* v. *Secretary of State for the Foreign and Commonwealth Office* [2005] QB 643 (CA). See also Ralph Wilde, 'The Extraterritorial Application of the Human Rights Act' in *Current Legal Problems* (2005, Vol. 58), 47–82.

123 *Re McKerr* [2004] 1 WLR 804 (HL); *R.* v. *Lambert* [2002] 2 AC 545 (HL); *R.* v. *Kansal (No 2)* [2002] 2 AC 69 (HL); *Wilson* v. *Secretary of State for Trade and Industry* [2003] 3 WLR 568 (HL).

124 On the retrospective effect of s. 3, see also *Wilson* v. *Secretary of State for Trade and Industry* [2003] 3 WLR 568.

125 On 30 Oct. 2003, the Secretary of State for Trade and Industry and Minister for Women, the Rt Hon Patricia Hewitt M.P., announced the Government's plans to create a Commission for Equality and Human Rights: HC Official Report, col. 17WS (30 Oct. 2003).

126 A survey conducted by YouGov for the Disability Rights Commission revealed that 70% of the British population could not name any of their human rights, but also that 62% thought it was a good thing to have an Act to protect everyone's human rights in Britain: YouGov Survey, 26–28 June 2006. See www.drc-gb.org/newsroom/news_releases/2006/70_per_cent_of_britons_don%e2%80%99t_k.aspx.

127 Institute for Public Policy Research, *Improving Public Services: Using a Human Rights Approach*, June 2005; Audit Commission, *Human rights: improving public service delivery*, September 2003; British Institute of Human Rights, *Something for Everyone: The impact of the Human Rights Act and the need for a Human Rights Commission*, December 2002. The Department for Constitutional Affairs Review suggests that the Human Rights Act has had a beneficial impact upon policy formulation, but also that there are widespread myths and misperceptions of the Act among the public: Department for Constitutional Affairs, 'Review of the implementation of the Human Rights Act', DCA 38/06, Jul. 2006.

128 Equality Act, s. 3.

and human rights enactments and about the likely effect of a proposed change of law;[129] conducting inquiries into any matter relating to its duties;[130] providing legal assistance to individuals;[131] and bringing and intervening in judicial review proceedings.[132]

The Commission will be a non-departmental public body, in keeping with the existing equality commissions. The Joint Select Committee on Human Rights strongly criticized this model,[133] and subsequently amendments were made to the Equality Act in the House of Lords to enhance the Commission's *de facto* independence.[134] The Equality Act also provides that the Commission will have funding which is 'reasonably sufficient' for the purpose of enabling it to perform its functions.[135] It will remain to be seen whether the Commission's annual budget (£70 million at the time of writing) is sufficient to cover the organisation's many activities.

DEFENDING THE HUMAN RIGHTS ACT

The Human Rights Act is arguably the greatest constitutional reform in the UK of the twentieth century. But it is under attack not just from the Conservative Party, and from the media, but also from the Labour Government which brought it into being. At the highest levels of government there is a continuing and deeply worrying failure to respect the culture of human rights that underpins the Human Rights Act. While the Government has since expressed its commitment to retaining the Act, and acknowledged that the Act has not had a significant impact on the Government's ability to fight crime, terrorism, or to deal with immigration,[136] repeated comments by the Prime Minister, Tony Blair MP, and other Government ministers have undermined the Act and its place within the British constitution.[137] The Government has not ruled out amending the Act to require particular regard to be paid to the right to life in Article 2 (in particular, the state's duty to maintain public security and safety), in a similar way to sections 12 and 13 in relation to freedom of expression and freedom of thought, conscience and religion, even though there is little evidence that this is necessary or would make any difference to the Act's operation.[138]

Assaults on the Human Rights Act and campaigns by the tabloid press to repeal the Act have shown the importance of entrenching rights in a written Constitution which defines the concept of citizenship in the UK for the twenty-first century. Now that there is to be a

129 Equality Act, s. 11. 130 Equality Act, s. 16. 131 Equality Act, ss 28–29.

132 Equality Act, s. 30.

133 Eleventh Report of Session 2003–4, 'Commission for Equality and Human Rights: Structure, Functions and Powers', Joint Committee on Human Rights, HL Paper 78, HC 536, published 5 May 2004, paras 108–143; Sixteenth Report of Session 2003–4, 'Commission for Equality and Human Rights: The Government's White Paper', Joint Committee on Human Rights, HL Paper 156, HC 998, published 4 Aug. 2004, paras 41–52; Sixteenth Report of Session 2004–5, 'Equality Bill', Joint Committee on Human Rights, HL Paper 98, HC 497, published 31 Mar. 2005, paras 27–30; Fourth Report of Session 2005–6, 'Legislative Scrutiny: Equality Bill', Joint Committee on Human Rights, HL Paper 89, HC 766, published 19 Dec. 2005, paras 21–27.

134 See Sched. 1, Part 4, para 42(3), Equality Act. See generally Anthony Lester and Kate Beattie, 'The New Commission for Equality and Human Rights' [2005] *Public Law*.

135 Sched. 1, Part 3, para 38, Equality Act.

136 'Review of the implementation of the Human Rights Act', n. 127 above. However, the Review does identify the European Court decision *Chahal* v. *UK* (1996) 23 EHRR 413 as affecting the Government's ability to deal with terrorist suspects by means of deportation or removal.

137 See generally 'The Human Rights Act: the DCA and Home Office Reviews', n. 52 above.

138 'Review of the implementation of the Human Rights Act', n. 127 above, p. 39.

Supreme Court for the UK,[139] it would be fitting if there were a supreme law which that Court could be charged with overseeing. Both the Labour Party[140] and the Conservative Party[141] have shown interest in bringing forth a British Bill of Rights. It is essential that any Bill of Rights provides equivalent or greater protection of human rights, not less protection than currently guaranteed by the Human Rights Act. There are also crucial questions to be answered about whether a Bill of Rights would be entrenched, and how it would relate to the Convention, to which the UK would (presumably) remain a party.

CONCLUSION

The Human Rights Act 1998 is a central pillar of the new British–Irish confederal and Scottish and Welsh quasi-federal systems of devolved government, securing minimum standards of protection of Convention rights throughout the UK as a whole. Under each system, Convention rights are given a special constitutional status. In Scotland, Convention rights are legally superior to Acts of the Scottish Parliament, and provide standards by which those Acts (as well as the acts of Scottish ministers) must be judged. In this way, 'the Convention will be pivotal to Scottish constitutional law'.[142] Prior to its suspension, the Northern Ireland Assembly had no power to legislate in a way which was incompatible with Convention rights.[143] The Welsh Assembly is required to exercise its powers as a public authority in ways compatible with Convention rights.[144] Only the Westminster Parliament remains free to exercise its non-judicial powers in ways which are incompatible with Convention rights.

Unless the present and future administrations recognize the Human Rights Act as no ordinary law, but a constitutional measure that, except in highly exceptional circumstances, takes precedence over ordinary legislation, there will be a powerful case to entrench human rights by means of a new constitutional settlement.

FURTHER READING

Clayton & Tomlinson *The Law of Human Rights* (2000).

Feldman, D. *Civil Liberties and Human Rights in England and Wales* (2nd edn, 2002).

139 As a result of changes enacted by the Constitutional Reform Act 2004 Cap 4.

140 The Labour Party consultation document *Bringing Rights Home: Labour's plans to Incorporate the ECHR into UK Law* (1996) anticipated a future UK Bill of Rights and Responsibilities (p. 14). However, the DCA Review expressed reservations about the merits of a British Bill of Rights: 'Review of the implementation of the Human Rights Act', n. 127 above.

141 Speech by the Rt Hon David Cameron MP, 'Balancing freedom and security – A modern British Bill of Rights', delivered to the Centre for Policy Studies, 26 June 2006; Speech by Dominic Grieve MP, 'Liberty and Community in Britain', 2 October 2006.

142 Lester and Pannick, n. 3 above, ch. 5 on Scotland, by Lord Reed.

143 Ibid., ch. 6 on Northern Ireland, by Brice Dickson. In the St Andrews Agreement of 13 October 2006 the Government committed itself to establishing a forum on a Bill of Rights for Northern Ireland, which will build on the work already undertaken by the Northern Ireland Human Rights Commission on a Bill of Rights.

144 Ibid., ch. 7 on Wales, by Kate Gallafent.

Institute for Public Policy Research *A British Bill of Rights* (2nd edn, 1996).

LAUTERPACHT, H. *An International Bill of the Rights of Man* (1945).

LAUTERPACHT, H. *International Law and Human Rights* (1950).

LESTER & PANNICK *Human Rights Law and Practice* (2nd edn, 2004).

WADHAM, MOUNTFIELD, EDMUNDSON & GALLAGHER *Blackstone's Guide to the Human Rights Act 1998* (4th edn, 2007).

USEFUL WEB SITE

www.odysseustrust.org

4

BRITAIN IN THE EUROPEAN UNION

Paul Craig

SUMMARY

Membership of the European Union raises a number of important issues in domestic constitutional law. In political terms, the fact that an increasing amount of legislation emanates from the Community means that we should be concerned about the method by which this legislation is made at Community level, and the way in which it is scrutinized in Parliament. In legal terms, Community law raises issues about sovereignty and how our membership of the Community has affected traditional conceptions of Parliamentary supremacy. Treaty articles and norms made thereunder often give rise to rights which individuals can use in their own name in national courts. Community law conceptions of fundamental rights are binding on member states and continue to be of relevance even after the passage of the Human Rights Act 1998. Membership of the Community has also had important constitutional implications for the judiciary, since national courts also function as Community courts. The discussion will conclude with consideration of the Constitutional Treaty.

INTRODUCTION

All aspects of national law have been affected to varying degrees by our membership of the European Union. Constitutional law is no exception. Indeed it is arguable that the effects of EU law on constitutional law have been particularly far reaching. This chapter will describe and evaluate this impact. The discussion will begin by considering the effect of the EU on the political order. There will be an analysis of the Community's legislative process, and the ways in which the Westminster Parliament has sought to accommodate this legislation. The focus will then shift to the effect of the EU on the constitutional legal order. There will be discussion of sovereignty, the constitutional importance of direct effect, the relevance of Community concepts of fundamental rights, and the changed role of national courts. The analysis will conclude with discussion of the Constitutional Treaty.

THE COMMUNITY AND THE NATION STATE

The idea of national identity played a powerful part in forging modern nation states out of principalities in both Germany and Italy in the second half of the nineteenth century. The nation-state was lauded in literature, philosophy, and music. The horrors of the Second World War were however believed by many to be the result of excessive nationalism. It was felt that the states within Europe should be organized so as to reduce the likelihood of further conflict.[1] This practical ideal lay behind the European Coal and Steel Community (ECSC) which was signed 1951. Coal and steel were the primary materials used in warfare. If production and distribution could be controlled by a centralized authority it would be far less possible for any country to develop a war machine which could be used against its neighbours. The success of the ECSC led pro-Europeanists to believe that more complete economic and political integration was feasible. Plans were drawn up for a European Defence Community (EDC). This was felt to require some form of wider European Political Community (EPC), which would coordinate foreign policy, as well as provide for economic and political integration.[2] Germany would be allowed a limited rearmament within the framework of the EDC. These plans proved to be too ambitious. The French left and right wings both objected, albeit for different reasons, to the idea of German rearmament, even within the EDC. The collapse of the EDC led also to the abandonment of ideas for the EPC.

This setback convinced advocates of European integration that a less overtly political step would be more likely to gain agreement. This was the rationale behind the European Economic Community (EEC) in 1957, the Rome Treaty. The focus was primarily on economic integration, bringing down trade barriers and ensuring free movement of economic factors of production. The architects of the original Treaty were however fully cognisant of the relationship between economics and politics. They realized that closer economic integration would bring closer coordination on social policy, as well as matters which had a more direct political impact.

There have been a number of important amendments to the Rome Treaty. The Single European Act 1986 had the principal objective of facilitating the completion of the single market. The Treaty on European Union, the Maastricht Treaty, which entered into force in 1993, was more far-reaching. It introduced the three-pillar structure. The First Pillar embraced the Community Treaties, and was supranational in nature. A number of important institutional and substantive changes were made, including an increase in the powers of the European Parliament, and the setting of a detailed timetable for economic and monetary union. The Second Pillar was concerned with Common Foreign and Security Policy, and the Third Pillar with Justice and Home Affairs. What distinguished the Second and Third Pillars was that decision making remained much more intergovernmental in nature, as compared to that which operates in the First Pillar. The member states dominated decision making under the Second and Third Pillars, largely to the exclusion of the

[1] J. Pinder, *European Community: The Building of a Union* (3rd edn, 1998); D. Urwin, *The Community of Europe: A History of European Integration since 1945* (2nd edn, 1995); M. Holland, *European Integration from Community to Union* (1993).

[2] The proposal for an EDC was made by France in 1950 and the EDC Treaty was signed, but not ratified, in 1952 by the six states of the ECSC. The French National Assembly refused to ratify the EDC Treaty. Plans for both defence and political union were then shelved.

Commission, the European Parliament, and the European Court of Justice. The Treaty of Amsterdam, which entered into force in 1999, brought further changes. The line between decision making within the Second and Third Pillars, and that within the First Pillar, was blurred. While the former remain intergovernmental in nature, they are now more infused with a supranational tenor than hitherto. The Treaty of Nice 2000 was designed primarily to deal with the institutional consequences of enlargement. More recently a Constitutional Treaty was drafted for the EU. This will be considered below.

The EEC as originally established had four major institutions. The Council of Ministers was composed of representatives from the member states. The Commission, consisting of members appointed from the states, who were, however, independent of their own country, represented the Community interest. The Assembly was originally an indirectly elected body representing the people. The Court of Justice was the fourth institution of prime importance. While the Community's institutional structure has, in formal terms, changed little since the original EEC Treaty, the powers accorded to the different institutions, and the way in which they interact, have changed markedly.

THE LEGISLATIVE AND DECISION-MAKING PROCESS

For the first 30 years of the Community's existence decision making was dominated by the Council and Commission. The Assembly had limited formal powers in the EEC Treaty. Its role in the legislative process was restricted: it only had a right to be consulted where a specific Treaty article stipulated that this should be so. The confined nature of the Assembly's powers was explicable in part because few if any international organizations had any democratically elected legislature which possessed real power at the international level. The explanation was also in part a reflection of the view of the Community held by its prime architects. Monnet, one of the principal founders, adopted a strategy of what has been termed elite-led gradualism.[3] It was hoped that popular consent would follow this lead, but the need to engage powerful business and labour organizations was accorded a much higher priority than the 'direct involvement of as yet uninformed publics'.[4] While Monnet was broadly in favour of a democratic Community 'he saw the emergence of loyalties to the Community institutions developing as a *consequence* of elite agreements for the functional organization of Europe, not as an essential *prerequisite* to that organization'.[5] Moreover, the legitimacy of the Community was to be secured through outcomes: peace and prosperity.

It was the Commission and the Council that dominated decision making during this 30-year period. The Commission was given a plethora of powers of a legislative, administrative, executive, and judicial nature.[6] Its legislative powers are of particular importance. The Commission has the right of legislative initiative, which means that it has a major influence over the development of the Community's legislative agenda. This, and its other powers, served to place the Commission at the heart of the Community.

[3] W. Wallace and J. Smith, 'Democracy or Technocracy? European Integration and the Problem of Popular Consent', in J. Hayward (ed.), *The Crisis of Representation in Europe* (1995) 140.

[4] Loc. cit.

[5] M. Holland, n. 1 above, p. 16. Italics in the original.

[6] P. Craig and G. de Búrca, *EU Law, Text, Cases and Materials* (3rd edn, 2002) ch. 2.

Notwithstanding this array of formal powers, the Council exerted increasing control over the Commission during this period. This was largely through institutional developments that were initially outside the strict letter of the Treaty, all of which served to increase the Council's influence over Community legislation.[7] The Luxembourg Accords ensured that decisions which affected important interests of a particular member state would not be taken unless that state agreed, even where the Treaty stipulated that voting was to be by qualified majority. Decision making was thus carried forward under the 'shadow of the veto' even when it was not formally invoked. The Committee of Permanent Representatives, the organ providing institutional support for the Council, developed its own working parties which enabled it to engage in a dialogue with the Commission over the details of legislative proposals. Management and regulatory committees emerged as the vehicle through which member state input could be ensured when decision making had been delegated to the Commission. Finally, the European Council, meetings of the heads of state, became an institutionalized forum through which member states could influence the overall direction of the Community at the highest level.

The Assembly, formally renamed the European Parliament (EP) by the Maastricht Treaty, pressed for greater powers in the legislative process, bolstered as it was by the fact that it had been directly elected since 1979. In the early 1980s it put forward radical proposals for a revision of the entire Treaty, which would have placed it in the centre of the legislative process. These proposals fell largely on stony ground. However, the Single European Act 1986 did afford the EP a real role in the legislative process for the first time. The cooperation procedure gave the EP power in the enactment of legislation, and made it necessary for the Commission, when drafting legislation, to take account of the EP's views.[8] The years since 1986 have seen the powers of the EP increase still further. The Maastricht Treaty[9] introduced the co-decision procedure, which gives more power to the EP than the cooperation procedure. The Amsterdam Treaty[10] further strengthened the EP's position under the co-decision procedure. It also extended its sphere of application, so that much important Community legislation is now subject to the co-decision procedure.

The details of the procedure are complex.[11] Suffice it to say for the present that the procedure accords the EP, in formal terms, coequal powers in the legislative process with the Council. A proposal is sent by the Commission to both the Council and the EP. The EP can if it wishes propose amendments at its first reading of the measure. If the Council approves of these then the proposed act can be adopted at that stage. The Council may however not agree with the EP's amendments, in which case the Council adopts what is known as a common position which is communicated to the EP. The EP then has three months to respond. It can at this Second Reading of the measure agree to the Council's common position, or not take a decision. The act will then be deemed to have been adopted in accordance with the common position. The EP may alternatively reject the common position in which case the act will not be adopted. It may however suggest further amendments. It is open to the Council to accept the EP's Second Reading amendments, in which case the act becomes law in the form of the common position as amended. If the Council does not approve of all the

[7] Ibid., 157–9.

[8] M. Westlake, *The Commission and the Parliament: Partners and Rivals in the European Policy-Making Process* (1994) and *A Modern Guide to the European Parliament* (1994).

[9] The Treaty on European Union, known as the Maastricht Treaty, entered into force in 1993.

[10] The Treaty entered into force in 1999.

[11] Craig and de Búrca, n. 6 above, pp. 144–7.

amendments then a meeting of the Conciliation Committee is convened. The Conciliation Committee has an equal number of representatives from the Council and the EP. Its task is to reach agreement on a joint text. If it is able to do, then this must be approved by the EP and the Council.

Although the co-decision procedure is complex it works and serves to accommodate the differing institutional interests of those concerned with the passage of Community legislation. The Commission will consult with the EP and the Council about the overall legislative programme for the coming year. It will also consult with the Council, or more accurately the Committee of Permanent Representatives, and the EP, or the relevant committee thereof, about a draft measure before it begins to go through the Article 251 procedure. The formal powers given to the EP by Article 251 enable it to propose changes at an early stage which, if accepted by the Council, can then be embodied in the measure which becomes law at that stage. The EP is then given further power if the Council does not accept all the EP's first reading suggestions. The EP can accept, reject, or propose further amendments to the Council's common position at the Second Reading stage. The bottom line, as one might say, is that an act will not be passed unless both the EP and the Council agree, hence the appellation co-decision.

THE NATURE OF THE COMMUNITY

It is important not to view the Community as if it were a nation-state, nor should one necessarily expect the form of institutional ordering to conform to that commonly found at the domestic level. Conceptions of the separation of powers, which play a marked role in the allocation of functions within domestic constitutions, do not have the same centrality within the EC. The legislative process is divided between the Council, the EP, and the Commission. This has a real impact on the relationship between the EP and the Council. The latter, for all its power, cannot dominate the former in the way that the executive dominates the legislature at Westminster. The EP will be run by the largest party, or a coalition, which will have its own agenda, albeit being mindful of what will be acceptable to the Council and the Commission. Responsibilities of an executive nature are exercised by the Commission, the Council, and the European Council. Administrative responsibility for the implementation of Community policy lies principally with the Commission, but it will often work through and with national bureaucracies. The EP does moreover have oversight powers through which it can call the Commission to account for the way in which Community policy is administered. It was the exercise of these powers that led to the appointment of the Committee of Independent Experts, whose report prompted the resignation of the Santer Commission in 1999.

Judicial power resides principally with the European Court of Justice (ECJ) and the Court of First Instance (CFI). The Commission does however have powers of a judicial nature. It will be the body that brings member states to court under Article 226 if they are in breach of the Treaty. The Commission will give the initial judicial decision on important issues such as competition law and state aids. The ECJ and the CFI have far-reaching powers of judicial review, which can be used to ensure that Community institutions do not exceed their power. The ECJ will adjudicate on important inter-institutional disputes between the principal Community organs. The ECJ has read into the EC Treaty general principles of law which are used to judge the legality of Community action. These principles include proportionality, legitimate expectations, principles of procedural legality and fundamental rights. It is the ECJ which will also adjudicate on disputes concerning subsidiarity, whereby member states will challenge the competence of the Community to act, arguing that the subject matter should have been left for resolution at state level.[12]

The theme which appears repeatedly in papers emanating from the Community is that of institutional balance, rather than separation of powers.[13] This refers to the desirability of preserving a proper balance of power between the Council, as representing the interests of the member states, the EP as representing the people, and the Commission as guardian of the overall aims of the Treaty. While classical ideas of the separation of powers are not therefore central to the institutional ordering within the EC, another constitutional principle, the Rule of Law, is of prime importance. Article 6 of the Treaty of European Union declares that the Community is founded on the respect for human rights, democracy, and the Rule of Law. Respect for these principles is made a condition of membership of the European Union.[14]

THE UNITED KINGDOM PARLIAMENT AND LEGISLATIVE SCRUTINY

It is clear that membership of the Community has significant implications for the Westminster Parliament, and also for the Welsh Assembly and the Scottish Parliament. We shall begin by considering the machinery introduced to deal with Community legislation, and then consider some more general issues concerning the relationship between Parliament and the EC.

In terms of machinery,[15] Committees of the House of Commons have been established to consider whether delegated legislation is necessary in order to implement, for example, an EC directive, and also to scrutinize proposals that emerge from the EC, in order to provide Parliament with information about impending European legislation. Concern that legislation emanating from Europe was not receiving proper attention led the House of Commons' Procedure Committee to propose the establishment of five standing committees. Only three were in fact established, in part because of the difficulty of finding MPs willing to staff more committees. The system works in the following way. The European Scrutiny Committee examines EU documents, such as draft proposals for legislation, and reports on the 'legal and political importance' of each document. It considers approximately 1,000 documents each year, half of which are deemed to be of legal or political importance, such that the Scrutiny Committee reports substantively on them. It recommends approximately 40 such documents per year for further consideration by one of the European Standing

[12] Case C–84/94, *United Kingdom* v. *Council* [1996] ECR I-5755; Case 233/94, *Germany* v. *European Parliament and the Council* [1997] ECR I-2405.

[13] P. Craig, 'Democracy and Rulemaking within the EC: An Empirical and Normative Assessment' (1997) 3 *ELJ* 105.

[14] Art. 49 TEU.

[15] T. St J. N. Bates, 'European Community Legislation before the House of Commons' (1991) 12 *Stat LR* 109; E. Denza, 'Parliamentary Scrutiny of Community Legislation' (1993) 14 *Stat LR* 56; The European Union Scrutiny System in the House of Commons(2005) available at www.parliament.uk/parliamentary_committees/european_scrutiny/the_european_scrutiny_system_in_the_house_of_commons.cfm.

Committees, and approximately three per year for debate on the floor of the House. The latter only occurs if the House decides that they should be considered in this way. The relevant European Standing Committee will consider the merits of the issues. The new regime has undoubtedly had a positive impact.[16] It has been hampered in part by the brevity of time left for discussion before the Community legislation is considered by the Council, and by the way in which such legislation is often drafted.[17] These problems are exacerbated by the fact that MPs are not overly eager to take on such unglamorous work, and by the fact that those who do participate in the standing committees are often extreme partisans on one side or the other of the domestic European debate.[18] It would nonetheless be wrong to underestimate the value of the work performed by the European Scrunity Committee itself. Its reports are clearly and succinctly presented.[19] They show an awareness of the legal and political importance of issues that are often complex. The committee's evaluation will sometimes support that of the relevant government minister, and will sometimes take a differing line. The very fact that there is a body within the UK looking at such issues, other than the relevant department of state, is undoubtedly beneficial. The European Scrutiny committee will also liaise where necessary with departmental select committees.

There is also a House of Lords' Select Committee on the European Union. It is chaired by a salaried officer of the House[20] and considers any Community proposal that it believes should be drawn to the attention of the House. The Committee functions through a number of subcommittees which are subject-matter based.[21] These subcommittees will co-opt other members of the House of Lords for the investigation of particular issues. The House of Lords' Select Committee is therefore different from that in the House of Commons. The latter will sift through Community legislation and refer matters on to the standing committee where this is warranted. The House of Lords' committee will produce its own valuable, detailed reports on particular issues.[22]

Having considered the machinery used to review Community legislation, we should now consider in more general terms the relationship between the UK Parliament and the EC. Space precludes analysis of the possible ways in which national parliaments might play a role within the Community.[23] The focus will rather be on the way in which Parliament views

16 The European Union Scrutiny System in the House, n. 15.

17 *Twenty-Seventh Report of the Select Committee on European Legislation*, HC 51-xxvii (1995–6).

18 A. Adonis, *Parliament Today* (2nd edn, 1993) 156.

19 See e.g. *Twenty Seventh Report of the Select Committee on European Scrutiny*, HC 34-xxvii (1999), dealing with diverse matters such as the extension to third-country nationals of social security rights, the decommissioning of nuclear research facilities, and the revision of Community competition law; *Third Report of the European Union Scrutiny Committee, The European Union's Annual Policy Strategy 2006*, HC 34-iii (2005); *Fourteenth Report of the European Union Scrutiny Committee, Aspects of the EU's Constitutional Treaty* HC 38-xiv-1 (2005).

20 The chairman will decide which issues are of sufficient importance to warrant scrutiny by one of the subcommittees.

21 There are seven such subcommittees which deal with: economic and financial affairs, trade and external relations; energy, industry, and transport; environment, public health, and consumer protection; agriculture, fisheries, and food; law and institutions; social affairs, education, and home affairs.

22 See e.g. *Third Report of the Select Committee on the European Communities*, HL 23 (1999), dealing with reforms to Comitology procedures; *Nineteenth Report of the Select Committee on the European Communities*, HL 101 (1999), dealing with the then forthcoming European Council meeting which was the first such meeting to deal with justice and home affairs.

23 E. Smith (ed.), *National Parliaments as Cornerstones of European Integration* (1996); P. Norton (ed.), *National Parliaments and the European Union* (1996).

the Community. This is of course affected by whether a particular MP is in favour of the EC or not. There is nonetheless a more general sense in which Parliament, as an institution, has been ambivalent about the allocation of power between the Community institutions. MPs have been concerned about the Community's 'democratic deficit'. One way to redress this deficit was to accord greater power to the EP, as has been done. Parliament has however been wary of further extending the EP's power. This is in part because there is a concern that the growing influence of the EP could lead to a diminution in that of the national Parliament, and in part because a Community with an empowered European Parliament will be that much more legitimate, not a conclusion favoured by 'Euro-sceptics'. The concern or ambivalence is also because an enhanced role for the EP would make it more difficult for Parliament to exert influence over Community decision making. When the EP was excluded from the legislative process, and when the Luxembourg veto applied to decision making within the Council, it was possible for the national Parliament to exercise, in theory at least, considerable control over the passage of EC legislation. The leading party in Parliament could tell the relevant minister to oppose a measure in the Council, and to use the veto as a last resort. Times have now changed. The political climate means that the use or threat of the veto is no longer acceptable in the way that it was. Qualified majority voting applies to almost all issues in the Council.[24] The EP, as we have seen, now has a significant role in the legislative process through the co-decision procedure. The final content of Community legislation will be shaped by negotiation between the states within the Council, by the interaction of the Council and the EP through the co-decision procedure, and by the mediating influence of the Commission. In these circumstances it is more difficult for Parliament at Westminster to have a real impact on Community decision making.

SOVEREIGNTY

THE TRADITIONAL DEBATE

A detailed analysis of sovereignty is provided by Anthony Bradley, above.[25] The present discussion will focus on sovereignty and the EC. It is however necessary to mention, albeit briefly, some of the background to the general sovereignty debate.

The debate over sovereignty has been characterized as a contest between the traditionalists, represented by Dicey[26] and Wade,[27] and upholders of the New View, represented by Jennings,[28] Heuston,[29] and Marshall.[30] The form of argument used by Sir William Wade is in fact very different from that advanced by Dicey, and therefore it is the views of Wade that will be considered here. No attempt will be made to consider the detail of the debate between Wade and the advocates of the New View.[31] The view of sovereignty advanced by Sir William Wade is captured in the following quotation.[32]

24 The member states are accorded differing numbers of votes within the Council.

25 Chapter 2.

26 A. Dicey, *An Introduction to the Study of the Law of the Constitution* (10th edn, 1967).

27 H. W. R. Wade, 'The Basis of Legal Sovereignty' [1955] *CLJ* 172.

28 Sir I. Jennings, *The Law and the Constitution* (5th edn, 1959), ch. 4.

29 R. F. V. Heuston, *Essays in Constitutional Law* (2nd edn, 1964), ch. 1.

30 G. Marshall, *Constitutional Theory* (1971), ch. 3.

31 For detailed discussion, see P. Craig, 'Parliamentary Sovereignty of the United Kingdom Parliament After *Factortame*' (1991) 11 *YBEL* 221.

32 N. 27 above, p. 174.

An orthodox English lawyer, brought up consciously or unconsciously on the doctrine of parliamentary sovereignty stated by Coke and Blackstone, and enlarged on by Dicey, could explain it in simple terms. He would say that it meant merely that no Act of the sovereign legislature (composed of the Queen, Lords and Commons) could be invalid in the eyes of the courts; that it was always open to the legislature, so constituted, to repeal any previous legislation whatever; that therefore no Parliament could bind its successors . . . He would probably add that it is an invariable rule that in case of conflict between two Acts of Parliament, the later repeals the earlier. If he were then asked whether it would be possible for the UK to 'entrench' legislation – for example, if it should wish to adopt a Bill of Rights which would be repealable only by some specially safeguarded process – he would answer that under English law this is a legal impossibility: it is easy enough to pass such legislation, but since that legislation, like all other legislation, would be repealable by any ordinary Act of Parliament the special safeguards would be legally futile. This is merely an illustration of the rule that one Parliament cannot bind its successors. It follows therefore that there is one, and only one, limit to Parliament's legal power: it cannot detract from its own continuing sovereignty.

This thesis has been vigorously challenged by the proponents of the New View, who argued that 'manner and form' provisions enacted in a particular statute would be binding, in the sense that a later statute dealing with the same subject matter could only alter the earlier statute if passed in accordance with the provisions of that earlier statute.[33]

THE JUDICIAL RESPONSE PRIOR TO *FACTORTAME*

On the traditional view of sovereignty as represented by Sir William Wade the latest will of Parliament must predominate; if there is a clash between a later and an earlier norm, then the latter is taken to be impliedly repealed or disapplied by the former. This view of sovereignty meant that there could be tensions between UK and EC law. The primacy of EC law over national law[34] was asserted by the ECJ early in its developing jurisprudence,[35] and extended by later case law.[36]

Prior to *Factortame* there were three differing strands within the UK jurisprudence. In some cases courts spoke in terms of the traditional orthodoxy on sovereignty.[37] The second, and dominant, line of cases sought to blunt the edge of any conflict between the two systems by using strong principles of construction: UK law would, whenever possible, be read so as to be compatible with Community law.[38] In the third type of case the courts accepted, in principle, the idea of purposive construction, but felt unable to read the UK legislation to be in conformity with the relevant EC norm.[39]

FACTORTAME, *EOC*, AND *THOBURN*

The leading decision is now *R.* v. *Secretary of State for Transport, ex parte Factortame Ltd.*[40] The applicants were companies which were incorporated under UK law, but the majority of the directors and shareholders were Spanish. The companies were in the business of sea

33 Nn. 28, 29, 30 above.
34 Craig and de Búrca, n. 6 above, ch. 7.
35 Case 6/64, *Costa* v. *ENEL* [1964] ECR 585, 593.
36 Case 106/77, *Amministrazione delle Finanze dello Stato* v. *Simmenthal Spa* [1978] ECR 629.
37 *Felixstowe Docks Railway Co.* v. *British Transport Docks Board* [1976] 2 CMLR 655, 664.
38 *Litster* v. *Forth Dry Dock* [1990] 1 AC 546.
39 *Duke* v. *GEC Reliance* [1988] AC 618.
40 [1990] 2 AC 85.

fishing and their vessels were registered as British under the Merchant Shipping Act 1894. The statutory regime governing sea fishing was altered by the passage of the Merchant Shipping Act 1988. Vessels that had been registered under the 1894 Act now had to register under the new legislation. Ninety-five vessels failed to meet the new criteria and the applicants argued that the relevant parts of the 1988 Act were incompatible with, *inter alia*, Articles 52, 58, and 221 of the EC Treaty.[41]

Whether the 1988 statute was in breach of EC law was clearly a contentious question. All the UK courts involved in the case agreed that a reference should be made to the ECJ under Article 177 (now 234). The issue in the first *Factortame* case concerned the status of the 1988 Act pending the ECJ's decision on the substance of the case. If the applicants could not fish in this intervening period they might well go out of business. The applicants sought therefore either for the 1988 Act to be 'disapplied' (i.e., not enforced) pending the decision of the ECJ; or, if the court did grant an interim injunction to the government to prevent the applicants from fishing, that the government should have to give a cross-undertaking to pay damages if it should lose in the main action before the ECJ. Their Lordships held that, as a matter of domestic law, interim relief against the Crown was not available.[42] The House of Lords then sought a preliminary ruling as to whether the absence of any interim relief against the Crown was itself a violation of Community law. The ECJ was therefore being asked to rule on whether a 'gap' in the availability of administrative law remedies in UK law constituted a breach of EC law.

The ECJ decided in favour of the applicants.[43] It reasoned from the *Simmenthal* case[44] where it had held that provisions of Community law rendered 'automatically inapplicable' any conflicting provision of national law. The *Simmenthal* decision gave a broad construction to the idea of a 'conflicting provision' of national law, interpreting it to cover any legislative, administrative, or judicial practice that might impair the effectiveness of Community law.[45] With this foundation the ECJ in the *Factortame* case concluded that:[46]

> [T]he full effectiveness of Community law would be just as much impaired if a rule of national law could prevent a court seised of a dispute governed by Community law from granting interim relief in order to ensure the full effectiveness of the judgment to be given on the existence of the rights claimed under Community law. It follows that a court which in those circumstances would grant interim relief, if it were not for a rule of national law, is obliged to set aside that rule.

The case then returned to the House of Lords to be reconsidered in the light of the preliminary ruling given by the ECJ, *R.* v. *Secretary of State for Transport, ex parte Factortame Ltd (No. 2)*.[47] Their Lordships accepted that, at least in the area covered by EC law, such relief would be available against the Crown. *Factortame (No. 2)* also contains dicta by their Lordships on the more general issue of sovereignty. The final decision on the substance of the case involved a clash between Articles of the EC Treaty, and a later Act of the UK Parliament, the Merchant Shipping Act 1988. The traditional idea of sovereignty in the UK is, as we have seen, that if there is a clash between a later statutory norm and an earlier legal provision the later statute takes precedence. The ECJ has repeatedly held that Community law must take precedence in the event of a clash with national law. Moreover, the conflict in

[41] Arts 43, 48, and 294 after the Treaty of Amsterdam renumbering.

[42] Such relief is now available: *M* v. *Home Office* [1994] 1 AC 377.

[43] Case 213/89, *R.* v. *Secretary of State for Transport, ex parte Factortame Ltd* [1990] ECR I-2433.

[44] N. 36 above. [45] Ibid., paras 22 and 23. [46] N. 43 above, para. 21. [47] [1991] 1 AC 603.

this instance was between national law and Articles of the Treaty itself. The ECJ has made it clear that in the event of such a clash EC law trumps national law. The duty of the national court was not therefore confined to seeing whether national law might be construed to be in conformity with Community law, as is the case in actions between individuals based on directives. The dicta of the House of Lords in *Factortame (No. 2)* are therefore clearly of importance. Lord Bridge had this to say:[48]

> Some public comments on the decision of the Court of Justice, affirming the jurisdiction of the courts of the member states to override national legislation if necessary to enable interim relief to be granted in protection of rights under Community law, have suggested that this was a novel and dangerous invasion by a Community institution of the sovereignty of the UK Parliament. But such comments are based on a misconception. If the supremacy within the European Community of Community law over the national law of member states was not always inherent in the EEC Treaty it was certainly well established in the jurisprudence of the Court of Justice long before the UK joined the Community. Thus, whatever limitation of its sovereignty Parliament accepted when it enacted the European Communities Act 1972 was entirely voluntary. Under the terms of the 1972 Act it has always been clear that it was the duty of a UK court, when delivering final judgment, to override any rule of national law found to be in conflict with any directly enforceable rule of Community law. Similarly, when decisions of the Court of Justice have exposed areas of UK statute law which failed to implement Council directives, Parliament has always loyally accepted the obligation to make appropriate and prompt amendments. Thus there is nothing in any way novel in according supremacy to rules of Community law in areas to which they apply and to insist that, in the protection of rights under Community law, national courts must not be prohibited by rules of national law from granting interim relief in appropriate cases is no more than a logical recognition of that supremacy.

Three aspects of this reasoning should be distinguished. One was essentially *contractarian*: the UK knew when it joined the EC that priority should be accorded to EC law, and it must be taken to have contracted on those terms. If, therefore, 'blame' was to be cast for a loss of sovereignty then this should be laid at the door of Parliament and not the courts. The second facet of Lord Bridge's reasoning was a priori and *functional*: it was always inherent in a regime such as the Community that it could only function adequately if EC law could take precedence in the event of a clash with domestic legal norms. The third factor at play was the existence of the European Communities Act 1972, which was said to impose a duty on national courts to override national law in the event of a clash with directly enforceable Community law.

The impact of *Factortame* was made clear in the *EOC* case,[49] which was concerned with the compatibility of UK legislation on unfair dismissal and redundancy pay with EC law. Under UK law[50] entitlement to these protections and benefits operated differentially depending upon whether the person was in full-time or part-time employment. Full-time workers were eligible after two years; part-time workers only after five. The great majority of part-time workers were women and the Equal Opportunities Commission (EOC) took the view that the legislation discriminated against them, contrary to Article 119.[51] The EOC sought a declaration that the relevant provisions of the UK legislation were in breach of EC law. The House of Lords held that the national legislation was in breach of Article 119 and the directives. The *Factortame* case was regarded as authority for the proposition

48 [1991] 1 AC 603, 658–9.

49 *R.* v. *Secretary of State for Employment, ex parte Equal Opportunities Commission* [1995] 1 AC 1.

50 Employment Protection (Consolidation) Act 1978.

51 Art. 141 after the Treaty of Amsterdam renumbering.

that it was open to a national court to declare provisions of a primary statute to be incompatible with norms of Community law.[52] The House of Lords also made it clear that this power to review primary legislation resided in national *courts*, not just the House of Lords.

The impact of the EU on traditional concepts of sovereignty was also considered in *Thoburn*.[53] Certain street traders were prosecuted for continuing to use imperial measures, rather than metric, when selling their goods. The obligation to use metric measures as the primary form of measurement derived from Community directives, and the UK Government had complied with this obligation through the enactment of a series of regulations, some of which were based on the European Communities Act 1972 (ECA 1972), section 2(2). The defendants argued, *inter alia*, that in this context the power to make such regulations through section 2(2) had been impliedly repealed by provisions contained in the Weights and Measures Act 1985. Laws LJ held that there was no inconsistency between the ECA 1972, section 2(2) and the Weights and Measures Act 1985, and therefore that no issue of implied repeal arose in the case. He held more generally that the constitutional relationship between the UK and the EU was not to be decided by the ECJ's jurisprudence: that case law could not itself entrench EU law within national law.[54] The constitutional relationship between the EU and the UK, including the impact of membership of the EU on sovereignty, was to be decided by the common law in the light of any statutes that Parliament had enacted.[55] The common law had, said Laws LJ, modified the traditional concept of sovereignty, in the sense that it had created exceptions to the doctrine of implied repeal. Ordinary statutes were subject to the doctrine of implied repeal. What Laws LJ referred to as 'constitutional statutes', which conditioned the legal relationship between citizen and state in some overarching manner, or which dealt with fundamental constitutional rights, were not subject to the doctrine of implied repeal.[56] The repeal of such a statute, or its disapplication in a particular instance, could only occur if there were some 'express words in the later statute, or by words so specific that the inference of an actual determination to effect the result contended for was irresistible'.[57] The ECA 1972 was regarded as just such a constitutional statute. It contained provisions that ensured the supremacy of substantive Community law in the event of a clash with national law, and was not subject to implied repeal.

SUPREMACY AFTER *FACTORTAME*, *EOC*, AND *THOBURN*: THE SUBSTANTIVE IMPACT OF THE DECISIONS

The decisions considered above generated much academic comment.[58] Space precludes a detailed analysis of the differing views. It is nonetheless clear that there are two issues of central importance. One concerns the substantive impact of these decisions on the previous orthodoxy concerning sovereignty. The other is as to the best way of conceptualizing what has occurred. The former will be considered here, the latter in the section that follows. The substantive impact of *Factortame*, and *EOC* and *Thoburn* may be described as follows.

52 [1995] 1 AC 1, 27. 53 *Thoburn* v. *Sunderland City Council* [2003] QB 151.

54 Ibid., paras 57–8. 55 Ibid., para. 59. 56 Ibid., para. 62. 57 Ibid., para. 63.

58 Craig, n. 31 above; Sir William Wade, 'Sovereignty – Revolution or Evolution?' (1996) 112 *LQR* 568; T. R. S. Allan, 'Parliamentary Sovereignty: Law, Politics and Revolution' (1997) 113 *LQR* 443.

First, in doctrinal terms these decisions mean that the concept of *implied repeal*, or *implied disapplication*, under which inconsistencies between later and earlier norms were resolved in favour of the later norms, will, subject to what is said below, no longer apply to clashes concerning Community and national law. This proposition is sound in terms of principle, whether viewed simply in terms of membership of the EU, or as part of a broader category of constitutional statutes that are not subject to implied repeal. There are good normative arguments for requiring the legislature to state expressly its intent to repeal or derogate from statutes of constitutional importance, and this is so notwithstanding the fact that there may be room for disagreement as to which statutes come within this category.

Second, if Parliament ever does wish to derogate from its Community obligations then it will have to do so *expressly and unequivocally*. The reaction of our national courts to such an unlikely eventuality remains to be seen. In principle, two options would be open to the national judiciary. Either they could follow the latest will of Parliament, thereby preserving some remnant of traditional orthodoxy on sovereignty. Or they could argue that it is not open to our legislature to pick and choose which obligations to subscribe to while still remaining within the Community. Which of these options our courts would choose will be dependent, to some extent at least, on the issues to be addressed in the next section.

Third, the supremacy of EC law over national law *operates in areas where EC law is applicable*, as is made clear from the dictum of Lord Bridge set out above. This may well be a statement of the obvious, but the point is more complex than might initially have been thought.[59] The problem being addressed here is often referred to as *Kompetenz-Kompetenz*: who has the ultimate authority to decide whether a matter is within the competence of the EC? The ECJ may well believe that it is the ultimate decider of this issue. However, national courts may not always be content with this arrogation of authority. This is particularly so given that the ECJ has, as is well known, often reasoned 'teleologically'[60] and expanded the boundaries of Community competence in a manner which has caused disquiet within some national legal systems. The German Federal Constitutional Court held that it will not inevitably accept Community decisions, including those of the ECJ, which it regards as crossing the line between legitimate Treaty interpretation and a *de facto* Treaty amendment.[61] The general tenor of Laws LJ's judgment in *Thoburn* is also inclined to the conclusion that the ultimate competence to decide on the scope of Community competence resides with the national court. While he does not address the point directly his reasoning to the effect that the fundamental legal basis of the UK's relationship with the EU rests with domestic, not European, law lends support to that conclusion. This is reinforced by his statement that if the EU were to enact a measure repugnant to a constitutional right guaranteed by UK law, it would be for the national courts to decide whether the general words of the ECA 1972 were sufficient to give it overriding effect in domestic law.[62]

59 P. Craig, 'Report on the United Kingdom', in A.-M. Slaughter, A. Stone Sweet, and J. Weiler (eds), *The European Courts and National Courts, Doctrine and Jurisprudence* (1998), ch. 7.

60 Teleological judicial reasoning connotes the idea that a court will reason in order to attain the end which it believes that the particular Treaty article was intended to serve.

61 *Brunner* v. *The European Union Treaty* [1994] 1 CMLR 57, paras 49, 99. More recent decisions do however indicate a 'softening' of approach by the German Court: Craig and de Búrca, n. 6 above, 297–8.

62 *Thoburn*, n. 53 above, para. 69.

SUPREMACY AFTER *FACTORTAME*, *EOC*, AND *THOBURN*: THE CONCEPTUAL BASIS OF THE DECISIONS

Commentators have been divided as to how best to conceptualize the impact of the courts' jurisprudence.[63] The issues here are complex, but the main features of the debate can be presented as follows.

It is possible to rationalize what the courts have done as a species of *statutory construction*. All would agree that if a statute can be reconciled with a Community norm through construing the statutory words without unduly distorting them then this should be done, more especially when the statute was passed to effectuate a directive. However the species of statutory construction being considered here is more far-reaching. On this view accommodation between national law and EC law is attained through a rule of construction to the effect that inconsistencies *will* be resolved in favour of EC law *unless* Parliament has indicated clearly and unambiguously that it intends to derogate from Community law. The degree of linguistic inconsistency between the statute and the Community norm is not the essential point of the inquiry. Provided that there is no unequivocal derogation from Community law then it will apply, rather than any conflicting domestic statute. Counsel for the applicants framed their argument in this manner in the first *Factortame* case.[64] This view was posited by Lord Bridge in the same case where he stated that the effect of section 2(4) of the European Communities Act 1972 was that the Merchant Shipping Act 1988 should take effect as if a section were incorporated that its provisions would be without prejudice to directly enforceable Community rights.[65] We have already seen that Lord Bridge relied on the 1972 Act in his argument in the second *Factortame* case.[66] A similar argument has been made judicially by Laws LJ in *Thoburn*.[67] Laws LJ voiced the same views extra-judicially,[68] as did Lord Hoffmann.[69] The construction view is said to leave the essential core of the traditional view of legal sovereignty intact, in the sense that it is always open to a later Parliament to make it unequivocally clear that it wishes to derogate from EC law. In the absence of such an explicit derogation, section 2(4) serves to render EC law dominant in the event of a conflict with national law. The attractions of this approach are self-evident. Clashes between EC law and national law can be reconciled while preserving the formal veneer of legal sovereignty. There are nonetheless a number of points to note about the construction approach.

(1) The doctrine of implied repeal or implied disapplication of an earlier statute was itself part of the traditional view of legal sovereignty, and in this sense the construction approach constitutes a modification of traditional doctrine. This is so even if one adopts Laws LJ's view that implied repeal should not generally apply to constitutional statutes.[70]

(2) The wording of section 2(4) is notoriously difficult to disentangle. The section is framed in terms of 'any enactment passed or to be passed . . . shall be construed and have effect' subject to Community rights. The very word 'construed' conveys the sense that the later statute must be capable of being read so as to be compatible with EC law without

63 Limits of space preclude coverage of all views on this issue. The sophisticated argument presented by Neil MacCormick can be found in *Questioning Sovereignty, Law, State and Nation in the European Commonwealth* (1999), ch. 6.

64 [1990] 2 AC 85, 96.

65 [1990] 2 AC 85, 140.

66 [1991] 1 AC 603, 658–9.

67 N. 53 above.

68 'Law and Democracy' [1995] *Public Law* 72, 89.

69 Lord Hoffmann, 'Europe and the Question of Sovereignty', the Second Lord Neill Lecture, 15 Oct. 1999.

70 *Thoburn*, n. 53 above.

thereby unduly distorting its meaning or rewriting it. This may well not be possible. It should be remembered that a statute might be seriously at odds with the requirements of EC law, even where Parliament has not, through any express wording, manifested its intent to derogate from the Community norm. It is doubtful whether section 2(4) was intended to cure all such absences of fit.

(3) Sir William Wade has argued forcefully that Lord Bridge's reasoning entails more than an exercise of construction as we normally understand that phrase. He contends that putatively incorporating section 2(4) of the 1972 Act into a later statute, such as that of 1988, 'is merely another way of saying that the Parliament of 1972 has imposed a restriction upon the Parliament of 1988', which is what 'the classical doctrine of sovereignty will not permit'.[71] Nor can this be countered simply by saying that the later Parliament could defeat the exercise of construction by expressly providing that the later statute is to prevail over any conflicting EC law. It is by no means clear that an express provision of the kind being postulated here would work, *given* the very reasoning of Lord Bridge. Such a statutory provision would itself be held to be contrary to EC law by the ECJ. This holding would be part of the 'Community law to which by the Act of 1972 the Act of 1988 is held to be subject'.[72] In order to overcome this argument the later statute would have to contain an express provision that it was to prevail over any conflicting EC law and also a provision rendering the relevant provisions of the ECA 1972 inapplicable to the subject matter covered by the later statute.

A second way to conceptualize what the courts have done is to regard it as a *technical legal revolution*. This is the preferred explanation of Sir William Wade who sees the courts' decisions as modifying the ultimate legal principle or rule of recognition on which the legal system is based.[73] On this view the 'rule of recognition is itself a political fact which the judges themselves are able to change when they are confronted with a new situation which so demands'.[74] Such choices are made by the judiciary at the point where the law 'stops'.[75]

There is however a third way in which to regard the courts' jurisprudence. This is to regard decisions about supremacy as being based on *normative arguments of legal principle the content of which can and will vary across time*. This is my own preferred view[76] and a similar argument has been advanced by Allan.[77] On this view there is no *a priori* inexorable reason why Parliament, merely because of its very existence, must be regarded as legally omnipotent. The existence of such power, like all power, must be justified by arguments of principle that are normatively convincing. Possible constraints on Parliamentary omnipotence must similarly be reasoned through and defended on normative grounds. This approach fits well with the reasoning of Lord Bridge in the second *Factortame* case. His Lordship did not approach the matter as if the courts were making an unconstrained political choice at the point where the law stopped. His reasoning is more accurately represented as being based on *principle*, in the sense of working through the principled consequences of the UK's membership of the EC. The contractarian and functional arguments used by Lord Bridge exemplify this style of judicial discourse. They provide sound normative arguments as to why the UK should be bound by EC law while it remains within the Community. These arguments would moreover be convincing and have force even if section 2(4) had never

71 Wade, n. 58 above, p. 570. 72 Ibid. 73 H. L. A. Hart, *The Concept of Law* (1961), ch. 6.

74 Wade, n. 58 above, p. 574. 75 Wade, n. 27 above, pp. 191–2.

76 Craig, nn. 31, 60 above, and P. Craig, 'Public Law, Political Theory and Legal Theory' [2000] *Public Law* 211.

77 Allan, n. 59 above.

been included in the 1972 Act. It may be that those who disagree with the courts' decisions in *Factortame* and *EOC* believe that they can counter the normative arguments presented by Lord Bridge.[78] They should then present such arguments since the discourse must be conducted at this level. Debates on such issues are of value.

DIRECT EFFECT

The doctrine of the supremacy of Community law has been one of the notable achievements of the ECJ. It has been a cornerstone in the building of a Community legal order. The ECJ's other principal contribution has been the doctrine of direct effect. Detailed analysis can be found elsewhere.[79] It is nonetheless important to understand the basic tenets of direct effect in order that its constitutional significance can be appreciated.

DIRECT EFFECT: AN OUTLINE

The meaning of direct effect is not free from ambiguity.[80] It does, however, most commonly connote the idea that individuals can bring actions in their own names within national courts in order to vindicate rights secured to them by the Treaty. It is in this sense a species of private enforcement of Community law. The Treaty makes explicit provision for public enforcement of Community norms, in Article 226 EC: the Commission is charged with the responsibility of bringing before the ECJ member states which have failed to comply with the Treaty. The Commission will bring the action in its own name against the member state and the ECJ will decide whether the member state has acted in breach of the Treaty or one of the legal norms made under the Treaty.[81] Whether the framers of the original EC Treaty intended for there to be direct effect is doubtful. It is however clear that private enforcement through direct effect provided a welcome supplement to public enforcement through the Commission, enabling Community law to be applied on a scale and in a manner that would not otherwise have been possible.[82] Moreover, the very fact that individuals were given rights that they could enforce in their own name transformed the very nature of the EC Treaty. It could no longer be viewed solely as the business of nation-states in the manner of many other international treaties. It was to be a form of social ordering in which individuals were involved in their own capacity. They were no longer to be passive receptors who had to await action taken on their behalf by others. They were now accorded rights that they could enforce in their own name.

The seminal case in the development of direct effect was *Van Gend en Loos*.[83] Dutch importers challenged the rate of duty imposed on a chemical imported from Germany.

[78] It might, for example, be possible to argue that on normative grounds priority should be accorded to an act of the domestic legislature which expressly derogates from a Community norm, even where the state remains within the Community. The nature of this argument would however have to be explicated clearly and it is by no means self-evidently correct.

[79] Craig and de Búrca, n. 6 above, ch. 5.

[80] Craig and de Búrca, n. 6 above, pp. 178–82.

[81] It is also possible for a member state to initiate an action against another member state under Art. 227 (formerly Art. 170), but this rarely happens.

[82] J. Weiler, 'The Community System: The Dual Character of Supranationalism' (1981) 1 *YBEL* 267; P. Craig, 'Once upon a Time in the West: Direct Effect and the Federalization of EEC Law' (1992) 12 *OJLS* 453.

[83] Case 26/62, *Van Gend en Loos* v. *Nederlandse Administratie der Belastingen* [1963] ECR 1.

They argued that a reclassification of the product under a different heading of the Dutch tariff legislation had led to an increase in the duty and that this was prohibited under Article 12 EC (now Article 25), which prohibits the imposition of any new customs duties on imports and also precludes any increase in existing rates. The Dutch court asked the ECJ whether Article 12 gave rise to rights that could be invoked by individuals before their national courts. The member states argued that the Treaty was simply a compact between states, to be policed in the manner dictated by the Treaty, through public enforcement at the hands of the Commission via Articles 169 and 170 (now Articles 226 and 227). They believed that direct effect would alter the nature of the obligations accepted by the signatories.

The ECJ disagreed. It held that the EEC was *not* simply to be viewed as a compact between nations. The 'interested parties' included the people. This was affirmed by the preamble and by the existence of institutions charged with the duty of making provisions for those individuals. It was this crucial conceptual starting point which laid the foundation for the now famous passage from the judgment, depicting the Community as a new legal order for the benefit of which states have limited their sovereign rights, with the consequence that individuals have rights and can be regarded as subjects of the Community. The ECJ emphasized that Article 12 was a natural candidate for enforcement by individuals through national courts. It stressed the negative nature of the obligation, the fact that it was unconditional, and that its implementation was not dependent on any further measures before being effective under national law.

The years immediately following *Van Gend en Loos* witnessed the application of the concept to a growing range of Treaty articles. The Court was keen to expand the concept given the advantages it possessed. In applying direct effect to other Treaty articles the ECJ began to relax the conditions for its application. Direct effect was applied in circumstances where it could not be said that the Treaty article in question created a negative obligation which was legally perfect, in the sense that no further action was required by the Community or the member states, and no real residue of discretion existed. The concept was applied to articles of the Treaty dealing with broad areas of regulatory policy, which were as much social as economic.[84]

It was inevitable that the ECJ should be asked whether Community legislation passed pursuant to the Treaty could also have direct effect. There are various types of such legislation. Regulations are defined in Article 249 EC as having general application. They are binding in their entirety and directly applicable in all member states. The ECJ had no reluctance in concluding that regulations were capable of having direct effect, provided that they were sufficiently certain and precise, which was normally the case.[85]

There has been more difficulty over directives. These are, according to Article 249, binding as to the result to be achieved while leaving the choice of form and methods to the states to which they are addressed. Moreover, while regulations are binding on all states, directives are only binding on the specific states to which they are addressed. Directives have proved to be a particularly useful device for legislating in an enlarged Community. Many areas of Community policy concern complex topics ranging from product liability to the environment, and from the harmonization of company law to the free movement of capital.

[84] Case 2/74, *Reyners* v. *Belgian State* [1974] ECR 631; Case 43/75, *Defrenne* v. *Sabena* [1976] ECR 455.

[85] Case 93/71, *Leonosio* v. *Italian Ministry of Agriculture and Forestry* [1973] CMLR 343; Case 50/76, *Amsterdam Bulb* v. *Produktschap voor Siergewassen* [1977] ECR 137.

If legislation could only be enacted in the form of regulations then it might be difficult to draft a measure with sufficient precision that it could be immediately applicable within the territories of all the member states. The directive enables the Community to specify the ends to be attained, often in great detail, while leaving a choice of form and methods of implementation to the individual member states.

However, the very nature of directives seemed to indicate that they could not have direct effect: they clearly require further action on the part of the member states, and they leave them with discretion as to methods of implementation. The ECJ nonetheless concluded that directives are capable of having direct effect. It held that it would be inconsistent with the binding effect of directives to exclude the possibility that they can confer rights.[86] The ECJ also drew on Article 234, which allows questions concerning the interpretation and validity of Community law to be referred by national courts to the ECJ. From the generality of this provision the Court concluded that questions relating to directives can be raised by individuals before national courts.[87] A further reason for according direct effect to directives is the estoppel argument: a member state that has not implemented the directive 'may not rely, as against individuals, on its own failure to perform the obligations which the directive entails'.[88] Provided, therefore, that the directive is sufficiently precise, that the basic obligation is unconditional, and that the period for implementation has passed, an individual can derive enforceable rights from a directive.

While the ECJ has been willing to give direct effect to directives it has, however, also held that they only have vertical as opposed to horizontal direct effect. Treaty articles and regulations give individuals rights that can be used both against the state, vertical direct effect, and against private parties, horizontal direct effect. Directives only have vertical direct effect. Thus, in the *Marshall* case[89] the ECJ held that Directive 76/207 on equal treatment could not impose obligations on individuals, but only on the state, either *qua* state or *qua* employer. The reason proffered by the court for this limitation was the wording of Article 249: the binding nature of the directive existed only in relation to 'each Member State to which it is addressed'. The correctness of this ruling and the rationale for this limitation of direct effect are by no means self-evident.[90] The existence of this limitation has however generated a very complex case law.

This is in part because the ruling that directives only have vertical and not horizontal direct effect requires some definition of the state for these purposes.[91] The complexity of the case law in this area is in part the result of the doctrine of indirect effect. The doctrine is associated with the important decision in *Von Colson*.[92] The applicants relied upon the provision of a directive in order to argue that the quantum of relief provided by German law in cases of discrimination was too small. The ECJ held that the provisions were not sufficiently

86 Case 41/74, *Van Duyn* v. *Home Office* [1974] ECR 1337, para. 12.

87 Loc. cit.

88 Case 148/78, *Pubblico Ministero* v. *Ratti* [1979] ECR 1629, para. 22.

89 Case 152/84, *Marshall* v. *Southampton & South West Hampshire Area Health Authority (Teaching)* [1986] ECR 723; Case C–91/92, *Faccini Dori* v. *Recreb Srl* [1994] ECR I-3325.

90 W. van Gerven, 'The Horizontal Direct Effect of Directive Provisions Revisited: The Reality of Catchwords', in T. Heukels and D. Curtin (eds), *Institutional Dynamics of European Integration, Liber Amicorum for Henry Schermers* (1994); P. Craig, 'Directives: Direct Effect, Indirect Effect, and the Construction of National Legislation' (1997) 22 *ELR* 519.

91 Case C–188/89, *Foster* v. *British Gas* [1990] ECR I-3133; D. Curtin, 'The Province of Government: Delimiting the Direct Effect of Directives in the Common Law Context' (1990) 15 *ELR* 195.

92 Case 14/83, *Von Colson and Kamann* v. *Land Nordrhein-Westfalen* [1984] ECR 1891.

precise to have direct effect. It went on, however, to hold that national courts had an obligation to interpret national law so as to be in conformity with the directive. The purpose of the directive was to provide an effective remedy in cases of discrimination, and if states chose to fulfil this aim through the provision of compensation then this should be adequate in relation to the damage suffered. National courts should, therefore, construe their own national law with this in mind. In *Marleasing*[93] the ECJ held that in applying national law, whether *passed before or after* the directive, a national court was required to interpret national law *in every way possible* so as to be in conformity with the directive.

While therefore an individual cannot, in a literal sense, derive rights from a directive in an action against another individual, it is possible to plead the directive in such an action. Once the directive has been placed before the national court, then the obligation to interpret national law in conformity with the directive where possible, derived from *Von Colson* and *Marleasing*, comes into operation. Where the directive encapsulates precise obligations, and where the national court is minded to interpret national law in the required fashion, this 'indirect' species of enforcement of a directive as between individuals will have much the same results as if the directive had been accorded horizontal direct effect.

The interpretative obligation does however create problems for courts and litigants alike.[94] It places national courts in some difficulty in deciding how far they can go in reconciling national legislation with Community norms while still remaining within the realm of interpreting, as opposed to rewriting or overruling, national norms. It places litigants in a difficult position since they will have to guess how far their national courts might feel able to go in reconciling national law with differently worded Community legislation. If directives had horizontal direct effect then at least the individual would know that in the event of any inconsistency between the two norms Community law would trump national law.

The jurisprudence in this area has become even more complex as a result of case law in which the ECJ has been willing to accord some measure of 'incidental horizontal direct effect' to a directive in actions between private individuals.[95]

DIRECT EFFECT: CONSTITUTIONAL IMPLICATIONS

It is necessary to understand the concept of direct effect, albeit in outline, in order to be able to appreciate the constitutional significance of the doctrine from the perspective of national law. There are two ways in which direct effect is of constitutional relevance, one of which is obvious, the other less so.

First, direct effect enables individuals to derive rights that are enforceable in their own national courts from norms derived from an international Treaty and legislation made thereunder. The general position in public international law is that individuals do not derive such rights, and this is so even where they are the beneficiaries of the norms laid down in an

93 Case C–106/89, *Marleasing SA* v. *La Commercial International De Alimentation SA* [1990] ECR 4135.

94 G. de Búrca, 'Giving Effect to European Community Directives' (1992) 55 *MLR* 215.

95 Case C–194/94, *CIA Security International SA* v. *Signalson SA and Securitel SPRL* [1996] ECR I-2201; Case C–129/94, *Criminal Proceedings against Rafael Ruiz Bernaldez* [1996] ECR I-1829; Case C–441/93, *Panagis Pafitis* v. *Trapeza Kentrikis Ellados AE* [1996] ECR I-1347; Case C–443/98, *Unilever Italia SpA* v. *Central Foods SpA* [2000] ECR I-7535. For discussion, see Craig and de Búrca, n. 6 above, pp. 220–7; J. Coppel, 'Horizontal Direct Effect of Directives' (1997) 28 *ILJ* 69; S. Weatherill, 'Breach of Directives and Breach of Contract' (2001) 26 *ELRev.* 177; M. Dougan, 'The Disguised Vertical Direct effect of Directives' [2000] *CLJ* 586.

international treaty.[96] There are instances where individuals have been held to have such rights, but they are exceptional and there has been nothing on the scale of the direct effect doctrine as developed by the ECJ. Indeed this was one of the reasons why the ECJ sought to distance EC law from general public international law in the *Van Gend* case. It wished to buttress the argument that because the EC Treaty was distinct from other international treaties, therefore it should not be thought strange that an individual derived rights from the former, even though he normally did not do so from the latter. There was clearly an element of circularity in this argument. The very decision as to whether direct effect did or did not exist was itself of crucial importance in deciding whether the EC Treaty really could be regarded as distinct from other international treaties. Major constitutional developments are not infrequently characterized by such reasoning. Be that as it may, direct effect is a central feature of EC law, and recognized as such by all the member states. In terms of national constitutional significance this means that law derived from sources other than Parliament and the common law will avail individuals before their own national courts in a way which has not been so on this scale hitherto.

The second reason why direct effect is of constitutional significance resides in the connection between this concept and the supremacy of Community law. The essence of this connection is that direct effect allows the supremacy doctrine to be applied at national level, and thereby makes it far more potent than it would otherwise have been. It would in theory be perfectly possible for the ECJ to have developed its supremacy doctrine even if it had never created direct effect. Community law would have been held to be supreme, and judicially enforceable through actions brought by the Commission under Article 226. The supremacy doctrine does of course operate in the context of such actions. Direct effect however enables supremacy of EC law to be enforced by individuals through their own national courts. This renders the supremacy of EC law all the more effective for a number of reasons. Member states might be more inclined to listen to their own national courts than to the ECJ. The national courts become Community courts in their own right, being able to pass judgment on national primary legislation in the context of an action brought by an individual. Direct effect spreads the workload of enforcing Community law, and its supremacy, across all the individuals and the national courts of the EC.

FUNDAMENTAL RIGHTS

There is little doubt that most claims to protect rights will now be brought under the Human Rights Act 1998 (HRA).[97] It will however still be open to claimants to use rights-based arguments derived from Community law.

An individual may draw on the *fundamental rights doctrine as developed by the ECJ*. The original EEC Treaty contained no list of traditional fundamental rights. The catalyst for the creation of such rights was the threat of revolt by the courts of some member states.[98] Individuals who were dissatisfied with a regulation would challenge it before their national court and contend that it was inconsistent with rights in their national constitutions. The ECJ denied that Community norms could be challenged in this manner. However, in order

[96] I. Brownlie, *Principles of Public International Law* (5th edn, 1998), ch. 24.

[97] See Chapter 3 above.

[98] Craig and de Búrca, n. 6 above, ch. 8.

to stem any national rebellion it also declared that fundamental rights were part of the general principles of Community law, and that the compatibility of a *Community norm* with such rights would be tested by the ECJ itself.[99] It is clear that *national norms* can also be challenged for compliance with fundamental rights. This will be so where member states are applying provisions of Community law which are based on the protection of human rights;[100] where they are enforcing Community rules on behalf of the Community or interpreting Community rules;[101] or where member states are seeking to derogate from a requirement of Community law.[102] The supremacy doctrine will apply with the consequence that national norms, including primary legislation, which are inconsistent with Community law can be declared inapplicable in the instant case. This is by way of contrast with the HRA where the courts are limited, in cases involving primary legislation, to making a declaration of incompatibility under section 4.

There is now also a *Charter of Fundamental Rights of the European Union*.[103] The direct catalyst for this development came from the European Council. In June 1999 the Cologne European Council[104] decided that there should be a Charter of Fundamental Rights to consolidate the fundamental rights applicable at Union level and to make their importance and relevance more visible to the citizens of the Union. It was made clear that the document should include economic and social rights, as well as traditional civil and political rights. The institutional structure for discussion about the Charter was laid down in the Tampere European Council in October 1999.[105] It was decided to establish a body called the Convention. It consisted of representatives of the member states, a member of the Commission, members of the EP, and representatives from national parliaments. The Convention was instructed to conclude its work in time for the Nice European Council in December 2000. The Charter was accepted by the member states, but its legal status was left undecided in Nice. This issue has now been addressed in the Convention on the Future of Europe, discussed below.

JUDICIAL ARCHITECTURE: NATIONAL COURTS AS COMMUNITY COURTS

Those who are not familiar with EC law are accustomed to think that there are only two Community courts: the European Court of Justice (ECJ) and the Court of First Instance (CFI). This belies reality. National courts have general jurisdiction over matters of Community law. This is a matter worthy of constitutional note. The explanation for this role played by national courts is to be found in a conjunction of two factors.

The first is the very concept of direct effect considered above . The fact that individuals are able to enforce their Community rights through national courts means that it will be the national judiciaries that frequently apply Community law doctrine.

99 Case 11/70, *Internationale Handelsgesellschaft* v. *Einfuhr- und Vorratstelle für Getreide und Futtermittel* [1970] ECR 1125, 1134.

100 Case 222/84, *Johnston* v. *Chief Constable of the Royal Ulster Constabulary* [1986] ECR 1651.

101 Case 5/88, *Wachauf* v. *Germany* [1989] ECR 2609; Case 63/83, *R.* v. *Kent Kirk* [1984] ECR 2689.

102 Case C–260/89, *Elliniki Radiophonia Tileorassi AE* v. *Dimotki Etairia Pliroforissis and Sotirios Kouvelas* [1991] ECR I–2925; Case C-159/90, *Society for the Protection of Unborn Children Ireland Ltd* v. *Grogan* [1991] ECR I-4685.

103 *Charter of Fundamental Rights of the European Union* [2000] OJ C364/1.

104 3–4 June 1999.

105 15–16 October 1999.

This first factor has been reinforced by a second. The ECJ made it clear that national courts should apply existing case law of the ECJ and the CFI. They should therefore only refer a case to the ECJ pursuant to Article 234 where the question before the national court had not already been adequately answered in a previous ruling given by the ECJ. This became clear from the seminal decision in the *Da Costa* case.[106] The facts in the case were materially identical to those in *Van Gend en Loos*,[107] as were the questions posed by the national court. The ECJ acknowledged that a national court of final resort was bound to refer a question to the ECJ, but then qualified this by stating that 'the authority of an interpretation under Article 177 already given by the Court may deprive the obligation of its purpose and thus empty it of its substance'.[108] This would especially be the case where the question raised was 'materially identical with a question which has already been the subject of a preliminary ruling in a similar case'.[109] The ECJ made it clear that the national court could refer the issue again if it had new questions to ask. It made it equally clear that if this was not so, then it would simply repeat the ruling which it had given in the original case from which the legal point arose. The *Da Costa* case, therefore, initiated what is in effect a system of precedent, whereby national courts would apply the prior rulings of ECJ. The ECJ extended this idea in *CILFIT*[110] where it held that the obligation to refer contained in Article 234(3) could also be qualified 'where previous decisions of the Court have already dealt with the point of law in question, irrespective of the nature of the proceedings which led to those decisions, even though the questions at issue are not strictly identical'. Provided that the point of law had already been determined by the ECJ, this should be relied on by a national court in a later case, thereby obviating the need for a reference. The application of precedent by national courts has enhanced the enforcement of Community law, and has eased the workload on the ECJ and the CFI. The Community system of adjudication could not have functioned as it has if the national courts had not been accorded this role.

The *EOC* case[111] considered earlier provides a good example of this process at work. Not only did the House of Lords make a declaration that provisions of a statute were incompatible with EC law. It did so without making a reference to the ECJ, having satisfied itself that the existing ECJ precedents meant that the national statute was indirectly discriminatory.

THE EUROPEAN CONSTITUTION

The Constitutional Treaty is very unlikely to enter into force, given the negative votes in the referenda in Holland and France. It is nonetheless important to have some idea of the origins of this constitutional initiative and the impact that it would have had on national constitutional law.

The *origins* of the Constitutional Treaty are to be found in the Nice Treaty. The discussions leading to the Nice Treaty left open four issues for deliberation at the Inter-Governmental Conference (IGC) in 2004. These were the 'delimitation of powers' between the EU and the member states, the status of the Charter of Fundamental Rights, simplification of the

[106] Cases 28–30/62, *Da Costa en Schaake NV, Jacob Meijer NV and Hoechst-Holland NV* v. *Nederlandse Belastingadministratie* [1963] ECR 31.

[107] N. 83 above.

[108] N. 106 above, p. 38.

[109] Ibid.

[110] Case 283/81, *Srl CILFIT and Lanificio di Gavardo SpA* v. *Ministry of Health* [1982] ECR 3415, para. 14.

[111] N. 49 above.

Treaties, and the role of the national parliaments. Matters, however, developed rapidly thereafter. The Laeken European Council in 2001 was crucial. It issued a Declaration that considerably broadened the range of matters that should be discussed concerning the future of Europe. No longer were there four 'discrete' issues. The Laeken Declaration placed just about every issue of importance concerning the future of Europe on the agenda for discussion, including major issues concerning the inter-institutional disposition of power within the EU. It also led to the setting up of the Convention on the Future of Europe, headed by the ex-French President, Giscard d'Estaing. It was certainly not preordained that this body would produce a Constitutional Treaty, but that is what it did.[112] The Constitutional Treaty was, after some hesitation and amendment, accepted by the member states. It then had to be accepted by all of the member states in accord with their constitutional traditions for treaty ratification. After the negative votes in the French and Dutch referenda the ratification process was however put on hold, and it is unlikely that the Constitutional Treaty will enter into force.

It is nonetheless important to understand something of its *structure*. The Constitutional Treaty was divided into four parts. Part I set out a number of the central principles that govern the operation of the EU, and its relations with the member states. Part II contained the Charter of Fundamental Rights. The main body of EU substantive law was contained in Part III, while Part IV addressed issues of transition, ratification, and the like.

In terms of *content*, there were a number of Articles in Part I of the European Constitution that were of direct interest for national constitutional law. Thus, the Charter of Fundamental Rights was made binding by Article I-9, with the main body of the Charter included in Part II of the Constitution. There were detailed provisions as to the division of competence between member states and the Union contained in Articles I-11–19. There was a supremacy clause in Article I-6, which provided that the 'Constitution, and law adopted by the Union's institutions in exercising competences conferred on it, shall have primacy over the law of the member states'. There were, however, a number of problems surrounding the interpretation of this provision. It was, for example, unclear whether it was intended to assert the supremacy of Union law over all national law, including national constitutions. If this was indeed the case then it was doubtful whether it would have proven to be constitutionally acceptable to many member states. The overall structure of the European Constitution, moreover, made it difficult for the EU to claim the ultimate authority to decide on the limits of Union competence. On a political level, there was a Protocol designed to enhance the role of national parliaments in the EU, and to ensure that they received proposals with sufficient time to comment on them before they became law. There was a further Protocol concerned with subsidiarity giving the national parliaments a greater role than hitherto in monitoring whether action at Union level really was required.

CONCLUSIONS

The Constitutional Treaty is unlikely to become a reality. In 2007 there were, however, initiatives to revive an abbreviated version of the Constitutional Treaty. The outcome remains to be seen. EU law nonetheless will continue to have a significant effect on national constitutional law, as it has done until now.

112 Treaty Establishing a Constitution for Europe [2004] OJ C310/1.

FURTHER READING

ANTHONY, G. *UK Public Law & European Law, The Dynamics of Legal Integration* (2002).

BIRKINSHAW, P. *European Public Law* (2003).

CRAIG, P. and DE BÚRCA, G. *EU Law, Text, Cases and Materials* (3rd edn, 2002).

LADEUR, K.-H. (ed.) *Europeanisation of Administrative Law: Transforming National Decision-Making Procedures* (2001).

MACCORMICK, N. *Questioning Sovereignty* (1999).

NICOL, D. *EC Membership and the Judicialization of British Politics* (2001).

PINDER, J. *The Building of the European Union* (3rd edn, 1998).

SLAUGHTER, A.-M., STONE SWEET, A. and WEILER, J. H. H. (eds) *The European Court of Justice and National Courts: Doctrine and Jurisprudence* (1998).

URWIN, D. *The Community of Europe: A History of European Integration since 1945* (2nd edn, 1995).

DE WITTE, B. 'Direct Effect, Supremacy and the Nature of the Legal Order' in Craig, P. and de Búrca, G. (eds), *The Evolution of EU Law* (1999) 177.

USEFUL WEB SITE

Web site for the European Union: **http://ec.europa.eu**

5

THE INTERNATIONALIZATION OF PUBLIC LAW AND ITS IMPACT ON THE UNITED KINGDOM

*David Feldman**

SUMMARY

Municipal public law is always influenced by foreign developments. The existence of a state depends at least partly on its recognition by other states. Political theories and legal ideas have always flowed across and between regions of the world. Yet any state has good reasons for controlling the introduction of foreign legal and constitutional norms to its own legal order. National interests and a commitment to the Rule of Law, human rights, and democratic accountability demand national controls over foreign influences. Ways of channelling and filtering foreign influences as they enter municipal public law may be more or less effective. This chapter considers the nature and legitimacy of the channels and filters, particularly as they apply in the UK, in the light of general public law standards.

INTRODUCTION

As in other countries, public law in the UK is affected by international law, and influenced by external and international considerations. Developments outside a territory have always affected its internal organization and external affairs. States surrender part of their autonomy in exchange for the benefits of cooperation, allowing them to pursue objectives

* I am grateful to many people for generously discussing these matters with me and offering many stimulating ideas and much information, particularly Professor John Bell, His Honour Ian Campbell, Professor Didier Maus, Professor Nicolas Maziau, Judge Tudor Pantiru, Professor Cheryl Saunders, Anna-Lena Sjolund, Christian Steiner, and Dr Rebecca Williams, and to Professor Dawn Oliver and Professor Jeffrey Jowell for many helpful comments on drafts of this chapter. However, the views expressed are my own, and do not necessarily represent those of any other person or body. Errors and idiosyncrasies are, of course, entirely my responsibility.

unattainable without coordination. International organizations can help to maintain peace, bolster social or economic stability, and foster free trade and open markets. At the same time, cooperation has significant costs for states. They must take account of internationally agreed objectives and values in their internal decision making. Sometimes they must subordinate their own interests to those of other states. This may compromise systems of accountability for the exercise of public power which are traditionally based on the political and legal processes operating within individual states. Traditional criteria for the legitimacy of state action, such as democracy, compliance with Rule of Law standards, or respect for fundamental rights, may be hard to apply when decision-making processes are shaped by international agreements or institutions which do not contain equivalent systems for control and accountability of the exercise of power. This leads some people to argue that a 'democratic deficit' in the EC and the European Union (EU) leads to a crisis of legitimacy which the draft EU Constitution might have ameliorated had it come into effect.[1]

This has consequences for UK public law. The structures of important state institutions are potentially challenged by such organizations as the Group of States against Corruption (GRECO), operating under the aegis of the Council of Europe,[2] and the European Charter of Local Self-Government,[3] which the UK ratified with effect from 1 August 1998. This chapter attempts to draw out three characteristics of the relationship between national systems of public law and international developments. The first is the importance of international influence over the very existence and fundamental structures of states. No state is an island (although some islands are states). Secondly, the channels between national and international planes normally permit influence to be exerted in both directions, and are usually subject to filters allowing states to preserve an element of autonomy, although the nature and effectiveness of the filters depends on national traditions and interests. Thirdly, the mechanisms by which states allow foreign influences to affect their systems of public law reflect their constitutional traditions and patterns of social interaction, and their legitimacy depends at least in part on their compatibility with those traditions and patterns.

THE IMPORTANCE OF FOREIGN INFLUENCES TO THE FOUNDATIONS OF PUBLIC LAW

An entity or group of entities may seek the status of statehood in a variety of circumstances: for example, following the break-up of an existing state, the attempted secession of part of a state, a merger of existing states, or an exercise of foreign control over a state. In such situations, the reaction of other states is of great consequence when deciding whether the entity has the necessary characteristics of statehood. International lawyers agree that recognition by other states is important, although they disagree about its strictly legal significance. Some

[1] See Chapter 4 of this work.

[2] GRECO, *First Evaluation Report on the United Kingdom* (Strasbourg: Council of Europe, 2001), criticized the UK Parliament's handling of complaints against members, for example because the Parliamentary Commissioner for Standards, who deals with the House of Commons, has not been put on a statutory basis, and there is no independent system for dealing with complaints against members of the House of Lords. See A. Doig, 'Sleaze fatigue: an inauspicious year for democracy' (2002) *Parliamentary Affairs* 389.

[3] European Treaty Series No. 122 (1985).

hold that recognition by other states is legally constitutive of the new state as a body with full personality in international law (the 'constitutive theory'). Others argue that recognition is politically and evidentially rather than legally important: it does not constitute the new state, but is a sign that other states accept that the new state already has that status in international law (the 'declaratory theory'). Whichever view is correct (and the balance of opinion currently tends towards the declaratory theory),[4] lack of recognition is at least persuasive evidence that an entity is not a state,[5] and international recognition may be crucial, as when the United Nations (UN) agreed to the establishment of the state of Israel in 1948. Sometimes, as in the case of Cyprus, the international community may intervene in the process of developing statehood, and effectively control the form and content of the new state's first constitution. If the international community uses armed force to end a conflict and secure a state's continued existence, it may impose a new constitution designed to protect the interests of the various parties to the conflict in order to give effect to the agreement which brings it to a close, as in Bosnia and Herzegovina in 1995.[6]

But there are no internationally accepted criteria for recognition. Individual states must decide on what grounds to recognize other entities as states. Most states look for an organized governmental authority exercising effective control over a permanent population and a defined territory, together with an ability to carry on external relations independently of other states and give effect to international obligations.[7] Other relevant factors may include: respect for the UN Charter, human rights, and established international frontiers; a commitment to peaceful resolution of international disputes; and respect for the rights of minorities.[8] None of these factors is necessarily decisive. For example, when the constituent parts of the former Yugoslavia broke up from 1992, the government of one of the republics claiming the status of a new state, Bosnia and Herzegovina, controlled only about half its territory when it was recognized by (among others) the UK. The remainder was under the control of anti-secessionist military groups. The integrity of the new state was secured only when military action by NATO ended three years of war, and the Dayton–Paris Accord of 1995 imposed a General Framework Agreement for Peace (GFAP) on the warring parties. Among other things, this set in stone an internationally agreed constitution, and put in place continuing international control through an international Peace Implementation Council and a High Representative with extensive powers. It has been argued that this external control makes it hard to accept that Bosnia and Herzegovina is an independent sovereign state, and calls in question the democratic legitimacy of its legislative system.[9]

It is some time since the UK has faced that level of external intervention in its affairs, but ideas from abroad have shaped its structure for centuries. Medieval feudalism was imported

4 See the discussions in James Crawford, *The Creation of States in International Law* (2nd edn, 2006) ch. 1, esp. 26–8; Ian Brownlie, *Principles of International Law* (6th edn, 2003) 86–8; Malcolm N. Shaw, *International Law* (5th edn, 2003) 367–76.

5 Shaw, *International Law*, n. 4 above, p. 372.

6 For an illuminating analysis of the kinds and consequences of international intervention in the formation of states and their constitutions, see Nicolas Maziau, 'L'internationalisation du pouvoir constituant' 2002 (3) *Revue Générale de Droit International Public* 549–79.

7 See e.g. Montevideo Convention on the Rights and Duties of States 1933, Art. 1; American Law Institute, *Restatement of the Foreign Relations Law of the United States*, 3rd edn, 1987, ß201.

8 See Shaw, *International Law*, n. 4 above, pp. 374–5.

9 See e.g. Gerald Knaus and Felix Martin, 'Lessons from Bosnia and Herzegovina: Travails of the European Raj' (2003) 14(3) *Journal of Democracy* 60–74.

from western Europe,[10] and overlay the pre-Norman structures to produce a system of government which made possible the growing central authority of the monarchy and the standardization of law across the country. Similarly, between the tenth and twelfth centuries, Scotland

was regulated by a complex patchwork combining a typically western European feudal framework with Celtic custom, which can be traced in many of its details to Irish law tracts of the seventh or eighth centuries. The result was what has been called a 'hybrid kingdom', and one of its marks was the emergence of a composite common law of Scotland by the end of the twelfth century.[11]

Public law and political theory in England and Scotland were essentially modelled on those of western European at that period. In the thirteenth century, the model was extended to Wales by military conquest. As elsewhere in Europe, there was a tension between the gradual centralization of law and bureaucracy and the vigorous desire of the nobility and a developing class of free men for an increased role in decision making.[12] The tension remained, but the structures of the constitution developed so as to accommodate both central and local authority and recognize the interests of a wider variety of free people than previously within the 'community of the realm',[13] encapsulated in such instruments as Magna Carta 1215 and the Statute of Marlborough 1267, which provided that writs should be issued freely against those who were alleged to have committed breaches of Magna Carta, putting the Charter of 1215 (or at least those parts of it which were capable of judicial enforcement) on the same footing as a statute.

By the sixteenth century, British public lawyers and administrators travelling to Avignon, Paris, Pavia, and other European universities to study Roman law and Greco-Roman political theory at the fountainhead of the Renaissance brought their learning home.[14] In the seventeenth century, the English state was effectively re-founded three times (in 1649 after the Civil War and the execution of King Charles I, at the end of the Protectorate in 1660, and after the flight of King James II in December 1688). The royalists in the lead-up to the Civil War relied on ideas derived from the law of nations (*ius gentium*) or natural law to bolster their claim to the divine right of kings,[15] and political philosophers, including Thomas Hobbes on the side of absolute monarchy and John Locke for constitutional monarchy, were part of major western European philosophical traditions.

In 1706–7, the Treaty of Union between England and Scotland led to the foundation of the United Kingdom of Great Britain. It was an instrument of international law, negotiated between the representatives of two sovereign nations and given effect in national law by a combination of Acts of their respective Parliaments and action taken by the monarch of each state (who happened by coincidence to be the same person).[16] Events on the international

[10] See R. C. van Caenegem, *An Historical Introduction to Western Constitutional Law* (1995) ch. 4.

[11] Michael Lynch, *Scotland: A New History* (1992) 53 (footnotes omitted).

[12] van Caenegem, n. 10 above, ch. 5.

[13] See Sir Maurice Powicke, *The Thirteenth Century 1216–1307* (2nd edn, 1962) 131–50, 216–18.

[14] W. Gordon Zeefeld, *Foundations of Tudor Policy* (1969), chs. I–VI, esp. pp. 20–2, 50–1, 79–80, 129–31; David Ibbetson and Andrew Lewis, 'The Roman Law tradition', in A. D. E. Lewis and D. J. Ibbetson (eds), *The Roman Law Tradition* (1994) 1–14.

[15] See e.g. J. W. Gough, *Fundamental Law in English Constitutional History* (1955) 12–174. The parliamentarians looked more to the pre-Norman period of English constitutional history: see Christopher Hill, 'Sir Edward Coke – Myth-Maker', in id., *Intellectual Origins of the English Revolution* (1972) 225–65.

[16] For discussion of the implications of this, see Elizabeth Wicks, 'A new constitution for a new state? The 1707 Union of England and Scotland' (2001) 117 *LQR* 109–26.

plane continue in the twenty-first century to help shape the UK's constitution through international human rights and other treaties, and participation in international organizations such as the UN, the Council of Europe, NATO, and the EC/EU. For example, the devolution legislation in 1998 allows the UK government in Westminster to prevent the devolved authorities from making or enacting legislation which would be incompatible with the UK's international obligations or Community law. International law is necessarily woven into the fabric of public law.[17]

INTERNATIONALIZATION AND PROTECTION FOR NATIONAL INTERESTS: INFLUENCES, CONTROLS, AND FILTERS

National authorities do not usually allow ideas from elsewhere to permeate national institutions unless two conditions are met. First, the state must have something to gain from accepting the ideas, either in terms of rationalizing or guaranteeing its own organization and security (as in the case of Bosnia and Herzegovina in 1995) or because of a promise of reciprocal benefits from other states. Second, unless the state faces irresistible armed force or economic sanctions it will insist on being able to influence the development and application of the ideas which it agrees to accept. Internationalization is thus a two-way street. Benefits must flow inwards to the nation, and the state must have the benefit of being able to influence or export as well as import ideas.

International law reflects this in that a treaty does not bind a state unless it has accepted the obligations arising under it. Internally, state constitutions usually impose filters to ensure that the state's legislative organs maintain control of the impact on municipal law of international treaties (binding agreements between two or more states), customary international law (those state practices internationally accepted as obligatory by most states),[18] and general principles of law.[19] Constitutions usually adopt a position lying somewhere between two poles, commonly known as 'monism' and 'dualism'. A 'monist' approach draws no clear division between national and international law, allowing both customary international law and treaties[20] to produce effects in national law without the need for national legislation to give effect to them. In civil law systems, the influence of classical Roman law ensured that *ius gentium*, or the law founded on human reason assumed to be common to all nations,[21] encouraged the adoption of constitutions which made at least some international obligations directly part of municipal law, treating national and international law as parts of a single, continuous fabric of law, rather than two entirely separate systems. This makes it easier to allow standards of civilized behaviour which form part of international law, including respect for human rights and prohibitions on genocide, torture, and other crimes against humanity, to take effect within states without the need for legislation, and to some extent to control inconsistent national laws.[22] Furthermore, if the existence of a state

[17] Government of Wales Act 1998, ss. 106, 108; Northern Ireland Act 1998, ss. 6, 7, and 14(5); Scotland Act 1998, ss. 29(2) and 35(1).

[18] Shaw, *International Law*, n. 4 above, pp. 68–88.

[19] Ibid., 92–103.

[20] Ibid., 88–92.

[21] See Barry Nicholas, *An Introduction to Roman Law* (1962) 54–9.

[22] See e.g. H. Lauterpacht, *International Law: Collected Papers*, vol. I (1970).

and its legal system depend on that state being recognized as meeting criteria for statehood set by international law (the 'constitutive theory' mentioned earlier), there can logically be no separation between national and international law.[23] Constitutions in civil law countries, and some common law countries like the USA which rebelled against British control, usually adopt some form of monism.

But there are sound reasons for having filters at national level to control the way in which the obligations affect national law- and policy-making. The principled reason is the desire to uphold constitutional guarantees, including the Rule of Law, and keep in the hands of the nations the democratic control of and accountability for national law and policy, in order to maintain the legitimacy of politics and public law in the state. The pragmatic reason is that international obligations may be contrary to the national interest and may derail important national objectives. 'Dualism' provides such a filter by treating national and international law as two separate systems. This prevents international law from directly affecting national law. The UK has traditionally adopted a broadly dualist approach.

However, in reality there is no sharp distinction between monist and dualist approaches. The principled and pragmatic considerations mentioned earlier ensure that few monist states are without controls over the incorporation of international law, while in dualist states the separation between municipal and international law has never been total. Monist states typically maintain essential national interests in the face of international pressure by providing that treaty obligations become enforceable through national law without national legislation only under strict conditions: they must be reciprocal obligations, binding on all the states parties to the treaty; and they must be compatible with the national constitution, which remains hierarchically superior to treaties as a matter of national constitutional law. For example, Article 25 of the *Grundgesetz* (Basic Law) of the Federal Republic of Germany makes the 'general rules of public international law' integral to federal law, creating rights and duties directly for inhabitants of the federal territory and taking precedence over national laws. This is an understandable reaction to the disregard, during the Third Reich, of the norms of public international law. On the other hand, under Article 59.2 treaties which regulate the political relations of the Federation or relate to matters of federal legislation must have the consent or participation, in the form of a federal statute, of the bodies which are competent to make such federal legislation, and treaties affecting federal administration must have the consent or participation of the competent bodies for federal administration. Even then the treaty has the status of a federal statute, and is of no effect if it is incompatible with a provision of the Basic Law, including the basic rights set out in Part I (Articles 1 to 19).[24]

Furthermore, the constitutional structures of monist states normally allow the legislature to control the exercise of treaty-making power by state institutions authorized by the constitution to exercise that power. For example, the Constitution of the USA provides that treaty obligations, together with the Constitution and federal laws made in pursuance of it, are the supreme law of the land,[25] but the President may make treaties only with the

[23] Hans Kelsen, *General Theory of Law and State* (1946) 363–80; id., *The Pure Theory of Law*, trans. Max Knight (1967) 328–47.

[24] *Internationale Handelsgesellschaft mbH* v. *Einfuhr- und Vorratstelle für Getreide und Futtermittel* [1974] 2 CMLR 540, BvfG; *Re the Application of Wünsche Handelsgesellschaft* [1987] 3 CMLR 225, BvfG; *Unification Treaty Constitutionality Case* (1991) 94 ILR 42, BvfG.

[25] US Constitution, Art. VI *bis.*

concurrence of two-thirds of the members of the Senate who are present.[26] The legislative arm has a veto – at least in theory – over the USA's treaty obligations, and so over the state of federal law, although executive agreements, such as those recognizing foreign states, do not require Congressional approval, and may allow federal authorities to enforce obligations arising from them despite the Tenth Amendment, which reserves to the States all powers not conferred by the Constitution on federal authorities.[27] In France, Article 52 of the Constitution of the Fifth Republic (1958) provides that the President of the Republic negotiates and usually also ratifies treaties, and under Article 55 once ratified or approved they prevail over legislation if the other state party reciprocally gives similar effect to the treaty obligations in its own law. But Article 53 preserves parliamentary control by providing that certain kinds of treaties may be ratified or approved only under an enactment, and take effect only after ratification or enactment.[28] What is more, no cession, exchange or annexation of territory is valid without the consent of the population of the territory.[29]

By the same token, in the UK dualism is only partial. Courts have long accepted that 'customary international law', the part of international law consisting of standards accepted by states by common consent without the need for multinational treaties or resolutions of international organizations, forms part of municipal law automatically, by incorporation, without the need for legislation, if sufficiently clear.[30] However, this is subject to the operation of certain filters. First, customary international law is incorporated only so far as it is compatible with national statutes and binding case law. For example, in *Al-Adsani* v. *Government of Kuwait*[31] the Court of Appeal held that torture was contrary to customary international law, but that the plaintiff, who claimed to have been tortured by Kuwaiti officials in Kuwait, could not sue the Government of Kuwait in English courts for torture committed abroad because the clear words of the State Immunity Act 1978 were interpreted as preventing the claimant from arguing that the violation of customary international law precluded the defendant from relying on state immunity. This was followed more recently in *Jones* v. *Ministry of the Interior of the Kingdom of Saudi Arabia and another (Secretary of State for Constitutional Affairs and others intervening)*.[32] The claimant alleged that he had been tortured in Saudi Arabia, and was met by a claim of state immunity. The House of Lords pointed out that state immunity was an important principle of international law. State immunity had been restricted by the Convention against Torture and other Cruel, Inhuman or Degrading Treatment or Punishment 1984 ('the Torture Convention') to allow criminal proceedings against state agents, but it had not been limited so as to allow civil proceedings against representatives of states for torture.

26 Ibid., Art. II.2 *bis*.

27 See *United States* v. *Belmont* 301 US 324 (1937) on the recognition by the USA of the USSR. See also *Breard* v. *Commonwealth* 248 Va. 68, 445 S.E. 2d 670 (1994), cert. denied 513 US 971 (1994).

28 The types of treaty are: 'peace treaties, trade treaties, treaties or agreements concerning international organizations, those which commit national resources, those which modify provisions of a legislative character, those concerning personal status, and those involving the cession, exchange, or annexation or territory': Art. 53, trans. in S. E. Finer, Vernon Bogdanor, and Bernard Rudden, *Comparing Constitutions* (1995) 229.

29 For further examples, see Shaw, *International Law*, n. 4 above, pp. 151–62.

30 See Shaw, *International Law*, n. 4 above, pp. 105–10; *Trendtex Banking Corporation* v. *Central Bank of Nigeria* [1977] QB 529, CA; *J. H. Rayner (Mincing Lane) Ltd* v. *Department of Trade and Industry* [1990] 2 AC 418, HL.

31 (1996) 107 ILR 536, CA.

32 [2006] UKHL 26, [2006] 2 WLR 1424, HL.

Secondly, crimes in customary international law do not automatically become crimes justiciable before domestic courts in England and Wales. The common law is no longer capable of generating new crimes, and there are good constitutional reasons for requiring parliamentary authorization for new crimes and extensions to the criminal jurisdiction of domestic courts.[33] The requirement preserves parliamentary sovereignty and the integrity of municipal common law and protects people against uncontrolled creation of criminal liabilities. The former rationale (though not the latter) justifies the decision of the House of Lords in *R. v. Jones (Margaret)*[34] that the international law crime of aggression was not part of English criminal law, so people charged with aggravated trespass and criminal damage after using force to try to prevent the UK's preparations for the attack on Iraq in 2003 could not claim by way of defence that they were using reasonable force to prevent an unlawful act (Criminal Law Act 1967, section 3). At the same time it demonstrates the strength of the moral argument for a more monistic approach in order to uphold international criminal law.

The interplay of customary international law, international treaty obligations, and UK statute is illustrated by *R. v. Bow Street Metropolitan Stipendiary Magistrate and others, ex parte Pinochet Ugarte (No. 3)*.[35] The applicant was a former President of Chile who was alleged to have authorized acts of torture and murder during his period in power, including some against Spanish citizens. A Spanish judge had issued an international arrest warrant seeking his extradition to Spain to face trial. The applicant had been arrested in England while on a visit to receive medical treatment. The question arose whether he could be extradited. An exceptional seven-judge appellate committee of the House of Lords held:

(a) unanimously, that a head of state would normally be entitled to claim immunity from legal process in the UK by virtue of a combination of customary international law and UK statutes dealing with state immunity and diplomatic immunity;[36]

(b) by a majority of four to three,[37] that torture (unlike murder) is an international crime against humanity by virtue of customary international law, and a peremptory norm of general international law (sometimes called *jus cogens*), defined in Article 53 of the Vienna Convention on the Law of Treaties 1969 as 'a norm accepted and recognized by the international community of States as a whole as a norm from which no derogation is permitted and which can be modified only by a subsequent norm of general international law having the same character', so that it overrides incompatible rules in customary international law or treaties;

(c) unanimously, that the Extradition Act 1989 in the UK prevented extradition for a crime which was not a crime in the UK (as well as in the state which has requested extradition of the suspect) at the time when it was committed (known as the 'double criminality rule');

[33] Roger O'Keefe, 'Customary international crimes in English courts' [2001] *BYIL* 293, 335.

[34] [2006] UKHL 16, [2006] 2 WLR 772, HL.

[35] [2000] 1 AC 147, HL.

[36] See State Immunity Act 1978, s. 20(1) read together with Diplomatic Privileges Act 1964, Sched. 1, para. 39 (giving effect to the Vienna Convention on Diplomatic Relations).

[37] Lords Browne-Wilkinson, Hope of Craighead, Hutton, and Saville of Newdigate. Lords Millett and Phillips of Worth Matravers dissented on the ground that conspiracy to murder in Spain was also an international crime for which no immunity would be available. Lord Goff dissented on the ground that the statutory immunity applied even in relation to torture.

(d) by a majority of four to three,[38] that torture committed outside the UK did not become a criminal offence in the UK until two conditions were met. First, there had to be legislation to make it a criminal offence. This was done by the Criminal Justice Act 1988, which came into force on 29 September 1988. Secondly, all the relevant states (Spain, Chile, and the UK) had to have ratified the International Convention against Torture and other Cruel, Inhuman or Degrading Treatment or Punishment 1984, which required states to recognize and provide in their own law for universal jurisdiction over offences of torture. In other words, every state party to the Convention was then obliged in international law both to accept jurisdiction over such cases in its own courts (wherever the torture was alleged to have been committed) and to recognize that other states' courts had similar jurisdiction. That happened on 8 December 1988; and

(e) by a majority of six to one, that after 8 December 1988 torture committed abroad was a criminal offence in the UK and so was an extradition crime.

This makes three constitutional principles clear. First, the UK operates a dualist filter not only in respect of treaties, but even in respect of a peremptory norm of general international law which establishes a crime against humanity. Only a legislature can authorize courts in the UK to impose criminal liability. Second, even when legislation is in place, English law[39] may recognize a treaty binding on the states involved in a case as an additional necessary step in establishing that there is international jurisdiction. In other words, English courts do not give effect to treaties as such, but may require a treaty before accepting that there is jurisdiction to extradite someone for an international crime against humanity, even when that crime has been shown to exist under statute and customary international law. Third, so far as UK statutes dealing with state and diplomatic immunity are designed to give effect to international treaties, they will be interpreted in the light of those treaties, which themselves may be subject to a peremptory norm of general international law.

Another recent decision establishes a further constitutional filter: the territorial principle. The scope of UK legislation is generally limited to the territory of the UK, even when giving effect to international obligations, although the legislation will be read in the light of those obligations, which may require courts to give limited extra-territorial effect to the legislation. For example, the Human Rights Act 1998 gives domestic effect to rights under the European Convention on Human Rights, which the European Court of Human Rights has interpreted as imposing obligations towards people in areas outside a state's territory if the state has actual control there. The 1998 Act therefore applies outside the UK, but only where agents of the UK have real control over the area where people claim to have suffered a violation of rights.[40]

Where international law operates as a source of domestic law, the courts have regard to the whole of public international law when establishing the scope of any right or obligation that is to have effect in domestic law. Elements cannot be examined in isolation. We have

38 Lords Browne-Wilkinson, Goff, Hope of Craighead, and Saville of Newdigate. Lord Hutton argued that it became an offence in the UK from the 29 September 1988 when s. 134 of the Criminal Justice Act 1988 came into force. Lords Millett and Phillips of Worth Matravers argued that it had been an international crime under customary international law before that, so there could be no immunity.

39 This is probably also the position in Northern Ireland. Nothing is said here about the applicability of the *Pinochet Ugarte (No. 3)* decision in Scotland.

40 *R. (Al-Skeini)* v. *Secretary of State for Defence (The Redress Trust and another intervening)* [2005] EWCA Civ 1609, [2006] 3 WLR 508, CA.

already seen one example of this: tort liability for torture is limited by the international law of state immunity unless it has been restricted by a treaty or *jus cogens*.[41] Other international law rules capable of limiting human rights obligations in international and domestic law include those concerning diplomatic immunity[42] and the overriding effect of decisions in UN Security Council Resolutions to preserve international peace and security by virtue of Article 103 of the UN Charter.[43] Dualism operates in the UK, but the division between municipal and public international law should be seen as a semi-permeable membrane, which allows rules to pass through it in different directions for different purposes.

The dualist filter has been most fully applied in the UK to rights and obligations arising from treaties, and from the action of international organizations established under treaties, to which the UK is a party. Usually, rights and obligations arising under treaties do not take effect in municipal legal systems with a dualist principle unless legislation has been passed to give effect to them. For example, rights under the European Convention on Human Rights, as a multilateral treaty, could not be directly litigated before courts in the UK, either as the basis for a claim for damages, declarations, or injunctions, or as a basis for challenging a decision or act in judicial review proceedings, until legislation had made them fully part of municipal law.[44] Thus, before the Human Rights Act 1998 came into force it was held that a journalist could not rely on the right to freedom of expression under ECHR, Article 10 to impugn the validity of a direction issued by the Home Secretary to broadcasters not to broadcast the voices of the representatives of proscribed organizations in Northern Ireland.[45] This has two effects. First, it prevents the Crown (in reality the government of the day, which conducts foreign affairs under the Royal Prerogative) from exercising its treaty-making prerogative in ways which change the law in the UK without the need for the approval of Parliament. In the absence of a statutory requirement, there is no need to obtain parliamentary approval before negotiating, signing, or ratifying a treaty.[46] This reduces democratic control, but to compensate for that dualism offers a safeguard against the use of the treaty-making prerogative to extend the legislative power of the executive, and protects the legislative supremacy of Parliament against attrition by the Royal Prerogative. Secondly, dualism protects both the government and Parliament against the direct imposition of the will of other states, contrary to the UK's national interests, through international treaties and the resolutions of international organizations. The UK Parliament can refuse to give effect to treaty obligations in municipal law. It, and the government of the day, can also refuse to accept that a treaty imposes any binding obligation. For example, the current government's view of economic and social rights arising under the International Covenant on Economic, Social and Cultural Rights and the Convention on the Rights of the Child is that

[41] *Jones* v. *Ministry of the Interior of the Kingdom of Saudi Arabia and another (Secretary of State for Constitutional Affairs and others intervening)* [2006] UKHL 26, [2006] 2 WLR 1424, HL.

[42] *R. (B.)* v. *Secretary of State for Foreign and Commonwealth Affairs* [2004] EWCA Civ 1344, [2005] QB 643, CA.

[43] *R. (Al-Jedda)* v. *Secretary of State for Defence* [2006] EWCA Civ 327, CA, currently under appeal to the House of Lords. See *A.* v. *Secretary of State for the Home Department (No. 2)* [2005] UKHL 71, [2005] 3 WLR 1249 at para. [29] *per* Lord Bingham of Cornhill.

[44] See e.g. *Malone* v. *Metropolitan Police Commissioner (No. 2)* [1979] Ch 344; *R.* v. *Ministry of Defence, ex parte Smith* [1996] QB 517, CA. See now the Human Rights Act 1998, the Scotland Act 1998, Government of Wales Act 1998, and Northern Ireland Act 1998.

[45] *R.* v. *Secretary of State for the Home Department, ex parte Brind* [1991] 1 AC 696, HL.

[46] See *JH Rayner (Mincing Lane) Ltd.* v. *Department of Trade and Industry* [1990] 2 AC 418, HL, at p. 500 *per* Lord Oliver of Aylmerton. Statutory requirements for parliamentary approval are rare. For an example, see

the obligations are aspirational rather than immediate, and do not require the state to guarantee an ascertainable level of protection at any one time.[47] Refusing to recognize or comply with treaty obligations makes the state liable to sanctions for breach of international law (if any sanctions are available), but it leaves the UK's legislatures ultimately in control of their own legal systems.

This protection for state autonomy can be attenuated. In some situations, Parliament has legislated to allow obligations imposed at EC or EU level to be enforced directly in courts and tribunals in the UK.[48] This means that government ministers, exercising powers under the Royal Prerogative, can agree in Brussels to change the law in the UK without parliamentary approval. There are some safeguards for national interests. When the supremacy of Community law was established by the Court of Justice of the European Communities (CJEC), the EC Council (the organization's main legislative body) had to agree to legislation unanimously. This has since changed. The range of decisions requiring to be adopted unanimously has steadily narrowed, and there is no legal protection for parliamentary sovereignty, although some procedural safeguards have been put in place. These include the 'scrutiny reserve' which usually prevents the UK government from agreeing to measures being adopted in Brussels until they have been scrutinized by the Houses of Parliament, a task performed with distinction by committees in both Houses.[49]

In relation to treaties which do not directly alter municipal law, Parliament's position is weak, despite (or because of) dualism. The two Houses normally have no right to be consulted before the text of a treaty is concluded, much less a veto over its signing or ratification. The government makes treaties, and is usually accountable to Parliament only afterwards. There is a constitutional convention that treaties will not be ratified until they have been laid before both Houses of Parliament. This, the so-called 'Ponsonby rule', derives from a statement to the House of Commons on 1 April 1924 by Arthur Ponsonby, then Under Secretary of State for Foreign Affairs in Ramsay MacDonald's Labour administration. The government, he said, wished Parliament to have 'an opportunity for the examination, consideration and if need be discussion of all Treaties before they reach the final stage of ratification'. They would be laid before each House for 21 days before the government ratified them. If a treaty did not require ratification, and was merely technical,[50] it would not be laid before Parliament. But 'the government shall inform the House of all agreements, commitments and undertakings which may in any way bind the nation to specific action in certain circumstances'.[51] However, the Ponsonby rule, which governments still accept today, gives

European Parliamentary Elections Act 1978, s. 6(1), which prevents the Crown from ratifying any treaty to increase the powers of the European Parliament unless approved by an Act of the UK Parliament.

47 For the government's position on the Convention on the Rights of the Child and criticism of it, see Joint Committee on Human Rights, Tenth Report of 2002–3, *The UN Convention on the Rights of the Child*, HL Paper 117, HC 81 (2003), paras 21–23.

48 European Communities Act 1972, s. 2, discussed further below.

49 See the resolutions of the two Houses at HC Debs, 17 Nov. 1998, col. 778 ff. and HL Debs, 6 Dec. 1999, col. 1019 ff.; K. M. Newman, 'The impact of national parliaments on the development of Community law', in F. Capotorti (ed.), *Du Droit International au Droit de l'Integration: Liber Amicorum Pierre Pescatore* (1987) 481–97; T. St. J. N. Bates, 'European Community legislation before the House of Commons' (1991) 12 *Stat. LR* 109–24.

50 'Technical' is not a technical term. It is capable of covering treaties establishing procedures for giving effect to already existing substantive obligations, and perhaps treaties concerned with the way states deal with fields in which their jurisdictions overlap, for instance in relation to double-taxation agreements.

51 HC Debs, 5th Ser., vol. 171, 1 April 1924, col. 2001.

Parliament no more than a right to receive information about the government's treaty-making activities.

Treaties by which the UK becomes a member of supranational or international organizations whose institutions have law-making powers give rise to an enhanced need to apply filters to protect the municipal legal systems against adverse effects, but also make it more difficult to secure that protection. The value of filters in such a system depends on the power of the state to influence the content of obligations imposed on it by treaty bodies. In 1973 the UK became a member state of the European Economic Community (EEC). This was originally an association of a small group of western European nations designed to remove national barriers to economic development and to turn the member states into a single market (the 'Common Market') in goods and services. At that stage, national interests were strongly protected by equal state representation on the main law-making body and (as noted earlier) a requirement for unanimity to make law. The veto power of each member state gave reasonable protection for the UK's national interests, making possible the UK's acceptance of the direct effect of some Community legislation and of the doctrine of the supremacy of Community law. Over time, however, the number of member states and the diversity of their interests increased, and the law-making activities of the institution grew in range and complexity. The EEC turned into the European Community (EC) and later the European Union (EU), dedicated to harmonizing a growing range of economic and social policies, including the regulation of police and judicial cooperation and other fields of common concern. Qualified majority voting was introduced, and the states came to have representation in rough proportion to their populations rather than on a basis of state equality. The range of matters on which an individual member state had a veto shrank to the point at which the EU Constitution, had it been adopted, would have removed the unanimity requirement from all law making but that which is most fundamental: the treaties establishing the institution and laying down the constituent rules about membership, law making, and governance. The safeguards for vital national interests, which originally justified relaxing the national filters by accepting the direct effect of Community law, are no longer in place.

Some international organizations never demand unanimity in decision making. From its establishment in 1946, the UN had such a large membership that unanimity was never a practical option. Each member state has a seat in the General Assembly, but that body's recommendations do not bind states in public international law except in relation to the internal governance of the UN[52] (although resolutions may be evidence of the emergence of binding rules of customary international law if they reflect state practice). The main power to impose obligations binding states in international law is conferred on the Security Council, which forms the executive group of the UN with special responsibility for preserving international peace and security.[53] Decisions of the Council (but not mere recommendations) bind all member states.[54] Only 15 states are members of the Security Council. Five of them, the 'great powers' of the period following the Second World War (China, France, Russia, the UK, and the USA), are permanent members. The other nine members are elected for a period of two years from among the remaining members of the General Assembly, as laid down by Article 23.2 of the UN Charter. Security Council Resolutions must be approved by an affirmative vote of at least nine members, but any of the permanent

[52] UN Charter, Art. 17. [53] Ibid., Arts 23, 24, 25, and 28. [54] Ibid., Art. 25.

members may veto any proposed resolution, except in relation to procedural matters (such as the agenda for sessions, or the states which should be given the opportunity to address the Council in matters affecting them), where there is no veto.[55] This offers asymmetric protection to national interests. Those of the five permanent members are well protected by their veto. Those of the non-permanent members can be subordinated to the interests of nine concurring members, although they may benefit from overlapping the vital interests of one of the permanent members. States without a seat on the Security Council are even less well protected. As members of the UN they can use diplomatic techniques in defence of their interests, but their success will depend significantly on the balance of power and the interests of the 'great powers'.

For historical reasons, the UK is a permanent member of the UN Security Council, so it has a measure of control over the most important decisions. In other international organizations, it has influence rather than control, and the extent of its influence depends on the arguments and pressure it can apply. By contrast, the USA, as a world superpower in terms of its military and economic might, can exercise great influence by offers of aid with strings attached, or by explicit or implicit threats of trade sanctions, withdrawal of aid, or in extreme cases invasion. Such influence does not depend on the quality of the superpower's arguments or the morality of its stance. It extends beyond organizations of which the USA is a member, although even a superpower must sometimes take account of other states' points of view, as the aftermath of the second Gulf War in 2003 has shown.

MECHANISMS FOR INTERNATIONALIZATION, CONSTITUTIONAL STRUCTURES, AND LEGITIMACY

Since a state is inevitably subject to international influences, they must be channelled into municipal law and contained within a structure which fits the state's constitutional law and traditions. How is this done?[56]

The most direct form of international (or at least supranational) influence arises when rules made by another state or states, or accepted at inter-state level, are automatically incorporated into the municipal legal system, without the need for any prior or subsequent legislative action. In the UK, the most straightforward example of this is the automatic incorporation of rules of customary international law subject to legislation and the doctrine of *stare decisis*, as mentioned in the previous section.

Marginally less direct, but more powerful, is the process whereby certain rules of EC and EU law become part of the municipal legal system. Section 2(1) of the European Communities Act 1972 creates what is in effect a statutory rule of automatic incorporation of what it calls 'enforceable Community rights'. Because of the doctrine of the supremacy of Community law over national law, this form of incorporation has a greater impact than the incorporation of customary international law. Enforceable Community rights need not be compatible with previous or subsequent parliamentary legislation. Instead, inconsistent

55 Ibid., Art. 27.

56 David Feldman, 'Modalities of internationalisation in international law' (2006) 18 *ERPL* 131.

parliamentary legislation must be disapplied to the extent that it is inconsistent with enforceable Community rights.[57]

In addition, section 2(2) of the Act allows her Majesty in Council or designated ministers and departments to give effect to or implement other Community obligations or rights (including those arising under Directives which do not have direct effect) in municipal law by way of statutory instruments, a form of subordinate legislation. These are usually subject only to the negative resolution procedure: they take effect unless either House passes a resolution annulling them.[58] Statutory instruments under section 2(2) can make any provision that could be made by Act of Parliament. They can even amend or repeal Acts of Parliament; and any provision of primary legislation is to be construed and to have effect subject to the provisions of the statutory instrument.[59] A subsequent Act of Parliament could revoke the statutory instrument, as long as that would not be incompatible with the enforcement of enforceable Community rights. Nevertheless, the filters protecting parliamentary control over the implementation of EC and EU law are limited: the negative resolution procedure is hardly a strong form of scrutiny or protection, and the best filter is the pre-adoption scrutiny of EC and EU measures by the House of Commons EU Scrutiny Committee and the House of Lords EU Committee and its subcommittees.[60] What is more, in some fields the member states have delegated power to the European Commission to negotiate treaties on their behalf with non-member states, including agreements on tariffs and trade and arrangements for extradition. The impact of such agreements on the rights and obligations of member states is as yet uncertain.[61]

Following the establishment of the United Nations in 1946, Parliament conferred power on the government to implement certain decisions of the UN Security Council by way of subordinate legislation, with limited or non-existent parliamentary oversight. When the Security Council, acting to preserve international peace and security under Chapter VII of the UN Charter, calls on the government to apply any measures to give effect to any decision of the Council under Article 41 of the UN Charter (that is, decisions not involving the use of armed force), section 1(1) of the United Nations Act 1946 allows Her Majesty by Order in Council to make 'such provision as appears to Her to be necessary or expedient for enabling the measures to be effectively applied'. The Order must be laid before Parliament forthwith after it is made, and, if it relates to a matter within the legislative competence of the Scottish Parliament, before that Parliament as well,[62] but neither Parliament can annul the Order save by means of an Act. Still less do such Orders require the approval of either House. The only control available is through judicial review. An Order can be quashed if it is outside the scope of the power conferred by the Act or is incompatible with a Community right (such as the right to be free of quantitative restrictions on free movement of goods)[63] or a Convention right under the Human Rights Act 1998. But if it acts compatibly with EC law and Convention rights the government has a very wide discretion as to the terms of the Order and the Treasury has a very wide discretion as to the manner of its implementation.[64]

[57] See Chapter 4, above. [58] European Communities Act 1972, Sched. 2, para. 2(2).

[59] Ibid., s. 2(4). [60] See discussion in Chapter 4 above.

[61] See Vienna Convention on the Law of Treaties between States and International Organisations 1986; Shaw, *International Law*, n. 4 above, pp. 671–3. [62] Ibid., s. 1(4), as amended by the Scotland Act 1998.

[63] See *R. v. HM Treasury, ex parte Centro-Com Srl* [1997] QB 863, CJEC.

[64] See *R. v. HM Treasury, ex parte Centro-Com Srl*, The Independent, 3 June 1994, CA, affirming (in relation to municipal law) [1994] 1 CMLR 109. On the implications of EC law, see the decision of the CJEC on the reference from the CA: [1997] QB 683, CJEC.

The scope of the power is enormous, and Orders can directly affect individuals. For example, after the terrorist attack on the World Trade Center on 9 September 2001 the UN Security Council passed Resolution 1373 of 28 September 2001, calling on the governments of member states to apply measures to give effect to decisions of the Council to combat terrorist activities. It required steps to be taken to freeze terrorist assets. In the UK, the Government implemented this by Orders in Council making it a criminal offence to make funds or financial services available to or for the benefit of people participating in acts of terrorism or to fail to report suspicions that people are intending to use funds for such a purpose, and allowing the Treasury to freeze the funds of such people whom the Treasury has reasonable grounds for suspecting may be holding funds for the purpose of committing, facilitating, or participating in acts of terrorism.[65] These Orders were subject to no parliamentary control or scrutiny either before or after they were made. In reliance on them, the Treasury froze the assets of several dozen people, and announced its action in press releases.[66] The Security Council resolution thus authorized a direct attack by the British Government on individuals' property, with very limited safeguards and filters within the jurisdiction for Rule of Law requirements and the democratic process.

Today, a provision like section 1(1) of the United Nations Act 1946 would face intensive parliamentary scrutiny. The House of Lords Select Committee on Delegated Powers and Regulatory Reform scrutinizes all provisions in Bills before Parliament which confer power to make delegated legislation. Proposed powers to make subordinate legislation rarely if ever survive unless the Committee is satisfied that sufficient safeguards are included in the power to ensure an appropriate level of parliamentary scrutiny of proposed subordinate legislation and to protect the Rule of Law and human rights. Where the proposed power could affect human rights or constitutional principles, that scrutiny is reinforced by the work of the Joint Select Committee on Human Rights and the House of Lords Select Committee on the Constitution respectively. It is noteworthy that the powers included in the Anti-terrorism, Crime and Security Act 2001 to permit EU Third Pillar (Police and Judicial Co-operation in Criminal Matters) initiatives to be given effect in the UK by way of subordinate legislation included far more safeguards than can be found in the United Nations Act 1946.[67] Even then the government agreed that legislation to implement the Framework Decision on the European Arrest Warrant would be introduced by way of a Bill (now Part 1 of the Extradition Act 2003) rather than by using the power to make subordinate legislation under the 2001 Act.[68]

Similar caution about authorizing subordinate legislation can be seen in the Human Rights Act 1998 and the devolution legislation to making rights under the European Convention on Human Rights (ECHR) ('the Convention rights') part of municipal law in the UK.[69] Section 1 of the Human Rights Act 1998, applied in the devolution legislation,[70]

65 Terrorism (United Nations Measures) (Channel Islands) Order 2001 (SI 2001/3363); Terrorism (United Nations Measures) (Isle of Man) Order 2001 (SI 2001/3364); Terrorism (United Nations Measures) Order 2001 (SI 2001/3365).

66 See e.g. Treasury Press Release 110/01, 12 October 2001, which includes a list of names.

67 See Anti-terrorism, Crime and Security Act 2001, ss. 111 and 112. For further primary legislation on cross-border cooperation see Crime (International Co-operation) Act 2003.

68 See Joint Committee on Human Rights, Second Report, 2001–2, *Anti-terrorism, Crime and Security Bill*, HL Paper 37, HC 372, para. 13.

69 See Chapters 3, 9, and 10 of this work.

70 See Government of Wales Act 1998, s. 107; Scotland Act 1998, ss. 29(2), 54(2), and 126(1); Northern Ireland Act 1998, ss. 6(2), 24(1), and 98(1).

appears to import the rights bodily from international law (the ECHR) to national law. However, the transplant is complicated by two factors. First, the rights in international law bind states, whereas in municipal law they bind public authorities within the state. This necessitated adjustments designed, among other things, to adapt the rights for municipal application and maintain consistency with constitutional principles such as parliamentary sovereignty and parliamentary privilege.[71] Second, there is a difference between formulating a right and understanding what it means when applied in practice. Both the scope of the Convention rights and the circumstances (if any) in which it is justifiable to interfere with them in international law depend on the extensive case law of the European Commission and the Court of Human Rights. Parts of it, such as the notion of the 'margin of appreciation', arise from the position of international tribunals *vis-à-vis* national authorities and cannot be transferred to municipal law. Even if a particular line of case law can be transferred to the municipal sphere, there may be good reasons for limiting its impact. Section 2 of the Human Rights Act 1998 therefore provides that courts and tribunals in the UK must take into account the case law of the Strasbourg organs when interpreting the Convention rights, but does not make it binding. Courts in the UK have on occasions declined to follow judgments of the European Court of Human Rights.[72] For example, the House of Lords has held that normal rules of precedent generally require a lower court in England and Wales to follow an earlier decision of a higher domestic court on the application of Convention rights in preference to a later, inconsistent decision of the European Court of Human Rights, unless it is clear that the policy justification for the earlier English decision no longer applies.[73] This introduces a filter into the channel by which the Convention rights enter municipal law: courts and tribunals in the UK are not required to follow decisions of international tribunals if they seem inappropriate to the structure of the domestic legal order or plainly wrong.

The Act also empowers ministers to make statutory instruments for various purposes, providing further channels for bringing municipal law into line with the ECHR. With relatively few preconditions or procedural filters a Secretary of State can make a statutory instrument adding an extra right to the list of Convention rights which became part of municipal law by virtue of section 1 of the Act. With equally little formal constraint, a Secretary of State can add a reservation to the newly recognized right to the list of reservations in section 1 of, and Part 1 of Schedule 3 to, the Act, or add a derogation from a Convention right to those recognized in section 1 of, and Part 2 of Schedule 3 to, the Act. Any UK court or tribunal interpreting a Convention right must then read it subject to the reservation or derogation in question. There have been two changes to the derogations recognized in the Act, both in relation to terrorism: the original derogation was repealed, and later a new one was inserted;[74] but the derogation order adding the new derogation was

[71] See e.g. the partial delimitation of the term 'public authority' in the Human Rights Act 1998, s. 6.

[72] On the circumstances in which courts in the UK should follow Strasbourg judgments, see e.g. *R. (on the application of Alconbury Developments Ltd)* v. *Secretary of State for the Environment, Transport and the Regions* [2001] UKHL 23, [2001] 2 WLR 1389, HL, at para. 26 *per* Lord Slynn of Hadley; *R.* v. *Spear* [2002] UKHL 31, [2003] 1 AC 734, HL; *R. (on the application of Anderson)* v. *Secretary of State for the Home Department* [2002] UKHL 46, [2003] 1 AC 837, HL, at para. 18 *per* Lord Bingham of Cornhill; David Feldman (ed.), *English Public Law* (2004), paras 7.30–7.31, 7.35–7.46.

[73] *Kay* v. *Lambeth LBC; Leeds City Council v. Price* [2006] UKHL 10, [2006] 2 WLR 570, HL.

[74] See Human Rights Act 1998 (Amendment) Order 2001 (SI 2001/1216), made when the Terrorism Act 2000 replaced the Prevention of Terrorism (Temporary Provisions) Act 1989, to remove the derogation from

subsequently held to be *ultra vires* because the measures concerned were not strictly required by the exigencies of the terrorist threat and consistent with the UK's other international obligations so as to meet the requirements of Article 15 of the ECHR,[75] so at present (as of May 2007) there is no designated derogation.

If the Strasbourg Court or a UK court decides that UK legislation is incompatible with a Convention right, section 10 of the Human Rights Act 1998 empowers the appropriate Secretary of State to make an Order in Council amending or repealing the incompatible provision, which is usually in an Act of Parliament. When the Human Rights Bill was before the House of Lords in 1997, the Select Committee on Delegated Powers and Deregulation[76] recommended that this 'Henry VIII' power should be hedged about with preconditions and procedural requirements, now contained in section 10 of and Schedule 2 to the Act, even though the purpose is to protect and extend, rather than to interfere with, human rights. This has the odd result that it is easier to make a statutory instrument which restricts rights by requiring courts in the UK to interpret Convention rights in the light of a reservation or new derogation than to extend rights by way of a statutory instrument (a remedial order) amending previously incompatible legislation.

Even where there is no express legislative authority for allowing international standards and treaties to influence municipal law, both treaties and the judgments of international and foreign tribunals can influence parliamentary and judicial decision making in the UK. Parliament and government departments are increasingly aware of the UK's obligations as a result of the work of the government's legal advisers, and select committees and individual members in Parliament. This is affecting both the content of legislation and the way in which scrutiny of government is conducted.[77] If it cannot yet be said that the influence is pervasive, it is at least significant and growing. The main constraint is the government's unwillingness to accept that economic, social, and cultural rights can impose immediate, binding, and justiciable obligations on the UK,[78] but this may change over time. This use of international standards is fully consistent with parliamentary democracy.

The judiciary too is a channel for allowing foreign influences into national public law systems. Judges in many countries round the world have a keen interest in foreign and international public law standards, including but not limited to human rights. In many common law jurisdictions they consider and draw illumination from public law judgments of courts

ECHR, Art. 5 which allowed detention of terrorist suspects without charge for up to seven days before they had to be brought before a judicial officer; and Human Rights Act 1998 (Designated Derogation) Order 2001 (SI 2001/3644), which purported to introduce a new derogation from Art. 5 to allow indefinite detention without trial of suspected international terrorists who were not UK nationals if they could not be removed abroad for legal or practical reasons, following the enactment of the Anti-terrorism, Crime and Security Act 2001.

75 *A.* v. *Secretary of State for the Home Department* [2004] UKHL 56, [2005] 2 AC 68, HL. Note that Lord Scott of Foscote expressed doubt as to the applicability of Art.15, as it was not one of the provisions made part of the legal systems of the UK by s. 1 of the Human Rights Act 1998, but the Home Secretary had conceded its relevance.

76 The forerunner of the Select Committee on Delegated Powers and Regulatory Reform.

77 See Lord Lester of Herne Hill, QC, 'Parliamentary scrutiny of legislation under the Human Rights Act 1998' [2002] *EHRLRev* 432; David Feldman, 'Parliamentary scrutiny of legislation and human rights' [2002] *PL* 323; id., 'The impact of human rights on the legislative process' (2004) 25 *Stat. L. Rev.* 91, id., 'Can and should Parliament protect human rights?' (2004) 10 *European Public Law* 635; Janet Hiebert, 'Parliamentary review of terrorism measures' (2005) 58 *MLR* 676; id., 'Interpreting a Bill of Rights: the importance of legislative rights review' [2005] *BJPS* 235; Carolyn Evans and Simon Evans, 'Legislative scrutiny committees and parliamentary conceptions of human rights' [2006] *PL* 785.

78 See n. 47 above.

elsewhere in the world. Judges do not simply adopt solutions or interpretations which have found favour elsewhere. The differences between constitutional and political structures in different countries make that undesirable: there may be no certainty that the solutions would fit a local context. Instead, they find it helpful to see how courts in different constitutional traditions have conceptualized and analysed the conflicting interests relevant to public law problems. This can help to crystallize issues and suggest approaches without dictating an outcome. Courts in the UK regularly use comparative law as a source of ideas for developing the common law and interpreting human rights. Senior British judges have long been familiar with different constitutional and human rights arrangements through sitting regularly as members of the Judicial Committee of the Privy Council on public law appeals. In recent years there have been three Lords of Appeal in Ordinary with South African backgrounds in the Appellate Committee of the House of Lords (Lords Hoffmann, Scott of Foscote, and Steyn), and for several years Lord Cooke of Thorndon, a former President of the Court of Appeal of New Zealand, sat regularly as a Lord of Appeal. Judges regularly participate in academic seminars and conferences concerning international and comparative law. The Judicial Studies Board increasingly involves academics in judicial discussions and seminars. A growing number of senior judges had previous experience as legal academics. Senior judges in different jurisdictions communicate extensively with each other, building up personal friendships and professional links through international conferences and colloquia and email. The Internet offers access to a huge archive of legal materials from many jurisdictions.[79] The Law Commission and other bodies entrusted with the task of law reform now routinely undertake comparative research on the areas of law under review. English judges have also become far readier than before to make use of international legal materials in their judgments, including opinions, recommendations and resolutions of experts and international bodies that do not bind states in public international law. This 'soft law' influences outcomes by establishing a normative framework which tends to favour one outcome of the 'hard law' dispute over another. In England and Wales, judges sometimes assume that its appropriateness is self-evident, but may in many cases be able to justify it on the ground that it represents customary international law. Where that is so, it is tenable to argue that treaty obligations should be interpreted in the light of the matrix of international obligations within which they operate, and 'if, and to the extent that, development of the common law is called for, such development should ordinarily be in harmony with the UK's international obligations and not antithetical to them.'[80] This open intellectual atmosphere, influenced by judges' experiences and by their growing familiarity with international and comparative methods through their work with the Human Rights Act 1998, various commercial law conventions and other sources, is likely to grow stronger. Judges will be keen to compare techniques of constitutional reasoning and hear how courts elsewhere approach such matters as the interpretation of legislation so as to make it compatible with human rights.

This approach offers benefits. But there are also dangers if we start to treat decisions as if they could simply be transplanted into different constitutional soil, or to elevate comparativism

[79] See A.-M. Slaughter, 'A global community of courts' (2003) 44 *Harvard International Law Journal* 191.

[80] *A.* v. *Secretary of State for the Home Department (No. 2)* [2005] UKHL 71, [2005] 3 WLR 1249, HL, at para. [27] *per* Lord Bingham of Cornhill; see also paras. [28]–[29]. See further, e.g., the speeches in recent cases on the implications for law in the UK of allegations of torture abroad: *Jones* v. *Ministry of the Interior of the Kingdom of Saudi Arabia (Secretary of State for Constitutional Affairs and others intervening)* [2006] UKHL 26, [2006] 2 WLR 1424, HL.

to the status of a judicial duty without constitutional authority. The decision of the Judicial Committee of the Privy Council in *Lange* v. *Atkinson and Australian Consolidated Press NZ Ltd*[81] illustrates this. Mr David Lange, a former Prime Minister of New Zealand, sued the defendants for libel in respect of a magazine article criticizing Mr Lange's performance as a politician and suggesting that he suffered from selective memory loss. The defendants pleaded, among other defences, that the article was 'political expression' and, as such, entitled to privilege against liability. They also pleaded qualified privilege (i.e. a protection against liability for libel as long as they had acted pursuant to a duty to bring the matters to the attention of the intended recipients, and had not acted maliciously). At first instance in the High Court of New Zealand, Elias J decided that political expression was not a separate ground of privilege at common law, but could be pleaded as a form of common law qualified privilege.[82] Mr Lange appealed. Before the Court of Appeal heard his appeal, the High Court of Australia, in a libel action brought by Mr Lange in Australia in relation to a publication of similar allegations there, decided that common law qualified privilege protected communications to the public of information, opinions, and arguments relating to governmental and political matters, as long as the publishers proved that they had acted reasonably.[83] When Mr Lange's appeal from Elias J reached the Court of Appeal of New Zealand, that court agreed with Elias J that such communications were entitled to qualified privilege, but, not following the High Court of Australia, held that the reasonableness of the publishers' conduct was irrelevant: at common law in New Zealand, only malice could deprive the publishers of the privilege.[84]

Mr Lange appealed to the Judicial Committee of the Privy Council ('the Board') against the decision of the Court of Appeal of New Zealand. After the Board had heard argument in the appeal, but before the Board delivered its judgment, the House of Lords had considered the same issue in relation to a libel action brought by Mr Albert Reynolds, a former Taoiseach of Ireland, over newspaper articles published in England which, he said, implied that he had deliberately misled the Dáil and his cabinet colleagues. The question was whether the defendants should be allowed to plead qualified privilege at a retrial. The House of Lords held that they could not, because at common law in England and Wales a publication was not privileged merely because it was about governmental or political matters. The publisher had to show that there was a duty to publish the material to its intended recipients (or, to put it another way, that publication was in the public interest).[85] In Mr Lange's appeal, the Board noted the differences between the Australian, New Zealand and English approaches to qualified privilege in respect of publications about political and governmental matters. There was no expectation that such issues would be settled in the same way in all common law jurisdictions. The Board accepted that 'striking a balance between freedom of expression and protection of reputation calls for a value judgment which depends upon local political and social conditions'. Furthermore, 'there is a high content of judicial policy in the solution of the issue raised by this appeal; . . . different solutions may be reached in different jurisdictions without any faulty reasoning or misconception . . .; and . . . within a

81 [2000] 1 NZLR 257, PC.

82 *Lange* v. *Atkinson and Australian Consolidated Press NZ Ltd* [1997] 2 NZLR 22.

83 *Lange* v. *Australian Broadcasting Corporation* (1997) 189 CLR 520, HC of Australia.

84 *Lange* v. *Atkinson and Australian Consolidated Press NZ Ltd* [1998] 3 NZLR 424, CA of New Zealand.

85 *Reynolds* v. *Times Newspapers Ltd* [2001] 2 AC 127, HL. On the meaning of a duty to publish, see now *Jameel* v. *Wall Street Journal Europe Sprl* [2006] UKHL 44, [2006] 3 WLR 642, HL.

particular jurisdiction the necessary value judgment may best be made by the local courts'. Nevertheless, the Board allowed the appeal and sent the case back for a further hearing because the New Zealand Court of Appeal had not had the opportunity to consider the English judgments in the *Reynolds* case before making its decision.[86]

This puts a high value on comparative law. While recognizing some limits, it comes close to imposing a duty on at least the top common-law courts to have regard to (though not to follow) each other's leading decisions. With respect, this seems to go too far. The Board's decision does not explain the legitimate basis for having regard to foreign authorities as guides to developing one's own public law, let alone justify allowing an appeal in order to force another court to do so. Using foreign legal material at all is not uncontroversial. Unstructured picking and choosing between sources can undermine or evade the filters which, for good constitutional reasons, constrain foreign influences on domestic legal systems. As noted earlier, this has not been much of an issue in the UK so far, or in Australia, Canada, India or New Zealand; but there has been heated disagreement in the USA about the propriety of taking account of either international law standards which do not form part of municipal law in the USA or decisions of courts in other common law countries. They are comfortable with comparative law techniques, as federal law must take account of dozens of state legal systems and constitutions. The real issue is the legitimacy of relying on international developments when taking a nation's constitutional jurisprudence in a new direction. In *Atkins* v. *Virginia*[87] the US Supreme Court, in a footnote to the majority judgment of Stevens J, adverted in passing to the fact that 'within the world community, the imposition of the death penalty for crimes committed by mentally retarded offenders is overwhelmingly disapproved' as evidence for an evolving standard of decency making such punishment cruel and unusual, and so contrary to the Eighth Amendment to the US Constitution.[88] The dissent by Rehnquist CJ (in which Scalia and Thomas JJ joined) argued that only standards within the USA, evidenced by federal and state legislation and decisions of juries, were relevant when deciding whether a punishment is cruel and unusual for constitutional purposes. It would be illegitimate to decide US constitutional law by reference to foreign standards. This does not mean that the dissentients are unaware of developments elsewhere. In *Lawrence* v. *Texas*,[89] the majority of the US Supreme Court held that there was no rational basis for a state law criminalizing homosexual sodomy and overruled *Bowers* v. *Hardwick*.[90] Scalia J's dissent (in which Rehnquist CJ and Thomas J joined) referred to a Canadian decision[91] as part of a 'slippery slope' argument, suggesting that judicially striking down laws which discriminate against homosexuals could lead to the judicial imposition on the legislature of homosexual marriage, which would be unacceptable under the US Constitution. Where the national constitution does not authorize courts to draw on foreign decisions, it may (as Rehnquist CJ pointed out in *Atkins* v. *Virginia*) be difficult to justify being guided from elsewhere in interpreting one's own constitution. As aids to articulating issues and becoming aware of possible approaches, not to mention a state's international obligations, comparative and international studies are hard to better, but in

[86] *Lange* v. *Atkinson and Australian Consolidated Press NZ Ltd* [2000] 1 NZLR 257, PC. For the further proceedings in the Court of Appeal of New Zealand, see [2000] 3 NZLR 385.

[87] 536 US 304 (2002).

[88] Ibid., fn. 21 of the judgment, referring to the Brief for the European Union as *Amicus Curiae* in *McCarver* v. *North Carolina*, O.T. 2001, No. 00–1727, p. 4.

[89] 539 US 558 (2003).

[90] 478 US 186 (1986).

[91] *Halpern* v. *Toronto* 2003 WL 34950 (Ontario CA).

the USA, unlike most other jurisdictions, the matter is being approached as one of constitutional principle.[92]

It is rare for a codified constitution either to authorize or to prohibit courts taking account of international legal standards or judgments of foreign or international tribunals when deciding municipal public law cases, but the 1996 Constitution of the Republic of South Africa is an exception. The Constitution is an outward-looking document. The formulation of the Constitution's Bill of Rights was heavily influenced by the examples of Canada, Ireland, India, and Nigeria, but the formulation of the rights and their constitutional status was a response to the particular needs of post-apartheid society. Section 39(1) of the 1996 Constitution provides that a court, tribunal or forum, when interpreting the Bill of Rights:

a. must promote the values that underlie an open and democratic society based on human dignity, equality and freedom;
b. must consider international law; and
c. may consider foreign law.

As a result, the judgments of the Constitutional Court of South Africa are a valuable repository of learning on international and comparative human rights law, and their constitutional legitimacy is beyond question.

Courts in the UK are not required to be as systematic as those in South Africa in their use of international and foreign law, but UK judges have regularly used both international and comparative law.[93] Treaties can be used to interpret legislation, on the assumption that Parliament does not intend to violate the UK's international obligations unless an intention to do so appears clearly.[94] Where a statute is designed to give effect to international obligations, the assumption is that Parliament intended to achieve that and nothing else.[95] A treaty may give rise to a legitimate expectation, enforceable in administrative law, that the government will act in accordance with the UK's international obligations, although this has been criticised as a 'constitutional solecism' amounting 'to a means of incorporating the substance of obligations undertaken on the international plane into our domestic law without the authority of Parliament'.[96] Treaties may provide a guide to the requirements of public

92 See, e.g., *Printz* v. *United States*, 521 US 898 (1997); *Foster* v. *Florida*, 537 US 990 (2002); *Roper* v. *Simmons*, 125 S Ct 1183 (2005); Norman Dawson, 'The relevance of foreign legal materials in US constitutional cases: a conversation between Justice Antonin Scalia and Justice Stephen Breyer' (2005) 3 *Int. J. Const. Law* 519 (also accessible on the Internet at www.wcl.american.edu); Ruth Bader Ginsburg, ' "A decent respect to the opinions of [human] kind": the value of a comparative perspective in constitutional adjudication' (2005) 64 *CLJ* 575.

93 Historically, Roman law (including the notion of *ius gentium*) had an influence on parts of the common law: see Andrew Lewis, ' "What Marcellus says is against you": Roman law and common law', in Lewis and Ibbetson, n. 14 above, ch. 12; Daan Asser, '*Audi et alteram partem*: a limit to judicial activity', ibid., ch. 13. Courts have also had regard to treaties, although only relatively recently in Scotland: see *T., Petitioner* 1997 SLT 734, Court of Session (Inner House), and above, text at n. 36 ff.

94 See e.g. *Waddington* v. *Miah* [1974] 1 WLR 683, HL.

95 See e.g. *R. (on the application of Mullen)* v. *Secretary of State for the Home Department* [2002] EWCA Civ 1882, [2003] 2 WLR 835, CA.

96 For the origin of the application of the doctrine to human-rights treaties see *Minister for Immigration and Ethnic Affairs* v. *Teoh* (1995) 183 CLR 273, HC of Australia; R. v. *Secretary of State for the Home Department, ex parte Ahmed and Patel* [1998] INLR 570; R. v. *Uxbridge Magistrates' Court, ex parte Adimi* [2001] QB 667, DC, esp. at p. 686 *per* Simon Brown L.J. For the criticism, see *Behluli* v. *Secretary of State for the Home Department* [1998] Imm AR 407 at p. 415 *per* Beldam L.J.; *R. (European Roma Rights Centre)* v. *Immigration Officer at Prague Airport (United Nations High Commissioner for Refugees intervening)* [2003] EWCA Civ 666, [2004] 2 WLR 147,

policy,[97] and can guide courts when exercising discretion in relation to such matters as levels of damages.[98] Where an administrative act or decision infringes a human right, courts will anxiously scrutinize it, applying a higher than usual intensity of review when deciding whether it is irrational.[99] However, UK courts retain a certain reserve in the face of treaties. Unless a treaty has been transformed into municipal law by legislation, like parts of the European Convention on Human Rights, they do not usually consider that they are under any obligation to take account of them:[100] for the UK lawyer, the dualism of the constitution means that treaties generally still exist as part of a different system of law. In cases reported in 11 leading series of law reports in 2001 and 2002, only three international conventions apart from the ECHR were considered: the Convention and Protocol relating to the Status of Refugees; the Convention on International Trade in Endangered Species of Wild Fauna and Flora; and the Convention on Jurisdiction and the Enforcement of Judgments in Civil and Commercial Matters. The last of these was considered only in private law and EC law cases. The first two were considered in a total of six public law cases.[101] UK courts feel no obligation to delve into a wide range of treaties such as is imposed on the South African judiciary in cases on constitutional rights.

It is therefore neither surprising nor disappointing to find that the direct application of foreign judgments in English courts in public law cases is limited, though they may have persuasive authority. One must leave aside decisions which have to be considered as a matter of law, such as foreign judgments in certain cases in the Privy Council, decisions of the Court of Justice of the European Communities and the Court of First Instance, and those of the European Court of Human Rights. In purely domestic cases reported in 2001 and 2002 in 11 leading series of law reports for England and Wales, the editors of *The Consolidated Index*[102] identified only 22 foreign cases which have received substantial consideration, in a total of 24 English cases. Of the 22 foreign cases, 13 related to public law issues, and all but one were decided by the Privy Council (which could almost count as a UK court), the sole exception being a decision of the Supreme Court of Canada.[103] They were discussed in the judgments in 17 English cases. The editors took the view that foreign decisions had been applied in six English cases,[104] considered in another four,[105] and distinguished in a further

CA, at paras [99] and [101] *per* Laws L.J., and see also Simon Brown L.J. at para. [51]. On appeal in the *Roma Rights* case, the House of Lords did not consider the issue.

97 See e.g. *Blathwayt* v. *Baron Cawley* [1976] AC 397, HL.

98 See e.g. *John* v. *MGN Ltd.* [1997] QB 586, CA.

99 See e.g. *Bugdaycay* v. *Secretary of State for the Home Department* [1987] AC 514, HL, and Chapter 3 above.

100 See e.g. *R.* v. *Secretary of State for the Home Department, ex part Brind* [1991] 1 AC 696, HL.

101 *The Consolidated Index 2001–2002 to Leading Law Reports* (2002) 347.

102 Op. cit., 241–313.

103 *Proprietary Articles Trade Association* v. *Attorney General for Canada* [1931] AC 310, PC, from which dicta of Lord Atkin at 324 were applied in *R. (McCann)* v. *Crown Court at Manchester* [2002] 3 WLR 131, HL.

104 *Attorney General of Hong Kong* v. *Nai-Keung* [1987] 1 WLR 1339, PC, applied in *In re Celtic Extraction Ltd* [2001] Ch. 475, CA; *Calvin* v. *Carr* [1980 AC 574, PC, applied in *Modahl* v. *British Athletic Federation Ltd* [2002] 1 WLR 1192, CA; *Darmalingum* v. *The State* [2000] 1 WLR 2303, PC, applied in *Porter* v. *Magill* [2002] 2 AC 357, HL; *De Freitas* v. *Permanent Secretary of Ministry of Agriculture, Fisheries, Lands and Housing* [1999] 1 AC 69, PC, applied in *R.* v. *Benjafield* [2002] 2 WLR 235, HL; *Kemper Reinsurance Co.* v. *Minister of Finance* [2000] 1 AC 1, PC, applied in *R. (on the application of Burkett)* v. *Hammersmith and Fulham London Borough Council* [2002] 1 WLR 1593, HL; and *Liyanage* v. *The Queen* [1967] 1 AC 259, PC, applied in *R. (on the application of Bancoult)* v. *Secretary of State for Foreign and Commonwealth Affairs* [2001] QB 1067, DC.

105 *Attorney General of Hong Kong* v. *Lee Kwong-Kut* [1993] AC 951, PC, considered in *International Transport Roth GmbH* v. *Secretary of State for the Home Department* [2002] 3 WLR 344, CA; *Darmalingum* v. *The State*

three.[106] Foreign dicta were applied in four English cases,[107] and considered in another one.[108] This suggests that the judges are taking a properly cautious approach.

That is not to say that foreign decisions have a minimal impact. Many more have been cited to and by courts, and might have influenced their thinking, without being expressly analysed, followed, or distinguished in judgments. Some public law principles have been shaped, at least partly, by foreign influences. The rule against anyone being a judge in his own cause derives from Roman law,[109] as does much else in the common law. The principle of proportionality, significant in national law because of its importance in the law of the EC, EU, and ECHR, might eventually seep into municipal administrative law by osmosis, just as coercive interim remedies against the Crown entered English law after they came to be available to protect Community rights in EC law.[110] There has also been some support for directly applying the proportionality test in preference to the strict *Wednesbury* unreasonableness principle in judicial review, even in cases not involving Community law or Convention rights.[111] At some point it could become impossible to justify maintaining different grounds for review in municipal administrative law depending on the source of the legal rights or obligations being litigated. In *R. (Association of British Civilian Internees: Far East Region)* v. *Secretary of State for Defence*, the Court of Appeal had 'difficulty in seeing what justification there now is for retaining the *Wednesbury* test', but considered that, since it had been applied on several occasions by the House of Lords, only that House could 'perform its burial rites'.[112] While the two tests often produce the same result, introducing proportionality in place of unreasonableness would alter the intensity of review in administrative law cases and would affect the result in some of them. Judges would need to consider carefully the way in which an enhanced standard of review in non-EC, non-ECHR cases would fit into the UK's political and constitutional setting.

[2000] 1 WLR 2303, PC, considered in *Dyer* v. *Watson* [2002] 3 WLR 1488, PC (a devolution case); *Prebble* v. *Television New Zealand Ltd* [1995] 1 AC 321, PC, considered in *R. (on the application of Asif Javed)* v. *Secretary of State for the Home Department* [2002] QB 129, CA; and *Winfat Enterprise (HK) Co. Ltd* v. *Attorney General for Hong Kong* [1985] AC 733, PC, considered in *R. (on the application of Bancoult)* v. *Secretary of State for Foreign and Commonwealth Affairs* [2001] QB 1067, DC.

106 *Attorney General of Hong Kong* v. *Ng Yuen Shiu* [1983] 2 AC 629, PC, distinguished in *R.* v. *Falmouth and Truro Port Health Authority, ex parte South West Water Ltd* [2001] QB 445, CA; and *Darmalingum* v. *The State* [2000] 1 WLR 2303, PC, distinguished in (1) *Attorney General's Reference (No. 2 of 2001)* [2001] 1 WLR 1869, CA, and (2) *Mills* v. *HM Advocate* [2002] 3 WLR 1597 (a devolution case).

107 Dictum of Lord Diplock in *Baker* v. *The Queen* [1975] AC 774, PC, at 788 applied in *R. (on the application of Kadhim)* v. *Brent London Borough Council Housing Benefit Review Board* [2001] QB 955, CA; dicta of Lord Clyde in *De Freitas* v. *Permanent Secretary of Ministry of Agriculture, Fisheries, Lands and Housing* [1999] 1 AC 69, PC, at 80 applied in *Gough* v. *Chief Constable of Derbyshire Constabulary* [2002] QB 1213, CA; dictum of Lord Atkin in *Eshugbayi Eleko* v. *Officer Administering the Government of Nigeria* [1931] AC 662, PC, at 670 applied in *R.* v. *Governor of Brockhill Prison, ex parte Evans (No. 2)* [2001] 2 AC 19, HL; and dicta of Lord Atkin in *Proprietary Articles Trade Association* v. *Attorney General for Canada* [1931] AC 310, PC, at 324 applied in *R. (on the application of McCann)* v. *Crown Court at Manchester* [2002] 3 WLR 131, HL.

108 Dicta of Wilson J. in *Perka* v. *The Queen* (1984) 13 DLR (4th) 1, SC of Canada, at 36 considered in *In re A (Children) (Conjoined Twins: Surgical Separation)* [2001] Fam. 147, CA.

109 See Asser, n. 93 above.

110 *R.* v. *Secretary of State for Trade and Industry, ex parte Factortame (No. 2)* (Case C–213/89) [1991] 1 AC 603, CJEC and HL; see now e.g. *R.* v. *Secretary of State for Health, ex parte Imperial Tobacco Ltd* [2002] QB 161, CA.

111 See e.g. *R. (Daly)* v. *Secretary of State for the Home Department* [2001] 2 AC 532 at 548–9 *per* Lord Cooke of Thorndon; *R. (Alconbury Developments Ltd)* v. *Secretary of State for the Environment, Transport and the Regions* [2001] 2 WLR 1389 at 1406–7 *per* Lord Slynn of Hadley.

112 [2002] EWCA Civ 473, [2003] QB 1397, at paras [34]–[37].

CONCLUSION

The internationalization of public law in the UK is a process of long standing and is continuing. It has benefits, but there are also risks. These are, first, that a borrowed solution will not be workable in a constitution with the special balance of power and democratic accountability found within the state, and, secondly, that reasoning relying on foreign thinking will not be regarded as a legitimate way of deciding public law cases under the constitution. The latter concern is evident in the Chief Justice's dissenting opinion in the US Supreme Court in *Atkins* v. *Virginia*, mentioned earlier. Where in the UK's constitutional rules are judges authorized to look for emerging standards abroad to guide UK public law? Statutes can authorize or require courts to look abroad, as the European Communities Act 1972 and the Human Rights Act 1998 show. But in the absence of such express provisions, there is a danger to the perceived constitutional legitimacy of judicial decisions if courts resort to foreign guidance without a legal basis in national law.

For these reasons, international influences must be treated with caution in developing the structures of an established state and constitutional arrangements. Filters are needed. If the relationship between national and international legal planes is not defined in a constitutional document (such as South Africa's 1996 Constitution) or statute, a case-by-case approach can lead to distinct oddities. We can conclude with two questions about the UK to illustrate this. First, how well are the fundamental values of representative democracy, executive accountability to Parliament, and parliamentary sovereignty protected against the inappropriate introduction to municipal law (either by the executive or by judges) of obligations derived from international law or EC or EU law? Second, why do UK judges seem more receptive to foreign judicial developments than to international treaties? One could argue that treaty obligations binding the UK in international law impose standards which should be respected by all organs of the state, including courts, and that there can be no justification in terms of UK constitutional law for having regard to judgments of foreign courts in jurisdictions which have no current constitutional link to the UK. This distinction is recognized by the Constitution of South Africa: there is a duty to consider treaties, but no duty to consider foreign judgments, in cases on constitutional rights. It will be interesting to see whether the influence of the ECHR and the European Court of Human Rights under sections 1 and 2 of the Human Rights Act 1998, bringing with it other treaties which the European Court of Human Rights uses to interpret the ECHR, will gradually lead UK courts to give greater weight to a range of treaties than they presently feel able to do.

FURTHER READING

The following suggestions are in addition to the sources cited in the footnotes above:

ALLISON, JOHN W. F. 'Transplantation and cross-fertilisation in European public law', in Jack Beatson and Takis Tridimas (eds), *New Directions in European Public Law* (1998) ch. 12.

BELL, J. 'Mechanisms for cross-fertilisation of administrative law in Europe', in Jack Beatson and Takis Tridimas (eds), *New Directions in European Public Law* (1998) ch. 11.

Brewer-Carrías, A. R. 'Constitutional implications of regional economic integration', in John Bridge (ed.), *Comparative Law facing the 21st Century* (2001) 675–752, on the way in which integration of markets between states depends on and in turn influences national constitutional structures and rules.

Chigara, B. 'Pinochet and the administration of international criminal justice', in Diana Woodhouse (ed.), *The Pinochet Case: A Legal and Constitutional Analysis* (2000) ch. 7, on the interaction of treaties, peremptory norms of customary international law, and the criminal law.

Dupré, C. *Importing the Law in Post-Communist Transitions: The Hungarian Constitutional Court and the Right to Human Dignity* (2003), especially ch. 2 on the importation by nascent or re-nascent states of constitutional law and constitutional values from other systems.

Ellis, E. (ed.) *The Principle of Proportionality in the Laws of Europe* (1999), for essays on the use of a single public law principle in a variety of legal systems.

European Review of Public Law, vol. 18 no. 1 (Spring 2006) at pp. 25–653 contains papers derived from a valuable colloquium of the European Group of Public Law in 2005 on the internationalization of public law, including general surveys and studies of particular European jurisdictions.

Fatima, S. *Using International Law in Domestic Courts* (2005), for full consideration of the various ways in which municipal legal systems can take account of different kinds of public international law.

Feldman, D. 'Monism, dualism and constitutional legitimacy' (1999) 20 *Australian Year Book of International Law* 105–26, discussing some ways in which international law shapes national constitutions and national law affects international law.

Henkin, L., Pugh, R. C., Schachter, O. and Smit, H. *International Law: Cases and Materials* (3rd edn, 1993), ch. 3 on the relationship between public international law and municipal law.

Smith, E. 'Give and take: cross-fertilisation of concepts in constitutional law', in Jack Beatson and Takis Tridimas (eds), *New Directions in European Public Law* (1998) ch. 8.

Zines, L. *Constitutional Change in the Commonwealth* (1991) ch. 1, on the development of the constitutional orders of Australia, Canada, and New Zealand towards autonomy from the UK.

USEFUL WEB SITES

Foreign and Commonwealth Office: **www.fco.gov.uk/**

The web site of the Foreign and Commonwealth Office includes a link to an Official Documents page, which allows further links to useful information, including an explanation of UK treaty practice and procedure, a Treaty Enquiry Service giving access to a searchable database of treaties to which the UK is a party, and the texts of the treaties.

Virtual Institute of the Max Planck Institute for Comparative Public Law and International Law: **www.virtual-institute.de/en/VI/EVI.cfm**

The web site of the Virtual Institute of the Max Planck Institute for Comparative Public Law and International Law offers a fine bibliographical resource together with papers and links to many other useful web sites.

Venice Commission: **http://codices.coe.int**

This web site, maintained by the European Commission for Democracy through Law (the 'Venice Commission') under the auspices of the Council of Europe, offers summaries of significant decisions of constitutional courts and other courts with similar jurisdictions in Europe and elsewhere.

United Nations: **www.un.org/**

The United Nations web site provides (among much other information and material) the text of the UN Charter, information about the working of the institutions of the UN including the General Assembly and the Security Council, the texts of many international treaties, and information about international tribunals.

www/worldlii.org/ This provides links to web-based sources on international and national law throughout the world. It includes decisions of international tribunals as well as constitutional texts and decisions of national courts.

6

MODELS OF DEMOCRACY: FROM REPRESENTATION TO PARTICIPATION?

John Morison

SUMMARY

The term democracy is used by many people in a whole range of ways. It can relate to processes of decision making and more widely to the substantive outcomes of decisions. An idea of democracy as involving two guiding principles of popular control and political equality from which can be drawn out a range of other principles such as openness, accountability, responsiveness, and participation has been developed. This allows an 'audit' of the quality of democracy in any given set of institutions. However, increasingly government and the exercise of public power now take place at levels and in formats that escape the traditional, formal state and it is necessary to consider the application of ideas of democracy to new forms of governance. In this context, theories of democracy can be used not only to claim legitimacy for the incumbent arrangements of power but also as a more radical, critical concept to challenge the exclusion of voices from formal decision making. A distinction may be drawn between democracy as a framework for decision making – aggregative democracy – and more radical ideas of democracy as a process for preference building – deliberative democracy. Ideas of heightened participation, particularly through increased consultation, have become important recently not only as a way of reinvigorating traditional, electoral democracy or even contributing towards better deliberation, but as part of the new, more consumer-based service delivery mechanisms that are associated with wider processes of modernization of government. Consultation and participation vary in quality from the cosmetic to full citizen control. Properly deliberative decision making is perhaps possible only in very limited circumstances.

INTRODUCTION

Democracy is a slippery word. And it is put to many uses. One result of this is that its meaning has become hollowed out and confused. At its simplest democracy can be a way of deciding or it can be a way of living. But this straightforward distinction between 'thinner' ideas about public decision making and 'thicker' notions about the terms on which people agree to live together conceals a whole range of issues and questions. For instance: What is good about democracy? Is democracy only about devising fair procedures for taking decisions or should it be concerned also about the outcomes of such decisions? How do ideas of democracy as the will of the majority square with ideas of self-determination where a section of the polity may not see itself as legitimately bound into a given political unit? Is it enough to have a liberal, constitutional system of democracy where virtually all adults have a right to vote along with rights of political expression, association, office holding, and access to diverse sources of information; where elected officials control public policy and citizens choose those officials, and hold them to account, through free and fair elections? Or is even this too much to expect? With government, or rather governance, now operating at a whole range of levels from the local, regional, and national to the transnational and global, is it realistic to expect to address even the formal democratic deficit that such structures bring? Or do new forms of governance involving a range of non-state agencies and delivery mechanisms require the reach of democracy to be extended beyond traditional ideas of the state? Are there other concepts of democracy that require more, for instance by way of substantive rights and equalities, in order to guarantee full political equality and equal participation? Is the state, at whatever level, to be entrusted with underwriting any version of democracy or is this something that belongs more comfortably with civil society operating as a counterweight to institutionalized power? Can the institutions of representative democracy ever be expected to provide a complete *framework* for decision making that can realize a full democratic vision? Is it necessary instead to focus on the *process* of decision making and develop ideas of more radical, direct, or deliberative democracy to reinvigorate democracy? While we might acknowledge as inspirational the ideal of ancient Athenian democracy with its small units of (free and male) citizens debating openly on the public good, is it practical or even desirable to attempt to construct a more modern version of this to capture those virtues of directness and deliberation that characterized the Greek *polis*? Could information and communication technology be harnessed to develop some idea of e-democracy that might widen and deepen participation and recover this ideal? How does democracy fit in with ideas of 'modernised government' where formal government has 'downsized' and services are delivered by multiple providers beyond the state within a complex regulatory framework? What is the relationship between democracy and those ideas of consultation and customer focus that are central to modernized government? Will democracy survive the threat of world-wide terrorism? Does democracy have a future at all or, at a time when the history of ideological conflict is supposed to be over – or at least re-cast into a clash of cultures – is democracy the only future on offer?

This chapter will raise some of these questions and attempt partial answers to a few of them. First it will look at a range of ways in which the term democracy is used and the sorts of meanings that are thereby invoked. Then there will be an exploration of the distinction between democracy as a framework for decision making and democracy as a process of decision-making. This will require examination of ideas and variants of representative democracy and their expression in various electoral systems. Consideration will then be given to ideas of democracy that emphasize the processes of decision making where the focus is less on ways to collect and aggregate choices and more on how a full range of voices can be included in a process of preference building. These ideas will be examined not just in the context of new participation strategies within particular initiatives such as the 'modernising government' programme but also more generally in order to determine if potentially they could provide a foundation for renewing democracy more widely. Some models of democratic decision making will be outlined and some examples of new forms of participation, including e-participation, will be given.

THE USES OF 'DEMOCRACY'

An appeal to 'democracy' can be used to promote the legitimacy of the incumbent institutions of government and their orderly management of general participation. It can also be deployed as a critical challenge to such institutions in a project of empowering excluded voices and developing ideas of civic virtue beyond the state. Here we look at a range of meanings that the term has attracted and consider briefly how some of those meanings have been used variously to legitimize, endorse, and critique existing institutions of government at many levels in the constitution.

The label 'democratic' can be used in a range of connected ways. There is the straightforward idea of majority rule – the idea that what most people want is what should prevail. But this notion of raw majoritarianism is also linked into more fundamental ideas about the importance and value of democracy as a way of living together. Thus we have Pericles in his celebrated funeral oration for the Athenian dead declaring that 'our constitution . . . is called a democracy because power is in the hands not of a minority but of the greatest number'.[1] In part this simply notes the power of the majority. But it also raises issues to do with fundamental cultural values connected to human dignity, respect for reason and freedom, and the whole civilizing inheritance of Europe. It suggests that democracy is commonly associated with more than just the decision-making power of the majority and is part of a wider, ethical idea about how to live together. Indeed, it is interesting that the controversial and ill-fated draft Treaty Establishing a Constitution for Europe written by Valéry Giscard D'Estaing quotes this remark of Pericles in order perhaps to indicate a democratic tradition of European public life dating back to Greece and Rome.[2] Other supranational constitutional documents also make reference to a wider democratic legacy. The preamble to the Charter of Fundamental Rights of the European Union refers to the Union's 'spiritual and moral heritage' and 'its foundation on the principle of democracy'.[3] The European Convention on Human Rights is predicated on an idea of democracy.[4] The Harare Commonwealth Declaration refers to 'the individual's inalienable right to participate by means of free and democratic political processes in framing the society in which he or she lives',[5] and the Copenhagen Criteria for candidate countries seeking membership of the European Union requires, in addition to a functioning market economy, 'stability of institutions guaranteeing democracy'.[6] A whole range of other international bodies from the

[1] Thucydides, *History of the Peloponnesian War* II, 37.

[2] See Draft Treaty Establishing a Constitution for Europe (CONV 850/03 July 2003). See also the EU's 'Human Rights and Democratisation Policy' at http://ec.europa.eu/comm/external_relations/human_rights/intro/index.htm.

[3] [2000] *Official Journal of the European Communities* C364/8.

[4] '. . . democracy is the only political model contemplated by the Convention and, accordingly, the only one compatible with it': *United Communist Party of Turkey v. Turkey* (1998) 26 EHRR 121, para. 45.

[5] The Harare Commonwealth Declaration 1991 (available at www.thecommonwealth.org/Internal/20423/34457/harare-Commonwealth-declaration).

[6] See http://ec.europa.eu/enlargement/enlargement_process/accession_process/criteria/index_en.htm.

World Bank, the group of industrialized countries known as G8, to the Organisation for Security and Co-operation in Europe (OSCE) are anxious to endorse the values of democracy and set out conditions of democratic sufficiency to countries that wish to join their clubs and enjoy what are presented as the benefits of free market capitalism. Reconstruction of the former Soviet bloc countries of central and eastern Europe and the progress of developing countries is, at least from the point of view of the West, unthinkable if it does not take place within a context of democracy and human rights (and an effective market economy).[7] Increasingly, ideas of 'good governance' are being developed in many contexts to underpin and extend democracy to government at many levels.[8] Indeed, there is even a view that a right to democratic governance and a democratic standard of governmental legitimacy today belong in international law.[9]

On this approach there can be very few constitutions, whether of transnational bodies or of individual countries,[10] that do not at least make some reference to democracy in an effort to capture some of the legitimacy that this term brings to particular arrangements of power. Undoubtedly the idea has power in this context. It speaks of control and ownership by the people of their government. In the emergent United States of America of 1789–91 rhetorical appeals by the framers of the Constitution to 'We the people' invoke notions of popular sovereignty and establish, perhaps for the first time, that the constitution is not a product of some divine order but rather the property of the people who retain ultimate authority through it. There is also the idea, often attributed to Abraham Lincoln, that democracy is government of the people, by the people, for the people. In an entirely different political context, ideas such as the People's Republic or the People's Courts or even the People's Army emerge.[11] Ideas of 'People Power', whether expressed in the mass demonstrations that brought change in the former Soviet bloc and elsewhere at the end of the last century or in vaguer ideas of popular movements against globalization or the war in Iraq, or in favour of hunting or even consumer boycotts, suggest other directions for such a use of the term democracy.

MEANINGS OF 'DEMOCRACY'

The word democracy is used in all sorts of often unexpected contexts too. For example, art may be described as democratic to indicate a degree of popularity or accessibility. In this

[7] Of course, as Amartya Sen warns us, it is important not to identify democratic values only with Europe but to consider too the contribution of other cultures including Asian traditions. See further 'Democracy and its Global Roots' *New Republic* (October 2003) and *Identity and Violence: The Illusion of Destiny* (2006). Cf. the discussion by Lord Darhendorf et al in *Democracy and Capitalism* (2006).

[8] For example the Commission of the European Union has developed five principles – openness, participation, accountability, effectiveness, and coherence – to establish 'more democratic governance'. These are to apply not just to the Union itself but 'to all levels of government – global, European, national, regional and local'. See Commission of the European Communities, *European Governance A White Paper*, Brussels, COM (2001) 428 Final, 25 July, p. 10. See also the work of the European Commission for Democracy through Law, better known as the Venice Commission at www.venice.coe.int/site/main/presentation_E.asp?MenuL=E.

[9] See S. Marks, *The Riddle of all Constitutions: International Law, Democracy and the Critique of Ideology* (2000) esp. ch. 2.

[10] See www.constitution.org/cons/natlcons.htm for English-language versions of many world constitutions.

[11] See for example the Constitution of China 1982 where Art. 1(1) establishes 'the People's Republic of China as a socialist state under the people's democratic dictatorship led by the working class and based on the alliance of workers and peasants', Art. 57 establishes the National People's Congress of the People's Republic of China as the highest organ of state power and Art. 123 states that the people's courts in the People's Republic of China are the judicial organs of the state.

way, for example, Andrew Lloyd Weber and Mozart are more democratic than Philip Glass or Stockhausen. Damien Hirst's pickled shark is more democratic/accessible than say, the *De Stijl* movement in inter-war Dutch abstract painting. Football is the people's game and the Late Princess Diana could even be described as 'the People's Princess'. Admitting more students to universities may be regarded as democratic, and, indeed, the whole activity of higher education may be considered as contributing to a wider democratic culture.[12] Good manners, or at least ideas of civility and civic virtue, may be part of democracy.[13] Buildings and public space too can be more or less democratic in the sense that they are accessible or welcoming. For example, contrast the approach of the new Scottish Parliament with its emphasis on accessibility with the Stormont building for the Assembly in Northern Ireland where a drive one kilometre long leads to a white stone monolith on a hill where passes must be produced and security clearance negotiated.[14] Part of this use of the term democratic concerns access but the idea here encompasses notions of openness too. Such ideas can be realized physically as in the London Authority building where the design of the glass-sided building is itself intended to be suggestive of openness and transparency generally in the government that takes place there.[15]

Of course such symbolic representations of the nature of public power as can be found in the architecture of government buildings are less important than the democratic quality of what occurs within them. Here, where power is being exercised directly, the term 'democratic' encompasses openness and access but also reaches out to include notions of responsiveness, interactivity, accountability, and proportionality. To what extent and on what grounds can the citizen have an input to power, or review and challenge those who exercise power on behalf of others? If, for example, we apply to a government agency for a driving licence we expect to know not only how to apply and what is required in terms of a completed form, test certificate, fee, etc., but also how to make queries and challenge any decision. A properly democratic system in this context might involve 'reachability' in so far as officials are capable of being contacted via web sites with dialogue boxes or hotlinks to email addresses or, more traditionally, through telephone hotline services, by post, or by personal appointment as appropriate. It might also require interactivity in so much as officials may be expected to engage in dialogue with applicants and be responsive in an open and transparent way.[16]

In reality 'democracy' is related to a whole variety of ideas and it has a range of meanings. These might involve, variously, accessibility, popularity, and inclusion as well as openness,

[12] See, for example, H. Giroux who argues for a link between democratic culture and critical learning and complains that 'obsessed with grant writing, fund raising, and capital improvements, higher education increasingly devalues its role as a democratic public sphere committed to the broader values of an engaged and critical citizenry' *Public Spaces, Private Lives: Democracy beyond 9/11* (2003) at p. 23.

[13] See further S. Carter, *Civility: Manners, Morals, and the Etiquette of Democracy* (1998).

[14] See the the Scottish Parliament at www.holyrood.tv/library.asp?title=Holyrood%20Building%20Tour§ion=45 and take a virtual, online tour of the Northern Ireland Assembly buildings at http://www.niassembly.gov.uk/vtour/vtour_index.htm.

[15] See www.london.gov.uk/gla/city_hall/city-hall-panos/index.jsp.

[16] It is an interesting feature of many local authorities that increasingly whole departments are being created to oversee 'democratic services'. See for example, Worcester County Council at http://worcestershire.whub.org.uk/home/wcc-mas-dsu or Conwy County Borough Council at www.conwy.gov.uk/section.asp?cat=619.

See also R. Blaug, 'Engineering Democracy' (2002) 50 *Political Studies* 102.) In part this is a response to the sort of modernized service delivery regime that, as is discussed later, requires formal structures of consultation. It is also related however to (more or less cosmetic) attempts to address a wider agenda of democracy at all levels of government.

transparency, responsiveness, civility, and other values. Using the word democracy also may bring in ideas that authority is not given simply by tradition but is to be justified or negotiated. Such an idea relates to reciprocity, the notion that people owe one another justifications for the mutually binding laws and policies that they collectively enact. While articulated most strongly in deliberative democracy, this essential value is present in many forms, although in more formal, liberal, constitutional, or procedural variations of democracy a similar value from the same fundamental source is more likely to surface in ideas of equal participation and accountability. This concept of accountability suggests that democracy applies not only at the input stage – where votes are cast – but also in relation to outputs: those who exercise power on others' behalf or who spend their money ought to be held to account for the discharge of those functions. In addition values such as participation and freedom may be called upon when the word 'democratic' is used. In particular, equality may be thought to have a particular relationship with democracy, whether this involves simply equal access to the machinery of choosing or more substantive ideas of equal influence.[17] Further consideration of how the term is used, maybe drawing on ideas more prevalent in continental Europe, might begin also to produce values of proportionality, mutuality, solidarity, and even subsidiarity. Indeed, as the examples of how the word democracy is used extend, the pervasiveness of the concept in a whole range of institutions and relationships is matched only by the elusiveness of its meaning.

'DEMOCRACY' AS A TOOL OF ASSESSMENT

Is it possible to tie down this concept more systematically? One approach, which allows us to see the interconnectedness of the values behind the idea of democracy, can be found with the *Democratic Audit*.[18] It seeks to provide an 'index' or scale of democracy by which to assess the quality of democracy and human rights in any country around the world. These audit criteria have been elaborated by David Beetham who outlined two basic principles of democracy from which it is possible to draw out or read off other principles which contribute to the realization of the democracy.[19] The first principle is that of *popular control* over the processes of decision making and the second principle is that of *political equality*. Beetham offers these two principles as 'a guiding thread' through the complexity of what a fully articulated idea of democracy involves. From the basic principle of popular control over decision making and decision-makers follows the subordinate principles such as openness, accountability, responsiveness, participation, and the Rule of Law. The basic principle of political equality produces ideas of representativeness, pluralism, and common citizenship.

17 See further R. Dworkin, 'Political Equality' reprinted as ch. 4 in his *Sovereign Virtue: The Theory and Practice of Equality* (2000). See also J. Jowell for the idea developed from Dworkin that 'the notion of equal worth' is a fundamental precept of our constitution because it gains its ultimate justification from ideas about how individuals should be treated in a democracy and is thus 'constitutive of democracy': 'Is Equality a Constitutional Principle?' (1994) *2 Current Legal Problems* 7 and Wojciech Sadurski, 'Law's Legitimacy and Democracy-Plus' (2006) 26 *Oxford J Legal Studies* 377–409.

18 This is a project begun in the early 1990s to inspect and evaluate the institutions of government in the UK, and developed by an intergovernmental body called International IDEA (Institute for Democracy and Electoral Assistance). See further www.democraticaudit.com/index.php/.

19 See further D. Beetham, *Auditing Democracy in Britain: Key Principles and Indices of Democracy*, Democratic Audit Paper No. 1 (1993) and S. Weir and D. Beetham, *Political Power and Democratic Control* (1999). See also www.democraticaudit.com/auditing_democracy/.

In this way the additional principles that are drawn out from the basic ones are not optional extras or supplementary add-ons but ways in which the main principles can and should be realized.

This is a sophisticated framework for understanding democracy. It also allows us to evaluate the democratic quality of the arrangements in any given state or government. Indeed, for example, a democratic audit has been carried out measuring Britain under New Labour across 18 indices of democracy.[20] This is interesting and useful. It even generates a modest agenda of further constitutional reform including such ideas as a written constitution, the introduction of proportional representation for elections to the House of Commons and to a new second chamber, and replacing Royal Prerogative powers with clearly defined statutory powers for ministers. But does such an approach, with its emphasis on the formal state and its conflation of government institutions with the sole or even main expression of democracy, exhaust the project of democracy? The description of democracy that Beetham outlines is one that can be applied usefully to instances of traditional public power or in relation to the discharge of governmental authority. But the idea of public now extends far beyond formal government and this introduces a new agenda for democracy. In the same way as 'public' (and all that this entails in terms of accountability, requirements to act unselfishly in the public interest, etc.) now no longer equates simply with 'state owned' or 'directly state controlled', so too the idea of state must now encompass more than the agencies of the formal state. This must be explored to uncover a fuller agenda of democracy and democratic renewal.

THE CONTEXTS OF DEMOCRACY

Resources held in common or belonging to the public sphere such as streets, squares, parks, and other civic spaces are by definition 'public' and clearly they may be described as more or less democratic depending on a range of factors including freedom of access for everyone together with equality in the use of such resources and the absence of additional restraints on activities carried out there. Such public, democratic spaces are often contrasted with private spaces such as homes, clubs and pubs or shopping centres which are owned by particular individuals or commercial companies. Here different standards may pertain, with access being restricted and certain conduct required or prohibited. But private spaces too may be democratic or not. For example, the workplace or even the family can be more or less democratic depending on how power is arranged and whose voices are heard.[21] Indeed there are those who see private space, especially where it is controlled by markets, as being *more* democratic than public space – particularly as regards giving effect to choices. (As is discussed further later, from such a perspective a willingness (or not) to pay for something involves asserting a choice in a way that may even be more effective than simply registering a vote.) Undoubtedly, nowadays we *require* some private spaces to be democratic in the

20 Ibid. See the latest findings published at www.democraticaudit.com/download/Findings7.pdf.

21 Indeed, Anthony Giddens, architect of the Third Way, sees close links between the wider project of democratizing the public sphere and re-imagining the family beyond its traditional condition. As he argues, the 'criteria are surprisingly close . . . [d]emocratisation in the context of the family implies equality, mutual respect, autonomy, decision-making through communication and freedom from violence': *The Third Way: The Renewal of Social Democracy* (1998) 93.

sense that they are inclusive or accommodating of difference. There is perhaps a new class of 'communal space' which is common to many people but is not public in the sense of being open to all citizens.[22] The erosion of the Victorian legacy of public parks, civic centres, and traditional city centres, and their replacement with an essentially private space of theme parks, leisure centres, industrial parks, and shopping malls, has changed how we experience interaction with others outside our homes and this has important democratic implications.[23] If the public space of a town centre, previously used in a whole variety of ways by a range of individuals – shoppers, protestors, football supporters, young people, the elderly, the unemployed, etc. – is 'privatized' in the sense that it is replaced by a commercial shopping mall or private development, there is a real danger that commercial criteria such as ability to pay will supersede more democratic, citizen-based requirements that it be equal, welcoming, inclusive, and accommodating of difference.[24]

Similarly where government functions that once belonged exclusively to the state are now discharged by the private sector through a whole network of partnerships, contracts and service agreements we demand 'democracy' in the sense of equality of treatment and a degree of control over and accountability for the expenditure of what remains public money. Indeed the migration of public power not only to the private sector but also upwards and outwards to other levels above and below the nation-state and its institutions provides a particular challenge to democracy. Power is recognized no longer to be the sole preserve of formal government structures, of parliaments and assemblies, cabinets and ministers, and civil servants and officials. Now it is seen as being exercised through a much wider process of governance involving not only the formal state at many levels but also the private sector, the community and voluntary sectors, and others.[25] While the state still 'steers' the 'rowing' is done by others.[26] Ideas of multi-level government have evolved from a simple recognition that there are layers beyond the national state to more sophisticated ideas of how power is dispersed into a multiplicity of sites, constituting nodes in a heterarchical network rather than layers in a hierarchical pyramid, which operate in a relationship of mutual influence rather than control.[27] The activity of government is complex and also

[22] See A. von Hirsch and C. Shearing, 'Exclusion from Public Space', in A. von Hirsh, E. Garland, and A. Wakefield (eds), *Ethical and Social Perspectives on Situational Crime Prevention* (2000) 77–96.

[23] This sort of private property with features that make it appear very like public space has been described as 'mass private property'. (See C. Shearing and P. Stenning, 'From the Panopticon to Disney World: The Development of Discipline', in A. Dobbs and E. Greenspan (eds), *Perspectives in Criminal Law: Essays in Honour of J Ll. Edwards* (1985) 335–49.) The emergence of virtual spaces in the form of Internet sites also provides a similar sort of space and a similar challenge in terms of its governance.

[24] In *CIN Properties* v. *Rawlins* [1995] 39 EG 148 (CA) a group of unemployed youths unsuccessfully challenged their exclusion from a shopping complex in the town of Wellingborough that was held by CIN Properties on a long lease from the local council as freeholder. As K. Gray and S. Gray argue in 'Civil Rights, Civil Wrongs and Quasi-Public Space' (1999) *EHRLR* 46, this case and others like it raise important issues about how to conduct democratic public life in modern urban space that increasingly is privately owned and governed by private-law ideas such as the 'arbitrary exclusion rule' that took precedence in this case over ideas of democratic inclusion and public-law rights.

[25] For discussion of the now familiar idea of governance see M. Bevir and R. A. W. Rhodes, *Interpreting British Governance* (2003) and the Special Issue of (2003) 81 *Public Administration*.

[26] See D. Osborne and T. Gaebler, *Reinventing Government* (1992).

[27] See, for example, N. Bernard, *Multilevel Governance in the European Union* (2002) or M. Keating's account of the 'reterritorialization of politics' as involving 'a dual process of sub-state mobilisation and supra-state integration' and a 'search for new levels of political action' in 'Europe's Changing Political Landscape', in P. Beaumont, C. Lyons, and N. Walker (eds), *Convergence and Divergence in European Public Law* (2002) 7.

multi-format. There are now many agencies and bodies from civil society and the private sector, as well as from government and quasi-government, that operate at every level from the local, regional, national, and European to deliver the policy and services of government. As well as formal institutions we need to examine networks, partnerships, and project groups and the activities of corporate bodies which now are emerging as significant agencies of governance in new market-based systems for delivering government services. Within such 'nodal' conceptions of government, the state is not necessarily given priority as the only or even the most important source of power. Ideas of 'governmentality' inform us that power is exercised indirectly and at a distance by a whole range of active subjects who not only collaborate in the exercise of power but also shape and inform it.[28] Given this, the democratic quality of governance depends on a whole range of other agencies beyond simply the formal state and the orthodox public sphere.

This is a significant challenge to ideas of democracy and their theatre of operation. David Held's idea of 'cosmopolitan governance' recognizes the scope of the project that is called for here.[29] In an influential work that widens the scope of democracy and constitutionalism significantly, Held contends that the future health of democracy depends upon the entrenchment of and defence of a common set of democratic rights and obligations at local, national, regional, and global levels. These do not operate at privileged national or sovereign levels, but deepen the capacity of people affected by decisions and actions which increasingly escape nation-state control to have a say in them. The rights to which Held refers – based on the principle of autonomy – range from traditional civil and political ones through to cultural and reproductive rights. In short, Held argues for 'a cosmopolitan model of democracy' which will require systems of accountability and control to operate at three levels at least. These include: (i) the relationships between domestic political institutions and key groups, agencies, associations, and organizations of the economy and civil society (both national and international); (ii) global issues beyond the control of nation states, including financial flows, environmental crises, security, new forms of communication, etc.; and (iii) those regional and global regulatory and functional agencies which make up part of the new international legal order. Held envisages new courts and parliaments operating at regional and global levels, entrenching and enacting these rights as part of 'a common structure of political action'. (Indeed, Held recognizes that his project may be even more wide ranging and require more even than new courts and parliaments where he insists that 'democracy can only be fully sustained by ensuring the accountability of *all* related and interconnected power systems, from economics to politics'.)[30] This sets the agenda very wide indeed. It perhaps maps the very edge of how the concept can be used. Democracy here is extended far

28 This governmentality approach, which is closely related to nodal conceptions of government, is based on key writings of Michel Foucault and some subsequent work including, particularly, N. Rose, *Powers of Freedom: Reframing Political Thought* (1999). Much of this thinking has been developed in a criminological context but it can be usefully applied to law and constitutional issues. As R. Cotterrell observes, 'the strength of Foucault's work for legal scholarship has been to emphasize the ubiquity of power . . . law, like power, should be seen as a resource operating routinely in innumerable sites and settings': 'Subverting Orthodoxy: Making Law Central' (2002) *Journal of Law and Society* 639. This sets an important agenda for constitutional scholarship as well as widening the focus of democracy.

29 D. Held, *Democracy and the Global Order* (1995); *Global Covenant* (2004).

30 Ibid., 267 (my emphasis).

beyond thin conceptions of procedural rules for decision making. It becomes central to a massively ambitious and optimistic project to 'constitutionalize' society at large.[31]

DEMOCRACY AND DECISION-MAKING

The preceding overview of the uses of the term democracy indicates that it has a range of meanings and applications. However as we proceed to consider more closely how democracy relates to decision making there remains an important distinction that needs to be considered further. This relates to the way in which democracy is seen as either being incumbent in traditional, liberal representative institutions or existing as a more radical, critical concept. This touches upon differences between 'constitutional' democracy and 'revolutionary' democracy,[32] procedural and substantive democracy,[33] aggregative as opposed to integrative approaches.[34] It relates also to distinctions between representational and direct democracy, top-down and bottom-up democracy, and adversary and unitary democracy.[35] Emerging from the very large literature on democracy, this distinction in part charts the movement from thin to thicker concepts,[36] but it also relates to distinctions between the ways in which democracy is experienced and the perspectives from which the institutions of democracy are viewed. It reflects, as Blaug argues, that democracy is 'a struggle over power, and as such, it provides an entirely different experience to those who hold power and those who do not'.[37]

Viewed from the centre of institutions of power, democracy appears as a set of structures where interests are represented and participation is channelled through institutionalized channels and by means of voting systems. This is incumbent democracy: it is a justificatory and legitimizing idea. Democracy here relates to a single political project to which all can be safely harnessed through the development and refinement of a set of institutions that are to be valued, protected, and, indeed, incrementally improved in a process whereby limited participation leads to the further institutionalization of accountable elite rule. Viewed from another perspective, at the periphery of the institutions of government, the powerless see democracy as a response to exclusion. Here democracy is critical and opposed to the top-down orientation of formal democracy. It is personal and developmental, located at the margins, and involves resistance to elite government. From this perspective, democracy becomes a means of challenging the orderly management of decision making and instead demanding that a whole range of power relationships be democratized as excluded voices are empowered in wider participatory processes.

31 See further I. Shapiro and C. Hacker-Gordon (eds), *Democracy's Edges* (1999) for sceptical accounts of some of the limitations of Held's approach.

32 See, for example, S. Wolin, 'Fugitive democracy' (1994) 1 *Constellations* 11.

33 A. Gutmann and D. Thompson, *Democracy and Disagreement* (1996).

34 See further, for example, C. Pateman, *Participation and Democratic Theory* (1989) or J. Dryzek, *Discursive Democracy: Politics, Policy, and Political Science* (1990).

35 See further J. Mansbridge, *Beyond Adversary Democracy* (1980).

36 It links in too with the distinction that Ronald Dworkin makes between majoritarian and 'partnership' democracy where the latter engages people in a collective political enterprise that can be best expressed in core principles about the value and responsibilities of a human life which in turn have very particular consequences on issues of today such as religion, taxation and the human rights of suspected terrorists. See *Is Democracy Possible Here? Principles for a New Political Debate* (2006).

37 R. Blaug, 'Engineering Democracy' (2002) 50 *Political Studies* 102 at 113.

From the perspective of incumbent democracy, the focus is on *frameworks* for decision making while more radical democracy is concerned with *process*. Elster describes the distinction by using the metaphor of the 'market' and the 'forum'.[38] With liberal, representative, or incumbent democracy there is a market for choices and the most popular policy or political party will win the competition for votes. Participation here is primarily instrumental. It is not about producing or shaping preferences but about aggregating them and giving effect to the most popular. In representative systems popular authorization generally extends only to the choice by citizens of representatives who will decide on the content of public decisions. In contrast a more deliberative approach is concerned with *preference building*. The emphasis here is on 'voice' and which argument is most persuasive in the forum of ideas and deliberation. It is an integrative as opposed to aggregative approach that sees society as an essentially social construct where preferences are endogenously produced and empowerment comes from participation in collective decision making about the actual substance of public action. Each of these general approaches will be considered in turn.

A FRAMEWORK FOR DECIDING – AGGREGATIVE DEMOCRACY

When considering frameworks for deciding in the context of democracy we usually think in terms of voting systems. However, there are frameworks for deciding that might be considered more or less democratic that predate the widespread franchise. In the UK it is these older constitutional structures that have been first colonized by limited electoral politics as the franchise spread in the nineteenth century, and then more generally inhabited by more recognizable democratic politics involving universal voting and the modern political party in the early twentieth century and subsequently.

In this way early ideas of democracy involve producing a framework or arrangement for rule.[39] The notion of *mixed constitution* that was dominant in the fourteenth century in England involved allowing each of the major interest groups of the time an institutional influence on the functioning of government. The mixed constitution idea allowed representation of distinct groups or classes. The three estates of the realm – 'clergy, barons and commons, those who pray, those who fight and those who work' according to the constitutional historian Maitland[40] – were all afforded a place in the 'parliamentum'. This arrangement had the advantage of ensuring that no one group was able to take absolute control over the others while allowing representation from each of the distinct classes. The partners in rule changed over time to become the King, Lords, and Commons but the essential idea was one of limiting government power and safeguarding individual liberty through an arrangement preventing any one element in society becoming overmighty.

The *balanced constitution* is a mid-seventeenth-century evolution of the mixed constitution idea. Here the function of government was seen as divided into two roles, legislative and executive, and the King, Lords, and Commons are seen as being balanced against each other in a framework for government. The Lords and the Commons were responsible for law making and the King for the executive function and within this overall arrangement each part kept in balance with the others and each organ was able to operate as a check on the

38 J. Elster, 'The Market and the Forum: Three Varieties of Political Theory' in J. Elster and A. Hylland (eds), *Foundations of Social Choice Theory* (1986) 103.

39 See further M. J. C. Vile, *Constitutionalism and the Separation of Powers* (1967).

40 *The Constitutional History of England* (1908) 70.

others. Variations on this idea of the balanced constitution remain important today. There are general notions about the constitution being a self-correcting mechanism where, for example, any executive excess can be repaired at election time when a new government is selected. There are also more specific ideas about settling the relative balance of power between the executive and the judiciary in relation to the judges' role in reviewing government decisions for their legality.[41] A range of ideas – from the doctrine of separation of powers, through federalism, devolution, and localism – relate to this idea of a framework for democracy.

This idea of a framework links into notions of civic republicanism, too. The checks and balances that permeate the constitution of the United States are designed not only to ensure limited government but to institutionalize more thoughtful government and ensure that public decisions are seen to be justified not by the fact simply that a majority is in favour but on the basis of reasons that have been debated in public deliberation.[42] This explains the judicial role too, which is to use its power creatively 'not to "block" democracy but to energize it' in an overall process where the role of the constitution is to combine political accountability with a high degree of reflectiveness and a general commitment to giving reasons.[43] Indeed, within this idea of constitutionalism providing a democratic framework for government, we are getting close to the sort of ideas that are considered below under the heading of *process*, where the constitution provides a framework for ongoing processes of democratic dialogue where each generation uses the framework it inherits in continuing struggles for recognition and inclusion.[44] Here constitutionalism is more than a simple framework guaranteeing what the US founding fathers described as 'life, liberty and the pursuit of happiness' – goals which are to be pursued by whatever means each individual wishes. Instead the constitution itself is to provide an operational framework creating institutional conditions that can exert pressure on society constantly to reorder itself in ways that emphasize participation, dialogue, deliberation, and mutual recognition as a means of renewing democracy.[45] Newer ideas of 'democratic experimentalism' also involve designing the conditions for decision making.[46] This approach is drawn from observing how pragmatic capitalist organizations react to coordinating decentralized decision making in volatile, complex, and rapidly changing environments. It suggests that the state re-engineers its processes to provide more localized strategies capable of permanent innovation within an overall approach where ideal standards are benchmarked and public and private actors are encouraged to develop ever more satisfactory procedures in a reflective, learning process.

41 See further, for example, R. Stevens, *The English Judges: Their Role in a Changing Constitution* (2002) and, more generally, C. Guarnieri and P. Pederzoli, *The Power of Judges: A Comparative Study of Courts and Democracy* (2002).

42 See further Cass Sunstein, *The Partial Constitution* (1993).

43 See Cass Sunstein, *Designing Democracy: What Constitutions Do* (2001) 241. See also J. Morison and M. Lynch, 'Litigating the Agreement: Towards a New Judicial Constitutionalism for the UK from Northern Ireland?' in J. Morison, K. McEvoy and G. Anthony (eds) *Judges, Human Rights and Transition* (2007).

44 For example Jurgen Habermas maintains that 'a constitution can be thought of as a historical project that each generation of citizens continues to pursue': *The Inclusion of the Other: Studies in Political Theory* (C. Cronin and P. de Greiff (eds), 1997) 203.

45 See further U. Press, *Constitutional Revolution: The Link Between Constitutionalism and Progress* (1995).

46 See further M. Dorf and C. Sabel, 'A Constitution of Democratic Experimentalism' (1999) 98 *Columbia LR* 267.

However the most important and obvious framework for democracy, and the one that is considered here, is the essentially *aggregative* decision-making method where individual preferences are counted in elections. This is the most basic expression of an institutional framework for collective decision making, and a system that can be said to be democratic broadly because it is possible to link the exercise of power with collective decisions of citizens, understood to be free and equal. Decision making here is collective, and from within this perspective of aggregative democracy it is important that the procedure gives equal consideration to each of the participants in the decision by giving their views equal weight. (Indeed, conventional rationales for the overall idea that the majority decision will be given effect within this system rest on this notion of equal consideration.) As suggested earlier there is a free 'market' of ideas and the role of the state is to ensure that there exists a fair framework for people to choose between these ideas and have their individual preferences counted equally and fairly in a process that aggregates all preferences in order to authorize representatives to govern.

In a sense this seems almost to involve a naive or at least an idealized view of how the constitution works where popular will is converted into government by means of a parliamentary and electoral mechanism.[47] For John Griffith there is a myth of the British constitution and it involves the idea of 'the will of the people transmitted through its elected representatives who make law instructing the Cabinet to administer affairs of state [in the public interest] with the help of an impartial civil service and under the benevolent wisdom of a neutral judiciary'.[48] On such a view the fact of an election is enough and the only issues concern what is the most effective way to regulate the contest and count the vote that gives effect to government.

Of course there are a number of very important matters here. First, there are issues over who is eligible to vote. The history here is one of incremental development where the right to vote gradually extended across property qualifications, age, sex, residence, and, most recently to the homeless, as popular, democratic politics comes to inhabit the traditional structures of the British constitution.[49] Historically there have been debates as to whether the ballot should be secret or in public.[50] Different views have been expressed as to whether a candidate should represent a constituency or interest or be an independent member of a wider deliberative body.[51] The degree to which a candidate should be representative or

47 For a good description of this idealized view see further L. Wolf-Philips, 'A Long Look at the British Constitution' (1984) 37 *Parliamentary Affairs* 385.

48 'The Political Constitution' (1979) 42 *Modern Law Review* 1–21.

49 On the history of the franchise see D. Butler, *The Electoral System in Britain since 1918* (2nd edn, 1963).

50 In the eighteenth century, J. S. Mill argued that a secret ballot would encourage voters to shirk their civic duty, pursue their own interest, and choose simply on the basis of 'interest, pleasure of caprice' rather than the common good. (See *Considerations on Representative Government* (1991) ch. 10.) J. S. Mill's father, James Mill, maintained that, without a secret ballot, the people would be unable to afford to deviate from the political views of their masters, and they would go through only the formalities of voting while the real power of choosing would be possessed by others: James Mill, *Political Writings* (ed. T. Ball, 1992) 227. These debates are now perhaps mirrored by disputes over whether voting should be compulsory as it is in a number of countries such as Australia, Belgium, Greece, and elsewhere.

51 As Edmund Burke famously argued, 'Parliament is not a congress of ambassadors from different and hostile interests; which interest each must maintain, as an agent and advocate, against other agents and advocates . . . You choose a member indeed; but when you have chosen him, he is not member of Bristol, but he is a member of *parliament*' ('Speech at the Conclusion of the Poll', in *Works* (1854) Vol. 1, p. 180).

reflective of those who vote has also been the subject of controversy.[52] There are issues too about how candidates and parties should be regulated. In the UK, as Ewing concludes, the Political Parties, Elections and Referendums Act 2000 is designed to 'transform British political parties from being one of the least to being one of the most highly regulated in Europe'.[53] Perhaps most controversially there are issues about which voting system is employed. There are several hundred electoral systems currently in use round the world. These divide into three broad families: the plurality-majority, the semi-proportional, and the proportional. As discussed elsewhere in this volume the UK uses variations of all three for elections to local authorities, the various devolved parliaments and assemblies, the House of Commons, and the European Parliament. The independent commission on the voting system for the House of Commons chaired by the late Lord Jenkins of Hillhead established in 1997 gave careful consideration to the alternatives, and recommended a rather complex mixed system, although this has not yet found favour with the government.[54]

Whatever rules are devised to ensure the fairness of the electoral context there are some people who maintain that the accepted mechanisms of political democracy can never be really effective in giving ordinary people any influence over collective decisions. This relates to the belief that the only real control that people exercise is over their own individual choices and that, therefore, the only effective mechanism for linking these choices to collective outcomes in a coherent manner is the free market. Within this approach the market alone allows people the option of taking their custom elsewhere (or 'exiting', as it is termed). It is this power only that can operate as an effective sanction and ensure that decision-makers are responsive to consumer choices. Such approaches are particularly important as increasingly governments everywhere are using market-based methods of supplying services. Also, as noted earlier, private, consumer-based arrangements and configurations are progressively replacing public services and public spaces. In this way it may be thought that market-based controls could be more effective in democratic terms than other forms of more politically based collective action. Of course such an approach linking purchasing power with participation through these new forms of political/consumer power ultimately amounts to a denial of the capacity of collective action to secure the 'good society' other than through a version of the market.[55] It also excludes those who are poor or 'flawed consumers'[56] who are unwilling or unable to engage as citizen/consumers.[57]

52 See the litigation surrounding the Labour Party policy of the 1990s to use all-women shortlists in *Jepson and Dyas-Elliot* v. *Labour Party* [1996] IRLR 116 (ET), the Sex Discrimination (Election Candidates) Act 2002 which now permits positive action, and A. Phillips, *The Politics of Presence* (1995) and R. Ali and C. O'Cinneide, *Our House? Race and Representation in British Politics* (2002).

53 K. D. Ewing, 'Transparency, Accountability and Equality: The Political Parties, Elections and Refendums Act 2000' [2001] *Public Law* 542.

54 See *Report of the Independent Commission on the Voting System* Cm 4090 (the Jenkins Report) (1998).

55 It should be pointed out that exit strategies *can* involve more than a simple belief in the instrumental rationality of the market and the force of consumer decisions there. See, for example, the associative democracy of P. Hirst, *Associative Democracy: New Forms of Economic and Social Governance* (1994) which emphasizes voluntarism and participation in and through the associational life of regions and localities. This asserts that 'the negative right to leave an association at one's choice, and the legal defence of that right by the public power, is more important than any positive interventions by the public power to ensure that the association is democratic' (p. 51).

56 See further Z. Bauman, *Postmodernity and its Discontents* (1997).

57 See further C. Shearing and J. Wood, 'Nodal Governance, Democracy, and the New "Denizens" ', (2003) 30 *Journal of Law and Society* 400 at 412–13. More generally the loyalty schemes that many supermarkets and other large stores operate provide an important illustration of this approach. These schemes involve data mining

A PROCESS OF DECIDING – DELIBERATIVE DEMOCRACY

Of course it is nearly always a caricature of representative democracy to see it as a giant aggregating machine, uncovering people's preferences and then translating them into law. Aggregative democracy has its thicker versions as well as its thin ones. On the one hand there are those who are pure proceduralists. For them democratic theories are separate from issues of distributive justice: democracy is about fair procedures, not about right outcomes. But even simple representative democracy can rarely be seen as exclusively procedural. Most democratic theories emphasize as a minimum the essential idea that what makes government democratic is that political authority is conferred though the mechanism of periodic competitive elections and that this is backed up by civil rights such as freedom of expression, and of assembly, etc., and a constitutional order dedicated to the Rule of Law and maintaining certain human rights.

However, there is a range of more developed ideas of democracy which suggest that the institutions and procedures of regular representative democracy do not exhaust the meaning of democracy. There is a range of theories of radical democracy that pick up the dissatisfactions that may be felt with the superficialities of mass democracy, where electoral outcomes are dependent on various arbitrary social and economic factors that may influence an election, and where a bare majority view on the general merits of one or other of the main political parties dominates.[58] These process theories of democracy are concerned with the creation of a public space where dialogue can take place beyond the placid limits of orthodox representative democracy and, indeed, where conflict can be expressed and accommodated.[59]

Instead of aggregative processes where a simple headcount determines policy, these approaches argue for a more deliberative method that is concerned with preference building

from a central register where individual and general consumer preferences are collected from the information given on the strip on the customers' card that registers purchases against centrally held personal information. See further J. Rowley, 'Customer Knowledge Management or Consumer Surveillance?' (2005) 7 *Global Business and Economics Review* 100. In some ways at least, these cards provide a perfect democratic system where choice is minutely monitored. (A marketing director from the UK supermarket Tesco described their Clubcard scheme as 'the most democratic organisation in the UK', claiming that 'customers vote with their Clubcard every week': *Guardian Weekend*, 19 July 2003, p. 19.) In the sense that the system is capable of registering very detailed preferences, it is highly 'democratic' in so far as it can ascertain actual choices accurately: if shoppers are not happy it will show on the card data and retailers must respond. Of course there are difficulties with this: 80% of supermarket profits come from the 20% of customers who have the largest disposable income and are most willing to 'consolidate' or be persuaded to spend more. Accordingly, the data mining will be directed towards satisfying this group, and lower-spending customers who perhaps buy only basic lines may find their needs catered for less sensitively. Within this approach there are inevitably difficulties when someone is not in a position to buy and therefore register an effective preference: it is necessary to be a consumer in order to be a citizen.

58 As B. Barber argues from the perspective of deliberative democracy, liberal democracy is a ' "thin" theory of democracy, one whose democratic values are prudential and thus provisional, optional, and conditional – means to exclusively individualistic and private ends. From this precarious foundation, no firm theory of citizenship, participation, public goods, or civic virtue can be expected to arise': *Strong Democracy: Participatory Politics for a New Age* (1984) 4.

59 For example, James Tully argues for both a philosophy and practice of constitutionalism that is informed by a spirit of mutual recognition, continuity, and consent, and the accommodation of cultural diversity. In living together in a post-imperial century which is marked by a series of intractable conflicts, Tully sees constitutionalism as being about the negotiation of claims for recognition through constitutional dialogues that can reach agreements about appropriate forms of accommodation of difference. (See *Strange Multiplicity: Constitutionalism in an Age of Diversity*, (1995).)

through closer participation in decision making.[60] In a sense such ideas reach back to the sort of direct democracy practised in the *polis* or city of classical Athens where each (free, male) citizen discussed and voted on policy in a deliberative way. Advocates of deliberative approaches often maintain that the process itself somehow mediates or transforms disagreements rather than simply minimizing or accommodating them.[61] There are various ways in which this is supposed to occur and this reflects the various perspectives within this general approach. Some approaches reflect the influence of Jurgen Habermas's ideas where the emphasis is on 'communicative action'.[62] Here the process of discussion itself, and the practical stance of being reasonable, willing to talk and listen will produce agreement. As Habermas puts it, 'the settling of political questions, as far as their moral core is concerned, depends on the institutionalisation of practices of rational public debate'.[63] Such debate takes place in the public sphere – in that space between the state and civil society – and although for Habermas it does not necessarily replace formal decision-making machinery, it does 'influence' it.[64]

Others suggest that democratic deliberation is more practical and that it offers new ways of actually making decisions. It works because it emphasizes politics as the public space where people demonstrate their plurality, and thinking in the presence of others produces an enlarged mentality which discourages individual self-interest and encourages altruism.[65] Other versions see deliberation as transforming preferences, inducing agreement, and producing a self-determining participatory democracy that transcends the narrow limits of traditional representative democracy and has application at every level.[66]

All of these ideas of deliberative or discursive democracy are however united by the emphasis that they put on the fairness of the debate that precedes the taking of any decision. The focus of constitutionalism moves away from the institutions and structures of traditional representative democracy and towards the processes that ensure and facilitate participation. In this way constitutionalism is about guaranteeing fair procedures, including free and equal access to the relevant deliberative arenas for the purposes of establishing procedures, setting the agenda, and making the final decision. All the standard, legally guaranteed liberties, such as freedom of speech, association, etc. are of course required but their basis

60 See further generally R. Blaug, 'New Theories of Discursive Democracy: A User's Guide' (1996) 22 *Philosophy and Social Criticism* 49; M. Saward, 'Reconstructing Democracy: Current Thinking and New Directions' (2001) *Government and Opposition* 559; A. Fung and E. Olin Wright, 'Deepening Democracy: Innovations in Empowered Participatory Governance' (2001) 29 *Politics and Society* 5–41; and Maurizio Passerin D'Entreves (ed.) *Democracy as Public Deliberation* (2006).

61 See further S. Thompson and P. Hoggett, 'The emotional dynamics of deliberative democracy' (2001) 29 *Policy and Politics* 351.

62 See particularly *Between Facts and Norms* (1996); *The Structural Transformation of the Public Sphere* (1989); and *The Theory of Communicative Action, Volume 2* (1989). For an introduction to Habermas in this general context see D. Cook, 'The Talking Cure in Habermas's Republic' (2001) 12 *New Left Review* 135.

63 J. Habermas, 'Further Reflections on the Public Sphere' in C. Calhoun (ed.), *Habermas and the Public Sphere* (1992) 447–8.

64 As Habermas puts it, 'discourses do not govern': 'Further Reflections on the Public Sphere' in Calhoun (ed.) op. cit. at 453. Instead they provide a sort of 'democratic countersteering' to help achieve a rational balance between the processes of the system and the life world. (See further Habermas, 'What Theories can Accomplish – and What they Can't' in *The Past as Future* (1994) 117.)

65 See H. Arendt, 'The Crisis in Culture', in *Between Past and Future* (1977) 220 and 'Truth and Politics', in *Between Past and Future* (1971) 241. See also M. Canovan, *Hannah Arendt: A Reinterpretation of her Political Thought* (1992) 229 ff.

66 See further Barber, *Strong Democracy*, n. 54 above, and J. Cohen and C. Sabel, 'Directly-Deliberative Polyarchy' (1997) 3 *European Law J* 313.

may be slightly different in so far as they are there to ensure participation.[67] Indeed, in their more radical forms, ideas of deliberative democracy bring in trenchant criticisms of existing state structures and rights complaining that these are not the sole or exclusive sites of public, civic interaction and that, furthermore, that they may even be exclusionary because they deny or swallow up other forms of public debate in civil society and structurally discriminate against full interaction along lines of race, class, and gender.[68] Beyond this there is the criticism that what counts as rational discourse for the purposes of this deliberative process may differ fundamentally from one group to another, with disadvantaged voices in particular being liable to exclusion on this ground.[69] More radical views of democracy may also take issue with the idea that democratic politics is inextricably linked to the emergence and consolidation of the modern state and national political communities. They question if democracy can continue to be viewed in exclusively national terms.[70] As the destiny of individuals living within national territories is increasingly shaped by decisions taken outside the framework of national political institutions, so there appears a need to develop democratic principles and processes in a global sense that will have effect in international and transnational contexts.[71]

CONSULTATION – A NEW AGENDA FOR DEMOCRACY

While some exponents of deliberative democracy regard it as a complete process for decision making at every level up to the global, others see it more modestly as contributing towards reviving democracy in its more formal sense. Indeed, the sort of heightened participation that is involved in deliberative democracy has attractions in the context of both traditional and more radical forms of decision making. This often surfaces in ideas of *consultation*. Indeed consultation sometimes appears as a panacea to deal with many of the problems of democracy which relate to failures of participation at every level from the transnational to the very local. Furthermore, consultation has application not just to decision taking and policy making but also as a way of democratizing citizen/consumer relations in the new mechanisms of service delivery.

67 See further J. Cohen, 'Discourse Ethics and Civil Society' (1988) 14 *Philosophy and Social Criticism* 315. See also J. Morison, 'The Case Against Constitutional Reform?' (1998) 25 *J Law and Society* 510, esp. 528–35 for discussion of some of the constitutional implications of these new democratic ideas.

68 For N. Fraser, in her critical engagement with what she perceives to be Habermas's failure in *The Structural Transformation of the Public Sphere* to fully recognize that status hierarchies of gender, race, and class preclude full interaction, the very idea of deliberation in its present, formal form is actually inimical to properly discursive interaction and can instead serve as a mask for domination. Indeed, as Fraser argues, 'the relationship between publicity and status is more complex than Habermas intimates . . . [and] declaring a deliberative arena to be a space where extant status distinctions are bracketed and neutralized is not sufficient to make it so' ('Rethinking the Public Sphere', in *Justice Interruption: Critical Reflections on the 'Postsocialist' condition* (1997) 74). See also J. Mansbridge, 'Feminism and Democracy' (1990) 1 *American Prospect* and S. Benhabib, *Situating the Self* (1991).

69 See further I. M. Young, *Inclusion and Democracy* (2000), particularly ch. 2.

70 See J. Dryzek, *Deliberative Democracy and Beyond* (2000).

71 See further, for example, M. Bookchin, *The Ecology of Freedom* (1982) or P. Laslett, 'Environmental Ethics and the Obsolescence of Existing Political Institutions', in J. Fiskin and P. Laslett (eds), *Debating Deliberative Democracy* (2003) 212, who argue that environmental issues particularly require a global approach to deliberation that is hugely challenging.

In terms of reinvigorating the traditional, representative machinery of democracy consultation seems to call in ideas of increased participation from civil society and this connects generally with the so-called third way approach and its mission to ensure, in the words of the Anthony Giddens, 'the democratisation of democracy'.[72] This process of democratic regeneration is to happen at every level and is to involve civil society generally. UN Agenda 21 calls for the 'broadest public participation' and urges 'active involvement of non-governmental organisations and other groups'. In Europe, the European Commission is currently engaged in a rather extraordinary process of addressing head-on the issue of lack of confidence in governments generally and the disconnectedness that many of its citizens feel with regard to the institutions of the European Union. In *European Governance: A White Paper*,[73] the Commission recognizes that 'democracy depends on people being able to take part in public debate' and it talks in terms of creating 'a transnational "space"' where such debate can take place.[74] Nationally, against a background of long-term downward trends in electoral turnout,[75] which have led to concerns about civic responsibility, and even to proposals for voting in supermarkets or via the Internet, consultation seems to give back the edge of participation which is missing from traditional representative democracy. The Independent *Power Inquiry* into the condition of Britain's democracy sees the problem as not being about political apathy as much as a weakening of effective dialogue between governed and governors which can be rebalanced by 'downloading' power to provide citizens with a more direct say over political decisions.[76] Devolution in particular has brought an increased awareness of the power of consultation, and ideas of consultation and increased participation are interwoven into the fabric of the new arrangements. For example, the so-called 'new politics' that is to guide Scottish devolution has been given expression in the key four principles which include reference to 'a participative approach to the development, consideration and scrutiny of polity and legislation.'[77] Section 144 of the Government of Wales Act 1998 contains a statutory duty on the National Assembly to consult with civil society while Northern Ireland perhaps prefigures the most extreme expression of a consultation culture with its Civic Forum and the duty in Section 75 of the Northern Ireland Act requiring all public bodies to develop an equality strategy through widespread consultation with certain

[72] A. Giddens, *The Third Way: The Renewal of Social Democracy* (1998) 70–86. See also D. Campbell and N. Lewis (eds), *Promoting Participation: Law or Politics?* (1999).

[73] COM (2001) 428 final 25 July. Of course such ideas create a whole set of new problems, as was discovered with the *Congress Online* project which ran in the USA from 2001 to 2005. See further www.congressonlineproject.org/. The unmanageable quantity of communications from citizens (more than 200 million in 2004) which Congress saw as a problem of overload was perceived by citizens as one of non-response.

[74] See further K. Armstrong, 'Rediscovering Civil Society: The European Union and the White Paper on Governance' (2002) 8 *European L J* 102.

[75] The overall trend in voter turnout at general elections since 1945 is generally downwards from a peak of 82% in 1950. The last three Westminster elections have seen a sharp decline from 71% in 1997 to 59.3% in 2001 and 61% in 2005. Elections to devolved bodies have a similar turnout but voting in local elections is in particular decline, with a figure of under 30% by no means exceptional. Perhaps most alarming is the fact that young people are most unlikely to vote with, for example, more than 6 out of 10 voters aged between 18 and 25 years not participating in the 2005 general election.

[76] *Power to the People. The Report of Power: An Independent Inquiry into Britain's Democracy* (2006). See also G. Stoker, *Why Politics Matters: Making Democracy Work* (2006) who similarly argues for a 're-engineering of representative politics' (ch. 10).

[77] See SPOR 1 (8), 9 June 1999, cols 367 ff., the Scottish Ministerial Code, para. 3.1.

individuals and groups.[78] Within devolution, and to an increasing extent within government at Westminster, every programme for government, along with almost every policy initiative, must be the subject of consultation. The days of simple green and white papers, followed by parliamentary debate and legislation seem now almost to belong to a different age.

Consultation applies not only to policy development and its expression in law, but also to the delivery of services, particularly in the new, partly marketized forms that these are presently taking. Services are provided by a range of state and non-state agencies in a variety of quasi-public, partly private, and market-based formats which require citizens to act as consumers in order to exercise a degree of accountability and control by virtue of their status as customers. This change in public sector provision is perhaps best described in terms of the modernization agenda. Modernization is a worldwide trend which shares several common elements based essentially on developing consumer focus, improving public sector performance, and taking advantage of new information and communication technology.[79] In the UK, modernization is a complex, constantly changing, and somewhat indistinct phenomenon. Essentially it involves a new approach or *style* in government operations which is oriented around reinvigorating public services by bringing in new concepts of efficiency, including elements of private sector efficiency, but without ceding control to the same extent as with earlier versions of privatization.[80] As the original key document, the White Paper *Modernising Government* expresses it, the aim is to ensure that the public sector will operate in a way that is 'as efficient, dynamic and effective as anything in the private sector'.[81] This ambitious strategy for changing the basis on which public services are delivered involves developing earlier ideas of the Citizen's Charter into programmes such as Service First, with its Quality Networks, Charter Marks, and Public Sector Benchmarking schemes.

The underlying general policy here is one of customer focus, which requires increasingly that services are targeted and delivery mechanisms monitored. This involves new levels and types of consultation. At the local government level both improved service delivery and enhanced consultation are central to modern approaches to local services.[82] For example, ideas about community leadership duties contained in the Local Government Act 2000 put an emphasis on articulating and developing a vision for the community to be obtained after

78 For Wales see L. Hodgson, 'The National Assembly for Wales, Consultation and Civil Society' (2004) 24 *Politics* 88. On s. 75 in Northern Ireland see further the work of the Equality Commission for Northern Ireland at www.equalityni.org/index.cfm and the Equality Coalition in Northern Ireland at www.communityni.org/index.cfm/section/article/page/Equality%20Coalition.

79 For the phenomenon of modernization generally see B. Charlton and P. Andras, *The Modernization Imperative* (2003) and for its application to UK government see J. Newman, *Modernising Government: New Labour, Policy and Society* (2001).

80 As Giddens describes this general phenomenon, 'the restructuring of government should follow the ecological principle of "getting more from less", understood not as downsizing but as improving delivered value': *The Third Way: The Renewal of Social Democracy* (1998) 74.

81 Cm 4310 (1999) para. 11. See also the second phase of the modernization programme, *Reforming Our Public Services: Principles into Practice* (2002) which offers four 'principles of public sector reform' centred on national standards; devolution and delegation; flexibility; and expanding choice. This has now been overtaken by the Prime Minister's Delivery Unit which is part of a 'Delivery and Transformation Group' which is to 'take[ ] forward the key themes of delivery, performance, capability and transformation'. (See further www.cabinetoffice.gov.uk/pmdu/).

82 See further D. Oliver, *Constitutional Reform in the UK* (2003) 43–6 and chs. 12 and 16 for details of how aspects of the general programme such as Best Value and Service First are developed both centrally and locally.

extensive dialogue and consultation. In addition the White Paper, *Strong and Prosperous Communities* envisages large-scale consultation to produce, variously, a Sustainable Community Strategy, a Local Development Framework and Local Area Agreements as the centrepieces for new partnership working at the local level.[83] The Best Value regime also involves commitment to consult all sections of the local community on key best value priorities and on the effectiveness of service delivery.[84] Here consultation occurs not so much on the basis of citizenship and participation in public decision making about what constitutes the good life lived together: rather participation is in consumer terms where delivery is focused and satisfaction monitored in an effort to improve services that are now delivered as commodities within a quasi-market-based mechanism where customer status is more significant than citizenship.

Within the modernization strategy the idea of using information and communication technology (ICT) has a particular appeal in so far as it seems to offer the potential of increasing participation and feedback.[85] The Democratic Engagement Branch within the Department for Constitutional Affairs has taken up the approach from an earlier consultation[86] and is working with the Hansard Society on a pilot programme, *Digital Dialogues*.[87] This involves using not only blogs, forums and webchats but also wikis, podcasting, file-sharing directories and virals to improve public participation in the policy making process. Indeed ICT is thought to have application not only for consumer-style participation but also more generally to reinvigorate formal representative democracy through online voting systems.[88] There are arguments about the potential for a 'civic commons in cyberspace' which would involve creating an enduring structure to fulfil the democratic potential of the new interactive media.[89]

THE LADDER OF CITIZEN PARTICIPATION

Consultation and participation are ideas whose time seems to have come – again. In a classic article published in 1969,[90] Arnstein commented on the ubiquity and fashionability of the terms at that time but wondered about the extent to which such ideas were mainly about allowing the powerful to claim that all sides were considered while acting in ways that benefit only some people. Arnstein developed a typology of eight levels of participation which represent a ladder moving from essentially non-participation to full citizen control (see Table 6.1).

[83] (2006) Cm 6939. See further Leigh at Chapter 12 of this volume.

[84] See the Communities and Local Government sponsored report by the Centre for Local and Regional Government Research, *The Long-term evaluation of the Best Value regime: Final Report* (2006).

[85] See further J. Morison, 'Modernising Government and the e-government Revolution: Technologies of Government and Technologies of Democracy', in N. Bamforth and P. Leyland (eds), *The Multi-Layered Constitution* (2003) 131 and W. Davies, *Modernising with Purpose: A Manifesto for a Digital Britain* (2005)

[86] *In Service of Democracy: A Consultation Paper for electronic democracy* (2002). Here the emphasis was on how e-technology could 'facilitate, broaden and deepen' participation.

[87] See further http://www.hansardsociety.org.uk/node/view/473.

[88] Experiments in the Republic of Ireland with online voting have not been encouraging, where problems were found with the secrecy and accuracy of software used in a pilot in two constituencies in a 2002 election. See further the *Second Report of the Commission on Electronic Voting* (2006).

[89] See Stephen Coleman of the Hansard Society, *Realising democracy Online: A Civic Commons in Cyberspace* (2001) and *Direct Representation: Towards a Conversational Democracy* (2005).

[90] S. Arnstein, 'A Ladder of Citizen Participation' (1969) *J. American Institute of Planners* 216.

Table 6.1 Eight Rungs on a Ladder of Citizen Participation

	Rung	
8	**Citizen Control**	Degrees of citizen power
7	**Delegated Power**	
6	**Partnership**	
5	**Placation**	Degrees of tokenism
4	**Consultation**	
3	**Informing**	
2	**Therapy**	Non- participation
1	**Manipulation**	

At the first stage there is cosmetic consultation where citizens may hear and be heard, although they lack the resources to ensure that their views will be taken into account. The ladder moves through various degrees of token consultation where the ground rules allow the consulted to advise but these rules retain, for those who hold power, the right to decide. Further up the ladder citizen power begins to develop, with partnership at stage 6 encouraging negotiation and trade-offs between the consulted and decision takers. At stages 7 and 8 citizens have obtained full managerial control and participation is complete and real.

Of course this eight-rung ladder is a simplification, but it does allow us to see that participation and consultation are very varied in their scope and effect. Full citizen control is quite a frightening prospect and it might in many instances be impractical. However, when government conjures up the genie of consultation as an adjunct to stimulate and revive incumbent democracy, or as a way of widening and deepening participation in making policy, or to sharpen the focus of new service-delivery mechanisms, it should be mindful of where on the ladder it wishes to place itself and how it wishes to respond to the demands and challenges this makes. Consultation that is worthy of the name does not mean that the policy is determined by the views of those who could be bothered to take part, any more than it means simply that the original policy is followed irrespective of the opinions of those consulted. At the same time it is quite possible that after considerable consultation there is simply no agreement. (Not even the most enthusiastic advocate of deliberative democracy would maintain that agreement is always possible.) However, it is important that the process of decision making is designed to maximize its participatory character and lead to a properly deliberative outcome. At the very least, and in order to give some substance to claims of democracy, it is necessary to develop models which hear all possible voices and give full consideration to views expressed. Agreement may not always be reached but ideas of reciprocity require as a minimum that justifications and explanations are offered for taking decisions that do not accord with the views of those consulted. Beyond this minimum there is a whole range of possible models for describing what properly deliberative decision making might look like[91] (and a variety of strategies, including simply voting, for deciding what to do when agreement

[91] In an article written with David Newman where this author was critical of the UK government's efforts to use the Internet for consultation, an example of a model for more democratic decision making was outlined. This was drawn from mediation processes which are designed to facilitate consensus despite initial divisions (and it has the additional advantage of being capable of being adapted for computer-supported deliberative decision making). See J. Morison and D. Newman, 'Online Citizenship: Consultation and Participation in New Labour's Britain and beyond' (2001) *International Review of Law, Computers and Technology* 171–94.

does not come). All such processes will share, however, the commitment to fairness and inclusion that characterizes a properly democratic approach where the process of decision making is given priority over the pursuit of any particular outcome from that process.

CONCLUSION

Democracy is a difficult concept to tie down. It has a role in legitimating incumbent institutions of democracy at every level from the subnational to the global, and a role in challenging existing frameworks of decision making through an emphasis on processes of decision making that maximize inclusion and encourage deliberation. Ideas of participation are becoming increasingly important, not just as part of the mission of deliberative forms of democracy to hear the voices of the excluded, but as a way of reinvigorating more traditional representative democracy and focusing the newer forms of service delivery that are associated more broadly with modernized government. However, participation, particularly when it is pursued through various mechanisms for consultation, can be very varied in quality. It might be possible to engineer full citizen control of public decision making such as would accord with the direct democracy of ancient Athens. However, it remains to be seen if such a highly developed version of democracy would be acceptable or practical.

FURTHER READING

CHOMSKY, N. *Failed States: The Abuse of Power and the Assault on Democracy* (2006).

CROUCH, C. *Post-Democracy* (2004).

DAHL, R. *Democracy and its Critics* (1989).

DRYZEK, J. *Deliberative Democracy and Beyond* (2000).

DWORKIN, R. *Is Democracy Possible Here? Principles for a New Political Debate* (2006).

FISKIN, J. and LASLETT, P. (eds) *Debating Deliberative Democracy* (2003).

HELD, D. *Democracy and the Global Order: From the Modern State to Global Governance* (1995).

The Power Inquiry, *Power to the People: The Report of Power: An Independent Inquiry into Britain's Democracy* (2006).

MULGAN, G. *Good and Bad Power: The Ideals and Betrayals of Government* (2006).

SAWARD, M. *Democracy* (2003).

SHAPIRO, I. *The State of the Democratic Theory* (2003).

SUNSTEIN, C. *republic.com* (2001).

STOKER, G. *Why Politics Matters: Making Democracy Work* (2006).

TULLY, J. *Strange Multiplicity: Constitutionalism in an age of Diversity* (1995).

YOUNG, I. M. *Inclusion and Democracy* (2000).

USEFUL WEB SITES

International Institute for Democracy and Electoral Assistance IDEA: **www.idea.int/**

Democratic Audit of the UK: **www.democraticaudit.com**

Electoral Commission: **www.electoralcommission.org.uk/**

Hansard Society: **www.hansardsociety.org.uk/**

The Consultation Institute: **www.consultationinstitute.org/**

Cabinet Office code of Good Practice for consultation: **www.cabinetoffice.gov.uk/regulation/consultation/consultation_guidance/consultation_guidance/index.asp**

Cabinet Office, e-Government Unit: **www.cabinetoffice.gov.uk/e-government/**

Website of the UK Government, DirectGov: **www.direct.gov.uk/Homepage/fs/en**

Governments across the world that are on the internet: **www.gksoft.com/govt/en/**

Democracies Online Newswire: **www.publicus.net/dowire.html**

The Power Inquiry: **www.Powerinquiry.org**

PART II

THE INSTITUTIONAL CONTEXT

Editorial note

The chapters in this part of the book are concerned with institutional matters.

Chapters 7 and 8 focus on institutional reform at UK level. Parliament itself has been going through a period of modernization, particularly of the procedures and working practices in the House of Commons. These have facilitated the processing of government business. The extent to which these reforms have strengthened the capacity of the House of Commons to hold government to account is debatable. The membership and committee structure in the House of Lords have also been going through changes. The composition of the House, the question of whether any of its members should be elected, and how any appointments should be made, have proved highly controversial, partly because of conflicting perceptions of the role and character of the second chamber. These are the subjects of Chapter 7.

The conduct of government itself has been affected by a range of theories about management, some imported from the private sector. These have resulted in institutional changes in the form of the creation of executive agencies within government departments. These have in turn altered relationships between ministers and civil servants, and between ministers and Parliament, and thus accountability arrangements. These changes have also produced an increased emphasis on effectiveness – on outputs and outcomes rather than inputs and procedures in government – and on the citizen as the 'consumer' of services. These are discussed in Chapter 8.

Other institutional reforms include devolution in Scotland, Northern Ireland, and Wales, and implications of these for England and for the UK as a whole. These form the subject of Chapters 9, 10 and 11. The arrangements for each country in the UK differ in response to the different needs of and pressures from Scotland, Northern Ireland, and Wales. In each of those three countries there are elected institutions – the Scottish Parliament, the Northern Ireland Assembly and the Assembly for Wales, with executives possessing extensive powers. Each of the devolution arrangements preserves the legislative sovereignty of the UK Parliament, discussed in Part I. But each changes the political climate in which the UK Parliament and government operate. And the powers of the Assembly for Wales are currently being increased, in response to pressure from Wales and experience of the devolution arrangements in the last few years.

Local government too has been undergoing a period of change, which goes back many years. Chapter 12 is concerned with the most recent reforms, intended to reinvigorate local democracy by institutional arrangements such as the use of cabinets instead of committees and, in some places, elected mayors, and by relaxing central control over local authorities which meet government-set criteria. We have here signs of a move towards more participatory and deliberative democracy such as was discussed in Chapter 6. Attempts by the Government to introduce elected regional tiers of government where local opinion was in favour came to an end after a referendum on the matter in the North East in 2004 failed to produce sufficient support.

Finally in this Part of the book, Chapter 13 discusses administrative justice, including judicial review, tribunals, ombudsmen and more informal methods of 'alternative dispute resolution'. In these mechanisms principles of constitutionalism and informality may come into conflict with one another. Administrative justice should be recognized as a constitutional principle, and informality should not be permitted to marginalize it.

7

THE 'MODERNIZATION' OF THE UNITED KINGDOM PARLIAMENT?

Dawn Oliver

SUMMARY

The ways in which we think of the two Houses of the UK Parliament are in a state of flux. To what extent are they channels for the giving of consent to government and legislation on behalf of the electorate? And to what extent are they constitutional watchdogs, civic forums, and institutions for the impartial scrutiny of government, its legislation, policy, and administration? How effective can they be? How central are they to the political process? The debate revolves around the relationships of the two Houses with one another and with the government and the place of party politics in our constitutional arrangements.

Since 1997 a number of 'modernizing' measures has been introduced in the House of Commons and more are currently under discussion. The reforms so far are designed largely to facilitate the passage of the legislation proposed by the Government, and to enable the House to perform its functions in holding government to account. However, the Government has also sought to marginalize the House of Commons in its legislative and accountability-imposing functions. And the Commons has begun to accept that its capacity to hold government to account is limited and to envisage transferring some accountability responsibilities to independent bodies. These trends have major constitutional implications.

As far as the House of Lords is concerned, there is general support for the ways in which the Lords perform their functions of acting as constitutional watchdogs, scrutinizing bills and draft bills, holding government to account, and providing a forum for the examination of matters of public interest. The composition of the House of Lords is however controversial and problematic. The patronage that the current arrangements create is not subject to any legal regulation. It raised concerns over the quality of appointments and 'cash for peerages' in 2006. And yet it has proved impossible so far to achieve the necessary support for any alternative arrangements, for instance for independent appointment and election.

INTRODUCTION

One of the recurring concerns in debates about the UK constitution for at least 40 years has been about the capacity, even the willingness, of the two Houses of Parliament[1] to discharge their constitutional functions. This concern has been coupled with a lack of clarity about what those functions are, what the two Houses' relationships with government and with one another should be, and their composition – whether it facilitates or hinders their performance.

Let us start with some of the common assumptions about Parliament, for if we understand that these are often mistaken we may find it easier to reach a view about whether, and if so how, Parliament needs to be reformed or modernized. A prevalent assumption is that Parliament is, and rightly so, at the heart or apex[2] of the political and governing processes in the UK. The emphases in constitutional orthodoxy on parliamentary sovereignty, parliamentary privilege, parliamentary self-regulation, the parliamentary executive, and ministerial responsibility to Parliament as being fundamental to the system imply this centrality.[3] Yet it is increasingly obvious that Parliament's centrality is declining for a number of reasons. The House of Commons is dominated by the Executive (normally referred to as the government), in whose hands real power and initiative lie.[4] To this extent the centrality of Parliament – as distinct from the centrality of the executive – is a myth and raises issues as to whether and how Parliament can reassert an independent and central role and, if it cannot or will not do so, whether alternative and supplementary arrangements should be made to hold the executive to account.

The devolution of power to the Scottish Parliament and the Welsh Assembly (and to the Northern Ireland Assembly, when it is able to operate) has removed both legal and political power from London[5] and created new bodies in those parts of the UK that are, in effect, operating under law-based, written constitutions. The UK Parliament – and the Executive – are having to share power with, defer to, or compromise with other bodies. Enactment of the Human Rights Act 1998 has reduced reliance on the two Houses as providing political protection against abuses of power by the Executive, and has increased legal, judicial protections against such abuses.[6]

The growing focus on law-based constitutionalism[7] in preference to 'the political constitution'[8] that flows from devolution, the Human Rights Act (and membership of the European

[1] The UK has a parliamentary executive: all members of Her Majesty's Government must be members of one or other of the two chambers of Parliament, i.e. the House of Commons or the House of Lords. The legislature is 'The Queen in Parliament': a Bill may become law only when it has the consent of the two Houses of Parliament and of the monarch. The exceptions to this are that under the Parliament Acts 1911 and 1949 the House of Lords may not amend or delay the passage of a 'money Bill', e.g. the annual Finance Act, and it has a one-year delaying power but no veto on the passing of other Acts of Parliament save an Act to extend the life of a Parliament beyond five years.

[2] See Report of the Hansard Society Commission on Parliamentary Scrutiny, *The Challenge for Parliament: Making Government Accountable* (2001).

[3] See for instance *Strengthening Parliament*, the report of the Conservative Party's Committee to Strengthen Parliament chaired by Lord Norton of Louth (2000).

[4] See Lord Hailsham, *Elective Dictatorship* (1976) and *The Dilemma of Democracy* (1978); *The Challenge for Parliament*, n. 1 above; Parliament First, *Parliament's Last Chance* (2003).

[5] See Chapters 9, 10 and 11.

[6] See Chapter 3.

[7] See D. Oliver, *Constitutional Reform in the UK* (2003).

[8] See J. A. G. Griffith, 'The Political Constitution' (1979) 42 *MLR* 1.

Union[9]) means that Parliament operates increasingly within legal and political constraints. The UK constitution has been trying to adapt to these new constitutional realities.[10] The role of the judiciary in holding the executive to account for its policies and administration, including for compliance with European law[11] and with the European Convention on Human Rights[12] is increasing in importance as the influence of Parliament appears to wane.[13] But constitutional adaptation has not taken the form of extra-parliamentary, US-style judicial review of legislation and executive action by a supreme court, or continental-style, pre-legislative constitutional or administrative scrutiny such as operates in France.[14] Instead, Parliament and government have been making internal adaptations to meet these new needs. Increasingly, the possibility of transferring some of the current functions of Parliament – for instance oversight of the security services and of the operation of the *Ministerial Code*, both noted below – to outside bodies is under consideration. Before turning to consider how this is happening in each House it will be helpful to consider their relationships with the government and with one another.

PARLIAMENT'S RELATIONS WITH GOVERNMENT

The relationships between the two Houses and the government are largely regulated by convention. For instance, it is a fairly settled tenet of the system that the government is entitled to get its business through the House of Commons, and to have it considered in the Lords. Whether it is entitled to have measures that were promised in its election manifesto given a fair wind in the House of Lords (the Salisbury convention[15]) is no longer clear. It is accepted that it is the sole prerogative of the Commons as the elected House and the chamber in which the Prime Minister sits, to withdraw confidence from the government so that a general election or resignation of the government followed by appointment of a new Prime Minister charged with producing a new administration should take place. Under the Parliament Act 1911, it is the sole right of the Commons to grant or refuse supply to the government, so that the Lords are not entitled to amend or delay – beyond a month – the passage of a money Bill.

It has for many years been accepted that changes to statutory provisions should generally be made by Act of Parliament. 'Henry VIII clauses', which grant ministers the power to change statutory provisions by order, are seen as undermining Parliament and thus being in need of strong justification. In January 2006 the Government introduced its Legislative and Regulatory Reform Bill in the House of Commons, and created a furore.[16] There had been no draft Bill for pre-legislative scrutiny. The Bill proposed to grant ministers the power by order to reform any public general Act of Parliament. It included very few conditions to prevent abuse of such power. Eventually the Bill was amended, for instance to require the minister proposing an order to be satisfied that the provision is not of constitutional

[9] See Chapter 4.

[10] See M. Elliott, 'Parliamentary sovereignty and the new constitutional order: legislative freedom, political reality and convention' (2002) 22 *Legal Studies* 340.

[11] See Chapter 4.

[12] See Chapter 3.

[13] See Chapter 13.

[14] This will be briefly discussed below.

[15] According to this convention, a 'manifesto' Bill, foreshadowed in the governing party's most recent election manifesto and passed by the House of Commons, should not be opposed by the second chamber on Second or Third Reading.

[16] See for instance the Third Report of the House of Commons Public Administration Select Committee, HC 1033, 2005–06.

significance, and giving parliamentary scrutiny committees a veto over Bills. But the Government had allowed no amendments until Report stage in the House of Commons, despite objections from select committees and others. The resulting Act still contains extensive powers for ministers to amend legislation by order. The Government gave undertakings that the Act would not be used for controversial changes to the law[17], but such undertakings are not, of course, enforceable, especially against a future government which might not feel morally bound by them. The point is that this was an attempt by government to marginalize Parliament. It suggests a divergence of culture between government and Parliament. The Government was either ignorant of an important constitutional principle, or arrogant in its disregard for Parliament, or out of touch with parliamentary culture and tradition.

Turning to the House of Lords' relations with government, the chamber generally accepts that its role is secondary, in recognition of the fact that the government and the Commons have democratic legitimacy flowing from election which the Lords have not been able to claim.[18] However, it has come to be accepted that the Lords have important functions in the revision of legislation, especially on technical or drafting points; functions in delaying legislation in order for the Commons or the government to reconsider a proposal where there are serious concerns, in the House of Lords or elsewhere, about its wisdom; a constitutional watchdog function; functions in the scrutiny of, for instance, the grant of delegated powers, of deregulation orders, and of European legislation; and generally functions in debating matters of public importance. The very fact that the Lords are not elected and are relatively independent of party, and that the House of Lords contains members with particular skills, expertise, and interests in these kinds of activity would serve to legitimate much of their activity if it took place outside somewhere called 'Parliament', such as a constitutional council or a council of state. But difficulties are undeniably caused by the fact that this is a 'House of Parliament' whose members are not elected. We shall consider these in due course.

RELATIONS BETWEEN THE HOUSE OF COMMONS AND THE HOUSE OF LORDS

The House of Lords is supposed to complement, rather than compete with or duplicate, the House of Commons in various ways. Since it is not elected, it cannot be part of its role to give or refuse consent to legislation on behalf of the electorate – or of any other body. It is not a body of 'representatives' though to an extent it is a body of 'voices' – a 'civic forum' – in the sense of a body of people who can contribute particular and significant perspectives to debate. (In this respect it may be an example of the deliberative model of democracy discussed in Chapter 6.) Although its consent is required to legislation other than money Bills (unless the Parliament Acts apply to facilitate the giving of Royal Assent to legislation without the consent of the Lords, normally after a year's delay) the Lords' power to withhold consent to legislation is in practice a mechanism for securing that the House of Commons (and the government) take seriously and respond to concerns expressed in the second chamber.

[17] HC Deb 9 February 2006, cols 1058–9.

[18] The composition of the House of Lords is discussed below.

Since the House of Lords Act 1999, which removed most hereditary peers from the second chamber, the House of Lords has been more assertive than previously in its relations with the Commons. This led to the establishment of a joint select committee on conventions, which reported in 2006.[19] The report noted that there was a range of views on what should be the proper role of the House of Lords in the legislative process, but agreed that in principle that House should consider government business in reasonable time, give a second reading to a manifesto Bill and not make 'wrecking amendments' to it, and give the Commons a reasonable time to consider Lords amendments. It proposed that resolutions to this effect should be passed by one or both Houses, but that these would simply be 'formulations' rather than codifications of conventions, which should not be regarded as rules.

We need to bear in mind at this point that giving (or refusing) consent to government policy and legislation are not the only checking functions that need to be performed in a democracy which accepts – as the UK seems to do – that majoritarianism can pose a threat to the principles which underlie most democratic arrangements. Uninhibited majoritarianism can undermine respect for minority and human rights and the operation of effective, often non-political, mechanisms for imposing accountability on government, such as constitutional review.[20] The question then is, where and how and by what criteria are such checking functions performed in the UK?

In most other democracies a written constitution provides the criteria for checking government. The legislature – often primarily the second or upper chamber or senate – and constitutional courts or councils or councils of state perform checking functions. The UK lacks such external, independent institutions. My suggestion is that the House of Lords is coming to fill this gap and to compensate for the fact that other non-parliamentary checking institutions commonly provided for in written constitutions do not exist in the UK.

With these background considerations in mind let us turn to examine the roles and functions of the two Houses of Parliament.

THE HOUSE OF COMMONS

THE ROLE AND FUNCTIONS OF THE HOUSE OF COMMONS

The role and functions of the House of Commons are relatively well settled, in theory at least. They are:

- to provide the government of the day (all ministers must by convention be members of one or other of the two Houses, and the Prime Minister and the Chancellor of the Exchequer must be members of the Commons);
- to sustain the government in power by passing its legislation;
- to give – or refuse – consent to taxation;
- to authorize and control public expenditure;

[19] HL 265, HC 1212, 2005–06. [20] See Chapter 1.

- to secure redress of constituents' grievances; and
- generally to hold the Executive to account for its policies and the conduct of government.

As it is the elected chamber it is natural that most of these functions are dominated by party political considerations. This is pre-eminently a political chamber. It is through elections that the electorate exercises its right to give or refuse consent to government, the most crucial function in a democracy. Elections inevitably produce party groupings, and the first past the post system of election to the House of Commons produces party discipline and partisanship in relations between parties. The system tends to produce majorities in Parliament even if, as is invariably the case, a majority of the voters did not support the winning party. It encourages competitive rather than cooperative relations between the parties.[21]

In the run-up to the 1997 general election the Joint (Labour Party–Liberal Democrat) Consultative Committee on Constitutional Reform committed the two parties to 'renewing Parliament' as a key to wider modernization of the UK's constitutional arrangements.[22] The main focus was on the House of Commons. The Report stated that 'the House of Commons no longer holds ministers to account and legislation is not given the scrutiny it requires'. The priorities in this agreement for modernizing the House of Commons were: to programme parliamentary business to ensure fuller consultation, more effective scrutiny of Bills, and better use of MPs' time; to improve the quality of legislation by better pre-legislative consultation and the use of mechanisms such as the special standing committee procedure where evidence is taken before legislation is passed; changing Prime Minister's Question Time to make it a more genuine and serious means of holding the government to account; to overhaul the process for scrutinizing European legislation so that decisions from the EU are more transparent and Parliament's role is more clearly defined; to strengthen the ability of MPs to make the government answerable for its actions; and to enhance the role of select committees in ensuring the accountability of departments. It is significant that the document was phrased largely in terms of what 'Parliament' should do and did not seek to distinguish between the roles of the two Houses. As we shall see, a distinction is essential if the roles of the Houses are to be properly understood.

After the 1997 election the Leader of the House, then Ann Taylor MP, chaired a newly created Modernisation Select Committee to consider what precise forms modernization should take. But despite the pre-election commitment of Labour and the Liberal Democrats, modernization of the House proved very difficult to achieve in the Parliament of 1997 to 2001. This was due in large part to the conservative ethos of both main political parties, lack of commitment on the part of Leaders of the House, a lack of trust in the government on the part of the opposition parties, and suspicion of its possibly ulterior motives in responding to modernization proposals. The fact of the matter is that the House of Commons is incapable of taking initiatives to modernize itself and depends on the approval of the government if any reforms are to be implemented.[23] However, after the 2001 election the former Foreign Secretary, Robin Cook, was appointed Leader of the House and

21 See A. King, *Does the United Kingdom have a Constitution?* (Hamlyn Lectures) (2001).

22 Joint Consultative Committee Report (1997) para. 64.

23 See A. Kennon, *The Commons: Reform or Modernisation* (2000).

he pushed the modernization programme forward with some success – and some failures. He resigned in April 2003 in protest at the Government's policy on Iraq. The pace of reform of the Commons slackened, though the Committee produced a lengthy report on the legislative process in September 2006, its only report since the general election the previous year. It will be useful to summarize briefly the principal reforms of the Commons that have been achieved since about 1997 and to consider whether they have in practice improved the Commons' performance of its functions.

INDIVIDUAL MINISTERIAL RESPONSIBILITY: GOVERNMENT'S DUTY TO PARLIAMENT

A major challenge has been, and remains, to give teeth to the convention of individual ministerial responsibility to Parliament. The classic version of the doctrine is that ministers are responsible to Parliament for all that happens in their departments, though they will only be regarded as culpable in respect of their own decisions or failures. They must give an account to Parliament, and they are expected to make amends if something has gone wrong.[24] The effectiveness, and content, of this convention had become a high-profile issue over a number of decades[25] but it crystallized in the Arms to Iraq Affair in the early 1990s. Certain defendants had been prosecuted for breach of the rules relating to the export of arms to Iraq, but it emerged during the trial that members of the government had known about the exports and had, in effect, allowed the prosecution to proceed in the knowledge that the defendants were at risk of wrongful convictions. The trial judge stopped the trial. Sir Richard Scott, then Vice Chancellor (Head of the Chancery Division of the High Court), was asked to report on the matter. His Report[26] made severe criticisms of ministers. These were debated in Parliament, ministers rejected the criticisms, and no ministers resigned. However, concerns about the basis and weaknesses of the conventions of ministerial responsibility that emerged from that affair were accepted as valid by the John Major government, and the requirement that ministers be accountable to Parliament was reaffirmed by both Houses and formalized through the resolutions on ministerial accountability passed by each House just before the 1997 general election. The House of Commons resolution provides:[27]

That, in the opinion of this House, the following principles should govern the conduct of ministers of the Crown in relation to Parliament:

(1) Ministers have a duty to Parliament to account, and be held to account, for the policies, decisions and actions of their Departments and Next Steps Agencies.
(2) It is of paramount importance that ministers give accurate and truthful information to Parliament, correcting any inadvertent error at the earliest opportunity. Ministers who

[24] See G. Marshall, *Ministerial Responsibility* (1989); D. Woodhouse, *Ministers and Parliament: Accountability in Theory and Practice* (1994); S. E. Finer, 'The Individual Responsibility of Ministers' (1956) 34 *Public Administration* 377; Hansard Society Commission on Parliamentary Scrutiny, *The Challenge for Parliament: Making Government Accountable* (2001).

[25] See for instance Lord Hailsham, *Elective Dictatorship* (1976); and *The Dilemma of Democracy* (1978).

[26] See *Report on the Export of Dual-Use Goods to Iraq*, HC 115 (1995–6) (the Scott Report); A. Tomkins, *The Constitution After Scott* (1998).

[27] See HC Debs, 19 Mar. 1997, cols 1046–7. The House of Lords resolution is in similar terms: HL Debs, 20 Mar. 1997, cols 1055–62.

knowingly mislead Parliament will be expected to offer their resignation to the Prime Minister.

(3) Ministers should be as open as possible with Parliament, refusing to provide information only when disclosure would not be in the public interest, which should be decided in accordance with relevant statute and the Government's Code of Practice on Access to Government Information.

(4) Similarly, ministers should require civil servants who give evidence before Parliamentary Committees on their behalf and under their directions to be as helpful as possible in providing accurate, truthful and full information in accordance with the duties and responsibilities of civil servants as set out in the Civil Service Code.

After the general election of 1997 and the change of government, these obligations were incorporated into the Ministerial Code by the new Prime Minister, Tony Blair, who accepted that the Prime Minister is responsible to Parliament for enforcing these rules. He also agreed to meet members of the House of Commons Liaison Committee (consisting of the chairs of select committees) twice a year. These concessions were only made, however, after sustained pressure from select committees in the House of Commons and expressions of press and public concern about the weak accountability of ministers to Parliament.[28] It does not of course follow from the passing of resolutions that the actual effectiveness of ministerial responsibility will improve. In the following sections of this chapter some indications will be given of how the convention is operating.

THE SCRUTINY OF LEGISLATION

A major problem over the scrutiny of legislation on the floor of the House of Commons or in its standing committees is that it is not conducted according to any particular criteria, but at large. Scrutiny tends to be highly politically partisan, aimed only partly towards improving the Bill and largely towards drawing attention to weaknesses in the Bill and opposing and harassing ministers.[29] As Feldman has pointed out, scrutiny should include the examination of measures against certain standards that are independent of the terms or subject matter of the measure itself.[30] These standards should include matters such as clarity of drafting, compatibility with international obligations and the Human Rights Act, and respect for various constitutional principles such as the independence of the judiciary, legal certainty, non-retroactivity, proportionality of penalty, and so on. This kind of scrutiny is not done well by the House of Commons,[31] dominated as it is by party.

A number of supposedly modernizing measures have been taken both to improve House of Commons scrutiny of legislation and to facilitate the passage of government legislation. The two objectives are commonly in tension with one another. The scrutiny of legislation has been improved by publication of explanatory notes with Bills and the introduction of pre-legislative scrutiny of some draft Bills. Acceptance of the carry-over of some Bills from

28 See for instance Liaison Committee, First Report, *Shifting the Balance: Select Committees and the Executive*, HC 300 (1999–2000); *Strengthening Parliament* (2000); and *The Challenge for Parliament: Making Government Accountable* (2001), above.

29 See Second Report of the Select Committee on Procedure, *Public Bill Procedure*, HC 49 (1984–5) para. 30.

30 See D. Feldman, 'Parliamentary scrutiny of legislation and human rights' [2002] *Public Law* 323.

31 But note the discussion of the Joint Committee on Human Rights, below and in Chapter 3.

one session to the next[32] would take the time pressure off scrutiny and could thus enable it to be done thoroughly if the will to do so existed among backbenchers. However, very few Bills have been carried over and the norm remains for scrutiny to be completed to enable Bills to receive Royal Assent before the end of the session. The establishment in 2002 of a Joint Committee on Human Rights[33] (on an initiative from the House of Lords) with the specific responsibility for scrutiny of legislation for compatibility with the Human Rights Act 1998 and the European Convention on Human Rights and for other human rights implications has produced focused, expert, and independent scrutiny of bills.

The House of Commons Modernisation Committee made a number of proposals in its 2006 report on *The Legislative Process*[34] but these did not include any proposals to build upon the standards-based scrutiny conducted by the Joint Committee and develop criteria, standards or checklists against which Bills could be scrutinised by other scrutiny committees. However, the Scrutiny Unit in the House of Commons, whose staff are mainly engaged in assisting House of Commons committees conducting pre-legislative scrutiny of draft Bills, is building up expertise and legislative standards statements, and the House of Commons Library staff are also developing some checklists when producing briefing material for MPs. This may lead to more objective scrutiny of draft Bills, but the use of standards and checklists[35] evidently does not appeal to MPs. The Modernisation Committee report did however propose replacing standing committee procedure with 'Public Bill Committees' that could take expert evidence (a proposal accepted by government but yet to be implemented), extending the use of pre-legislative scrutiny to more, and controversial, Bills and various other detailed changes.

Modernizing measures purportedly designed to facilitate the legislative process include the timetabling or programming of Bills. However, a Deputy Speaker of the House expressed the view in 2003 that the more comprehensive introduction of programming had not led to Bills being scrutinized more thoroughly or completely than hitherto; programming was capable of being used constructively, but, short of any more fundamental approach, detailed programming should not be left in the hands of the usual channels, and in effect all that had been achieved thus far was legislation in a hurry. In general, he felt, the process continues to be attended by recrimination and, unless some radical initiative were to be taken the prospects for improved scrutiny were not encouraging.[36]

THE SELECT COMMITTEES

Some reforms have been designed to increase the influence and powers of the House of Commons' select committees and thus the effectiveness of individual ministerial responsibility. The departmental and other investigative select committees have the function of monitoring the expenditure, administration, and policy of government and its departments.

[32] See HC Debs, 29 Oct. 2002, cols 688–828. Normally if a Bill does not complete its parliamentary passage by the end of the parliamentary session each year it is 'lost'. The government will have to reintroduce the Bill in the following session and start the parliamentary process over again. 'Carry over' enables the Bill to continue its parliamentary passage from one session to the next.

[33] See Chapter 3.

[34] HC 1097 (2005–06).

[35] See D.Oliver 'Improving the scrutiny of Bills: the case for standards and checklists' [2006] *Public Law* 219.

[36] See First Report from the Select Committee on the Modernisation of the House of Commons, HC 1222, (2002–03) relating to the Programming of Bills, Memorandum from Sir Alan Haselhurst, Deputy Speaker.

These committees now have an agreed, explicit set of core objectives, extending beyond the long established role of imposing direct ministerial responsibility to tasks such as monitoring performance against targets in public service agreements, taking evidence from independent regulators and inspectorates, considering the reports of Executive Agencies,[37] considering major appointments made by ministers, and examining treaties within their subject areas.[38] However, in practice committees remain autonomous in how they interpret these core tasks. Several have refused to take on scrutiny of draft Bills, for instance. The fact of the matter is that parliamentarians are not interested in performing this often technical function. They may not have the time or skills to do so. When they do engage in the textual scrutiny of Bills or draft Bills, they rely heavily on expert assistance from committee clerks, members of the Scrutiny Unit, or legal and other advisers. A question arises whether the role of experts and lawyers ought not to be institutionalized in some way, for instance in an extra-parliamentary advisory committee which would report to Parliament and government on Bills and draft Bills. A model might be New Zealand's Legislation Advisory Committee.[39]

The government accepts that it has an obligation to respond to select committee reports within two months of their publication. Government responses are published by the House of Commons. In some cases proposals from select committees have first been rejected outright and then ultimately, after a long campaign, been accepted: the Prime Minister's agreement to meet the Liaison Committee twice a year is an example of a concession won only after determined persistence on the part of that Committee.

The Public Administration Select Committee (PASC) provides an example, unfortunately atypical, of what could be achieved by select committees. Under the particularly energetic leadership of Tony Wright, the PASC has produced reports proposing reforms and pressing the government to meet concerns about many issues concerning machinery of government and accountability. Topics have included the accountability of quangos (quasi-autonomous non-governmental organizations) and regulators,[40] maintenance of the public service ethos,[41] the use of political advisers as 'spin doctors',[42] the system for making public appointments,[43] the use of public service targets,[44] control of the Royal Prerogative[45] and Public Inquiries.[46] But other House of Commons select committees have been less energetic and it cannot be said that there has been systematic improvement of committee work in the House of Commons.

Although the Public Administration Select Committee has an important role in holding ministers to account for the operation of the *system* and has been an energetic and relatively

37 See Chapter 8.

38 See Modernisation Committee, First Report, *Select Committees*, HC 221 (2001–02); Liaison Committee, Second Report, *Select Committees: Modernisation Proposals*, HC 692 (2001–02); approved HC Debs, 14 May 2002, cols 648–730.

39 See D. Oliver, 'Improving the scrutiny of Bills' supra.

40 Sixth Report from the Select Committee on Public Administration, *Quangos*, HC 209 (1998–9).

41 Select Committee on Public Administration, Seventh Report, *The Public Service Ethos*, HC 263 (2001–02).

42 Public Administration Select Committee, Eighth Report, *These Unfortunate Events*, HC 303 (2001–02).

43 See Public Administration Select Committee, *Government by Appointment: Opening up the Patronage State*, HC 165, Fourth Report (2002–03).

44 Public Administration Select Committee, Fifth Report, *On Target? Government by Measurement*, HC 62 (2002–03).

45 Public Administration Select Committee Fourth Report, *Taming the Prerogative*, HC 422 (2003–04).

46 Public Administration Select Committee First Report, *Government by Inquiry*, HC 51 (2004–05).

effective committee, a row blew up in 2006 over the responsiveness of ministers to reports of the Parliamentary Ombudsman to the PASC. The Parliamentary Ombudsman had found[47] that the Government had been guilty of maladministration in producing misleading information and not warning people about the risks of private pension schemes not being able to provide pensions if wound up with insufficient funds. She recommended that the Government should consider whether to make arrangements for the restoration of full pensions to those who had lost out from the winding up of schemes. The Department of Work and Pensions rejected both the recommendation and the finding of maladministration. The Public Administration Select Committee responded in a report expressing concern about the constitutional implications not only of the Government's rejection of this report but of what appeared to be a trend for the Government to reject Ombudsman reports.[48] The point is that the Ombudsman reports to Parliament, in particular the PASC; there being no legal redress for maladministration, the effectiveness of ministerial responsibility to Parliament is crucial for the workability of the system, and for the victims of maladministration. The PASC noted that this was one of four special Ombudsman reports rejected by the Government over the years, but that it was the second in that year. The Committee commented that the Government's relationship with the Ombudsman was changing, that there appeared to be an emerging attitude in government that they could properly and with impunity reject any independent assessment of their actions and findings of maladministration,[49] and stated that, 'It would be extremely damaging if Government became accustomed simply to reject findings of maladministration. . . . It would raise fundamental constitutional issues about the position of the Ombudsman and the relationship between Parliament and the Executive.'[50]

The performance of select committees in questioning effectively those appearing before them or obtaining the documents they need is unsatisfactory in a number of respects. MPs do not have the time to conduct lengthy and complex inquiries, especially where the evidence is challenged; few MPs have experience in examining and cross-examining witnesses; the committee memberships are large in number, members have varying agendas, some pro-government and others anti; the chairs do not appear to coordinate the handling of witnesses; the committees do not have the power to compel the attendance of witnesses or the production of documents if the government is unwilling; the government permits civil servants to appear before select committees only on behalf of and at the direction of ministers.

These weaknesses in select committee capability were particularly apparent at the times of the Arms to Iraq affair in 1993–4, noted above, and again in the investigation into the alleged 'sexing up' of the government's dossier on the risk of an attack by Iraq in the run-up to the attack by the USA-UK coalition on Iraq in Spring 2003. In each case select committees had conducted their own inquiries into the issues, but they were much less successful in extracting documents and evidence from witnesses and making authoritative findings of

47 Trusting in the pensions promise: government bodies and the security of final salary occupational schemes: HC 984 (2005–06).

48 *The Ombudsman in Question: the Ombudsman's report on pensions and its constitutional implications* HC 1081 (2005–06).

49 At para. 66.

50 At para. 78. The Government's position was debated in the House of Commons, but the government refused to alter its position: HC Deb. 7 December 2006, cols 512–50. The cost to government of making good the loss to pensioners would have run into billions of pounds.

fact than the related inquiries subsequently conducted by Sir Richard Scott[51] and Lord Hutton.[52] These inquiries elicited documents and information which would certainly have been denied select committees, they subjected witnesses to some skilful cross-examination, and made detailed findings of fact. No select committee could possibly achieve this quality of investigation and report. However, even where inquiries are independently and professionally conducted and critical findings of fact are made, it is all too easy for ministers to escape responsibility in the sense of acknowledging culpability. Thus, as we have noted, ministers disputed some of the adverse findings of the Scott Report and, with the government majority in Parliament, were able to escape formal censure or resignation.[53]

The Hutton Report exonerated the government from 'sexing up' the dossier published in September 2002 on the case for attacking Iraq. But the press and public opinion were not convinced by these findings,[54] and a further inquiry was established by the Foreign and Commonwealth Office under Lord Butler of Brockwell[55] in February 2004 to investigate intelligence in the lead-up to the war. This report was far more critical, though written in civil service code sometimes known as 'Mandarin'. It is not easy to pin responsibility on a government that claims that it has not erred. Again, this raises questions about the capabilities and capacities of select committees in holding government to account. Should some of these accountability functions be transferred to independent expert bodies reporting to Parliament? And, given the current concerns about the Government's response to Ombudsman reports, what clout could or should such bodies and parliamentary committees have if this were done?

Parliamentary committees have themselves expressed concern about their capacity or capability in holding government to account – in imposing ministerial responsibility. The Joint Committee on Human Rights called for the establishment of an independent organization to oversee the security services, MI5 and MI6, after the director general of MI5 refused to answer their questions about counter-terror laws, and also to examine claims by government based on intelligence information.[56] In August 2006 the PASC published a report calling for an *independent* investigation into the *Ministerial Code*.[57] A strong body of evidence is building up to the effect that it is beyond the capacity, perhaps beyond the wish, of MPs, to carry out the detailed scrutiny of government (and its Bills and statutory instruments) that modern conditions require, and that independent non-political bodies, possibly with coercive powers, may be better placed to perform this function.

The ways in which departmental select committees are composed has attracted criticism over the years. By convention each committee has a majority of government party members,

51 See Sir Richard Scott, *Report on the Export of Dual-Use Goods to Iraq*, HC 115 (1995–96); see also articles on this report in [1996] *Public Law*.

52 *Report of the Inquiry into the Circumstances Surrounding the Death of Dr David Kelly C.M.G. by Lord Hutton*, HC 247, 28 Jan. 2004.

53 See for instance D. Oliver, 'The Scott Report' [1996] *Public Law* 357; see also A. Tomkins, *The Constitution After Scott* (1998).

54 For Lord Hutton's response to media criticism of his report see Lord Hutton 'The media reaction to the Hutton Report' [2006] *Public Law* 807.

55 *Review of Intelligence on Weapons of Mass Destruction*, HC 898 (2004–05).

56 See Joint Committee on Human Rights 24th Report 2005–06 *Counter-Terrorism Policy and Human Rights: Prosecution and Pre-Charge Detention*, HL 240, HC 1576, para. 164.

57 *The Ministerial Code: the case for independent* investigation HC 1457 (2005–06).

and each party's whips decide which of their own party members shall be nominated to each committee. The parties make their own arrangements as to consultation on the selection of members of committees drawn from their number. The chairs are shared between the political parties in rough proportion to the balance in the House. By convention certain committees are chaired by opposition backbenchers. The Modernisation Committee proposed[58] that nomination to committee membership should be made by a select committee that would be independent of the whips, but this was rejected by the House. These committees remain therefore vulnerable to manipulation by the party machines.

In October 2003 the House of Commons resolved that the chairs of the investigative committees should receive additional salaries of £12,500 per annum in recognition of the extra workload they carry, and with a view to providing an alternative career path for backbenchers who might otherwise seek or accept government appointment. But it was also agreed that committee chairs would serve for only two Parliaments. A difficulty here is that the chairs' reliance on the whips for their reappointment to committees after an election, and thus the additional salary, may undermine their independence. The extent of the patronage of the whips is increased by this provision, contrary to the spirit of the Modernisation Committee report. And it would be surprising if a Committee chair were to turn down an offer of a government appointment simply for the sake of the salary that goes with the chair.

ASSESSMENT OF HOUSE OF COMMONS REFORM

On the face of it there has been a great deal of reform of the House of Commons since the election of 1997, and indeed since 1979 (when a new system of departmental select committees was introduced). But it is questionable whether the reforms overall have really increased the effectiveness of the House in holding the government to account. Some – such as timetabling of Bills, noted above – have undermined it. With a large majority a government has little to fear for its legislation from the Commons and can weather the embarrassment of criticism from select committees.

Unless the ethos and politics of the House of Commons and its members are to change, reform is likely to add up to little more than tinkering. Robin Cook, former Leader of the House, noted that the House is highly tribal, and that the parties which make up the tribal groupings, though they are rivals and competitive with one another, are attached to and defensive of the tribal system itself.[59] There is no real sense that the House of Commons is or ought to be autonomous in its relations with government or independent of the parties that operate in the House.[60] As we have seen, in 2002 the House deliberately rejected an opportunity to increase independence by reforming the process for appointment of members of select committees. Unlike the Scottish Parliament, which has its Parliamentary Bureau,[61] the House of Commons places its business in the hands of the Leader of the House (a member of the Cabinet appointed as Leader by the Prime Minister) in informal consultation with the whips through the 'usual channels'.

58 First Report, HC 221 (2001–2).

59 *Parliament and the People: Modernisation of the House of Commons*, Hansard Society (2002).

60 See B. Winetrobe, 'The Autonomy of Parliament', in Oliver and Drewry (eds), *The Law and Parliament* (1998).

61 See Chapter 9.

The politics of the House cannot change radically unless elections produce small majorities or hung parliaments, and these outcomes are unlikely without proportional representation – or party splits. Neither seems likely in the foreseeable future. It is, in other words, unrealistic to believe that the elected chamber could perform all the functions commonly expected of it. Party politicians who rely on election and their parties for their positions can only perform party political functions. Those functions, of giving or refusing consent to legislation, providing a forum for opposition and a training ground for an alternative government, are essential in a democracy. But so is the performance of other, non-partisan, functions of standard-based scrutiny of legislation, inquiry into and report on complex issues, remedying of maladministration. These have to be performed elsewhere and by people with different qualities.

It seems likely that governmental desires to marginalize Parliament and recognition of the limitations in the capacities and capabilities of MPs to hold government to account will lead to calls for independent expert bodies to be involved in the accountability system. However, some of the concerns about the House of Commons and its relationship with government may influence proposals for reform or modernization of the House of Lords, to which we now turn.

THE HOUSE OF LORDS

The House of Lords is undoubtedly a constitutional anachronism. The membership consists of hereditary peers and life peers, and archbishops and bishops of the Church of England (who are not peers and serve until retirement). The Prime Minister decides how many new members should be appointed to the House, how many new members each party should have and consequently the party balance, and how many new cross-benchers (members who do not take a party whip) there should be. There is no statutory or other formal regulation of this power, which is an exercise of the Royal Prerogative. As a matter of practice when appointing peers from other parties, the Prime Minister does so on the nomination of the leader of that party. These party nominees are expected to take their party whip. There is no regulation of the ways in which the parties select these members, although there is a general understanding, not always observed, that award of a peerage is an honour which should normally only be granted to people who have achieved distinction in their lives. Nor are there any other formal criteria (e.g. merit or the needs of the House of Lords for particular experience or expertise in its membership) for these appointments.

Before nominees are appointed they are subject to scrutiny, for propriety only, by a non-statutory Appointments Commission that was established in 2000.[62] In 2006 concerns were raised that persons who had made loans to parties before the 2005 general election had been nominated for peerages as rewards for the financial support. The concerns were raised by the Appointments Commission, partly because the making of loans had not been disclosed to them. There was also public concern that criminal offences may have been committed. As of May 2007 the Director of Public Prosecutions is considering whether there is evidence sufficient to justify prosecutions. But the Appointments Commission has no veto on appointments even if it is not satisfied as to propriety. The Appointments Commission is

[62] See House of Lords Appointments Commission website www.lordsappointments.gov.uk.

also charged with nominating independent members for appointment to the House of Lords. The Prime Minister however reserves the right to make some independent appointments, for instance of immediate past holders of public positions including the Speaker of the House of Commons, the Cabinet Secretary, the Chief of the Defence Staff, the Queen's Principal Private Secretary, and the Archbishops of Canterbury and York.

As of January 2007 the membership of the House of Lords was as follows: 92 hereditary peers; up to 26 archbishops and bishops of the Church of England; 608 life peers, appointed by the Queen on the advice of the Prime Minister, to be members of the House for life.

The life peers included:[63]

Members taking the Labour whip	207
Members taking the Conservative whip	159
Members taking the Liberal Democrat whip	73
Lords of Appeal in Ordinary and retired Lords of Appeal	26
Other cross-benchers who take no party whip	176
Others	11

The presence of hereditary peers and archbishops and bishops of the Church of England requires explanation. Until 1999 membership included some 750 hereditary peers. The House of Lords Act 1999 removed all hereditary peers from membership of the House, save for 75, who were elected by the body of hereditary peers in proportion to the then party allegiance or cross-bench membership of all hereditary peers, two hereditary Great Officers of State, and a further 15, elected to membership by all the then members of the House to serve as office holders, for example as deputy speakers. When one of the 75 hereditary members elected by hereditary peers dies, runners-up from the 1999 election take their place. When one of the 15 holders of office dies (as happened in 2003) the whole House elects a replacement from among the hereditary peers who wish to stand for election. The Clerk of the Parliaments (a permanent official of the House) maintains a register of those peers.[64]

Up to 26 archbishops and bishops of the Church of England become members of the House of Lords by seniority of appointment as bishops, and they serve until retirement, normally at 70. They are not life peers. They sit on the Bishops' Benches as Lords Spiritual.

The overall allegiance of members of the House of Lords (including hereditary peers) as of January 2007 was as follows:[65]

Conservative	206
Labour	211
Liberal Democrat	78
Crossbench	202
Bishops	26

63 See www.parliament.uk/directories/house_of_lords_information_office.

64 Lord Weatherill introduced the House of Lords (Amendment) Bill (HL 32) in the House of Lords in Feb. 2003, which if enacted would have ended the system of replacing hereditary peers by election. The number of hereditary peers in the House of Lords would thus, over time, diminish.

65 See Parliament web site, supra.

These figures excluded seven 'others' and 12 peers on leave of absence.

Thus, no one party has a majority in the House of Lords. Party affiliation is not proportionate to the level of support for the parties in the 2005 election; nor indeed is it rationally or explicitly related to any other measure.

Despite its anomalies, the House of Lords is in many respects a highly regarded and effective chamber in much of what it does. It is one of the busiest parliamentary chambers in the world.[66] Although its members are part-time it is a full-time house. Increasingly its best work is done in committees and is of a non-partisan, technical, expert, or constitutional kind.

CONCEPTUALIZING THE ROLE AND FUNCTIONS OF A SECOND CHAMBER

It is not easy to reconcile the facts that the House of Lords' members are for the most part party aligned and are not elected, and yet that it is an effective chamber, with democratic principles. At root the problem is how we conceptualize institutions called 'chambers of parliament', and how we conceptualize the House of Lords in particular. Generally chambers of Parliament are bodies through which consent is given on behalf of the electorate or, in the case of second chambers in federal systems, on behalf of the members of the federation, to legislation proposed by the government and to the granting of supply. Consent to legislation and supply is in practice given or refused conditionally upon the government maintaining the confidence of the chamber through discharge of its duties to give an account of its conduct of government and its policies. Chambers of Parliament are elected for the very reason that, in a democracy, only the people through their elected representatives have the right to give consent to legislation. The House of Lords does not fit this model at all.

This is not however a full picture of the consent-giving – or perhaps more appropriately, consent-refusing – processes in democracies operating under the Rule of Law. We have already noted that in some countries other bodies besides the Parliament have the right to refuse consent to legislation or to set aside legislation passed by the parliament. For instance, supreme courts in many countries may strike down or disapply legislation on grounds of unconstitutionality. Constitutional councils or councils of state pronounce on matters such as the constitutionality or workability of legislation or draft legislation and this may affect the eventual validity of laws.[67] Arrangements of this kind exist even in countries with elected second chambers, such as France, suggesting perhaps that elected bodies are not suited to the performance of these functions and so additional institutions should play a part in the legislative process. Consent-refusing activity carried out by such independent, unelected, expert bodies is a central part of the democratic arrangements in those countries: democracy there is not taken to mean that elected legislators in the Parliament are entitled to pass, on bare majorities of those present and voting, any law they wish, regardless of its compatibility with the constitution, human rights, or international obligations. Such consent-refusing activity by external institutions is not possible in relation to primary legislation

66 See for instance its Annual Report, e.g. HL Paper 41, 2004–05.

67 See for instance, in relation to France, J. Bell, *French Constitutional Law* (1992); J. Massot, 'Legislative drafting in France: The Role of the Conseil d'Etat' (2001) 22 *Statute Law Review* 96–107.

passed by the UK Parliament because of the almost uniquely British doctrine of parliamentary sovereignty.[68]

Second chambers in countries with federal systems normally have special functions in representing the regions, states or provinces and concerning themselves principally with federal matters. In a non-federal state like the UK, whose devolution arrangements are asymmetrical and evolving,[69] the potential role of a second chamber in representing and protecting the interests of the nations and regions is less clear than in federal states. In most bicameral states, all of which have written constitutions, second chambers also have functions as constitutional watchdogs, their consent being required to constitutional amendments and other constitutional measures, often with a requirement for a special majority in each House.[70] Given the fact that the UK, almost uniquely, has no written constitution and a sovereign Parliament (in the special sense that its legislation on any subject matter will be given effect to by the courts, unless it is incompatible with European Community law),[71] it would not be possible for the UK's second chamber to perform the same kind of watchdog role as can second chambers in states with written constitutions. Nonetheless it is natural that the House of Lords, being less political than the House of Commons, should have come to be looked to as a kind of constitutional watchdog. This is strongly reflected in its committee work. And given the operation of the electoral and party systems, which, as has been noted, mean that almost invariably the government has a safe majority in the House of Commons, the House of Lords is accepted as having a role in making the government and the House of Commons think again about controversial legislation and about the quality of legislation – drafting, workability and so on.

The capacity of the House of Lords to perform its relatively apolitical functions has been incrementally increased in important ways in recent years. This is because the party-aligned members are relatively free from party pressures, being there for life; they have their careers behind them and thus normally have no ambitions for a future career in politics. The presence of members mostly of distinction and with experience and expertise in matters coming before the House has enabled its debates to be authoritative and well informed. Cross-benchers will often hold the balance in the House, and this means that the parties seeking the support of cross-benchers – as will often be the case since no one party has a majority in the House – have to argue the issues on the merits rather than appeal to party loyalty.

THE HOUSE OF LORDS IN ACTION

The House of Lords has established important and influential select committees to perform some watchdog functions. We have already noted the role of the Joint Committee on Human Rights, established in February 2001, in scrutinizing all Bills and draft Bills for human rights implications and generally commenting on human rights issues.[72] The House of Lords Constitution Committee was formed in 2001 in response to the recommendation of the Royal Commission on Reform of the House of Lords that the role of the second

[68] See Chapter 2. The exception to the doctrine of parliamentary sovereignty is that European law prevails over inconsistent UK legislation: see Chapters 2 and 4.

[69] See Chapters 9, 10 and 11.

[70] For a comparative study of second chambers see M. Russell, *Reforming the House of Lords: Lessons from Overseas* (2000); S. C. Patterson and A. Mughan, *Senates: Bicameralism in the Contemporary World* (1999).

[71] See discussion in Chapters 1, 2 and 4.

[72] See also discussion in Chapter 3.

chamber as a constitutional 'longstop' should be increased, not by increasing the formal powers of the House to delay or veto legislation but through the establishment of a Constitutional Affairs Committee which would monitor legislation for constitutional issues and generally keep a watching brief on the constitution.[73]

The House of Lords' European Union Committee undertakes in-depth scrutiny of selected items of EU business, through its six subcommittees. The reports are widely regarded in Europe as being of extremely high quality and are capable of having a significant influence on European policy development. The Delegated Powers and Regulatory Reform Committee scrutinizes proposals in Bills for the delegation of powers and reports to the House whether the provisions of any Bill inappropriately delegate legislative power, or whether they subject the exercise of legislative power to an inappropriate degree of parliamentary scrutiny. (There is no parallel in the House of Commons with the scrutiny of delegated powers functions of the Lords, so this is a function, essentially constitutional in nature, performed uniquely by the Lords.) The Committee's functions were extended into the scrutiny of deregulation orders under the Deregulation and Contracting Out Act 1994 and the Regulatory Reform Act 2001. They will be further extended as the Legislative and Regulatory Reform Act 2006 comes into force.

What has been happening in the UK, then, is that functions performed by supreme or constitutional courts or councils of state or constitutional councils in other countries are being institutionalized and internalized in the second chamber. They are intra-, not extra-parliamentary. But the ability of the chamber to perform those functions, and the legitimacy of its doing so, depend upon its composition and in particular the degree of party political penetration of its intrinsically apolitical, constitutional, functions.

Self-restraint on the part of the politicians in the House is necessary to counter the predictable allegations of illegitimacy that will be made where Commons Bills are opposed by unelected members on party political rather than constitutional or other non-partisan grounds.[74] Ultimately, under the Parliament Acts 1911 and 1949 a Bill may receive the royal assent without the consent of the House of Lords.[75] The Royal Commission on Reform of the House of Lords considered whether further conventions might be elaborated to give effect to a principle that the second chamber should be cautious about challenging the clearly expressed views of the House of Commons on any public policy issue, whether or not contained in the election manifesto of the governing party. But it felt that it was not possible to reduce this principle to a simple formula, and proposed that the second chamber should pragmatically work out a new convention reflecting the principles.[76] If necessary a new conciliation mechanism should be developed through a joint committee. Neither of these proposals has been implemented. We have already noted the recommendations of the Joint Committee on Conventions which reported in November 2006 that one or both Houses should pass resolutions recording formulations of the understandings between Parliament and the government. No conciliation mechanism has been proposed.

73 *A House for the Future*, Cm 4534 (2000).

74 A degree of self-restraint is observed under the Salisbury convention, noted earlier.

75 See for instance *Jackson* v. *Attorney-General* [2006] 1 AC 262.

76 Royal Commission, Report on the Future of the House of Lords, noted above, at pp. 40–1.

MATCHING FUNCTION AND COMPOSITION IN THE HOUSE OF LORDS

Despite general agreement that the House of Lords performs important functions well and that it should continue to do so, and that these are functions that ought to be performed in any democratic system, the composition of the House, in the sense of the routes by which members arrive there and the terms on which they serve, is controversial. This is because they are not elected, and yet the House is conceptualized as an orthodox chamber of Parliament. The natural starting point or assumption in a democracy is that a second chamber – at least a conventional second chamber – should be elected: its members have powers in the legislative process and ought to be dismissible by the electorate, and they ought to reflect the electorate's views about the government's legislative programme. But there is also a common assumption that election of some or all of the members of the second chamber would not have any impact on the performance of the house in legislative scrutiny. In my view this assumption is misplaced. As we shall see there is no consensus in favour of election of all or even part of the House of Lords. I think this is largely because of a realisation, perhaps unarticulated, that election would have a negative effect on the performance of its scrutiny functions by the second chamber.

Ways of 'modernizing' the appointment process will be discussed below. Before doing so it is worth exploring the implications of these natural assumptions in favour of election to the second chamber. Election of a substantial proportion of the members of the second chamber would create severe problems in the British constitution. First, the Commons is the pre-eminent chamber because it provides the government and can remove it and because it has sole responsibility for the raising and spending of taxation. What would be the point of a wholly or substantially elected second chamber? Its position in relations with the Commons and with government could either be as a pointless rubber stamp for government decisions, or as a body that, having democratic legitimacy from election, could hold up government legislation for partisan party political reasons.

Secondly, an elected or substantially elected house would not, in my view, add value to the legislative process. A second chamber that was able to paralyse on party political grounds a government supported by a majority in an elected first chamber would tip the balance too far away from effectiveness and towards populism. The balance would not be right. It may well be that the House of Commons should be further reformed, for instance, through the introduction of proportional representation. But introducing a substantial elected element into the House of Lords will not make up for the defects in the House of Commons.

Lastly, in my view elected members would not be well fitted to perform the important scrutiny and watchdog functions that the House of Lords performs. These functions require substantial numbers of impartial and expert members not only among the cross-benchers but also among party-aligned members. If party lists were drawn up by the parties regionally it is likely that they would be dominated by people from the region and with special interests and expertise in the affairs of the region, but without the other qualities required for the exercise of the second chamber's functions. Further, people who do have the necessary combination of qualities would be unlikely to be willing to stand for election on a party ticket. Many such people are not politically committed and are not aligned with political parties, or if aligned would not want to go through the process of submitting themselves for selection to stand for election and then standing for election. The point, already made, is that many of the functions the House of Lords performs are of the kind that are performed in other countries, and rightly so, by independent non-politicians with particular expertise and experience often outside politics. The present arrangements do provide people with the required expertise and impartiality, and they work in conditions which promote and respect that impartiality and do not expose them to undue party political pressure. Election could not in my view be expected to provide sufficient numbers of appropriately qualified people.

PROPOSALS FOR REFORM OF THE COMPOSITION OF THE SECOND CHAMBER

The Royal Commission on the Reform of the House of Lords recommended in 2000 that the hereditary members should be removed, and the Prime Minister should no longer have the right to appoint to the Second Chamber. The Church of England's representation should be reduced to 16. An independent statutory Appointments Commission should be established with responsibility for appointments. Membership should include up to 35 per cent elected people, 20 per cent independents and the rest appointed party aligned members. Overall the party membership should reflect the proportion of the vote won by parties at the most recent general election. The Appointments Commission should move towards a gender and ethnic balance, secure that a range of 'voices' were in the second chamber, and use 10 places for members of Christian denominations other than the Church of England and other faiths.[77] These proposals did not find favour on a number of grounds. The parties did not want 'their' nominees to be subject to the Appointments Commission. And public opinion seemed to favour election (while at the same time not wanting partisan party politics in the second chamber). In February 2003 both Houses debated and voted on a range of possible options for reform of the composition of the second chamber, ranging from a wholly elected through various percentages of elected members to a wholly appointed House. There was a majority in the House of Lords for a wholly appointed House, and no majority in the House of Commons for any of the options put to it, though overall there was more support for a substantially elected House than for a wholly or substantially appointed one.

In March 2007 both Houses debated the proposals in the Government's White Paper *The House of Lords: Reform.*[78] These were put forward by the Leader of the House of Commons, Jack Straw, who had sought cross-party support for the reform of the composition of the House. The proposals envisaged the House continuing to perform is present functions, but altering the composition by removal of the remaining hereditary peers, reducing the number of Church of England Bishops and Archbishops, providing for election of 50 per cent of the members, and putting the Appointments Commission on a statutory basis. It would be charged with responsibility for appointment of 20 per cent of the members as cross-benchers, and of the remaining party members.

Each House voted on a range of proportions of elected members. The preference of the House of Commons was for 100 per cent elected. This was unexpected since there had seemed to be general agreement that a proportion of the members should be cross-benchers. The preference of the House of Lords was for 100 per cent appointed.

[77] *A House for the Future* Cm 4534, January 2000, Chapter 12.

[78] Cm 7027.

As of May 2007 it is not clear whether, when or how the Government will take the matter of reform of the second chamber forward, but it seems unlikely that further legislation will be introduced by the Government until after the next general election, expected in 2009, when proposals for reform may be included in party manifestos. The 'mandate' that election is said to provide may then help to break the deadlock.

A number of general points need to be noted. The major concerns are that the House should have legitimacy, that it should continue to be able to perform its functions in relation to the scrutiny of legislation and policy and as a constitutional watchdog as well as it does currently, and that it should be a representative civic forum for many aspects of society, as the Royal Commission had proposed.

The role of the proposed independent statutory Appointments Commission in relation to party nominations needs to be clarified, if one is established, especially in the light of the 'cash for peerages' concerns which arose in 2006 when it was disclosed that in the 2005 general election loans had been made to parties by persons who were in due course nominated for peerages. The loans had not been disclosed to the Appointments Commission or to the Electoral Commission and it was alleged that peerages had been offered in exchange for these financial contributions. In my view what are commonly regarded as 'Nolan principles'[79] of appointment on merit in relation to appointments generally should be followed. The parties seem to assume that they should be entitled to have those they nominate appointed to any vacancies, subject only to vetting for propriety, and that this is a matter for the exercise of patronage outside any criteria to do with the job to be done or the needs of the House, or to do with the qualities or suitability of the person put forward for appointment.

If the parties themselves are not placed under any kinds of obligation or pressure to put forward nominations that will enable the House overall to reflect the make-up of society (for instance as to gender or ethnic balance, or national or regional interests, or occupation or experience) or meet the needs of the House (for instance for particular expertise to enable it to perform its functions), the Appointments Commission would not be able to do so from the relatively modest proportion of appointments of independent members for which it would have responsibility. It would be entirely possible for the parties to put forward only members with track records of making donations to the party or of party political activity in, for instance, local government or the House of Commons, and not people with expertise which the House might need, for instance in (in alphabetical order) the arts, commerce, constitutionalism, culture, the economy, ethics, European matters, foreign affairs, human rights, law, medicine, national and regional interests, social policy, and so on. In other words, the House might not be able to perform its functions if party patronage is not regulated under a new statutory scheme. This could result in a need to 'externalize' many of the functions currently performed by the second chamber through, for instance a council of state, or a constitutional council, or a US or German style supreme or constitutional court.

This consideration points either to the parties themselves being placed under explicit statutory obligations to bring forward appropriate nominations to meet the needs of the House and merit criteria, or to the Appointments Commission imposing some kind of a

79 See Chapter 17 and Reports of the Committee on Standards in Public Life, First Report (*Seven Principles of Public Life*) and Sixth Report (*Public Appointments*).

veto or filter process over party nominations to secure that those appointed meet the needs of the House and merit criteria as well as the needs of the parties.

It is worth observing at this point that such a filtering or veto power could in practice suit the parties or their leaders since they would be able to resist pressure from members seeking the exercise of party patronage in their favour to confer the status of a peerage and membership of the House, on the ground that they were required to take account of the general needs of the House and their own needs for spokespersons on particular issues as well as the intrinsic merits of those aspiring to appointment.

A further difficulty would arise if members of the second chamber were entitled to retire from it and then stand for election to the House of Commons or the European Parliament. The Royal Commission strongly recommended that it should not be possible for people who had served in the second chamber to stand for election, or to do so save after a period in quarantine after leaving the House, as they considered that it would be contrary to the relatively non-partisan ethos of the House for members to be able to treat it as a stepping stone to a subsequent political career.

Overall the possible reforms of the composition of the House of Lords will have important repercussions for the UK's 'political constitution'. If the ability of the House of Lords to perform its functions is undermined by new provisions as to its composition, then inevitably a need will arise, and be argued for, for those functions to be entrusted to external bodies of the kinds mentioned above. Indeed if a reformed House of Lords were less able to perform its legislative scrutiny work it is not unthinkable that the courts might feel justified in dealing with provisions that they consider to be contrary to fundamental constitutional principles[80] by either declaring them to be unconstitutional (though valid) or refusing to give effect to them.[81] That would not be the best way of dealing with constitutionality in the absence of a written constitution but it might be better than leaving matters to a Parliament that lacks the capacity and commitment to prevent such laws being passed.

CONCLUSIONS

The 'modernization' of Parliament means many things. The House of Commons' committee system has been modernized, in the sense of being better resourced. The legislative process has been modernized so as to facilitate the passage of the government's legislation. However there is growing concern that the Commons lacks the capacity, even the will to carry out the legislative scrutiny and accountability tasks it has been expected to perform. Modernization has failed to deal with the principal modern problem, the facts that the government is not sufficiently accountable to the electorate via Parliament for its conduct of government and that there are few mechanisms other than electoral accountability to secure good government and good legislation. This is largely because of the domination of the House of Commons by the governing party.

The chamber that is not dominated by the party of government – and which the government admitted in establishing the Royal Commission should not be so

[80] See Chapters 1 and 2. [81] See *Jackson* v. *Attorney-General* [2006] 1 AC 262.

dominated – is the House of Lords.[82] 'Modernization' by way of a system of independent appointments could mark the move to a new, more modern, concept of democracy and representation than is implicit in the often sterile concentration on election, mandates, and majorities.[83] A well-designed independent appointment system, coupled perhaps with election of a proportion of members by regions and nations, could secure a membership that included the expertise and experience that the House needs to fulfil its legislative scrutiny functions. It could secure a House that was reflective of the voices of sectors of society that are not heard in the Commons. It could move towards a more deliberative, participatory style of democracy such as was discussed in Chapter 6. It would allow independence of judgement in that chamber. Such independence could encourage rational rather than partisan debate and bring out the constitutional and human rights implications of much legislation which are not always obvious or palatable to ministers. The legitimacy of such a House should not be problematic so long as it develops explicit conventions to determine when it will defer to the elected House and when it will not do so. The implication of recent developments is that the two Houses are diverging, the Commons becoming the party political House through which consent is given or refused to government and its measures, the Lords becoming a hybrid between a council of state, a civic forum,[84] and a modified political House. This evolution is a rather typical and in many respects serendipitous British compromise. The House of Lords performs important functions which the House of Commons cannot be expected to perform. However, the signs are that the government, members of the House of Commons, and the press are rejecting this path. The general preference seems to be for election and/or a patronage-based, not merit-based, system of appointment for all but the independent members.

The continuation of reasonably amicable and workable relationships between the two Houses and between them and the government depends upon self-restraint on all sides and in particular on the House of Lords limiting its party political activity and emphasizing its constitutional role. If this does not happen it is inevitable that moves will be made towards another kind of 'modernization', the election of all or a substantial part of the House. The pros and cons of this have been noted above. But a point to bear in mind is that if the House of Lords were to become substantially politicized through elections, there would be a major new lacuna in our constitutional checks and balances. In my view the case for moving to a written constitution with a supreme court with power to strike down unconstitutional legislation, and a constitutional council or council of state with powers of pre-legislative scrutiny of draft Bills for workability and compatibility with important constitutional principles, would then become overwhelming. This would reduce the freedom of action of the House of Commons and the government. In other words, the trend from a political to a law-based constitution would be accelerated by politicization of the House of Lords.

[82] The terms of reference of the Royal Commission are set out at the beginning of the Report, Cm 4534 (see n. 59 above).

[83] See discussion in Chapter 6.

[84] See T. Wright and A. Gamble, 'Is the party over?' (2002) 73 *Political Quarterly* 123.

FURTHER READING

Blackburn, R. and Kennon, A. (eds) with Sir Michael Wheeler-Booth *Griffith and Ryle on Parliament. Functions, Practice and Procedures*, (2nd edn, 2003).

Erskine May, *Parliamentary Practice*, (22nd edn, 1997).

Hansard Society Commission on the Legislative Process *The Challenge for Parliament. Making Government Accountable* (2001).

Report of the Royal Commission on the Reform of the House of Lords *A House for the Future*, Cm 4534 (January 2000).

Rogers, R. and Walters, R. *How Parliament Works* (6th edn, 2006).

Russell, M. *Reforming the House of Lords. Lessons from Overseas* (2000).

The House of Lords: Reform (Cm 7027).

USEFUL WEB SITES

www.parliament.uk

www.cabinet-office.gov.uk

8

THE EXECUTIVE: TOWARDS ACCOUNTABLE GOVERNMENT AND EFFECTIVE GOVERNANCE?

Gavin Drewry

SUMMARY

We sometimes talk about modern constitutions as if there is a clear-cut distinction between 'executive', 'legislative', and 'judicial' functions. This way of thinking originated in the notion of separation of powers, formulated by Montesquieu in the eighteenth century. But, today, even in the USA, the tripartite division of 'powers' is far from watertight. The UK constitution is based upon a fusion between executive and legislative powers, in which ministers are also members of the legislature.

The traditional British view of the executive needs to be revised in line with new models of decision making based on sectoral policy networks and policy communities. How much of the eighteenth-century concept of an 'executive' has survived the growth of complex bureaucracies, in which the boundary between the respective functions of ministers and civil servants has become increasingly blurred?

Locating the latter boundary has become more difficult in the wake of a New Public Management (NPM) revolution that has transformed the public services of many developed countries, including the UK. Governments, influenced by free market economic theories, have, on the one hand, sought to diminish the scale of state intervention and, on the other, have increasingly questioned the efficiency of traditional bureaucracy and have come to prefer more market-orientated, performance-driven and 'business-like' modes of public service delivery. In the UK there has been a long series of important public sector reforms, including privatization, contracting out and the Citizen's Charter, subsequently incorporated into a wider agenda of public service modernization. One of the UK's most significant NPM reforms was the Next Steps programme, launched in 1988, which transferred many of the functions of central government departments to semi-independent agencies, headed by chief executives employed on short-term contracts – many of them recruited from outside the civil service.

Cumulatively, all these reforms have had very important implications for ministerial responsibility, for parliamentary scrutiny of government, and for the structure of the civil service itself. This is one reason for welcoming the Blair Government's commitment – albeit slow in implementation – to formalizing the position of civil servants through the enactment of a Civil Service Act.

INTRODUCTION

The familiar word 'executive' which features in the title of this chapter is more problematical that might at first be supposed. Much constitutional discourse still revolves around traditional 'separation of powers' distinctions between executives, legislatures, and judiciaries. But, as this chapter will show, in an age in which traditional notions of 'government' have given way to the broader and more flexible concept of 'governance', and as policy making is seen as a complex and evolving process, conducted in an array of specialized policy networks with varied and shifting memberships, it has become unfashionable to depict the modern executive function as being confined merely to presidents, prime ministers, and cabinets and (by extension) their civil servants.

This shift in the terminology is linked to the growing complexity of the relationship between political and bureaucratic office holders – ministers and civil servants. The comfortingly democratic idea that the 'policy' decisions that matter are taken by ministers, accountable to citizens via the ballot box (and in the UK, to Parliament), while civil servants merely play a subordinate 'administrative' role has long been recognized as a myth. The constitutional doctrine of ministerial responsibility suggests that ministers should account to Parliament for all the actions of their officials, but in an era of 'big government' in which ministries are large, fragmented, and decentralized, this too is largely a mythical aspiration. This gap between fact and fiction has, as we shall see, been exacerbated (or at least consolidated) in recent years by 'new public management' (NPM) developments, such as the Next Steps agency programme.

So today – for reasons that this chapter will seek to explain – the meaning of the term 'executive', and the constitutional character of the executive function, have become afflicted by much doubt and confusion. And this ambiguity poses particular difficulty when we seek to determine who is responsible for what, and who is to be held accountable, and by what means, for the deeds and misdeeds of a government.

THE EXECUTIVE AND SEPARATION OF POWERS – THE HISTORY OF AN IDEAL

Everyday usage of the term executive often refers to a mechanism or an office-holder *in charge* of an organization or a process, responsible for making sure that things run efficiently and that goals are met. Thus, we encounter various species of executive officers, chief executives, and executive committees, running bodies of various types – private companies, hospitals, and local authorities; and most UK civil servants now work in 'Next Steps' executive agencies (discussed later in this chapter), responsible for the delivery of major central government services and headed by agency chief executives. The word is also associated with the function of 'execution', particularly in legal contexts: for instance, the execution of a warrant or of a death sentence, or being the executor of a will. But this meaning is quite different from being 'in charge'; on the contrary, it has much more to do with carrying out the instructions of a higher authority.

The meaning of the term executive and the nature and the boundaries of executive office and of the executive function become even more complex and elusive when applied to national governments and considered in the context of a 'changing constitution'. Those familiar with the doctrine of separation of powers – associated originally with the writings of the eighteenth-century French philosopher, Montesquieu, and then enshrined in the United States Constitution – have probably become accustomed to structuring their thinking about governmental arrangements around the ostensibly simple tripartite array of 'legislatures', 'executives', and 'judiciaries'. But even 250 years ago, when Montesquieu wrote his famous work, *The Spirit of the Laws*, this constitutional model begged a lot of questions.

The modern usage of the term began with the founding and early development of the US Constitution – and with discussions among the founding fathers about 'separation of powers' and ways of safeguarding liberty under the law. But there is an important *pre-history* of that debate wherein the meaning of the term executive became entangled with the early intermixing of 'executive' and 'judicial' (and indeed 'legislative') functions in the absolute monarchies of feudal Europe.

The doctrine of separation of powers may in fact be traced back to the ancient Greek and Roman belief in 'mixed government': ordered in such a way as to ensure the accommodation of different social orders and interests – foreshadowing the more modern constitutional notion of checks and balances enshrined in the US Constitution. Centuries later, medieval writers began to refer to a distinction between *making* law and *putting it into effect*: but in those days the latter was usually taken to refer to the role of the courts in applying the law (we must remember in this context that English absolute monarchs used to dispense justice in their high court of Parliament).

This interpretation of executive power in judicial terms survived in the work of John Locke, writing in context of the seventeenth-century English conflicts between Parliament and monarchy. His *Second Treatise on Government* (1690) moved on from the Greek notion of mixed government, by advocating a two-way institutional/functional separation between legislative and executive powers (though the latter was still essentially seen in the 'judicial' sense, just described).

Institutional developments in the aftermath of the seventeenth-century Cromwellian interregnum paved the way for a more developed notion of executive power in the modern sense of applying the law by *administrative* rather than judicial means. This was the sense in which Montesquieu used the term in *The Spirit of the Laws*, first published in 1748:

> Where the legislative and executive powers are united in the same person or body there can be no liberty, because apprehensions may arise lest the same monarch or senate should enact tyrannical laws to execute them in a tyrannical manner.

This argument was taken up by James Madison in one of *The Federalist Papers*[1] which argued the case for ratification of the US Constitution. Madison had to concede that in

[1] The generic title of the 85 essays, written by Alexander Hamilton, John Jay, and James Madison, that were published in New York newspapers between autumn 1787 and spring 1788. The one referred to here is essay XLVII, Feb. 1788.

England the legislative, executive, and judicial branches were far from being as separate and as distinct from one another as Montesquieu had claimed, but he argued (somewhat tendentiously) that Montesquieu clearly can only have meant:

> No more than this, that when the *whole* power of one department is exercised by the same hands which possess the *whole* power of another department, the fundamental principles of a free constitution are subverted.

Madison went on to show that none of the existing constitutions of the then American States, working to formulate and agree the new federal constitution, while they might pay lip-service to separation of powers, displayed in fact a complete functional separation. And he went on to develop the notion of checks and balances between the constituent branches, summed up in one of the earlier Federalist essays,[2] which begins:

> To what expedient, then, shall we finally resort, for maintaining in practice the necessary partition of power among the several departments, as laid down in the Constitution? The only answer that can be given is, that as all these exterior provisions [such as setting out functional boundaries in the Constitution, and hoping everyone abides by them] are found to be inadequate, the defect must be supplied, *by so contriving the interior structure of the government as that its several constituent parts may, by their mutual relations, be the means of keeping each other in their proper places.* [emphasis added]

The founding fathers linked their perception of the need to avoid combining the legislative and executive functions to their concerns about preserving the Rule of Law. If the same institution/ruler both makes the laws and interprets/applies them, then those laws can be redefined according to the whim and caprice of that ruler, and no citizen can be certain about the limits of lawful conduct. And this poses a fundamental threat to liberty – the right of the individual to do whatever is not prohibited by law.

SEPARATION OF POWERS IN THE UK?

But of course the constitutional picture was and is very different in England (unsurprisingly so, given that the American founding fathers wanted to create a republican constitutional order that would be an improvement on that to which they had been subjected under the English monarchy prior to the War of Independence). In his classic work, *The English Constitution*, published in 1867, Walter Bagehot rejected traditional eighteenth-century accounts of British politics, deploying his famous distinction between the 'dignified' and the 'efficient' parts of the constitution. The former (the monarch and the House of Lords) merely 'impressed the many' and secured popular support for the system. But behind this dignified façade lay the 'efficient secret' of the English Constitution, 'the close union, the nearly complete fusion, of the executive and legislative powers'. The key to this fusion was a hitherto largely unrecognized assemblage of Her Majesty's ministers, the cabinet. This arrangement is of course the very antithesis of American-style separation of powers, which prohibits officers of the executive branch, headed by the President, from sitting in Congress; in Britain, ministerial members of the executive must (by constitutional convention) be selected either from the elected House of Commons or from the non-elected House of Lords – and nowadays, on democratic grounds, mainly from the former. Bagehot attached

2 Federalist essay LI.

particular importance to the constitutional position of the House of Commons, which had what he called the 'elective' function of making and unmaking cabinets.

A lot has happened to the constitutional structure since 1867, and some of it happened quite soon after Bagehot's commentary was published. Written in an age of small-scale government, his analysis predated the development of a large, complex, and decentralized civil service. In the 1860s the functions of government were very largely to do with war, peace, diplomacy, trade, and the running of the Empire: government was not concerned with the provision of public services like education, health care, pensions, or urban planning. Local government existed then only in a very rudimentary form.

And the growth of the electorate in the second half of the nineteenth century led to the rise of party machines to compete for the popular vote. In the same period, following the industrial revolution, governments were becoming more interventionist with regard to issues like public health, factory safety, and policing. Party labels became much more important to candidates standing for election to Parliament, and MPs became increasingly subject to party discipline in the House of Commons as governments sought to mobilize their majorities to enact ever larger and more ambitious programmes of legislation. The position of the Prime Minister as party leader and the party's chief media spokesman, as the selector of his (or, later, her) ministerial team and as chair of cabinet became ever more dominant. In an introduction to a new edition of Bagehot's *The English Constitution*, Richard Crossman argued that cabinet government had been superseded by prime ministerial government.[3] The growing role of prime ministers as big players on the international stage has further encouraged this view. Experience of the administrations of Margaret Thatcher and Tony Blair has fuelled debates about whether we now have, in essence if not in strict constitutional form, a 'British Presidency'.[4]

FROM GOVERNMENT TO GOVERNANCE

Nowadays the old tripartite distinction between the different 'powers' looks crude and out of date, though it is still an important part of the vocabulary of constitutional discourse. It has in any case become increasingly fashionable to try to break free of traditional constitutional and institutional categories by thinking in more flexible and wide-ranging terms about what institutions are (the 'new institutionalism'[5] has become an important concept in political science) and by employing the concept of 'governance' instead of 'government'. In the mid-1990s a working group of the International Institute of Administrative Sciences came up with the following working definition of governance:

- Governance refers to the process whereby elements in society wield power and authority, and influence and enact policies and decisions concerning public life, and economic and social development.

[3] R. H. S. Crossman, Introduction to Walter Bagehot, *The English Constitution* (1963) 1–57. Cf. John P. Mackintosh, *The British Cabinet* (3rd edn, 1977).

[4] The arguments are extensively and cogently reviewed in Michael Foley, *The British Presidency* (2000).

[5] See B. G. Peters, 'Political Institutions, Old and New', in R. E. Goodin and H.-D. Klingemann, *A New Handbook of Political Science* (1996) 205–20.

- Governance is a broader notion than government, whose principal elements include the constitution, legislature, executive, and judiciary. Governance involves interaction between these formal institutions and those of civil society.
- Governance has no automatic normative connotation. However, typical criteria for assessing governance in a particular context might include the degree of legitimacy, representativeness, popular accountability, and efficiency with which public affairs are conducted.

Nowadays, the word governance is commonly used, not only by academic political scientists but also by politicians and international agencies (as in the phrase, 'good governance', widely used by aid agencies, such as the World Bank). At the same time, the processes of government and governance, including policy decision making, have come to be seen as crossing traditional institutional boundaries and involving wider communities and networks of actors both from inside government and from outside, whose composition varies from one policy sector to another. There is no place in this chapter to explore the interesting ramification of the extensive policy networks/communities literature, but the following passage captures some of the flavour:

> A policy network (or policy community) is a systematic set of relationships between political actors who share a common interest or general orientation in a particular area. These relationships typically cut across formal institutional arrangements and the divide between government and non-governmental bodies. A policy network may therefore embrace government officials, key legislators, well-placed lobbyists, sympathetic academics, leading journalists and others. The recognition of the existence of policy networks highlights the importance of informal processes and relationships in policy making and particularly in policy initiation.[6]

THE CORE EXECUTIVE

The debates about 'prime ministerial' versus 'cabinet' government and about the possible emergence of a 'British presidency' still attract scholarly interest, but – in similar vein to the movement from government towards governance – some political science commentators have begun to move away from traditional notions of a British 'executive' comprising Prime Minister and cabinet by employing the broader and more flexible term, *core executive*. Thus, Professor Rod Rhodes has written as follows:

> In fact, what constitutes the executive varies from policy area to policy area. Departments take important policy decisions with little or no reference to the cabinet and Prime Minister. Equally, central co-ordination, for example the Treasury's role in economic policy making, is not a function solely of Prime Minister and cabinet. The term 'executive' is used here to refer to *the centres of political authority which take policy decisions*. In other words, the executive institutions are not limited to Prime Minister and cabinet but also include ministers in their departments. The term 'core executive' refers to *all those organisations and procedures which coordinate central government policies, and act as final arbiters of conflict between different parts of the government machine*. In brief, the 'core executive' is the heart of the machine, covering the complex web of

6 A. Heywood, *Politics* (3rd edn, 2007) 432.

institutions, networks and practices surrounding the Prime Minister, cabinet, cabinet committees and their official counterparts, less formalised ministerial 'clubs' or meetings, bilateral negotiations and interdepartmental committees.[7]

One feature of this approach is that it both implicitly ('all those organisations and procedures') and explicitly ('and their official counterparts') draws civil servants into the ambit of the core executive, alongside ministers. Traditional UK constitutional analysis draws a clear demarcation line between the role and the status of *elected* ministerial members of the political executive, both members of and answerable to Parliament, and the *non-elected* civil servants who advise them. That line was relatively easy to identify in the first half of the nineteenth century when the government and its agendas, and the bureaucracy that supported it, were very small. But it became ever more blurred and more permeable as we moved into the complexities of the twentieth-century interventionist state. And the blurring has become more noticeable with the new public management programmes that began after Mrs Thatcher's first election victory in 1979.

It is to these matters that we now turn our attention.

FROM EXECUTIVE POWER TO THE ADMINISTRATIVE STATE

Discussion of executive functions has been complicated by the rise of modern, economically and politically developed administrative states, with large and complex bureaucracies. The 'executive' functions of presidents, prime ministers, and cabinets have come to be shared with salaried administrators – and the boundaries of the executive function have expanded and become blurred. One by-product of this is the endless debate in public administration about the 'policy'/'administration' dichotomy, and about the division of responsibility for 'policy' and 'operational' matters.

Many early writers on the phenomenon of bureaucracy depicted it as an unqualified evil, at odds with democratic government. But others (notably the German scholar Max Weber)[8] came to recognize bureaucracy as a ubiquitous and effective organizational model, essential to developed social systems underpinned by rational-legal forms of authority. Decades before Weber, John Stuart Mill's classic essay on representative government, published in 1861, had acknowledged the need for trained officials, so long as the ultimate control lies with representative institutions:

Government by trained officials cannot do, for a country, the things which can be done by a free government; but it might be supposed capable of doing some things which free government, of itself, cannot do . . . There could not be a moment's hesitation between representative government among a people in any degree ripe for it, and the most perfect imaginable bureaucracy. But it is, at the same time, one of the most important ends of political institutions, to attain as many

[7] R. A. W. Rhodes, 'From Prime Ministerial Power to Core Executive', in R. A. W. Rhodes and P. Dunleavy (eds), *Prime Minister, Cabinet and Core Executive* (1995) 12.

[8] See in particular M. Weber, *The Theory of Social and Economic Organisation* (1947), translated and edited by A. M. Henderson and T. Parsons. For more general discussion of the development of the concept of bureaucracy see M. Albrow, *Bureaucracy* (1970); A. Dunsire, *Administration: The Word and the Science* (1973).

of the qualities of the one as are consistent with the other; to secure as far as they can be made compatible, the great advantage of the conduct of affairs by skilled persons bred to it as an intellectual profession, along with that of a general control vested in, and seriously exercised by, bodies representative of the entire people.[9]

But Mill was, of course, writing in an age of 'small government', when the nominal size of the civil service (in 1851) was around 39,000.[10] Central government ministries were very small, and the great majority of civil servants were copy clerks and messengers who have no modern counterparts in an age of word processing, photocopiers, telephones, and emails. Nearly all government offices were centrally located in and around Whitehall. Ministers were able, and were expected, to be personally involved in all the key decisions in their ministries – and to shoulder the responsibility in Parliament, if things went wrong (although, even then, they often managed to side-step parliamentary criticism). A century later the size of the civil service had swelled tenfold; the functions of government had expanded far beyond the grasp of day-to-day ministerial control; senior civil servants, not directly accountable to Parliament, not subject, as ministers are, to periodic re-election, and operating largely out of the public eye, had – both by default and by deliberate delegation – acquired a great deal of power in their own right.

Though the role of some senior civil servants involves working closely with ministers on matters of policy, the great majority of civil servants are involved in delivering public services – paying welfare benefits, issuing passports, licensing road vehicles, collecting taxes, etc. But whatever their role, it is a firm principle that all civil servants are politically neutral. They give loyal service to the government of the day, of whatever party. Serving civil servants, particularly senior ones, are required to refrain from active involvement in party politics – campaigning or standing as candidates for elected office. And the spectacle that occurs in Washington, DC whenever there is a change of presidency, of thousands of political advisers moving out and being replaced by the appointees of the new incumbent, has no parallel in the UK when there is a change of Prime Minister.

Civil service neutrality means serving ministers of any government currently in office with non-partisan loyalty. Thus, when a Labour government came to power in May 1997, under the premiership of Tony Blair, civil servants who, for eighteen years, had served Conservative administrations, headed first by Margaret Thatcher and then by John Major, stayed in post following the transition (apart from ones who would have moved jobs anyway). Some temporary 'special advisers' (see below) replaced the advisers who had been serving the outgoing government, but their numbers were small.

The problem of ensuring that public bureaucracy serves rather than usurps democratic government, and gives good and cost-effective service to the taxpayer (who funds it) and to the consumer of public services (who is in most cases also a taxpayer), acquires new urgency in an age of large-scale, interventionist government. And in the 1980s and 1990s, government concern about the 'bigness' of government and the scope and cost of its activities became a key item on the agenda of political debate.

9 J. S. Mill, *Considerations on Representative Government*, ed. R. B. McCallum (1948) 180.

10 See G. Drewry and T. Butcher, *The Civil Service Today* (2nd edn, 1991) 48.

MODERNIZING GOVERNMENT: FROM PUBLIC ADMINISTRATION TO PUBLIC MANAGEMENT

The election of the Thatcher Government in 1979 marked the beginning of a period of rapid and radical change in UK public administration. The process continued under Margaret Thatcher's Conservative successor, John Major – and was further developed and repackaged by Tony Blair's Labour Government. Public administration has been displaced – at least in part – by, a 'new public management' (NPM) which rejects traditional bureaucratic methods and structures in favour of market-based and business-like regimes of public service.[11] The radical nature and extent of the NPM phenomenon is summarized by Owen Hughes:

> Since the mid-1980s there has been a transformation in the management of the public sectors of advanced countries. The rigid, hierarchical, bureaucratic form of public administration, which has predominated for most of the twentieth century, is changing to a flexible, market-based form of public management. This is not simply a matter of reform or a minor change in management style, but a change in the role of government in society and the relationship between government and citizenry.[12]

As Hughes observes, variations on the NPM theme can be found in the recent administrative histories of many developed countries. He goes on to characterize this as 'a new paradigm in the public sector', though whether it is sufficiently universal to amount – as is sometimes suggested – to a new '*global* paradigm', seems much more questionable.[13]

NPM has seen the growth of new relationships between the public sector and the private and voluntary sectors. Public bodies have striven for managerial accolades of quality, like Chartermark, Investors in People and the Business Excellence Model. A new public service vocabulary has been invented: privatization, contracting out, market testing, internal markets, public-private partnerships – and, in the late 1990s, 'joined-up government'. So far as the civil service is concerned, the beginning of the 1980s was marked by tough new managerial policies.[14] Substantial cuts in manpower were announced by the Thatcher government: in 1979 there were 732,000 civil servants; ten years later the figure stood at 570,000; by the beginning of the new millennium it was around 450,000. Following the reports of two efficiency reviews, chaired, respectively, by Sir Peter Gershon[15] and Sir Michael Lyons[16], the Blair Government adopted an ambitious programme to cut public

[11] There is a very large literature on the nature and development of NPM. See, in particular, Owen Hughes, *Public Management and Administration* (3rd edn, 2003); N. Flynn, *Public Sector Management* (4th edn, 2002); B. G. Peters and D. J. Savoie (eds), *Taking Stock: Assessing Public Sector Reforms* (1998); S. Horton and D. Farnham (eds), *Public Management in Britain* (1999); D. Oliver and G. Drewry, *Public Service Reforms: Issues of Accountability and Public Law* (1996); C. Pollitt, *Managerialism and The Public Services* (2nd edn, 1993); S. Zifcak, *New Managerialism: Administrative Reform in Whitehall and Canberra* (1994); J. Stewart and K. Walsh, 'Change in the Management of Public Services' (1992) 70(4) *Public Administration*, 499–518; C. Hood, 'A Public Management for All Seasons' (1991) 69(1) *Public Administration*, 3–20; M. Barzelay, *The New Public Management: Improving Research and Policy Dialogue* (2000).

[12] Hughes, op. cit., 1.

[13] See Christopher Hood, 'Contemporary Public Management: a New Global Paradigm?' (1995) 10(2) *Public Policy and Administration* 104–17.

[14] G. Drewry and T. Butcher, *The Civil Service Today* (2nd edn, 1991) 164–6.

[15] *Releasing resources to the front line*, the Treasury, July 2004

[16] *Well Placed to Deliver? – Shaping the Pattern of Government Service*, the Treasury, March 2004.

service manpower and to move a lot of government jobs out of London and the South East of England.

The early Thatcher years saw a substantial squeeze on civil service pay, and subsequently there have been moves in many parts of the public sector away from traditional, more or less automatic incremental pay increases towards more performance-related pay regimes. Pay and conditions of service in the civil service, below the small number of top grade posts in the Senior Civil Service, have since been decentralized to departments and agencies. Unprecedented friction between the Thatcher Government and its civil service reached a climax in the litigious confrontation between the Prime Minister and the civil service unions in the Government Communications Headquarters (GCHQ) case[17] – a cause célèbre of modern judicial review.[18]

During the Thatcher years there were also – as we shall see later – important changes in the management and organizational culture of the civil service. Ministers were attracted to ideas, and management nostrums imported from the private sector, designed mainly to improve cost effectiveness and value for money. The transformative process culminated, in 1988, in the launch of the radical Next Steps initiative, a development aptly described by the Commons Treasury and Civil Service Committee as 'the most far-reaching since the Northcote–Trevelyan reforms in the nineteenth century'.[19] The Next Steps initiative has effected a transformation of the structure and culture of the civil service, and has had a massive impact upon the organizational arrangements of government departments.[20] It is only one aspect of the much wider NPM agenda, but we will pay particular attention to it in this chapter, not least because of the important questions it has raised about the principles and mechanisms of public accountability.

Subsequently, in 1991, we saw the launch of the Citizen's Charter, with its promise of improved services and enhanced consumer sensitivity throughout the public service; and a big market-testing initiative in central government[21] – and then a re-launch of the Charter initiative by the Blair Government, in 1998, under the new title, 'Service First'. This was followed by a White Paper on *Modernising Government*, that appeared in May 1999.[22]

It might of course be argued that the arrangements for delivering public services – such as welfare, education, and health – are not a 'constitutional' matter at all, being concerned with administrative superstructure rather than with those fundamental principles of government that are the essence of a constitution. The Next Steps white paper, for instance, was not itself regarded as, or presented as, a 'constitutional' document, neither was the Blair Government's *Modernising Government* white paper. However, both these documents – particularly the former – have important implications for 'the changing constitution'. Although the Thatcher Government insisted from the outset that existing constitutional principles (particularly those relating to ministerial responsibility) would remain undisturbed,

[17] *Council of Civil Service Unions* v. *Minister for the Civil Service* [1985] AC 374. The Prime Minister, as Minister for the Civil Service, had removed union membership rights from civil servants working at GCHQ. The unions' challenge to the decision failed in the Appellate Committee of the House of Lords, having succeeded at first instance.

[18] The Blair government has largely restored trade union rights at GCHQ.

[19] Eighth Report from the Treasury and Civil Service Committee, 1987–8, *Civil Service Management Reform: The Next Steps*, HC 494, vol. I, para. 1. The Northcote-Trevelyan Report of 1854 was a landmark in the process of establishing a modern and independent civil service, recruited by merit rather than by ministerial patronage.

[20] See P. Dunleavy, 'The Architecture of the British Central State', (1989) 67(3), 67(4) *Public Administration* 249–75 and 391–417.

[21] *Competing for Quality: Buying Better Public Services*, Cm 1730 (1991).

[22] *Modernising Government*, Cm 4310 (1999).

the Next Steps programme has had a significant impact on the relationships between civil servants and ministers and between ministers and Parliament – and indeed on the shape and functions of the civil service itself.

The *Modernising Government* proposals consolidated and developed changing ideas about the relationship between the citizen, as consumer of public services, and the state as a service provider (or, in many contexts, a facilitator of service provision through contractual and quasi-contractual partnerships with the private and voluntary sectors). And of course the Blair Government's wider programme has featured major items of constitutional reform that both form a backcloth to and feed into the micro-agenda of public service and public management reform: devolution, for instance, adds extra layers and varieties of bureaucracy to what was already there, and has implications both for local government and for the traditional unity of the UK civil service; the Freedom of Information Act 2000 has added some extra 'teeth' to the transparency promised by the Citizen's Charter and Service First.

Let us now look in more detail at some important features of the New Public Management reforms and at some of their implications for the position of civil servants in a broadly defined core executive.

THE NEXT STEPS PROGRAMME

In November 1986 the Cabinet Office Efficiency Unit embarked upon a service-wide scrutiny exercise, to take stock of the progress already made in managerial reform of the civil service under the Thatcher Government (in particular, the Financial Management Initiative) and to report on what further measures should be taken. The outcome of this review was a prospectus for radical changes in the structure and culture of the civil service, published in February 1988, under the title, *Improving Management in Government: the Next Steps*.[23]

The report was based on more than 150 interviews with civil servants (including 26 permanent secretaries) and with ministers. It found, among other things, that most civil servants concerned with the delivery of government services (about 95 per cent of all staff) welcomed earlier moves to define management tasks more clearly and to devolve budgetary responsibilities, and that most civil servants were conscious that senior management is dominated by people with policy skills and who have little experience of managing or working in the area of service delivery.

A key paragraph of the report read as follows:

> The aim should be to establish a quite different way of conducting the business of government. The central Civil Service should consist of a relatively small core engaged in the function of servicing ministers and managing departments, who will be the 'sponsors' of particular government policies and services. Responding to these departments will be a range of agencies employing their own staff, who may or may not have the status of Crown servants, and concentrating on the delivery of their particular service, with clearly defined responsibilities between the Secretary of State and the Permanent Secretary on the one hand and the Chairmen or Chief Executives of the agencies on the other. Both departments and their agencies should have a more open and simplified structure.[24]

[23] Published by the Cabinet Office. [24] Ibid., para. 44.

At the heart of the Next Steps report was a formula for institutionalizing that crucial, though in practice elusive, distinction between the functions of 'administration' and 'policy making' in government. It distinguished between ministerial support and policy functions (performed by about 20,000 civil servants, working closely with ministers) and executive, or service delivery functions. The latter would progressively be transferred to semi-autonomous executive agencies. These agencies, headed by chief executives, would be managed, within an agreed policy framework (which would normally be published), operating at arm's length from day-to-day ministerial control.

On the day of publication, the Prime Minister made a House of Commons statement endorsing the recommendations.[25] She said that the new agencies would 'generally be within the Civil Service, and their staff will continue to be civil servants'. Mrs Thatcher made clear that the convention of ministerial responsibility (discussed below) would still apply to agencies, which would remain within the purview of parliamentary select committees, the National Audit Office, and the Parliamentary Ombudsman.

This first batch of agencies employed a total of about 71,000 civil servants, nearly half of them from the Employment Service. Apart from the latter, most of the new agencies were small, and most of them covered specialized, and in some cases commercial, aspects of departmental work that were already more or less semi-detached (e.g. the Meteorological Office, Her Majesty's Stationery Office (HMSO), and the Queen Elizabeth II Conference Centre). The biggest 'next step' was taken when the massive Social Security Benefits operation of the Department of Social Security (DSS) became an agency in April 1991.[26] At the same time, a Social Security Contributions Agency, with 9,000 staff, became responsible for the administration of National Insurance contributions (it has since become part of the Inland Revenue). And in April 1993, another Social Security agency – the Child Support Agency – came into existence.[27]

In April 1991, another very large department, Customs and Excise (25,000 staff) was reorganized into 30 executive units, 'on Next Steps lines'; and Inland Revenue (63,000 staff), subdivided into 34 executive offices, followed a year later.[28] The Prison Service (some 38,000 staff) became an agency in April 1993. The largest examples of agencies created subsequently include the Lord Chancellor's Department's Court Service, with just over 9,000 civil servants, which gained agency status in April 1995, and the Crown Prosecution Service, which became an agency (or more accurately, was reorganized 'on Next Steps lines') in March 1997, with 5,665 staff. In April 2000, 12 years after the launch of the Next Steps programme there were 105 agencies in the Home Civil Service, plus Inland Revenue and Customs, the Crown Prosecution Service, and the Serious Fraud Office, operating 'on next steps lines': these bodies covered nearly 78 per cent of the civil service.

25 HC Debs, 18 Feb. 1988, cols 1149–56.

26 Most DSS functions and agencies were transferred in June 2001 to the new Department for Work and Pensions. In April 2002, a new agency, Jobcentres Plus, was created from a merger of the Employment Service and parts of the Benefits Agency.

27 The Agency never functioned satisfactorily and, in July 2006, the Government announced a major overhaul of the child support scheme, including the prospective replacement of the CSA by a completely new agency: HC Debs, 24 July 2006, col 597 ff. And see the white paper, *A New System of Child Maintenance*, Cm 6979, December 2006.

28 In April 2005 the two organizations were merged to form HM Revenue and Customs.

AGENCY CHIEF EXECUTIVES

Recalling our earlier discussion of the meanings of 'executive', one interesting aspect of Next Steps is the basis upon which agency chief executives (ACEs) have been appointed. In the upper echelons of many parts of the public sector there has been a steady movement away from permanent career appointments, automatic salary increments, and internal promotions, towards filling higher-level posts by open competition, performance-related pay, and short-term service contracts whose renewal depends upon proven capacity to achieve stipulated targets. The performance targets of Next Steps agencies are published in the form of framework agreements.

Historically, the UK higher civil service has been a world of lifetime tenure, annual incremental salary rises, and steady progression up the promotion ladder for those who have passed through the tough graduate recruitment programme (usually in their early twenties) and found their perch on the bottom rung. This culture has been changing for some time, and the Next Steps programme has markedly accelerated the process of change.

The Next Steps ACEs have been appointed on three- to five-year contracts; most have been recruited by open competition, and most of the latter have come from outside the civil service. Historically, open competition and security of tenure have substantial constitutional significance, in signalling the neutrality and the independence of a minister's senior official advisers, and rejection of a US-type 'spoils' system based on political patronage. Of course running an agency (the service delivery end of civil service activity) is different – no less important, but generally less politically sensitive – from being a top ministerial adviser. But in practice the distinction is far from absolute: the powerful chief executive of a large agency may be expected to have lines of direct communication with ministers, and the latter may turn to ACEs for 'advice'. And ACEs have had to become accustomed to operating, from time to time, in the very public glare of media and select committee scrutiny – as successive former heads of the Child Support Agency, and of the Prison Service, and Passport agencies would no doubt ruefully confirm.

NEW PUBLIC MANAGEMENT, AGENCIES, AND MINISTERIAL RESPONSIBILITY

In an essay on ministerial responsibility, contributed to an earlier edition of this book, Colin Turpin wrote that, while ministerial responsibility is an 'essential' feature of the constitution, it 'is something malleable and precarious in practice, depending as it does upon procedure and custom, upon intangible understandings and traditions, and upon political circumstances'.[29] This malleability has proved particularly significant – conducive both to useful adaptiveness to change and to problematical uncertainties about who is responsible for what – in the context of NPM reforms. Turpin noted elsewhere in his essay that hiving off and privatizing public services, key items in the NPM agenda, 'entails a further truncation of ministerial responsibility as governmental activities are transferred to the private sector'.[30]

[29] C. Turpin, 'Ministerial Responsibility', in *The Changing Constitution* (3rd edn, 1994) 150.
[30] Ibid., 145.

Next Steps executive agencies – although remaining embedded within government – have provided some particularly vivid and interesting illustrations of the malleability and precariousness of these constitutional principles. From the outset, questions have been raised as to whether Next Steps really is compatible with the traditional principles and mechanisms of ministerial responsibility that Margaret Thatcher, in 1988, insisted would remain intact.

The logic of Next Steps, strengthening and making more explicit the existing division between the functions of and responsibility for 'policy making' and 'administration', seemed tacitly to recognize a point made earlier in this chapter – that the practical workings of ministerial responsibility are divorced from the theory. And can ministers resist the temptation to interfere in 'operational' matters in circumstances where agency performance that is perceived (by the media and/or Parliament) to be substandard, or the misconduct or maladministration of agency staff, threatens to cause them political embarrassment? The chequered history of the former nationalized industries – most of them now privatized – supposedly operating at arm's length from ministerial control but in practice subject to frequent interference, reinforced some of these concerns.[31]

Meanwhile, Parliament – the forum in which constitutional theories about ministerial responsibility are supposed to be translated into action – has had to adapt to the arrival of Next Steps.[32] The Select Committee on Procedure noted in its 1990 report on the select committee system that: 'as their numbers and scope grow, scrutiny of executive agencies, and of their relationships with their parent Departments, ought to play an increasingly important part in the work of select committees'[33] and a glance at the web pages of the House of Commons committees confirms that they have done so. MPs were from the outset encouraged to establish direct contact with agency chief executives on operational matters and, following some persistent lobbying by MPs, letters from ACEs replying to MPs' written questions have, since October 1992, been included in *Hansard*.

The National Audit Office (NAO) has also investigated agencies,[34] and early in the life of the Next Steps initiative it was decided (following a recommendation by the Treasury and Civil Service Committee) that ACEs could appear before the Public Accounts Committee as agency accounting officers.[35] Early in 1992 the NAO published its first report on a Next Steps Agency, the Vehicle Inspectorate; and in May that year the Chief Executive of the Agency gave evidence to the Public Accounts Committee (PAC), sitting alongside the Permanent Secretary of the Department of Transport. The accountability of ACEs is particularly problematical. According to the Cabinet Office's guidelines for civil servants appearing before select committees (the so-called Osmotherly Rules):

> Where a Select Committee wishes to take evidence on matters assigned to an Agency in its Framework Document, ministers will normally wish to nominate the Chief Executive as being the official best placed to represent them. While Agency Chief Executives have managerial authority to the extent set out in their Framework Documents, like other officials they give evidence on behalf of the minister to whom they are accountable and are subject to that minister's instruction.[36]

[31] See NEDO, *A Study of UK Nationalised Industries* (1976).

[32] See P. Giddings (ed.), *Parliamentary Accountability: A Study of Parliament and Executive Agencies* (1995).

[33] 1989–90, HC 19, paras 42, 44.

[34] *The Next Steps Initiative*, Cm 410 (June 1989).

[35] *The Financing and Accountability of Next Steps Agencies*, Treasury, Cm 914 (1989), ch. 5.

[36] Para. 43. See www.cabinet-office.gov.uk/central/1999/selcom/role.htm.

The Treasury and Civil Service Committee objected to this approach from the very beginning of the Next Steps programme and recommended that Chief Executives should be made *directly* responsible to select committees.[37] Six years later, the same committee repeated its earlier recommendation:

> We do not believe that ministerial power to intervene in the actions and decision of Agencies justifies the retention of ministerial accountability for the actions and decisions of Agencies for which the Chief Executives are responsible . . . The delegation of responsibility should be accompanied by a commensurate delegation of accountability. We recommend that Agency Chief Executives should be directly and personally accountable to Select Committees in relation to their annual performance agreements. Ministers should remain accountable for the framework documents and for their part in negotiating the annual performance agreement, as well as for all instructions given to Agency Chief Executives by them subsequent to the annual performance agreement.[38]

Rejecting this proposal, the Government argued:

> a minister is 'accountable' to Parliament for everything which goes on within his Department, in the sense that Parliament can call the minister to account for it. The minister is responsible for the policies of the Department, for the framework through which those policies are delivered, for the resources allocated, for such implementation decisions as the Framework Document may require to be referred or agreed with him and for his response to major failures or expressions of Parliamentary or public concern. But a minister cannot sensibly be held responsible for everything which goes on in his Department in the sense of having personal knowledge and control of every action taken and being personally blameworthy when delegated tasks are carried out incompetently, or when mistakes or errors of judgement are made at operation level.[39]

In recent years, governments have sought to address the tricky problem of how to maintain some credibility for the classical doctrine of ministerial responsibility in an age of 'big government' by claiming – as in the passage just cited – that there is a clear distinction between *responsibility* (the job one is charged with doing) and *accountability* (the duty to explain, or render an account of what has or has not been done).[40] Thus, in the present context, ACEs are *responsible* for the operational performance of their agencies (and liable to shoulder the blame when things go wrong); ministers are *responsible* for the policy framework within which agencies operate and – in accordance with the rules of ministerial responsibility – *account* to Parliament and the electorate both for that policy and for matters that fall within the responsibility of the ACE.

This anxiety of ministers to steer clear of blame for operational failure by distinguishing between responsibility and accountability was vividly exhibited in the row over the escape of prisoners from Parkhurst prison in January 1995. The Home Secretary, Michael Howard, maintained that he was not responsible for operational matters such as ensuring that prisons were secure. In his statement to the House of Commons he

[37] Eighth Report from the Treasury and Civil Service Committee, *Civil Service Management Reform: The Next Steps*, 1987–8, HC 494, para. 46.

[38] Fifth Report from the Treasury and Civil Service Committee, *The Role of the Civil Service*, 1993–4, HC 27, para. 171.

[39] *Taking forward Continuity and Change*, Cm 2748 (1995), p. 28.

[40] See Oliver and Drewry, op. cit. (n. 11 above), ch. 1.

claimed that:

With regard to operational responsibility, there has always been a division between policy matters and operational matters. That has existed not only since the introduction of agencies – it has been recognised for years, and indeed for generations.[41]

He was responsible for matters of policy regarding prison security, funding, and so on, but as there was no criticism of those matters he could not be held to blame – and therefore had no duty to resign. His accountability meant that he was required to ascertain the relevant facts, to explain them to Parliament – and to ensure that security was improved.

The next episode in the saga came with the publication in October 1995 of the Report of the Learmont Inquiry into prison security, which concluded bleakly that the Parkhurst escapes 'revealed a chapter of errors at every level and a naivety that defies belief'.[42] In a House of Commons statement, the Home Secretary noted that Learmont had not found that any decision of his had, directly or indirectly caused the escape, and he then announced that the Director General of the Service, Derek Lewis, had 'ceased to hold his post with effect from today'.[43]

Derek Lewis – a man with a private sector background, and refreshingly uninhibited by the polite mandarin reticence of more traditional senior civil servants – did not take this lying down. He and other critics were quick to point out that Learmont had also found that the Director General had been regularly distracted from his operational responsibilities by constant ministerial demands for information and advice: the Report called for an in-depth study of the relationship between the Home Office and the Prison Service Agency 'with a view to giving the Prison Service the greater operational independence that Agency status was meant to confer'.[44] Questions were also raised about the recent transfer of the Governor of Parkhurst, it being alleged that the Home Secretary had put pressure on the Director General to take this 'operational' decision. An Opposition motion in the Commons, deploring the Home Secretary's unwillingness 'to accept responsibility for serious operational failures', was comfortably defeated.[45] But this did little to dispel unease, in Parliament and elsewhere, about the artificiality of the policy/operational distinction, particularly in an area of high political sensitivity in which the Home Secretary had staked his political reputation on a hard-line penal policy.

In the 1995–6 parliamentary session the Commons Public Service Committee launched an inquiry into Next Steps agencies, with particular reference to the relationship between ministers and chief executives, and the controversy surrounding the Lewis case. Following publication of and debate on the Scott Report on Arms Sales to Iraq early in 1996, the Committee widened the scope of its inquiry to cover broader issues of ministerial accountability to Parliament. In January 1997, the Committee produced a further report on the same subject, following the Government's response to the earlier report.[46] The two reports were debated in the Commons a few weeks before the general election, and both Houses of Parliament passed resolutions on ministerial responsibility.[47] The House of Commons

[41] HC Debs, 10 Jan. 1995, col. 40.

[42] The Learmont Report, *Review of Prison Service Security in England and Wales and the Escape from Parkhurst Prison on Tuesday 3rd January 1995*, Cm 3020 (1995), para. 2.257.

[43] HC Debs, 16 Oct. 1995, cols 31–3.

[44] Learmont Report, para. 3.87.

[45] HC Debs, 19 Oct. 1995, cols 502–50.

[46] 1996–7, HC 234.

[47] HC Debs, 12 Feb. 1997, cols 273–93.

resolution read as follows:

That, in the opinion of this House, the following principles should govern the conduct of ministers of the Crown in relation to Parliament:

(1) Ministers have a duty to Parliament to account, and be held to account, for the policies, decisions, and actions of their Departments and Next Steps Agencies.
(2) It is of paramount importance that ministers give accurate and truthful information to Parliament, correcting any inadvertent error at the earliest opportunity. Ministers who knowingly mislead Parliament will be expected to offer their resignation to the Prime Minister.
(3) Ministers should be as open as possible with Parliament, refusing to provide information only when disclosure would not be in the public interest, which should be decided in accordance with relevant statute and the Government's *Code of Practice on Access to Government Information* (second edition, January 1997).
(4) Similarly, ministers should require civil servants who give evidence before Parliamentary Committees on their behalf and under their directions to be as helpful as possible in providing accurate, truthful and full information in accordance with the duties and responsibilities of civil servants as set out in the *Civil Service Code (January 1996)*.

Soon after the 1997 election the new Home Secretary, Jack Straw, told the Commons that, in his judgement, his predecessor's reputation had been 'deeply damaged by his refusal to accept proper responsibility for the Prison Service, and his arcane and unconvincing attempts to distinguish between policy and operations'.[48] He said that, in future, 'as a first step towards restoring proper ministerial responsibility' all parliamentary questions about the Prison Service would be answered by ministers, and not by the Director General, adding that, 'I regard it as essential that ministers should answer personally to the House for what is done in our prisons and not leave the matter to their civil servants'.

In the same debate, Mr Howard was denounced by one of his own former ministerial colleagues, Anne Widdicombe, who said, with reference to his denial that he had put pressure on Derek Lewis to suspend the Governor of Parkhurst, that he had 'dug a hole for himself over policy and operations'.[49] She also suggested that

> We demean our high office if we mistreat our public servants. As hon. Members, we demean ourselves if we come to the House to indulge in a play of words and make statements which, although they may not be untrue . . . may be unsustainable.[50]

She now regretted that she had not resigned as a minister over the episode. Mr Howard was later to become Leader of the Opposition.

NEW LABOUR, THE CIVIL SERVICE, AND THE NEW PUBLIC MANAGEMENT

The election of the Labour Government in May 1997 marked the end of 18 years of Conservative government, during which time public service reform, rather than being seen as a *means* to enabling government to realize its key objectives with the minimum of cost

48 HC Debs, 19 May 1997, col. 396. 49 Ibid., col. 406.
50 Ibid., col. 408. Mr Howard's reply is at cols 461–7.

and difficulty, had been an *end* in its own right – at the very top of the government's substantive policy agenda. This writer has argued elsewhere that the civil service inherited by Tony Blair and his colleagues in 1997 'was in a transitional state, between old and new – caught between "continuity and change" '[51] – the latter being the interestingly evocative title of two white papers published during the John Major years.

Labour, certainly in the later years of its long stint in opposition, had not, by and large, contested the main elements of the NPM reform programme in principle – and once in office it showed no inclination to reverse them. Indeed, given the decision to adhere to the previous government's public spending targets, unravelling reforms that emphasized performance measurement and greater financial discipline would have made no sense.

The smoothness of the civil service's transition in 1997 from serving one government to serving another was in itself an illustration of the 'continuity' that has survived the NPM revolution. In the run-up to the election John Major gave opposition frontbenchers nearly 18 months' access to senior civil servants to discuss the machinery for implementing Labour's objectives. And after the election, apart from some early tensions between the Government's own partisan 'spin doctors' and the neutral civil servants in the Government Information Service,[52] the civil service settled down quickly and apparently comfortably to the task of serving the incoming administration.

The Blair Government, a very different animal from its Old Labour ancestors, eschewed the Harold Wilson device of reformist royal commissions and committees of inquiry into aspects of the public service. But, although by 1997 most of the principles underlying the NPM agenda had become matters of consensus politics, the new government did have its own substantial reform programme – focusing upon decentralization (including devolution and local government reform),[53] the further improvement of public service standards, and 'joined-up' government. These were summarized in a white paper on *Modernising Government*, published in March 1999,[54] which stated three main aims:

- Ensuring that policy making is more joined up and strategic.
- Making sure that public service users, not providers, are the focus, by matching services more closely to people's lives.
- Delivering public services that are high quality and efficient.

Much of the Blair agenda for public service reform and modernization can trace its ancestry to the 'new right' politics of the Thatcher years, though this rather embarrassing lineage has been camouflaged by the New Labour rhetoric of a 'third way'. But where do things stand in that complex, and sometimes ambiguous, relationship between ministers and their civil servants, discussed earlier in this chapter?

[51] Gavin Drewry, 'The Civil Service', in R. Blackburn and R. Plant (eds), *Constitutional Reform: The Labour Government's Constitutional Reform Agenda* (1999) 154–72, at 162.

[52] Drewry, 'The Civil Service', ibid.

[53] See the white paper, *Modern Local Government: In Touch with the People*, Cm 4014 (1998), the Local Government Act 2000, and Chapters 9, 10, and 11.

[54] See n. 22, above.

MINISTERS AND CIVIL SERVANTS: TIME FOR A CIVIL SERVICE ACT?[55]

Unlike the civil services of most other countries, the position and status of the UK civil service is largely non-statutory. The Northcote–Trevelyan Report of 1854 said that the newly reformed civil service should be put on to a statutory footing, but this has never happened. There is the Civil Service Order in Council 1995 (subsequently amended) which covers day-to-day-employment and management issues. And, since January 1996, the constitutional framework within which civil servants work, and the values they are expected to uphold, have been set out in a non-statutory code,[56] modelled on a draft originally proposed by the House of Commons Treasury and Civil Service Committee,[57] and revised in May 1999 to take account of devolution to Scotland and Wales.

But is a non-statutory code good enough – particularly given the immense cumulative impact of New Public Management reforms, such as Next Steps, which have exacerbated ambiguities in the role of civil servants vis-à-vis ministers? It is true that orders in council do have statutory status, but they are issued under the Royal Prerogative and are not subject to parliamentary scrutiny: the Wicks Committee on Standards in Public life has described their use in this context as 'inherently unsatisfactory'.[58] Episodes like the Derek Lewis/Michael Howard row (see above), the 'arms to Iraq' saga in the 1990s,[59] and more recently the suicide, in July 2003, of the civil servant, Dr David Kelly[60] (see p. 172 supra) have raised real concerns about the adequacy of the present framework. The waters have been muddied further, and the perceived need for clarification intensified, by the continuing proliferation of special advisers in government departments.[61]

The Labour and Liberal Democrat parties went into the 1997 general election with a joint commitment to enacting a Civil Service Act, and that has ostensibly remained the formal position of the Blair government. In 2000, the Committee on Standards in Public Life called for a timetable to implement this commitment.[62] The same committee revisited the issue in 2003 and took extensive evidence. Some of that evidence was negative. The Labour peer, Lord Donoughue, said that he was

55 The arguments for and against enacting a Civil Service Act are usefully summarized on a website, 'How to be a Civil Servant', www.civilservant.org.uk/csact.shtml, and the links to be found therein.

56 The latest version can be found on the Cabinet Office web site, at www.cabinet-office.gov.uk/central/1999/cscode.htm.

57 See D. Oliver and G. Drewry, *Public Service Reforms* (1996) ch. 6.

58 9th Report of the Committee on Standards in Public Life, Cm 5775 (April 2003), para. 10.7.

59 There is a good overview of many of the issues discussed here, written in the wake of the Scott Report on Arms to Iraq, in Adam Tomkins, *The Constitution after Scott* (1998) ch. 2.

60 David Kelly, an official in the Ministry of Defence, was publicly identified as one of the sources used by a BBC journalist who claimed that the Government had put improper pressure on the Joint Intelligence Committees to 'sex up' their assessment of Iraq's military capabilities in the run-up to the 2003 invasion. The report of an inquiry into his death, by Lord Hutton (HC 247, 2003–4) did little to dampen the speculation and controversy that surrounded this episode.

61 The role of special advisers lies beyond the scope of this chapter, but there is a good discussion of some of the issues in the 9th Report of the Committee on Standards in Public Life, loc. cit., ch. 7.

62 6th Report, ch. 5.

not clear what the problem is: what is the need for legislation? I can see all the disadvantages . . . For a start a Civil Service Act would be constitutionally significant . . . The Civil Service traditionally works for the Crown . . . You have a big statutory Act and they are actually under Parliament.[63]

Other witnesses warned about the inflexibility that would accompany a new Act. The Head of the Civil Service, Sir Andrew Turnbull, seemed to be in favour, though his tone was rather lukewarm:

I do not know that it would make a huge difference. I think it is seeking the reassurance that the long-standing kind of values and structure cannot be changed by stealth. In the actual day-to-day practice, I do not think there would be a great deal changed . . . . But an Act would underpin [the Civil Service Code] . . . it would give reassurance that, over 10 or 20 years, you will not suddenly wake up and find you have got a world that you did not like and you do not quite know how you got there.[64]

But the balance of the evidence was positive. Baroness Prashar, the then First Civil Service Commissioner,[65] suggested that an Act

will disentangle what I call the constitutional position of the Civil Service from what I call the organisation development and the reform of the Civil Service. So, it will free that up and I do not see the Act in any way interfering with the development and the reform of the Civil Service. . . . I think the disadvantage at the moment is the minute you talk about reform . . . people start talking about the values.[66]

The Wicks Committee Report (noted previously) reported concern in some quarters that the government appeared to have been dragging its feet on the issue of a Civil Service Act, and it reiterated its previous call for a consultative timetable: 'the Government should begin an early process of public consultation on the contents of a draft Bill. The Bill should receive pre-legislative scrutiny by a Joint Committee of both Houses of Parliament.'

In its response to the Report, the government confirmed that it still accepted the case in principle for legislation, but said that 'any legislation has to compete for its place alongside many other priorities'. Meanwhile, the House of Commons Public Administration Select Committee had renewed its call for legislation,[67] and it later published its own draft Bill[68] which, *inter alia*, would put the Civil Service Code onto a proper statutory footing, give new powers to the Civil Service Commissioners and clarify the role of special advisers. On 15 November 2004 the Government published its own draft Bill, accompanied by a consultation document.[69] Its version was along similar lines to that of the Select Committee, though without the extended powers for the Civil Service Commissioners. Referring to the consultation exercise, the newly-appointed Cabinet Secretary and Head of the Civil Service, Sir Gus O'Donnell, told the Public Administration Committee in October 2005 that he was 'in favour of anything which entrenched the traditional [civil service] values of honesty, objectivity and impartiality' – but that the Government had 'more important' legislative priorities.[70] So, at the time of writing, there seems little likelihood of much forward movement in the immediate future.

63 9th Report, para. 10.8. 64 Ibid., para. 10.10.

65 The Civil Service Commissioners are responsible for maintaining the principle of civil service recruitment by merit through open competition and for upholding core civil service values. Details can be found on their website, www.civilservicecommissioners.gov.uk/. 66 Ibid., para. 10.12.

67 8th Report, 200 1–2, published on 19 July 2002. 68 Published on 5 January 2004.

69 Cm 6373, 2004. 70 HC 513-I, 200 5–6, Q. 120.

While accepting that a new Act would not be a panacea for all that ails this area of the constitution, this writer believes that the case for legislation has, on balance, been overwhelmingly made, and that further foot-dragging – speciously sustained by hoary old half-truths about limited parliamentary time – are simply not good enough. As one commentator has aptly put it:

> Parliament should assert its primary authority on the regulation of the civil service. Parliament should legislate to demarcate a new, clearer constitutional function for the civil service. The cloak of the crown, so convenient to the government, should be stripped away, and the civil service should be clothed in a new parliamentary garb.[71]

CONCLUSIONS

Not all of the issues discussed in this chapter are particularly new in themselves. Narrow definitions of the 'executive' function, founded on eighteenth-century constitutional theory, have long been recognized as providing, at best, an incomplete basis for understanding the complexities of modern government and governance. And the largely fictional character of ministerial responsibility in an era of large-scale government and huge public bureaucracies has been increasingly apparent since the latter part of the nineteenth century – even though a lot of the fiction has been preserved, largely for the convenience of ministers who are only too happy to accept the credit for successful initiatives (even if they are quick to pass the buck to their officials when things go wrong).

What is new is that recent and continuing reform agendas – New Public Management and 'modernization' programmes – have thrown some of these longstanding issues and concerns into much sharper relief. The NPM reforms have blurred the line between 'public' and 'private' services, and heavily compromised the traditional Weberian model of public bureaucracy. Next Steps executive agencies have spawned a new species of public service hybrid – the agency chief executive – whose accountability, and whose relationship to ministers, is sometimes ambiguous. This chapter has supported proposals to put the civil service on to a firmer, statutory footing. But it must be conceded that statute law operates only at the margins of a public service. The practicalities of achieving an appropriate balance between 'efficiency, effectiveness and economy' (watchwords of NPM) and democratic accountability are to be found much more in the evolutionary and incremental development of a organizational culture and in the fine-tuning of constitutional conventions than in the imposition of formal legal norms.

[71] Tomkins, op. cit., 94.

FURTHER READING

FLYNN, N. *Public Sector Management* (4th edn, 2002).

FOLEY, M. *The British Presidency* (2000).

HEYWOOD, A. *Politics* (3rd edn, 2007).

HUGHES, O. *Public Management and Administration* (3rd edn, 2003).

KAVANAGH, D., RICHARDS, D., SMITH, M., and GEDDES, A. *British Politics* (5th edn, 2006), chapters 10–13.

NEWMAN, J. *Modernising Governance, New Labour, Policy and Society* (2001).

RHODES, R. A. W. and DUNLEAVY, P. (eds) *Prime Minister, Cabinet and Core Executive* (1995).

TOMKINS, A. *The Government After Scott* (1998).

USEFUL WEB SITES

www.cabinet-office.gov.uk

www.parliament.uk/parliamentary_committees/public_administration_select_committee.cfm

9

SCOTTISH DEVOLUTION: DEVELOPING PRACTICE IN MULTI-LAYER GOVERNANCE*

Barry K. Winetrobe

SUMMARY

The passage of the Scotland Act 1998 was an early and major step in the Labour government's package of constitutional reform for the UK. Constitutions and politics are essentially about relationships, which exist to provide a governmental structure as efficient as possible in delivering the accepted aims and norms of the general polity. The first two sessions of the Scottish Parliament from 1999 to 2007 provide a living experiment in multi-layer democracy, through the efforts of governments, parliaments, and people of the UK and of Scotland to adjust to this novel situation. Central government has tried to ensure that it retains the ultimate reins of power, so that the degree of decentralization in Scotland and elsewhere provided by devolution does not produce such policy and institutional diversity as to hinder or undermine its own key priorities and policies. At the same time, devolved Scotland is, from an internal perspective, both an exercise in effective, more 'local' governance and also, a form of 'new politics' more open, participative, and inclusive than is traditional in the UK. How all these potentially conflicting tensions operate depends largely on the functioning of the network of relationships that has developed.

INTRODUCTION

Devolution is the latest structural development in the long constitutional history of Scotland. In two senses relevant to this chapter, that history has an impact on the current operation of Scottish devolved governance.

* This chapter does not provide a narrative of the campaign for Scottish devolution, its implementation in the later 1990s, or its first years of operation. Such background information is well covered in the existing literature, such as those cited in the Further Reading at the end of this chapter. I am extremely grateful to all those colleagues who commented so helpfully on earlier drafts of this text and of the chapter in the 2004 edition on which it is based.

First, Scotland since 1707 has retained a considerable degree of cultural and institutional distinctiveness.[1] This fostered demands over the last three centuries for changes to these constitutional arrangements, whether through independence or by means of some form of realignment within the Union. Therefore, devolution in Scotland is not just part of the current constitutional modernization package. It is also an attempt to address the demands for due regard to be paid to Scotland's unique governance background and needs. The fact that the present devolution scheme in Scotland is broader and deeper than that in Wales[2] is testament to the two countries' very different constitutional and governmental history.

Secondly, the more recent governmental history of Scotland shaped the current scheme in distinct, potentially contradictory, ways. For the Labour Party, its 18 years in opposition after 1979 and awareness that its support in Scotland was stronger than that in England brought it to a more positive view of the desirability of the diffusion of power through devolution, as a brake on unsympathetic central government control. Further, in attributing its long period out of office in part to its own ideological and other splits, Labour determined that any such diffusion of power would not reopen the door to any repeat of these damaging impressions of division and ungovernability of the early 1980s. By the time it returned to government in 1997 as 'New Labour', the party's commitment to constitutional reform was irrevocable. Implementation would have to take account of the perceived dangers of diversity and division inherent in any decentralization policy.

Within Scotland during these years, however, the constitutional question was being shaped by developments which involved more than just the Labour Party. Though the Liberal Democrats and the SNP had very different ultimate solutions to the problem of unaccountable, unresponsive centralized government, both to differing degrees could go along with Labour's more cautious approach. This spirit of cooperation helped to build the momentum through the 1980s and 1990s that led to the achievement of the current scheme of devolution.[3] The cooperative constitutional policy making that produced the proposals on which the devolution legislation was eventually based generated much rhetoric, some of which remains. For example, there was much 'popular sovereignty' language, encapsulated in the 1988 *Claim of Right* and in the Scottish Constitutional Convention, reflecting a view that devolution arose out of the will and efforts of the Scottish people, even if formally granted through UK institutions.[4] This 'popular sovereignty' rhetoric[5] brings with it an expectation of some constitutional entrenchment, and protection from central interference.

The other main rhetorical strand was that any devolution scheme would be based on a 'new type of politics', very different from that practised in Westminster and Whitehall. It would replace adversarial, confrontational politics with an emphasis on a more consensual, participative way of doing political business. This aspirational model was bound to influence how devolved relationships evolved.[6]

[1] James Mitchell, *Governing Scotland* (2003).

[2] Notwithstanding the more expansive devolution scheme in the Government of Wales Act 2006.

[3] Bob McLean, *Getting it together: the history of the Campaign for a Scottish Assembly/Parliament* 1980–1999 (2005); Kenyon Wright, *The people say yes* (1997).

[4] 'We, gathered as the Scottish Constitutional Convention, do hereby acknowledge the sovereign right of the Scottish people to determine the form of government best suited to their needs'. See the Convention's final report, *Scotland's Parliament, Scotland's Right* (Nov. 1995).

[5] In his foreword to the 2005–06 Annual Report of the Parliament, the Presiding Officer, George Reid, describes Holyrood as 'the People's Parliament'.

[6] Defenders of this approach argue that consensus did not at all mean an absence of vigorous political argument, or of fundamental policy disagreements between parties. See Alice Brown, 'Designing the Scottish

These two notions, of 'popular sovereignty' and 'new politics', were given formal expression within a series of key principles, which were originally formulated for the Parliament but have now become generally accepted as applicable to Scottish devolution as a whole.[7] These four key principles were devised by the Consultative Steering Group (CSG), which had been established by the UK Government to devise a blueprint for the operation of the Parliament:[8]

- *Sharing the Power* – 'The Scottish Parliament should embody and reflect the sharing of power between the people of Scotland, the legislators and the Scottish Executive.'
- *Accountability* – 'The Scottish Executive should be accountable to the Scottish Parliament and the Parliament and Executive should be accountable to the people of Scotland.'
- *Access and Participation* – 'The Scottish Parliament should be accessible, open, responsive and develop procedures which make possible a participative approach to the development, consideration and scrutiny of policy and legislation.'
- *Equal Opportunities* – 'The Scottish Parliament in its operation and its appointments should recognise the need to promote equal opportunities for all.'

The idea that governmental institutions, especially parliamentary ones, should operate within the framework of published principles is relatively novel in the UK. It echoes modern techniques of mission statements, targets, aims and objectives, and the like, which now abound in the public sector.[9] The CSG principles could easily have become a relatively meaningless set of pious aspirations, gathering dust on the devolution shelf. In practice, certainly from the perspective of the Parliament, they have significantly informed the operation of devolved governance; have provided the Parliament with a distinct and clear sense of purpose, and have become entrenched in its development.[10] So identified have they become with the Parliament that its Procedures Committee recommended that they 'should be known and understood as the Parliament's principles' rather than the 'CSG principles'.[11]

So, modern Scottish devolution comes with a lot of baggage. It reflects tendencies of both decentralization and central oversight and control. It seeks to answer a specific Scottish situation within a broader package of constitutional change. It tries to adhere to notions of 'new politics' and 'popular sovereignty' while operating essentially within the 'old constitution' of parliamentary sovereignty, representative democracy and adversarial party politics.

Parliament' (2000) 53 *Parliamentary Affairs* 542 and, for an external critique, see James Mitchell, 'New Parliament, new politics in Scotland' (2000) 53 *Parliamentary Affairs* 605.

7 The Parliament agreed 'that its operations should embody the spirit of the CSG key principles': SPOR vol. 1 no. 8, 9 June 1999 cols 367ff. The Executive unilaterally adopted the Principles in its dealings with the Parliament by incorporating them into successive editions of the *Scottish Ministerial Code*, para. 3.1.

8 *Shaping Scotland's Parliament*, HMSO, Jan. 1999.

9 It also has some resonance with developing notions of objective measurement criteria for particular governmental tasks, such as legislative scrutiny. See Dawn Oliver, 'Improving the scrutiny of Bills: the case for standards and checklists' [2006] *Public Law* 219.

10 Barry Winetrobe, *Realising the Vision: a Parliament with a Purpose* (2001), and, for a detailed internal analysis, *The founding principles of the Scottish Parliament*, 3rd Report, 2003, of the Procedures Committee, March 2003, SP Paper 818. Himsworth takes a more sceptical view. See Chris Himsworth, 'The domesticated executive of Scotland' in Paul Craig and Adam Tomkins, *The Executive and Public Law* (2006) 192 at 209.

11 Procedures Committee, (n. 10 above), vol. 1 para. 1001. It also recommended that it was imperative that the Executive remain committed to the CSG principles: paras 54–5.

This is quite a challenge. Experience of central-local relations in recent decades suggests that what the House of Commons Scottish Affairs Committee in December 1998 neatly described as 'multi-layer democracy',[12] especially where one layer holds most of the trump cards, can be a recipe for disagreement, conflict, and even gridlock. For multi-layer democracy not just to survive, but to produce 'better government', there must be a robust, effective, and inclusive network of relationships, delineating the relevant 'rules of engagement'.[13] It is this network that this chapter sets out to describe and examine.

FORMAL GOVERNMENTAL COMPETENCE

The obvious starting point for this examination is the relationship between the two governance tiers of the UK and of devolved Scotland, in terms of their respective powers. The Scotland Act 1998 explicitly preserves the traditional notion of the legislative supremacy of the UK Parliament: 'This section does not affect the power of the Parliament of the UK to make laws for Scotland.'[14] Thus, the position of the Scottish Parliament as a subordinate Parliament within the UK, created by a UK statute, is made clear, and this has been accepted by the courts in London and Edinburgh in the limited jurisprudence that has so far emerged.[15]

The division of legislative power between Edinburgh and London is achieved by delineating the areas of public policy (mainly expressed in broad terms, rather than by listing all relevant statutory and other provisions) which are not devolved. The residue is presumed to be within the 'legislative competence' of the Scottish Parliament. 'Legislative competence' is set out in three parts of the Scotland Act:

- *Sections 29–30*, which define what would be regarded as outwith legislative competence; guidance on the interpretation of these provisions, and the means of amending the boundary of legislative competence;
- *Schedule 4* (legislation protected from modification by the Scottish Parliament, such as all or part of core constitutional statutes like the 1706–7 Union legislation, the European Communities Act 1972, the Human Rights Act 1998, and the Scotland Act itself); and
- *Schedule 5* (reserved matters, such as defence, social security, taxation, and aspects of energy, transport, and home affairs).

A purported Act of the Scottish Parliament will not be valid law if any of its provisions fall within any of the following five grounds:[16]

- it would form part of the law of a country or territory other than Scotland, or confer or remove functions exercisable otherwise than in or as regards Scotland;

12 Scottish Affairs Committee, *The operation of multi-layer democracy*, 2nd report of 1997–8, HC 460.

13 See House of Lords Constitution Committee, *Devolution: inter-institutional relations in the United Kingdom*, 2nd report of 2002–3, HL Paper 28, Jan. 2003, and, generally, Dawn Oliver, *Constitutional Reform in the United Kingdom* (2003).

14 S. 28(7). See, generally, Anthony Bradley, Chapter 2, above.

15 *Whaley* v. *Lord Watson of Invergowrie* 2000 SC 125 and 340; *Anderson, Reid & Doherty* v. *Scottish Ministers* 2002 SC (PC) 63; Iain Jamieson, 'Challenging the validity of an Act of the Scottish Parliament' 2002 *SLT (News)* 71; Barry Winetrobe, 'Scottish devolved legislation and the courts' [2002] *Public Law* 31.

16 See the exact provisions of s. 29(2).

- it relates to any reserved matters set out in Schedule 5;
- it is in breach of the restrictions on legislation protected from modification as set out in Schedule 4;
- it is incompatible with any of the Convention rights in Schedule 1 to the Human Rights Act 1998 or with European Community law;
- it would remove the Lord Advocate as head of the systems of criminal prosecution and investigation of deaths in Scotland.

In colloquial language, the division of legislative power is often described as being between 'devolved matters' and 'reserved matters'. However, the Act does not use the term 'devolved matters', and its use of the term 'reserved matters' covers just one, albeit the most important in practice (contained in Schedule 5), block of matters which are not devolved.

The area of executive responsibility of the Scottish Executive (known as 'devolved competence') is primarily defined by reference to the Parliament's legislative competence.[17] It also covers other functions specifically transferred to the Executive, in areas where the Parliament has no legislative power (known informally as 'executive devolution').[18] As an executive institution under the Crown, the Executive can also exercise appropriate Royal Prerogative powers within its remit.[19]

Much of the initial focus on this division of powers has been on the legal implications. How are the divisions delineated, defined, and amended? How are disputes resolved? While this is of fundamental importance,[20] it should not overshadow the more political issue of the operational efficacy of the divisions of responsibilities, and the extent to which they enable or restrict the ability of the Executive and the Parliament to 'govern' devolved Scotland. For so long as the constitution of Scotland itself remains a live political issue, any blurring of responsibilities provides scope for those who challenge the present devolution scheme as being either too limited or too wide. The potential for blurring has arisen when a policy area is only partly devolved (e.g. rail transport[21]); where reserved and devolved matters interact (especially in social security with various aspects of social services provision, such as personal care for the elderly); where there is a strong EU component (e.g. agriculture and fisheries); or where a cross-cutting devolved area impacts on otherwise reserved matters (e.g. the law and order aspects of drugs policy).

In practical and consequently electoral terms, the policy area where the division of powers is most crucial is the broad economic field. Fiscal, macroeconomic, employment, competition, and related policies are reserved matters, leaving the devolved institutions with limited scope to influence the Scottish economy directly. The Labour–Liberal

[17] S. 54.

[18] S. 63. The main package of functions so transferred was contained in a 1999 Order, and relates mainly to administrative matters, such as public appointments: Scotland Act 1998 (Transfers of Functions to the Scottish Ministers etc.) Order 1999 (SI 1999/1750).

[19] See s. 53(2)(a) and Sched. 5 para. 2(1)(a). For an account of the Royal Prerogative see Anthony Bradley and Keith Ewing, *Constitutional and Administrative Law* (14th edn, 2007) ch. 12 parts D and E.

[20] See the provisions on 'devolution issues' in s. 98 and Sched. 6, and *Stair Memorial Encyclopaedia of the Laws of Scotland, Constitutional Law reissue* (2002), paras 468–79. See also Robert Hazell and Richard Rawlings, *Devolution, Law Making and the Constitution* (2005).

[21] See for example Holyrood's Local Government and Transport Committee's decision to recommend rejection of a Member's Bill, *Provision of Rail Passenger Services (Scotland) Bill*, as being outwith the Parliament's legislative competence and unlikely to be capable of being brought within competence by amendments: cols 4163–8, 24th meeting, 2006, 24 October 2006.

Democrat Executive does have ministers for finance and enterprise, and 'growing the economy' is stated in the 2003 coalition agreement to be its 'top priority'. However, as that document implicitly admits, the devolved input, though wide ranging, is often indirect and secondary.[22] The whole area of finance and taxation has been a thorny issue throughout the development of the devolution scheme.[23] While there have been efforts to make the Scottish budgetary process a genuinely inclusive, transparent, and accountable exercise,[24] the Chancellor of the Exchequer's Budget and Comprehensive Spending Review statements,[25] and the preservation of arrangements such as the non-statutory Barnett Formula (which regulates the share of money paid to the Scottish Parliament from the Treasury by reference to spending south of the border),[26] are still of greater importance in shaping Scotland's economy and public services. The devolved institutions' financial responsibilities are mainly restricted to 'expenditure' issues, rather than the 'income/revenue' side of the public accounts. This creates a skewing of fiscal responsibility and of public transparency and accountability for policy delivery.

In more direct constitutional terms, the key area of division of power relates to the structure of the devolution scheme itself, which remains Westminster-based. Many executive and parliamentary functions are reserved to Westminster. The Executive's officials remain UK home civil servants; and the rules for the appointment and removal of ministers, and the size and electoral system of the Parliament are all governed by Westminster legislation. From a London perspective, there are good reasons for devolution itself being a non-devolved matter which it is not open to the Scottish Parliament itself to change, but this fact entrenches the conceptualization of the devolved institutions as subordinate bodies with limited authority and discretion rather than as bodies 'sharing' sovereignty with the UK level, for instance. The Parliament's first Presiding Officer, Lord Steel of Aikwood, has criticized the fact that the Parliament cannot amend many of its main structural and procedural arrangements, even those relating to the number of Deputy Presiding Officers.[27] Much of the formal effect on the Executive of the civil service being a reserved matter is diluted by a broad delegation of authority to the First Minister,[28] much as was granted to the Scottish Secretary in the pre-devolution era. The Parliament's Procedures Committee, nevertheless, takes the view that it could restrain the Parliament from setting down novel accountability 'rules of engagement' between it and Executive officials.[29] Some loosening of the restrictions of the Scotland Act in these areas would seem to be a necessary precondition for the Parliament taking sufficient control of its own destiny to enable it to develop further.

22 *A partnership for a better Scotland* (May 2003) s. 1 (pp. 6 ff.).

23 Witness Labour's sudden decision in 1996 to subject the proposed '3p in the £' income tax-varying power to a separate referendum question, and the assurances by the Executive parties, fearful of an electoral backlash, that they would not resort even to these very limited fiscal levers.

24 Arthur Midwinter, 'Budgetary Scrutiny in the Scottish Parliament: an Adviser's View' (2005) 21 *Financial Accountability & Management* 13.

25 See Chapter 15.

26 See paras 535–6, *Stair Memorial Encyclopaedia* (2002) op. cit. (n. 20 above).

27 The Parliament's Procedures Committee concluded that 'the time is ripe for the Parliament to take control of its own proceedings': Procedures Committee report, op. cit. (n. 10 above), para. 830.

28 Civil Service Order in Council 1995, as amended. See the explanation in Pt II of the *Concordat between the Cabinet Office and the Scottish Administration* (Nov. 1999). For the first time, a Scottish Executive version of the Civil Service Code was published in June 2006, alongside the revised UK version, though it is almost entirely identical to the UK text.

29 Procedures Committee report, op. cit. (n. 10 above), paras 513–48.

THE EXECUTIVE–PARLIAMENT RELATIONSHIP

One of the most important devolution relationships is that between the Parliament and the Executive, as it sets the tone of devolved governance itself. Devolution policy making in the years before 1999 suggested that a novel relationship, very different from that between Whitehall and Westminster, was necessary for successful and effective devolved governance. Yet in a devolution scheme that was devised and enacted within UK legislation and institutions (many of whose politicians and officials would transfer into the new devolved institutions), it was almost inevitable that an essentially 'Westminster model' of governance would emerge. The UK Government made no secret of its intentions in this regard, and its July 1997 white paper clearly stated that 'the relationship between the Scottish Executive and the Scottish Parliament will be similar to the relationship between the UK Government and the UK Parliament'.[30]

This Westminster-based approach was adopted from the outset by the new Scottish Executive, whose own guidance documents retained traditional notions of ministerial responsibility, confidentiality of internal administrative proceedings, and the like. Those new Members of the Scottish Parliament (MSPs) who might have not fully appreciated the effect of this approach, and took much of the 'new politics' rhetoric at face value, were rapidly disabused of their error. In particular they learned that the Scottish Executive's civil servants were not directly available to assist the Parliament and its members in some form of new cooperative governance arrangements (perhaps akin to the traditional form of local government with which many of them were familiar), but were to remain responsible only to their ministers.[31]

The CSG Report itself[32] encapsulated the potential conflicts and paradoxes in these two approaches. By virtually ignoring the role of party in the Parliament (and the whipping and discipline that went with it), it underestimated the degree to which the familiar, adversarial nature of parliamentary proceedings would result. Its detailed proposals did not adequately provide for a Parliament intended to operate through consensual, inclusive procedures, facilitating instead a system in which the Executive would have the sort of leading and initiating role that the UK Government has in the House of Commons. Ambiguity emerged as to crucial issues such as the allocation between the executive and non-executive sides of parliamentary time not otherwise specified by standing orders. The Executive appeared to assume (as does the UK Government of the day in relation to the UK Parliament) that the Parliament existed primarily as an assembly for the discussion and approval of its policies, a platform for the announcement of its initiatives, and a forum for the controlled scrutiny of its policies and conduct within accepted UK notions of parliamentary accountability.

A telling example of this was the practical exercise of the Parliament's mechanisms for scrutinizing the Executive. As at Westminster, the Parliament generally gathers its information from the Executive and others through agreement and by invitation, rather than by formal demands. The Scotland Act has provided the Parliament with significant information-gathering powers, within its devolved remit. Since they are set out in UK legislation,

30 *Scotland's Parliament*, Cm 3658, para. 2.6.

31 Barry Winetrobe, 'Public accountability in Scotland' in A. McHarg and T. Mullen, *Public Law in Scotland* (2006).

32 See n. 8 above.

these powers should be more readily enforceable in practice than the notionally unfettered 'privilege-based' powers of the UK Parliament, for instance to call for evidence. However, when the first serious breakdown in consensual information gathering by parliamentary committees appeared in late 2000, concerning inquiries into a schools examinations crisis, the Executive managed to persuade the Parliament to accept (without any detailed scrutiny or consultation, through the Procedures Committee or otherwise) a resolution defining the practical exercise of these powers. This 'self-denying ordinance' provided limitations of the Parliament's formal statutory powers, similar to those which apply at Westminster, and incorporated familiar notions of ministerial responsibility and parliamentary accountability.[33]

However, after more than seven years the relationship between the young Parliament and the more experienced Executive (the latter being essentially a continuation of the Scottish Office, with its accumulated experience of dealing with Westminster) is developing into a more equal relationship. Notwithstanding the impression the Scottish public may get from the Scottish media, the Executive does not 'run' the Parliament, initiate proposals for changes in its procedures, or arrange its business, to the same extent as the UK Government does in the House of Commons. There is no 'Leader of the House', and the 'usual channels' are more institutionalized and inclusive, especially through the Parliamentary Bureau (the Parliament's business committee). Nevertheless, through its parliamentary majority, the Executive does inevitably have a leading, and often initiating, role in plenary and committee proceedings, and in key bodies such as the Bureau.[34] Pressures of executive administration, coalition government, public policy delivery, and party politics will provide temptations for the Executive to wield that majority to shape the Parliament, its structures, and procedures, to its own convenience.

THE EXECUTIVE COALITION

After the election in 1999, the new Scottish Executive ministerial team, as the government of devolved Scotland, had to devise rules and guidance for its operation, both internally affecting ministers and officials, and in its dealings with the public and the Parliament. The fact that it was a coalition government of Labour and the Liberal Democrats was an added complication, and made clarity essential in the relationships and responsibilities between ministers of the two coalition partners, and between all ministers and their officials. The arrangements have been delivered through two key Executive documents, the *Scottish Ministerial Code*, and the *Guide to Collective Decision Making*.[35] While the *Code* is, in essence, an adaptation of the UK *Ministerial Code*,[36] the *Guide* is a novel document,

33 Ss. 23–6, Scotland Act; parliamentary resolution on 'Executive accountability to Parliament', SPOR vol. 8 no. 14, cols 1197 ff., 1 Nov. 2000.

34 See Meg Russell & Akash Paun, *Managing Parliament Better? A Business Committee for the House of Commons* (2006).

35 The latest editions were published in Aug. 2003 following the general election: www.scotland.gov.uk/library5/finance/smcc-00.asp and www.scotland.gov.uk/library5/finance/gcdm-00.asp respectively.

36 Mark Shephard, 'Lessons from Westminster: The Scottish Executive and New Improved Codes of Conduct?', in J. Fleming and I. Holland (eds), *Motivating Ministers to Morality* (2001) 61–74.

setting out the appropriate ministerial and official relationships under devolved coalition governance.

In particular, the key device for achieving what the Guide calls 'the efficient and effective conduct of business within the Executive' is the doctrine of collective responsibility. Indeed, 'the Scottish Executive operates on the basis of collective responsibility', which is defined for these purposes as:[37]

- All the business of the Executive, including decisions, announcements, expenditure plans, proposed legislation and appointments, engages the collective responsibility of the Executive as a whole and must be handled with an appropriate degree of consultation and discussion so as to ensure the support of all ministers;
- Ministers have the opportunity to express their views frankly as decisions are reached;
- Opinions expressed and advice offered within the Executive remain private;
- Decisions of the Executive are binding on and supported by all ministers;
- Mechanisms for sharing information and resolving disputes are followed.

Given the centrality of collective responsibility as a means of maintaining coalition governance – what may be termed *collective coalition responsibility* – it was ironic that the greatest apparent breach of the doctrine arose as a familiar case where a minister openly disagreed with a major Executive policy. This was the case of Mike Watson, the Culture Minister and a Labour constituency MSP in Glasgow, who appeared to campaign publicly against a hospital reorganization in that city. Though defended by his First Minister, and retaining his Cabinet post at the time, he was not appointed to the Executive after the 2003 election.[38]

The relationship between the First Minister and the Deputy First Minister is an interesting one. The former is a statutory post, defined in the Scotland Act,[39] and has been held since 1999 by whoever is the leader of the Labour Party in Scotland. The latter is an entirely administrative creation, to provide a sufficiently senior title for the leader of the 'junior' coalition party, the Scottish Liberal Democrats.[40] The relationship between the two posts is not entirely one of head of government and deputy, and in some respects resembles the 'co-equal' model in Northern Irish devolution.[41]

An essential priority for the two coalition parties thus far has been maintaining support for the coalition and all its policies among the Liberal Democrat parliamentary party. A minority of these MSPs was sceptical of the initial coalition, and of the speedy, private way in which the coalition negotiations were conducted in May 1999. They expressed their disquiet during the first session over various policies (such as student finance, fishing, and free personal care for the elderly) by threats of what would have been damaging rebellions in key parliamentary votes. The original coalition arrangements on maintaining party and

[37] *Guide*, preface and see further para. 1.2. The definition was set out initially in the 1999 and 2003 coalition agreements between the two parties.

[38] Barry Winetrobe, 'Collective responsibility in devolved Scotland' [2003] *Public Law* 24.

[39] See especially ss. 45–6.

[40] As such, any change in the leadership of the Liberal Democrats automatically feeds through to the Deputy First Ministership, as when Nicol Stephen took over from Jim Wallace in June 2005.

[41] See generally S. 5 of the 2003 coalition agreement, *A partnership for a better Scotland*; S. 2 of the *Guide*, and, for ministerial and other appointments, S. 4 of the *Code*. And see Chapter 8, below.

inter-party discipline were relatively loose,[42] but these have been tightened up in the post-2003 election coalition agreement.[43]

INTERGOVERNMENTAL RELATIONS

On the introduction of devolution, the UK Government promulgated a series of concordats, under an overarching *Memorandum of Understanding*, with the devolved executives.[44] These are designed to set out the arrangements for 'good communications' between them: 'The primary aim is not to constrain the discretion of any administration but to allow administrations to make representations to each other in sufficient time for those representations to be fully considered.'[45]

The concordats attached to the *Memorandum of Understanding* also cover EU policy coordination; financial assistance to industry; international relations; and statistics.[46] There are also bilateral concordats between the devolved administrations and individual UK government departments and related bodies,[47] as well as other guidance on the operation of devolution.[48] These arrangements are bolstered by regular (or, at least intended to be so[49]) intergovernmental meetings,[50] including those, such as the British–Irish Council, which arise as a result of the Belfast Agreement machinery. In addition, the continued existence of the UK Cabinet post of Secretary of State for Scotland, supported by a relatively small Scotland Office (since June 2003, as part of the Department for Constitutional Affairs), was intended to provide further means of liaison between the devolved Scottish Executive and the UK Government.

These arrangements provided an elaborate network linking the administrations in London and Edinburgh. In practice, the relationship has not always been so cooperative and mutually supportive as was originally intended.[51] The guidance retains many of the traditional notions of British governance, such as the confidentiality of much core central government activity (even from the eyes and ears of the supposed partnership administrations in Edinburgh,

42 A particular problem was in parliamentary committee activity, where coalition whipping formally did not take place.

43 See the segment of S. 5 of the May 2003 partnership agreement, entitled 'The Partnership Parties' support for the Executive in Parliament'. This refers, for example, to a Backbench Liaison Group of ministers and MSPs from the two party groups.

44 See generally Richard Rawlings, 'Concordats of the constitution' (2000) 116 *LQR* 257.

45 *Memorandum of Understanding*, Cm 5240, Dec. 2001, para. 4.

46 *Supplementary agreements B–E*, Cm 5240.

47 The Scottish Executive has concordats with departments such as Health, Defence, and Trade and Industry, and bodies such as the Forestry Commission and the Health & Safety Executive: www.scotland.gov.uk/concordats/.

48 See the lists on the Department for Constitutional Affairs web site: www.dca.gov.uk/constitution/devolution/index.htm.

49 Alan Trench, 'Devolution: the withering away of the Joint Ministerial Committee' [2004] *Public Law* 513–17.

50 See, in particular, the Joint Ministerial Committee system, set out in *Supplementary Agreement A* to the *Memorandum of Understanding*, n. 45 above.

51 For an annual overview of intergovernmental relations under devolution, see the relevant chapter of the Constitution Unit's *State of the Nations* devolution yearbook, as well as the useful description and commentary in the House of Lords Constitution Committee report, op. cit. (n. 13 above).

Cardiff, and Belfast), and the supposition that governments can routinely control and speak for 'their' parliaments.

A controversial example of the latter tendency has been the Sewel Convention, by which the UK Parliament will not normally legislate on matters within the legislative competence of the Scottish Parliament, without the consent of that Parliament through what was commonly known as a 'Sewel Motion'. Though described in terms of the two parliaments, it was set out initially by a junior Scottish Office minister during the passage of the Scotland Bill in 1998, and the UK Government's guidance on it makes it clears that application of the Convention and resort to the consent process is primarily on the initiative of the two governments.[52] The Convention generally, and the scale of its application through Executive-sponsored Sewel Motions in the Parliament, became a significant issue in the practical development of devolved governance in Scotland.[53] Eventually, both Parliaments examined the issue by way of committee inquiry. The Scottish Parliament's Procedures Committee proposed a series of changes to the Holyrood end of the process, including renaming it as 'Legislative Consent', which were adopted in late 2005, and the Scottish Affairs Committee at the House of Commons followed up with its own inquiry, reporting in 2006. As well as a good example of the two governments and especially the two parliaments being willing to cooperate to reform a sensitive aspect of the initial devolution scheme, it seems that there is a fair chance that the reforms will largely defuse the controversy over the operation of the Sewel Convention.[54]

Viewed from Scotland, the intergovernmental arrangements have generally been seen as the UK Government maintaining central control and oversight of devolved governance, but failing to reflect developing political realities. The Scottish Secretary and Scotland Office themselves rapidly became perceived as virtually redundant, as the First Minister and the Executive increasingly were regarded as the government of Scotland, and relations generally being conducted bilaterally between equivalent departments or offices, rather than through the conduit of the Scotland Office. The initial intergovernmental relationship was altered when in June 2003 a new UK Department for Constitutional Affairs was created – absorbing, *inter alia*, the Scotland and Wales Offices, though retaining the two Secretaries of State – and a UK Supreme Court was proposed.[55] One cabinet minister now shares the job of Scottish Secretary with another ministerial portfolio (to date, that of Transport Secretary), and the current junior Scottish minister is also a junior Northern Ireland minister. Significantly, in view of the supposed communication function of the network of intergovernmental relations, the changes appeared to be as much of a surprise to the First Minister and his team as to everyone else, and the episode serves as a salutary reminder of how the structure and operation of Scottish devolution ultimately depends on decisions in London.

[52] Lord Sewel, HL Debs, vol. 592, col. 791, 21 July 1998; *Memorandum of Understanding*, para. 13; *Post devolution primary legislation affecting Scotland*, Devolution Guidance Note 10, Nov 2005 update.

[53] Paul Cairney. and Michael Keating. (2004) 'Sewel motions in the Scottish Parliament' (2004) 47 *Scottish Affairs* 115; Barry Winetrobe. 'A partnership of the Parliaments? Scottish law-making under the Sewel Convention at Westminster and Holyrood' in Hazell and Rawlings (n. 20 above).

[54] Scottish Parliament Procedures Committee 7th report 2005 *The Sewel Convention*. Vol. 1. SP Paper 428, October 2005; House of Commons Scottish Affairs Committee *The Sewel Convention: the Westminster perspective*. 4th report, HC 983, 2005–06, June 2006, and Government response in 2nd Special Report, HC 1634, 2005–06, October 2006.

[55] Now enacted in Constitutional Reform Act 2005, Part 3.

INTER-PARLIAMENTARY RELATIONS

Relations between the various parliaments and assemblies within the UK (and beyond[56]) have been rather neglected by academic commentators, perhaps because they are not buttressed by an extensive network of written guidance and regular meetings, such as exists between the four administrations in the UK.[57] Nevertheless, they comprise an important strand in the overall devolution network.

The distribution of legislative power between Westminster and Holyrood has led to the development of conventions and 'Speaker's rulings'[58] on the admissibility of particular types of business relating to matters primarily within the competence of the 'other' parliament. Though Westminster has generally adhered to a self-denying ordinance on devolved matters, there is nothing, for example, in the devolution legislation to restrict the Scottish Parliament from discussing non-devolved matters. It has debated reserved matters ranging from the Act of Settlement 1701 to foreign affairs such as Iraq, as well as those directly affecting current Scottish public policy, such as the treatment of asylum seekers in Scotland or the future of nuclear power.

Generally, thus far, the impact of devolution on Westminster has not been dramatic.[59] As from the 2005 general election, the number of MPs from Scotland has been cut from 72 to 59, but the now-diminished Scottish Secretary still answers oral Scottish Questions in the House of Commons, and the Scottish Affairs Committee and the Scottish Grand Committee have continued to operate, mainly dealing with primarily non-devolved issues, though the latter has not met since November 2003. The incendiary potential of the 'West Lothian Question' – which broadly exposes the asymmetrical nature of devolution in the UK by asking why Scottish MPs can participate in matters affecting England when they cannot deal with the same matters applying to Scotland because they are devolved to the Scottish Parliament[60] – has not yet blown devolution off course, despite instances of Scottish MPs' participating and voting in Westminster proceedings on controversial policy matters such as student finance, foundation hospitals, and proposed bans on hunting. The tighter parliamentary arithmetic after the 2005 Westminster election has revived discussion of the Question, especially within the UK Conservative Party, but the huge gap between 'sound bite' solutions like 'English votes for English laws' and procedurally sound and politically acceptable answers remains.[61]

[56] Like the Executive, the Parliament has a substantial external relations strategy, engaging especially with national and sub-national parliaments around the world. For a summary, see the Parliament's web site at www.scottish.parliament.uk/corporate/elu/index.htm.

[57] Barry Winetrobe, 'Inter-Parliamentary relations in a devolved UK: an initial overview', House of Lords Constitution Committee report, op. cit. (n. 13 above), Appendix 5, pp. 59–69.

[58] For the House of Commons, see, in particular, the Speaker's statement of 12 July 1999 (HC Debs, vol. 335, cols 21–2), and the resolutions agreed on 25 Oct. 1999 (HC Debs, vol. 336, cols 761 ff.), following the report of the Procedure Committee, *The procedural consequences of devolution*, 4th report of 1998–9, HC 185, May 1999.

[59] Meg Russell, Guy Lodge and Oonagh Gay, 'The Impact of Devolution on Westminster: If not now, when?' in Alan Trench (ed.), *Has Devolution made a Difference?: The State of the Nations 2004* (2004).

[60] It is so called because it was first, and frequently, asked by the anti-devolutionist Labour MP for West Lothian, Tam Dalyell, during the devolution debates of the late 1970s.

[61] See Robert Hazell, *The English Question* (2006), the brief consideration by the Scottish Affairs Committee in its Sewel report of June 2006, paras 45–50 (see n. 54 above) and Chapter 9 below.

On a more positive note, there has been much informal interaction between committees, members, and staff of the two parliaments, often as part of wider inter-parliamentary relations. In particular there is a growing willingness for each parliament to learn from the experience of its counterpart and from public policy developments generally.[62] The Scottish Affairs Committee has even suggested recently that there might be merit in a 'Super' Scottish Grand Committee, comprising Scotland's MPs, MSPs and MEPs.[63] The Scotland Act's linkage of the size of the Scottish Parliament and the number of MPs from Scotland, devised to reduce the number of Scottish MPs and of MSPs, was a symbol of the early tensions between and within the two parliaments However, the UK Government resisted pressure from MPs, including its Scottish backbenchers, and accepted the arguments from both the Scottish Executive and Scottish Parliament to retain the existing number of MSPs, while proceeding with the cut in the number of Scottish MPs.[64] The tensions between the Scottish MPs and MSPs remain, and especially on the Labour benches, though these now focus on the electoral system for, rather than the size of, Holyrood, especially the regional (or 'list') element, which is largely made up of opposition members.[65]

THE EXECUTIVE, THE PARLIAMENT, AND THE PEOPLE

As has already been noted, the relationships between the devolved government and the Parliament with the Scottish public were intended to adhere to the CSG principles. These stress a positive, open, and inclusive approach to the participation of the Scottish people in devolved governance. Both the Executive and the Parliament, in their own ways, have tried to devise procedures and practices which give meaningful effect to this aspiration. The Executive has done this primarily through substantive consultation on policy and legislative proposals, and an open approach to public information through, for example, information technology (IT) and the Freedom of Information (Scotland) Act 2002 which came fully into effect in 2005.

The Parliament has devised innovative forms of public engagement through, for example, its public petitions system, committee meetings outside Edinburgh, webcasting of proceedings, online discussion forums, and other IT means of information provision and interactive participation, the development of an extensive cross-party group system, and so on.[66] Research commissioned by the Parliament suggests that those who do engage with the Parliament – as visitors, witnesses, or constituents – have a more positive view of it than do the general public, who receive more negative images from the media and elsewhere.[67]

However, genuine public engagement in devolved governance is low, even in terms of participation in elections, with turnout at the 2003 Scottish Parliament election dipping below 50 per cent. Generally, the Parliament and the Executive have not coordinated their public engagement activities, which can cause difficulties when they each hold their own

[62] An example of open acknowledgement by Westminster of what is happening north of the border was the report in July 2003 of the Select Committee on the Lord Chancellor's Department, *Judicial appointments: lessons from the Scottish experience*, 2nd report of 2002–3, HC 902.

[63] Sewel report of June 2006, paras 45–50 (see n. 54 above) paras 34–44.

[64] Scottish Parliament (Constituencies) Act 2004.

[65] Discussed below.

[66] See its *Participation Handbook* (2004): www.scottish.parliament.uk/vli/participationHandbook/index.htm.

[67] Procedures Committee report, op. cit., Annex F (see n. 10 above).

separate consultation exercises at different stages of the policy-making process over what may be seen by the public as the same policy proposals. This has led to complaints from interest groups of 'consultation overload'. The Executive has its own policy programme and timetable derived from its electoral mandate and coalition agreement, including an apparent desire to maintain an annual legislative cycle, notwithstanding the four-year sessional arrangements in the Parliament. These create pressures against meaningful parliamentary and public engagement in public policy making.

Understandable public focus on practical outcomes rather than enhanced processes has meant that dissatisfaction with policy delivery and with various political 'scandals' since 1999[68] have tended to diminish public faith in the devolved institutions and politicians.[69] Ironically the very transparency of devolved governance makes it more, not less, open to destabilizing media criticism, and also more at risk of capture by professional, organized pressure groups and lobbyists. Both the Executive and the Parliament are aware of the difficulties of achieving genuine inclusiveness and involvement in governance of those beyond the 'usual suspects' who are otherwise ignored or unheard. One study of interest groups in devolved Scotland concluded that 'while the language of People and Parliament has a decent ring to it, the necessary reality of contemporary policy making may well continue to be Groups and Government'.[70]

There is always the risk, as the devolved institutions move on from their early days, that initial enthusiasm for innovation and genuine public engagement will wane in the face of the daily grind of governance. This is particularly acute for the Parliament, where the pressures of business, especially that which is Executive-initiated, may make transparent and inclusive procedures and practices seem to busy members and staff as unnecessary add-ons, which can be diluted or dispensed with. This tendency seems to be creeping in especially when the Parliament is considering what it regards as 'internal' or housekeeping matters, such as, at the time of writing, the Standards and Public Appointments Committee's review of the Members Code of Conduct or the Committee Conveners Group's attempt to have the Standing Orders requirement for committee to publish annual reports abolished. Maintaining initial momentum for a distinctive parliamentary culture, which remains justifiably much admired, will be a major challenge for Holyrood.

MEMBERS OF THE SCOTTISH PARLIAMENT

The rules governing the conduct of MSPs are generally familiar to students of the Westminster Parliament, subject to the fundamental distinction that the devolved Parliament enjoys no parliamentary privilege in the Westminster sense. The opportunity

68 These include various '-gates', such as Lobbygate (concerning allegations in late 1999 about improper lobbying and access to ministers) and Officegate (concerning office expenses of the First Minister, Henry McLeish, which led to his resignation in late 2001), and most damagingly, the Holyrood Project on the new parliamentary building, which was significantly delayed and over budget, the subject of a very public inquiry chaired by a former Conservative Law officer, Lord Fraser of Carmylie, which reported in September 2004, just after Holyrood was finally open for parliamentary business (www.holyroodinquiry.org/FINAL_report/report.htm).

69 See generally the quarterly devolution monitoring reports on the Constitution Unit web site, the current series of which since 2006 is at http://www.ucl.ac.uk/constitution-unit/research/devolution/devo-monitoring-programme.html.

70 Grant Jordan and Linda Stevenson, 'Redemocratizing Scotland: towards the politics of disappointment', chap. 12 of Alex Wright, *Scotland: the challenge of devolution* (2000) 171.

Table 9.1 Results of 1999 and 2003 elections

	1999 election		2003 election	
	Total MSPs	Constituency – regional MSPs	Total MSPs	Constituency – regional MSPs
Labour	56	53–3	50	46–4
SNP	35	7–28	27	9–18
Conservative	18	0–18	18	3–15
Liberal Democrat	17	12–5	17	13–4
Green	1	0–1	7	0–7
SSP	1	0–1	6	0–6
D Canavan	1	1–0	1	1–0
Senior Citizens	–	–	1	0–1
'Others'	–	–	2	1–1
Total	129	73–56	129	73–56

was taken in the late 1990s to ensure that the lessons of 'political sleaze' were learned, so that MSPs are subject to very strict ethical regulation and only limited 'privilege'-type protections.[71] However, in the particular area of relationships between elected members, the (sometimes unintended) impact of novel constitution making can be seen.

It might have been thought that, when the Additional Member System of proportional representation was devised for the Parliament through what the final report of the Scottish Constitutional Convention in 1995 described as 'long and detailed discussions', the politically-aware negotiators would have appreciated its potential for confusion and conflict between constituency and regional MSPs. However, this does not seem to have been the case, as the focus then was almost entirely on providing a greater degree of proportionality and broader representation in elections to the new devolved Parliament than could be achieved under the traditional 'first past the post' system. Of the 129 MSPs, 73 were to be elected in the 72 single-member Westminster constituencies (with the split of the Orkney and Shetland constituency into two Scottish Parliament seats), and 56 in 8 regions (representing the former European Parliament electoral regions), with 7 members to each region.

The 1999 and 2003 elections resulted in very different proportions of constituency and regional ('list') MSPs in the various political parties, with the skewing within and between the parties only very marginally reduced in 2003 (see Table 9.1).

[71] Ss. 39–43, Scotland Act 1998. The transitional regulatory scheme on members' interests has been replaced by an Act of the Parliament, the Interests of the Members of the Scottish Parliament Act 2006. See Chapter 17, below.

Not surprisingly, the parties often tended to view the relative importance and role of constituency and regional members in terms of their own proportions of each. So, for example, Labour championed the rights of constituency MSPs as the primary representatives of people within their constituencies, while the Scottish National Party (SNP) often had relatively greater concern for regional MSPs. This was exacerbated by Labour's belief that Opposition parties were not placing their regional MSPs' offices in geographically convenient locations, but within their 'target' Labour-held constituencies in the region. When the Parliament first met in early 1999, MSPs and parties had virtually no official guidance on how these two types of MSPs should operate in practice, and tensions were publicly exposed when the Parliament debated a draft Members' allowances scheme, including financial provision for constituency and regional offices, in June 1999. The acrimonious debate dealt a significant blow to the hopes of a new form of non-adversarial politics so early in the life of the Parliament.[72]

Continuing problems between constituency and list MSPs led the Presiding Officer to convene an informal working group of MSPs plus a Westminster MP, to draw up guidance for the interaction both of list and constituency MSPs, and of MSPs and Scottish MPs. A set of principles for the former relationship was prepared by this group, and, once subjected to prolonged consultation with, and significant amendment by, the party business managers and parliamentary groups, was agreed formally by the Parliament in July 2000 and incorporated into the Members' Code of Conduct, as Annexe 5. There were five principles, which can be summarized as:

- constituents have eight MSPs (one constituency and seven regional);
- constituents' wishes are paramount;
- all MSPs are equal;
- MSPs should not misrepresent the basis of their representation;[73] and
- MSPs should not deal with matters outside their area.

These provisions, originally designed to be general guidance for the assistance of MSPs and the citizens and bodies they deal with, have proved to be rather bureaucratic in their application and enforcement.[74] The 2003 Procedures Committee CSG principles report examined the issue and recommended that the existing guidance should be reviewed and clarified so as to ensure cooperative working between MSPs for the benefit of their constituents.[75] This issue became linked with the questions of the size of the Parliament and the numbers of Scottish MPs (discussed above), and the Scotland Office set up an independent inquiry in 2004, which reported in 2006.[76] Unfortunately for Labour, the report refused to support significant changes to the electoral system, including a ban on 'dual candidacy', whereby candidates would be prevented from standing in both the constituency

72 SPOR, vol. 1 no. 7, col 280, 8 June 1999.

73 For example, an MSP should not claim that he or she is the sole or main representative of a particular locality.

74 Jonathan Bradbury & Meg Russell, *The Local Work of Scottish MPs and MSPs: Effects of Non-coterminous Boundaries and AMS* (2005).

75 Procedures Committee 2003, op. cit., paras 842–6 (see n. 11 above).

76 *Putting Citizens First* (Arbuthnott Report), January 2006, and see Scottish Affairs Committee, Third Report, 2005–06, HC 924, May 2006.

and regional ballots.[77] As these matters are, like the West Lothian Question or the Sewel Convention, surrogates for the political and constitutional tensions in the devolution scheme, they are unlikely to fade away, and some revisiting of the Holyrood electoral system may be expected in the medium term.

ASSESSMENT

This chapter has examined some of the main strands of the network of Scottish devolution relationships. Through a variety of devices – including statute; concordats and other more informal written arrangements; regular meetings and discussions; fiscal, legal, and administrative levers; underlying principles and other conventions – the devolution scheme has held together thus far, in the sense that devolved Scottish governance appears to have become a recognized and accepted feature of the constitution. It has not been subject to interruptions or structural collapse, as in Northern Ireland, nor, unlike the Welsh situation, have its essentials been the subject of widespread, fundamental questioning or reform.

This is not to pronounce Scottish devolution since 1999 an unequivocal success, however that may be measured or assessed. Any positive verdict relates more to the robustness of its structures and procedures than to the substance of policy delivery (better public services and so on) or substantially greater participation in government. That the scheme has survived so far relatively unscathed may be due not so much to the quality of the scheme or of its actors, as to the degree of consensus-building that preceded it, and to the generally favourable political, economic, and legal circumstances in which it has operated.

The general unity of purpose between the governments in London and Edinburgh has been a key factor in this survival, despite a number of internal upheavals at the top of Scottish Labour, tensions between MSPs and Scottish MPs, and a series of major policy differences. In both party-political terms and as the creator of the devolution scheme itself, it is clearly in the UK Government's interests for devolution to be seen to succeed. Devolved intergovernmental relations will, however, be more severely tested when there are governments of different party colours in London and Edinburgh.[78]

Just as important for the relative stability of devolved governance has been the generally positive economic and financial position in the UK since 1999, ensuring substantial growth in the overall resources available for the devolved institutions' pursuit of their policy objectives. This has masked both the inherent limitations on the devolved institutions' ability to use economic or fiscal levers to affect policy in Scotland, and their refusal thus far to use such tools as they do have, such as the power to vary the standard rate of income tax by up to 3p.[79] It has also moderated disquiet in other parts of the UK over the fairness or otherwise of the territorial distribution of public money, through the Barnett Formula. A sustained period of financial restraint or outright 'cuts' could well expose the fragility of

[77] Such a prohibition was, however, included in the Government of Wales Act 2006 s. 7, in response to similar pressure from Labour in Wales.

[78] This chapter has been written before the Holyrood general election of May 2007, which may presage clearer differences between the two governments, and so provoke or encourage some of the tensions or fissures in the devolution scheme that have not hitherto emerged in any serious way.

[79] Part IV (ss. 73–80), Scotland Act 1998.

these arrangements, and the substantial structural 'irresponsibility' of devolved institutions as primarily spending bodies (especially in areas, such as health and education, where there has been some clear divergence from UK/English policy). Opposition parties, though often for different political reasons, have called for greater powers to be devolved in these key areas, and it is possible that a British government may become tempted by the greater degree of direct fiscal and policy responsibility that this may impose on the devolved institutions, and away from itself.

A further factor in the period of relative stability has been the absence of any serious legal challenge to the devolution scheme.[80] Few major 'devolution issues' have arisen, other than in the human rights field,[81] and many of these, arguably, would have arisen even without devolution. No legislation of the Parliament has yet been overturned by the courts or even challenged before Royal Assent by UK ministers.[82] While such jurisprudence as does exist has reinforced the notion that the Parliament, as a creature of statute, is fully subject to the courts, this has not yet led to a flood of disruptive challenges to its proceedings and internal actions. It remains to be seen whether this relative legal calm is a result of the quality of the initial devolution scheme (including its detailed disputes resolution arrangements), and of its operation thus far, or because these early years have been an untypical honeymoon period. A direct challenge by UK ministers to the *vires* of a Bill passed by the Parliament, or the disapplication of a statutory provision by the courts, could well transform the situation into a more confrontational one between the devolved institutions on the one hand, and the UK authorities and/or the courts on the other.

Finally, it has been noted that the devolution settlement has not been subject to substanive amendment thus far, with any changes concentrating on the margins of areas like legislative competence. Wider changes may be proposed for the Parliament's electoral system, and other structural changes have been floated by commentators, even for some form of quasi-bicameralism for the Parliament. Quite how the existing scheme would cope with such proposed changes, or how destabilizing the very reopening of the fundamentals of the Scotland Act scheme would be, remains to be seen.

Space does not permit detailed consideration of two important aspects of the new multi-layer democracy in Scotland. One is local government, described by one commentator in 2000 as 'the forgotten layer.'[83] The other is Europe, though this is a tier where devolved Scotland has little direct influence or power. Both the Executive and the Parliament have established a presence in Brussels to ensure that at least their distinctive voices are heard in the corridors of European power. The Parliament's European and External Relations Committee has produced a number of valuable reports on Scotland's role in the developing Europe, while experiencing the same problems as any parliamentary 'European Affairs' committee, of keeping track meaningfully of EU documents and legislation.[84]

80 Hazell & Rawlings, (n. 20 above).

81 See *Stair Memorial Encyclopaedia of the Laws of Scotland* (2002), op. cit. (n.20 above) paras 475–6.

82 Ss. 32–5, and, for related powers over administrative action (including subordinate legislation), s. 58, 1998 Act.

83 John Fairley, ' "Layers of democracy": making home rule work', ch. 7 of Wright, op. cit., (see n. 70 above) p. 92; Michael Bennett, John Fairley and Mark McAteer, *Devolution in Scotland, the impact on local government* (2002).

84 For a good overview, see the Committee's *2005–06 Annual Report*, 2nd Report, 2006, SP Paper 570, May 2006.

The Executive inevitably has to maintain a twin-track approach domestically to EU matters, liaising with both the Parliament and with the UK Government.

In practical policy terms, EU primacy has been demonstrated in a number of areas of particular importance to Scotland, such as agriculture and fisheries and economic development and support. Europe has become a focus of the continuing debate over the Scottish constitution, especially between the SNP and its 'unionist' opponents, as Scotland's subsidiary position to the UK in EU matters has become apparent. This tension is likely to increase following enlargement of the EU, when more small countries of comparable size to Scotland became full member states of the EU, with seats at the top tables of decisionmaking.

CONCLUSIONS

Much of the reformist thesis of 'what is wrong with the British constitution' has tended to concentrate on the stultifying centralization of government in the UK. Solutions therefore tend to focus on mechanisms which would diffuse power to other governance centres and to the people themselves. Devolution, as a major decentralizing technique, provides a significant opportunity for observation of diffusion in practice. This chapter is not the place to discuss whether this thesis is accurate, or even whether diversity, and any consequential policy differentiation, is a 'good thing'.[85] However the assumption that diffusion of power brings policy diversity, and, ultimately, better overall governance does seem to be implicit in examinations of the British constitution, and of the devolution schemes. This makes assessments of the Scottish scheme difficult in so far as the media and the public, as well as politicians, often approve of policy diversity in some cases but seek uniformity in others.

As UK experience since 1997 has demonstrated (especially in areas such as freedom of information or human rights), constitutional reform is a form of radical policy-making that, even if successfully delivered, may produce all sorts of unexpected and unintended consequences. So it has been with Scottish devolution which, as a policy pledge, was delivered relatively smoothly between 1997–99, but which, as a novel form of working governance, has thrown up many constitutional and political challenges. Some of this, as this chapter has illustrated, is due to the inherent interlocking nature of constitutional issues, but it is also a result of the often shallow and confused constitutional understanding by significant actors in the devolved institutions and in their UK counterparts. A good example of this has been the ad hoc growth in devolved Scotland of 'parliamentary commissioners', a constitutional design applied to certain constitutional watchdogs such as the Public Services Ombudsman and Information and Children Commissioners, so as to ensure their independence of the Executive by making the Parliament their 'sponsoring body'. The practical and constitutional complexities inherent in this model, as devised in various Acts, only emerged gradually, but when they did it was in the full glare of the media (who feasted on stories of allegedly profligate and unaccountable 'tsars'), and when the Commissioners made decisions uncongenial to the MSPs and ministers who had so enthusiastically created them.[86]

Nevertheless, even at this relatively early stage in the life of Scottish devolution, it seems to have become accepted as an integral and 'permanent' feature of Scottish and UK governance.

85 See Michael Keating, *The Government of Scotland: Public Policy-Making after Devolution* (2005).

86 Oonagh Gay & Barry Winetrobe, *Officers of Parliament; transforming the role* (2003); Scottish Parliament Finance Committee, *Accountability and governance*, 7th report, 2006, September 2006.

This is no mean achievement, and it can be contrasted with the position in Wales and Northern Ireland. However, it may well face greater challenges in the years to come, and its long-term viability and success will depend on many factors, some of which are outwith the direct influence and control of the devolved institutions themselves. The effectiveness of a robust network of relationships, such as those described in this chapter, will be a precondition for that viability. Successful relationships will be those which adhere to the spirit and culture of the founding principles, as has been described. They can facilitate not just continuing devolution in Scotland, but a form of devolution that can produce better government.

FURTHER READING

Bates, T. (ed.) *Devolution to Scotland: the legal aspects* (1997).

Bromley, C. et al. (eds) *Devolution – Scottish answers to Scottish questions?* (2003).

Hassan, G. and Warhurst, C. *Tomorrow's Scotland* (2002).

Himsworth, C. and Munro, C. *The Scotland Act 1998* (2nd edn, 2000).

Keating, M. *The Government of Scotland: Public Policy-Making after Devolution* (2005).

Mitchell, J. 'Scotland: devolution is not just for Christmas', in Trench, A. (ed.) *The Dynamics of Devolution: the State of the nations 2005* (2005) (and equivalent chapters in earlier editions of this annual series).

Murkens, J. et al. *Scottish independence: a practical guide* (2002).

Stair Memorial Encyclopaedia of the Laws of Scotland Constitutional Law reissue (2002).

Winetrobe, B. *Realising the vision: a Parliament with a purpose*, Constitution Unit (2001).

Wright, A. (ed.) *Scotland: the challenge of devolution* (2000).

USEFUL WEB SITES

Scottish Parliament: **www.scottish.parliament.uk**

Scottish Executive: **www.scotland.gov.uk**

Scotland Office: **www.scotlandoffice.gov.uk/**

Scottish Civic Forum: **www.civicforum.org.uk**

Audit Scotland: **www.audit-scotland.gov.uk**

Scottish Public Services Ombudsman: **www.scottishombudsman.org.uk**

Scottish Information Commissioner: **www.itspublicknowledge.info**

Scottish Affairs Committee: **www.parliament.uk/parliamentary_committees/scottish_affairs_committee.cfm**

Hansard Society Scotland: **www.hansardsociety.org.uk/programmes/hansard_society_scotland**

Constitution Unit UCL (devolution): **www.ucl.ac.uk/constitution-unit/research/devolution/index.htm**

Institute of Governance, Edinburgh University: **www.institute-of-governance.org/**

10

NORTHERN IRELAND AND THE BRITISH CONSTITUTION SINCE THE BELFAST AGREEMENT

*Christopher McCrudden**

SUMMARY

Two approaches tend to dominate constitutionalism: a pragmatic empiricist approach, which is traditionally British, and a more ideological constitutional approach, more prevalent, for example, in the United States and Canada.

The twentieth-century history of Northern Ireland demonstrates that the pragmatic approach, the then dominant Westminster model of British political and constitutional practice, was not a successful transplant in Northern Ireland between the 1920s and the 1960s. A tradition based on pragmatic empiricism was unable to cope with a major challenge to the legitimacy of government and the state.

Since the early 1970s an approach based on constructing a more ideological constitutionalism has been adopted in relation to Northern Ireland, concentrating on the development of explicitly normative principles and the construction of institutional arrangements designed to mesh these with local needs.

To some extent British constitutional thought may also be in the process of modifying its pragmatism more generally and moving towards a more defined and ideological constitutionalism. This development is still somewhat nascent in Britain, and ideological constitutionalism in the UK is, thus far, most clearly reflected in the Belfast Agreement between the British and Irish Governments and most of the main political parties in Northern Ireland.

Within the more consciously ideological approach to constitutionalism, there are several differing and competing approaches. It appears that even though both the Northern Ireland and British approaches to constitutional issues may be *converging* in adopting a more

* Grateful thanks to Maggie Beirne, Christine Bell, Brian Barrington, Neil Faris, Brigid Hadfield, Stephen Livingstone, Vincent McCormack, John McGarry, Paul Mageean, Austen Morgan, Martin O'Brien, Brendan O'Leary, Dawn Oliver, Brian Simpson, John Morison, Colin Harvey, and Gerard Quinn, for extensive comments on an earlier draft.

consciously ideological approach to constitutionalism, at the same time they may be *diverging* as to which ideology to adopt. On the spectrum between more communitarian and more individualist ideological approaches, Northern Ireland is located, perhaps, more towards the former than is Britain.

Experience in Northern Ireland therefore raises many issues that go to the heart of the British constitutional tradition, both as it was and as it might become.

INTRODUCTION

Since the time when it was finalized, on Good Friday, 10 April 1998, the Belfast Agreement[1] has dominated the political life, and constitutional development, of Northern Ireland. It was, and remains, an enormously ambitious attempt to establish a constitutional process that will enable both sides in the Northern Ireland dispute – nationalists, who prefer a united Ireland independent of the UK, and unionists, who prefer continued membership of the UK – to participate in government together. To enable this to occur, it is necessary to address (not to solve, but to address) all of the major contentious issues in Northern Ireland politics and constitutional debate. The Belfast Agreement can be seen as having two major functions: first, as a major part of a peace process aimed at securing a permanent move away from the use of armed force as an ever-present element in Northern Ireland politics; and, second, as a detailed framework for a form of devolved government in Northern Ireland that would differ considerably from that in Scotland and Wales. The first aim is further along the road of being achieved than the second, which still hangs in the balance. The purpose of this chapter is to explain the current constitutional debate concerning Northern Ireland and how it differs from that in the rest of the UK in significant respects.

One of the themes of this chapter, then, is the contrast between the developing Northern Ireland constitutional model, as encapsulated in the Belfast Agreement, and British constitutional practice, both past and present. To justify and illustrate this assessment, it will be useful to introduce at this point a brief discussion of two contrasting approaches to constitutional thinking. The first is a pragmatic empiricist approach. An important theme running through British legal thought concentrates on history and tradition when evaluating the processes by which political and legal decisions are made. The results of these processes are assessed pragmatically. Problems are solved, in this empiricist tradition, on the basis of experience. Solutions are what works and what lasts. Institutions should therefore operate flexibly, learn from the past, and develop to suit the conditions of their time. This is the essence of a common-law approach, in which principle is often sacrificed to pragmatism.[2] The British *constitutional* tradition is also heavily imbued with this approach. Several of the principles which are said to describe, inform, and underpin the British constitution, such as majoritarian democracy, parliamentary supremacy, and constitutional conventions, may be seen as the embodiment of this tradition, concentrating as they do on 'the authority

[1] 'The Belfast Agreement: An Agreement Reached at the Multi-Party Talks on Northern Ireland, April 10, 1998' (hereafter, 'the Agreement'), Cm 3883 (1998).

[2] P. S. Atiyah, *From Principles to Pragmatism* (1978).

of experience and the continuity of practice'[3] and ensuring the flexibility of the process by which decisions are made.[4] In this tradition, authoritative constitutional structures are thought to *evolve*; they are seldom *made*.

An alternative model of constitutional practice may be simply stated. Imagine a constitutional tradition which concentrates first and foremost on setting out a number of values which political and legal institutions are required to promote. Imagine further that the decisions these institutions reach are assessed on the basis of their conformity to this set of values, and are to that extent constrained and confined. What counts in this alternative more ideologically driven constitutional approach are the values captured by the processes of decision making and furthered by particular decisions, rather than the fact that the process has simply survived. In this context, constitutional settlements are explicitly constructed, often as a result of a period of major political upheaval.

The distinction between these two constitutional approaches is not unproblematic, however. The British constitutional tradition has frequently evidenced rich seams of normative thinking. The English common law is clearly not devoid of principles. Nor does the constitutional thinking of other countries, such as Canada or the United States, demonstrate a single-minded espousal of a more ideological approach to constitutionalism. From its establishment, there has been a competing pragmatic tradition of legal thought in American constitutionalism. More generally, the dualism inherent in the distinction may be criticized at a more fundamental level as too stark, given the interplay between these approaches.

Yet, despite these complexities, the distinction between the pragmatic and the more ideologically driven constitutional approaches is useful to an understanding of Northern Ireland constitutional developments in two respects. Elements of the arrangements for the government of Northern Ireland, in operation from 1921 until 1972, when they collapsed, may provide evidence of an approach that differed from traditional British approaches. (Examples include the establishment of devolved government, legal protections against discrimination, and the role of the Privy Council in scrutinizing legislation by the devolved Parliament). In practice, however, the dominant constitutional approach adopted was a modified British constitutional approach.[5] The failure of this earlier experiment in devolved government illustrates the difficulty this tradition has in being able to handle fundamental challenges to legitimacy arising in a divided society. This approach has, since the collapse of the devolved government in 1972, been replaced with attempts to devise political and legal arrangements based on an ideological constitutionalism more attuned to coping with a divided society. Northern Ireland has become an important laboratory in which to assess the strengths and weaknesses of these two approaches. It provides a case study, first, of the limits in Northern Ireland of the British constitutional tradition, and secondly, of the difficulties of constructing new arrangements on the basis of constitutional idealism. It is thus of importance in any assessment of the extent to which the British constitution reacts

[3] M. Loughlin, 'Tinkering with the Constitution' (1988) 51 *MLR* 531, 536.

[4] This theme runs through many analyses of British constitutional and political thinking, see e.g. I. Jennings, *The Law and the Constitution* (5th edn, 1973); P. Norton, *The British Polity* (1984); S. H. Beer, *Modern British Politics* (3rd edn, 1982); I. Harden and N. Lewis, *The Noble Lie* (1986).

[5] This is not to say that the act of constituting Northern Ireland, and the adoption of the dominant British approach, was not itself driven by ideology in some quarters. What was pragmatic in Britain was ideological in Northern Ireland.

to a crisis of political legitimacy.[6] One of our tasks will be to identify where the Belfast Agreement and the constitutional settlement that grew out of it depart from this constitutional tradition, and where it diverges from the models of devolution adopted for Scotland and Wales.

There is, however, another important aspect of ideological constitutionalism that is important to an analysis of the relationship between the current Northern Ireland constitution and the British constitution. In the UK, the pragmatic model of constitutional practice used to be so deeply embedded in the British legal and political tradition that it required a leap of the imagination for British constitutional lawyers to consider any fundamentally different arrangement as appropriate. Now, however, proposals to adopt a more ideological model of British constitutional practice are much more acceptable, and this is reflected in the constitutional reforms of the Labour Government, in power since 1997. Devolution to Scotland and Wales, the adoption of the Human Rights Act 1998 (*de facto* incorporating the European Convention on Human Rights into UK law), the changing composition of the House of Lords, and the proposed formal separation of the judiciary from the legislature, each reflect ideological constitutional tendencies. Perhaps most particularly, ideological constitutionalism is reflected in the adaptations required by membership of the European Community, itself a prime example of such constitutionalism in the making, and in the way in which judicial review has developed since the 1960s. To some extent, therefore, developing a more ideological constitutionalism in Northern Ireland is consistent with, and indeed reflects, the drift of recent British constitutional thinking.

But there is no one model of ideological constitutionalism. Though perhaps most clearly associated with those political traditions (such as that of the United States) which purport to place liberal individual rights at the core of the values which are protected, this need not be the case. An ideological constitutional approach may equally well seek to promote what might seem more intangible values, such as creating a stable political community from a number of diverse groups, or furthering a particular type of participatory process of political decision making,[7] or providing a set of specific collective goods, such as health or housing. The Canadian and South African attempts to further political and social integration through new constitutional arrangements are recent examples of this variant of constitutional idealism.[8] Relatively crudely put, the ideals adopted in an ideological constitutional approach may be either traditional liberal values of individualism and autonomy, or more communitarian values of fraternity and the recognition of community identity.

To the extent that the British constitution now shows signs of developing a more ideological form of constitutionalism, one of our other tasks will be to identify where the Belfast Agreement and the Northern Ireland constitutional settlement adopt contrasting ideological approaches. We shall see that the Belfast Agreement is an uneasy mix of liberal

[6] Considered more generally in S. H. Beer, *Britain Against Itself* (1983).

[7] See discussion in Chapter 6 above.

[8] See e.g. P. H. Russell, 'Canada's Charter of Rights and Freedoms: A Political Report' [1988] *Public Law* 385. For an extensive consideration of various comparative dimensions, see J. McGarry, 'Political Settlements in Northern Ireland and South Africa' (1998) 46(5) *Political Studies* 853–70; J. McGarry (ed.), *Northern Ireland and the Divided World: Post-Agreement Northern Ireland in Comparative Perspective (2001).*

and more communitarian values, in contrast to the more undiluted liberalism of recent British constitutional reforms.

OVERVIEW OF THE NEW INSTITUTIONS OF THE NORTHERN IRELAND CONSTITUTION PROVIDED FOR IN THE BELFAST AGREEMENT

Before going into these issues more deeply, we need first to develop a basic map of the Northern Ireland constitutional terrain. In negotiations since 1972 designed to reach an acceptable accommodation,[9] three interlinking 'strands' were developed, to encapsulate and reflect the diverse set of priorities and interests involved. From the early 1990s, in the negotiations preceding the Belfast Agreement, these three 'strands' were formalized. Strand One involved relationships within Northern Ireland (internal). Strand Two involved relationships between Northern Ireland and the Republic of Ireland (north–south). Strand Three involved the relationships between Britain and Ireland (east–west). In the Agreement, institutions were developed under each of these strands to reflect these interlinking relationships.

We shall discuss the detail of these institutions subsequently, but for the purposes of exposition a brief outline of what the Agreement envisaged will be useful at this point.

A new Northern Ireland Assembly would be elected by proportional representation. The members of the Assembly would choose which of three broad groups (nationalist, unionist, or 'other', explained below) they would join, and the most important decisions would require substantial agreement between the nationalist and unionist groups. From the Assembly members, a Northern Ireland Executive would be formed on the basis of party strength, using the so-called d'Hondt method (to be discussed subsequently) thus ensuring the establishment of a cross-community government bridging the political divide. In practice, it was likely that the nominee of the largest nationalist party and the nominee of the largest unionist party would lead the Executive jointly as First and Deputy First Minister, who were to be equal in everything except their titles. Cross-border institutions (particularly a North/South Ministerial Council) would be established to carry out limited executive functions and provide a forum for continuing discussions between the Northern Ireland Executive and the Irish government. In addition, institutions would be established (particularly the British-Irish Intergovernmental Conference) to provide an East-West forum for discussions on Northern Ireland between the British and Irish Governments. Vital to the success of the Agreement, however, was the inclusion of other provisions dealing with the constitutional status of Northern Ireland, the decommissioning of paramilitary weapons, the release of paramilitary prisoners, and human rights and equality. The Agreement, therefore, had an explicitly consociational character,[10] supplemented by provisions evidencing

[9] For a brief discussion of previous negotiations, see Christopher McCrudden, 'Northern Ireland and the British Constitution', in Jeffrey Jowell and Dawn Oliver (eds), *The Changing Constitution* (3rd edn, 1994) 323.

[10] On consociationalism in general, see B. O'Leary, 'Consociation', in A. Kuper and J. Kuper (eds), The *Routledge Encyclopaedia of the Social Sciences* (3rd edn, 2004). On consociationalism in the Agreement, see J. McGarry and B. O'Leary, *The Northern Ireland Conflict: Consociational Engagements* (2004); J. McGarry and B. O'Leary, 'Consociational Theory, Northern Ireland's Conflict, and its Agreement. Part One. What

strong adherence to rights, corrective and distributive justice, and including some elements that some thought of as federal or confederal.[11]

The approach adopted in the Agreement was the result of painstaking negotiations undertaken since 1972. Many of the major institutional elements in the Agreement were modifications of approaches developed in earlier, failed attempts to arrive at stable government: power sharing between the two communities, the use of proportional representation, the use of referenda, the openness to Northern Ireland becoming part of a united Ireland, and the development of North–South institutions. All these elements of the Agreement had been foreshadowed in earlier attempts to negotiate a settlement.[12] From this perspective, the major change in constitutional thinking dates from the early 1970s, when these innovations were first crystallized in the Sunningdale Agreement of 1973, resulting in the establishment of a short-lived cross-community power-sharing government, which collapsed in 1974.

However, to view the 1998 Belfast Agreement simply as 'Sunningdale for slow learners'[13] is to miss a highly significant constitutional aspect of the Belfast Agreement, namely, that it is not only an agreement between most Northern Ireland political parties but also a bilateral Agreement between the British and Irish Governments, whose role in the negotiations was crucial. This internationalization of Northern Ireland constitutional development clearly marks it out not only from Sunningdale, but also from the devolution arrangements elsewhere in the UK.

Under UK law, however, if the Agreement is to have any real domestic legal force, the provisions of the Agreement have to be incorporated into UK law, by statute; in legal terminology, the Agreement was not self-executing. The implementation of the Agreement by ordinary statutes not only has symbolic meaning, but also has consequences that go beyond the symbolic. For UK lawyers, the Agreement is arguably of secondary importance, an interpretative tool rather than itself the prime source of authority. In cases of conflict between any statute implementing the Agreement and the Agreement itself, the former prevails under UK law. Such statutes are also subject to ordinary repeal and amendment by subsequent Parliaments.

There are multiple sources of legal support for the Agreement in international, UK, and Irish law. A bilateral Treaty, the British–Irish Agreement, was formally concluded between the UK and the Republic of Ireland, and is binding in international law.[14] The Northern Ireland Act 1998 and the Northern Ireland Assembly Act 1998 provided the basic legal framework for establishing the institutional aspects of the Agreement in UK law. The Irish

consociationalists can learn from Northern Ireland' (2004) *Government and Opposition*; B. O'Leary, 'The 1998 British-Irish Agreement: Consociation Plus' (1999) 26(Winter) *Scottish Affairs* 1–22.

[11] B. O'Leary, 'The Belfast Agreement and the British-Irish Agreement: Consociation, Confederal Institutions, A Federacy, and a Peace Process', in A. Reynolds (ed.), *The Architecture of Democracy: Constitutional Design, Conflict Management and Democracy* (2002) 293–356; B. O'Leary ('Complex Power-Sharing in and Over Northern Ireland: A Self-determination Agreement, a Treaty, a Consociation, a Federacy, Matching Confederal Institutions, Inter-Governmentalism and a Peace Process', in M. Weller (ed.), *Resolving Self-Determination Disputes Using Complex Power-Sharing* (2004, in press).

[12] For a discussion of these earlier attempts, see McCrudden, op cit., n. 9 above.

[13] As Mr Seamus Mallon, then Deputy Leader of the SDLP, was reported to have described the Belfast Agreement. See Mary Holland, 'A very Good Friday', *The Observer*, Sunday 12 April 1998.

[14] Four other treaties were concluded in 1999 on various aspects of the arrangements agreed in the basic British-Irish Agreement.

Constitution was amended. This collection of instruments, domestic and international, together with the Agreement itself, essentially became the Northern Ireland constitution. Each part of the Agreement was regarded as mutually reinforcing and necessary for the other parts. The British–Irish Agreement would not come into force until legislation had been enacted implementing the institutional aspects of the Agreement, and until the amendments to the Irish Constitution had been approved in a referendum.

CONSTITUTIONAL STATUS OF NORTHERN IRELAND

With this brief overview in mind, we can now turn to consider the new constitutional arrangements in more detail. The constitutional status of Northern Ireland is, clearly, one of the most important and most difficult issues underlying the conflict, with a clear majority of the population in favour of the union of Northern Ireland with Great Britain (unionists, mostly Protestants), but a sizeable proportion equally in favour of unification between Northern Ireland and the rest of Ireland (nationalists, mostly Catholics). The rest of Ireland had gained a form of Dominion status with a substantial degree of autonomy from the UK in 1921(and was known as the Irish Free State). It subsequently renounced this status, however, and adopted an essentially republican constitution in 1937, declaring itself formally as having the status of a Republic in 1948 (calling itself Ireland or, in the Irish language, Éire).[15] The 1937 Constitution envisaged a state comprising the whole of the island of Ireland, whilst accepting that until that took place, the Constitution would not apply to Northern Ireland. The Belfast Agreement, essentially, accepted the legitimacy of the aspirations both of unionists and of nationalists, recognizing that the majority want Northern Ireland to remain part of the UK, but established procedures to enable any future change in that position to be implemented. This was a demonstration of the British Government's position that it was willing for Northern Ireland to join a united Ireland, if that was the wish of its inhabitants. These provisions were incorporated in the British–Irish Agreement[16] as provisions legally binding on the Republic of Ireland and the UK in international law.

First, all participants recognized[17] 'the legitimacy of whatever choice is freely exercised by a majority of the people of Northern Ireland with regard to its status, whether they prefer to continue to support the Union with Great Britain or a sovereign united Ireland'.[18]

Second, all participants recognized 'that it is for the people of the island of Ireland alone, by agreement between the two parts respectively and without external impediment, to exercise their right of self-determination on the basis of consent, freely and concurrently given, North and South, to bring about a united Ireland, if that is their wish, accepting that this right must be achieved and exercised with and subject to the agreement and consent of a majority of the people of Northern Ireland.'[19]

[15] Republic of Ireland Act 1948. In UK law, this was recognized in 1949.

[16] British-Irish Agreement, to which the Multi-Party Talks Agreement is annexed, see op. cit., n. 1 above.

[17] Technically, the participants only 'endorsed the commitment made by the British and Irish governments that in a new British-Irish Agreement they [i.e. the two governments] will' recognize.

[18] Agreement, Constitutional Issues, 1(i).

[19] Agreement, Constitutional Issues, 1(ii).

Third, the participants acknowledged 'that while a substantial section of the people in Northern Ireland share the legitimate wish of a majority of the people of the island of Ireland for a united Ireland, the present wish of a majority of the people of Northern Ireland, freely exercised and legitimate, is to maintain the Union and, accordingly, that Northern Ireland's status as part of the UK reflects and relies upon that wish; and that it would be wrong to make any change in the status of Northern Ireland save with the consent of a majority of its people.'[20]

Fourth, the participants affirmed 'that if, in the future, the people of the island of Ireland exercise their right of self-determination . . . to bring about a united Ireland, it will be a binding obligation on both Governments to introduce and support in their respective Parliaments legislation to give effect to that wish.'[21]

Fifth, whatever choice is made by a majority of the people of Northern Ireland, the power of the sovereign government with jurisdiction there 'shall be exercised with rigorous impartiality on behalf of all the people in the diversity of their identities and traditions and shall be founded on the principles of full respect for, and equality of, civil, political, social and cultural rights, of freedom from discrimination for all citizens, and of parity of esteem and of just and equal treatment for the identity, ethos, and aspirations of both communities.'[22] All the people of Northern Ireland have the right 'to identify themselves and be accepted as Irish or British, or both, as they may so choose.'[23] Their right to hold both British and Irish citizenship is accepted by both governments and will not be affected by any future change in the status of Northern Ireland. The British Government repealed previous legislation relating to the constitutional status of Northern Ireland, in particular section 75 of the Government of Ireland Act 1920, in the 1998 Act. Articles 2 and 3 of the Irish Constitution, relating to the claim by the Republic of Ireland to Northern Ireland, were repealed by a referendum amending the Constitution.

There is much in the Agreement that broke new institutional ground in British constitutional terms, as we shall see. However, the commitment by the parties in the Agreement to the principle of consent, and the acceptance by the British Government that it was willing to relinquish a part of the UK went well beyond the institutional innovations of the Agreement. While it is true that somewhat similar declarations had been made by British Governments in the past, beginning with the Anglo Irish Agreement of 1985, these provisions of the Agreement are, in constitutional terms, of considerable significance, since they impose legal obligations on the British Government in domestic law to enter into negotiations on a united Ireland in certain contexts, indicating the extent to which the constitutional position of Northern Ireland is different from the position of Scotland and Wales. There has as yet been no formal acceptance by a British Government of a similar right of either the Scots or the Welsh to secede, and certainly no underpinning of any such acceptance in specific terms in an international agreement.

20 Agreement, Constitutional Issues, 1(iii).

21 Agreement, Constitutional Issues, 1(iv).

22 Agreement, Constitutional Issues, 1(v).

23 Agreement, Constitutional Issues, 1(vi).

ESTABLISHING THE ASSEMBLY AND EXECUTIVE

The future constitutional status of Northern Ireland was, however, only one of the essential elements in the Agreement. The purpose of the Agreement was also to enable stable government to be constructed as soon as possible, on the basis of consent. One of the essential ingredients in the Northern Ireland conflict, however, is the absence of trust between the two communities. Concluding the Agreement was but one step along a long road to the creation of sufficient trust to enable the Agreement to function effectively in practice. In the discussions leading to the Agreement, and in the Agreement itself, considerable attention was paid, therefore, to the process of implementation, to ensure that such trust as had been generated through the process of the negotiations would not be endangered by allegations of bad faith in the implementation of the Agreement in the first few months after it was concluded.

At first, the pieces of the jigsaw fell into place in the way they were intended to do. The first stage was securing popular support for the Agreement. Only if majorities in both Northern Ireland and the Republic of Ireland were seen as having approved the Agreement, would it be implemented. Following the conclusion of the Agreement, and under its terms, a referendum was held separately in both the Republic of Ireland and Northern Ireland on the same day (22 May 1998). The result was seen politically as expressing overwhelming approval of the Agreement in the Republic of Ireland, and among the nationalist population of Northern Ireland. Among the unionist population in Northern Ireland, however, although it appeared that a majority voted in favour, there was a significant group of anti-Agreement unionists, an indication of trouble to come.[24]

On 25 June 1998, elections were held to the new Assembly, consisting of 108 members elected by the single transferable vote system of proportional representation (PR(STV)), in contrast to the 'winner-takes-all' system of voting prevalent in UK elections.[25] In these Assembly elections, the Ulster Unionist Party (UUP) and the Social Democratic and Labour Party (SDLP) emerged as the largest unionist and nationalist parties respectively. Together with the Democratic Unionist Party (DUP) and Sinn Féin, these comprised the four largest parties. Of these parties, only the DUP was formally opposed to the Agreement. However, among the Ulster Unionist Party members of the Assembly there was a significant group of members elected who were in varying degrees sceptical of the Agreement, creating potential difficulties for the operation of the 'cross-community' voting requirement. In these results, we can identify another feature of Northern Ireland that stands in marked contrast to politics in the rest of the UK: the absence of UK-wide political parties among the most popular parties. While the Conservative Party has fielded candidates, they have attracted little support. The Labour Party, until 2003, refused to accept members from Northern Ireland and, at the time of writing (November 2006) prohibits people in Northern Ireland from organizing in Labour Party branches there, let alone field Labour Party candidates there.

[24] For the results of the referendums and of the elections discussed subsequently, see www.ark.ac.uk/elections.

[25] A type of proportional representation allowing voters to vote for candidates in order of preference.

If the voting system adopted, and the parties elected, mark out Northern Ireland as different from elsewhere in Britain, the decision-making process in the Assembly confirms this even more clearly. As we shall see, however, the initial formation of the Executive was initially much delayed and, once established, the operation of the Assembly and the Executive was punctuated thereafter by periods of (constitutionally controversial) suspension in February 2000, in August and September 2001, and continuously since October 2002. When it did operate, safeguards were in place to ensure that both parts of the community could participate and work together in the operation of the Assembly. Members of the Assembly are, controversially as we shall see, required to register a designation of identity (nationalist, unionist, or other) for the purposes of measuring cross-community support in Assembly votes.[26] Key decisions are taken on a cross-community basis. This involves either 'parallel consent', that is, a majority of those members present and voting, including a majority of the unionist and a majority of the nationalist designations present and voting; or a weighted majority (60 per cent) of members present and voting, including at least 40 per cent of each of the nationalist and unionist designations present and voting. Key decisions requiring cross-community and concurrent majority support include the election of the presiding officer (equivalent to the Speaker) of the Assembly, the election of the First Minister and Deputy First Minister, the adoption of standing orders, the exclusion of a person or party from ministerial office, and budget allocations. In other cases, a 'petition of concern' brought by at least 30 Assembly members could trigger decisions requiring cross-community support.

A Committee for each of the main executive functions of the Northern Ireland Administration was established to shadow what became the ten Northern Ireland Departments. The Chairs and Deputy Chairs of the Assembly Committees were allocated proportionally, using the d'Hondt system.[27] Membership of the Committees was in broad proportion to party strengths in the Assembly to ensure that the opportunity of Committee places was available to all members. The Northern Ireland Act 1998 identified three categories of functions, 'excepted,'[28] 'reserved',[29] and 'transferred'.[30] In only the latter two had the Assembly any powers to legislate, and only in the case of transferred functions did the Assembly have full authority to pass primary legislation for Northern Ireland, subject to the European Convention on Human Rights and European Community law.[31] Decisions were normally to be taken by a simple majority of members voting, except when a decision on a cross-community basis was required. The Assembly was able to seek to include Northern Ireland provisions in UK-wide legislation in the Westminster Parliament, especially on devolved issues where parity is normally maintained (e.g. social security law). The Assembly had authority to legislate in reserved areas with the approval of the Secretary of State and subject to the overall control of the Westminster Parliament. The courts decided disputes

[26] Failure to register an identity results in the member being treated as 'other'.

[27] A method of allocating seats on the basis of the proportional representation achieved by political parties, named after a Belgian mathematician.

[28] Northern Ireland Act 1998, Sched. 2, including the Crown, Parliament, international relations, defence, nationality, taxation, appointment and removal of judges, *inter alia*, among excepted matters.

[29] Northern Ireland Act 1998, Sched. 3, including maintenance of public order, control of the police, external trade, minimum wage, competition law, intellectual property, *inter alia*, among reserved matters.

[30] Northern Ireland Act 1998, s. 4(1) provides that a 'transferred matter' means any matter which is not an excepted or reserved matter.

[31] Among other limitations, see Northern Ireland Act 1998, s. 6.

over legislative competence. Draft legislation was subject to detailed scrutiny and approval in the relevant Departmental Committee. These requirements were intended to ensure that both communities in Northern Ireland support Assembly decisions and prevent the simple majoritarianism that operated prior to 1972 in Northern Ireland, and currently operates in Westminster.

The Agreement specified that once it had met and established an Executive, the Assembly would exercise full legislative and executive authority in respect of those matters within the responsibility of the Northern Ireland Government Departments, with the possibility of taking on responsibility for other matters as detailed elsewhere in the Agreement. After the 1998 elections, therefore, the Assembly met initially in a 'shadow' mode, without legislative or executive powers, to resolve its standing orders and working practices, and make preparations for its effective functioning. The formal establishment of the North/South Ministerial Council, implementation bodies, the British-Irish Council, and the British–Irish Intergovernmental Conference, together with the assumption by the Assembly of its legislative and executive powers would take place at the same time on the entry into force of the British–Irish Agreement.

The Agreement provided for how the Executive was to be formed, and the Northern Ireland Act 1998 duly enacted these provisions. A Northern Ireland Executive was provided for, to consist of a First Minister and a Deputy First Minister and up to ten ministers with departmental responsibilities. In addition, the Northern Ireland Act 1998 provided for additional junior ministers to be appointed. The First Minister and Deputy First Minister were to be jointly elected into office by the Assembly voting on a cross-community basis, according to the 'parallel consent' method, that is a majority of those members present and voting, including a majority of the unionist and nationalist designations present and voting. Although it was technically possible that members from the smaller nationalist and unionist parties could occupy the positions, or indeed two people from the same unionist or nationalist party, in practice the requirement for cross-community support meant that these positions were always likely to (and, subsequently, indeed, did) go to the nominees of the largest nationalist and unionist parties.[32] Following the election of the First Minister and Deputy First Minister, the posts of ministers were to be allocated to parties on the basis of the d'Hondt system, that is by reference to the number of seats each party has in the Assembly. Ministers were to be allocated in proportion to numbers of Members of the Assembly, and in sequential order.[33] The Executive was to be convened, and presided over jointly, by the First Minister and Deputy First Minister, whose functions were to include dealing with and coordinating the work of the Executive and the response of the Northern Ireland administration to external relationships. Here again, we see the importance attached to the need to ensure cross-community support in the establishment of an inclusive government, and the creation of a dual-headed leader of the Executive. Both are major constitutional innovations in UK constitutional practice.

[32] Interestingly, however, these nominees were not consistently the Party leaders, except in the case of the Ulster Unionist Party. Indeed, it is noteworthy that for a considerable period the leaders of Sinn Féin, the SDLP, and the DUP did not choose even to become members of the Executive.

[33] For further details, see B. O'Leary, B. Grofman, and J. Elklit, 'Divisor Methods For Sequential Portfolio Allocation In Multi-party Executive Bodies: Evidence From Northern Ireland and Denmark' (2005) 49(1) *American Journal of Political Science* 198.

In July 1995, the Assembly met for the first time and duly elected the First and Deputy First Ministers. Mr David Trimble, leader of the UUP, was elected First Minister and Mr Seamus Mallon, deputy leader of the SDLP, was elected Deputy First Minister. However, in a move that had not been anticipated in the Agreement, but which reflected the unease about the Agreement felt by a sizeable group within the Ulster Unionist Party in the Assembly, Mr Trimble refused to agree to the next step, the appointment of an Executive, until weapons decommissioning by the IRA had begun. The Assembly therefore continued operating on a 'shadow' basis, since no executive or legislative powers could be transferred to it, until the Executive had been established. There was no timetable provided in the Agreement or in the Northern Ireland Act for the establishment of the Executive. However, the Agreement envisaged the establishment of a Northern Ireland transitional administration whose representatives would identify by 31 October 1998 the 12 subject areas for North–South cooperation and implementation in the shadow North/South Ministerial Council. Only in December 1998 did the First and Deputy First Ministers reach agreement on the structure of government departments in Northern Ireland, and on cross-border bodies.[34] Mr Trimble was adamant that progress on decommissioning was necessary before an Executive was formed. Although after elections to the Assembly, inaugural meetings were also supposed to take place of the British–Irish Council and the North/South Ministerial Council in their transitional forms, only the latter met in December 1998.

THE AGREEMENT AS A 'PEACE AGREEMENT'

The Agreement was not simply a new constitutional settlement, it was also (as importantly) a peace agreement, part of a larger 'peace process' designed to bring to an end the murders, rioting, and political violence that had characterized Northern Ireland continuously since at least the early 1970s, and periodically since it was established in 1921. The pre-Agreement negotiations were founded on a principle of inclusivity, the involvement of all the major actors (including those involved in violence) in reaching a historic compromise. Nationalist parties had a particular interest in policing, criminal justice and security policy, what Sinn Féin called 'demilitarization'. Those with links to paramilitary activity, especially Sinn Féin and the smaller loyalist parties such as the Progressive Unionist Party, pressed for the release of prisoners and would have found it difficult to gain the agreement of their constituency for the constitutional aspects of the Agreement, if these issues had not been addressed. This led to a long process of negotiations, leading to the declaration by the major illegal paramilitary groups associated with unionism and nationalism, including the illegal Irish Republican Army, the IRA, of an end to violence by them. Some time after, the political parties associated with these groups (including Sinn Féin, associated with the IRA) were permitted to join the negotiations. The DUP was so opposed to the admission of Sinn Féin to the talks process that it had walked out of the negotiations, while the UUP had remained at the table. In return, it was essential for the UUP that the Agreement address the issue of violence, an issue of considerable importance to other parties as well. The unionists and the

34 Joint Statement issued by the First Minister, Mr David Trimble, and the Deputy First Minister, Mr Seamus Mallon on the accommodation reached regarding future Northern Ireland Government Departments, and cross-border bodies, 18 Dec. 1998.

British Government were most concerned to ensure that those associated with illegal paramilitary activity in the past would use only peaceful and democratic methods to advance their aims in the future. This required addressing the issue of decommissioning.

Negotiations over decommissioning had been an important part of the peace process prior to the final stages of the negotiations leading to the Agreement and came close to being a deal-breaker in the final days. For unionists, it was to prove the issue that tested the resolve of Sinn Féin to pursue peaceful means in the future. A significant difficulty in including Sinn Féin representatives was the close link between the party and the illegal IRA. In an attempt to provide a structure for inclusion of parties associated with paramilitary groups, an international body on arms decommissioning was established by the British and Irish governments in 1995. This had an international membership, including US Senator George Mitchell, and Canadian General John De Chastelain. In 1996, the body reported and set out the so-called Mitchell Principles. These included 'the total disarmament of all paramilitary organisations'.[35] Acceptance of the Mitchell Principles became a *sine qua non* for participation in the negotiations. In August 1997 the two governments concluded a formal agreement to establish an Independent International Commission on Decommissioning (IICD).[36] The participants in the negotiations agreed in September 1997 'that the resolution of the decommissioning issue is an indispensable part of the process of negotiation'.[37] As far as UK law was concerned, the Northern Ireland Decommissioning Act 1997 set out the modalities under which paramilitary groups could decommission their weapons, including benefiting from an amnesty in relation to the possession of such weapons, if they did so within a set period.[38]

In the Agreement itself, all participants reaffirmed 'their commitment to the total disarmament of all paramilitary organisations,' but this was in the context of the implementation of the Agreement as a whole.[39] They also confirmed their intention to 'continue to work constructively and in good faith with the Independent Commission,'[40] and to 'use any influence they may have, to achieve the decommissioning of all paramilitary arms within two years following endorsement in referendums North and South of the agreement and in the context of the implementation of the overall settlement'.[41] The IICD would monitor, review and verify progress on decommissioning of illegal arms, and would report to both governments at regular intervals.

As we have seen, the UUP, led by Mr Trimble, was substantially split between those in the party who generally supported the Agreement, and those who did not. To retain the support of those who generally supported the Agreement, Mr Trimble needed to show that progress

[35] *Report of the International Body on Arms Decommissioning* (the Mitchell Report), 24 Jan. 1996 (Belfast, Northern Ireland Office), para. 20.

[36] Agreement between the Government of Ireland and the Government of the UK establishing the Independent International Commission on Decommissioning, 26 Aug. 1997.

[37] Agreement, Decommissioning, para. 1.

[38] Since 1997, the amnesty period has been successively extended, see e.g. Northern Ireland Arms Decommissioning (Amendment) Act 2002; Northern Ireland Arms Decommissioning Act 1997 (Amnesty Period) Order 2003 (SI 2003/426).

[39] Agreement, Decommissioning, para. 3. The provision reads: 'All participants accordingly reaffirm their commitment to the total disarmament of all paramilitary organisations. They also confirm their intention to continue to work constructively and in good faith with the Independent Commission, and to use any influence they may have, to achieve the decommissioning of all paramilitary arms within two years following endorsement in referendums North and South of the agreement and in the context of the implementation of the overall settlement.'

[40] Agreement, Decommissioning, para. 3.

[41] Ibid.

was being made in the post-Agreement period over the highly emotive issue of decommissioning. Not only was Mr Trimble under pressure from members of his own party, but the UUP was also in competition with the DUP, led by the Revd Ian Paisley. As we have seen, the DUP was solidly anti-Agreement, having left the negotiations when Sinn Féin was first admitted to the talks, and the party did not endorse the Agreement. Given the salience of decommissioning to the unionist electorate, progress towards decommissioning was important, therefore, if Mr Trimble was to retain support from his own party and if the UUP was to retain electoral support from the unionist electorate. There was, however, another consideration, particularly relevant to the decommissioning of IRA weapons: unlike the other paramilitary groups, the IRA was, arguably, represented through Sinn Féin in the Executive, and it was unsurprising that greater pressure would be exerted on the IRA than on other groups to decommission because of this.

For the paramilitary groups, particularly the IRA, decommissioning also presented a substantial problem, involving the necessity of ensuring that no substantial part of the movement would split off and form a separate group dedicated to keeping the 'armed struggle' alive. To achieve this, a belief had to be established within the movement that the Agreement was 'working', and that meant that the implementation of the policies on policing, security policy, criminal justice, equality, human rights, and prisoners was often subjected to close analysis. Of these, probably the most contentious was policing. Discussions on these issues were therefore continually linked to the negotiations on decommissioning. There does also seem to have been a difference in perception between Sinn Féin and unionists as to what was evidence of progress on decommissioning. For unionists, progress should be tested against the Agreement's goal of complete disarmament. For Sinn Féin, any movement away from paramilitary activity by the IRA should be seen as a major achievement. Whether the bottle was seen as half-full or half-empty was a crucial difference in perception.

ESTABLISHMENT AND INITIAL OPERATION OF THE ASSEMBLY AND THE EXECUTIVE

Mr Trimble's refusal to agree to the establishment of the Executive remained in place until November 1999, well over a year after the election of the First and Deputy First Ministers. Following an 11-week review by Senator Mitchell, during which the parties were understood to have re-committed themselves to decommissioning by May 2000, as provided in the Agreement,[42] and after the appointment by the IRA of a person to liaise with the IICD, the Assembly reconvened on 29 November for the purpose of running the d'Hondt procedure for nominating ministers. Following this, events then moved swiftly under the choreography established by the Agreement. The next day the Secretary of State for Northern Ireland moved Orders in the Commons, with devolution of powers to the Assembly to come into effect on 2 December.[43] The same day, the Government of the Republic of Ireland

42 Statement by Senator George Mitchell in Belfast, concluding the Review of the Northern Ireland Peace Process, 18 Nov. 1999.

43 SI 1999/3208 and SI 1999/3209, bringing the relevant parts of the Northern Ireland Act 1998 into operation on 2 Dec. 1999.

brought into effect the changes to the Irish Constitution agreed in the referendum. On 2 December, the Northern Ireland Executive met for the first time. By the end of December 1999, then, the Assembly and the Executive were both in operation, finally. The North/South Ministerial Council and the British–Irish Council were both formally established, meeting later that month in Armagh and London respectively.

NORTH–SOUTH INSTITUTIONS

Not only did the agreement to the formation of the Executive allow the formal transfer of legislative and executive devolution of power to the Assembly and the Executive, it also led to the establishment of the important North–South institutions. There were, essentially, three differing manifestations of North–South governmental activity formalized in the Agreement. The principal institutional manifestations of such cooperation involved the establishment of a North/South Ministerial Council. The second was the setting up of new cross-border 'implementation bodies' with responsibilities for particular issues that were considered likely to benefit from cross-border cooperation, but unlikely to be particularly controversial.[44] The North/South Ministerial Council and the Northern Ireland Assembly were mutually interdependent; one 'cannot successfully function without the other'.[45] In fulfilment of an 'absolute commitment' the two Governments made sure that these bodies were functioning at the time of the transfer of powers to the Assembly and the Executive, with legislative authority for these bodies transferred to the Assembly soon after. A third, rather looser arrangement was the provisions for agreed cooperation between bodies with jurisdiction over designated functions in each of the two jurisdictions.

The North/South Ministerial Council brought together those with executive responsibilities in Northern Ireland and the Irish Government. The Council's role was to develop cooperation and action within the island of Ireland, including through implementation on an all-island and cross-border basis, on matters of mutual interest within the competence of these administrations. All Council decisions were by agreement between the two sides. Northern Ireland was led in plenary meetings, which set the work programme, by the First Minister, the Deputy First Minister and any relevant ministers. The Irish Government was represented by the Taoiseach (Irish Prime Minister) and relevant ministers. In sectoral meetings, where the work programme set out by the plenary was carried out, both governments were represented by relevant ministers, although, as we shall see, this became a contentious issue. It took decisions by agreement on policies for implementation separately in each jurisdiction, in relevant areas within the competence of both Administrations. It took decisions by agreement on policies and action at an all-island and cross-border level. Such decisions were to be implemented by the 'implementation bodies'.

44 British-Irish Agreement 1999, 8 March 1999, implemented for the UK by the North-South Co-operation (Implementation) Bodies (Northern Ireland) Order 1999 (SI 1999/859). See Neil Faris, 'Juggling the Jurisdictions: the Legal Basis for the Cross-Border Implementation Bodies', (2001) 49(2) *Administration* 56.

45 Agreement, Strand Two, para. 13.

BRITISH–IRISH INSTITUTIONS

Strand Three, which considered 'east–west' relationships, also resulted in significant institutional developments. Two institutions were established: a British–Irish Council (BIC) and a British-Irish Intergovernmental Conference (BIIC). The BIC was established 'to promote the harmonious and mutually beneficial development of the totality of relationships among the peoples of these islands.'[46] Unionists saw it as important in situating the conflict in a broader context than the Irish context. Membership of the BIC comprised representatives of the UK and Irish Governments, devolved institutions in Northern Ireland, Scotland, and Wales, and representatives of the Isle of Man and the Channel Islands. Of considerably greater practical importance, however, a standing British–Irish Intergovernmental Conference was also estabished. This subsumed both the Anglo–Irish Intergovernmental Council, and the Intergovernmental Conference established under the earlier 1985 Anglo–Irish Agreement, much despised by unionists. The BIIC was a forum in which the British and Irish Governments formally discussed Northern Ireland. Unlike the other institutions discussed up to this point, the BIIC was not suspended when the Executive and Assembly were suspended. Indeed, the role and importance of the BIIC increased significantly during these periods.

DECOMMISSIONING AND SUSPENSION

In January 2000, a large spanner was thrown into the workings of all these institutions by a report from the IICD that no decommissioning by the IRA had yet taken place, and that the IRA had not even made any commitments to decommission. The IICD reported that it had 'received no information from the IRA as to when decommissioning will start'.[47] The IRA had earlier made clear that any move on decommissioning would depend on a dramatic reduction in the British military presence in Northern Ireland.[48] Mr Trimble threatened to resign if decommissioning had not begun by February. A subsequent last-minute presentation by the IRA of new proposals on the modalities for decommissioning to the Decommissioning Commission and a report by General de Chastelain that 'valuable progress'[49] had been made in this respect, did nothing to prevent the suspension of the institutions on 11 February by the Secretary of State and the restoration of direct rule from Westminster.

This suspension required new UK legislation to be enacted, the Northern Ireland Act 2000. The Act provided for executive responsibility for Northern Ireland to revert to the Secretary of State, and for the legislative power of the Assembly to be exercisable by Order in Council during the suspension period. The Secretary of State could end the period of suspension by Order, having taken into account the outcome of a review undertaken by the UK and Irish Governments, initiated by the UK Government.[50]

46 Agreement, Strand Three, para. 1.

47 Report of the Independent International Commission on Decommissioning, 31 Jan. 2000, para. 3.

48 IRA Statement, 6 Jan. 2000.

49 Report of the Independent International Commission on Decommissioning, 11 Feb. 2000, para. 5.

50 Subsequently modified by the Northern Ireland Act 2000 (Modification) Order 2003 (SI 2003/1155) and the Northern Ireland Act 2000 (Modification) (No. 2) Order 2003 (SI 2003/2592).

The suspension of the Assembly by the Secretary of State was important not only because it demonstrated the uncertain political situation, and the central importance of decommissioning to the unionists, but also because it brought to the fore the vexed issue of the constitutional relationship between Northern Ireland and the rest of the UK. Procedures were established to ensure suitable coordination, and avoid disputes between the Assembly and the Westminster Parliament. Assembly representatives and the Government of the UK agreed terms to ensure coordination and Northern Ireland input into national policy making, including policy making on EU issues.[51]

But these detailed arrangements, enacted in the Northern Ireland Act 1998, were the tip of a constitutional iceberg. Despite all the arrangements for consultation, and the elaborate attempts to ensure that neither government stepped on the toes of the other, the Secretary of State for Northern Ireland continued to occupy a crucial position of power. The Secretary of State remained responsible for those matters that were the responsibility of the Northern Ireland Office which had not been devolved to the Assembly. In addition, the Secretary of State approved and laid before the Westminster Parliament any Assembly legislation on reserved matters, and represented Northern Ireland's interests in the UK Cabinet. The Westminster Parliament legislated for non-devolved issues. It retained authority to legislate as necessary to ensure the UK's international obligations were met in respect of Northern Ireland.

The first suspension went much further, however, in demonstrating that the UK government was prepared to act *outside* the confines of the specific procedures set out in the Agreement. This was important for what it said about the British Government's approach to the Agreement. It demonstrated that the then British Government viewed the Agreement as a means to the end of achieving a pragmatic settlement, rather than as embodying a specific ideology to which the Government was itself committed. We shall see this essentially pragmatic approach to the Agreement coming to the fore on several occasions subsequently. The Agreement had provided that the UK Parliament's power to legislate for Northern Ireland was to 'remain unaffected'.[52] From the perspective of the British Government, parliamentary sovereignty remained legally undiminished. The British Government saw the act of suspension as an example of the ultimate constitutional authority of the Westminster Parliament over Northern Ireland in UK law.

Others, however, with a broadly nationalist perspective, took a very different view of the legality of suspension. The Agreement, it was argued, contained no provision giving the Secretary of State the power of suspension. '[A]nything that alters the [A]greement, especially its institutions, without the consent of the parties that negotiated the [A]greement and the institutions established under it, is a breach of the spirit and letter of the [A]greement.'[53] The Agreement had limited the ability of the UK Parliament to alter the constitution of Northern Ireland as set out in the Agreement, without the consent of the devolved Assembly (which had been accorded the right to dissolve the Assembly under the Agreement) using the cross-community consent procedure. In this respect, the Agreement,

[51] See, for example, Memorandum of Understanding and supplementary agreements between the UK government, Scottish ministers, the Cabinet of the National Assembly for Wales, and the Northern Ireland Executive Committee, Dec. 2001, Cm 5240.

[52] Agreement, Strand One, para. 33.

[53] Brendan O'Leary, *Irish Times*, 5 Feb. 2000, p. 10. See also the argument in rebuttal by Austen Morgan, 10 March 2000, p. 14.

ratified by the British–Irish Agreement, was a binding commitment to respect the right of the people of Ireland to self-determination.

The suspension attracted opposition from both the Irish Government and the nationalist parties in Northern Ireland. Indeed, from that point on, it became an issue in each of the further sets of talks, under the heading of the 'stability of the institutions', code words for the desire to try to ensure that UUP would not walk out of the Executive in the future. Perhaps surprisingly, given the extensive use of judicial review to address controversial developments under the Agreement, no application for judicial review was made challenging the suspension, perhaps an indication that such a challenge would be unlikely to succeed legally, or that there was no other advantage to be gained.

On 15 February the IRA announced that it would withdraw from talks with the IICD in protest at the suspension.[54] On 6 May 2000, however, after several days of talks, the IRA issued a statement that, for the first time, contained an unequivocal commitment to put its arms 'completely and verifiably' beyond use.[55] Mr Trimble interpreted the statement as indicating a commitment that the IRA would disarm. On this basis, he agreed to restore the Executive on 22 May, and having done so received the support of his ruling Ulster Unionist Council on 27 May. In June, the weapons inspectors appointed to oversee the process announced that some IRA arms dumps had been inspected and sealed.[56] On 30 May 2000, the British government restored devolved powers to the Assembly and the Executive.[57] In June, the Northern Ireland Assembly met for the first time since it had been suspended in February. A further inspection of IRA arms dumps was announced by the weapons inspectors in October,[58] and the IRA stated that its representative would resume talks with General De Chastelain, head of IICD.[59]

The decommissioning issue, like the IRA, had not gone away, however. At the end of October 2000, at a meeting of the Ulster Unionist Council, the policy-making body of the UUP, there was a further attempt by anti-Agreement unionists to constrain Mr Trimble's room for manoeuvre. In order to head off a motion calling on Mr Trimble to leave the Executive if the IRA failed to decommission, Mr Trimble proposed a different motion that would commit him to preventing Sinn Féin ministers from taking part in the meetings of the North–South Ministerial Council established under the Agreement, until the IRA had fully engaged with the IICD. Mr Trimble won the motion by 445 votes to 374, and subsequently put the exclusion into practice. This, in turn, resulted in a successful challenge, by way of judicial review, by the two excluded Sinn Féin ministers, supported by the SDLP Deputy First Minister.[60] This illustrates how judicial review was increasingly being used by political parties to attempt to achieve political gains.[61]

We have seen that the strict proportionality in ministerial appointments was modified somewhat by the provision in the Northern Ireland Act permitting the appointment of

[54] Statement issued by the IRA, 15 Feb. 2000. [55] Statement issued by the IRA, 6 May 2000.

[56] Martii Ahtisaari and Cyril Ramaphosa, *Report on the First Inspection of IRA weapons dumps*, 26 June 2000, London. [57] Northern Ireland Act (Restoration of Devolved Government) Order 2000 (SI 2000/1445).

[58] Martii Ahtisaari and Cyril Ramaphosa, *Report on the Second Inspection of IRA weapons dumps*, 26 Oct. 2000, London. [59] IRA statement on Arms Inspections, 25 Oct. 2000.

[60] *In the Matter of Applications by Bairbre De Brún and Martin McGuiness for Judicial Review* (NI Court of Appeal, 5 Oct. 2001) [2001] NI 442.

[61] Sinn Féin unsuccessfully challenged the refusal to award money to the party under the Political Parties, Elections and Referendums Act 2000: *In the Matter of an Application by Sinn Féin for Judicial Review; In the Matter of S. 12 of the Political Parties, Elections and Referendums Act 2000* (NI QBD, 10 Apr. 2003).

junior ministers. In practice, only two junior ministers were appointed, one from the UUP and one from the SDLP, and both served in the 'Office of the First and Deputy First Minister', a single department headed jointly by UUP and SDLP ministers. However, even with these modifications, there were considerable difficulties in operating the Executive. The Agreement envisaged that the Executive would provide a forum for the discussion of, and agreement on, issues which cut across the responsibilities of two or more ministers, for prioritizing executive and legislative proposals and for recommending a common position where necessary (for example, in dealing with external relationships). The Executive would also be responsible for agreeing each year a programme incorporating an agreed budget linked to policies and programmes, subject to approval by the Assembly, after scrutiny in Assembly Committees on a cross-community basis. Ministers would, however, have full executive authority in their respective areas of responsibility, within any broad programme agreed by the Executive Committee and endorsed by the Assembly. Although there was a requirement of collective ministerial responsibility, no effective mechanism of enforcing it emerged, a marked contrast with the operation of British cabinet government.

Indeed, the Executive included a party, the DUP, that was implacably opposed to the Agreement in its then form and demanded its renegotiation. The DUP had two ministers in the Executive. Despite being committed ministers in other respects, they refused to participate in meetings of the Executive due to the presence of Sinn Féin ministers. As a condition of appointment, ministers, including the First Minister and Deputy First Minister, had been required to affirm the terms of a Pledge of Office undertaking to discharge effectively and in good faith all the responsibilities attaching to their office. Participation in the North/South Council was also one of the responsibilities attaching to relevant posts in the Executive. Despite this, DUP ministers never attended such meetings. If a holder of a relevant post would not participate 'normally' in the Council, the First and Deputy First Minister were to be able to make 'alternative arrangements'.[62]

While they regarded themselves as able to exclude *themselves* from full participation, the DUP was prepared to use judicial review to resist their exclusion by others from full participation. The party challenged action taken by the First and Deputy First Ministers in 2000–2001, as part of an attempt to discipline DUP ministers who accepted ministerial portfolios but were regarded by the First and Deputy First Ministers as parading their contempt for the Agreement. Having initially taken the view that statements by the party indicated that DUP ministers did not regard the ministerial Code of Conduct as binding, nor information regarding the Executive as confidential, the First and Deputy First Ministers had withheld Executive papers from the two DUP ministers.

A successful application for judicial review was ultimately[63] made against this decision, resulting in a declaration that the decision was unlawful.[64] Although the First and Deputy First Ministers were entitled to withhold confidential papers, the DUP ministers had a

62 Agreement, Strand Two, para. 2.

63 Initially, an application for leave to apply for judicial review was dismissed: *In the Matter of an Application by Maurice Morrow and Gregory Campbell for Leave to apply for Judicial Review* [2001] NI 261. The Northern Ireland Court of Appeal allowed an appeal against this refusal, [2006] NI 1.

64 *In the Matter of an Application by Maurice Morrow and Gregory Campbell for Judicial Review* (No. 2) [2006] NI 2.

legitimate expectation that 'in so doing, [they] would act in accordance with a fair, rational and clearly articulated policy when implementing any such decision'. The First and Deputy First Ministers had failed to do so, in particular by subsequently introducing a new factor to justify withholding the papers, viz. the failure of the DUP ministers to participate in meetings of the Executive.

Meanwhile, further talks to try to resolve the decommissioning issue were held between January and March 2001. In a dramatic move, Mr Trimble announced on 8 May that he would resign as First Minister on 1 July if the IRA did not decommission by that date. The threatened resignation did not save the UUP in the Westminster General Election and the local government district council elections, both held on 7 June. Both the DUP and Sinn Féin made significant gains, at the expense of the UUP and the SDLP respectively.[65] Following the elections, the two Governments held further talks with representatives of the three main pro-Agreement parties, but this was not enough to prevent Mr Trimble's pre-announced resignation coming into effect on 1 July. The effect of this resignation was significant, in that, under the Northern Ireland Act 1998, the resignation of either the First or the Deputy First Minister triggered the start of a six-week period for the election of a replacement. In the absence of any agreement on decommissioning, any election would be bound to fail since the election of the First and Deputy First Minister required support under the parallel consent requirement. The British Government was, therefore, faced with three options, each unpalatable. If this six-week deadline could not be met, then new elections to the Assembly could be called, as provided in the Agreement. Or, it could suspend the Assembly and reintroduce direct rule for the foreseeable future, as it had done in the past. Or, it could temporarily suspend the Assembly with the effect of extending the period of negotiations. In order to buy time in which negotiations could resolve the decommissioning issue, this third option was adopted. The Secretary of State suspended the Assembly on two separate occasions (on 11 August and 21 September) for a period of 24 hours on each occasion.[66] This enabled the clock on the six-week requirement to be re-set; following each 24-hour suspension, another six weeks began to run.

Meanwhile, several days of intense negotiations in July 2001 failed to reach agreement. These have been called the 'Weston Park' negotiations, after the location in which they were held. On 1 August, the British and Irish Governments announced a package of measures addressing issues of policing, security normalization, 'stability of the institutions', and decommissioning of paramilitary weapons.[67] The political parties were given until Monday 6 August 2001 to give their response to the proposals. On 6 August, a statement was issued by General De Chastelain, in which he announced that an IRA representative had proposed a method for decommissioning. General De Chastelain said in the statement that, '[b]ased on our discussions with the IRA representative, we believe that this proposal initiates a process that will put IRA arms completely and verifiably beyond use'.[68] But this did not convince Mr Trimble, and the UUP subsequently rejected both the Implementation Plan and the moves on decommissioning.

65 For the results, see www.ark.ac.uk/elections.

66 SI 2001/2884; SI 2001/2895; SI 2001/3230; SI 2001/3231.

67 Northern Ireland Office and Department of Foreign Affairs, Implementation of the Good Friday Agreement, 1 Aug. 2001.

68 Statement by the Independent International Commission on Decommissioning, 6 Aug. 2001: www.nio.gov.uk/pdf/010806dc-nio.pdf.

At this point, international events appear to have affected developments in Northern Ireland. During August, three Irish citizens, later identified as having close connections with Sinn Féin, were arrested in Colombia on suspicion of involvement with FARC, a group with links to political violence and illegal drug dealing in Colombia, and designated a terrorist group by the United States State Department. The full significance of this would only become apparent after the destruction of the New York World Trade Centre, the attacks on the Pentagon, and the crash of another plane bound for Washington DC, on 11 September 2001, together with the subsequently declared United States' 'war on terrorism'. After that, any connections between the IRA and US-declared terrorist organizations was problematic for Sinn Féin, given the extent to which it had depended on American goodwill in the past, not least in the process leading up to the talks that led to the Agreement.

Further pressure was brought to bear on 22 September 2001, when Mr Trimble announced that his party would table a motion in the Northern Ireland Assembly to exclude Sinn Féin ministers from the Executive and that, if the motion failed, the UUP would withdraw its ministers from the Executive, bringing down power sharing. Under the Northern Ireland Act 1998, an individual minister could be removed from office if he or she lost the confidence of the Assembly, voting on a cross-community basis, for failure to meet his or her responsibilities, including those set out in the Pledge of Office.[69] This Pledge required that those who held office should use only democratic, non-violent means. By 2 October, the UUP had secured the 30 signatures needed to allow it to table a 'petition of concern'. On 8 October, the Assembly debated the motion, which was supported by Unionist members of the Assembly but was not supported by Sinn Féin (unsurprisingly) or the SDLP. Due to a lack of cross-community support, the attempt failed. Following the debates, the UUP announced that its three ministers would withdraw from the Executive. They formally resigned on 18 October, but agreed to return if there was a start to decommissioning by the IRA. The two DUP ministers also resigned. In that event, the Secretary of State had seven days in which to decide what action to take.

On 23 October, following intensive behind the scenes activity, the IICD reported that a decommissioning event, which it regarded as 'significant',[70] had taken place by the IRA, and had been witnessed by the head of the IICD. Following this, Mr Trimble announced that he would recommend that the UUP ministers should retake their seats on the Northern Ireland Executive, a position subsequently supported by his party's executive. On 25 October, the DUP reappointed its two ministers to the Executive. Mr Trimble was ready to resuscitate the Executive by standing for election as First Minister, but was faced with the problem of having to secure sufficient votes on a cross-community basis to ensure that he would be re-elected, together with Mr Mark Durkan (the soon-to-be-elected leader of the SDLP) as Deputy First Minister.

There were now insufficient numbers of pro-Agreement unionists in the Assembly willing to support sharing power in an Executive in which Sinn Féin was represented for the cross-community requirement to be satisfied. At the first attempt, on 2 November, the motion to elect both failed. In order to ensure sufficient 'unionist' votes to satisfy the

[69] Additional provisions regarding exclusion from ministerial office were enacted in the Northern Ireland (Monitoring Commission etc.) Act 2003.

[70] Statement by the Independent International Commission on Decommissioning, 23 Oct. 2001: www.nio.gov.uk/pdf/iicd1001.pdf.

cross-community requirement, the two members of the Women's Coalition, who had previously designated themselves as 'other', redesignated themselves, following an amendment of Assembly Standing Orders, one as 'unionist' and the other as 'nationalist'. Despite this additional 'unionist' vote, the motion to elect failed by one vote to attain cross-community support. Since an election would have to take place before 4 November, six weeks after the institutions had last been suspended for 24 hours on 22 September, time was running out. At a second attempt on 6 November, Mr Trimble and Mr Durkan were elected, but only after some Alliance Party members of the Assembly redesignated from 'other' to 'unionist'.

This was a particularly bitter pill for the Alliance Party to swallow, since it regards itself as the main cross-community centre party in Northern Ireland, having both Protestants and Catholics among its supporters. Although unanimously agreed by the parties to the Agreement, several aspects of these arrangements were resented by several of the smaller parties, particularly the Alliance Party on the ground that the votes of 'others' had less weight in practice than the votes of nationalists or unionists. In particular, some perceived the requirement that Assembly members should designate themselves as nationalist, unionist, or other, as perpetuating the sectarian divide, given the close association between nationalism and the Catholic community and between unionism and the Protestant community. In part to assuage their concerns, it was agreed, after Alliance pressure, that there would be a review of these arrangements, including the details of electoral arrangements and of the Assembly's procedures, with a view to agreeing any adjustments necessary in the interests of efficiency and fairness. The matter was ultimately remitted for consideration as part of the wider review to take place in 2004, as discussed below. The issues highlighted by these developments were important, involving the question of whether such aspects of the Agreement as the need for cross-community support, and the need for members of the Assembly to designate themselves as 'nationalist', 'unionist', or 'other,' should be seen as pragmatically recognizing the realities of a divided society in order to secure a stable future government acceptable across both communities, or as an unacceptable strengthening and underpinning of division. Given the centrality of these arrangements to the operation of the institutions, this debate is of considerable significance.

There was, however, another difficulty with the election. The election had taken place some days after the six-week period had elapsed and was thus apparently in breach of the provisions of the Northern Ireland Act. This resulted in a challenge to the election by the DUP by way of judicial review of the Secretary of State – a challenge ultimately rejected by the House of Lords.[71]

On 30 November, a meeting of the British–Irish Council was held in Dublin, the first meeting of the council since December 1999. Other meetings had been not been held as a result of the problems in the peace process. A meeting of the North/South Ministerial Council was held in Dublin the same day, involving ministers from the Northern Ireland Executive and the Irish Government. This was the first meeting since Mr Trimble had imposed his ban, in October 2000, on Sinn Féin ministers attending these meetings.

[71] *Robinson* v. *Secretary of State for Northern Ireland* [2002] UKHL 32, [2002] NI 390. See the discussion by B. Hadfield, in N. Bamforth and P. Leyland (eds), *Public Law in a Multi-Layered Constitution* (2003).

On 3 December, the second revised programme for government was agreed by the Executive and presented to the Assembly.

The devolved institutions operated from November 2001 until the autumn of 2002, the longest single period of uninterrupted activity. Yet again, however, on 14 October 2002, the devolved institutions were suspended by the Secretary of State, originally for six months,[72] following reports of continued IRA paramilitary activity, culminating in allegations of involvement by the IRA in a break-in at the central police intelligence centre at Castlereagh, and revelations of an alleged IRA spy ring operating at Stormont, the home of the Assembly and the heart of the administration in Northern Ireland. During 2003, political minds concentrated on the next elections to the Northern Ireland Assembly, scheduled for May 2003. There was considerable jockeying for party political advantage. It seemed likely that an election that took place in a context where there was no decommissioning and no devolved government, would benefit the DUP and Sinn Féin as both communities moved towards more extreme positions, with the consequence that agreement to form a power-sharing government would prove even more difficult after the election. Talks were held, therefore, during March and April 2003 to attempt to secure a more explicit commitment on arms decommissioning and an end to paramilitary activity by the IRA. In March, over the objections of several political parties, the elections were postponed for six weeks initially to give more time,[73] with the Assembly finally dissolved on 28 April. On 1 May, a joint declaration was issued by the two governments, setting out their positions,[74] and the British Government announced a further suspension of the elections until later, probably in the autumn, when it was hoped that the necessary trust between the parties would have been re-established.[75] On 6 May, the IRA announced that it had agreed that it would resume contact with the decommissioning body.[76] Following further talks, particularly between Mr Trimble and Sinn Féin, it appeared that by the end of October 2003 an agreement had been reached on decommissioning that would enable the elections to the Assembly, now scheduled for 26 November 2003, to be held in the expectation that an Executive could be formed following them. A further act of decommissioning took place in October by the IRA, witnessed by the IICD.[77] The deal foundered, however, when the lack of transparency of what had occurred became evident.[78] Further damage may also have been done to the confidence of unionists in decommissioning when no details were forthcoming of any further acts of decommissioning. The election took place in November 2003, considered in more detail subsequently, with no agreement in prospect.

72 SI 2002/2574, followed by SI 2003/1155 extending the six-month suspension period until 14 Oct. 2003.

73 Under the Northern Ireland Assembly Elections Act 2003.

74 Joint Declaration by the British and Irish Governments (April 2003); Agreement between the British and Irish Governments (April 2003).

75 Enacted in the Northern Ireland Assembly (Elections and Periods of Suspension) Act 2003.

76 Statement by IRA on the Peace Process, 6 May 2003.

77 *Report of the Independent International Commission on Decommissioning*, 21 Oct. 2003: www.nio.uk/pdf/iicd2.pdf.

78 Statement by Mr David Trimble, leader of the UUP on decommissioning, 21 Oct. 2003.

LINKAGES AND THE LARGER CONTEXT OF BRITISH CONSTITUTIONAL DEVELOPMENTS BETWEEN 1998 AND 2004

For the purposes of exposition, we have concentrated so far in our analysis mostly on the vexed issues of decommissioning and the establishment of the institutions of devolved government. This picture of a trade-off between the two, with the UUP seeking decommissioning in exchange for permitting Sinn Féin to participate in devolved government, captures only part of a much more complex process of post-Agreement implementation, albeit the part that has attracted most public attention, both inside and outside Northern Ireland. In truth, however, these aspects of post-Agreement constitutional politics in Northern Ireland are the tip of the iceberg, with much else of vital constitutional significance happening below the waterline.

It is important to understand how the other issues addressed in the Agreement were dealt with post-Agreement for two, related, reasons. First, the more successfully these other issues were handled, the more positive was the political atmosphere. This strengthened the case for decommissioning, and encouraged confidence that the establishment of the devolved institutions could be resolved satisfactorily. It is important to remember that the Agreement was constructed in such a way as to make each part of it interconnected with all the other parts. It was, therefore, difficult to prevent difficulties with the operation of one part of the Agreement from adversely affecting the other parts of the Agreement as well. In the recurring talks described previously, these other issues were frequently addressed as an integral part of the process. In fact, each of these sets of talks was similar in many ways to the negotiations leading to the Agreement itself, in linking all the issues together, even where one was the subject of prime attention.

There is, however, an important additional reason for considering these issues. Understanding how these issues were handled illustrates further the extent to which the constitutional scene in Northern Ireland looks different from that in the rest of the UK. When the institutions developed in the Belfast Agreement were operating, it was to be expected that tensions would be resolved politically in the context of those institutions. When these institutions were suspended, however, and this was for most of the time since the Agreement was concluded, other actors came to the fore. We have already identified the critical role of the Secretary of State for Northern Ireland. Two other institutional actors were particularly important in this context. The first was the judiciary. The second was the civil service. How would these institutions react to these developments? Of these, there is much better information available on the former than the latter,[79] not surprisingly since the former operate more in public than the latter. We have seen already that at various points in the post-Agreement phase, the judiciary was called on to review issues of central importance to the operation of the Agreement.[80] Indeed, it is no exaggeration to say that the judiciary is

[79] But see P. Carmichael and R. Osborne, 'The Northern Ireland Civil Service Under Direct Rule and Devolution' (2003) 69 *Int. Rev. Adm. Sci.* 205.

[80] See Gordan Anthony, 'Public Law Litigation and the Belfast Agreement', (2002) 8 *European Public Law* 401. See also Kieran McEvoy and John Morison, 'Constitutional and Institutional Dimension: Beyond the "Constitutional Moment": Law, Transition, and Peacemaking in Northern Ireland' (2003) 26 *Fordham Int. Law J.* 961.

now a central element in the post-Agreement architecture, addressing tensions between constitutional pragmatism and the differing forms of ideological constitutionalism.

We can, however, consider these issues only briefly in the following pages, concentrating on the aspects of particular importance to British constitutional lawyers.

POLICE REFORM

An important aspect of 'normalization' involved the creation of a police force which all sections of the population could recognize as legitimate, and to which they could give their consent and support. The Royal Ulster Constabulary (RUC) was not accepted by a significant group of nationalists as such a body; it had the abiding respect and commitment of most unionists but was regarded as illegitimate by a significant section of the Catholic population, and had been a source of grievance since the 1920s. The participants in the Agreement committed themselves to 'a new beginning to policing in Northern Ireland with a police service capable of attracting and sustaining support from the community as a whole.'[81] They also believed that the Agreement offered 'a unique opportunity to bring about a new political dispensation which will recognise the full and equal legitimacy and worth of the identities, senses of allegiance and ethos of all sections of the community in Northern Ireland'.[82] They considered that 'this opportunity should inform and underpin the development of a police service representative in terms of the make-up of the community as a whole and which, in a peaceful environment, should be routinely unarmed'.[83]

Following the Agreement, an Independent Commission on Policing was established, chaired by Mr Chris Patten (since 2005, Lord Patten of Barnes), to make recommendations for future policing arrangements in Northern Ireland including means of encouraging cross-community support for these arrangements. After widespread consultation throughout Northern Ireland, the Patten Commission reported in September 1999.[84]

Policing and some of the Commission's recommendations were to prove to be among the most divisive issues in the post-Agreement period. On the one hand, the changes proposed by the Patten Commission were controversial, particularly among unionists, because they sought to create a new police service, making a break with the past. On the other hand, the nationalist parties accepted Patten and insisted on its full implementation. They regarded the British Government's response to the proposals as set out in the Government's first Implementation Plan[85] and adopted in the Police (Northern Ireland) Act 2000 as selective and subversive of the reforms proposed. The implementation of the Patten reforms was, therefore, the subject of long and often bitter controversy in the successive talks surrounding decommissioning and the devolution of powers to the Assembly and Executive. As a

81 Agreement, Policing, para.1.

82 Agreement, Policing, para.1.

83 Agreement, Policing, para.1.

84 *Report of the Independent Commission on Policing for Northern Ireland* (Patten Commission) (Sept. 1999): www.belfast.org.uk/report.htm. See further J. McGarry, 'Police Reform in Northern Ireland' (2000) 15 *Irish Political Studies* 183–92; C. Shearing, 'A "New Beginning" for Policing' (2000) 27 Journal of Law and Society 386; J. M. McGloin, 'Shifting Paradigms - Policing Northern Ireland' (2003) 26 *Policing* 111; J. McGarry and B. O'Leary, 'Policing Reform in Northern Ireland', in J. McGarry and B. O'Leary (eds), *Essays on the Northern Ireland Conflict: Consociational Engagements* (2004).

85 The Patten Report: Updated Implementation Plan 2001 (March 2000): www.nio.gov.uk/pdf/patten2001.pdf.

result of these discussions, and following the July 2001 Weston Park talks, the British Government produced a second revised Implementation Plan,[86] including detailed commitments to new legislation, subsequently enacted in the Police (Northern Ireland) Act 2003. In response, the SDLP joined the new Policing Board.

The new Policing Board[87] was established with broad powers to hold the police accountable.[88] The name of the police force was effectively changed from the Royal Ulster Constabulary to the Police Service of Northern Ireland[89] (with new symbols and a new uniform). A system of District Policing Partnerships was established at district council level. An Oversight Commissioner was appointed to report on progress in implementation of the Patten recommendations. And a new system of recruitment was initiated.

The purpose of the new recruitment methods was to ensure that the new police service would be more representative of the community as a whole. Although Catholics represented more that 40 per cent of the population of Northern Ireland, they comprised only 7 per cent of the RUC. The Patten report recommended that in order to achieve a more representative police force, generous financial terms should be offered to existing officers to retire, and in future recruitment exercises, Catholics and Protestants should be recruited on a 50–50 basis to increase Catholic representation to 30 per cent in ten years. This latter proposal was particularly controversial, leading to an unsuccessful legal challenge being mounted under the Human Rights Act 1998, on the ground that the recruitment methods were contrary to the European Convention on Human Rights.[90] Essentially, this controversy involved a clash between liberal individualism and the more communitarian approach prevalent in the Patten approach.

CRIMINAL JUSTICE REFORM AND SECURITY NORMALIZATION

As regards 'demilitarization', the British Government had committed itself in the Agreement to making progress 'towards the objective of as early a return as possible to normal security arrangements in Northern Ireland, consistent with the level of threat'.[91] Following the Agreement, it published an overall strategy dealing with the reduction of the numbers and the role of the Armed Forces deployed in Northern Ireland to levels compatible with a normal peaceful society. Successive negotiations around the issue of decommissioning led to the removal of some security installations, the modification of some emergency powers operating in Northern Ireland, and continuing reductions in troop levels, except during the most contentious 'marching seasons'.[92]

As well as police reform and 'demilitarization', the Agreement provided that there would be a wide-ranging review of criminal justice (other than policing and those aspects of the

[86] The Patten Report: The Government's Implementation Plan August 2001: www.nio.gov.uk/pdf/implan.pdf.

[87] Northern Ireland Policing Board: http://nipolicingboard.org.uk/index.htm.

[88] This was in addition to the earlier established Police Ombudsman (dealing with complaints against the police).

[89] Police Service of Northern Ireland: http://.psni.police.uk/.

[90] *In the matter of an Application by Mark Parsons for Judicial Review* [2002] NI 378; an appeal against this judgment was subsequently dismissed by the Northen Ireland Court of Appeal [2003] NICA 20; [2004] NI 38.

[91] Agreement, Security, para. 2.

[92] The current programme is in Annex 1 to the Joint Declaration, fn. 75 above.

system relating to the emergency legislation) to be carried out by the British Government through a mechanism with an independent element, in consultation with the political parties and others. More generally, the British Government stated that it was ready, in principle, to devolve responsibility for policing and justice issues to the Assembly and Executive.

A Criminal Justice Review Group was established in June 1998 to conduct this review. The Group reported in March 2000, somewhat later than had been agreed, recommending a wide range of reforms to the criminal justice system in Northern Ireland.[93] Among the 294 recommendations, some were intended to address the particular circumstances of Northern Ireland in innovatory ways. Among these were proposals to establish an independent commission to oversee the appointment of judges which should aim to develop a judiciary reflective of Northern Ireland society (in particular its religious and ethnic background and gender), the establishment of a independent Public Prosecution Service for Northern Ireland, the removal of symbols from the interior of courtrooms, and the integration of restorative justice into the justice system. Here, too, we see the development of distinctive approaches encouraging greater participation of citizens in public life and greater representativeness in the composition of public institutions.

The publication of the report led to a six-month period of consultation. What the nationalist parties saw as the dilatory response by the British Government to some of the recommendations brought the issue into the July 2001 Weston Park talks. Following pressure there, the British Government confirmed that it would bring forward a response to enhance implementation of the Review's recommendations, which it did in November 2001.[94] Those elements in the Government's response that required legislation were introduced by the Justice (Northern Ireland) Act 2002. In June 2003, following further discussion of these issues in the talks process, the government published an updated Criminal Justice Review Implementation Plan.[95] In addition, a Justice Oversight Commissioner was appointed to report on the implementation of the changes set out in the revised Implementation Plan. A Chief Inspector of Criminal Justice in Northern Ireland was appointed to assist in the establishment of a new independent Criminal Justice Inspectorate for Northern Ireland. A new Justice (Northern Ireland) Bill amending the 2002 Act was enacted in 2004.

PRISONERS

The issue of prisoners was particularly important and controversial for both communities.[96] For those parties associated with paramilitary activities, the release of their prisoners had a special symbolic significance. Opposition to the Agreement from this part of the movement would be likely to lessen the likelihood that the Agreement would be accepted by the broader constituency. The approach taken in the Agreement was that both governments agreed to put in place mechanisms to provide for an accelerated programme for the release of prisoners convicted of offences arising out of the political conflict in Northern Ireland.

93 *Review of the Criminal Justice System in Northern Ireland*: www.nio.gov.uk/pdf/mainreport.pdf.

94 Draft Justice (Northern Ireland) Bill and Implementation plan, Nov. 2001.

95 *Criminal Justice Updated Implementation Plan 2003*: www.nio.gov.uk/pdf/cjimp2003.pdf.

96 See in general K. McEvoy, *Paramilitary Imprisonment in Northern Ireland: Resistance, Management and Release* (2001).

Should 'the circumstances' allow it, any qualifying prisoners who remained in custody two years after the commencement of the scheme would be released at that point.

The Northern Ireland (Sentences) Act 1998 provided the legal framework for the implementation of this aspect of the Agreement. As an incentive for paramilitary groups to remain on ceasefire, however, the Agreement had provided that 'prisoners affiliated to organisations which have not established or are not maintaining a complete and unequivocal ceasefire will not benefit from the arrangements'.[97] Release dates would be set for all qualifying prisoners. The review process established following the Agreement provided for the advance of the release dates of qualifying prisoners 'while allowing account to be taken of the seriousness of the offences for which the person was convicted and the need to protect the community'.[98] Prisoners eligible for release were those convicted of offences scheduled under emergency legislation, provided that the paramilitary group with which the prisoner was associated was on ceasefire at the time of the release. The legislation specified, however, that the Secretary of State for Northern Ireland had discretion to return the released prisoner to prison under certain circumstances, including where the paramilitary group went back to violence, or the individual was seen as posing a risk to public safety, a discretion that was exercised to return a particularly prominent Loyalist activist to prison.[99] There was, therefore, a powerful incentive for paramilitary groups to remain on ceasefire, and most did (at least formally).

For those opposed to violence for political ends, however, in particular for those who (or whose family members) had suffered from it, the prisoners were also a potent symbol. The decision by the Secretary of State to release IRA prisoners early was unsuccessfully judicially reviewed on the application of the daughter of one of two of the victims of an IRA bomb. She argued that the decision of the Secretary of State not to 'specify' the IRA under the Northern Ireland (Sentences) Act 1998, which would have meant that a prisoner associated with the IRA would not be eligible for early release, was unlawful on the ground that the IRA was not in fact maintaining a complete and unequivocal ceasefire. The application was dismissed by the Northern Ireland High Court, a decision upheld by the Northern Ireland Court of Appeal.[100]

PARADES, FLAGS, SYMBOLS, AND OATHS OF ALLEGIANCE

Parades and the use of flags and other symbols demonstrating allegiance to one community or other in Northern Ireland, or to the UK or the Republic of Ireland, have long been flashpoints, sometimes occasioning rioting and often creating tensions. For much of the period immediately before and after the conclusion of the Agreement, for example, an annual parade by a Portadown Lodge of the Orange Order (the main Protestant parading organization, with a long history of involvement in Northern Ireland politics) became the focus

97 Agreement, Prisoners, para. 2. 98 Agreement, Prisoners, para. 3.

99 Unsuccessfully challenged in *In the matter of an application by John Adair for Judicial Review* [2003] NIQB 16. For a later challenge to the use of this power see *In the matter of an application by Stephen James McClean for Judicial Review* [2003] NIQB 32; [2005] NI 21.

100 *In the Matter of an Application by Michelle Williamson for Judicial Review* [2000] NICA 281.

of attention. Tension had arisen because the housing estates bordering part of the Lodge's 'traditional' route had (through population changes) become predominantly Catholic and nationalist and the people there were hostile to the parade. In 1996, the RUC had re-routed the parade away from the Catholic area, leading to massive disorder across Northern Ireland, resulting in the reversal of the police decision. The Government commissioned the North Report[101] to consider the issue of parades and make recommendations.

The issue of parades is highly complex, seen by many as involving conflicting rights. On the one hand, there is the right to freedom of speech, to freedom of association, and to freedom of peaceful assembly. On the other hand, there is the right to be free from intimidation and discrimination. The report's recommendations included a proposal to create an independent body to take decisions on whether, and where, parades could be conducted. These recommendations were implemented in the Public Processions Act 1998, which established the Parades Commission.[102] The approach adopted has several innovatory elements that distinguished it from the approach adopted in the rest of the UK to contentious parades. The Commission is given responsibility for making decisions on parades, taking over the role of the police in this respect. The considerations that the Commission may take into account in regulating parades include, in addition to the usual time, place and manner issues, an additional criterion of 'impact on relationships within the community.'[103] Perhaps of central importance, however, is the Commission's role in mediating local disputes, facilitating local agreement on how contentious parades should take place, and creating conditions whereby the contending groups resolve the issues themselves, with the aid of the Commission.[104] The theory is, therefore, to encourage citizen participation. These arrangements contributed to a substantially peaceful summer 'marching season' in the spring and summer of 2003. However, several local groups (particularly the Orange Order) refused to participate officially in such discussions, and the Parades Commission remained controversial among sections of the Protestant population. Following the discussions at Weston Park, the Government announced a review of the operation of the Parades Commission and the 1998 legislation. This review, conducted by Sir George Quigley, was established in November 2001, and his report was issued for consultation in 2002.[105]

A related issue in Northern Ireland is the use of symbols and emblems that are associated with particular communities. Flying the Union flag, the Irish tricolour, and the use of the harp and crown, are controversial and potentially highly divisive. The Agreement acknowledged the sensitivity of the use of symbols and emblems for public purposes, and the need in particular in creating new institutions of government to ensure that such symbols and emblems would be used in a manner that promoted mutual respect rather than division.[106] Regulating the use of flags was a matter transferred to the Assembly. In the absence of agreement on the issue by local politicians, however, the Secretary of State introduced the Flags (Northern Ireland) Order 2000 during suspension of the devolved institutions, regulating the flying of flags over public buildings. After the devolved institutions became

[101] *Report of the Independent Review of Parades and Marches* (North Report), 29 Jan. 1997.

[102] Northern Ireland Parades Commission: http://paradescommission.org.

[103] Public Processions (Northern Ireland) Act 1998, s. 8(6)(c).

[104] The Commission has also been subject to judicial review, see e.g. *Re Farrell* [1999] NICA 7. On the composition of the Commission, see *Re White* (Northern Ireland High Court, unreported, 20 May 2000).

[105] *Review of the Parades Commission* (Sir George Quigley CB PhD), 27 Sept. 2002, www.nio.gov.uk/pdf/quigreport.pdf.

[106] See also Agreement, Constitutional Issues, para. 1 (v).

operative again, in May 2000, there was still no agreement forthcoming in the Assembly or the Executive. The Secretary of State then made Regulations coming into effect in November 2000, on the ground that it would be inappropriate for individual ministers to decide whether or not the Union flag should be flown, with practices differing from government building to government building. The Regulations specified, therefore, the days on which the Union flag should be flown. An application was made for judicial review, but it failed.[107] The decision of the Secretary of State was found by the courts not to be discriminatory, nor did it fail to take into account relevant considerations, nor was it inconsistent with the undertakings of the British Government in the Agreement, nor was the Secretary of State restricted to making such Orders only when the devolved institutions were suspended, despite the issue being a transferred matter.

The issue of oaths of allegiance came to the fore in judicial review proceedings by a Sinn Féin Member of (the Westminster) Parliament. Sinn Féin's policy was (and is) to refuse to swear any oath or to make any affirmation of allegiance to the Crown. A challenge was brought, asking for a declaration that legislation limiting access to public funding to political parties that could satisfy certain conditions was incompatible with the Human Rights Act 1998. It was argued that, apart from the requirement that, in order to be eligible for funding, the party's MPs should swear an oath of allegiance or affirm, Sinn Féin would be eligible for such funding. The requirement of an oath was, it was argued, contrary to Articles 10 and 14 of the Convention, and Article 3 of the First Protocol to the ECHR. Concentrating on the Article 14 issue, it was held that Sinn Féin was not in an analogous position to the other political parties in that it would, irrespective of whether it was required to take the oath of allegiance, refuse to take its seats in Westminster, and that the refusal to allocate public funding was not therefore discriminatory in comparison with the treatment accorded other parties.[108]

EQUALITY AND HUMAN RIGHTS

Issues of human rights and equality are important parts of the Agreement. Arrangements were agreed that, again, were unique in British law. In addition to equivalent human rights legislation to that applicable in the rest of the UK, and, in particular, the passage of the Human Rights Act 1998, which also applies in Northern Ireland, there exists a raft of additional human rights and equality protections which have no equivalent in the rest of the UK. Much of this owes its existence or its current form to the Agreement, and the implementation of this legislation has therefore become an important element in the post-Agreement constitutional landscape.

Alongside the human rights concerns relating to policing and criminal justice that have already been discussed, the Northern Ireland Act 1998 introduced other important provisions to implement the Agreement, including the establishment, unlike the situation in the rest of the UK, of an independent Northern Ireland Human Rights Commission (NIHRC) with an enforcement role.[109] The House of Lords upheld the Northern Ireland Human

107 *In the Matter of an Application by Conor Murphy for Judicial Review* (NI QBD, 4 Oct. 2001) [2001] NI 425.

108 *In the matter of an Application by Sinn Féin for Judicial Review* [2003] NIQB 27.

109 Northern Ireland Human Rights Commission: www.nihrc.org.

Rights Commission's ability to seek to intervene in cases before the courts in order to make submissions on relevant human rights issues.[110] In addition, the UK Government was required to commission from the new Human Rights Commission advice on whether any rights additional to those in the Convention were necessary in the 'particular circumstances' of Northern Ireland. The operation of the Human Rights Commission has become increasingly contentious, not least because of perceptions that it has mishandled its enforcement functions and failed to produce coherent, acceptable proposals for a future Bill of Rights,[111] leading to several resignations. During 2003, these issues increasingly featured in the various political talks discussed previously, resulting in an agreement between the two governments and some of the political parties to establish an additional forum for consideration of a possible Bill of Rights for Northern Ireland, comprising local politicians and civil society.[112]

A Human Rights Commission was also established in the Republic of Ireland as a result of the Agreement. A joint committee of representatives of the two Human Rights Commissions, North and South, was established as a forum for consideration of human rights issues in the island of Ireland. The joint committee is considering, at the time of writing, the possibility of establishing a charter, open to signature by all democratic political parties, reflecting and endorsing agreed measures for the protection of the fundamental rights of everyone living in the island of Ireland.

Equality and discrimination issues also featured significantly in the Agreement.[113] Two equality agendas were addressed. One agenda related to national equality between the two different allegiances, one Irish, the other British, what came to be called 'parity of esteem'. This equality agenda is reflected in many of the institutional provisions such as those attempting to ensure equal representation and fair practices in the Assembly and Executive,[114] and the establishment of North–South institutions. Beyond these arrangements, however, the parties affirmed a list of important rights: the right of free political thought; the right to freedom and expression of religion; the right to pursue democratically national and political aspirations; and the right to seek constitutional change by peaceful and legitimate means. In addition, there are new duties on government to encourage the use of the Irish language. A new Bill of Rights, supplementing the European Convention on Human Rights, is envisaged. This would reflect the principles of 'mutual respect for the

110 *Re Northern Ireland Human Rights Commission* [2002] UKHL 25.

111 See NIHRC, Bill of Rights Consultation Document, Sept. 2003. See also Brendan O'Leary, 'The Protection of Human Rights under the Belfast Agreement', (2001) 72(3) *Political Quarterly* 353; 'Symposium, Proposed Bill of Rights for Northern Ireland', (2001) 52 *Northern Ireland Legal Quarterly* 230.

112 Joint Communiqué, British–Irish Intergovernmental Conference, 2 July 2003, Annex, para. 5; Joint Communiqué, British–Irish Intergovernmental Conference, 22 Jan. 2004, para. 11.

113 See R. D. Osborne, 'Progressing the Equality Agenda in Northern Ireland', (2003) 32 *Journal of Social Policy* 339.

114 However, other innovations suggested by the Agreement were not adopted. The Agreement had proposed 'arrangements to provide that key decisions and legislation are proofed' to ensure that they do not infringe the ECHR and any future Bill of Rights for Northern Ireland (Agreement, Strand One, para. 5(c)). The Assembly 'may appoint a special Committee to examine and report on whether a measure or proposal for legislation is in conformity with equality requirements, including the ECHR/Bill of Rights' (Agreement, Strand One, para. 11). The Assembly 'shall then consider the report of the Committee and can determine the matter in accordance with the cross-community consent procedure'. It would also be 'open to the new Northern Assembly to consider bringing together its responsibilities for these matters into a dedicated Department of Equality' (Agreement, Rights, Safeguards and Equality of Opportunity, para. 7). Neither of these proposals was, however, adopted in the post-Agreement period.

identity and ethos of both communities and parity of esteem'.[115] Here, too, post-Agreement litigation has been important. A decision by the Lord Chancellor to retain a requirement for new Queen's Counsel to make a declaration promising to serve Her Majesty the Queen was successfully challenged, although not on grounds directly related to the Agreement.[116]

The Agreement is also forthright on social equality, i.e. equality between communities defined by characteristics other than nationality: religion, ethnic affiliation, race, disability, gender, and so on. The parties affirmed 'the right to equal opportunity in all social and economic activity, regardless of class, creed, disability, gender or ethnicity; . . . and the right of women to full and equal political participation'.[117] The Northern Ireland Act implemented the decision to create a new Equality Commission,[118] bringing together all of the then-existing separate bodies with anti-discrimination enforcement functions.[119] The Fair Employment and Treatment Order 1998 continued and deepened the innovatory approach to tackling inequality between the two communities in employment previously adopted in the Fair Employment Act 1989. Furthermore, section 75 of the Northern Ireland Act implemented the Agreement's proposals with regard to a new statutory duty on public authorities, requiring such bodies to promote equality of opportunity on a wide set of criteria (not just race; disability and gender, as in the rest of the UK), and good community relations in exercising their functions. Public bodies are required to draw up statutory schemes showing how they would implement this obligation. As part of the equality duty to be imposed on public bodies, they are required to include arrangements for policy appraisal, including an assessment of impact on relevant categories of people. The fair employment legislation and the equality duty represent an important shift away from relying on the operation of traditional anti-discrimination law, and illustrate the development of a broader based approach based on achieving substantive equality, developing regulatory mechanisms to address structural inequalities, and the use of participatory processes to ensure that substantive equality is delivered. In 2003, arising from the political talks on devolution, the British Government agreed to review the operation of section 75, in order to make it more effective.[120]

Also in contrast to the approach of the Westminster Government, which has not accepted that British anti-discrimination legislation should be brought together into a single piece of legislation, when the Northern Ireland Executive launched its Programme for Government in October 2000, it indicated that it would begin consultation on a Single Equality Bill that would harmonize all existing anti-discrimination laws applying to Northern Ireland that were within the jurisdiction of the Executive. The responsibility for taking this forward lay with the Office of the First and Deputy First Minister. The intention to enact such legislation during 2002 obviously fell foul of the problems over the devolved institutions, but work continued and (as with each of the issues considered in this section) featured in discussions on the restoration of devolved government.

115 Agreement, Rights, Safeguards and Equality of Opportunity, para. 4.

116 *Re Treacy's Application for Judicial Review* [2000] NI 330 (QBD, Crown Side).

117 Agreement, Rights, Safeguards and Equality of Opportunity, para. 1.

118 Equality Commission for Northern Ireland: www.equalityni.org.

119 The Fair Employment Commission, the Equal Opportunities Commission (NI), the Commission for Racial Equality (NI), and the Disability Council.

120 See Joint Communiqué, British-Irish Intergovernmental Conference, 2 July 2003, Annex, para. 9, discussing the formation of an advisory group to review s. 75.

DEALING WITH THE PAST

It is not uncommon for 'peace agreements' to include provisions to enable the past history of conflicts to be brought out into the open in the hope that by establishing a mechanism to address past horrors, reconciliation in the future might be more likely to emerge. A classic example of this approach is to be found in the establishment and operation of the Truth and Reconciliation Commission in South Africa, as part of the post-apartheid settlement. No equivalent body was established by the Belfast Agreement. There were, however, echoes of this approach in the establishment of ad hoc and piecemeal initiatives both before and after the Agreement.[121] A Victims' Commission had been established in October 1997 with the task of examining 'possible ways to recognise the pain and suffering felt by victims of violence arising from the troubles of the last 30 years'. The Commission reported in April 1998.[122] In January 1998, again in the run-up to the Agreement, the government established a judicial inquiry into 'Bloody Sunday', when British security forces killed 14 men in 1972.[123] An Independent Commission for the Location of Victims' Remains was established by agreement between the two governments in April 1999. Protection was given to information provided to the Commission, and any evidence that came to light as a result, about the whereabouts of the remains of victims of political violence.[124] The government established a police investigation into alleged security force collusion with Loyalist paramilitary murders.[125] A Canadian judge (Judge Cory) was also appointed to investigate allegations of collusion between the security forces and paramilitary groups in several controversial cases.[126]

Here again, the role of judicial review has been critical and the Bloody Sunday inquiry has involved considerable litigation, mostly under the Human Rights Act 1998. Relatives of those killed on Bloody Sunday, for example, failed to obtain an order quashing the decision of the Tribunal to allow certain security force personnel to give evidence to the Tribunal from behind screens,[127] while retired and serving soldiers due to give evidence to the inquiry successfully challenged a decision of the Tribunal that soldier witnesses would be identified by their full names,[128] and that they should give evidence in Londonderry rather than some other venue in Britain.[129]

121 Christine Bell, 'Dealing with the Past in Northern Ireland' (2003) 26 *Fordham Int. Law J* 1095.

122 Report of the Northern Ireland Victims Commissioner, Sir Kenneth Bloomfield KCB, 'We Will Remember Them' (May 1998): www.nio.gov.uk/pdf/bloomfield.pdf.

123 Official Bloody Sunday Inquiry web site: www.bloody-sunday-inquiry.org.uk.

124 Northern Ireland (Location of Victims' Remains) Act 1999.

125 *Stevens Enquiry: Overview and Recommendations*, 17 Apr. 2003: www.met.police.uk/commissioner/MP-Stevens-Enquiry-3.pdf.

126 Implementation of the Good Friday Agreement, supra fn. 67, paras 18 and 19.

127 *In the Matter of an Application by the Next of Kin of Gerard Donaghy for Judicial Review and the Matter of a Decision of the Bloody Sunday Inquiry* (NICA, 8 May 2002).

128 *R.* v. *Lord Saville of Newdigate, ex parte A* [2000] 1 WLR 1855.

129 *R. (on the application of A and others)* v. *Lord Saville of Newdigate and others (No. 2)* [2001] ECWA Civ 2048. See also *R.* v. *The Bloody Sunday Inquiry, ex parte B and others, The Times* 5 Apr. 1999 (CA).

ELECTORAL SUPPORT FOR THE AGREEMENT

We can see, therefore, that the Agreement and post-Agreement implementation led to several developments that point to the distinctive character of Northern Ireland within the UK, in particular the central role of a particular form of constitutional idealism and the establishment of institutions and provisions to develop this. Ultimately, however, given the rules for operating the Assembly and the Executive, the Agreement must attract the support of the majorities of the electorate in both communities or it will die, however sophisticated the thinking that lay behind it, and however much effort has gone into the process of implementation.

We saw that, in the referendums that approved the Agreement, the Northern Ireland electorate supported the Agreement by an overwhelming majority. That result hid, however, the disquieting fact that the Agreement has proven much more popular among nationalists and Catholics than among unionists and Protestants, and this divide has been demonstrated consistently in opinion polls taken since that referendum, although with significant variations over time.[130] Given the need for cross-community support if the devolved institutions are to function, there is a need for majorities in both communities to support the Agreement. However, given the choice between pro-Agreement unionists and anti-Agreement unionists, the unionist community appeared in November 2003, as demonstrated in the Assembly elections held then, increasingly to support the latter. Of the 108 Assembly seats, there were 30 DUP, 27 UUP, 24 Sinn Féin, 18 SDLP, 6 Alliance, with two seats to smaller unionist parties and 1 independent.[131] However, in January 2004, three defections by UUP Assembly members to the DUP reduced the UUP to 24, equal with Sinn Féin, and increased the DUP to 33, nine more than any other single party.[132]

Within the nationalist community, the issue was somewhat different. Both of the major nationalist parties (the SDLP and Sinn Féin) supported the Agreement. For nationalist voters the question was rather which party was thought most likely to be successful in sustaining the Agreement in the face of the perception of increasing unionist opposition. The November 2003 Assembly elections appeared to show that increasingly Sinn Féin was replacing the SDLP as the party of choice among nationalists.

The apparent political polarization of nationalists and unionists evident in the November 2003 election was replicated in each of the subsequent elections held in Northern Ireland between 2004 and 2006. The European Parliamentary election on 10 June 2004, but even more the Westminster and local government elections in 2005, confirmed the electoral ascendancy of the Democratic Unionist Party over its rival the UUP and, though somewhat less dramatically, Sinn Féin over the SDLP. The following table shows, in particular, the extent to which the DUP replaced the UUP as the dominant voice of unionism. In terms of the parties, the electorate has polarized, with both communities opting for the more traditionally extreme of the two parties seen as claiming their allegiance. Perhaps not surprisingly, one of the casualties of this trend was David Trimble, who resigned from leadership of the UUP soon after the Westminster elections.

130 G. Evans and B. O'Leary, 'Northern Irish Voters and the British-Irish Agreement: Foundations of a Stable Consociational Settlement?' (2000) 71(1) *Political Quarterly* 78–101.

131 The first preference vote shares were DUP 26%, Sinn Féin 24%, UUP 23%, SDLP 17%, Alliance 4%, leaving 6% for smaller parties. Contrast this result with the results of the earlier 1998 elections to the Assembly. In 1998, of the 108 Assembly seats, there were 20 DUP, 28 UUP, 18 Sinn Féin, 24 SDLP, 6 Alliance, with 12 seats to smaller parties. See www.ark.ac.uk/elections/.

132 *Financial Times*, 6 Jan. 2004.

Table 10.1 Votes and vote shares of the major parties: 1997–2005[133]

Election	DUP N %	UUP N %	SDLP N %	SF N %
1997 Westminster	107348 13.6	258349 32.7	190814 24.1	126921 16.1
1997 local	99651 15.8	175036 27.9	130387 22.6	106934 16.9
1998 assembly	145917 18.0	172225 21.3	177963 21.9	142858 17.6
2001 Westminster	181999 22.5	216839 26.8	169865 20.9	175392 21.7
2001 local	169477 21.4	181336 22.9	153424 19.4	163269 20.6
2003 assembly	177944 25.7	156931 22.7	117547 16.9	162758 23.5
2005 Westminster	241856 33.7	127314 17.7	125626 17.5	174530 24.3
2005 local	208278 29.6	126317 18.0	121991 17.4	163205 23.2

POLITICAL NEGOTIATIONS AFTER NOVEMBER 2003

Given that the DUP had gone into that election pledged not even to negotiate, let alone to share power, with Sinn Féin, the prospects of devolved government in Northern Ireland looked bleak. Given that the DUP and Sinn Féin were the two leading parties in their respective communities, there were three possibilities. The first strategy that might have been adopted would have been to attempt to reach agreement between the more 'moderate' parties (the UUP and the SDLP) and only *one* of the more 'extreme' parties (DUP and Sinn Féin), leaving the remaining more extreme party out in the cold. So far that strategy has not been seriously pursued, not least because the SDLP refused to contemplate the establishment of a devolved government without the participation of Sinn Féin. A second strategy would have been for the two governments to accept that the prospects for agreement involving all the parties looked unlikely, put the idea of devolved government in cold storage, and operated a system of government in Northern Ireland based on continuing direct rule but with an increased role for the Republic of Ireland. The third strategy, which is the one that has been pursued up to the time of writing (November 2006), has been to attempt to negotiate an agreement that would include all four of the major Northern Ireland parties in a coalition of devolved government of a type envisaged under the Agreement.

Pursuing this third approach is no easy task. On the one hand, it involves securing a commitment by the DUP to sharing power with Sinn Féin and the SDLP. Given its traditional hostility to nationalism and the sectarianism of the DUP leadership historically, sharing

[133] Taken from: Devolution Monitoring Report: Monitoring Report, July 2005, p. 5.

power with the two parties that represented the bulk of Catholic, nationalist voters would require a major cultural and policy shift in the DUP. Increasingly, after November 2003, the DUP articulated its unease with participating in a devolved coalition government as directed solely at Sinn Féin because of its unwillingness to decommission its weapons and support the police. On the other hand, for Sinn Féin, an equally important cultural and policy shift would be needed if the DUP were not to have continuing reasons to refuse to share power. In particular the 'armed struggle' would have to cease, weapons would have to be decommissioned completely, involvement in criminality stopped, and support given to the police (for a long time seen as representing the traditional enemy). Both Sinn Féin and the DUP were potentially vulnerable to internecine conflicts if their respective leaderships moved too fast or were seen to compromise too much. For the two governments, much would also be required in keeping some momentum going, building confidence in these two parties that a devolved government was preferable to direct rule, and ensuring that the traditional supporters of the two parties saw that they were gaining from being involved in continuing negotiations.

Knowing that the DUP could and would veto the election of a first and deputy first minister if the Assembly were to be convened after the November 2003 election, the Secretary of State for Northern Ireland decided not to convene the Assembly since to do so would have started the clock on another Assembly election within six weeks. The Assembly has effectively been kept in mothballs since November 2003 awaiting political agreement.

REVIEW OF THE AGREEMENT

The participants in the negotiations leading to the Agreement were anything but naive; most had been involved in the minutiae of previous negotiations and well understood the potential difficulties, though few would have anticipated all that has occurred since the conclusion of the Agreement. Not surprisingly, therefore, the Agreement included provisions for reviewing aspects of the Agreement. Each institution would be able to review any problems that arose for its operations. However, if difficulties arose which required remedial action across the range of institutions, or otherwise required amendment of the British–Irish Agreement or relevant legislation, the process of review would fall to the two governments in consultation with the parties in the Assembly. In addition, the two governments and the parties in the Assembly would convene a conference four years after the Agreement came into effect, to review and report on its operation.

In the wake of the November 2003 elections, the four-year review of the Agreement provided for under the Agreement, tentatively set to begin at the end of January 2004, became a major reassessment. On the day following the election, the Irish and British Governments agreed, however, that the Agreement 'remains the only viable political framework that is capable of securing the support of both communities in Northern Ireland. We are determined that its wide ranging provisions will continue to be implemented.' The governments agreed that the 'fundamentals' of the Agreement must remain and that those were not open to renegotiation.[134] But what *are* the 'fundamentals' that characterize the Agreement? The problem is, as we have seen, that each set of interests involved in the original negotiations leading to the Agreement identified something different in the Agreement as 'fundamental'.

134 Joint Statement by the British and Irish Governments, 28 Nov. 2003.

The review of the Agreement was opened in February 2004 jointly by the British and Irish Governments but this was suspended only a few months later when it appeared that the prospects for agreement were bleak. In part, this suspension was precipitated by the report of the Independent Monitoring Commission, a group of four individuals appointed by the British and Irish Governments. Arising out of the negotiations conducted during 2003, resulting in the Joint Declaration by the British and Irish Governments,[135] it had been agreed that an Independent Monitoring Commission (IMC) would be established.[136] The primary function of this body would be to report on the extent to which the ceasefires of the loyalist paramilitary groups and the IRA were being complied with, and the degree to which security normalization being adopted by the British Government met its commitments.[137] The Northern Ireland (Monitoring Commission etc) Act 2003 was then passed to implement this proposal. In its first report, published in April 2004, the IMC described in some detail the continuing links between paramilitary activity and organized crime in Northern Ireland and, of most significance politically, the continuing state of readiness of the IRA and its links at the highest level to Sinn Féin.[138] In a later report, the IMC reported that the IRA had 'engaged in a lower level of violence than in the preceding period, committing fewer paramilitary shootings and assaults', but concluded that it showed 'no signs of winding down its capability'. There was 'no fundamental change in the capacity of the organisation or its maintenance of a state of preparedness'.[139]

In the wake of the European Parliament election, the two Governments set a new deadline of September 2004 for talks to try to achieve the restoration of devolution. A new round of discussions at Lancaster House in June 2004, followed by two and a half days of negotiations at Leeds Castle in September, co-hosted by the Irish and British prime ministers, produced no new breakthrough. In the continuing absence of an agreement between the parties, in early December 2004, the two Governments published their own proposals to restore a power-sharing devolved administration.[140] The proposals detailed institutional and procedural reforms to all three strands of the Belfast Agreement, and proposed further acts of decommissioning by the IRA.

Two important events shortly after the publication of these proposals further reduced the likelihood that these proposals would be accepted by the parties. First, twelve days after the proposals, the IRA was blamed for the biggest bank robbery in UK history, stealing £26.5 million from the Northern Bank in Belfast. At the end of January 2005, members of the IRA were alleged to have been involved in the murder of a Catholic, Robert McCartney, and then to have engaged in the intimidation of witnesses to prevent them giving evidence to the police. A campaign by the five sisters of the murdered man, criticizing the IRA and the Sinn Féin leadership for it failure to ensure cooperation with the police, was highly publicized, particularly in the United States, contributing further to a weakening of tolerance for the Republican position there.

135 Joint Declaration, 1 May 2003.

136 Draft Agreement on Monitoring and Compliance between the British and Irish Governments, 1 May 2003.

137 Agreement between the UK and Ireland on the establishment of the IMC, Command Paper 6068, 3 December 2003. The IMC came into operation in January 2004, following an exchange of letters between the British and Irish governments.

138 Available at www.nio.gov.uk/pdf/imcreport.pdf.

139 www.nio.gov.uk/3rd_report_of_the_imc.pdf, at p. 13.

140 'Proposals by the British and Irish Governments for a Comprehensive Agreement', 8 Dec. 2004 (www.nio.gov.uk/proposals_by_the_british_and_irish_governments_for_a_comprehensive_agreement.pdf).

In February, the IMC reported that the IRA had been behind the Northern Bank raid, as well as three other robberies in 2004. Had the Assembly been sitting, the commission concluded, it would have recommended the exclusion of Sinn Fein ministers from office.[141] Subsequently, the House of Commons voted to suspend £400,000 worth of allowances to the four Sinn Fein MPs, in addition to the £120,000 assembly research grant, originally withdrawn following an earlier IMC report. In May 2005, the IMC issued its fifth report.[142] The report stated that the IRA remained 'a highly active organisation'. It was 'determined to maintain its effectiveness, both in terms of organised crime, control in republican areas, and the potential for terrorism'. The IMC had 'no present evidence that it intends to resume a campaign of violence . . . but its capacity remains should that become the intention'.[143]

In July 2005, however, the position of the IRA appeared to have changed significantly. The IRA 'ordered an end to the armed campaign', instructed all units 'to dump arms', ordered 'all Volunteers to assist the development of purely political and democratic programmes through exclusively peaceful means,' and insisted that they 'not engage in any other activities whatsoever'.[144] In September 2005, the Independent International Commission on Decommissioning concluded 'that the IRA has met its commitment to put all its arms beyond use'.[145] Two independent witnesses confirmed this view, issuing a parallel statement at the IICD press conference, affirming that 'beyond any shadow of doubt, the arms of the IRA have been decommissioned' and that 'decommissioning is now an accomplished fact'.[146] This, in turn, was followed by a statement from the IRA that: 'The IRA leadership can now confirm that the process of putting arms beyond use has been completed.'[147] Much would ride on the verdict of the IMC. Near the end of April, the IMC published a (mostly) favourable report on the absence of IRA activity.[148]

With decommissioning by the IRA finally addressed, the stage was set for a new political initiative. In April 2006, the two governments agreed that there should be a further, and apparently final, attempt to achieve devolved government in Northern Ireland.[149] The two prime ministers stipulated that if the political parties were unable to agree to form a power-sharing executive by 24 November, the Assembly would be dissolved. Direct rule would be the form of government for the foreseeable future, and the Republic of Ireland would be involved more closely. The Northern Ireland Assembly was to be convened in 'shadow' form on 15 May for an initial six weeks, without any legislative powers, to enable the establishment of an inclusive Executive Committee. Should that fail, as was expected, the Assembly would cease to sit and a new round of negotiations would take place over the summer. The Assembly would be recalled in September for another 12-week period, to agree an inclusive administration. If this was unsuccessful, the salaries and allowances paid to the current cohort of assembly members (MLAs) would cease and the next Assembly election, due in

141 Available at www.independentmonitoringcommission.org/documents/uploads/HC%20308.pdf.

142 *Fifth Report of the Independent Monitoring Commission*, HC 46, 24 May 2005 (www.independentmonitoringcommission.org/documents/uploads/IMC_Report.pdf).

143 Ibid.

144 BBC News Online (28 July 2005).

145 Report of the Independent International Commission on Decommissioning, 26 September 2005, at: www.nio.gov.uk.

146 BBC News Online (26 September 2005).

147 RTE News (26 September 2005).

148 *Tenth Report of the Independent Monitoring Commission*, HC 1066, 26 April 2006, at: www.independentmonitoringcommission.org/documents/uploads/ACFEF3.pdf.

149 *Joint Statement by the Prime Minister and the Taoiseach*, 6 April 2006, at: www.nio.gov.uk/media-detail.htm?newsID=12944.

May 2007, would effectively be abandoned, in which case the British and Irish Governments would develop partnership arrangements to develop the structure and functions of the Belfast Agreement.

A principal focus in the period between April and November 2006 was on the issue of criminal justice in various guises. For the DUP the focus was on the extent to which Sinn Féin would agree to support the police and, in particular, demonstrate that support by joining the Policing Board and the District Policing Partnerships, which were established to oversee the operation of the PSNI. The DUP insisted that no power-sharing devolved administration would be formed with Sinn Féin unless and until it actively supported the police. Sinn Féin, however, argued that a timetable for criminal justice and policing to become transferred matters, under the control of the Assembly, should be established. Sinn Fein's position was that it would not join the Policing Board or the District Partnerships until the reform of the police had been completed and criminal justice and policing had been devolved to the Assembly.

Legislation was introduced at Westminster in April to reconvene the Assembly members as planned and established the 24 November deadline for agreement on renewed devolution. In May, the Bill became law after a speedy process through both Houses. On 8 May 2006, the Northern Ireland Act 2006 received Royal Assent. The Act recalled the members of the Northern Ireland Assembly to sit in a '2006 Assembly' to provide a forum for the parties to begin preparations for devolved government. It set a deadline of 24 November 2006 for the parties to have made sufficient progress to allow for devolution to be fully restored. On 15 May, the Assembly met for an initial plenary session. Soon after, the DUP leader, the Reverend Ian Paisley, rejected his nomination by the Sinn Féin president, Gerry Adams, as first minister. In June, the prime ministers visited Northern Ireland, to stress the finality of the 24 November deadline. Failure to reach agreement by that date would lead to new British-Irish 'partnership arrangements . . . to ensure the effective joint stewardship of the Good Friday Agreement'.[150] During the period in which the Assembly sat, a committee, optimistically named the 'Preparation for Government Committee' deliberated across a wide range of issues that needed to be addressed and resolved before an agreed devolved coalition government could be established.

In the second week of October, the two Governments convened a three-day meeting of the parties in Scotland to attempt to agree on the way forward. In the absence of agreement, the two governments published their own proposals, termed the 'St Andrews Agreement'.[151] They believed 'that the agreement we are publishing today clears the way to restoration' of the devolved institutions.[152] The St Andrews Agreement put forward several changes to the future operation of the devolved institutions. The British Government committed itself to introduce legislation in Parliament before the statutory November deadline to enact these changes, once parties had endorsed the St Andrews Agreement and agreed definitively to restore the power-sharing institutions. As regards the issue of policing, the two governments set out that they considered,

> that the essential elements of support for law and order include endorsing fully the Police Service of Northern Ireland and the criminal justice system, actively encouraging everyone in the

150 NIO news release, 29 June 2006.

151 Agreement at St Andrews, 13 Oct. 2006, www.nio.gov.uk/st_andrews_agreement.pdf.

152 Para. 2.

community to co-operate fully with the PSNI in tackling crime in all areas and actively supporting all the policing and criminal justice institutions, including the Policing Board.[153]

The Governments requested the parties to continue discussions

> so as to agree the necessary administrative arrangements to create a new policing and justice department. It is our view that implementation of the agreement published today should be sufficient to build the community confidence necessary for the Assembly to request the devolution of criminal justice and policing from the British Government by May 2008.

With this wording, the two Governments hoped to satisfy the demands of both Sinn Féin and the DUP. In several annexes, other proposals were made on other matters, including future financial assistance, and human rights issues. The St Andrews Agreement set out a 'fixed timetable' for the implementation of that Agreement and the governments asked the parties, 'having consulted their members, to confirm their acceptance by 10 November.' Following endorsement of the St Andrews Agreement by the parties, the Assembly would meet to nominate the first and deputy first minister on 24 November. Between then and restoration of the Executive on 26 March 2006 the new Programme for Government Committee would 'agree all the necessary arrangements relating to ministerial responsibilities',[154] and ensure that the Executive would operate immediately after the election of the first and deputy first minister. The Governments made clear 'that in the event of failure to reach agreement by the 24 November we will proceed on the basis of the new British Irish partnership arrangements to implement the Belfast Agreement.'[155]

By 10 November, the political parties had made sufficient statements of (highly qualified) support for the St Andrews Agreement for the two governments to accept that the next stage (the convening of the Assembly to nominate a shadow first and deputy first minister) could go ahead. Legislation was introduced on 16 November at Westminster, passed through all its stages on 21 and 22 November and received Royal Assent on 23 November 2006, prior to the planned first meeting of the Transitional Assembly on 24 November.[156] The Act repealed the previous Northern Ireland Act 2006 enacted earlier in the year and created a further 'Transitional Assembly' which would operate between the coming into force of the Act and 26 March 2007, which was set as the target date for restoration of the Northern Ireland Assembly. The Northern Ireland Act 1998, which provided the necessary legislative basis for the Belfast Agreement, was amended in accordance with the terms of the St Andrews Agreement, with these amendments coming into force if (and only if) devolved government were to be restored on 26 March 2007. A new Ministerial Code was enacted and a duty was placed on ministers and junior ministers to act in accordance with the provisions on ministerial accountability of the Code. Changes to the Code must be agreed by the Executive Committee and then proposed to the Assembly by the first and deputy first ministers. Any changes would have effect once endorsed by cross-community support there. The Assembly was provided with the power to refer important ministerial decisions to the Executive Committee, by enabling 30 members of the Assembly to initiate such a referral within seven days of a ministerial decision or notification of the decision. The pledge of office, which all

153 St Andrews Agreement, para. 6 154 Para. 10. 155 Para. 12.

156 For a useful summary of the Bill as introduced, see House of Commons Library, Research Paper 6/56, The Northern Ireland (St. Andrews Agreement) Bill, 17 Nov. 2006, http://www.parliament.uk/commons/lib/research/rp2006/rp06–056.pdf.

ministers must make before taking up office, was amended to require commitments to: uphold the rule of law, including support of the police; to promote the interests of the whole community represented in the Assembly; to participate fully in the Executive Committee, the North-South Ministerial Council (NSMC) and the British Irish Council (BIC); and to observe the joint nature of the offices of the first and deputy first ministers. New arrangements were provided for the appointment of the first and deputy first ministers, who were to be nominated by the largest parties in each of the two largest designations within the Assembly, rather than jointly as under the 1998 Act. The provisions of the 1998 Act that deal with the NSMC and BIC were also amended to set out the arrangements that would apply in circumstances where the responsible minister or junior minister did not intend to attend or where there was a dispute over who was responsible. The Act placed a duty on the restored Assembly to report to the Secretary of State before 27 March 2008 on progress towards the devolution of policing and justice matters. Importantly, however, although the proceedings to be conducted by the Transitional Assembly include the making of nominations from among its members of persons to hold office as first minister and deputy first minister, there is no reference to the 24 November deadline of the 2006 Act. This deadline became therefore one of political, rather than legal, significance.

The Transitional Assembly was convened on 24 November and over the next few days the DUP leader, over the apparent objections of some in his own party, indicated that, if Sinn Féin agreed to support the police and legal system, he would agree to being nominated as first minister and enter into an Executive that included Sinn Féin. For its part, Sinn Féin indicated that it would be holding an *ard fheis*[157] to consider changing its position on cooperation with the police, provided that there was a timetable for the devolution of police and criminal justice issues. This (again highly conditional) agreement enabled the Secretary of State to declare that there was sufficient progress to continue the process of negotiations and he convened the Programme for Government Committee as a Committee of the Transitional Assembly to act as one important forum for continuing discussions. Elections to a new Assembly were held in March 2007, followed by the formation of a devolved administration.

CONCLUSION

What is the significance for British constitutional law and practice of these developments in Northern Ireland? Discussion of the Belfast Agreement has often focused on several central areas of dispute over its particular meaning and implications for Northern Ireland politics and law.[158] In the context of this chapter, however, there are three issues concerning the interpretation of the Agreement that are of particular importance to British constitutional lawyers more generally.

The first issue is whether the Agreement is essentially 'devolution plus'[159] (with the implication that the constitutional settlement reached in the Agreement is a development that

157 This is the national delegate conference and the ultimate policy-making body of the party.

158 See references to discussion of the Agreement in the Further Reading at the end of this chapter.

159 The phrase is taken from B. O'Leary, *The 1998 British-Irish Agreement: Power-Sharing Plus* (1998). See also Elizabeth Meehan, 'The Belfast Agreement - Its distinctiveness and points of cross-fertilization and the UK's devolution programme', (1999) 52(1) *Parliamentary Affairs* 19.

grows out of and is consistent with devolution arrangements in the rest of the UK), or does the Agreement represent a settlement whose resemblance to devolution in Scotland and Wales is merely skin deep, masking an essentially *sui generis* constitutional arrangement? It should be clear from the preceding discussion that in my view the Agreement establishes a unique constitutional settlement that differs significantly from the other devolution arrangements discussed in this book, not least because it is embodied in an international agreement between two sovereign, independent countries.

Second, should the Agreement be seen as underpinning the Union, or be seen as instituting a process by which Northern Ireland will become increasingly detached from the rest of the UK?[160] My view is that the Agreement is neutral as to the future in this respect, allowing the communities in Northern Ireland to agree to disagree, but establishing a context in which each side can attempt to persuade the other to their point of view.[161] It remains essentially unresolved, however, whether in this period of continuing debate, the Agreement should be seen as instituting a bi-national future, in which both traditions in Northern Ireland can see their traditions reflected in the public sphere on an equal basis, or a future in which the public sphere is made neutral, reflecting neither tradition explicitly, or a future that is essentially British in its symbols and allegiances until there is agreement on any alternative constitutional arrangements. It is likely that this will continue to generate heated debate.

The third issue is more complex. To what extent does British constitutional practice *conflict* with the constitutional arrangements for Northern Ireland established in the Agreement? The role of the constitution differs significantly depending on what part of the UK (Britain or Northern Ireland) we consider. In Britain, or at least in England, the constitution is the outward manifestation of a substantial degree of consent, or at least acquiescence.[162] Traditionally, constitutional procedures in Britain derive from that consent or acquiescence, rather than attempt to construct it. In Northern Ireland, given the absence of consent from a significant proportion of the population in the recent past, it has been necessary to attempt to construct consent in part on the basis of constitutional guarantees. The role of the constitution in Northern Ireland is thus much closer to the one which constitutions are sometimes thought to play in countries other than Britain, in particular those nations that attempt to construct a constitution on the basis of an ideology. The Agreement therefore provides a constitution for Northern Ireland that is based on the ideological constitutionalism discussed in the Introduction, although one operating in practice with a heavy dose of pragmatism.

This brings into perspective why issues that might be thought irrelevant to constitutional law in Britain are of critical constitutional significance in Northern Ireland, and why the Belfast Agreement is so complex and multifaceted. There are differences between what is needed to help resolve the Northern Ireland conflict by constitutional means, and both the British constitutional tradition of pragmatic empiricism and the emerging idealist constitutionalism characteristic of New Labour. Not only has pragmatism as an end in itself been

160 See also Brigid Hadfield, 'The Belfast Agreement, Sovereignty and the state of the Union' [1998] *Public Law* 599.

161 See also B. O'Leary, 'The Nature of the Agreement' (1999) 22(4) *Fordham J. Int. Law* 1628–67; B. O'Leary 'The Nature of the British-Irish Agreement' (1999) 233 (Jan.-Feb.) *New Left Review* 66–96.

162 See the discussion by B. Crick, 'Northern Ireland and the Concept of Consent', in C. Harlow (ed.), *Public Law and Politics* (1986).

rejected, so too the model of constitutional idealism adopted in Northern Ireland diverges from the model of idealism emerging from the Labour government's constitutional reforms in Britain. At the risk of considerable oversimplification, we can identify several elements in the New Labour approach: the importance of equality of opportunity, the need to resuscitate the institutions of representative democracy, the key role of liberal individualism realized in the protection of civil and political rights, and an increased role for the market as a mechanism for wealth creation and distribution. In contrast, we have seen that, in Northern Ireland, while these ideas also play an important role, they are balanced by sometimes complementary, sometimes contrasting ideas: the importance of substantive equality, the role of participatory democracy, the key role of community identification, and the appropriate role of government in limiting the operation of the market and ensuring distributive justice.

There is, however, a possible constitutional scenario: where the approach to constitutionalism evident in Northern Ireland becomes a model for emerging British constitutionalism. Several issues of growing importance in Britain (such as the appointment of judges, the treatment of minorities, the role of participatory democracy, police reform, voting procedures) may well benefit from deeper consideration of Northern Ireland developments. In practice, however, it is striking how little influence the Northern Ireland experience seems to have in Britain, and this seems unlikely to change.

To the extent that there are such differences, then, is the British constitution a barrier to devising and maintaining Northern Ireland constitutional politics, becoming Ireland's British problem, or could it be said to assist such constitution building?[163] In my view, it is too soon to reach a definitive judgement, given that the institutions established to handle such tensions have operated so sporadically. A tentative answer, however, may be attempted. British constitutional pragmatism has been generally permissive of the Northern Ireland ideological constitutionalism we have identified, while clearly not reinforcing it. The more recently emerging British ideological constitutionalism may well also have enabled certain parts of the Agreement to be seen as less controversial than they otherwise might.

It is clear, however, that the traditional and emerging British constitutional approaches are likely over time to reassert themselves, submerging the *sui generis* aspects of the Northern Ireland constitution unless the latter are continually safeguarded and reinforced. We have seen consistently in our consideration of the Northern Ireland constitutional developments post-Agreement, that where constitutional pragmatism came to the fore, the *sui generis* ideological aspects of the Agreement were constantly under pressure. We have seen, too, that aspects of New Labour constitutional ideology, especially perhaps the Human Rights Act 1998, have been used (mostly unsuccessfully, so far) to attempt to reshape some of these *sui generis* elements to become more consistent with the constitutional ideology emerging in the rest of the UK.

However, to date, there is no clear indication that the existing or emerging British constitutional approaches are so *essentially* antagonistic to the principles underpinning the Agreement as to give rise to unresolvable problems in the future.

[163] Cf. T. Hadden, Book Review [1982] *Public Law* 676. See further Colm Campbell, Fionnuala Ní Aoláin, and Colin Harvey, 'The Frontiers of Legal Analysis: Reframing the Transition in Northern Ireland', (2003) 68 *Modern Law Review* 317.

FURTHER READING

BELL, C. *Peace Agreements and Human Rights* (2003).

HARVEY, C. (ed.) *Human Rights, Equality and Democratic Renewal in Northern Ireland* (2001).

MCGARRY, J. (ed.) *Northern Ireland and the Divided World* (2001).

MCGARRY, J. and O'LEARY, B. *The Northern Ireland Conflict: Consociational Engagements* (2004).

MORGAN, A. *The Belfast Agreement: a practical legal analysis* (2000).

RUANE, J. and TODD, J. (eds) *After the Good Friday Agreement: Analysing Political Change in Northern Ireland* (1999).

'Symposium, Analysis of the Northern Ireland Peace Agreement', (1999) 22(4) *Fordham Int. Law J.*

WILFORD, R. *Aspects of the Belfast Agreement* (2001).

WILSON, R. *Agreeing to Disagree?: A Guide to the Northern Ireland Assembly* (2001).

USEFUL WEB SITES

University of Ulster, Conflict Archive on the Internet (CAIN) (material on the Northern Ireland conflict 1968 to present): **http://cain.ulst.ac.uk**

Northern Ireland Elections: **www.ark.ac.uk/elections**

Nations and Regions: The Dynamics of Devolution: Quarterly Monitoring Reports (Northern Ireland): **www.ucl.ac.uk/constitution-unit/leverh/monitoring.htm**

ESRC Devolution and Constitutional Change Programme: **www.devolution.ac.uk**

BBC Northern Ireland: A State Apart (An interactive chronicle of the Northern Ireland conflict): **www.bbc.co.uk/northernireland/learning/history/stateapart/**

Northern Ireland Office: **www.nio.gov.uk/**

Irish Department of Foreign Affairs: **www.irlgov.ie/iveagh**

Irish Department of the Taoiseach: **www.irlgov.ie/taoiseach/default.htm**

Criminal Justice System Northern Ireland: **www.cjsni.gov.uk**

11

DEVOLUTION AND THE CHANGING CONSTITUTION: EVOLUTION IN WALES AND THE UNANSWERED ENGLISH QUESTION

*Brigid Hadfield**

SUMMARY

The enactment of the Government of Wales Act 2006 formalizes a clearer division between the Welsh Assembly and the Welsh Assembly Government, provides for enhanced legislative powers for the Assembly from May 2007 and, after a referendum to be held at some future unspecified date, facilitates the devolution of primary legislative powers to the Assembly. This Act, therefore, brings the model of Welsh devolution closer to the general principles of devolved executive and legislative power contained in the Scotland Act 1998 and the Northern Ireland Act 1998. Meanwhile, although there is increasing public interest in the English Question, the Government does not share this interest and any attempt by it to answer the Question seems remote. This chapter looks at the evolution of Welsh devolution and the effective stagnation of the English Question in terms of it moving towards a resolution, as issues in their own right. The chapter also, however, compares the institutional dynamism created by devolution to Wales with the institutional stasis in England as the UK Parliament maintains its sole grip on national policy formulation and law making for England. The two classic *leitmotifs* of the sovereignty of the Westminster Parliament and executive domination infuse all national decision-making for England; they also underpin Welsh devolution. The key question in terms of the principles of the UK's changing constitution, is what is the difference in real consequences between to 'infuse' and to 'underpin'? The answers at the constitutional level have yet to emerge. The answers emerging at the level of the political and institutional levels created by devolution show a new dynamic.

* My thanks are due to Professor Richard Rawlings for his very helpful comments on an earlier draft of this chapter.

INTRODUCTION

The phrase the 'devolved United Kingdom' has entered the constitutional lexicon with little exposition of its essential appositeness. The same may be said of the all-intrusive qualifying adjective: 'asymmetrical', which has gained ground over terms such as 'multi-textured'[1] that seem to open up more exciting possibilities in a consideration of the changing constitution.

There is indeed actual, or potential, devolution to three of the four nations[2] of the UK, but the omission of any devolution at all to England raises the question whether the phrase 'the devolved United Kingdom' has any constitutional import beyond the fact that some parts of the UK, constituting only 15 per cent of the population, possess some devolved powers. What constitutional significance, if any, this has beyond the devolved nation itself and, therefore, for the whole UK must be explored more fully. Likewise, the principles and the details of the three devolved systems are different but, beyond the devolved nation itself, what does this fact reveal about the changing constitution of the UK?

Devolution has been presented by successive Labour Governments in terms of the needs to preserve the union, on the one hand, and, on the other, to enhance accountability, responsiveness, inclusiveness and transparency as reflected in new forms of governance for the devolved nation. The introduction of devolution responds to an identifiable and identified wish within the devolved nation for greater control and influence over their own laws and policies. This then has to be balanced by the retention of institutions to decide those laws and policies, for example major taxation, foreign affairs and defence, which relate to the UK as a whole.

The need to maintain the union is currently a political given and, although not all share that commitment, the present state of devolution is examined here within the perimeters that this commitment creates. Two brief points should, however, be made about this. First, with regard to devolution to Northern Ireland, cross-community power sharing, parity of esteem and cross-border relations with the Republic of Ireland are key and distinctive components. These combine with an express statutory duty on the UK Government to terminate the union between Great Britain and Northern Ireland and, with the Irish Government, to introduce legislation to establish a united Ireland. This duty arises only when there is majority consent within Northern Ireland for an alteration in its national status.[3] There is here no possibility that devolution has been introduced to preserve the union between Great Britain and Northern Ireland. The oft-repeated emphasis on the need to preserve the union, therefore, is confined to England, Wales and Scotland. Devolution is not ineluctably unionist in its essence.[4] Secondly, although Northern Ireland may indeed be regarded as 'different', it is also far too soon for it to be assumed that devolution to Scotland and Wales has weakened the nationalist vote and has thus strengthened the union.

As far as asymmetry is concerned, this factor, especially when combined with political pressure for change, may be used, perhaps paradoxically, to seek greater similarity between the devolved nations as well as to maintain difference. This is particularly pertinent for

1 N. Burrows, *Devolution* (2000) 1.

2 For ease of reference the word 'nation' is used for each of the component parts of the United Kingdom.

3 Northern Ireland Act 1998, s. 1 and Sched. 1.

4 For a fuller analysis of devolution throughout the twentieth century, see B. Hadfield, 'The United Kingdom as a Territorial State' in V. Bogdanor (ed.), *The British Constitution in the Twentieth Century* (2003).

devolution to Wales when compared with Scotland, but asymmetry should not become a mask for unreasoned change in either direction. The asymmetrical devolved arrangements are regarded both as a 'settlement' and as a 'process rather than an event'. Change is possible but change, at least in the absence of an affirming referendum, is thus to be confined to what may be defined as non-fundamental change, namely that which is a part of an outworking of the foundation principles of 1997–8, but is not an alteration of them.

As much published work shows, including two other chapters in this book, devolution has made significant changes to the political and constitutional climates of the devolved nations. It does not follow that the UK constitution, *a fortiori* the English constitution, has likewise changed. In order to pursue these issues together, therefore, the larger part of the chapter is concerned with devolution to Wales and focuses on those aspects of devolution which both highlight the main features of the evolution of Welsh devolution and which also point to the contrast with England, where there is a paucity of channels to address the English Question as defined in terms of who legislates for England, a factor of not inconsiderable concern in a representative parliamentary democracy. New channels too may be needed to revivify the 'English constitution' so that in England too new principles of accountability, responsiveness, inclusiveness and transparency may feature in the formulation of laws and policies for England.

WALES: NEW DAWNS AND FUNDAMENTAL CHANGE

There have been two major Acts of Parliament providing for devolution to Wales, the Government of Wales Act 1998, following a referendum in September 1997 on the Government's key proposals, and the Government of Wales Act 2006, which was not preceded by a referendum. The latter Act re-enacts about three-quarters of the 1998 Act with only minor changes but amends the remaining provisions of the 1998 Act in several key respects. Specifically it alters the relationship between the Assembly and the Welsh Assembly Government and it enhances the Assembly's legislative powers from the original devolution scheme to, in essence, a power to ask the Westminster Parliament for 'more of the same'. These legislative changes supplement or formalize other important changes wrought administratively both by the Assembly itself and by the UK Government. The Government did not regard the immediately operative changes in the 2006 Act[5] as being so significant as to require the holding of a referendum. The Secretary of State for Wales classified the first alteration as one to the 'internal architecture' of the 1998 devolved arrangements so to provide for 'enhanced democratic accountability'. The expansion of the Assembly's legislative powers provides a 'stronger and quicker mechanism' for the Assembly to achieve its legislative priorities, so likewise constituting a 'development of the current settlement and not a fundamental change'.[6]

[5] Government of Wales Act 2006, s. 161 brings most of the Act into force after the Assembly election in May 2007. The coming into force of the provisions on Assembly Acts is controlled by ss. 105 and 161(7).

[6] Mr Peter Hain, the Secretary of State for Wales, on the Second Reading of the Government of Wales Bill, HC Debs, 9 Jan. 2006, cols 31–2.

The 2006 Act does provide for the further enhancement of the Assembly's legislative powers, making them closer, but not identical,[7] to the model of the primary legislative powers of the Scottish Parliament but these provisions cannot be brought into force without the holding of a referendum that neither Government expects to take place for several years. The timing of that referendum is, under section 104 of the 2006 Act, dependent upon the support of a two-thirds majority of the Assembly members and the majority of both Houses of Parliament. The evolution of Welsh devolution from 1998 thus raises important questions about the use of the referendum both in terms of what constitutes fundamental change and in providing an indication that the Government does regard the holding of a referendum as *de rigueur* in at least some constitutional situations. New dawns are for Parliament to provide; fundamental change is for the electorate.[8]

It is important to note the considerable and widespread debate that took place between the Acts of 1998 and 2006 on the way forward for Welsh devolution, the significance of this debate being heightened by the absence of a constitutional convention preceding devolution to Wales in 1998–9. Of major import is the publication in March 2004 of the highly significant and comprehensive report of the Richard Commission on *The Powers and Electoral Arrangements of the National Assembly for Wales*.[9] The First Minister of the then Labour–Liberal Democrat coalition executive had established the Commission in July 2002 under the chairmanship of Lord (Ivor) Richard. The report was not implemented in full by the UK Government, (notably the Government rejected its proposals to change the electoral system for an enlarged Assembly to the single-transferable-vote) but it was a highly important report not only in its substance but also in the opportunities that it gave to the wider public to engage in the debate on the nature and development of Welsh devolution. This wide-ranging debate continued with the publication in June 2005 of the Government's White Paper entitled *Better Governance for Wales*[10] that preceded the 2006 Act. This was considered by, among others, an ad hoc Assembly Committee[11] and the House of Commons Select Committee on Welsh Affairs.[12] The presence of devolved institutions is thus significant not only in terms of the delivery of policies but also as providing a catalyst to debate the nation's political structures.

DEVOLUTION TO WALES: MARK 1

Constituency and Regional Assembly members

The Government of Wales Act 1998 ('the 1998 Act') was enacted after the referendum held in Wales in September 1997, in which the principles of the Government's proposed package

[7] Cf. s. 108 of the 2006 Act (specified powers will be transferred to the Assembly) and s. 29 of the Scotland Act 1998 (plenary legislative power is granted subject to specified exceptions).

[8] Mr Peter Hain, e.g., writing in the *Western Mail*, 8 Dec. 2005, the day of the First Reading of the Bill: 'This is an historic day for Wales, opening up another new dawn for devolution like that famous one in September 1997'. See also HC Debs cited in n 6, col. 45.

[9] Available from www.richardcommission.gov.uk.

[10] Cm 6582, June 2005.

[11] Committee on the Better Governance for Wales White Paper, National Assembly for Wales, Sept.2005. Part of the Committee's remit was to: 'take evidence from organisations and individuals with a direct interest in the proposed new structure of the Assembly and its proposed legislative powers'.

[12] First Report, HC 551 (2005–06) and Third Special Report (the Government's response), HC 839 (2005–06).

for devolution to Wales were narrowly approved. On a turnout of 50.1 per cent of the electorate, 50.3 per cent of those voting voted in favour of the establishment of a Welsh Assembly, 49.7 per cent voted against. Only 6,721 votes divided the two camps. The principles of the Government's proposals for a Welsh Assembly, contained in the White Paper *A Voice for Wales*, published in July 1997,[13] were thus submitted to the electorate for their endorsement in advance of the legislation. Consequently, after the referendum, these principles formed the basis of the 1998 Act. That Act established the following electoral system, which also applied (in principle but with different detail) to the Scottish Parliament. A 60-member Assembly, the National Assembly for Wales, was elected in both 1999 and 2003 under the additional member electoral arrangements that were detailed in Annex C to the White Paper and in section 2 and Schedule 1 of the 1998 Act. Forty members represent single-member constituencies, elected under the first-past-the-post electoral system. The elector also casts a second, or party, vote and the remaining 20 assembly members (four from each of the five Welsh regions) are elected from the closed regional party lists in proportion to the votes cast within that region, after first allowing for the number of seats gained by each party on the first or constituency votes in that region. This system seeks to enhance party proportionality in the outcome of the election.

All Assembly members, elected by the constituency or through the regional list, are of equal standing. As promised in the 1997 White Paper, however, political parties have been permitted to nominate individuals simultaneously both for direct election in the constituency and for the list of potential additional members. Consequently it has been possible for an unsuccessful constituency candidate to be returned as a regional list Assembly member, raising difficult questions as to who should represent the constituency interests in the Assembly: the successful constituency candidate or their unsuccessful opponent who had been returned as a regional member. As devolution inevitably engenders 'questions', this anomaly has become known as the Clwyd West Question. The constituency member returned in the 2003 election for Clywd West was the Labour party candidate. Three of his defeated political opponents (from the Conservative, Plaid Cymru and Liberal Democrat parties) were all, however, at the top of their parties' regional lists for the North Wales region and, therefore, all were returned as Regional Assembly members. The question of back-door election, which is not confined to Clwyd West, may be also be addressed in democratic deficit terms: some candidates who have received between, say, only 8–16 per cent of the votes cast in the constituency poll may nonetheless become Assembly members.

The National Assembly and the Welsh Government

Although the Labour Party has been the largest party in Wales after both elections, it had no overall majority in 1999 and this led to a coalition government with the Liberal Democrats between then and the next election in 2003 but not subsequently. The term 'government' or, technically, originally at least, 'executive committee'[14] has, however, to be narrowly understood for the following reasons.

The form of devolution embodied in the 1998 Act is usually referred to, somewhat misleadingly, as 'executive' devolution to contrast it with the legislative devolution found in both the Scotland Act 1998 and the Northern Ireland Act 1998. Both the Scottish Parliament and the Northern Ireland Assembly have been endowed with those fuller legislative powers

[13] Cm 3718, July 1997.

[14] Government of Wales Act 1998, s. 56.

that are often termed primary law-making powers, although they are not the equivalent of the sovereign legislative powers of the Westminster Parliament. This is not the case with the National Assembly for Wales. This stems from two key principles of the White Paper of 1997 and the 1998 Act, namely the institutional form of the Assembly and the limited extent of its law-making powers.

The Assembly was established as a unitary or single body corporate with no legal distinction between the legislature and the executive. As the Richard Commission stated, the body was 'a single executive body, setting and implementing policies in Wales within the frameworks created by primary legislation passed in Westminster, and accounting to the people of Wales for delivery'.[15] This pulled sharply against the normal UK pattern of at least a *de facto* separation between the legislature and a Cabinet-style government, with the concomitant methods of accountability within the Parliament or, here, Assembly. The *de jure* form of the 1998 Act was quickly adapted, through certain changes of nomenclature and practice, to a more familiar separation of responsibilities. This was a move greatly facilitated by the Assembly Review of Procedure that was initiated within the Assembly itself in July 2000 and which reported in February 2002.[16] All this happened as follows.

Under the 1998 Act section 22, those powers, both administrative and subordinate legislative powers, which had previously been the responsibility of the Secretary of State for Wales, were conferred directly on the Assembly. The 18 broad areas capable of being devolved are specified in Schedule 2 to the Act and included: agriculture, culture, economic development, education and training, the environment, health and health services, housing, industry, local government, social services, sport and recreation, tourism, town and country planning, transport and the Welsh language. The Assembly under section 62(1)(b) was in turn empowered to delegate those powers to the Assembly First Secretary or to any committee of the Assembly or, indeed, to retain them for plenary decision.

The First Secretary is elected from among the Assembly members and, as is to be expected, has always been the leader of the largest party in the Assembly (the Labour party). Under section 53(2), the First Secretary was given the power to appoint Assembly Secretaries from among the members of the Assembly. The committees of the Assembly divide between the 'executive committee', which alone could be either a single party or a coalition committee depending on the outcome of the Assembly elections, and the cross-party subject committees. At the heart of this division lies a tension, unresolved by the 1998 Act itself, between the Assembly 'as an executive body subordinate to Westminster and the aspirations of a body with its own democratic mandate'.[17]

Section 56, the provision requiring the establishment of an 'executive committee', defined its composition as the First Secretary and the Assembly Secretaries to whom the former allocated accountability 'in the fields in which the Assembly has functions'. The First Secretary was accountable to the Assembly for the exercise of the executive committee's functions. The Assembly, however, unlike the Scottish Parliament, was considerably closer to the local government model of governance through committees; section 57 of the Act required the establishment of the same number of cross-party subject committees as there were in the executive committee Assembly Secretaries with allocated responsibilities. These

15 Richard Commission, para. 4.10.

16 Report available from www.wales.gov.uk/cms/1/AssemblyReviewOf Procedure.

17 Richard Commission, para. 4.12.

subject committees were consequently led or headed by an Assembly Secretary but at the same time had the responsibility of scrutinizing the discharge of his or her responsibilities. The fact that the members of the executive committee were thus members of the subject committees was a potentially inhibitory factor on their work of policy formulation and scrutiny.[18] The White Paper, *A Voice for Wales*, had envisaged that 'much work'[19] would be done in the subject committees, which could have been the direct recipients of delegated power from the Assembly.

What in fact happened was that the Assembly delegated all its powers to the First Secretary who then retained some of those powers but largely, under section 62(5), delegated most of them to the relevant Assembly Secretary and hence retained control of them within the executive committee. The chain of accountability, Assembly control over and indeed awareness of the full gamut of the substance of its delegation to the executive committee, and the respective functions of the Assembly and the 'executive', however, within the body corporate were not clear, given the mixture of the *de facto* and the *de jure*, and caused particular problems for the supporting officials of the Assembly.

This admixture of the possibilities of the formal legal position (a powerful plenary Assembly and influential subject committees) and the factual concentration of powers in the hands of the First Secretary and the executive committee was further muddied by the changes of nomenclature introduced early in the Assembly's existence. By October 2000 and particularly after the publication of the report of the Assembly Review of Procedure in February 2002 and the consequent changes in Standing Orders, the First Secretary had become known as the First Minister (as is the case under the legislation in both Scotland and Northern Ireland), the Assembly Secretaries as ministers, the executive committee as the Assembly Cabinet, and the government as a whole as the Welsh Assembly Government. These changes were in time additionally given greater physical and administrative manifestations because the executive and their civil servants are now based in the Cathays Park area of Cardiff, and the Assembly itself and the now distinct Assembly Parliamentary Service, which serves all Assembly Members and the subject committees, are now located in the new Senedd building in Cardiff Bay, which building was opened on St David's Day 2006. Electronically too a distinction is made: the Assembly and the Welsh Assembly Government have their own separate web sites, originally accessed through the same page.[20]

The first phase of Welsh devolution is thus marked by the emergence of what Professor Richard Rawlings appositely termed a 'virtual Parliament' and the development 'within the formal legal shell of the corporate body of a divide between the executive and the representative institution as a whole' combined with 'a hardening and political thickening of the political and administrative core' that is the Welsh Assembly Government.[21]

The Assembly's law-making powers

The above *de facto* developments, working within the framework of the 1998 Act, must be placed alongside both the very limited law-making powers that the Act devolved to the

[18] Richard Commission, paras 4.33–37 and 6.30; and *Better Governance for Wales*, Cm 6582, paras 2.14 and 2.15.

[19] Cm 3718, para. 4.16.

[20] www.wales.gov.uk. See now: www.assemblywales.org and www.new.wales.gov.uk.

[21] R. Rawlings, 'Law making in a Virtual Parliament' in Rawlings and Hazell (eds.), *Devolution, Law Making and the Constitution* (2005) 71.

Assembly and the piecemeal and ad hoc nature of the transfer, factors which, like the corporate nature of the Assembly, also became pressure points for change.

The form of devolution that the Act contained is usually called executive devolution for this reason. The Assembly was established as an executive body for the scrutiny and implementation of certain Westminster and Whitehall laws and policies rather than a body with *suo motu* legislative and major policy powers. No primary legislative powers were devolved by the 1998 Act. The Assembly rather inherited the powers previously vested in the Secretary of State for Wales to reach administrative decisions and (much less frequently) to make secondary legislation under powers conferred by an Act of the Westminster Parliament. Furthermore, there was no generic delegation of powers within the eighteen subject areas listed in Schedule 2 to the 1998 Act, as the heading to Schedule 2 itself indicated by the carefully chosen phrase: 'fields *in which* functions are to be transferred by the first Order in Council'. Article 2 of that first Order, the National Assembly for Wales (Transfer of Functions) Order 1999[22] is, in part, a model of clarity: it states that, except as provided in the Order itself, 'all functions of a minister of the Crown under the enactments specified in schedule 1 are, so far as exercisable in relation to Wales, transferred to the Assembly'. Its Schedule 1, however, headed 'enactments conferring functions transferred by article 2', then lists in chronological order beginning in 1841 some 330 public and general Acts (in whole or, usually, in part only), about 10 local and private Acts and approximately 50 statutory instruments.

As the Richard Commission pointed out,[23] the schedule neither requires the first transfer Order to include all matters within all of the listed functions nor precludes functions in other areas being subsequently conferred on the Assembly. Responsibility for animal welfare, fire and rescue services and student support, for example, has subsequently been transferred to the Assembly. So to the presentational muddle of the first transfer Order must be added the fact that it has been amended and added to both by subsequent Orders and by Acts of Parliament. In addition a few later Acts have directly conferred powers upon the Assembly. The whole picture rapidly came to lack both a comprehensive document listing the full range of the Assembly's powers and also cohesive clarity with regard both to what had been devolved and what might be devolved. What should be noted, however, is that 'the creation of the Assembly has given a very strong push to the momentum to extend the boundaries of devolution into new areas'.[24] The factors leading to pressures for the devolution of additional powers include a particular set of circumstances (for example the foot and mouth disease outbreak in 2001) and the Assembly's wish to have a more holistic set of powers in any given area.[25] The overall picture, however, is both confused and unprincipled. The matter has been well expressed thus: 'in Scotland there is a picture of the full puzzle (for example, agriculture) from which some pieces may be removed. In Wales, by contrast there is no picture; only pieces.'[26] Transparency in governance is not assisted by opacity in and inaccessibility of legislation.

The Assembly's actual output from this mosaic of legislative empowerment is good, also bearing in mind the long history of Wales and England as one legal jurisdiction in contrast

22 SI 1999/672. 23 Para. 9.5. 24 Richard Commission, chap. 9, *Findings*, p. 195.

25 Ibid., para. 9.10.

26 Evidence of Cardiff Law School to the Welsh Affairs Select Committee on The Primary Legislative Process as it affects Wales, HC 79, (2002–03) para. 8.

with the separate corpus of Scots law prior to devolution to Scotland. Under the Government of Wales Act 1998, sections 64 to 66, the main type of devolved laws take the form of Assembly statutory instruments (some of which may also be made with the Secretary of State for Wales) and approximately 1,550 such instruments have been made.[27] The distinctiveness of such legislation is, of course, a separate issue, and much of it does replicate English provisions. Research has shown that approximately a quarter of Assembly legislation is non-replica law; this is a significant contribution from a virtually non-existent baseline in 1998–9.[28]

While it is possible to argue that there were at least pragmatic reasons for this initial form of devolved power[29] and that the Assembly has worked well within the limitations of the original devolution settlement, the potential of the Assembly's delegated legislative powers depends heavily upon the style of the drafting of future parent Acts. Obviously a highly detailed Act would have been more constricting than a genuine framework Act, but the former was more likely than the latter, not least because the Westminster Government might be reluctant to confer too wide powers on the Assembly, over the perhaps unforeseen exercise of which it would retain no control. Additionally, as the parent Act might confer delegated powers not only on the Assembly but also upon a Secretary of State to make subordinate legislation for England where greater freedom would be constitutionally undesirable, there is an inevitable tension between the constitutional requirements for England and those for the effective and democratic operation of executive devolution in Wales. If devolution for Wales is to have any substantive consequences, however, and if the differences between a single Secretary of State and a 60-member directly elected Assembly are not to be discounted, the need arises to make separate and different provision, in major or minor regards, for England and Wales in the same framework Act. One solution is to produce 'two-part' Acts of Parliament, each relevant part drafted substantively differently for Wales and for England; or to draft separate sections for each jurisdiction within the same Act. The Secretary of State for Wales in January 2006 referred to 34 Bills in eight years that had made specific provision for Wales[30] (in addition to the Wales-only Acts mentioned below) but these Acts contain no uniform method of provision.

Legislation and Inter-Governmental Arrangements

These needs of Welsh devolution here confront both the demands of (and variations in) Parliamentary drafting and also the omission from the 1998 Act itself of any reference to most inter-governmental relations between London and Cardiff.[31] The need for the Welsh Assembly and Government to be consulted on both the substance and the form of the framework Act as prepared and drafted by the UK Government is central to the effective operation and development of Welsh devolution. The 1998 Act does not deal with this matter; rather the Memorandum of Understanding between the UK and the devolved Governments,[32] and also the UK Government's Devolution Guidance Notes set out the main principles.[33]

[27] Rawlings, nn. 21, 93. See also www.opsi.gov.uk/legislation/wales/w-stat.htm.

[28] Rawlings, nn. 21, 97.

[29] See the quotation from Mr Ron Davies, the then Secretary of State for Wales, in the Richard Commission, para. 5.11.

[30] HC Debs. cited in n. 6, col. 31.

[31] Welsh Affairs Select Committee, HC 79, (2002–03), paras 13–17.

[32] The latest version is Cm 5240, Dec. 2001.

[33] These Guidance Notes are found on www.dca.gov.uk/constitution/devolution/guidance.htm.

The current version of Devolution Guidance Note (DGN) 1 on 'Common Working Arrangements', in paragraph 33 states that when Whitehall departments prepare primary legislation, 'consideration will always be given to the arrangements for Wales'. This consideration requires consultation with the Welsh Assembly Government, especially on Bills that will confer new powers on, or alter the existing functions of, the Assembly. This requirement to consult is further elaborated on in DGN 9, which concerns specifically post-devolution primary legislation affecting Wales and which in its latest form (November 2005) reflects an important non-legislative change. The key principle of the present version of DGN 9, not found in the earlier versions, is the keenly won agreement from the UK Government that Parliamentary Bills 'should be drafted in a way which gives the Assembly wider and more permissive powers to determine the detail of how the provisions should be implemented in Wales'. The background history to this provision is instructive in and of itself for Wales but it is also provided in order to illustrate, for comparative purposes regarding the English Question, the advantages which devolution may provide for political dialogue and constitutional change. The new DGN 9 principle (along with the provisions of the 2006 Act) may also point the way towards a growing separation of English and Welsh laws, which separation might provide further insight into a resolution of the English Question.

The history of this new principle is as follows. In the Report of the Assembly's Review of Procedure, published in February 2002,[34] Annex V, Professor Richard Rawlings articulated several principles which, he counselled, should be adopted in the drafting of Bills which affect Wales. The principles were subsequently adopted by the plenary of the Welsh Assembly[35] and endorsed by the House of Lords Select Committee on the Constitution,[36] and the principles both reflected and engendered considerable support for the need for more flexible grants of power to the National Assembly. The fifth of these principles was that where 'a Bill gives the Assembly new functions, this should be in broad enough terms to allow the Assembly to develop its own policies flexibly'. In spite of widespread support for this principle, the UK Government was reluctant to accept it. In evidence in December 2002, to the House of Commons Select Committee on Welsh Affairs, in the course of its investigation into the primary legislative process as it affected Wales, the Secretary of State for Wales, stating that the issue of flexibility was decided on the merits of each case, explained:

> I think that the tension arises really between this flexibility and Parliament's need to understand how legislation will be applied when it approves that legislation, so Assembly ministers have been happy to provide assurances to government ministers which they can repeat on the floor of the House in order for that certainty to be inspected by members of the House.

He also added that such assurances of a Government minister to the House could bind neither the Welsh Assembly Government nor the Assembly itself. Such difficulties, he explained, stood in the way of the acceptance of Rawlings' principle 5.[37]

The issue also surfaced in the consideration by the House of Lords Select Committee on the Constitution of the inter-institutional relationships in devolution. In its report of January 2003 it recommended that: 'greater consistency be introduced into the process by which Westminster legislates for Wales' an objective which, it stated, could be achieved by

[34] N. 16 above. [35] February 2002, Plenary 2001–02, (50).

[36] Second Report: Devolution; Inter-Institutional Relations in the UK, HL 28, (2002–03), paras 119–25.

[37] Uncorrected Evidence, HC 79-i, (2002–03) Q 160.

adherence to the Rawlings principles.[38] In its response in March 2003 to the Committee's report, the Government stated its agreement with the desirability of greater consistency, its willingness to consider expanding the guidance contained in the then extant DGN on legislation for Wales and its acceptance that the Rawlings principles were a 'useful contribution to that consideration'.[39]

Meanwhile, however, in July 2002, the First Minster had appointed the Richard Commission to review the scope of the Assembly's powers and their adequacy for meeting the needs of Wales. It published its highly significant report in July 2004. In chapter 13, the Commission propounded as one possible way of developing Welsh devolution the value of a commitment to be given by the UK Government to framework Bills which 'would bestow upon the Assembly the widest possible legislative competence within devolved areas'.[40] The following month, August 2004, the Welsh Labour party produced a policy document entitled *Better Governance for Wales*, co-signed by both the First Minister and the Secretary of State for Wales.[41] It made only brief references to the Richard Commission recommendations on electoral reform and reform of devolution, which were very comprehensive, but it set out its own agenda for the moving forward of Welsh devolution. The proposals, it stated, were to become a part of Labour's manifesto for the next general election (which, as it happened, was held in 2005) and then to be subsequently implemented. In paragraph 19, however, it did refer to the Richard Commission's proposal on broad framework legislation and referred to it as a 'valuable way of building the Assembly's legislative capacity and political autonomy'.

After the May 2005 General Election, the Labour Government in its White Paper of June 2005, also entitled *Better Governance for Wales*, stated its commitment to more consistency in the drafting of legislation for Wales and added:

> It also recognises that legislation made by the Assembly is subject to scrutiny by Assembly members using procedures at least as rigorous as those available to Members of Parliament. In light of that, the Government now intends for the future to draft Parliamentary Bills in a way that gives the Assembly wider and more permissive powers to determine the detail of how the provisions should be implemented in Wales.[42]

As this principle required no legislation, it came into immediate effect and has found a home in DGN 9.

The extent of the legislative freedom originally devolved to the Assembly was, therefore, potentially very limited or potentially very expansive. Several years of the experience of devolution has seen a formalized but non-statutory move towards the latter. This may be illustrated by section 17 of the National Health Service Redress Act 2006, the side note to which is simply ' framework power'. It is a one-section provision for Wales; there are 16 substantive sections applying to England. This should be a foretaste of the drafting style to come. The explanatory memorandum to the clause, referring to the White Paper

38 N. 36 above, para. 124(a).

39 House of Lords Committee on the Constitution, 10th Report, The Government's Response to the Second Report of the Select Committee on the Constitution, Cm 5780, March 2003, para. 21.

40 Richard Commission, para. 13.15. See generally paras 13.13–20.

41 Better Governance for Wales: A Welsh Labour Policy Document, August 2004. Available from http://image.guardian.co.uk/sysfiles/Politics/documents/2004/08/04/Better_Governance_for_Wales.doc.

42 Cm 6582 , para. 3.12. This commitment was also given by the Secretary of State for Wales, Mr Peter Hain, when he presented the White Paper to the House of Commons: HC Debs 15 June 2005, col. 263.

commitment, stated that section 17 gives to the National Assembly 'a broad power to make regulations establishing arrangements for redress in respect of Wales'.[43]

The Westminster Parliament, of course, also remains free to legislate for Wales only, rather than the much more usual application of its Acts to both England and Wales, but time constraints, a seemingly invariable feature of the political landscape, pre- and post-devolution, militate against anything other than an occasional use of that power. Under section 31 of the 1998 Act the Secretary of State for Wales is required to undertake such consultation with the Assembly about the (Westminster) government's 'legislative programme for the session as appears to him to be appropriate'. In fact under devolution mark 1, the Westminster Parliament enacted only six Wales-only Acts, not including the Government of Wales Act 2006, which will be considered below. The six Wales-only Acts were the Children's Commissioner for Wales Act 2001; the Health (Wales) Act 2003; the Public Audit (Wales) Act 2004; the Public Services Ombudsman (Wales) Act 2005, and two Acts in 2006: the Transport (Wales) Act and the Commissioner for Older People (Wales) Act.

The publication of Wales-only Bills in draft form facilitates pre-legislative scrutiny and enhances input not least from the Assembly itself and the House of Commons' Select Committee on Welsh Affairs. This practice should continue in the absence of very strong countervailing factors to the contrary.

DEVOLUTION TO WALES: MARK 2: THE GOVERNMENT OF WALES ACT 2006

As Rawlings stated above, the early years of the Assembly are best remembered for the rapid emergence of a 'virtual parliament' but a 'virtual' parliament is one that lacks substance.[44] The question as to how the legal form came to be aligned with the altered reality and also in turn altered it further relates to another key factor in the evolution of Welsh devolution. Given the central role of the Scottish Constitutional Convention[45] as a prelude to devolution to Scotland, dealt with in Barry Winetrobe's chapter, together with its legal, constitutional and political history, devolution to Scotland was strongly but not solely autochthonous and it was built upon stronger and more distinctive foundations than that for Wales. By contrast, the legal, constitutional and political history of Wales, especially with regard to England and the English legal system, precluded, or seemed to preclude, a stronger form of devolution. In Wales, there had been no particular preparation for, or groundswell in support of, devolution in 1997–8 (or possibly for the limited form of devolution being offered), as the outcome of the referendum itself showed. This was so even though the referendum in Wales was held a week after the referendum in Scotland and, therefore, it was hoped, would be influenced by, as correctly anticipated, the decision favourable to devolution to Scotland.[46] The eight years since the commencement of devolution have seen something of a sea

43 The explanatory memorandum is available from www.opsi.gov.uk/acts.htm.

44 N 21 above at 71 and 73.

45 The Claim of Right for Scotland adopted by the Convention in March 1989 begins: ' We, gathered as the Scottish Constitutional Convention, do hereby acknowledge the sovereign right of the Scottish people to determine the form of Government best suited to their needs . . . '. Its report published in 1995 'Scotland's Parliament, Scotland's Right' is available from www.alma.co.uk/business_park/scc/scc-rpm.htm.

46 Referendums (Scotland and Wales) Act 1997, ss 1 and 2.

change, in terms of at least the creation of an institutional dialogue. This has led to greater autochthony and a heightened sense of Welsh ownership of the evolution of devolution.

The case for devolution to Wales in 1997–98 was not a deeply held or widely embedded one. This is a point reinforced by the low turnout in both of the Assembly elections, in 1999 (46 per cent) and 2003 (38 per cent). This factor is now being addressed. Consequent upon the enactment of section 5 of the Political Parties, Elections and Referendums Act 2000, the Electoral Commission is under a duty to prepare and publish reports on the administration of elections to the National Assembly for Wales. In its report on the 2003 election, the Commission drew attention to the fact that the Assembly lacked the requisite legal powers both to develop a communications and information strategy concerning its own responsibilities and achievements and also to address the information deficit concerning the conduct of elections.[47] The Electoral Commission, concerned about the low turnout, also commissioned and, in September 2006, published a further report on public attitudes towards Assembly elections and ways of encouraging voter participation.[48]

In response to the Electoral Commission's recommendations after the 2003 election, the Government had in its 2005 White Paper promised an increase in these powers of the Assembly[49] and, under the Government of Wales Act 2006, section 27 and Schedule 2, paragraph 5, the new Assembly Commission now has the powers to promote public awareness of the current or any pending system of the election of Assembly members and also of devolved government in Wales. The Assembly Commission may also carry out programmes of education and information in these regards.

The success of such an encouragement of public participation, however, is, in part, dependent upon public acceptance that the Welsh Assembly has such powers as to make voting for it a worthwhile exercise. This is relevant to both its democratic mandate and its powers. The Government of Wales Act 2006 has made certain key amendments to the factors discussed above and they will come into effect after the next Assembly election in May 2007.

Constituency and Regional Assembly members

The West Clwyd Question has been given a very specific answer by the 2006 Act, an answer criticized by, among others, the Electoral Commission.[50] Under section 7, a party's submission of its list of candidates for return as Regional Assembly members cannot now include a person who is a candidate to be the constituency member for an Assembly constituency. A similar preclusion applies to an independent who is seeking to be a Regional Assembly member, although so far there have been no successful individual regional members. This reform does not address the comparative status of regional and constituency members, although there is a requirement in section 36(6) of the 2006 Act, under the heading of 'integrity', for the Assembly's new standing orders to include provision about (or to provide

47 The Electoral Commission: The National Assembly for Wales Elections 2003, Nov. 2003, chs 2 and 3.

48 The Electoral Commission: Wales: Poll Position. Public Attitudes towards Assembly Elections. Sept. 2006.

49 Cm 6582, para. 4.8.

50 The Electoral Commission; White Paper: Better Governance for Wales: The Electoral Commission's response. Sept. 2005, paras 9–31, their conclusion, at para. 31, being that 'the case for change has not been made out'. For a full consideration of all the arguments see the excellent paper from the Electoral Reform Society: Briefing Paper (for the House of Lords debate on the Government of Wales Bill) 22 March 2006. The Society also came out against the ban on dual candidacy.

for a Protocol on) the different roles and responsibilities of the constituency and regional members and precision in their description. The Government supports the need for 'clearer guidance' on the relationship between the regional and constituency members.[51] In an Assembly with enhanced powers the tension between the two groups may become greater.

There has been some heated political debate about the West Clywd Answer and it became the main sticking point between the Government and the Conservative Opposition, not least in the House of Lords' debates on the Government of Wales Bill for the following reasons. The Labour party won one regional seat in the 1999 Assembly election and in the 2003 election none, all its seats otherwise being constituency seats. This fact led to some suggestions that the UK Government was motivated by partisan rather than disinterested concern for the issues of the fairness of constituency representation *per se*. This impression was heightened when, in response to a request from a Conservative Assembly Member under the Freedom of Information Act 2000 in April 2006, the First Minister stated that 'officials have not uncovered any information matching your request' about the existence of evidence of abuse by the regional list Assembly members, such as targeting a constituency in their region with the aim of unseating a candidate who defeated them in the constituency election.[52]

This dual candidacy question is, of course, a relatively small part of the much larger whole concerning both the proliferation and the appropriateness of the voting systems in use in the UK and a relatively specific resolution of this issue avoids the UK Government addressing what is for them a thorny issue. There has been no shortage of contrary advice. Part of the remit of the Richard Commission concerned the electoral arrangements of the National Assembly, and its fully reasoned recommendation for the election of an enlarged 80-member Assembly under the single-transferable-vote system[53] has been endorsed by the Electoral Reform Society.[54] The increase in the size of the Assembly and the recommended change in the electoral system were not totally unrelated. The UK Government in its White Paper on *Better Governance for Wales* briefly stated (but did not reason) its disagreement with the Richard Commission's proposals as not being the 'right way forward'. It then stated its intention, reflected now in the provisions of the 2006 Act, to retain the present system, amended only to address 'issues which have emerged in the course of two sets of Assembly elections in 1999 and 2003'.[55]

This is now a point of difference, asymmetry in the standard term, between Wales and Scotland. In Scotland the same electoral system is used as in Wales but the proportion of the constituency seats is greater. In Wales the ratio of constituency seats (40) to regional seats (20) is 67 per cent to 33 per cent. In Scotland the figures are, respectively, 73 seats (57 per cent) to 56 seats (43 per cent). In the Welsh Assembly election of 2003, 17 of the 20 regional members were unsuccessful constituency candidates (85 per cent).[56] In the 2003 Scottish

51 See also the Government's views rejecting alternatives to the ban on dual candidacy and also supporting the need for clearer guidance on the relationship between the two classes of members in Appendix 2 to the House of Lords Select Committee on the Constitution, 10th Report, (2005–06), Government Response to a Report on the Government of Wales Bill, April 2006, HL 168.

52 This is, e.g., referred to in HC Debs, 18 July 2006, col. 201–02.

53 Chap. 12.

54 Electoral Reform Society, n. 50 above and its report *Much* Better Governance for Wales: the ERS's views of the White Paper June 2005, available from www.electoralreform.org.uk/publications/briefings.

55 Cm 6582, para. 4.3.

56 Richard Commission, para. 12.22.

Parliament elections, 88 per cent of the regional members of the Scottish Parliament were unsuccessful constituency candidates.[57]

The Secretary of State for Scotland in the summer of 2004 set up a Commission, under the chairmanship of Sir John Arbuthnott, to report on boundary differences and voting systems in Scotland. It reported in January 2006.[58] It recommended that candidates for election to the Scottish Parliament should not be prohibited from standing in a constituency and on a regional list at the same election.[59] The Government has no plans to amend the Scotland Act in this regard and certainly not before the 2007 Scottish Parliament elections.[60]

It is outside the remit of this chapter to enter into a comparative debate on the merits of the full arguments from the Richard and Arbuthnott Commissions and on the Government's respective stances *vis à vis* Wales and Scotland. The points being made are that: (1) asymmetry should not be allowed too easily to mask unreasoned inconsistency; (2) the presence of devolution renders it easier at least to have constitutional issues aired; and (3) it still remains the case even with what may be termed a 'written constitution' for Wales (and Scotland) that political arguments may be, or may be perceived as being, a dominant concern. It is not necessarily the case that devolution has engendered a clearer demarcation between the political and the constitutional.

The National Assembly and the Welsh Assembly Government

The 2006 Act makes such changes to the institutional design of the Assembly and the Welsh Assembly Government as the early experience of the operation of the provisions of the 1998 Act showed to be necessary and which have been anticipated by administrative and other changes prior to the 2006 Act. Primarily these changes effect a separation between the legislative and the executive arms of Welsh devolution. The Government's White Paper preceding the 2006 Act sets out the reasons why this formalization was necessary: accountability was confused; the civil service had been expected to serve both the ministers and the Assembly in its scrutiny work with a consequential confusion of loyalties; and as ministers remained technically delegates of the Assembly, their authority could be withdrawn at any time by a narrow majority vote of the Assembly, constituting 'far too insecure a foundation on which to build effective government for Wales'.[61] The statutory reconciliation of the *de facto* with the *de jure* was the abolition of the corporate status of the National Assembly for Wales, indeed formally the abolition of the National Assembly for Wales itself, and the establishment of both a new National Assembly for Wales[62] and of a distinct Welsh Assembly Government,[63] which exercises its functions on behalf of the Crown and not by delegation from the Assembly.[64]

57 The Arbuthnott Commission, *Putting Citizens First: Boundaries, Voting and Representation in Scotland* (Jan. 2006), para. 4.21. The Commission noted that in Scotland this may be called the 'Cunninghame South Question'.

58 N. 57.

59 See its recommendations in ch. 4.

60 See, e.g., The House of Commons Standard Note on the Arbuthnott Commission, SN/PC/3918, Feb. 2006, pp. 9–10.

61 Cm 6582, para. 2.4. See also the pre-emptive resignation in February 2000 of the then First Minister Alun Michael, before an Assembly vote of no-confidence supported by all three opposition parties (specifically around EU funding for Wales but of wider import). The vote was still taken and was carried by 31 votes to 27 with one abstention.

62 Government of Wales Act 2006, s. 1.

63 Ibid., s. 45.

64 Ibid., s. 57(2).

The 2006 Act provides for the conferment of separate ministerial powers, for example, under section 58 on the transfer of ministerial functions. Service as a member of staff of the Welsh Assembly Government is service in the Home Civil Service.[65] By contrast, the new Assembly Commission, which is itself a body corporate, has the statutory duty under section 27(5) of ensuring that the Assembly is provided with the property, staff and services required for the Assembly's purposes and under Schedule 2, paragraph 3 (3), these members of staff are not civil servants. Somewhat controversially the Secretary of State for Wales is given the power by Schedule 12, paragraph 20 of the 2006 Act to make the Assembly's new standing orders to replace the current ones. This must be done by March 2007 in time for the next Assembly elections. The Secretary of State must comply with certain statutory requirements and, under Schedule 11, subparagraphs 20(3) and (5), must give effect to Assembly proposals passed on an overall two-thirds majority vote. Additionally the Act gives statutory sanction to the change of nomenclature, such as First Secretary to First Minister, used from the early days of devolution. What thus has happened in general terms is the closer approximation of Welsh devolution not only to the Scottish model but also more generally to the traditional Westminster model of a functionally separate Government and legislature with (through standing orders) clear if not necessarily effective lines of accountability.

The Assembly's law-making powers

Drafting style apart, section 33 of the 2006 Act leaves unaltered the substance of section 31 of the 1998 Act, which required the Secretary of State to undertake such consultation with the Assembly as he considers appropriate about the UK Government's legislative programme for each session. The move to consistently genuine, rather than nominal, framework Acts of Parliament is dealt with above and is currently regulated by DGN 1 and DGN 9. DGN 9, as was seen, includes the significant commitment by the Government that Bills will be drafted in such a way as to secure wider powers for the Welsh Assembly. The Richard Commission had recommended this greater legislative freedom as a direct 'bridge', with no other intermediate stage, to eventually full legislative competence for the Assembly, comparable to that already possessed by the Scottish Parliament.[66]

The advantage of what is now the commitment in DGN 9, this new 'legislative partnership', was, the Commission stated, 'maximum scope for the Assembly to exercise its secondary legislative powers to implement its policies without further recourse to Westminster'. It added:

> This would require Whitehall and Westminster to accept the logic of devolution in framing legislation: that the process of delegating executive powers under primary legislation should take account of both the Assembly's status as an elected body and of its procedures for the scrutiny of secondary legislation. It would also allow the Assembly to continue to develop its expertise in formulating policy in broad fields and in drafting secondary legislation.... Provided Westminster could accept such a potentially far-reaching change in the way it frames primary legislation, this approach would enable the Assembly to continue to develop its capacity and would provide for a smooth transition to a legislative Assembly.[67]

65 Ibid., s. 52(2). 66 Para. 14.24. 67 Paras 14.25 and 14.28.

The Government, while no doubt accepting this reasoning, decided that the platform to take the weight of the eventual transfer of primary powers should be constructed in two stages not the one stage recommended by the Commission. In addition to the important, if extra-statutory, first stage now in DGN 9, the 2006 Act confers upon the Assembly from May 2007, as the second stage, the 'enhanced' power to make Assembly Measures.

This intermediate power comes into effect subsequent to the next Assembly election in May 2007 and this is the stage that was not part of the Richard Commission's recommendations. A Measure will be enacted when the Assembly has passed it and the Queen in Council has approved it. It is thus a form of subordinate legislation. Under section 94 an Assembly Measure has the power to make the same provision as may be made by an Act of Parliament. This power, of course, includes the power to amend an existing or future Act of Parliament or to make new legislative provision. This is thus the conferment by Parliament upon the Assembly of a particularly extensive and continuous power, commonly known as a 'Henry VIII' type of power: the power for subordinate legislation to amend primary laws.

The Assembly's legislative competence, that is the substantive extent of the legislative provision that may be made by Measure, is controlled by section 94 and Schedule 5. Its power to enact Measures can be exercised with regard only to any one or more matters falling within the 20 fields specified in part 1 of Schedule 5 to the 2006 Act (an amended and widened version of the list originally found in Schedule 2 of the 1998 Act, especially concerning the devolution of public administration). Schedule 5 can be amended, under section 95, by the Westminster Parliament's own (modified) procedures for delegated legislation. Under that section this process is triggered by a request from the Assembly itself. Thus the intermediate position gives the Assembly the power to ask the Westminster Parliament to use its modified affirmative resolution procedures for delegated legislation to grant it additional powers (or to restrict its powers) over the devolved responsibilities without having to wait either for Parliament to have the time to legislate by Wales-only Act or to find another appropriate Act on which to tag the Welsh requirements. This thus frees the development of the Assembly's policies from the constraints of Parliament's own legislative priorities. The Secretary of State may under section 95(7)(b) refuse to lay the requisite draft of the Order (incorporating the Assembly's request) before each House of Parliament, with reasons for the refusal being given to the First Minister. The UK Government has justified the conferment of this discretion not only on *vires* grounds but also on grounds of substance: the Order may be regarded as 'defective, unworkable or premature'.[68] The Assembly's own procedures for dealing with Measures are to be regulated by standing orders. Illustrations given by the Government of statutory provisions that could have been dealt with under this procedure, had it been available earlier, include the establishment of the social housing ombudsman and the public services ombudsman, the local health boards and the Welsh Audit Office.[69]

The third stage power of *primary* law-making ('Assembly Acts') closer to that possessed by the Scottish Parliament and the Northern Ireland Assembly is indeed provided for in the 2006 Act but devolution of this power is dependent upon the outcome of a referendum. It is regarded as fundamental and not incremental change. The Act provides no timetable on this

[68] Op.cit., n. 12, HC 839, Appendix, para. 30.

[69] See Deposited Paper in the House of Lords' Library, 15 June 2005, HINF2005/271, provided as the Annex to House of Commons Standard Note (on the White Paper 2005) SN/PC/3717.

matter. The fact that the referendum cannot even take place without a two-thirds majority support of all votes in the Assembly (not simply of those voting) and the agreement of the Secretary of State and both Houses of Parliament, and the fact that those procedures cannot happen until the Secretary of State has undertaken such consultation as he considers appropriate show that the decision of the two Governments will determine when that question will be put to the Welsh electorate.[70] It is the opinion of both Governments that no adequate consensus exists in Wales for the implementation of primary law-making powers for the Assembly at the present time.[71] Given the powers of the Assembly to stimulate public interest in the current or pending system of devolved Government in Wales and given the fact that as in 1997 there needs to be only be a very slight majority on a low turnout for fundamental change to occur, the Governments' prediction that it might be 10 years before public opinion favours full legislative devolution could, with political will, be tested much earlier. Repeat referendums may take place under section 103 of the 2006 Act without the need for any further legislation. The referendum question itself is not provided in the Act and it will be dealt with in subsequent delegated legislation.[72]

The grant of the power to pass Assembly Acts and that to pass Assembly Measures is, under sections 93(5) and section 107(5), preceded by the classic phrase found also in the Scotland Act 1998 and the Northern Ireland Act 1998: 'This Part (of the 2006 Act) does not affect the power of the Parliament of the United Kingdom to make laws for Wales'; that is, the Act re-balances 'legislative authority towards the Assembly, without affecting the overall constitutional supremacy of Parliament as regards Wales within the United Kingdom'.[73] Even with expanded devolution, the *leitmotifs* of the UK constitution are clearly present, if not always insistent: the dominance of the UK Government and the sovereignty of Parliament. If devolution ever moves beyond dialogue between politically compatible central and devolved Governments (and yes, Northern Ireland is different), these fundamental principles will then, and only then, be put to the test.

WHAT ABOUT ENGLAND?: THE ENGLISH QUESTION IGNORED

There is no devolution in England, unlike Wales and Scotland and Northern Ireland. There may be many English Questions (and many ways of phrasing the same question) but the most important question raised by devolution to Wales, Scotland and Northern Ireland coupled with the absence of devolution to England is this: which institutions should make laws and policies for England? The three devolved systems are patently not identical but if a Scottish Parliament makes laws for Scotland in the devolved areas, and a National Assembly for Wales likewise makes laws for Wales, and a Northern Ireland Assembly likewise (subject to it not being suspended) makes laws for Northern Ireland, then who should make laws for England in these comparable fields? This question is not answered at all by the creation of English regional assemblies, which address a totally different set of issues. After the comprehensive defeat of the referendum in the north-east of England in

70 See ss 103–04 and Sched. 6 to the Government of Wales Act 2006.

71 See, e.g., HC Debs, 28 Feb. 2006, cols 192–5, on a rejected clause seeking to control the timing of the referendum.

72 S. 103 and Sched. 6(3) of the 2006 Act, and s. 104(4) of the Political Parties, Elections and Referendums Act 2000.

73 Cm 6582, para. 3.6.

November 2004,[74] the distractions of this answer to the main English Question should be off the political agenda.

The answer given by the present Government (in so far as it wishes to address the question) is that the UK Parliament remains the sole legislature for England and that all Members of Parliament, wherever their constituency is, may, if they wish, vote on any English Bill.[75] This applies even if the matter of the English Bill is devolved elsewhere. So, to give the standard and real, illustrations: student fees and foundation hospitals are matters devolved to the Scottish Parliament and are decided there without any 'English' input. The issues of student fees or foundation hospitals in England are decided by all members of the House of Commons, including those representing Scottish Westminster constituencies and, depending upon the party balance, the votes of Scottish MPs may be decisive over the wishes of the MPs representing English constituencies. The UK Parliament is the sole legislature for England and, as a corollary, the principle of the parity of MPs prevails over what may be the wishes of the majority of English Members.

This position, this treating of the English Question as a non-Question, raises serious questions about the democratic nature of law making for England in the devolved UK and these concerns are not answered by resort to false parallels from the pre-devolved era. As the Labour party draws not inconsiderable strength from the votes of MPs from Scottish and Welsh constituencies, and this may on an English issue be decisive strength, the party may be regarded as having a vested interest in the non-resolution of the English Question.[76]

The Conservative opposition also has a vested interest in a particular resolution of this matter. That party draws its strength now almost exclusively from the English constituencies and, indeed, in the 2005 general election received 65,000 more English votes than the Labour party although 92 fewer English seats. Conversely the party returns very few if any MPs from Scotland and Wales. Currently the party has one Scottish MP and three Welsh MPs. The Conservative party is increasingly committed to 'English votes for English laws', that is, that any Bill for England on a matter that is devolved elsewhere, particularly to Scotland, should be voted on only by MPs representing English constituencies. The counter-arguments to this proposal include the concern that this would create a (UK Labour) Government that might be unable to secure the enactment into the law of England of its key policies (because of English Conservative votes). This is starkly phrased as a (potential) inability to govern because of variable majorities and minorities for a Government on UK, Great Britain and English MPs' votes. A further concern is that this would create a *de facto*

[74] On a turnout of 47.8%, 78% of those voting voted against the proposal for a non-legislative, deliberative regional assembly. See more widely the chapter by Ian Leigh.

[75] Strictly speaking this is an England and Wales Bill or Act; this still being one legal jurisdiction. See C. Himsworth, para. 25 in App. 1 on 'The general effects of devolution upon the practice of legislation at Westminster'; Appendix to the Select Committee on the Constitution, 15th Report, 2003–04. The main issue here is the one of substance rather than legislative form.

[76] This is a summary of arguments. Additional reading includes: the Secretary of State for Constitutional Affairs Speech to the ESRC Devolution and Constitutional Change Programme, 10 March 2006; available from www.dca.gov.uk/speeches/2006/sp060310.htm. The House of Commons, Standard Note, 26 June 2006 on the West Lothian Question, SN/PC/2586, is a very good review of all the various arguments. See also the various party contributions in the House of Lords on the Second Reading of Lord Baker's Private Member's Bill (Conservative), Parliament (Participation of Members of the House of Commons) Bill, HL Debs, 10 Feb. 2006, cols 902–56. See further the House of Commons (Participation) Bill, HC Debs, 9 March 2007, cols 1777–848. See also HC Research Paper 07/24.

English parliament that, given the size of England, would become a rival to Parliament in its UK manifestations. *A fortiori*, the establishment of a totally separate devolved English Parliament is also rejected, as is a federal UK. All these arguments are sometimes wrapped up in terms of peril to the union, although this point rarely leaves the arena of assertion or stated preference. Perhaps rethinking the constitution in confederal terms may assist in the way the issues are conceptualized: power resides in all the component nations of the UK and central power itself is a derived and not original source of power.[77]

There is also the practical and non-partisan but highly important argument that it is virtually impossible to draft (or to identify for voting purposes) a Bill that applies solely to England, but the increasing implementation of the Government of Wales Act 2006 may assist in this process by more clearly separating laws for England and Wales. This drafting or 'identification' point, whatever its strengths might have been, may be of diminishing import.[78]

It is also sometimes argued that there is little popular support for a separate (devolved) English Parliament, although this proposition has never been put to an actual test (as opposed to public opinion polls and surveys). No referendum has been held in England either about devolution for England or about its willingness to accept its own actual experiences of the present devolved settlement-cum-process, which at the law-making and policy-formation levels conflates England and the UK. Working from the Welsh referendum precedent in 1997, public support as low as 25 per cent could be regarded as sufficient to engender even fundamental change, with all the dynamism for further change that flows from that.

There is also a subset of issues arising from the non-resolution of the English Question and these too have to be posited against the problems of seeking to resolve it. First, the *sole* legislature for England is (*pace* the European union) a sovereign Parliament; although the three devolved legislatures have (or may receive) what is termed a primary law-making power, that power is one of restricted competence under the devolution Acts not least with regard to the protection of the rights guaranteed by the European Convention of Human Rights. The dynamics of the judicial/political dialogue with regard to devolved laws and human rights is different. The Human Rights Act, by contrast, assiduously seeks to preserve the sovereignty of the Westminster Parliament, leaving the response to a successful challenge to an Act of Parliament applying to England (or England and Wales) in the political or moral domains. This may be regarded as a 'bad' or a 'good' thing but this difference needs clearer justification.

Secondly, one purpose behind devolution is the revitalization of governance: devolution seeks to secure better accountability, inclusiveness, responsiveness and transparency in the formulation and delivery of laws and policies. Many aspects of the UK constitution may have changed over the last 10 years but reform (as opposed to partial and incomplete

77 The Steel Commission, *Moving to Reform – A New Settlement for Scotland*, Report to the Scottish Liberal Democrat Spring Conference March 2006, e.g., employs the language of 'founding partners' in the UK (p. 60), a phrase which opens up the possibilities of a confederal analysis of the union.

78 This technical issue, although it may have been overstated, is nonetheless a difficult question to resolve not least with uneven devolved powers in the UK and at times (regarding Northern Ireland) partially inoperative devolution, and with the frequent use of the Sewel convention discussed in Barry Winetrobe's chapter. There is no good reason, however, why the issue should not be approached seeking to resolve the greater anomaly (if only in terms of population affected) of the English Question in the devolved era rather than other anomalies concerning the devolved nations.

modernization) of the House of Commons is not one of them. This inevitably impacts upon the enactment of laws and policies for England. These processes for England need reforms comparable to those taking place in the devolved nations.

Thirdly, there is a lack of institutional interest in constitutional change in England. The dynamo is not there. It is an obvious point, but the establishment of devolved institutions means not only new politics (and new politicians) but also new forums for engagement with the public, new forums for issues to be aired, new powers to establish commissions (the Richard Commission) and new focal points for national bodies (the Electoral Commission and Parliamentary Select Committees) to engage in debates engendered by devolution. As the Welsh experience considered above shows, there is a plethora of bodies to take the initiative, to respond, to engage in dialogue, to move the agenda along, to act as a counterpoise (but not necessarily an equally powerful one) to the evaluation or wishes of the UK Government. By contrast, England suffers from the dead-hand combination of Government domination and a sovereign Parliament.

What is needed for England is the establishment of a wide-ranging and inclusive convention comparable to the Scottish Constitutional Convention that was set up in the aftermath of the 1987 general election and that did such significant work in Scotland in the 1990s as the prelude (as it happened) to Scottish devolution. Certainly that was a spontaneous not official body but post-devolution there does need to be in England a new engagement between the political elites and those whom they represent concerning modes and principles of governance. The opinions and experience of political parties, religious leaders and the faith communities, civil society at local, regional and national levels, voluntary organisations, academic opinion and pressure groups needs to be harnessed. The English Question, whatever answer emerges, needs to be widely addressed for the sake of the English constitution and for the revitalization of English politics and popular engagement with questions of constitutional concern.

CONCLUSION

The UK constitution has not been changed by devolution. Certainly *de facto* the work of the Westminster Parliament is less extensive geographically, although the pressures on its time are stated to be as intense as ever. Certainly intergovernmental processes have been put in place, but they have not really been tested, given the absence of party differences among the UK, Scottish and Welsh Governments, although this is not to state that their policies or ethos have been identical.[79] The constitutions of the three devolved nations have been changed by devolution but not the English constitution (except negatively) and not the UK constitution.[80] Indeed the capacity for devolution to develop in Wales and Scotland is in many ways held back by the elision of 'English' and 'United Kingdom' at the heart of the UK's legislative and executive structures. No new thinking has there emerged to counteract or diminish the assumptions of the 'rightness' of Government dominance and of the

[79] See, e.g., M. Keating, L. Stevenson and J. Loughlin, *Devolution and Public Policy: Divergence or Convergence*, ESCR Devolution and Constitutional Change Programme, March 2005.

[80] See further D. Feldman, 'None, one or several: Perspectives on the UK's constitution(s)' (2005) 64 *Cambridge Law Journal* 329.

manipulation of constitutional questions for partisan advantage. Devolution shows both how much change is possible and how little is likely for as long as the Government dominates a sovereign Parliament.

FURTHER READING

Rawlings, R. and Hazell, R. *Devolution, Law Making and the Constitution* (2005).

Hazell, R. (ed.) *The English Question* (2006).

Hadfield, B. 'Towards an English Constitution' (2002) 55 *Current Legal Problems* 151.

Hadfield, B. 'Devolution, Westminster and the English Question' (2005) *Public Law* 286.

USEFUL WEB SITES

www.assemblywales.org
www.new.wales.gov.uk
www.parliament.uk
www.richardcommission.gov.uk

12

THE NEW LOCAL GOVERNMENT

Ian Leigh

SUMMARY

Since coming into office in 1997 the Labour Government has instituted the most important programme of local government reform in decades. This chapter evaluates the programme of reform aimed at reinvigorating local democracy after decades of central–local conflict, dwindling local powers, and declining interest from the electorate. It discusses the various interlocking strands in the reform programme: the relaxation of the *ultra vires* rule to enable councils to fulfil their new mission as 'community leaders' or 'place-shapers'; the introduction of powerful leaders and cabinets and scrutiny committees, which radically alter the role of councillors; the creation of new offices of directly elected mayors, especially in London; and changes to the electoral system. It asks, finally, whether these changes will be sufficient to secure the future of local democracy in the face of demands for regional government and in a changing constitution.

THE NATURE OF LOCAL GOVERNMENT

Local government has an image problem. In the popular imagination municipal often equates with mundane. Somehow the governance of town halls does not capture the imagination in the same way as more high-profile constitutional reforms. This is unjust for two reasons.

First, most of a citizen's daily contact with the state and its officials is with local authorities, rather than government departments. Councils are responsible for services on which the well-being of individuals and communities depend such as education, social services, roads, swimming pools and leisure centres, libraries, and planning, as well as more mundane, but nonetheless vital, matters like refuse collection and disposal.

Secondly, local government has been the site of much of the constitutional innovation of the last quarter century, although it has rarely been labelled as such. Examples include the right of council tenants to buy their homes, rate capping, the abolition of the Greater London Council and metropolitan counties, the introduction of compulsory competitive tendering, and the community charge ('poll tax') and its replacement with the council tax.

During the 1980s much central–local conflict, especially over finance, found its way to the courts.[1] In place of legal battles, the Labour Government that was elected in 1997 has consciously sought a new cooperative partnership with local authorities. A forum for discussion of issues of joint concern – the Central Local Partnership – has been established. Under its auspices regular meetings have been held between ministers and the representatives of local authorities to promote better understanding, consultation and joint working.[2]Although powers for central government to limit local council tax ('rate capping' was first introduced under the Rates Act 1984) remain on the statute book in a modified form, they have been used sparingly. The much-hated compulsory competitive tendering regime introduced by the Conservative administrations, which required some functions to be 'market tested' by inviting tenders before they could be provided by council employees,[3] has been lifted also. It has been replaced with a more flexible 'Best Value' system in which councils have a duty to demonstrate the economy, efficiency, and effectiveness of the way they have chosen to organize their services, subject to periodic inspection.[4]

Other aspects of the Labour Government's contributions to this process are discussed in greater detail below. These include: the creation of the Greater London Authority and the office of Mayor of London, the introduction of elected mayors and local cabinets, local electoral experiments, and new statutory powers for councils to become 'community leaders'.

Why has this not been thought of as 'constitutional' reform? An obvious, if misleading, answer would be that in the absence of a written constitution local government enjoys no formal constitutional status or protection. In the UK there is no legal restraint on central government enlisting Parliament to abolish local government altogether, still less reforming its essential characteristics. From an international perspective this is anomalous: references to local government abound in written constitutions the world over.[5] They do so because the idea has been found useful and important.

This idea is no less important in the UK, although for clues to the constitutional significance of local government one must look to different sources. Two can be cited: a little-noticed treaty ratified in 1998 and official reports.

The treaty is the European Charter of Local Self-Government 1985. It defines the constitutional status to be given to local government by the signatory states.[6] The Charter contains some important principles, though broadly expressed. These include 'subsidiarity', a democratic principle stipulating that decisions should be taken at the nearest feasible level to those who are affected by them. For example, Article 4, paragraphs 3–5 state:

3. Public responsibilities shall generally be exercised, in preference, by those authorities which are closest to the citizen. Allocation of responsibility to another authority should weigh up the extent and nature of the task and the requirements of economy and efficiency.

1 For example: *Nottinghamshire CC* v. *Secretary of State for the Environment* [1986] AC 240; *Hammersmith and Fulham* v. *Secretary of State for the Environment* [1990] 3 All ER 589. See generally M. Loughlin, *Legality and Locality: the Role of Law in Central-Local Relations* (1996).

2 www.communities.gov.uk/index.asp?id = 1133646.

3 Local Government Planning and Land Act 1980 and Local Government Act 1988. S. Arrowsmith, *The Law of Public and Utilities Procurement* (1996) chs 12–14.

4 Local Government Act 1999, s. 3. The Government announced plans to reform the inspection system in the Local Government and Public Involvement in Health Bill 2007, Pt. 8, chapter 2.

5 See, for example: Constitution of the Fifth Republic 1958, Art. 72 (France); Basic Law of the Federal Republic of Germany, Art. 28.

6 C. Crawford, 'European Influence on Local Self-Government', (1992) 18(1) *Local Government Studies* 69.

4. Powers given to local authorities should normally be full and exclusive. They may not be undermined or limited by another, central or regional, authority except as provided for by the law.
5. Where powers are delegated to them by central or regional authority, local authorities shall, insofar as possible, be allowed discretion in adapting their exercise to local conditions.

In addition, Article 9 guarantees the freedom to determine expenditure priorities and to raise adequate resources. The UK Government's decision to ratify this treaty in 1998 is of greater symbolic than legal significance. The Charter is binding between member states only (local authorities cannot invoke it on the international stage) but it is of tangential domestic legal significance: it is open to a court to refer to it in order to help resolve statutory ambiguity.

So far as official domestic recognition of the importance of local government is concerned, the following statement – from the report in 1986 of the Committee on the Conduct of Local Authority Business (the Widdicombe Committee) – is hard to improve upon as a summary of constitutional values:

[T]he value of local government stems from its three attributes of:

(a) pluralism, through which it contributes to the national political system;
(b) participation, through which it contributes to local democracy;
(c) responsiveness, through which it contributes to the provision of local needs through the delivery of services.[7]

Several characteristics are usually said to distinguish British local government: that it is elected, that councils have a measure of statutory discretion and financial autonomy, and that they have multiple local functions. In recent decades each of these features has come under some strain, so much so that at times central government (especially during the Conservative administrations from 1979 to 1997) has been accused of acting unconstitutionally in rebalancing them. It is worth briefly considering these further before moving on to discuss the reforms that have been introduced in an attempt to reinvigorate local democracy.

Local authorities have been elected since the 1880s, with the introduction under the Local Government Act 1888 of elected county councils (earlier legislation gave a right for householders only to vote). The changes since then have been not so much to the democratic character of local government but rather a regular process of adjusting its structures. The most prominent examples were reforms of the Local Government Act 1972, establishing a two-tier system of elected counties and districts over much of the country, but with variations in the split of functions between the tiers in the metropolitan areas,[8] and the creation in 1963 of the Greater London Council (abolished in 1986). Since a further reorganization of local government in 1992–6 most of England and all of Scotland and Wales now have a single tier of elected local authorities. In places these are district, borough, or city councils and in others county councils. In parts of rural England, however, the two tiers of counties and districts introduced in the Local Government Act 1972 survive, with functions divided between them.[9] In London, borough councils exercise most of the

[7] *The Conduct of Local Authority Business, Report of the Committee of Inquiry Into the Conduct of Local Authority Business*, Cmnd 9797 (1986), para. 3.11.

[8] Metropolitan county councils were subsequently abolished, however, by the Local Government Act 1985.

[9] In its 2006 White Paper *Strong and Prosperous Communities*, Cm. 6939–1 (2006) the Government has signalled a preference for unitary authorities by proposals to make it easier for councils to seek this status by agreement.

functions of unitary councils but a new elected strategic body, the Greater London Authority, came into operation in 2000.[10]

The independent electoral approval that local councillors enjoy underlines the claim that this is local *government*, rather than local administration. The latter would suggest local implementation of centrally determined policies for merely practical reasons. The former implies that locally elected politicians have some degree of democratic legitimacy and discretion and control over how local functions are performed. Without such discretion local elections would be a meaningless exercise. The elected nature of local authorities inevitably imports into their business party political conflict (although it is still common to find some independent councillors in a council). It also creates the possibility of conflict between the politics of the council and of central government, with each claiming their own electoral mandate.

Significantly, less than a decade after the introduction of popularly elected local authorities the courts could be seen deferring to the new bodies in a case in which a local by-law was unsuccessfully challenged, on the grounds that it was made by councillors who had been elected as local representatives and who must be presumed to have knowledge of local conditions.[11] In modern times, however, judges have been generally less deferential to local democracy. In a 1995 judgment declaring unlawful the decision of Somerset County Council to prevent deer hunting on land controlled by it, Laws J. specifically rejected the council's argument that its statutory powers to manage land should be given a wider interpretation because elected council members were entitled to reflect local feelings on the issue.[12] Nor have councillors been allowed to use popular endorsement of their local manifesto policies by electoral success as cover for otherwise unlawful decisions:[13] to do so would in effect allow them to enlarge their own powers by making reckless electoral promises. On the other hand, the courts have been sensitive to local democracy in preventing councils from suing for defamation on the grounds that to do so would inhibit free discussion and public accountability.[14] Taken together these decisions tend to show the judiciary recognizing the value of local democracy as a mechanism for accountability to local people but, somewhat paradoxically, restricting the powers that elected councillors can wield.

It would be misleading, however, to suggest that local authorities are models of representative democracy. Electoral apathy is a serious and longstanding concern. Local elections have rarely produced turnouts of more than 40 per cent for decades, unless coinciding with a General Election, but when, during the 1990s, voting dropped to around 10 per cent in some parts of the country the legitimacy of local democracy was seriously called into question.

The powers of local authorities and their democratic legitimacy are inextricably linked. Why bother to vote in local elections if councils are powerless to change anything? Equally, however, why should bodies that are ignored by the electorate be trusted with new powers by Parliament or deferred to by the courts? The Labour Government's 10-year programme

[10] See pp. 306–8 below. A Bill to reform the powers of the Greater London Authority was announced in the Queen's Speech in November 2006.

[11] *Kruse* v. *Johnson* [1898] 2 QB 91, 98–9 (Lord Russell) and 104 (Sir F. H. Jeune), Mathew J dissenting.

[12] *R.* v. *Somerset CC, ex parte Fewings* [1995] 1 All ER 513, 529; the Court of Appeal affirmed the decision on slightly different grounds: [1995] 3 All ER 20.

[13] *Bromley* v. *GLC* [1983] 1 AC 768, especially Lord Wilberforce at 814; cf. *Secretary of State for Education and Science* v. *Tameside MBC* [1977] AC 1014, holding that the council's manifesto commitment (to retain grammar schools) was relevant to the reasonableness of the minister's intervention.

[14] *Derbyshire CC* v. *Times Newspapers* [1993] AC 534.

of reform to revive local democracy, ushered in by the Local Government Acts 1999 and 2000, was intended to break this conundrum. In Laurence Pratchett's words, the aim was to deal with the 'electoral apathy', 'functional impotence', and 'arcane decision-making structures'[15] afflicting local democracy. We will examine the reforms to local powers and executive structures in turn, paying less attention to the electoral reforms.

POWERS

The aim of the reform of local government powers was to meet the changing role of local authorities. The perceived shift was from councils acting as the primary providers of local services to coordinating and leading a range of public, private, and voluntary bodies. To some extent this had been foreshadowed in the fashionable notion of the 1980s – the 'enabling council' (i.e. enabling rather than doing) – although that was associated with an ideological bias in favour of contracting out the delivery of council services. A broader, communitarian, vision involving 'partnership' between councils, other local agencies, voluntary bodies, and the private sector was first articulated by Professor John Stewart.[16] It influenced an important report by a House of Lords Select Committee, *Rebuilding Trust*, the work of the self-styled Commission for Local Democracy, and the incoming Labour government.[17]

The 1998 White Paper endorsed this vision of 'community leadership' as follows:

> Among all our public institutions councils have a special status and authority as local, directly-elected bodies. They are uniquely placed to provide vision and leadership to their local communities.... Councils need to listen to, lead and build up their local communities. We want to see councils working in partnership with others, making their contribution to the achievement of our aims for improving people's quality of life.[18]

This has remained the dominant theme of Government policy although the current vogue terminology has changed: reports now speak of the council's role in 'place-shaping'.[19]

The legal regime was felt to be inadequate for this new role in being merely a collection of diverse statutory functions, powers, and duties with no indication of what the sum of the parts amounted to. Moreover, the *ultra vires* rule created some artificial barriers to partnership working between local authorities and other bodies. Since it prevented as unlawful the delegation of power from a council to another body, the rule inhibited cooperative working with other agencies in the public, voluntary, and private sectors and the establishment of free-standing, arm's-length, enterprises (such as companies) for such joint work. All cooperative enterprises of this kind were under the shadow that the courts might find them to be unlawful if they exercised powers entrusted by Parliament to the local authority or if the council was unable to point to explicit legal authority for its participation.

[15] L. Pratchett, 'Introduction: Defining Democratic Renewal', (1999) 25 *Local Government Studies* 1, 3.

[16] E.g. J. Stewart and G. Stoker (eds), *Local Government in the 1990s* (1995) ch. 14.

[17] See *Report of the House of Lords Select Committee on Relations Between Central and Local Government 'Rebuilding Trust'*, HL 97 (1995–96); Commission for Local Democracy, *Taking Charge: the Rebirth of Local Democracy* (1995); Labour Party, *Renewing Democracy, Rebuilding Communities* (1995).

[18] Department of the Environment, Transport and the Regions, *Modern Local Government: In Touch With the People*, Cm 4014 (July 1998), Foreword and Introduction by John Prescott.

[19] Lyons Inquiry into Local Government, *Place-shaping: a shared ambition for the future of local government* (March, 2007).

The *ultra vires* rule had come to be seen as increasingly rigid. It had developed lineally from nineteenth-century legal doctrines concerning the powers of corporations, whether public or private (such as companies). Whereas in relation to companies it was applied increasingly liberally in the early twentieth century and was finally abolished by legislation, for public corporations it became an increasingly potent method of judicial control.[20]

As Laws LJ put it in the *Fewings* decision:

> any action to be taken must be justified by positive law. A public body has no heritage of legal rights which it enjoys for its own sake; at every turn all of its dealings constitute the fulfilment of duties which it owes to others; indeed it exists for no other purpose.... It is in this sense that it has no rights of its own, no axe to grind beyond its public responsibility: a responsibility which defines its purpose and justifies its existence. In law this is true of every public body. The rule is necessary in order to protect the people from arbitrary interference by those set in power over them.[21]

Central government can influence the parliamentary process to obtain wide grants of discretionary power and is only rarely subjected to detailed duties. This is not the case with local government. The legacy, then, for local authorities is that each action and decision, however minor, must be shown to rest on explicit statutory authority.[22] The courts, moreover, have compounded the situation by often interpreting narrowly even apparently widely drafted statutory powers when the actions of the council could adversely affect local taxpayers by causing financial liability for an unsuccessful transaction[23] or where private rights or interests would be affected.[24] A particularly controversial judicial construct is the fiduciary principle, by which the courts have treated a local authority as a type of trustee of money received from local taxpayers.[25] Under the guise of this dubious doctrine some decisions involving council expenditure have been held to be unlawful in giving too little weight to taxpayers' interests.[26]

Recent attempts at reform are an attempt to undo some of these negative implications of *ultra vires*. They have taken three main forms.[27]

First, expanded discretionary powers to enter into partnership arrangements with other local bodies or agencies have been introduced by sections 2(4) and 4 of the Local Government Act 2000.[28] These were intended to remove the uncertainty over the legality of some of these cooperative ventures. In the spirit of 'joined-up' government various programmes have

20 The turning point came in *Ashbury Railway Carriage Co.* v. *Riche* (1875) LR 7 HL 653 when the House of Lords rejected the argument that statutory corporations should be regarded as having the legal attributes of a natural person except to the extent that the statute expressly or impliedly restricted them. See: M. Stokes, 'Company Law and Legal Theory', in W. Twining (ed.), *Legal Theory and Common Law* (1986); H. Rajak, 'Judicial Control: Corporations and The Decline of Ultra Vires', (1995) 26 *Cambrian Law Review* 9.

21 *R.* v. *Somerset CC, ex parte Fewings* [1995] 1 All ER 513, 524.

22 All local authorities now enjoy their powers solely under statute: Local Government Act 1972, ss. 2(3), 14(2), and 21(2). The Act extinguished the claim that boroughs created under royal charter possessed the powers of an ordinary person and so were not subject to *ultra vires*; and see *Hazell* v. *Hammersmith LBC* [1992] 2 AC 1, 39–43 *per* Lord Templeman.

23 As in *Hazell* (above) and *Credit Suisse* v. *Allerdale BC* [1996] 4 All ER 129, CA.

24 E.g. *Fewings* (above).

25 Loughlin, op. cit. (n. 1 above), ch. 4; I. Leigh, *Law, Politics and Local Democracy* (2000) 131–9.

26 *Roberts* v. *Hopwood* [1925] AC 578; *Prescott* v. *Birmingham Corp.* [1955] Ch. 210; *Bromley LBC* v. *Greater London Council* [1983] AC 768.

27 A fourth measure, the Local Government (Contracts) Act 1997, aimed to remedy some of the disadvantages where a contract involving a local authority was held void because it was *ultra vires* (as in the *Hazell* and *Allerdale* cases), is less important here.

28 The community initiative power includes specific ability to give financial assistance, to enter into arrangements or agreements, to cooperate with, or facilitate, or coordinate the activities of any person, to exercise on

been introduced to stimulate local authorities to work in partnership, both with other public authorities and with the voluntary and private sectors. Local Area Agreements are three-year agreements setting out the priorities for a local area made between central government (through the relevant regional office), the lead local authority and other key partners.[29] Strategic Service-delivery Partnerships are similar collaborative agreements aimed at improving the delivery of services in the locality. Local authorities play a leading role in Local Strategic Partnerships – forums to bring together the public sector as well as the private, business, community and voluntary sectors at a local level, so that initiatives and services support each other and work together. The Government intends to develop these arrangements further by imposing duties on the public sector partners to work together in developing and delivering the priorities under Local Area Agreements.[30]

Secondly, there is a power of 'community initiative'. This was intended to enshrine in law the role of the council as 'the elected leader of their local community'.[31] Its introduction should be set against a growing chorus of calls throughout the 1990s for the introduction of a power of 'general competence', which, in the more radical versions proposed, would have abolished *ultra vires* entirely.[32] Rather than following that route the Labour Government proposed to give enhanced recognition to the position of local government through what was described as an 'over-arching' or under-pinning duty, with a linked power of community initiative – a type of quasi-constitutional mission statement which would give structure and purpose to the many specific powers and duties of councils.[33]

In the form ultimately introduced these proposals were diluted, however: the legal power is supplementary, rather than fundamental, and the duty was omitted. All local authorities now have power to do anything which they consider is likely to promote or improve the economic, social, or environmental well-being of their area.[34] When exercising the power (or considering whether to do so) an authority must consider the effect on the achievement of sustainable development in the UK.[35] Linked to the power is a specific duty to 'prepare a strategy for promoting or improving the economic, social and environmental well-being' of the authority's area (s. 4(1)). In so doing the council may consult widely and must have regard to ministerial guidance. The strategic plan is intended to provide focus for the leadership and coordinating aspects of the community leadership role. Apart from a specific power to incur expenditure, detailed powers to enter partnerships also feature prominently[36]

Although the power of community initiative is undoubtedly useful it hardly constitutes a fresh start for local authorities. There are various limitations: the power cannot be used to override restrictions in other more detailed legislation on the council's powers.[37] Where a

behalf of any person any functions of that person, and to to provide staff, goods, services, or accommodation to any person: s. 2(4), LGA 2000.

[29] Local Government Association *Leading Localities: Local Area Agreements* (London, 2005).

[30] *Strong and Prosperous Communities*, Cm. 6939–1 (2006). LGPIH Bill pt. 5, ch. 1.

[31] *Modern Local Government In Touch With the People* (n. 16 above), para. 8.9.

[32] For a full account of the various alternatives: see Leigh (n. 5 above) ch. 2.

[33] See Department of the Environment, Transport and the Regions, *Modernising Local Government: Local Democracy and Community Leadership* (Green Paper, Feb. 1998), ch. 8 and the earlier Labour Party policy document, *Renewing Democracy, Rebuilding Communities* (n. 7 above).

[34] S. 2(1), LGA 2000.

[35] S. 2(3), LGA 2000.

[36] S. 2(6), LGA 2000.

[37] Anything subject to a 'prohibition, restriction or limitation on their powers which is contained in any enactment' is specifically excluded under s. 3(1). This applies to existing and future legislation ('whenever passed or made') and to subordinate legislation also (subs. 3(6)).

council hopes to vary national limitations due to local circumstances it is necessary to seek ministerial relaxation under the Beacon scheme (below). Ministers also have a wide power to exclude activities by delegated legislation.[38]

Overall, the community initiative power is less impressive than the 'over-arching' provision initially promised by the government. This becomes clearer if we consider possible alternatives. A statutory statement of the rationale for local government could certainly be devised. It has been in the case of the new Greater London Authority, which works within a statutory statement of its purposes,[39] underlying the myriad of more specific powers and duties of the Authority. An alternative to a mission statement of this type would be a direction to the courts concerning the importance of local democracy when specific provisions in local government legislation fall to be construed. An interpretive provision of this kind could be the equivalent for local democracy of section 3 of the Human Rights Act 1998.[40] Compared with either of these possibilities, the much more prosaic formulation of the new power reveals its altogether more modest ambitions.

The attitude of the judiciary towards the new power will be a key issue. In the great majority of cases councils will continue to act under specific, detailed, and limited statutory powers. The question then will be how these specific powers and the new general power fit together. Attempts in the past to liberalize *ultra vires* by giving broad powers to local authorities have foundered at this stage.[41] Further relaxation of *ultra vires* is likely to be most useful at the boundaries of what local authorities do, in permitting experimental and joint projects to tackle social exclusion and promote economic development, in crime control and community health programmes. The (very little) evidence to date is more encouraging perhaps than might have been expected. In *R. (J)* v. *Enfield LBC*[42] one of the questions was whether the Council could give financial assistance towards rental to an asylum seeker who was specifically barred under other legislation from being offered accommodation as such. The court held that the power under section 2 of the 2000 Act was capable of being so interpreted, although it would be exceptional to apply it to an individual case in this way.

The third strand of reform of powers involves relaxation of legal and ministerial controls over local authorities. The original idea was the 'Beacon council' scheme[43] whereby ministers would relax controls for authorities that could demonstrate that they deserved greater freedom because of their strong existing performance. This is an adapted version of the 'Free Local Government' initiatives which have been introduced in Scandinavia.[44] The Beacon

[38] S. 3(3), LGA 2000.

[39] The Greater London Authority Act 1999, s. 30 states that the principal purposes of the Authority are to promote economic and social development, wealth creation, and the improvement of the environment in Greater London and the Authority has power to do anything which it considers will advance these purposes.

[40] See Chapter 3, above.

[41] See especially decisions in relation to s. 111 of the Local Government Act 1972 which allows a council to do anything 'which is calculated to facilitate, or is conducive or incidental to, the discharge of any of their functions'. As examples of restrictive interpretations of s. 111: *Hazell* v. *Hammersmith and Fulham LBC* [1991] 1 All ER 545; *McCarthy and Stone* v. *Richmond upon Thames LBC* [1991] 4 All ER 897; *Credit Suisse* v. *Allerdale BC* [1996] 4 All ER 129; *Credit Suisse* v. *Waltham Forest LBC* [1996] 4 All ER 176; *Morgan Grenfell* v. *Sutton LBC* (1996) 95 LGR 574; *Allsop* v. *North Tyneside MBC* (1992) 90 LGR 462.

[42] [2002] EWHC 432 (Admin); [2002] LGR 390.

[43] DETR, *The Beacon Council Scheme: Prospectus* (Feb. 1999).

[44] H. Kitchin, 'A Power of General Competence for Local Government', in L. Pratchett and D. Wilson, *Local Democracy and Local Goverrnment* (1996); L. Rose, 'Nordic Free-Commune Experiments: Increased Local Autonomy or Continued Central Control?', in D. King and J. Pierre (eds), *Challenges to Local Government* (1990).

Scheme has turned into a periodic grant competition, according to thematic priorities, in which authorities identified as performing strongly in particular services (or, exceptionally, overall) are commended and encouraged to share best practice with other authorities, through open days, seminars, staff exchanges, and so on.[45] A second route for relaxation of controls is through positive review in the audit and inspection process: ministers have power to set aside legal constraints on forms of service delivery by local councils where these cut across 'best value'[46] and also to remove or amend enactments which they think prevent or obstruct local authorities from exercising their community well-being power.[47] Additionally, the Government has signalled in its 2006 White Paper an intention to relax ministerial control for all local authorities over some matters (such as the approval of local by-laws or the granting of Parish Council status).

From reform of powers we turn now to the reform of local government executive structures.

NEW FORMS OF GOVERNANCE

THE PROBLEM

The elected nature of local government inevitably gives rise to the presence of party politics: in most local authorities there are caucuses of councillors grouped according to party affiliation in imitation of the arrangements at Westminster. This is a longstanding feature, although it appears that party politics at the local level became more intense during the 1970s and 1980s.[48]

Traditionally, councils have organized themselves quite differently, however, from the central state. Legally speaking, the whole council (all the councillors of whatever political affiliation) was responsible for the authority's decisions. In practice most decisions were delegated to committees of elected members with smaller areas of responsibility or, in the case of purely administrative matters, to council employees, the officers. The officers, however, served the council as a whole, rather than the majority group of councillors.

The mismatch between these two features – the political nature of local government and the legal responsibility of the whole council – became acute in a number of local authorities during the 1980s. The Widdicombe Committee found in 1986 that 85 per cent of local authorities were organized on political lines with party groups meeting outside the council's structure to determine political strategy.[49] These party groups, however, had no formal place within the decision-making process. Attempts to regularize the position by giving the majority

45 Government Response to the Review of the Beacon Council Scheme (Office of the Deputy Prime Minister, 2005)

46 Local Government Act 1999, s. 16(1); ministers may also confer additional powers on authorities by order where it is considered to be necessary or expedient in order to permit or facilitate compliance with best value: ibid., s. 16(2).

47 Under s. 5 of the 2000 Act.

48 J. Gyford, S. Leach, and C. Game, *The Changing Politics of Local Government* (1989); K. Young, 'Party Politics in Local Government: an Historical Perspective', in *Aspects of Local Democracy, Research Volume IV, Report of the Committee of Inquiry into the Conduct of Local Authority Business* (1986) 81–105.

49 *The Conduct of Local Authority Business*, Cmnd 9797 (1986), paras 2.37–2.40. See also the follow-up study: K. Young and M. Davies, *The Politics of Local Government Since Widdicombe* (1990).

party group an official decision-making power were held to be unlawful in depriving opposition councillors of access to information.[50] On the other hand, unless they were guaranteed a secure environment in which to reach policy decisions there was no incentive for a controlling majority of councillors to bring policy formulation out of closed party group meetings and into the council as such.

Consequently, the legal constitution of local government was founded on a bizarre and unhealthy silence about its most visible attribute – party politics. Decisions would be reached behind closed doors in the group meeting of the majority party, to be rubber-stamped in public council meetings.[51] Furthermore, the legal framework still clung doggedly to the fiction that all councillors were of equal importance, regardless of political affiliations. In many local authorities, however, the chairmen of committees had assumed a role that paralleled at the local level the function of a Secretary of State, with political direction and control of an area of the council's work. This too was of dubious legality.[52]

An obvious solution to these problems would have been to acknowledge the political realities by allowing for the legal creation of a political executive with effective balancing mechanisms. Instead, in its Local Government and Housing Act 1989, the Conservative government focused on outlawing political abuses – a duty that all council committees must reflect the political balance of the parties was introduced.[53]

REFORM

More radical proposals for reform came about because of dissatisfaction with the system of decision-making by committees that operated in local authorities and because of the need to reinvigorate local politics in the light of dwindling participation rates in local elections.

To combat electoral apathy many councils have attempted to broaden their engagement with the public by use of 'deliberative' (rather than 'representative') democratic devices: local referendums, citizens' juries, service user panels, questionnaires, focus groups, and so on. A council is now permitted to conduct polls to ascertain local views on any matter concerning its services, expenditure on those services, or with its power to promote well-being of its area.[54] The council has discretion over who to consult and how.

Experimental attempts have also been introduced to tackle voter turnout more directly. Legislation now permits councils to apply for permission to use alternative electoral arrangements to the traditional single day voting in person at polling station.[55] These schemes have included the use of postal ballots, rather than polling stations, electronic

50 *R.* v. *Sheffield City Council, ex parte Chadwick* (1985) 84 LGR 563.

51 In *R.* v. *Amber Valley DC, ex parte Jackson* [1984] 3 All ER 501 it was held that the mere fact that a planning application had been discussed in a prior party group meeting of the majority group did not mean that the council could not later determine it fairly. In *R.* v. *Waltham Forest Borough Council, ex parte Baxter* [1988] 2 WLR 257 there was an unsuccessful attack on a decision reached after councillors, who had voted against the policy in closed group meeting but lost, later followed the party whip and supported it in a council meeting; on the facts the Court of Appeal found that their discretion not been fettered.

52 The Local Government Act 1972 did not permit a council to delegate functions to an individual councillor, and where an officer acted under the instruction of a committee chairman this might be held unlawful: *R.* v. *Port Talbot BC, ex parte Jones* [1988] 2 All ER 207.

53 LG and HA 1989, s. 15; the Local Government (Committees and Political Groups) Regulations 1990 (SI 1553/1990).

54 Local Government Act 2003, s. 116.

55 Representation of the People Act 2000, s. 10.

voting, and the use of non-conventional polling stations such as supermarkets and doctor's surgeries. At the same time councils have moved to a cycle of more frequent elections – a third of councillors stand for re-election in three years out of a four-year cycle in an attempt to make councils more responsive to the local electorate. More radical reform, such as the introduction of proportional representation for local elections, has been rejected for England and Wales. In Scotland, however, following the report of the MacIntosh Committee, proportional representation was introduced in local government by the Local Government (Scotland) Act 2004.

So far as the system of decision-making is concerned, the problem was the lack of separation of policy formulation, implementation, and scrutiny – the council as a whole was responsible for all of these functions. Consequently, the decision-making processes were confusing and lacked transparency. Instead of focusing on their representation and scrutiny roles councillors were involved in close management of tasks better left to officers.[56]

A consultation paper from the Department of Environment, published in 1993, argued for recognition of political executives on several grounds: 'they provide clear political direction for the authority; make clear where accountability lies; provide a more efficient, quicker and coordinated decision-making process; and provide a confidential forum for the ruling group to test the range of policy options with its official advisers'.[57] Moreover, the change would enable councillors who were not members of the executive to take on stronger scrutiny and constituency roles. The proposal that the government should allow experimentation with different forms of political executive did not appeal to the ministers at that time. However, the concept of a political executive became an accepted feature of later reform models[58] and, ultimately, part of the Labour Government's programme in the Local Government Act 2000.

The legislation required councils to review their administrative arrangements and to adopt one of three forms (the status quo was not a permitted option): a Leader and cabinet system, an elected Mayor and cabinet, or an elected Mayor and council manager (a powerful officer).[59] Not surprisingly, most councils have opted for the Leader and cabinet, since it 'represents the formalisation of already existing group-dominated political processes'.[60] A much smaller number have adopted the elected Mayor and cabinet model.

Under the Leader and cabinet model[61] the Leader is chosen by councillors[62] and is removable by them without reference to the electorate. Except in 'hung' authorities (those where no party has overall control), where the election of the Leader may become a semi-transparent process, normally the leadership and membership of the cabinet will be decided in the group meeting of the majority party and then presented to the Council meeting for endorsement. The council may either allow the Leader to decide on the size and responsibilities of the cabinet (the so-called 'strong Leader') or may do so itself (the 'weak Leader').[63] Removal of the Leader or any member of the cabinet is left to the council to determine

[56] E.g. Commission For Local Democracy, *Taking Charge: The Rebirth of Local Democracy* (1995), chs 3 and 4.

[57] *Community Leadership and Representation: Unlocking the Potential* (1993), para. 5.22.

[58] *Modernising Local Government: Local Democracy and Community Leadership* (1998) ch. 5; *Modern Local Government: In Touch With the People*, Cm 4014 (1998) ch. 3.

[59] The account here concentrates on the first two, since these are the most prevalent forms.

[60] C. Copus, 'The Party Group: A Barrier to Democratic Renewal', (1999) 25(4) *Local Govt Studs* 76, 89–90.

[61] S. Leach, 'Introducing Cabinets into British Local Government', (1999) 52(1) *Parl. Affs.* 77.

[62] Local Government Act 2000. s. 10(3)(a).

[63] LGA 2000, s. 13(3) and (4) respectively.

under its standing orders; a 'strong' Leader might have the power to dismiss other members of the cabinet, whereas a 'weak' one would not.

In its 2006 White Paper[64] the Government has proposed a significant strengthening of the position of the leader, by introducing the possibility of *directly elected* leaders. Even where a council chose to retain an indirectly elected Leader, the position would be strengthened since the leader would choose the other members of the cabinet, not the council. In all cases leaders would serve a four-year fixed term, making them much less vulnerable to by-election turbulence and allowing a sustained programme to be put forward. In a radical break with tradition it is proposed that all the legal powers of the council be vested in the leader.

In the current arrangements the political executive is balanced by overview and scrutiny committees.[65] The purpose of these committees is, first, to scrutinize the discharge of executive functions and, secondly, to provide a policy role in reporting and making recommendations to the authority or the executive about the discharge of their functions and on matters which affect the authority's area or inhabitants.[66]

Overview and scrutiny committees have the power to require members of the executive and officers to attend and answer questions (and there will be a corresponding duty on them to do so) and to invite other people.[67] The government clearly envisages that reviews of policy should be carried out by overview and scrutiny committees in a way which will allow the committee to investigate the impact of the policy on users of council services and other partners of the council in delivering them. There will be a natural link between such reviews and community planning and performance review under the best value regime.

The division between executive and scrutiny councillors is based on a parliamentary select committee model. Separation from the executive is enforced by a provision preventing oversight and scrutiny committees from including members of the executive.[68] However, as with parliamentary select committees, there is a majority of councillors who are from the same party as the executive. Critics argued that unless the reforms addressed the hidden influence of the party group they would prove ineffective.[69] Studies suggested that there may be a reluctance among councillors on scrutiny committees to criticize party colleagues[70] and that it might have been preferable to require scrutiny committees to be chaired by an opposition councillor, an omission from the legislation. There are indications that in some councils 'backbench' councillors have struggled since these reforms to find a worthwhile role, now that they have been formally excluded from the policy process.[71] The Government has brought forward proposals to address this and to reinvigorate the role of councillors as 'Democratic Champions'. These include the possibility of single councillor constituencies and strengthening the powers of Oversight and Scrutiny Committees by requiring councils to consider and publicly respond to their recommendations and by giving them powers to question and influence other public service providers in the locality.[72]

64 *Strong and Prosperous Communities* (2006), ch. 3; LGPIH Bill, pt. 3.

65 A council opting for a Mayor and cabinet model (below) is required to have overview and scrutiny arrangements also.

66 S. 15(1).

67 S. 15(3) and (4).

68 S. 15(2).

69 Copus, op. cit., 76, 88–9.

70 M. Cole, 'Local Government Modernisation: the Executive and Scrutiny Model', (2001) 72(2) *Pol Q* 239; R. Ashworth, 'Toothless Tiger? Councillor Perceptions of the New Scrutiny Arrangements in Welsh Local Government', (2003) 29 *Local Govt Studs* 1.

71 Cole, op. cit., 241–2.

72 *Strong and Prosperous Communities* (2006), ch. 3; LGPIH Bill, pt. 5, ch. 2.

ELECTED MAYORS

The more innovative model is the directly elected mayor. This is an imported office: mayors are common in local government overseas, especially in the cities of the USA, France, Italy, and Germany.[73]

In the UK the idea was first championed by Michael Heseltine as Secretary of State for the Environment, and then taken up by the Campaign for Local Democracy.[74] It was first officially proposed as an option for the proposed new London Authority.[75] The idea was approved in a referendum held in Greater London in May 1998 and the Greater London Authority Act 1999 gave effect to these proposals, with the first elected mayor, Ken Livingstone, returned in May 2000.

In the case of councils outside London a 1999 white paper proposed that councils should be placed under a duty to consult local people about the form of government they wished to see, with an elected mayor as one of the options. Fearing resistance from councillors to the idea, the government proposed that there would be a possibility of a referendum being triggered to put the elected mayor option to the electorate, even where this was not the council's preferred choice.[76]

Advocates of the idea of a directly elected mayor hoped that it would bring about functional separation in the council between the executive (comprising a directly elected mayor or leader and the council's staff) and the elected assembly of councillors. Moreover with an elected mayor, instead of the political leadership of council being determined by the party group, it is a matter directly for the electorate. The idea was to bring about a working tension which might increase public knowledge about local government and weaken party dominance. This has been partially successful: three of the 11 mayors elected to date are independent[77] and in other cases the mayorship and the majority on the council are in the hands of different parties.

Low turnout rates however (between 11 and 42% of the electorate) suggest that generally the experiment has failed to revive significant public interest in local democracy.[78] The significant exception was the campaign to elect a Mayor for London in 1999–2000 which dominated the news for months and attracted as candidates three former government ministers (Frank Dobson, Glenda Jackson, and Steve Norris), a former Leader of the Greater London Council (Ken Livingstone), and a former Deputy Chairman of the Conservative Party (Lord Archer). The failure of other major cities to follow London's lead is disappointing, especially since one aspiration was that elected mayors would be figureheads who would represent their communities nationally and in Europe.

[73] See H. Elcock, 'Leading People: Some Issues of Local Government Leadership in Britain and America', (1995) 21(4) *Local Govt Studs* 546; G. Stoker, 'The Reform of the Institutions of Local Representative Democracy: Is there a role for the mayor-council model?' (CLD Research Report No. 18, London, 1996); G. Stoker and H. Wolman, 'Drawing Lessons from US Experience: An Elected Mayor For British Local Government', (1992) 70(2) *Public Admin.* 241.

[74] Commission for Local Democracy, *Taking Charge: the Rebirth of Local Democracy* (1995) ch. 4.

[75] *A Mayor and Assembly for London*, Cm 3897 (1998).

[76] *Local Leadership, Local Choice*, Cm. 4298 (1999) ch. 2.

[77] Strictly only Hartlepool, Mansfield, and Middlesbrough qualify. In Stoke on Trent however Mike Wolfe, representing the Mayor4Stoke Party, was elected in October 2002.

[78] See further Electoral Commission, *Reinvigorating local democracy? Mayoral referendums in 2001* (January 2002).

By late 2006 only 31 referendums had been held (6 of them as a result of petitions) and only in 11 instances was the result in favour of an elected mayor.[79] After a flurry of interest in 2001 and 2002, none has been held since the (unsuccessful) referendum in Ceredigion in May 2004. Ministers, however, remain more interested in the idea than the general public appears to be and published proposals in 2006 intended to make it easier for a council to promote a change to an elected mayor without a referendum.[80] It is questionable whether many elected councillors will opt to diminish their own role and influence in this way and it would appear that only in a very few cases is the electorate interested or well organized enough to force this change upon them.

LONDON

In comparison with these the creation of a Mayor and a new strategic authority for London in the Greater London Authority Act 1999[81] can be counted a success in raising the profile of issues affecting London as a whole. The Authority comprises two elected institutions with complementary roles, the Mayor and the London Assembly. Elections are held for both simultaneously every four years.[82] The Mayor is elected under the supplementary vote system. This, if there are three or more candidates, allows voters to express a first and second preference among the candidates. At the counting stage unsuccessful candidates are eliminated and second preferences are redistributed if no candidate achieves more than 50 per cent of first preferences. (If there are fewer than three candidates, the 'first past the post' voting system is applied.) Ken Livingstone, who was elected as the first Mayor, in May 2000, as an Independent, and then re-elected in 2004, having been re-admitted to the Labour Party, has become the recognizable figure-head for the metropolis.

There are 25 Assembly members, chosen by a mix of electoral methods: 14 represent constituencies and 11 are chosen for London-wide seats, according to the Additional Member system using the electoral strengths of the respective political parties.

The Mayor is the most visible face of the new Authority and is the main source of initiatives in policy affecting London as a whole, as well as being responsible for coordinating other agencies and bodies across the capital. As well as running new transport and economic development bodies, the Mayor works closely with (and makes appointments to) the new Metropolitan Police Authority and London Fire and Emergency Planning Authority, and is responsible for setting the overall framework for the development of London, within which Borough councils deal with planning. He also has a coordinating role to improve the environment and air quality in London, in other environmental issues such as waste and noise, and encouraging local initiatives. The Mayor prepares a series of strategies to deal with various matters: transport, economic development and regeneration, spatial development, biodiversity, municipal waste management, air quality, ambient noise, and culture.

79 www.electoralcommission.gov.uk/referendums/mayoralrefresults.cfm (searched on 16 Nov. 2006). Mayors were elected in Bedford, Doncaster, Hartlepool, Mansfield, Middlesbrough, North Tyneside, Stoke on Trent, and Watford and in the London Boroughs of Hackney, Lewisham, and Newham. See also N. Rao, 'Options for Change: Mayors, Cabinets or Status Quo?' (2003) *Local Govt Studs* 1.

80 Department for Communities and Local Government, *Strong and Prosperous Communities* (October 2006), Cm 6939–1, para. 3.27.

81 M. Supperstone and T. Pitt-Payne, 'The Greater London Authority Bill', [1999] *Public Law* 581; B. Pimlott and N. Rao, *Governing London* (2002).

82 GLA Act, ss. 1 and 2 and Sched. 1.

There are proposals for legislation to extend the Mayor's powers.[83] The Greater London Authority Bill 2006–07 proposes the addition of important new fields to the powers and duties of the Mayor and the Assembly. These include the preparation of a housing strategy and a similar strategy to address health inequalities in London. Particularly innovative are a bundle of provisions on climate change that underline the place of the Authority in carrying through the national goals of reducing emission of greenhouse gases. Under the Bill the Mayor and Assembly will be required to prepare strategies both for climate change mitigation and energy and for adaptation to the effects of climate change in Greater London. These proposals may well be the forerunners of more widespread legal duties to address climate change.

The Mayor and the Assembly operate clearly within the pattern of English local government and in that respect they perhaps compare unfavourably with their counterparts in major cities elsewhere in the world. Finance, for example, is derived from Council tax and central grant: there is no power to raise money by local income tax. Although accountability for policing in the metropolis has been removed from the Home Secretary and a new Metropolitan Police Authority has been established,[84] the Mayor's power is indirect and in keeping with arrangements for police authorities elsewhere in the UK,[85] compared, for example, to the more interventionist powers of a US mayor.

The Mayor's most high-profile contributions to date have come in the field of transport.[86] There was a protracted, acrimonious, and unsuccessful legal battle with the government over the use of public-private partnerships in the funding of the London Underground which was reminiscent of central–local conflict in the 1980s.[87] More positively, in 2003 London became the first major conurbation in the world to introduce a system of congestion charging on the capital's roads. This is the type of bold policy initiative that perhaps could only be taken forward by a powerful mayor operating at a strategic level. Undoubtedly also the successful bid for the 2012 Olympics to come to London owed much to collaborative efforts of the Mayor and national government.

The Assembly comprises paid, full-time politicians, with a scrutiny and policy remit. The Assembly keeps the Mayor's exercise of statutory functions under review[88] and has power to investigate, and prepare reports about, any actions and decisions of the Mayor or any of the Authority's staff, and matters in relation to which statutory functions are exercisable by the Mayor. It may also investigate matters relating to the principal purposes of the Authority or any other matters which the Assembly considers to be of importance to Greater London. The Assembly may submit proposals to the Mayor, to which he is required to make a formal response.[89] It can amend the Mayor's overall budget and plans, although it requires a two-thirds majority to do so. It also exercises oversight over the performance of the functional bodies, for transport and economic development, the police and fire authorities. It also has power to consider any other issues that it believes are important to Londoners.

The Mayor is accountable to the Assembly through several mechanisms. A written report must be given by the Mayor to the Assembly at least three clear working days prior to each of its monthly meetings, dealing with the significant decisions taken, with reasons, and

[83] Proposals for a new Greater London Authority Bill were announced in the Queen's Speech on 15 November 2006.

[84] GLA Act, Pt VI.

[85] Police Act 1996, Pt 1.

[86] Pimlott and Rao (n. 81 above) ch. 7.

[87] See n. 1 above.

[88] GLA Act, s. 59.

[89] GLA Act, s. 60.

responses to any formal proposals made by the Assembly.[90] The Mayor attends the Assembly's meetings to answer questions but is not be obliged, however, to disclose advice received from the staff of the Authority or from functional bodies or their staff.[91] The Assembly has powers to summon such people, but, in the same way, they are not obliged to disclose advice given to the Mayor. This is a move towards treating such officers more in the mould of civil servants than has been customary with local government officers (similar restrictions apply to civil service evidence to parliamentary select committees) and follows, perhaps inevitably, from the formal recognition of a distinct political executive. The Assembly meetings, the Mayor's reports, the text of questions and answers, and the minutes of the meetings are open or available to the public.[92] The Mayor is required to prepare an Annual Report assessing progress on implementing strategies, including the achievement of any targets and giving any information which the Assembly has asked to be included before the beginning relevant year. The report is followed by an annual State of London debate.[93] In addition, a 'People's Question Time' must be held twice yearly.[94] A more radical proposal for accountability – that the Assembly be able to impeach the Mayor – was, however, rejected.

The overall scheme of the Act carries through the objective of creating a strong Mayor's office – most power vests in the Mayor and there are few formal restraints. Nevertheless, cooperation between the Mayor and the Assembly is necessary since the Assembly has strong powers to review the work of the Mayor. Its powers to block initiatives or policies are weaker: the necessary two-thirds veto by the Assembly is unlikely to be obtainable in practice, especially within an Assembly elected at the same time as the Mayor. The Mayor, therefore, is clearly in the stronger position.

The success of the arrangements in London has stimulated interest in strong leadership models for other cities. The past decade has also seen significant interest in the possibility of English regional government. The potential implications of this for local government are explored in the next section.

THE CHALLENGE OF REGIONALISM

Apart from electoral apathy, perhaps the main challenge to the position of local authorities as 'community leaders' or 'place-shapers' has come from those advocating regional government. Were regional government to be introduced in England there could be real rivalry for strategic leadership of an area. Moreover, as the pattern of devolution in Scotland and Wales already demonstrates, the introduction of regional government would imply corresponding structural reform of local government, with an inevitable move towards unitary authorities. This section describes how regional government became a fashionable policy option and its subsequent decline.

90 GLA Act, s. 45.

91 See GLA Act, ss. 61–5 for the attendance of witnesses at Assembly meetings and production of documents to it.

92 Subject to the exceptions for confidential and other exempt material set out in Pt VA of the Local Government Act 1972.

93 GLA Act, s. 47.

94 GLA Act, s. 48.

The main pressures for the introduction of regional government stem from dissatisfaction with central, rather than local, government. The principal arguments are that regional government would allow for a sense of political identity to be recognised even where the central government at Westminster failed to reflect the political mood of the regions. Regional government might therefore counteract a feeling of political disenfranchisement. A further argument relates to the lack of regional democratic accountability for central government offices dispersed regionally and regional quangos. Oversight of such bodies featured prominently in the proposals for regional government from the Constitution Unit, for example.[95] However, the subsidiary arguments for regional government relate more strongly to issues about local government functions and focus on the need for strategic planning in such areas as land use and transportation and the need for co-ordination at the regional level of economic development and bids for and implementation of EU funding.

In theory, three options exist for regional-local relations in the UK. Firstly, a pattern of regions could be superimposed upon a consistent layer of local government, with the competence of both tiers fixed from the centre: this would be like the post-1972 dual-tier local government writ large. Secondly, a variable geometry of regional and local government might be imposed from above. Thirdly, the composition of local government could itself be one of the devolved responsibilities of regional government, as in the devolution legislation for Scotland and Northern Ireland. In the second and third scenarios different regions might develop significantly differing patterns of local government. However, there is an important difference: in the second scheme, regional variations in local government would result from national legislation and be under the control of central government, whereas in the third they would be a product of regional initiative and experimentation. Any of these arrangements could incorporate something lacking from present central-local relations: the powers of regional authorities over local government might also be limited, so providing a form of constitutional guarantee for local authorities.

Viewed in the light of these possible scenarios the Government's attitude to regional government has been remarkably unambitious. The Regional Development Agencies Act 1998 established agencies for London and eight regions[96] responsible for regional economic development. These are business-led and dominated boards, although the membership also contains local authority members and representatives of other regional interests, such as the education and voluntary sectors. The Government intended that one-third of members should be drawn from local councillors in the region that the agency serves, to reflect the size of local authorities, the geographical spread, and political balance. The RDAs replaced a number of existing quangos (English Partnerships, Training and Enterprise Councils, and Urban Development Corporations, for example) and are the lead agencies in coordinating bids for funding for regional EU funding. In addition, the legislation envisages the possibility of further transfer of central government functions to the RDAs by ministers where

[95] Constitution Unit, *Regional Government in England*, (London, 1996). For earlier proposals see the minority dissenting memorandum to the report of the Role Commission on the Constitution, suggesting that the House of Lords be amended to include a strong provincial presence, which would give it an indirectly elected character by being drawn from regional assemblies: *Report of the Royal Commission on the Constitution 1969/73*, volume ii: Memorandum of Dissent, Cmnd. 5460-i (1973).

[96] Regional Development Agencies Act 1998, s.1 and Sched. 1. The regions are the East Midlands, Eastern, North East, North West South, East South West, West Midlands and Yorkshire and Humberside. With the exception of the North West Region, the boundaries are intended to mirror the existing areas of the relevant Government Regional offices.

expedient to do so.[97] This opens the possibility of uneven or asymmetrical development between English regions: where an individual RDA consents, functions may be delegated to it without being given to RDAs generally.[98]

Obviously absent from these arrangements was a layer of democratic accountability. To address this, legislation provides for ministerial designation of regional chambers 'if the Secretary of State is of the opinion.... that there is a body which is representative of those in a regional development agency area and with an interest in its work' and which is 'suitable to be given the role'.[99] Where a regional chamber is designated the RDA is under a duty to consult it. The Government has recognized eight regional assemblies: East of England Regional Assembly; East Midlands Regional Assembly, North East Assembly, North West Regional Assembly, South East England Regional Assembly, South West Regional Assembly, West Midlands Regional Assembly and Yorkshire and Humber Assembly. They are grouped together in an umbrella organization, the English Regions Network.

These, however, are *indirectly*-elected consultative assemblies drawn mainly from members of the local authorities in the region: about two-thirds of members of the regional assemblies are councillors (some also include MPs and MEPs). The remaining members are from local business, voluntary, charitable, educational and religious organizations.

In comparison with the directly-elected chambers in other parts of the UK, the RDAs and regional assemblies are poor relations, subject to ministerial powers and patronage and lacking any powers over central government regional offices. The Government was prepared to consider elected regional government in parts of England that could demonstrate a demand for it[100] – this would have produced an asymmetric form of regionalism in practice. The initial step in assessing demand was to hold regional referendums, and legislation was enacted to allow for these in 2003.[101]

However, the policy ran aground following the first referendum, held in November 2004, in which the electorate in North East England voted against an elected assembly. On a turnout of 47.8 per cent of the region's voters (the vote was conducted entirely by postal ballot), 78 per cent voted against and 22 per cent in favour. Since the Government had anticipated that, if anywhere, demand was strongest in the North East because of proximity to Scotland, distance from London and a strong regional identity, effectively the outcome killed the prospects of further regional campaigns. In the aftermath critics were divided over whether the voters were disinterested because the proposals for an assembly had been too expensive and unnecessary, or because it lacked sufficient powers to be worth establishing as an elected body – it lacked law-making powers or the range of executive functions of the National Assembly for Wales, for instance.

In its current mild form regional government is scarcely a threat to a local government. Indeed, in England, the Association of District Councils and the Association of Metropolitan Authorities have been supporters of regional government. Regional Chambers are dominated by local authority representatives, rather than supervising or taking over their powers. Elected regional assemblies, on the other hand, would have posed

[97] Regional Development Agencies Act 1998, s. 8(1).

[98] RDA Act, s. 6(3). Delegation of functions may be made simultaneously to all RDAs without their consent. Equally, however, delegation may be withdrawn, provided (where an RDA does not consent) it is withdrawn from all RDAs simultaneously: s. 6(4).

[99] RDA Act, s 8(1).

[100] See the White Paper, *Your Region, Your Choice*, Cm 5551 (May 2002).

[101] Regional Assemblies (Preparations) Act 2003.

a threat since they would have had their own electoral legitimacy, would have been independent of local councils, and might even have taken over the task of allocating funding to local authorities. That possibility appears to have receded for the foreseeable future.

CONCLUSION

The Labour Government programme of reform to revitalize local democracy is now well-advanced. On a sober assessment some of the reforms delivered have been less dramatic than was promised. The new power of community initiative adds useful flexibility to local authorities' powers but is less than the quasi-constitutional power that was initially proposed. Reform of executive structures has resulted in most councils adopting a Leader and cabinet model, with very few local referendums to approve the arrangements. This has not sharpened accountability as much as the Government had hoped. Fewer still authorities have taken the bold step of introducing an elected mayor, although experience in London suggests that strong leadership may have advantages for other major cities also.

On the positive side, two decades of central–local conflict have come to an end, to be replaced with a new era of partnership working, However, until electors see local authorities responsible for the bulk of local finance (most still comes through central government grant) or with greater discretion over key local services, they may stay away from polling stations. The electorate has not yet become sufficiently animated for turnout in local election to improve substantially, although a further series of reforms proposed in 2006 aims to strengthen leadership and devolve some power to local authorities.

Local government has emerged relatively unscathed from the challenge posed by possible elected regional assemblies. These would have tended to 'draw up' functions from local councils as much as drawing them down from central government. There remains, however, pressure to move to a system of unitary authorities across all England, as has happened in Scotland and Wales, although, for the time being the Government is content to encourage rather than to compel this development.

Nevertheless, as constitutional reform proceeds, one useful reform to consider is some form of constitutional protection for local democracy.[102] The idea was proposed in the early 1990s by the Institute of Public Policy Research.[103] Whether as part of a written constitution or in freestanding legislation, the point of the proposal would be to set out the virtues of political pluralism, local participation, and responsiveness to local communities. Delineating the boundaries of local government's sphere as against central or regional government might be difficult, as would questions of local taxation, but these have not proved an insuperable barrier to reform in the devolution legislation. Certainly the idea merits consideration if we are serious about preserving local democracy.

[102] See further I. Leigh, *Law, Politics and Local Democracy* (2000) ch. 1.

[103] Institute of Public Policy Research, *A Written Constitution for the United Kingdom* (1991) 95 and 221–2.

FURTHER READING

ARDEN, A., MANNING, J. and COLLINS, S. *Local Government Constitutional and Administrative Law* (1999).

BAILEY, S. *Cross on Principles of Local Government Law* (3rd edn, 2004).

Commission for Local Democracy *Taking Charge: The Rebirth of Local Democracy* (1995).

COPUS, C. *Party Politics and Local Government* (2004).

COPUS, C. *Leading the Localities: Executive Mayors in English Local Governance* (2006).

LEIGH, I. *Law, Politics and Local Democracy* (2000).

LOUGHLIN, M. *Legality and Locality: the Role of Law in Central-Local Relations* (1996).

PIMLOTT, B. and RAO, N. *Governing London* (2002).

PRATCHETT, K. and WILSON, D. (eds) *Local Democracy and Local Government* (1996).

STEWART, J. and STOKER, G. (eds) *Local Government in the 1990s* (1995).

USEFUL WEB SITES

Audit Commission: **www.audit-commission.gov.uk/**

Commission for Local Administration (Local Government Ombudsmen): **www.lgo.org.uk/**

Department of Communities and Local Government **www.communities.gov.uk/**

English Regions Network: **www.ern.smartregion.org.uk/page.asp?id** = 1

Greater London Authority (the Mayor of London and London Assembly): **www.london.gov.uk/**

INLOGOV (The Institute of Local Government Studies, University of Birmingham): **www.inlogov.bham.ac.uk**

(Local Government) Improvement and Development Agency: **www.idea.gov.uk**

Local Government Information Unit: **www.lgiu.gov.uk/**

Local Government Association: **www.lga.gov.uk**

Lyons Inquiry into Local Government **www.lyonsinquiry.org.uk**

PART III

REGULATION AND THE CONSTITUTION

Editorial note

Regulation has become an increasingly important element in the UK's constitutional arrangements. This has been particularly the case in relation to privatized industries, public expenditure, access to official information, and standards of conduct in public life. Thus the regulation of power is the focus of this part of the book. Before the privatization of many industries in the 1980s and 1990s, much regulation was internal to government: government itself regulated, often in an informal manner, the industries that were publicly owned. Since privatization regulation has been formalized, statutory, and external to those industries. Independent expert regulatory bodies have been created to take on these tasks. Chapter 14 examines the implications of this development. However, much of government activity remains largely internally regulated. The control of public expenditure (which is the focus of chapter 15) is the paradigm example: the Treasury regulates government departments' spending in various ways. The National Audit Office and Parliament do so too, but Parliament's role is increasingly formal only.

Sunshine can be a powerful disinfectant, and the accountability of public bodies is enhanced by openness about their activities. Chapter 16 considers the impact of the Freedom of Information Act 2000, which provides for and regulates rights of access to information.

Finally in this part of the book, the regulation of standards of conduct in public life is considered in Chapter 17. As a result of a number of scandals in the 1990s and a loss of trust in politicians and others in public life, standards of conduct have been increasingly subject to regulation. A range of techniques are discussed in this chapter, including self-regulation with or without independent elements, the adoption and publication of codes of conduct, even the criminalization of some breaches of rules relating to conduct and conflicts of interest. Overall the chapters in this part show that the system is becoming increasingly rule bound, regulated, and juridified.

Editorial note

13

COURTS, TRIBUNALS, OMBUDSMEN, ADR: ADMINISTRATIVE JUSTICE, CONSTITUTIONALISM AND INFORMALITY

Andrew Le Sueur

SUMMARY

An important aspect of the principle of administrative justice is that citizens can challenge the decisions of public authorities. The concept and practice of administrative justice is undergoing far-reaching reform. Two sets of values – associated with constitutionalism and informality – underpin the reforms. These values express laudable aims, but they also give rise to tensions and contradictions. Where this happens, the values of constitutionalism ought to prevail. Administrative justice should be recognized as a constitutional principle.

INTRODUCTION

- Watchdog [the Local Government Ombudsman] slams council planners: a Plymouth man fed up with dust and noise from lorries going to a golf course development has won his fight against the city council.
- Ring road plan faces legal battle: plans to turn Reading's ring road into a giant one-way system face being scuppered by a last-minute High Court challenge.
- Cancer patient wins drug access: a lung cancer patient has said he is 'over the moon' after winning an injunction [in a judicial review claim] to receive the drug Tarceva.
- Pension for nuclear testing widow: a widow whose husband campaigned for a military pension has been granted his wish [by the Pensions Appeal Tribunal], three months after he died.'

As these headlines show,[1] in a constitutional democracy, it is important that people can challenge the wrongful decisions, actions and omissions of public authorities. There are various ways of seeking to get things put right. Most commonly, and away from the gaze of

[1] Taken from the BBC News website http://news.bbc.co.uk/.

journalists, citizens manage to do this by themselves by simply asking the public authority to think again. In relation to some functions, public authorities have been required or encouraged to set up complaints systems and internal appeal mechanisms to facilitate this.[2] Elected representatives – MPs and councillors – often get involved in disputes through their constituency casework.[3] Some agencies and their sponsor departments have created 'independent' complaints handling agencies to receive and seek to resolve complaints (such as the Independent Case Examiners' Office dealing with child support and the Adjudicator's Office dealing with tax).[4] Beyond these avenues of redress are three types of external mechanism for challenge – courts (especially through claims for judicial review), appeals to tribunals under various Acts of Parliament, and the work of the public sector ombudsmen.[5]

Together, these avenues of challenge form a major part of the administrative justice system (a term that will be examined in the next section). The administrative justice system is currently undergoing far-reaching reform led by the Ministry of Justice (formerly the Department of Constitutional Affairs).[6] This chapter is about the two sets of values or currents – constitutionalism and informality – which underpin the reform agenda.[7]

One current – implemented for example by the Constitutional Reform Act 2005 and the Tribunals, Courts and Enforcement Act 2007[8] – seeks to promote the values associated with constitutionalism.[9] The aim here is to put the governance of courts and tribunals on a new statutory footing, with a greater independence from government and more transparency in their organizational structures. Thus, relatively informal ways of working (such as the 'tap on the shoulder' judicial appointments system based on 'secret soundings') have been replaced by more formal, transparent, and accountable institutional structures and processes (for example the Judicial Appointments Commission of England and Wales using a competence-based approach in open competitions). The values of constitutionalism include the idea that citizens are holders of legally-enforceable rights and entitlements. It is

[2] See D. Cowan and S. Halliday, *The Appeal of Internal Review* (2003).

[3] As well as helping constituents by writing letters to public authorities, MPs also (controversially) continue to control access to the Parliamentary Ombudsman, who is able to investigate complaints of maladministration by central government bodies only if a case is referred by an MP.

[4] See n. 12 below.

[5] In quantitative terms, the tribunal system is by far the most significant arena for citizen-state dispute resolution, handling nearly 500,000 cases a year (of which the biggest categories are social security, immigration and asylum, tax and VAT, and mental health). The two main ombudsmen – the Parliamentary Ombudsman (dealing with central government bodies) and the Local Government Ombudsmen – together receive over 20,000 requests to investigate alleged injustice caused by maladministration each year. About 4,500 people a year seek permission to bring a judicial review claim in the Administrative Court, though the court ends up giving a full hearing to fewer than 400.

[6] www.justice.gov.uk/.

[7] I do not suggest that either trend is entirely new; it is possible to identify aspects of them at work in previous decades and in other contexts apart from administrative justice.

[8] This chapter was completed in January 2007, when the Tribunals, Courts and Enforcement Bill had been introduced to the House of Lords but not yet considered by the House of Commons. It has been assumed that the Bill will be enacted in broadly the form it was introduced. The author is legal adviser to the House of Lords Constitution Committee, but the views expressed in this chapter are of course entirely personal ones.

[9] This is not the place to examine the scope and meaning of constitutionalism in detail: see further J. Steyn, 'The Weakest and Least Dangerous Department of Government' [1997] *Public Law* 84, 87–8 (where he refers to 'political theory as to the type of institutional arrangements that are necessary in order to support the democratic ideal. It holds that the exercise of government power must be controlled in order that it should not be destructive of the very values which it was intended to promote. It requires of the executive more than loyalty to the existing constitution. It is concerned with the merits and quality of constitutional arrangements').

part of the constitutional paradigm that disputes – especially between the state and the citizen – should be adjudicated upon by independent and impartial judges (not civil servants); and it follows that access to justice is to be improved by better quality and better funded legal services. There is understood to be a public – not merely a private – interest in calling public authorities to account for their errors and omissions. The citizen's 'day in court' (or a tribunal) is celebrated as an opportunity for open and impartial justice. Many facets of these values are, as will be discussed below, expressed or implied by Article 6 of the European Convention on Human Rights (ECHR).

The other current within the reforms seeks to promote the values of informality. Internal dispute resolution inside public authorities is seen as a major way of dealing with disputes. Where this fails, the values of informality encourage, perhaps even insist upon, a range of alternative dispute resolution (ADR) techniques,[10] such as mediation, in place of formal adjudication before judges (in the case of courts and tribunals) and formal investigations and reports (in the case of the ombudsmen). These reforms – in and of themselves and in the way they are being introduced – will result in a more informal, less public, and more discretionary dispute resolution system. The values associated with informality reject a one-size-fits-all approach to resolving disputes; flexibility and innovation in dispute resolution are to be encouraged, as these will help ensure that there is greater practical access to justice. Administrative justice is conceived of as a service to be delivered to the public, effectively and efficiently. The figure of an independent judge is not seen as either a necessary or sufficient part of the equation needed to achieve justice; indeed, a day in court (or the tribunal) far from being a matter of pride, is portrayed as a stressful experience that most citizens wish to avoid, or perhaps cannot even cope with.[11] Public accountability – revealing what has gone wrong – is not seen as an important aspect of the dispute resolution process as other mechanisms (such as audits and inspections) are better attuned to that task.

The Ministry of Justice presents the reforms that are taking place to the administrative justice system as a seamless whole. A rather different view is taken in this chapter: that in several ways the values of constitutionalism and informality sit uneasily together. Where there is tension or contradiction, it is argued, the values of constitutionalism ought to prevail.

ADMINISTRATIVE JUSTICE

Before looking at the currents and cross-currents of reform, something needs to be said about the concept and practice of administrative justice. This chapter focuses on one part of administrative justice: the redress of grievances against public authorities. It needs to be acknowledged, however, that administrative justice has a much wider reach, covering internal decision-making by public authorities and the need to prevent disputes arising in the first place.[12]

[10] ADR techniques are not *necessarily* informal in character (some involve highly structured decision-taking); but much ADR is far more informal than hearings before courts and tribunals.

[11] See n. 12 below, paras 2.7, 6.20 and 6.23.

[12] DCA White Paper, *Transforming Public Services; Complaints, Redress and Tribunals*, Cm 6243, July 2004, para. 1.6 (administrative justice 'embraces not just courts and tribunals but the millions of decisions taken by thousands of civil servants and other officials').

One problem with making sense of administrative justice in the sense of redress of grievances has been the lack of any overarching concept, reflected in the haphazard development of a myriad of avenues of complaint and challenge and criteria for assessing the wrongfulness of administrative action. Writing in 1994, Martin Partington lamented that despite all the changes from the 1960s on – with the creation of public sector ombudsmen, the expansion of the tribunal system, and the development of judicial review – 'there has been no official inquiry or review into the structure of administrative justice as a whole to see how the various constituent parts are or are not hanging together'.[13] The Citizen's Charter initiative in 1991 might for a while have seemed capable of providing some steer to the system, but 10 years later it had withered away.[14]

PROPORTIONATE DISPUTE RESOLUTION

In 2004, the DCA published a White Paper, *Transforming Public Services; Complaints, Redress and Tribunals*.[15] This fell short of providing a comprehensive vision of administrative justice (little is said about judicial review or the constitutional context) but it did go a long way towards explaining the Government's diagnosis and prescription for a better system. The White Paper coins the phrase 'proportionate dispute resolution' (PDR) to explain the idea that will guide future reforms:[16]

> Our strategy turns on its head the Department's traditional emphasis first on courts, judges and court procedure, and second on legal aid to pay mainly for litigation lawyers. It starts instead with the real world problems people face. The aim is to develop a range of policies and services that, so far as possible, will help people to avoid problems and legal disputes in the first place; and where they cannot, provides tailored solutions to resolve the dispute as quickly and cost effectively as possible. It can be summed up as 'Proportionate Dispute Resolution'.[17]

In practical terms, the broad strategy of PDR consists of a series of more specific reform initiatives.[18] These include:

(1) a commitment across central government to make the framework of law defining people's rights and responsibilities as 'fair, simple and clear as possible';

(2) to give people better information about their rights and responsibilities and where they can go for help when problems arise;

13 'Rethinking the structure of administrative justice in Britain', ch. 5 in O. Mendelsohn and L. Maher (eds), *Courts, Tribunals and New Approaches to Justice* (1994) 109. Non-official inquiries include the JUSTICE/All Souls Review published as *Administrative Justice: Some Necessary Reforms* (Oxford, Clarendon Press, 1988), witheringly criticized by C. Harlow, 'The JUSTICE/All Souls Review: Don Quixote to the Rescue?' (1990) 10 *Oxford Journal of Legal Studies* 85; and the University of Bristol conference on administrative justice held in 1997, papers from which were published in M. Partington and M. Harris (eds), *Administrative Justice in the 21st Century* (1999).

14 G. Drewry, 'Whatever happened to the Citizen's Charter?' [2002] *Public Law* 9.

15 See n. 12 above.

16 A 'ghastly slogan', as one minister acknowledged: Lord Filkin, 'New Routes to Justice', 14th Annual Denning Lecture, 9 June 2004; he explained that 'By PDR we really mean . . . you don't want to have a highly costly adversarial system dealing with issues that could be dealt with more quickly, simply and cheaply by means that are good enough for the disputees'.

17 See n. 12 above, para. 2.2; see also DCA Strategy 2004–09, *Delivering Justice, Rights and Democracy* 55–61.

18 See n. 12 above, para. 2.3.

(3) to 'ensure that people have ready access to early and appropriate advice and assistance when they need it, so that problems can be solved and potential disputes nipped in the bud long before they escalate into formal legal proceedings';

(4) to 'promote the development of tailored dispute resolution services, so that different types of dispute can be resolved fairly quickly, efficiently and effectively without recourse to the expense and formality of courts and tribunals where this is not necessary'.

(5) 'to deliver cost-effective court and tribunal services, that are better targeted on those cases where the hearing is the best option for resolving the dispute or enforcing the outcome'.

We will return to aspects of the reforms later.

The Government's attraction to PDR can be explained in several different ways. One explanation is that it represents the triumph of the alternative dispute resolution (ADR) movement, a way of thinking about dispute resolution whose advocates have been hugely successful in bringing its philosophy and practices into mainstream policy-making about court and tribunal reform in recent years.[19] The trend away from adjudication is apparent not only in the UK but in other countries;[20] and even international courts have seen the attractions of PDR as a way of controlling case-loads.[21] A different explanation may be that PDR fits into the practical priority of the current Government for citizen-centred service delivery: making access to dispute resolution services easier could be seen as part of this. Another explanation may be that the Government is motivated by concerns about escalating public expenditure in this area, especially on legal aid. It should not be assumed, however, that redressing grievances outside courts and tribunal hearings will *necessarily* be cheaper.

CATEGORIES OF WRONGFULNESS

If, in a practical and straightforward way, administrative justice involves putting things right when a public authority goes wrong, we need to know what 'wrongful' means in this context. As the avenues of challenge to official decisions have expanded beyond the courts (ombudsmen from the 1960s onwards and an expansion in the number of tribunals matching the expansion of the welfare state from the 1940s), three broad categories of wrongfulness have come to be recognized.

The first is unlawfulness. Public officials must properly understand the scope of their legal powers, use fair procedures, avoid irrational or disproportionate use of powers and (since 1973) act in conformity with European Community law and (since October 2000) the rights set out in the Human Rights Act 1998. In England and Wales it is typically the Administrative Court which is responsible for adjudicating on these alleged failures through claims for judicial review. Appeals to tribunals may also involve arguments about lawfulness.

[19] See S. Roberts and M. Palmer, *Dispute Processes: ADR and the Primary Forms of Decision-Making* (2nd edn, 2005).

[20] See S. Boyron, 'The Rise of Mediation in Administrative law Disputes: Experiences from England, France and Germany' [2006] *Public Law* 320.

[21] See Lord Woolf et al, *Review of the Working Methods of the European Court of Human Rights* (2005), available at www.echr.coe.int.

The second is maladministration leading to injustice. This is typically investigated by the various public sector ombudsmen – which now include in relation to England and Wales: the Parliamentary Commissioner for Administration (more often referred to as 'The Parliamentary Ombudsman', dealing with complaints against central government departments and bodies); the Health Services Commissioner for England ('The Health Service Ombudsman', for complaints about the NHS); the Commission for Local Administration in England ('The Local Ombudsman', dealing with local authorities); Public Services Ombudsman for Wales; and, offering similar grievance-handling services, the Housing Ombudsman Service; the Independent Police Complaints Commission; Independent Review Service for the Social Fund; the Information Commissioner; Office of the Independent Adjudicator for Higher Education; and some of the work of the Office of Communications (Ofcom).[22]

Maladministration has not been given a statutory definition. Speaking when the Parliamentary Ombudsman was established in 1967, Richard Crossman MP, the minister responsible for the legislation, famously set out what has come to be known as the 'Crossman catalogue' of examples of maladministration: 'bias, neglect, inattention, delay, incompetence, ineptitude, perversity, turpitude, arbitrariness and so on' – 'a long and interesting list'.[23] In 1993, the then Parliamentary Ombudsman (Sir William Reid, a former senior civil servant) expanded the list:

> rudeness (though that is a matter of degree); unwillingness to treat the complainant as a person with rights; refusal to answer reasonable questions; neglecting to inform a complainant on request of his or her rights or entitlement; knowingly giving advice which is misleading or inadequate; ignoring valid advice or overruling considerations which would produce an uncomfortable result for the overruler; offering no redress or manifestly disproportionate redress; showing bias whether because of colour, sex, or any other grounds; omission to notify those who thereby lose a right of appeal; refusal to inform adequately of the right of appeal; faulty procedures; failure by management to monitor compliance with adequate procedures; cavalier disregard of guidance which is intended to be followed in the interest of equitable treatment of those who use a service; partiality; and failure to mitigate the effects of rigid adherence to the letter of the law where that produces manifestly inequitable treatment.[24]

The third category of wrongfulness is that the original decision-maker has gone wrong on the merits of the matter. Merits review is a process by which a person other than the original decision-maker, reconsiders the facts, law or policy aspects of the initial decision, and determines what the correct or preferable decision ought to be. The process of review is often described as 'stepping into the shoes of the primary decision-maker.' Merits review is typically the province of internal appeals or complaints systems (where a different, probably more senior official has a second look at a decision at the request of the citizen affected)[25] and of some tribunals appeals.

[22] Several ombudsman-type systems have been set up by statute to deal with complaints private sector enterprises (e.g. the Financial Services Ombudsman, the Office of the Immigration Services Commission, and the Pensions Ombudsman) and business sectors have also set up similar systems themselves (e.g. Telecommunications Ombudsman (Otelo) and the Press Complaints Commission).

[23] HC Hansard, Vol. 734, col. 51, 18 Oct. 1966.

[24] Annual Report 1993.

[25] See D. Cowan and S. Halliday, *The Appeal of Internal Review: Law, Administrative Justice and the (non-emergence) of disputes* (2003).

These three categories are increasingly beginning to overlap. For example, some of the grounds of judicial review – which are to do with lawfulness – are strikingly similar in scope to some aspects of maladministration, due to the expansion of judicial review. As Henry L.J. put it:

> What may not have been recognized back in 1974 [when the Local Government Ombudsman was set up] was the emergence of judicial review to the point where most if not almost all matters which could form the basis for a complaint of maladministration are matters for which the elastic qualities of judicial review might provide a remedy.[26]

An aggrieved person may therefore be faced with two options – judicial review and ombudsmen investigation. An illustration of this is the campaign against the way in which the Ministry of Defence set up a compensation scheme for civilians interned in the Far East during World War II. Eligibility criteria depended on the closeness of a British detainee's links with the UK (which had the effect of excluding British people who had been born and brought up in places such as India and Hong Kong). The Parliamentary Ombudsman issued a damning report on the scheme, finding that maladministration had caused injustice, less than a week after the High Court ruled upheld the lawfulness of the scheme.[27] The boundaries between the ombudsman and court system are under conceptual strain, even if in practice both institutions seek to avoid taking jurisdictional points.[28]

There are other signs of the categories of wrongfulness overlapping. In the past it was anathema for the Administrative Court in hearing a judicial review claim to carry out 'merits review' and to seek to stand in the shoes of the original decision-maker and form its own view of the underlying facts and the proper outcome.[29] The Human Rights Act 1998 and the developing case law of the European Court of Human Rights are requiring national courts to increase the intensity of review. What that means varies between different Convention rights. In relation to Article 5 (deprivation of liberty) judicial controls must, in the context of restrictions placed on people under the mental health legislation, be 'sufficiently intrusive to constitute an adequate examination of the *merits* of the relevant medical decisions'.[30] In relation to Article 2 (right to life), the Court of Appeal has speculated that the best approach may be:

[26] *R* v. *Local Commissioner for Local Government for North and North East England ex parte Liverpool City Council* [2001] 1 All ER 462.

[27] See Parliamentary Commissioner, *A Debt of Honour: The ex gratia scheme for British groups interned by the Japanese during the Second World War* (HC 324, 2004–05); *R. (Association of British Civilian Internees: Far East Region)* v. *Secretary of State for Defence* [2002] EWCA Civ 473; [2003] QB 1397 (holding that the Secretary of State's decision to include birth in the UK as a factor was not as a matter of law irrational).

[28] The Parliamentary Ombudsman is barred from investigating 'any action in respect of which the person aggrieved has or had a remedy by way of proceedings in any court of law' subject to the proviso 'that the Commissioner may conduct an investigation notwithstanding that the person aggrieved has or had such a right or remedy if satisfied that in the particular circumstances it is not reasonable to expect him to resort or have resorted to it' (Parliamentary Commissioner Act 1967 s. 5(2)). Similar provisions apply to the Local Government Ombudsman.

[29] See e.g. *R* v. *Somerset County Council ex parte Fewings* [1995] 1 All ER 515 (Laws J.): '. . . the judicial review court is not concerned with the merits of the decision under review. The court does not ask itself the question, "Is this decision right or wrong?". Far less does the judge ask himself whether he would himself have arrived at the decision in question . . . The only question for the judge is whether the decision taken by the body under review was one which it was legally permitted to take in the way that it did.'

[30] *HL* v. *United Kingdom* (2005) 40 EHRR 32.

for the court *to make its own judgment* as to whether there would be an interference with the right to life under Article 2, rather than making a judgment as to the reasonableness of the decision made by the Prison Service

albeit that:

even were it to be the case that it is for the court to make that *primary judgement*, the reality is that the court would have to attach considerable weight to the assessment of risk made by those with professional involvement in the areas with which the case was concerned.[31]

It is not only the courts which are said to be straying into merits review: this accusation has also been levelled against the ombudsmen.[32]

Though in many respects far-reaching, the reforms discussed in this chapter do little to clarify these category confusions and uncertainties. The glimmer of hope is that the Government is sympathetic to the idea of reforms to the overlapping jurisdictions of the courts, tribunals and ombudsmen.[33]

CONSTITUTIONALISM

Having introduced some aspects of administrative justice, we can now move on to look at the first current within the reform strategy – the promotion of constitutionalism. This has a wide reach, extending beyond citizen and public authority disputes. The reforms to the judicial system brought about by the Constitutional Reform Act 2005 embrace all courts, not only those dealing with administrative adjudication. Part 1 of the Tribunals, Courts and Enforcement Act 2007 affects tribunals (such as employment tribunals and the Lands Tribunal) that deal with citizen-citizen disputes as well as those concerned with grievances against public authorities. At a general level we can say that the aim of this revitalization of the judicial system and tribunals is to promote greater openness and transparency and to emphasize independence from government. These goals have an especial importance when a public authority is one of the parties.

THE CONSTITUTIONAL REFORM ACT 2005

In the summer of 2003, in a U-turn of policy, the Labour Government embarked on a major programme of judiciary-related constitutional reform. The previous edition of this book considered the evidence for various explanations of the reasons for this change of view – pragmatic factors to do with changing roles of judges, external pressure from the Council of Europe, constitutional principles, and the specific personalities and events of that time.[34]

31 *R. (on the application of Bloggs 61)* v. *Secretary of State for the Home Department* [2003] EWCA Civ 686; [2003] 1 WLR 2724 at [81]–[82] (Keene L.J.).

32 For an early example, see the K.C. Wheare, *Maladministration and its Remedies* (1973) 153.

33 During the passage of the Tribunals, Courts and Enforcement Bill. See HL Hansard, 31 Jan. 2007, cols 303–5 (Baroness Ashton of Upholland); HC Public Bill Committee, 27 March 2007, col. 246 (Vera Baird). The Law Commission of England and Wales is considering the issue as part of its project on remedies in public Law.

34 A. Le Sueur, 'Judicial Power in the Changing Constitution', ch. 13 in J. Jowell and D. Oliver (eds), *The Changing Constitution* (5th edn, 2004).

Whatever may have been the immediate impulse for timing of change, the reforms are now taking hold and have created a new set of constitutional relationships.

- The office of Lord Chancellor has been redefined. He is no longer head of the judiciary and does not sit as a judge (or as Speaker of the House of Lords). But although the Lord Chancellor – currently Lord Falconer – is now a more 'mainstream' minister, he retains important constitutional responsibilities to defend the independence of the judiciary. He continues to have a role in judicial appointments (though less influence than before) and judicial discipline. Since 2003, the office of Lord Chancellor has been combined with that of Secretary of State for Constitutional Affairs (Secretary of State for Justice after May 2007).
- The Lord Chief Justice of England and Wales – currently Lord Phillips of Worth Matravers – has become Head of the Judiciary.[35] The enlarged areas of responsibility attached to the role of the Lord Chief Justice have been accompanied by provision of new administrative support, including a Judicial Communications Office. It remains to be seen how the Lord Chief Justice and Lord Chancellor will share their leadership roles.
- The system for appointing judges in England and Wales has been reformed with the creation of a new Judicial Appointments Commission (chaired by Baroness Prashar), the role of which is to run selection exercises and make recommendations to the Lord Chancellor.[36] The Lord Chancellor has limited power to reject recommendations or to require the selection panel to reconsider the selection.
- In October 2009, the country's top-level court will cease to be the Appellate Committee of the House of Lords sitting in the Palace of Westminster (and, for devolution issues, the Judicial Committee of the Privy Council) when the new UK Supreme Court begins to operate.
- The relationship between the judges and Parliament is changing. Those members of the senior judiciary who hold peerages (the Lords of Appeal in Ordinary, retired law lords, and some other senior figures such as the current Lord Chief Justice of England and Wales) will lose their right to take part in the scrutiny and legislative work of the House of Lords.[37] The Lord Chief Justice of England and Wales, the Lord Chief Justice of Northern Ireland and the Lord President of the Court of Session now have a right to make written representations to Parliament on matters that appear to them 'to be matters of importance relating to the judiciary, or otherwise to the administration of justice, in that part of the United Kingdom'.[38] Senior judges appear to give evidence before parliamentary select committees more frequently than in the past.

In these various ways, a new constitutional settlement is being established between the judiciary, Parliament and Government.[39]

TRIBUNALS, COURTS AND ENFORCEMENT ACT 2007

A second area in which the processes of constitutionalism can be seen is in reform of tribunals. Introducing the Tribunals, Courts and Enforcement Bill to the House of Lords in

[35] S. 7. [36] Part 4. [37] S. 135. [38] S. 5.

[39] The House of Lords Constitution Committee is assessing this; a report is expected in mid-2007. See www.parliament.uk/parliamentary_committees/lords_constitution_committee.cfm.

November 2006, the Lord Chancellor was clear about the aim:

First and foremost, Chapter 1 of Part 1 puts it beyond doubt that the tribunal judiciary are independent from the Executive, and that the tribunals themselves are independent of the departments which make the decisions under review. It is right that this has happened and it strengthens our commitment to increasing public confidence in tribunals. It is a vital part of the Bill.[40]

Over the years, Acts of Parliament have attached tribunals to many administrative schemes run by central government, their agencies and local authorities. The main reasons for establishing tribunals have been to provide a less costly, more expert and informal alternative to the courts. Prior to the 2007 Act, there were more than 70 separate tribunals hearing appeals against decisions of these various public authorities. The largest 10 dealt with a total of over 133,000 cases a year. The Appeal Service is by far the largest tribunal, hearing appeals in relation to welfare benefits. Other major tribunals deal with mental health issues, immigration and asylum, income tax and value added tax, schools, and criminal injuries compensation.

Part 1 of the Tribunals, Courts and Enforcement Act 2007 'creates a new, simplified statutory framework for tribunals which provides coherence and will enable future reform'.[41] The background to the Act is a review carried out by Sir Andrew Leggatt, a retired judge, into the tribunal system in England and Wales.[42] In a far-reaching report he lamented that the quality of the 70 or so tribunals (the case load of which varied from nil to hundreds of thousands) 'varies from excellent to adequate'.[43] There was a lack of coherence, with no unified administrative support for the various tribunals and widely differing procedural rules. The report provided a blueprint for a new institutional structure. The DCA's White Paper *Transforming Public Services* accepted the gist of the Leggatt recommendations, though not all aspects of the detail and in one important respect – the focus on ADR – it went much further.

The 2007 Act creates two overarching or 'generic' tribunals, the First-tier Tribunal and the Upper Tribunal (the main role of which is to hear appeals from the First-tier), into which various existing tribunal jurisdictions are transferred. The First-tier and Upper Tribunals are to be arranged into 'chambers' according to subject matter or geographical area, or both. When, in the future, a right of appeal to a tribunal is created by an Act of Parliament, it will no longer be necessary to spell out the detail of the composition and procedure of that tribunal – jurisdiction will be conferred on the First-tier and Upper Tribunal. As before, panels hearing cases will often consist of both legally-qualified members (to be called judges) and non-legally-qualified members able to provide expertise (for instance people with a background in healthcare in cases dealing with disability benefits or mental health).

A Tribunal Service, an executive agency of the Ministry of Justice, will provide a unified system of administrative support to the tribunals (in ways similar to that of the Her Majesty's Court Service in relation to courts). Judicial leadership for the new tribunal system comes in the form of a new office, that of the Senior President of Tribunals (the first holder of which is Sir Robert Carnwath, a Lord Justice of Appeal).

The 2007 Act provides for a clearer and more flexible system for challenges to the lawfulness of tribunal decisions, allowing transfer of cases between the Administrative Court (to which a dissatisfied party may claim judicial review)[44] and the Upper Tribunal. The Upper

40 Lord Falconer, HL Hansard, 29 Nov. 2006, col. 761.

41 Explanatory Notes to the Tribunals, Courts and Enforcement Bill, para. 5.

42 Report of the Review of Tribunals by Sir Andrew Leggatt: *Tribunals for Users – One System, One Service* (2001), www.tribunals-review.org.uk/. For discussion see A. Bradley, 'The tribunals maze' [2002] *Public Law* 200.

43 P. 5. 44 Or the Court of Session in Scotland.

Tribunal is given powers of 'judicial review' (the quotation marks are in the Act), enabling it to make all the remedial orders and apply the grounds of review previously confined to the Administrative Court on claims for judicial review.

The Upper Tribunal is a superior court of record, giving it a status similar to that of the High Court. A uniform right of appeal from the Upper Tribunal (subject to permission being granted) to the Court of Appeal in England and Wales is created, replacing the perplexing array of appeal routes that existed previously.

As well as seeking to create a clearer system, the Act seeks also to promote separation of powers between tribunals and Government. The statutory guarantee of judicial independence, created by the Constitutional Reform Act 2005 in relation to the courts, is extended to tribunals. The function of making procedural rules for tribunals is transferred from the Lord Chancellor and other ministers to a new Tribunal Procedure Committee. A new public body, the Administrative Justice and Tribunals Council, has the role of keeping the new tribunals and the whole administrative justice system under review.[45] The Senior President of Tribunals is required to publish his policy on the deployment of judges and members to the various chambers 'to ensure openness and transparency' and to seek the concurrence of the Lord Chancellor 'to ensure appropriate executive accountability to Parliament'.[46]

INFORMALITY

At the same time as it is pursing policies designed to promote values associated with constitutionalism through the creation of a more formal and transparent constitutional status for courts and tribunals, the Government is following a policy of informality in dispute resolution. This emphasis on informality can be seen in three main areas.

NIPPING DISPUTES IN THE BUD

First, the proportionate dispute resolution strategy announced by the DCA in 2004 seeks to encourage the resolution of disputes and complaints at an early a stage by the public authority against which the grievance has arisen. This can happen in several ways. At its most informal, this involves situations where the aggrieved citizen simply asks for a decision to be looked at again. In other circumstances, the internal processes for handling complaints are regulated by policies or legal frameworks. Examples of the latter are disputes about decision-making to do with homeless persons. Part VII of the Housing Act 1996 was an attempt to steer challenges in this context away from judicial review claims; the Act creates a right to request a review of the decision by an appropriately senior person in the authority (and, if the complainant is still dissatisfied, there is an appeal on a point of law to the county courts). The rationale for diverting homeless people's complaints away from judicial review was that they often turned on factual and judgement disputes (for example, whether the accommodation offered was suitable) rather than issues of law, and such disputes were best dealt with locally by the authority itself if possible, or failing that an ordinary court in easy reach of the claimant and local authority:

'Nipping disputes in the bud long before they escalate into formal legal proceedings'[47] has a commonsense attraction that is hard to resist. Clearly it is sensible to put things right as

45 Replacing the Council on Tribunals.

46 Explanatory Notes, n. 41 above.

47 N. 12 above, para. 2.3.

soon as possible and no one would suggest that lawyers or other third parties need to be involved in all cases. But while internal dispute resolution has many advantages it needs also to be acknowledged that – from the constitutional point of view – it does little to promote the rule of law or legal values.[48] Empirical evidence suggests that officials involved in dealing with internal complaints can have a very low opinion of lawyers – in one context, even expressing the cynical view that local solicitors got involved in homeless persons cases only when conveyancing work was slow and that lawyers lacked expertise of the law and system.[49] Commentators (writing in 1998) formed the view that 'we must come to the depressing conclusion that such systems have become a cheap way of denying justice'.[50]

When challenges to the lawfulness of attempts at internal dispute resolution have been brought to the courts, they have been wary of over-judicializing the process. The Court of Appeal has held that there is no apparent bias where a reviewing officer in a homeless persons unit looks at successive requests for review by the same person, a situation that arises in over 10 per cent of cases in some local authorities.[51] The House of Lords considered whether, in order to comply with the requirements of ECHR Article 6 (giving people a right to an independent and impartial tribunal whenever a 'civil right or obligation' is determined), a local authority deciding homelessness cases should have some mechanism for obtaining independent findings of fact (for example contracting out that function to a third party), and held – contrary to the Court of Appeal – that no such requirement should be imposed.[52] So while the actual decisions reached in internal review processes are subject to judicial control by judicial review claims (or in the case of homelessness decisions, by appeals to the county court), the law is slow to intervene to insist on legal controls of the processes beyond those spelt out in any legislative framework governing them.

THE TWILIGHT ZONE: NON-STATUTORY COMPLAINTS HANDLERS

A second manifestation of the values of informality is the plethora of non-statutory 'independent' grievance-handling bodies that have been established by public authorities to handle complaints at arm's length. They include the following bodies, which may make recommendations in the form of suggesting that an apology be made or that compensation be paid:

- the Adjudicator's Office, formed in 1993, investigates complaints relating to HM Revenue & Customs, The Valuation Office Agency, The Public Guardianship Office, and The Insolvency Service;[53]

48 For a valuable analysis of the different 'normative modes' of administrative justice see M. Adler, 'A Socio-Legal Approach to Administrative Justice' (2003) 25 *Law & Policy* 323. On the rule of law as institutional morality, see J. Jowell, ch.1 above.

49 See D. Cowan and J. Fionda, 'Homelessness Internal Appeals Mechanisms: Serving the Administrative Process – Part One' (1998) 27 *Anglo-American Law Review* 66, 77. See also S. Halliday, 'Internal Review and Administrative Justice: some evidence and research questions from homelessness decision-making' (2001) 23 *Journal of Social Welfare and Family Law* 473.

50 Cowan and Fionda, n. 49 above, 185.

51 *Feld* v. *Barnet LBC* [2004] EWCA Civ 1307; [2005] H.L.R. 9.

52 *Runa Begum* v. *Tower Hamlets LBC* [2003] UKHL 5; [2003] 2 AC 430 at [40] (Lord Hoffmann), disapproving of *Adan* v. *Newham LBC* [2001] EWCA Civ 1916; [2002] 1 WLR 2120.

53 www.adjudicatorsoffice.gov.uk/ (currently led by Dame Barbara Mills QC, a former Director of Public Prosecutions). It explains its remit as follows: 'we compare what they have done against their own published standards' and that most complaints involve 'mistakes, delays, poor or misleading advice, inappropriate staff behaviour, and use of discretion'.

- the Independent Case Examiners' Office, formed in 1997, provides a review and resolution service in relation to the Child Support Agency and the Northern Ireland Social Security Agency.[54] Its mission statement is 'Judging the issues without taking sides';
- the Independent Complaints Adjudicator for Ofsted and the Adult Learning Inspectorate;[55]
- the Independent Complaints Reviewer, originally set up in 1998, investigates complaints about the Land Registry, the National Archives, the Charity Commission and the Housing Corporation.[56]

The focus of these bodies is on maladministration, though as we have seen the boundaries between maladministration and issues of lawfulness are often hazy. For example a failure to follow published guidelines may be both bad administration and legally flawed as failing to give effect to a legitimate expectation.

While the values of informality promote the innovation of these bodies, and the ease of access to them for complainants, the values of constitutionalism prompt some probing questions. Although these bodies are careful to label themselves 'independent', that independence is of a different character from that enjoyed by judges in courts and tribunals (now protected by section 3 of the Constitutional Reform Act 2005). The people making recommendations in these bodies have no security of tenure comparable to that of judges and are in the main accountable to ministers for their work. Their non-statutory nature means that Parliament has had no opportunity to check, debate and approve of their status and methods of operation. Scrutiny of their work by Parliament is rather haphazard and confined mainly to written answers by ministers to MP's questions.

THE RISE AND RISE OF ADR

A third way in which we can see informality is in the seemingly inexorable rise of interest in the use of alternative dispute resolution (ADR) associated with claims for judicial review, appeals to tribunals and ombudsmen. ADR includes resolution techniques such as:[57] negotiation, arbitration; conciliation; early neutral evaluation; mediation; and negotiation. Interest in ADR is neither new nor confined to the administrative justice. The ADR movement has its origins in the 1960s and 70s with the rejection of adversarialism and a loss of confidence in the professionalism of lawyers. More recently, ADR has come into the mainstream. What may originally have been a desire to see the transformation of human relationships through new methods of dealing with disputes has become closely tied into the work of courts. In England and Wales ADR plays a growing role in ordinary civil litigation since the adoption of the Civil Procedure Rules in 1999. The CPR reformed the procedural rules covering the conduct of litigation, increasing the role of judges as case managers and encouraging parties to settle cases at the earliest opportunity rather than at the door of the court.

What is new is the emphasis that is being placed on ADR in the context of administrative justice. There remain doubts as to the applicability of ADR to public law matters. The

54 www.ind-case-exam.org.uk/, currently led by Ms Jodi Berg (a solicitor and arbitrator). During 2005 the ICE made 1,512 recommendations (HC Hansard, 27 Feb 2006, col. 243W).

55 www.ofsted-aliadjudicator.co.uk/.

56 www.icrev.demon.co.uk/, again led by Ms Jodi Berg.

57 *Transforming Public Services*, n. 12 above, para. 2.11.

Government seems to have changed its mind about the extent to which ADR may be used in public law. The 'Pledge Commitments for Settlement of Government Disputes through Alternative Dispute Resolution' published in March 2001, conceded that 'There may be cases that are not suitable for settlement through ADR, for example cases involving . . . abuse of power, public law, human rights'.[58] Today none of those categories are ruled out as intrinsically unsuited to ADR. To date, academic analysis of the scope for ADR in public law cases has been mixed – ranging from scepticism, through cautious welcome, to generally positive responses.[59] The White Paper emphasizes the fact that there are known unknowns in the context of tribunals: the use of ADR 'may mean a significant reduction in the number of cases which require a full judicial determination or they may turn out to be just another step in the process, adding cost and slowing things down'.[60]

ADR AND TRIBUNALS

The White Paper *Transforming Public Services* makes clear the Government's policy for a transformation in how tribunals operate away from adjudication to refocus on an array of dispute resolution techniques:

> The organisation [the new tribunal system] will inherit existing jurisdictions and procedural rules but its overarching mission will be dispute resolution and we expect it, in conjunction with departments, users and representatives, to develop new ways of operating. We believe this to be possible even where the issue is one of entitlement rather than compensation. In many cases appellants succeed before tribunals because they bring new evidence, possibly as a result of advice, or because they are more articulate orally than on paper and the tribunal is the first opportunity they have had to explain their case. In other cases the tribunal accepts evidence which the original decision maker was not prepared to accept. These are benefits that flow from having a tribunal hearing but it is possible to imagine ways in which the same benefit could be achieved without the stress and formality of a hearing. And where it is clear to the tribunal that there is likely to be a particular outcome to a case it must be helpful to everyone if reconsideration can be prompted before a hearing takes place.[61]

The White Paper suggests that civil servants or government lawyers employed by the Tribunal Service, not necessarily judges, will have key roles:

> Staff working on behalf of and with delegated powers from the judiciary could well have an important role to play in such a process. This will mean new skills for staff, different working arrangements for judiciary and staff and new powers for both.[62]

58 Available on the Ministry of Justice website.

59 E.g. M. Adler writes 'Because, in administrative disputes, citizens may settle for a lot less than they are entitled to, I am somewhat sceptical about the contribution of mediation and conciliation (and likewise of negotiation) to the resolution of administrative disputes and I argue that tribunal hearings may be needed to protect the interests of the citizen': 'Tribunal Reform: Proportionate Dispute Resolution and the Pursuit of Administrative Justice' (2006) 69 *Modern Law Review* 958. G. Richardson and H. Genn have sought to develop categories of tribunal case in which oral hearings are and are not essential: 'Tribunals in Transition: Resolution or Adjudication?' [2007] *Public Law* 116. Supperstone et al have been more upbeat in mapping out the scope for ADR in relation to judicial review claims, though even they concede that 'the use of ADR in public law disputes is considerably less straightforward than it might be in many other areas of law': M. Supperstone, D. Stilitz and C. Sheldon, 'ADR and Public Law' [2006] *Public Law* 299, 319.

60 See n. 12 above, para. 6.22.

61 See n. 12 above, para. 6.20.

62 See n. 12 above, para. 6.21.

OMBUDSMEN AND ADR

The appetite for ADR is not confined to the new tribunal system. It is seen as having a role in relation to the work of the ombudsmen (whose role is to investigate maladministration leading to injustice rather than lawfulness). The relationship between the public sector ombudsmen and ADR is a curious one. On the one hand they are sometimes presented *as a form of ADR*. The White Paper lists them as such.[63] The courts have also suggested from time to time that an ombudsman investigation would be a preferable route for a claimant than continuing with a claim for judicial review.[64] On the other hand, the ombudsmen are important grievance-handing organizations in their own right, which, like courts and tribunals, may wish to use *ADR techniques* in fulfilling their roles in addition to formal investigations and publishing reports.

The legal powers of the ombudsmen are typically expressed in the following terms: to carry out investigations, to make formal reports, and to recommend action that ought to be taken by the public authority to rectify injustice where it is found to have occurred. No specific provision is made in the legislation for informal resolution of complaints, though this is often attempted by the ombudsmen before a formal, in-depth investigation is launched, using the evidence submitted by the citizen and telephone calls to the public authority. The Collcutt report into the ombudsmen system in England, commissioned by the Cabinet Office in 2000, called for a refocusing in the present arrangements: there should, the report recommended, be an express statutory requirement for the ombudsmen to try informal dispute resolution before a formal investigation, and the legislation should be amended to reflect this:[65]

> Informal resolution . . . [is] used by the ombudsmen to get a 'quick fix' but their status under current legislation is rather uncertain. Any new legislation should be based around the concept of the ombudsman seeking resolution, by an agreed settlement if possible, with investigation and the ability to make recommendations as an option. The process should be sufficiently flexible to allow proportionate effort and any approach which is judged appropriate by the ombudsman.

ADR AND JUDICIAL REVIEW

Despite a slow start, there are signs that ADR will become important in relation to potential or actual claims for judicial review. For many years, the courts hearing judicial review claims have insisted that claimants use all other convenient redress routes before bringing the matter to court. A pre-action protocol requires that any internal complaints system be used before proceedings are started, or reasons for not doing so revealed to the court.[66] If a tribunal appeal exists, that must generally be used in preference to judicial review.[67]

The claim for judicial review procedure in the Administrative Court is a two-stage process: a claimant must first obtain the permission of the court, which is granted or withheld on the basis of the claimant's written case and any reply the defendant public authority chooses to

63 See n. 12 above, para. 2.11.

64 See e.g. *R. (on the application of Anufrijeva)* v. *Southwark LBC* [2003] EWCA Civ 1406; [2004] QB 1124.

65 *Review of the Public Sector Ombudsmen in England: A Report by the Cabinet Office* (London, Cabinet Office, 2000), para. 6.36.

66 www.dca.gov.uk/civil/procrules_fin/contents/protocols/prot_jrv.htm.

67 *R.* v. *Secretary of State for the Home Department ex parte Swati* [1986] 1 WLR 772.

submit to the court; if permission is granted, the claim proceeds to a full hearing. A large proportion of claimants are refused permission to proceed at the first stage, and of those that are granted permission a significant number are withdrawn before trial. It seems plausible to suggest that the permission stage has in effect evolved into a form of 'early neutral evaluation' (a type of ADR). Anecdotal evidence suggests that some public authorities show little inclination to negotiate with a claimant until after permission has been granted, and that the view of the court that there is an arguable case acts as an incentive to settle before trial.

A more explicit move towards the use of ADR was made by the Court of Appeal in 2001;[68] pronouncements were made about the need for litigants and their legal advisers to use ADR methods rather than judicial review. Mr Cowl and other residents challenged the lawfulness of the council's decision to close a residential care home. The scenario was sadly familiar: the council needed to prune almost £1 million from its social services budget but the residents of the home argued that promises of a 'home for life' had been made and that they accordingly had a legitimate expectation that the premises would remain open. Their claim for judicial review was refused by the Administrative Court, holding that there was insufficient evidence to establish a 'home for life' promise and that at the time of the closure decision it was not irrational for the council to proceed on the basis that there was no such promise. The Court of Appeal dismissed an appeal. The importance of the judgment lies in the general guidance issued by the court on the importance of ADR. Lord Woolf C.J. complained that 'insufficient attention' has been paid 'to the paramount importance of avoiding litigation wherever possible' in disputes with public authorities. ADR was generally, he said, capable of meeting the needs of the parties and the public and saved time, expense and stress. The Court of Appeal said that the legal aid authorities should cooperate with the Administrative Court 'to scrutinise extremely carefully' claims for judicial review so as to ensure that parties tried 'to resolve the dispute with the minimum involvement of the courts'. Ample powers existed under the Civil Procedure Rules (CPR) for the Administrative Court to hold, on its own initiative, an *inter partes* hearing at which both sides could explain what steps they had taken to resolve the dispute without the courts' involvement using complaints procedures and other forms of ADR. The lawyers in the case were not criticized since they were 'merely following the unfortunate culture in such litigation of over-judicialising the processes which were involved'. Today, sufficient should be known about ADR 'to make the failure to adopt it, in particular when public money is involved, indefensible'. There is now a 'heavy obligation' to resort to litigation only if it is really unavoidable. If litigation is necessary, the courts should deter the parties from 'adopting an unnecessarily confrontational approach to the litigation'.

The impact of *Cowl* has been modest so far. There are many unresolved questions as to which cases in principle are amenable to ADR, how ADR is to be funded, how the use of ADR relates to the strict and short time limits that apply in judicial review claims, and who will carry out the ADR and where. According to one generally optimistic analysis (by members of the public law Bar who are trained mediators) 'the use of ADR in public law disputes is considerably less straightforward than it might be in many other areas of law'.[69]

68 *Cowl* v. *Plymouth CC* [2001] EWCA Civ 1935.

69 M. Supperstone, D. Stilitz and C. Sheldon, 'ADR and Public Law' [2006] *Public Law* 299, 319.

A CLASH OF VALUES?

It is too early to provide any sort of definitive assessment of the administrative justice reform agenda and its implementation. The institutional and structural changes brought about by the Constitutional Reform Act 2005 and Part 1 of the Tribunals, Courts and Enforcement Act 2007 have either only recently or not yet been brought into force. The expansion of informal dispute resolution – in judicial review, tribunal hearings and in relation to the ombudsmen – has yet to be put into practice on a large scale. What can be attempted, however, is an assessment of the values that underlie the reforms. What has been suggested in this chapter is that there are two currents – changes associated with the promotion of constitutionalism and changes designed to implement values associated with informality. It is paradoxical that just at a time when courts and tribunals, traditionally the arenas for adjudication by judges, are being put on new and firmer constitutional footings so – simultaneously – there are attempts to steer disputes away from them. If the 'informalization' project is as successful as its supporters hope, fewer cases will be decided by judges finding facts and applying the law, and more by civil servants and third-parties through negotiation, mediation, early neutral evaluation and so on. This final section of the chapter outlines two of the main constitutional risks in this and suggests that one way to help minimize these risks is to recognize that administrative justice is a constitutional right not merely a service to be delivered.

BEHIND CLOSED DOORS: MIND THE TRANSPARENCY GAP

Courts and tribunal hearings are normally open to the public and press and much of their legitimacy stems from the fact that reasoned justifications are given for findings (justice is not only done but seen to be done). ADR by contrast is almost always a private affair. While in citizen–citizen disputes that may be acceptable, it is open to question whether that is so where a public authority is one of the parties. In place of a reported and reasoned decision, the most that we get to know about ADR proceedings is usually at best a brief anonymized summary published by a public authority. For example:

> The claimants brought an action for damages for unlawful detention, sex and race discrimination and negligence arising from the immigration detention. Significant and sensitive issues concerning policy and procedure in immigration were raised. The matter was successfully mediated.[70]

It needs to be recognized that the pursuit of informality risks creating a transparency gap. There is a public, not merely a private, interest in challenges brought by citizens against public authorities. Under the Tribunals, Courts and Enforcement Act 2007, the Administrative Justice and Tribunals Council (the successor to the Council on Tribunals) has duties to formulate a programme of work, to 'keep the administrative justice system under review' and make an annual report. It is imperative that internal complaints and appeals schemes and the deployment of ADR by public authorities, courts and tribunals do not fall beneath the radar and that adequate information about informal dispute resolution is included.

[70] DCA, *Annual Report 2005/06 Monitoring the Effectiveness of the Government's Commitment to using Alternative Dispute Resolution* (available on the Ministry of Justice website).

COMPULSION OR CHOICE?

In its traditional form in the public law context, the principle of access to justice means that citizens should not be impeded in their attempts to challenge the lawfulness of public authorities' decisions. The Government's proportionate dispute resolution strategy starts from the assumption that for most people's disputes, achieving a ruling from an independent judge sitting in a court or tribunal is unnecessary; and that justice has a broader meaning and can be delivered in a variety of forms. In the rush towards informality what must not be overlooked however is the existence of a fundamental right to access to a court or tribunal.[71] Parliament and the courts generally decry attempts by government to oust the jurisdiction of the courts, as without formal hearings the constitutional principle of the rule of law cannot be given practical effect.[72] So long as ADR is offered as an option there is perhaps little risk that it will hinder access to an independent judge. But what if its use is to be made compulsory or refusal to use it made subject to sanctions? The White Paper acknowledged this:

> Of course the rights of participants have to be safeguarded and in many cases a hearing will be unavoidable. None of these proposals is intended to result in any individual receiving less than the entitlement or remedy they would obtain from a full judicial determination, nor, conversely, is it intended to distort duties which a department owes to all its clients, the tax payer and the community.[73]

Such assurances are however no substitute for legal clarity. There may be signs that the Government may view formal justice as an inconvenience. In a letter to the House of Lords Constitution Committee, a minister said:

> In the tribunal context, I do not see 'ADR' as an 'adjunct' to formal proceedings. The tribunals have a duty to be accessible. Formal proceedings may well hamper that objective. I see 'ADR' not as an alternative but as potential ways of providing justice in a more practical and effective manner . . . '[74]

When published in draft form,[75] before formal introduction to Parliament, the Tribunals, Courts and Enforcement Bill contained the following clause:

> A person exercising power to make Tribunal Procedure Rules or give practice directions must, when making provision in relation to mediation, have regard to the following principles –
>
> (a) mediation of matters in dispute between parties to proceedings is to take place only by agreement between those parties;
>
> (b) where parties to proceedings fail to mediate, or where mediation between parties to proceedings fails to resolve disputed matters, the failure is not to affect the outcome of the proceedings.

By the time the Bill was introduced to the House of Lords to begin its legislative process, the Government had decided to remove that clause. It was re-inserted only following a report of the Constitution Committee[76] and an amendment moved by a backbench peer.[77]

[71] ECHR Art. 6, discussed below. [72] See ch. 1 above. [73] See n. 12 above, para. 6.23.

[74] Letter from Baroness Ashton of Upholland to the House of Lords Constitution Committee, Nov. 2006.

[75] The DCA published the Bill in draft in July 2006, but undermined one of the main aims of draft Bills (to enable parliamentary scrutiny ahead of the formal legislative process) by doing so on the day that Parliament rose for its summer recess. The DCA later declined to make public the responses received to the draft Bill.

[76] Select Committee on the Constitution, 1st Report of Session 2006–07, HL Paper 13.

[77] Lord Goodlad, HL Hansard, 31 Jan. 2007, col. 254. Lord Thomas of Gresford, the Liberal Democrat spokesman, said 'people should not be pushed into mediation. They should always have at the back of their

ECHR Article 6 guarantees that 'in the determination of his civil rights and obligations or any criminal charge against him, everyone is entitled to a *fair and public hearing* within a reasonable time by *an independent and impartial tribunal established by law*' and that 'judgment shall be *pronounced publicly*' (emphasis added). Thus the Convention sets up the independent judicial body as the paradigm dispute-resolution mechanism: there is a fundamental right to formal adjudication and access to court. Many citizen–state disputes involve a 'civil right', though that category is notoriously difficult to define.[78] Where a Convention right (rather than a 'civil right') is in issue, Article 13 provides comparable protection in relation to Convention rights.[79] A person with an arguable claim must have an 'effective remedy before a national authority', though that remedy does not have to be in the form of a judicial body. What *is* required however is that the body – whether a judicial body or otherwise – must have adequate powers of investigation and the capacity to make binding orders. The rights guaranteed by Articles 6 and 13 do not stand in the way of ADR, so long as ADR is offered or encouraged as an option to the aggrieved citizen rather than acting as a restriction on access to adjudication by a court. That should be recognized in UK legislation.

A STATUTORY BASIS FOR ADR

It is important that courts, tribunals, ombudsmen and other institutions engaging in ADR have a clear statutory basis for doing so. Similarly, thought should be given to placing the non-statutory dispute resolution bodies established in recent years, such as the Adjudicator's Office, the Independent Case Examiners' Office, and the Independent Complaints Reviewer, on a firmer legal foundation. Not only will this enable Parliament to place constraints on use of ADR in situations where there may be unfairness (see above) but a statutory basis will enable proper post-legislative scrutiny to take place, monitoring this important development in policy towards administrative justice.

ADMINISTRATIVE JUSTICE AS A CONSTITUTIONAL RIGHT

It has been suggested in this chapter that where there is tension or conflict between the values of constitutionalism and informality, the former ought to prevail because this will better ensure that citizen's rights are protected in an open and accountable manner. One way of helping achieve this would be to recognize that administrative justice is a constitutional principle, not merely a service to be delivered.

Some constitutional systems have expressly acknowledged the existence of a specific right to justice in relation to administrative action. For example, section 33 of the South African Constitution provides that 'Everyone has the right to administrative action that is lawful,

mind that they are entitled to a hearing within the structure of the tribunal system and that an independent judge will decide. The problem with mediation is that you have the Government or a similar body on the one side and the individual on the other, and the bargaining power is not equal' (col. 258).

[78] Thus the European Court of Human Rights has held that the revocation of professional and trading licenses, disputes about planning permission and some social security disputes and state pensions are 'civil rights' for the purposes of Art. 6; but the following are not – disputes relating to elections, tax liability (*Ferrazzini* v. *Italy* [2001] STC 1314) and situations where there is a broad discretion rather a defined entitlement.

[79] Art. 13 was not expressly incorporated into domestic law by the Human Rights Act 1998, but the duty on the courts under s. 2 of the HRA to have regard to the case law of the European Court of Human Rights means that it has often had decisive influence on the courts' approach.

reasonable and procedurally fair' and requires legislation to be enacted 'to provide for the review of administrative action by a court or, where appropriate, an independent and impartial tribunal'.

As we have seen, the European Convention on Human Rights (ECHR), drafted in the 1950s before we were so attuned to the need for specific rights against the administrative state, makes no express reference to administrative justice. Article 6 guarantees a right to formal adjudication for any dispute that involves a 'civil right or obligation' but this fits uneasily in the context of decision-making by public authorities as not all administrative disputes involve such rights and obligations. Some other Convention rights require public authorities to act proportionately and with legal authority,[80] both aspects of administrative justice. Beyond the ECHR, the Council of Europe has developed a range of conventions, resolutions and recommendations that more explicitly engage with various aspects of administrative justice.[81] The European Union, in Article 41 of the Charter of Fundamental Rights, recognizes a 'right to good administration'.

How might a constitutional right to 'administrative justice' or 'good administration' be given effect in UK law? One option that may be on the horizon would be to include a right to administrative justice in any British Bill of Rights that may be adopted in years to come.[82]

A different tack would be for English common law to recognize administrative justice as one of the fundamental rights protected (subject to parliamentary sovereignty) by the courts.[83] In the English legal system, principles of administrative justice have developed in the form of the grounds of judicial review – illegality, irrationality and procedural impropriety.[84] There are signs that an overarching right to good administration may be adopted. Laws L.J., in a recent judgment about legitimate expectations (the rule that where a person has been assured he will be treated in a particular way by a public authority, he must be so treated unless there is a pressing reason of the public interest to do otherwise), described:

> a requirement of good administration, by which public bodies ought to deal straightforwardly and consistently with the public. In my judgment, this is a legal standard which, although not found in terms in the European Convention on Human Rights, takes its place alongside such rights as fair trial, and no punishment without law. That being so there is every reason to articulate the limits of this requirement – to describe what may count as good reason to depart from it – as we have come to articulate the limits of other constitutional principles overtly found in the European Convention.[85]

[80] E.g. Art. 8–11, where a public authority interfering with a right must do so only 'in accordance with the law' and so far as it is 'necessary in a democratic society', which involves a proportionality test.

[81] See www.coe.int/t/e/legal_affairs/legal_co-operation/Administrative_law_and_justice/. For a useful overview, see R. Benitez, 'Administrative Justice in a World in Transition: Pan-European Values in Administrative Justice' (2001) 30 *Common Law World Review* 434. See further below.

[82] There is growing interest in such a project from all three main political parties. During early 2007, the all-party group Justice is conducting an inquiry in the content of such a Bill of Rights and the means by which it might be adopted.

[83] Others include e.g. the right of access to a court (*R.* v. *Lord Chancellor ex parte Witham* [1998] QB 575), freedom of expression (*Derbyshire CC* v. *Times Newspapers* [1993] AC 534) and prohibition on torture (*A* v. *Secretary of State for the Home Department* [2005] UKHL 71; [2006] 2 AC 221).

[84] See ch. 1 above.

[85] *R. (on the application of Nadarajah)* v. *Secretary of State for the Home Department* [2005] EWCA Civ 1363 at [68].

What is the point of labelling something a 'constitutional right' in the UK? It means less than it does in other countries. In the absence of a codified constitution, any prescribed legislative process for constitutional legislation, or a specialized constitutional court, to say something is or ought to be regarded as 'constitutional' in the UK operates mainly as a warning that care needs to be taken in legislating or adjudicating on an issue.

Where legislation deals with a constitutional right, special attention needs to be paid to the express aims and also any unintended consequences of the Government's proposals. This has been recognized by the fact that the House of Lords has a select committee on the constitution, which examines all Bills for their constitutional implications and draws to the attention of that House any matters of concern.[86] In the House of Commons, where a Bill is of 'first class' constitutional importance, the normal procedure is altered, and such a Bill may have its clause-by-clause scrutiny in a committee of the whole House rather than in a standing (or Bill) committee. Robert Hazell has recently argued that a better constitutional protection would be for Bills of clear constitutional significance to be subject to proper consultation and pre-legislative parliamentary scrutiny (in which a committee considers a draft of the Bill before it begins its formal legislative process through Parliament).[87] If administrative justice is a constitutional matter we can expect and demand a greater degree of care in legislating about it.

A second area in which care is taken when constitutional rights are at stake is in the courtroom. If it is correct (as Laws L.J. suggests) to say that there is a fundamental right to administrative justice recognized by the common law, the court's approach to adjudication may be modified in three important ways. First, the principle of legality will apply:

> A power conferred by Parliament in general terms is not to be taken to authorise the doing of acts by the donee of the power which adversely affect the legal rights of the citizen or the basic principles on which the law of the UK is based unless the statute conferring the power makes it clear that such was the intention of Parliament.[88]

This is a technique of statutory interpretation designed to protect constitutional rights from being circumscribed by implication. If Parliament (for which read 'the Government') wishes to restrict, alter or otherwise affect the rights of citizens to seek justice in disputes with public authorities, the legislation attempting to do that must spell out the intended consequences in plain and blunt terms.

A second way in which a court may modify its method where a constitutional right (in the British sense) is in issue is where a claimant for judicial review argues that a public authority's decision is unlawful on the grounds that it is irrational (or unreasonable). Where this is so, the court adopts an 'anxious scrutiny' approach, meaning that to a considerable extent the burden is shifted away from the citizen having to demonstrate that the decision was unreasonable and onto the public authority to provide a cogent justification for its action.[89] And thirdly, if a legislative provision is classified as 'constitutional', it is immune from implied (and therefore possibly unintended) repeal.[90]

[86] www.parliament.uk/parliamentary_committees/lords_constitution_committee.cfm.

[87] R. Hazell, 'Time for a New Convention: Parliamentary Scrutiny of Constitutional Bills 1997–2005' [2006] *Public Law* 247.

[88] *R.* v. *Secretary of State for the Home Department ex parte Pierson* [1998] AC 539 at 575 (Lord Browne-Wilkinson).

[89] A. Le Sueur, 'The Rise and Ruin of Unreasonableness' [2005] *Judicial Review* 32.

[90] *Thorburn* v. *Sunderland City Council* [2002] EWHC 195; [2003] QB 151.

So for both Parliament and for the aggrieved citizen, labelling something 'constitutional' has practical benefits.

FURTHER READING

Department for Constitutional Affairs, *Transforming Public Services: Complaints, Redress and Tribunals*, Cm 6243.

USEFUL WEB SITES

www.justice.gov.uk/

www.tribunals.gov.uk/

www.tribunals-review.org.uk/

14

REGULATION, MARKETS, AND LEGITIMACY

Tony Prosser

SUMMARY

Although governments have to a large degree withdrawn from ownership of the economy, debate over public regulation has increased in recent years. This chapter examines the institutions and techniques used, concentrating on regulation of the public utilities such as telecommunications, energy, water, and rail. It is suggested that regulation has a number of rationales, notably control of natural monopoly, creating and policing competitive markets, and social goals such as ensuring the provision of universal service. Nationalization attempted to implement similar goals but suffered from a lack of their definition and from institutional confusion, particularly on the legitimate role of government. The arrangements adopted for regulating the utilities after privatization are more promising, especially as a result of reforms introduced since 2000, though the regulators' work has proved much more complex than originally thought. Regulatory procedures were seriously neglected in the statutes establishing the regulatory bodies, but the regulators themselves have done much to open up their procedures; recent reforms will reinforce this, although the means available for challenging regulatory decisions remain inconsistent and untidy. There may also be a greater concern with matters of legal principle in regulation as a result of European developments.

INTRODUCTION

There is a widely accepted view that the 1980s and 1990s were the epoch of a withdrawal of the state in favour of the marketplace. Yet, paradoxically, there is also a perception that regulation has grown enormously during this period, so much that some writers now consider us to live in a 'regulatory state'.[1] Regulation is far more visible than in earlier times, its extent inspires considerable public debate, and regulatory authorities themselves have a much higher profile than when government took a greater role in delivering services. Regulation is central to economic life, for example through the role of competition law and the regulation

[1] See e.g. G. Majone, 'The Rise of the Regulatory State in Europe' (1994) 17 *West European Politics* 77–101; M. Moran, *The British Regulatory State: High Modernism and Hyper-Innovation* (2003).

of the public utilities, and also in relation to social provision, both public and private, notably in the health and education sectors. The paradox is, however, apparent rather than real. Even where government has withdrawn from direct provision of services, markets cannot be seen simply as the products of non-intervention, for they must be actively created and policed by public authorities. Even where public provision retains a role, there has been a marked stress on consumer empowerment through setting standards and inspecting performance against them, and in some areas regulators still take decisions on social principles rather than facilitating markets. These roles all raise constitutional issues of the legitimacy of regulatory decisions, issues that have only recently been fully addressed in British constitutional scholarship.

In this chapter I shall adopt an institutional approach, examining some of the key institutional forms used by public actors to replace, shape, or intervene in markets and concentrating on the utility regulators. This will mean the neglect of many important areas; in particular the crucially important one of 'self-regulation' will not be considered.[2] Nor will it be possible to consider the institutions implementing general competition policy in detail, and I shall also not be able to cover the new social regulators in areas such as healthcare. I hope that there will be compensation for this loss of scope through the advantages of a focus on institutional issues; after all, institutional design is one of the key concerns of constitutional lawyers.

RATIONALES FOR REGULATION

There are several different rationales for regulation; these in themselves raise constitutional issues relating to the balancing of different principles and to the best institutional arrangement for resolving conflicts between them. Some rationales for regulation are based on economic principle. The first of these seeks to prevent the profit maximization of natural monopolies from distorting the efficient distribution of goods; the second seeks to resolve the problems which arise when markets operate freely, such as so-called 'externalities' which occur when the unregulated price of a good does not fully reflect its true cost to society (for example, the cost of pollution caused in its manufacture).[3] A further, and very different, rationale is that of regulating for competition, where the regulator does not limit the operation of markets but develops and encouraging them. This may take the form of encouraging the creation of competitive markets in previously monopolistic areas; a notable example is that of energy supply. Just as important is the policing of markets after they have come into existence. This is of course primarily a task for general competition law, implemented both by the general competition authorities and by the sectoral utility regulators. In addition to the economic rationales, there is a quite different tradition of what is rather unhelpfully dubbed 'public interest regulation' based upon more general social or

[2] For good discussions of the complexity of self-regulation see I. Ayres and J. Braithwaite, *Responsive Regulation* (1992); J. Black, 'Constitutionalizing Self-Regulation' (1996) 59 *MLR* 24 and 'Decentring Regulation: Understanding the Role of Regulation and Self Regulation in a "Post-Regulatory" World' (2001) 54 *Current Legal Problems* 103.

[3] See e.g. S. Breyer, *Regulation and its Reform* (1982) 15–35; C. Foster, *Privatization, Public Ownership and the Regulation of Natural Monopoly* (1992) esp. ch. 9; A. Ogus, *Regulation* (1994) Pt I, and R. Baldwin and M. Cave, *Understanding Regulation* (1999) Pt I.

distributive principles. For example, in the UK rationales for nationalization were characterized largely by opposition to the motive of pure profit and by reference to a seemingly self-evident concept of 'the public good', while also containing more specific elements such as improving working conditions and providing some form of representation for consumers other than their influence through markets.[4] More recently, some types of regulation, such as that of broadcasting, may be based on the protection of citizenship rights, for example to balanced news coverage, or on the promotion of social solidarity.[5]

Some of the most important regulatory innovations of recent years have been the arrangements adopted for the privatized utilities, notably telecommunications, gas and electricity, water, and railways. In the very limited official discussion available the original rationale seems to have been conceived as primarily economic, concentrating on the control of monopoly.[6] However, if one examines the legal sources for the regulators' powers, the privatization statutes, and the licences of the utilities in question, one finds that in every case a predominantly economic rationale limited to requiring regulators to maximize economic efficiency seemed to play only a secondary role and broader public interest considerations loomed large, for example ensuring that services were made available to meet all reasonable demands, including potentially unprofitable services, and that special consideration was given to the needs of vulnerable groups such as pensioners and the disabled.[7]

As mentioned above, regulation for competition has also played an increasing role, and primary duties to promote competition or to secure effective competition were included in later statutes relating to electricity and gas.[8] The Utilities Act 2000 was intended to replace the untidy mix of duties on the regulators by a new single competition-based primary duty, although it was only applied to the energy regulator. The new primary duty is to protect the interests of consumers, wherever possible by promoting effective competition; subsidiary duties in respect of the elderly, disabled, and chronically sick are also included, and the Secretary of State has new powers to issue guidance on social and environmental objectives to which regulators will be required to have regard.[9] Similar provision is made for the water regulator in the Water Act 2003, and the Communications Act 2003 recasts the duties for regulation of telecommunications and broadcasting. Thus even in an area where apparently economic regulation predominates, there is in fact a mix of regulatory rationales, making it particularly important to secure legitimacy for the resolution of conflicts between the different principles involved. This means that institutional design is of considerable constitutional importance.

[4] For a seminal text see H. Morrison, *Socialisation and Transport* (1933); T. Prosser, *Nationalised Industries and Public Control* (1986).

[5] See for example the citizenship duty applying to the Office of Communications in the Communications Act 2003, s. 3(1)(a); see also T. Prosser, 'Regulation and Social Solidarity' (2006) *J. of Law and Society* 364.

[6] See the two official Littlechild reports: S. Littlechild, *Regulation of British Telecommunications' Profitability* (1984) and *Economic Regulation of Privatised Water Authorities* (1986).

[7] For further details see T. Prosser, *Law and the Regulators* (1997) 15–24 and e.g. Telecommunications Act 1984, s. 3(1)(a). See also *R. (T-Mobile (UK) Ltd, Vodafone Ltd, Orange Personal Communication Services Ltd)* v. *The Competition Commission and the Director General of Telecommunications* [2003] EWHC 1566 (QBD).

[8] Electricity Act 1989, s. 3(1)(c); Gas Act 1995, s. 1, inserting a new s. 4(1)(c) into the Gas Act 1986.

[9] Utilities Act 2000, ss. 9, 10, 13, 14.

REGULATORY INSTITUTIONS

NATIONALIZATION

Regulation has a long history in the UK, through a variety of different institutions including the courts, Parliamentary committees, and special commissions.[10] In the case of the public utilities, however, the choice made for much of the twentieth century was of nationalization rather than independent regulation, most famously through the major nationalizations under the Labour government elected in 1945.[11] The enterprises were established as public corporations at 'arm's length' from government, managed by a board appointed by the minister. The boards were to be autonomous as regards day-to-day administration but ministers would have some power to determine matters of policy and to engage in general economic control. Thus, apart from the power of appointment of board members, ministers were given power to issue general directions to the boards with which the latter were obliged to comply.[12] In some limited circumstances ministers also had the power to issue specific directions, and, more importantly, the boards needed the approval of the minister for capital investment programmes.[13] It very soon became apparent that ministerial control was not to be exercised through the use of statutory directions; they would have to be published and this would imply an open acceptance of ministerial responsibility. Instead, informal measures were used extensively, and secretly. The confusion of responsibilities here was increased by the vagueness of the statutory duties of the corporations.[14] Nor did this confusion of responsibilities run only one way, for there is evidence that the industries themselves were able to restrict effectively the abilities of ministers to impose unwelcome policies in certain areas.[15] Indeed, it can be suggested that in some crucial matters the industries were more autonomous under nationalization than was the case when regulated after privatization. Thus the key challenge was the development of a system which would allow a sufficient degree of autonomy to the enterprises while still ensuring that they were in some way held accountable.[16] This was never successfully achieved under nationalization.

THE STATUS AND FUNCTIONS OF UTILITY REGULATORS AFTER PRIVATIZATION

Nationalization raised in an acute form the question of the legitimate relationship between government and other public bodies. Similar concerns have surrounded the arrangements adopted in the 1980s and 1990s for regulating privatized enterprises. New regulatory

[10] See Prosser, *Law and the Regulators*, n. 7 above, ch. 2.

[11] The main statutes were the Coal Industry Nationalisation Act 1946, the Civil Aviation Act 1946, the Transport Act 1946, the Electricity Act 1947, the Gas Act 1948, and the Iron and Steel Act 1949.

[12] See e.g. Coal Industry Nationalisation Act 1946, s. 3(1).

[13] See e.g. Coal Industry Nationalisation Act 1946, s. 3(2), (3).

[14] E.g., on pricing, the standard provision was to the effect that the industry was under a duty to 'secure that the combined revenues . . . are not less than sufficient to meet their combined outgoings properly chargeable to revenue account taking one year with another': Electricity Act 1947, s. 36(1); the coal legislation used the phrase 'on an average of good and bad years'.

[15] Foster, op. cit., (n. 3 above), 79–86.

[16] The most convincing critique of accountability is National Economic Development Office, *A Study of UK Nationalised Industries* (1976).

agencies were established in relation to the public utility industries which seemed unlikely to operate in fully competitive markets. The specialist agencies were the Office of Telecommunications (Oftel), the Office of Gas Supply (Ofgas), the Office of Electricity Regulation (Offer) (these latter two were later merged into the Office of Gas and Electricity Markets or Ofgem), the Office of Water Services (Ofwat), and the Office of the Rail Regulator (ORR). Similar powers in relation to the major airports were given to the Civil Aviation Authority (CAA), the long-established regulator of civil aviation. Each agency (except for the CAA which is a commission) was headed by a director-general in whom the powers were vested personally; in this one sees a reflection of the highly personal style of UK government through ministers, and it was a key influence on the way in which regulation operated, at least in its early years. However, the agencies were deliberately distanced from ministerial responsibility through the adoption of the status of 'non-ministerial government department', a notion which seems curious given the centrality of ministerial responsibility in the UK constitution, but does seek to prevent accusations of political interference which could discredit the achievement of privatization. Most agency staff were seconded from the ordinary civil service for periods of about three years.

These arrangements have now undergone a process of reform, commencing with the Utilities Act 2000.[17] This established a new regulatory commission for the energy sector in the form of the Gas and Electricity Markets Authority.[18] A commission model has been adopted also for postal services, and the telecommunications and broadcasting legislation created Ofcom in a commission form.[19] Provision was made to convert the Office of the Rail Regulator into a commission in the Railways and Transport Safety Act 2003, and the Water Act 2003 did the same for Ofwat. The commission model for regulation has now convincingly won in comparison to the older model of giving powers to an individual director-general. As we shall see below, this is linked to other changes which would justify us in identifying a second model for regulatory institutions since the 1997 change of government.

A further important change is that this model of regulation has been extended to some of the few enterprises which remain in public ownership. The most important example is that of the Post Office. Under the Postal Services Act 2000, its status was changed to that of a public limited company wholly owned by government. It is however regulated by an independent commission, the Postal Services Commission (Postcomm) which has responsibilities for price control, competition issues, and for ensuring the provision of a level of universal service defined by statute. In part this reform is due to European liberalization of postal services which requires, for example, definition of universal service and separation of regulation from operation.[20] However, it also reflects the use of independent regulation for privatized enterprises, as do the arrangements adopted for regulation of the publicly owned Scottish water industry under the Water Industry Act 1999 by the Water Industry Commission for Scotland.[21]

[17] The background is the Labour government's review of utility regulation: Department of Trade and Industry, *A Fair Deal for Consumers: Modernising the Framework for Utility Regulation*, Cm 3898 (1998) and *A Fair Deal for Consumers: The Response to Consultation* (1998).

[18] See Pt I and Sched. 1.

[19] Communications Act 2003, s. 1.

[20] See the Postal Services Directive (97/67/EC), [1998] OJ L15 14; and the amending Directive 2002/39/EC, [2002] OJ L176 21.

[21] Water Industry Act 1999, ss. 12–13, Sched. 2; see also now the Water Industry (Scotland) Act 2002, Pt I, the Water Services etc. (Scotland) Act 2005, and T. Prosser, 'Regulating Public Enterprises' [2001] *Public Law* 505, 514–20.

Finally, the effects of European liberalization have not been confined to postal services. Telecommunications regulation is now based on the 2002 regulatory package of directives, and part of the requirements of the directives is that national regulatory authorities be established independent of those providing services in the sector; this does not necessarily prevent regulation by a government department, but if the government retains a presence in providing services there must be effective structural separation of the regulator from this.[22] The role of independent regulation is regularly supervised at a European level.[23] Similar provisions apply in the energy sector.[24] Because of these developments cooperation between the various regulatory authorities in Europe has become increasingly important, although so far no unified European regulator has been established for any utility sector. It is these European Community law requirements which are the most important for the spread of independent regulatory authorities beyond the UK, and for ensuring their guaranteed future.

Although the problems associated with nationalization have been avoided in the new regulatory regimes as the new regulatory agencies have been clearly distanced from direct government control in their day-to-day operation, it is essential to remember that the government had the key role in shaping the environment in which the privatized enterprises operate. Ministers are responsible for important matters of general policy (for example, the broad mix of different sources of electricity generation). Apart from the fact that ministers appoint the regulators, it was ministers who initially possessed the major powers of deciding on the degree of competition which the enterprises would meet, through issuing licences (called authorizations in the case of gas and appointments in the case of water companies) necessary for the enterprises to do business; it is the conditions of these licences that determined the fundamental constraints in which the enterprises operate. The regulatory agencies were given the function of enforcing these conditions together with a number of other tasks, which include drawing up service standards (for example, relating to failure to maintain electricity supply or to meet agreed appointments with consumers) and monitoring performance by the utilities against them.[25]

This apparent division of labour was however made less neat by the fact that the agencies have functions relating to the modification of the licences, normally by agreement with the enterprise itself but, if this cannot be obtained, through a reference to the Competition Commission (formerly the Monopolies and Mergers Commission). The agencies thus have a role in setting the basic rules of the game as well as monitoring their implementation, and it is this which has probably aroused the greatest controversy. In addition, government continues to possess important concurrent powers, especially in the case of electricity where, for example, the minister was given a power of veto over licence modifications.[26] In gas and

[22] Directive 2002/21/EC on a common regulatory framework for electronic communications networks and services, [2002] OJ L108/33, art. 3(2).

[23] See, e.g. Commission of the European Communities, *European Electronic Communications Regulation and Markets 2005 (11th Report)*, COM(2006)68 final.

[24] Directive 2003/54/EC concerning common rules for the internal market in electricity, [2003] OJ L176/37, art. 23; Directive 2003/55/EC concerning common rules for the internal market in natural gas, OHL176/57, art. 25

[25] See the Competition and Service (Utilities) Act 1992.

[26] Electricity Act 1989, ss. 11(4), 12(5); a similar veto power was added for gas by the Gas Act 1995, Sched. 3 inserting new ss. 23(5) and 24(4A) into the Gas Act 1986. For the ability of a minister to require licence modification in the special case of the use of a regulation under different statutory powers see *Mercury Personal Communications* v. *Secretary of State for the Department of Trade and Industry*, [2000] UK CLR 143.

electricity, however, the power to issue licences has been given to the regulators rather than the minister and in the case of telecommunications European Community law has severely limited discretion in the licensing process through providing a general entitlement to provide electronic communications services without the need for individual licences but subject to general conditions drawn up by Ofcom.[27]

The powers of the regulators to modify licence conditions have been extremely important as these powers have enabled regulators to amend the basic rules under which regulated enterprises operate. For example, regulators periodically set new price controls that limit the amounts regulated enterprises can charge for important services; they have also made rules requiring enterprises to trade fairly, and to meet social objectives such as avoiding disconnection of supply. Where such a licence modification is proposed by a regulator, the enterprise may choose to accept it or, if it refuses, the regulator may then refer the proposal to the Competition Commission that issues a report on the basis of which a licence modification may be imposed on the enterprise. This is often seen as a form of appeal against the regulator's proposal; however, the power to require a reference is available only to the regulated enterprise itself and not to third parties such as consumers or competitors who may be adversely affected by the proposed licence modification. For such third parties, a legal obligation to consult them only comes into play after agreement has been reached with the regulated enterprise.[28] Moreover, the original legal structure did not facilitate the making of collective licence modifications to a number of licences held by different enterprises in the same market; a single company could veto such a modification irrespective of the views of the others. This reflected the original position where a single privatized enterprise dominated a market, but not the more recent development of competition so that a number of different enterprises supply services. The arrangements have thus now been reformed, with arrangements for standard licence conditions and collective licence modifications if a large majority of licence holders agree in electricity and gas; the new approach in telecommunications mentioned above is fundamentally different, and sets general conditions for all market operators without the need for licence conditions for each company.[29] For example, these will set out the requirements of universal service to ensure that telecommunications services are made available to all.

The duty to protect the interests of consumers is an important requirement for all the regulators (except in rail, where this is primarily the responsibility of the Department for Transport), although the combination of roles as consumer champion and impartial arbiter between consumer and other interests is a potentially very difficult one. In terms of institutional arrangements for implementing consumer protection, there was initially a striking lack of consistency, ranging from a large number of local committees in telecommunications to a single national Gas Consumers' Council. Important changes took place as part of the Labour Government reforms, with the creation of new, independent consumer bodies in energy, posts and water.[30] In communications, Ofcom is also obliged to establish a Consumer Panel, although, unlike the other new consumer councils, it is not appointed

[27] Gas Act 1995, s. 5; Utilities Act 2000, s. 30; Communications Act 2003, Pt 2 and Directive 2001/22/EC, [2002] OJ L249 21.

[28] Telecommunications Act 1984, s. 12; Gas Act 1986, s. 21; Electricity Act 1989, s. 11; Water Industry Act 1991, s. 13.

[29] Gas Act 1986, s. 8; Electricity Act 1989 s. 11A; Communications Act 2003, ss. 45–51.

[30] See the Utilities Act 2000, s. 2 and Sched. 2; Postal Services Act 2000, s. 2 and Sched. 2, and the Water Act 2003, s. 35 and Sched. 2. The new bodies adopted the titles Energy Watch, Postwatch, and Water Voice.

independently of the regulatory body.[31] However, further reform is now also being undertaken, which will replace the specialist bodies in energy and posts with ombudsman schemes, with the first calling point for complaints being the general body Consumer Direct and consumer representation lying with the new general body Consumer Voice.[32]

The key points about the regulatory institutions are thus that, while strongly distanced from governmental intervention in their ordinary operation, they work within a framework created by governmental decisions at the time of privatization, they have responsibilities determined by the privatization of particular industries rather than by a coherent sectoral approach (except in the case of electronic communications where the initiative has come from Brussels), and the original structure of individual directors-general reflected the personalized model characteristic of British government without as yet a clear procedural code. Nevertheless, we have seen some gradual moves towards a more coherent and consistent model since 2000, with the adoption of the commission model as standard and some clarification of the regulators' statutory duties, although uncertainty remains on the most appropriate means of consumer representation.

REGULATING THE PRIVATIZED UTILITIES IN PRACTICE

These then are the basic tasks and institutional structures of the utility regulators. How have they operated in practice? The nearest thing to a clear statement of regulatory philosophy can be found in the two reports commissioned from Professor Littlechild, later to become the first Director-General of Electricity Supply, concerning the arrangements for regulating the telecommunications and water industries.[33] The key principles underlying these reports were, first, the superiority of competition over regulation, and, secondly, the need to avoid a necessarily unpredictable form of regulation based on discretionary assessments by regulators; he felt that regulatory systems should work in as predictable a way as possible. Thus the stress was on the opening up of markets so as to make regulation necessary only in the short rather than the long term (regulation 'is a means of "holding the fort" until competition arrives'[34]) and rejection of the United States approach to price regulation based on the assessment of a fair rate of return on capital employed by the regulated enterprises. Instead, it was proposed that regulation through formulae linked to changes in the retail price index (RPI), thus in most cases limiting increases to a figure below general inflation, be adopted to limit the scope of discretionary judgement by regulators. This approach was implemented through conditions in the licences.

Both principles have shown themselves to be of limited value. First, the regulation of natural monopoly has turned out to be much more complex in practice than originally envisaged and the second theme of the Littlechild report, that of the minimization of regulatory discretion, has also proved to be unrealistic. It has influenced, as mentioned above, the licence conditions linking price increases to the RPI. However, the application of the

[31] Communications Act 2003, s. 16.

[32] Department of Trade and Industry, Strengthen and Streamline Consumer Advocacy: Summary of Responses and Government Response to Consultation (2006).

[33] Littlechild, (1984) and (1986), n. 6 above.

[34] Littlechild, (1984), n. 6 above, para. 4.11.

formulae has been anything but automatic, mainly because they must be made subject to periodic review. This has occurred for a number of reasons; in some cases due to their being set for a period of five years which then ended, but in others due to unduly generous formulae adopted at privatization permitting politically unacceptable profits for the regulated enterprises. The first striking example was that of British Telecom. The initial control was of RPI-3 (broadly, the controlled prices could rise by a figure three per cent below the rise in the retail price index measuring the prices of a range of products) applying to line rentals and local and national call charges from 1984. This was subject to threatened tightening at least three times during the initial five years. In 1989 it was amended to RPI-4.5 and applied also to operator assisted calls, special controls applying to connection charges. In 1991 the cap was tightened to RPI-6.25 with international calls added, and in 1993 it was further tightened to RPI-7.5 and its scope was further widened. As a result, the volume of British Telecom turnover covered by the formula increased from 48 per cent to 71 per cent. A further revision came into effect in 1997, with major changes to the form and coverage of the control, and new controls were introduced once more in 2002, focussed on the lowest-spending 80 per cent of residential consumers. Retail price control was finally abolished in 2006, although wholesale price controls were retained, applying to the charges BT makes to competitors for interconnection. Thus price control has turned out to be a complex matter involving detailed periodical investigation of the regulated enterprise's finances.

In the case of the other utilities, price control also proved complex. For example, in water the formula was complicated by the need to allow for the companies to finance investment needed to meet enhanced environmental and water quality requirements under UK and European Community law. Perhaps the most striking problem occurred in the case of the electricity distribution price review in 1994–5. Proposals were announced by the regulator in August 1994, but in December a takeover bid was launched for one of the companies. It mounted a defence showing that it was considerably better off financially than the regulator had assumed in setting his proposals. Just before the end of the formal consultation period the proposals were withdrawn and replaced by tighter controls. This caused considerable problems, particularly as the announcement was made one day after the government's sale of its residual stake in the electricity generating companies. Although these companies were not directly affected by the distribution controls, their shares fell sharply in value and institutional holdings commenced trading below the offer price. The regulator (Professor Littlechild himself) justified his reopening of the controls on the basis of 'what appears to be widespread public concern about whether the price control proposals are sufficiently demanding . . . and whether they represent an appropriate balance between the interests of customers and shareholders'.[35]

However, in some areas the scope of price control has become much smaller as competitive markets have been created; thus the last retail price controls for electricity and gas were lifted in 2002 and the last retail controls for telecommunications in 2006. Of course, price controls will remain indefinitely for areas of natural monopoly such as bulk transmission of electricity or gas transportation, or access to the rail network. In these contexts the price controls work in the wholesale market; in other words, they set periodic limits to increases in the amount which a monopoly enterprise can charge companies to use the network it

[35] His statement is reproduced in full as 'Widespread Public Concern Over Planned Price Controls', *Financial Times*, 8 March 1995.

owns, for example to transport gas for supply to consumers or to provide train services for the public. Any expectation that regulation will wither away in these areas is quite unrealistic. Some retail price controls also remain where there is monopoly in supply to consumers, for example in water services and certain rail fares. Moreover, as suggested earlier, the stark opposition of regulation and competition in the Littlechild reports has been shown to be misleading. A major role, indeed probably *the* major role, of the regulators has been the creation and policing of competition, and they played a key part in opening up the energy supply markets to competition during the 1990s. As mentioned earlier, the provisions of the Competition Act 1998 now provide concurrent powers for the regulators to enforce the prohibitions on anti-competitive agreements and abuse of a dominant position contained in the Act, and the Enterprise Act 2002 gives them power to undertake market investigations and to investigate 'super-complaints' from designated consumer bodies.[36] A particular advantage of this change is that it gives stronger enforcement powers to the regulators, permitting, for example, fines for past conduct and the granting of interim relief; the general enforcement powers of the regulators themselves have also been made more effective. It should also be stressed that the development of competitive markets fits in well with European Union policy and European Community law which have moved rapidly to liberalize telecommunications markets and rather less rapidly to liberalize those in energy and postal services.[37]

Economic regulation is thus very different from the mere application of rules controlling natural monopoly. The picture is further complicated by the fact that the regulators have also undertaken forms of social regulation. This type of regulation reflects the fact that public utilities are different from ordinary companies in that they provide essential services; access to these is seen as required by rights of citizenship rather than simply being a matter for market provision. Thus universal service in various forms has been the underlying reason for such regulation. Social regulation has often been regarded with some suspicion on constitutional grounds; it is claimed that it is more appropriately the task of elected government and that the regulators should confine themselves to economic tasks. A particularly important early role was to restrict the conditions in which suppliers of utility services can disconnect supply for non-payment of Bills. This has been undertaken with some success, and for example in the case of electricity in 2000 the number of disconnections was only 300 as compared to 70,000 before privatization, although the numbers have increased more recently. The Water Industry Act 1999 now bans the disconnection of water and sewerage services from domestic premises.[38] A further concern in energy has been to prevent 'cream skimming' in which the competitive market only benefits the most profitable consumers; the government has required the energy regulator to develop a social action plan to protect the position of the most vulnerable consumers, re-launched in 2005 as the Social Action Strategy.[39] In the case of telecommunications, a broader approach has been taken,

[36] Competition Act 1998, s. 54 and Sched. 10; for discussion see T. Prosser, 'Competition, Regulators and Public Service', in B. Rodger and A. MacCulloch (eds), *The UK Competition Act – A New Era for UK Competition Law* (2000) 225. For the extension of regulators' enforcement powers, see e.g. Utilities Act 2000, ss. 59, 95. See also the Enterprise Act 2002, ss. 204–5, Sch. 9 Pt. 2; the Enterprise Act 2002 (Super-complaints to Regulators) Order 2003 (SI 2003/1368).

[37] For a summary see T. Prosser, *The Limits of Competition Law – Markets and Public Services* (2005), ch. 8.

[38] S. 1.

[39] Ofgem, *The Social Action Strategy* (2005). The regulator also publishes annual reviews of progress in implementing the strategy.

concentrating on the requirements of universal service and reflecting similar trends at a European level. This included requiring the provision of special tariffs for low users and protecting the availability of public call boxes in rural areas.[40] Once more, the work of the regulators parallels that taken at a European Union level.[41] There are now also powers for government to issue social and environmental guidance to which the regulators will be required to have regard in the energy, water and postal sectors. Such guidance should do something to tidy up the present rather uncoordinated approach regulators have taken to social regulation.[42]

RAIL: A REGULATORY FAILURE?

This account suggests that the utility regulators have been broadly successful in undertaking a range of tasks. The difficulties have come from decisions taken by government at the time of privatization, notably the setting of price formulae which were too generous and the failure to encourage more competition through, for example, splitting up British Gas. This also does much to explain other areas of regulatory difficulty, notably that of the railways, where the system was split up into an infrastructure company, 25 operating companies, three rolling stock leasing companies, and a large number of maintenance companies. Unsurprisingly, the system has been characterized by grave problems of coordination. This was complicated further by an initial overlap of regulatory responsibilities between the Rail Regulator and Office of Passenger Rail Franchising, the latter being responsible for the setting and monitoring of franchise conditions. After devastating criticism from the House of Commons Transport Committee, plans for reform of rail regulation were published in 1998, and were implemented in the Transport Act 2000.[43] The Act replaced the Franchising Office with a Strategic Rail Authority in the form of a commission with new responsibilities to engage in strategic planning of the network as a whole and to work closely with other transport and planning bodies. The Rail Regulator was retained and has responsibility for setting the conditions and charges for access to the monopoly infrastructure by companies providing rail services, but is made subject to guidance from the Secretary of State.[44] Further reform took place under the Railways Act 2005, which abolished the Authority and passed its responsibilities to the Secretary of State for Transport. The frequent reform reflects the serious problems which have been encountered on the railways, including the collapse of Railtrack (the privatized infrastructure company) and its replacement by Network Rail (a public interest company with no shareholders), and an astonishing escalation of costs for infrastructure work, in part due to contracting out of maintenance and renewal of lines to a large number of contractors and sub-contractors.[45] It would seem unfair to blame these on the regulatory

[40] See Oftel, *Review of the Universal Service Obligation* (2005).

[41] Directive 2002/22/EC on universal service and users' rights relating to electronic communications networks and services, [2002] OJ L108/51.

[42] Department of Trade and Industry, *Social and Environmental Guidance to the Gas and Electricity Markets Authority* (2004); *Social and Environmental Guidance to the Postal Services Commission* (2001).

[43] Environment, Transport and Regional Affairs Committee, *The Proposed Strategic Rail Authority and Railway Regulation*, HC 286, 1997–8; Department of the Environment, Transport and the Regions, *A New Deal for Transport: Better for Everyone*, Cm 3950 (1998), and *A New Deal for the Railways* (1998); Transport Act 2000, Pt IV.

[44] Transport Act 2000, s. 224(6).

[45] For detailed discussion see T. Prosser, 'The Privatisation of Britain's Railways: Regulatory Failure or Legal Failure?' 57 *Current Legal Problems 2004*, Jane Holder et al. (ed.) (2005), 213.

structures adopted or on deficiencies in performance of the regulators; rather, it seems fundamentally due to the fragmented structure adopted for the privatized railways where responsibility for infrastructure and operations were separated and basic functions extensively contracted out, together with a failure of government to set a clear strategy. The principle of separating regulatory and funding responsibilities is obviously sound, and the 2005 Act does something to clarify responsibilities by making ministers unambiguously responsible for strategy and the overall level of financial support. Much of the blame for the problem lies with the assumption that replacing a single, hierarchically organized rail network by many actors linked by contract and coordinated by economic incentives would result in a system which was effectively self-regulating. In fact, coordination by a public authority has proved necessary, both for planning services and for regulating their delivery. Moreover, as the former Rail Regulator, Tom Winsor, has consistently stressed, independent regulation is essential as a guarantee of stability for private investors in the industry.[46]

REGULATORY ACCOUNTABILITY

It is evident then that regulation involves difficult judgements based on a variety of factors, both social and economic. What are the procedures by which these judgements are made? The regulators are not elected nor are they subject to that most attenuated form of accountability, ministerial responsibility to Parliament. They therefore lack direct democratic legitimacy. Nor do they apply a coherent body of rules which have parliamentary approval; as we saw earlier their statutory duties are vague and often contradictory, and remain difficult to interpret even after the new single primary duty. Issues of regulatory accountability are thus of great constitutional importance.[47]

One way to achieve accountability may be, while accepting the inevitability of discretionary decisions, to design accountable decision-making procedures, as has been attempted in the USA.[48] It is argued that the legitimacy of the regulators' decisions would be increased through the requirement of open hearings involving the participation of affected interests, the giving of detailed reasons for decisions, and the availability of judicial review as a form of check on decision making. The underlying rationale is a kind of pluralist one; the truth (if indeed such a thing exists) best emerges through the open testing of as many different conceptions of it as possible.[49]

The US practice was not however taken seriously in the design of the British regulators; it is fair to say that it was seen as a threat which would straitjacket regulators in legal complexities.[50] Yet the other extreme, which was adopted, of a near-total absence of mandatory

[46] See e.g. 'The Future of the Railways: Sir Robert Reid Memorial Lecture 2004', (2003–4) 13 *Utilities Law Review* 145. For the difficult relations between regulator and minister at the time of the failure of Railtrack see *Weir v Secretary of State for Transport* [2005] EWHC 2192 (Ch), discussed in P. Leyland, 'The *Railtrack* Case: Mainly on the Wrong Track?' (2004/5) 14 *Utilities Law Review* 213.

[47] For a particularly useful analysis of the accountability issues see the House of Lords Select Committee on the Constitution, 'The Regulatory State: Ensuring its Accountability' HL 68, 2003–4.

[48] See e.g. C. Graham and T. Prosser, *Privatizing Public Enterprises; Constitutions, the State and Regulation in Comparative Perspective*, (1991), ch. 7; S. Breyer and R. Stewart, *Administrative Law and Regulatory Policy* (6th edn, 2006); G. Palast et al., *Democracy and Regulation* (2003).

[49] For a detailed discussion of this argument see R. Stewart, *The Reformation of American Administrative Law*, (1975) 88 *Harvard Law Review*, 1669.

[50] See e.g. Foster, op.cit, n. 3 above, 259–67.

structured procedures in regulation, faced considerable criticism. A couple of caveats need to be made here. First, the creation of the regulators has resulted in considerably greater openness than was the case under nationalization, through imposing a form of external supervision which, as we have seen, did not exist previously. Second, individual regulators have been, by the standards of British public bodies, exceptionally open in reaching their decisions.

The most striking case was that of Oftel. From the outset, the first Director General of Telecommunications promised an open approach, although he was criticized for failure to give proper reasons for his first interconnection decision for fear of legal challenge.[51] During the directorship of Don Cruikshank during the mid-1990s further important steps were taken to ensure openness. An operating plan and work programme were published annually and the most important innovations concerned consultation procedures. It was already the practice to publish frequent consultation documents and to invite representations, but from March 1995 it was announced that all responses to consultations would be made public unless clearly marked confidential; the latter type of response might be given lesser weight by the regulator. Consultation would also incorporate a second stage; after representations had been received the Director General would be prepared to receive further comments on them for a period of 14 days, thus permitting review of submissions by others. Full explanations would be given for decisions, including references to the arguments of the parties consulted and a summary of views submitted.[52] In addition, public hearings would be employed as part of the consultative process. All these procedural innovations have been used in decisions relating to price control, fair trading, and universal service. Regulation of telecommunications passed to Ofcom from the end of 2003; it has also made a commitment to consult widely before reaching decisions, and is subject to various procedural duties under the Communications Act 2003, for example to review regulatory burdens, to carry out impact assessments, to publish promptness standards, and to establish, and consult, a consumer panel.[53] It has consulted extensively on major issues including public service broadcasting and telecommunications markets.

The other utility regulators also did much to open up their procedures, although it is fair to say that none went so far or developed such consistent procedures as Oftel.[54] More consistent arrangements were developed in the Utilities Act 2000 and in the later utilities statutes. Thus, for example, the energy regulator is required to develop a forward work programme annually after consultation and to give reasons for a wide range of decisions, including revocation and modification of licences and for enforcement action.[55] It is also under a duty to have regard to best regulatory practice, including accountability and proportionality.[56] Though divergencies are to some degree inevitable in substantive decisions made within any system of regulation which includes discretion, this is not necessarily the case in relation to procedures, where US experience shows that it is possible to adopt a reasonably standardized set through the Administrative Procedure Act.[57] A key point is that the US legislation adopts different approaches to rule making and adjudication. Relatively

[51] See Oftel, *Annual Report 1985*, HC 461, 1985–6, para. 1.27.

[52] Oftel, *Consultation Procedures and Transparency* (1995).

[53] Ss. 6–8, 12, 16.

[54] For details see Prosser, *Law and the Regulators*, n. 7 above, 83–6, 113–15, 144–7, 177–8, 198–9.

[55] Ss. 4, 42, 87.

[56] Energy Act 2004, s. 178.

[57] See Graham and Prosser, n. 48 above, 220–4, 256–7, and I. Harden and N. Lewis, *The Noble Lie* (1986) 302–10.

formal procedures, normally involving hearings with cross-examination, are prescribed for adjudication. Rule-making, while less formally prescribed, is also, however, subject to a number of structured procedural requirements, including as a minimum giving notice of the proposed rule and receiving comments on it, a minimum which has been supplemented in a variety of ways by agencies and courts.[58] In the UK, the Oftel model has gone a considerable way towards the US approach to rule making; another model is that of the Financial Services Authority which falls under a requirement to adopt a sophisticated procedure of consultation where it makes rules, including publishing cost–benefit analysis and its response to representations. In relation to more individualized decisions, legislation has also imposed duties to give reasons on the regulators in determining a number of types of individual disputes[59] and the exercise of adjudicative functions by the regulators falls under the informal supervision of the Council on Tribunals.[60] Moreover, many of the general administrative reforms of recent years will apply to the utility regulators; thus, as non-ministerial government departments they fall within the scope of the Freedom of Information Act 2000 and the jurisdiction of the Parliamentary Ombudsman; the Code of Practice on Consultation will also apply to them.[61] We do appear to be moving towards a more coherent procedural regime for regulatory decisions. The same is not true, however, for appeals against regulatory decisions.

APPEALS AND JUDICIAL REVIEW

A further important element of accountability is the existence of opportunities to check the decisions of the regulators through appeal or judicial review; this is an area where there is extreme inconsistency at present.[62] Perhaps the most important example of such checking is at first sight contained in the role of the Competition Commission; it will be recalled that licence modifications to which the company does not consent involve a reference to the Commission.[63] In one sense this could be seen to represent an appeal from a preliminary decision of the Director-General that such a modification is required. However, the main role of this procedure has in practice been to put pressure on companies to agree to modifications so as to avoid such a reference and the resulting delay and heavy commitment of management time; for example, in the case of telecommunications up to August 1992, 25 voluntary modifications had been made with only one reference to the Commission.[64] There have been a number of high-profile references in other cases; indeed, such a reference was crucial to preparing the ground for the opening up of the gas market to competition. The threat of referral has great advantages as a sanction for the regulator. However, as

58 See Harden and Lewis, ibid., and for an example of rule making on universal service under the US Telecommunications Act 1996 see Prosser, *Law and the Regulators*, n. 7 above, 281–6.

59 Competition and Service (Utilities) Act 1992, ss. 1, 5(1), 6(1), 7(1), 11, 16, 17, 23, 34, 36.

60 Council on Tribunals, *Annual Report 1991–2*, HC 316, 1992–3, para. 2.10, and see S. K. Bailey, 'Council on Tribunals and the Utilities', (1993) 4 *Utilities Law Review* 51–2.

61 Better Regulation Executive, *Code of Practice on Consultation* (2004).

62 For a detailed analysis see T. Prosser, 'The Place of Appeals in Regulation: Continuity and Change' in Centre for the Study of Regulated Industries, *Regulatory Review 2004/5* (2005).

63 Telecommunications Act 1984, ss. 12–15; Gas Act 1986, ss. 22–7; Electricity Act 1989, ss. 12–14; Water Industry Act 1991, ss. 14–16.

64 National Audit Office, *The Office of Telecommunications: Licence Compliance and Consumer Protection*, HC 529, 1992–3, para. 2.42.

mentioned above, the ability of the regulated firm to veto a licence modification made without a Commission reference privileges that firm above others affected, such as competitors or consumers who have no such 'appeal' rights. The introduction of collective licence modification procedures may reduce the effect of such a veto where standard licence conditions apply to a number of holders, but it does not improve the position of third parties. as the 'appeal' right will continue to be available only to those who hold a licence. Licence modification references continue to go to the Commission in its reporting function, not to the Competition Appeal Tribunal. This means that third party rights of appeal to the tribunal will not be available.[65]

A 'mish-mash' of different arrangements exists in relation to other decisions. The most important development has been in the case of telecommunications licensing, where a right of appeal on the merits to the Competition Appeal Tribunal is provided by the Communications Act 2003 for any person affected by the decision, and the Tribunal has received a couple of such appeals each year since then.[66] This right is due to the special requirements of European Community law in relation to the liberalization of telecommunications.[67] There is a further appeal on a point of law for a party or anyone else with a sufficient interest to the Court of Appeal.[68] In addition, where the regulators exercise concurrent powers under the Competition Act, there is also a right of appeal on the merits to the Competition Appeal Tribunal and on a point of law to the Court of Appeal; provision is also made for third party appeals by a person with a sufficient interest.[69] Such appeals have played an important role. Thus in one third party appeal, the Court of Appeal noted the breadth of the appeal right to the tribunal, permitting the latter, where it differs from the regulator on questions of law, fact or evidence, to remit a decision or substitute its own decision; it did not however have the power to instruct the regulator how to proceed if the case was remitted. The Tribunal and the Court of Appeal in this case also considered arguments based on the European Convention on Human Rights, arguments which are likely to be increasingly important in relation to regulatory decisions.[70] Yet another different model applies where financial penalties are imposed by a regulator; here there is a right of appeal to the High Court against the penalties and their amount on grounds similar to judicial review.[71] To complete the jigsaw, certain decisions of the energy regulatory in relation to the organization of the wholesale markets may be appealed to the Competition Commission on specified grounds.[72]

In other cases judicial review will be the only remedy against regulatory decisions, for example after a licence modification has been made.[73] Once more, the United States experience has in the UK been seen as offering lessons as to what should be avoided, and so there

65 Competition Act 1998, s. 47.

66 S. 192. Such an appeal also applies in competition-based broadcasting decisions: s. 317.

67 Directive 2002/21/EC on a common regulatory framework for electronic communications networks and services [2002] OJ L108/33, art. 4(1).

68 S. 196.

69 Competition Act 1998, ss. 46–9, as amended by the Enterprise Act 2002, s. 17.

70 *Office of Communications* v. *Floe Telecom Ltd* [2006] EWCA Civ 768. For a rehearing involving detailed economic analysis, see *Albion Water Ltd* v. *Water Services Regulation Authority* [2006] CAT 23.

71 Utilities Act 2000, ss. 59 and 95; Postal Services Act 2000, ss. 30–7; Transport Act 2000, s. 225; Water Act 2003, s. 48.

72 Energy Act 2004, ss. 173–7.

73 For a comprehensive account of the early role of the courts see C. Scott, 'The Juridification of Relations in the UK Utilities Sector', in J. Black, P. Muchlinski and P. Walker (eds), *Commercial Regulation and Judicial Review* (1998) 19–61.

has been a reluctance to accept that the courts should play a central role in establishing principles for the operation of the regulatory bodies. Experience so far suggests that there will not be automatic resort to judicial review by those disappointed by regulatory decisions, despite the willingness of the courts to accept such challenges not only by judicial review but, in certain cases where contracts are involved, by private law action.[74] This has not resulted in a flood of cases from those regulated despite initial fears that it might do so.

In the US, over-enthusiastic judicial review of issues of substance rather than of procedure has been identified as a major cause of the 'ossification' of the rule-making process.[75] The UK courts have in general intervened in matters of procedure while not double-guessing regulators on matters of substance. In the first case of judicial review of a utility regulator, judicial review was sought of a refusal by the Director General of Gas Supply to order reconnection of gas to the applicant's home after allegations of meter tampering.[76] The application was successful on the ground of procedural impropriety because the applicants had been given no opportunity to comment on evidence obtained by the Director General from a meter reader, although all grounds alleging substantive illegality were rejected. The court stressed the broad discretion conferred on the Director General and his autonomy as regards questions of fact. A similar stress on the breadth of the substantive discretion of the regulator appeared in later cases attempting to challenge the regulator's substantive discretion.[77] Thus, in the frequent situation of a conflict between different statutory duties of the regulator, 'he is given the choice how that conflict is to be resolved, and to decide priorities, and so long as he bears in mind the entirety of his duties, has a predisposition to fulfil all the duties so far as this is practicable and with those duties in mind makes a decision which promotes one or other of the objectives specified (and is rational), his decision stands and is not open to challenge'.[78] In the context of rail, making a decision which had particularly important implications for the role of competition in the industry, the Administrative Court emphasised that given the regulator's expertise in a highly technical field, it would be 'very slow indeed' to impugn the regulatory decision, and that it was no part of the Court's function to substitute its own view on matters of economic judgment.[79]

In other cases the courts have taken a more interventionist approach, for example in a decision relating to the different treatment of two electricity licence holders.[80] Although it has correctly been criticized as misunderstanding the role of the (then) Monopolies and Mergers Commission in the licence modification process, the decision does at least appeal to a principle of equal treatment rather than simply reassessing the substantive merits of the

74 *Mercury Communications* v. *Director General of Telecommunications* [1996] 1 All ER 575 (HL); see also A. McHarg, 'Regulation as a Private Law Function?' [1995] *Public Law* 539.

75 T. McGarity, 'Some Thoughts on "Deossifying" the Rulemaking Process' (1992) 41 *Duke LJ* 1385 at 1400, 1410–28.

76 *R.* v. *Director General of Gas Supply, ex parte Smith*, CRO/1398/88, QBD, 31 July 1989.

77 *R.* v. *Director General of Telecommunications, ex parte British Telecommunications plc*, CO/3596/96 (QBD), noted by C. Scott at (1997) 8 *Utilities LR* 120; *R.* v. *Director General of Telecommunications, ex parte Cellcom Ltd.* [1999] ECC 314; *R. (T-Mobile (UK) Ltd, Vodafone Ltd., Orange Personal Communication Services Ltd.)* v. *Competition Commission and Director General of Telecommunications* [2003] EWHC 1566 (QBD).

78 *Ex parte Cellcom*, ibid., para. 25, *per* Lightman J.

79 *Great North Eastern Railway Ltd v the Office of Rail Regulation* [2006] EWHC 1942.

80 *R.* v. *Director General of Electricity Supply, ex parte Scottish Power*, noted at (1997) 8 *Utilities LR* 126. See also A. McHarg, 'A Duty to be Consistent? *R.* v. *Director General of Electricity Supply, ex parte Scottish Power*' (1998) 61 *MLR* 93.

regulatory decision.[81] Similarly, a decision of the Northern Ireland Court of Appeal relating to licence modification was once more concerned with process values, in this case the relationship between different regulatory bodies.[82] A decision that the use of prepayment devices in water was unlawful is also best understood as preventing the by-passing of the rigorous procedural safeguards applying to the disconnection of water supply.[83] Thus these decisions are not simply examples of over-detailed judicial intervention in the substance of regulatory discretion. Indeed, it is the establishment of expert regulators with discretionary powers which has done most to prevent such 'ossification' of decision-making.[84]

It remains to be seen whether there will be a substantial increase in the number of cases brought as a result of growing liberalization and of the move towards competition law prohibitions more susceptible to judicial enforcement.[85] A further issue of importance is the question of whether, in those areas where judicial review is the only remedy available against regulators, this is sufficient to comply with Article 6 of the European Convention on Human Rights giving the right to a determination of civil rights by an independent and impartial tribunal established by law. The attitude of the UK courts so far is that the current law, as developed after the Human Rights Act 1998 to permit more searching review, is adequate to do so, but the cases in which this has been determined may be distinguished either as concerning matters of policy where there is a legitimate role for a minister accountable to Parliament, or as not involving the determination of a freestanding Convention right.[86] By contrast, regulatory decisions do not necessarily involve matters of policy in this sense, and the right to peaceful enjoyment of possessions under Article 1 of the First Protocol to the Convention may be at issue, for example where a regulatory decision affects freedom of an enterprise to trade. We are likely to see some interesting attempts to challenge regulatory decisions in the courts over the next few years; moreover, the background of a Convention right is likely to result in more searching review, notably on the basis of proportionality.[87] Meanwhile, the mess of different types of procedures for challenging decisions by the regulators needs urgently to be cleared up; a general appeal right on the merits to the Competition Appeal Tribunal is the obvious answer, and would avoid the possibility of successful challenge for breach of Article 6. Such an appeal right was in fact proposed by the House of Lords Constitution Committee, but was one of its few recommendations to be rejected by the Government.[88]

81 See McHarg, ibid.

82 *Re Northern Ireland Electricity plc's Application for Judicial Review* [1998] NI 300, and see A. McHarg, (1999) 10 *Utilities LR* 164–8.

83 *R.* v. *Director of Water Services, ex parte Lancashire County Council and Others, The Times*, 6 March 1998, noted *sub nom R.* v. *Director of Water Services, ex parte Oldham Metropolitan Borough Council*, D. Legge in [1998] 9 *Utilities LR* 123.

84 For a grossly inappropriate judicial role in the substance of economic regulation in the absence of a regulator in New Zealand, see the decision of the Privy Council in *Telecom Corporation of New Zealand* v. *Clear Communications Ltd* [1995] 1 NZLR 385; cf. *Albion Water Ltd* v. *Water Services Regulation Authority* [2006] CAT 23 before the Competition Appeal Tribunal.

85 For liberalization as a spur to greater use of challenge in the courts, see C. Scott, 'The Juridification of Relations in the UK Utilities Sectors', n. 73 above, 56–7, 60.

86 *R. (on the application of Alconbury Developments Ltd)* v. *Secretary of State for the Environment, Transport and the Regions* [2001] UKHL 23; *Runa Begum* v. *Tower Hamlets London Borough Council* [2003] UKHL 5.

87 But cf. *R (on the application of Pro-Life Alliance)* v. *BBC* [2003] UKHL 23.

88 'The Regulatory State: Ensuring its Accountability', n. 47 above, paras 219–32; 'The Regulatory State: Ensuring its Accountability: The Government's Response' HL 150 (2003–4), paras 60–73.

Another possibility is the use of private law actions, for example in misfeasance in public office, against regulators. Such a case was brought against the Bank of England in its former regulatory role in relation to the banking system, where statute explicitly provided immunity for anything done by the Bank in its regulatory role in the absence of bad faith. The case was discontinued on the direction of the court part way through with no liability being found on the part of the Bank; the hearing had by then run for 255 days, with opening speeches by counsel of 90 and 119 days, at a cost of £100 million (not including earlier hearings on points of law, which had resulted in the litigation overall lasting for a period of 12 years).[89] The heavy criticism by the judge of the conduct of the case may well deter such actions in the future.

CONCLUSIONS

Many of the problems described above result from the difficulty of fitting bodies such as the regulators into the constitutional structure; accountability has traditionally been based almost exclusively on ministerial responsibility to Parliament and, despite the long history of regulatory boards not headed by ministers, other means for accountability have not been developed with any degree of sophistication. What was particularly striking on the establishment of the utility regulators was the personalized nature of regulation; the assumption seemed to be that appointing an acceptable personality as regulator would ensure a high-quality result. This in turn reflected the traditionally highly personalized traditions of constitutional government in the UK, once more based around ministerial responsibility rather than any stronger concept of the state and of administrative law.[90] The reforms undertaken since 2000 have moved away from the personalized model to commissions and towards a more coherent system of procedural requirements for the regulatory process. However, as we have seen with the procedures for challenging regulatory decisions, considerable inconsistency remains, especially in relation to appeal rights.

A further source of problems has been the lack of a coherent regulatory philosophy and the failure to establish adequate criteria for regulation at the time of privatization. Such attempts as there were to do so, especially in the Littlechild reports, have been shown by experience to be unsatisfactory; nor would the solution sometimes suggested of adopting economic efficiency as the key criterion resolve many of the regulatory problems outlined. Once more, the absence of normative principle reflects a more general problems of constitutional thought in the UK,[91] and the absence of clearly applicable constitutional norms of due process has encouraged the highly pragmatic approach described, though again there are signs of a more coherent approach since 2000.

Some proposed solutions are unlikely to be more successful. Thus suggestions for a rule-based system of regulation are unlikely to be effective given the impossibility of reducing the range of regulatory principles to any form of determinate rules. This would also have the effect of limiting severely the ability of regulators to respond to the rapidly changing environments in which they operate. Similarly, proposals for requiring that the decisions of

89 *Three Rivers District Council v. The Governor and Company of the Bank of England* [2006] EWHC 816.

90 See K. Dyson, *The State Tradition in Western Europe* (1980).

91 See T. Daintith, 'Political Programmes and the Content of the Constitution', in W. Finnie, C. Himsworth, and N. Walker (eds), *Edinburgh Essays in Public Law* (1991) 41.

regulators be based as far as possible on economic rather than social criteria do not reflect the range of objectives as defined by statute; if anything there has been a tendency for regulators to move towards accepting a greater role for social considerations in their decisions rather than the reverse and this is recognized both in the reforms since 2000 and in broader European developments.[92] A further uncertainty is in relation to challenge in the courts and the role of the Human Rights Act; although private law actions are less likely after the failure of that against the Bank of England over BCCI, it is possible that the use of judicial review will increase and that the Act will both encourage more searching judicial scrutiny and require further procedural development by the regulators themselves.

What is needed can perhaps be summarized as a greater concern with procedural and substantive principle. I have stressed that initially it was at the level of procedure that the regulatory arrangements seemed at their weakest as a matter of law, but here the recent reforms, building on best practice of the regulators themselves, may be the beginning of moves towards a more principled system. Indeed, there is a growing concern within government about regulatory procedures and there have been attempts to develop more coherent procedural systems across regulation in general, not just the utilities, although there has been reluctance to incorporate them in legislation.[93] The time is ripe for incorporating the lessons learned into a more general Regulatory Reform Act setting out standardized procedures for regulation, especially for consultation and for challenge of decisions.

Secondly, we need to develop further substantive principles of regulation in place of the highly empirical approach taken so far. Unresolved questions include: What is regulation for? What is the relationship between economic and social goals? What rights to services are implied by the statutory arrangements?[94] Impetus to this approach may be given by the increasing amount of regulatory intervention in these areas at the European level, which may lead to a less pragmatic and more litigious approach to regulation in the future and so may force these issues to be more effectively confronted than has been the case in UK domestic law.[95] Already utility liberalization has been accompanied by a clearer definition of concepts of universal service, notably in telecommunications but also in postal service where, for the first time, UK law has needed to provide such a definition. Indeed, it can be argued that this is the source of a growing body of public service law reflecting both continental traditions of public service and the necessary conditions to make market liberalization politically and socially legitimate.[96] It is also striking that it is through the implementation of European obligations that a more satisfactory appeal process is being provided in telecommunications. Similarly, European developments have led to a rationalization of the historically highly pragmatic arrangements for the policing of competition in the UK, and have also created a specialist court in the form of the Competition Appeal Tribunal. As a result of these developments, we now have the foundations for undertaking a discussion of regulation in terms of constitutional principle, something not characteristic of previous UK debate. It is certainly much needed.

[92] Cf. Foster, n. 3 above, ch. 9.

[93] See the work of the Better Regulation Executive in the Cabinet Office at www.cabinetoffice.gov.uk/regulation/index.asp (consulted 2 November 2006).

[94] For an attempt to tackle these issues, see T. Prosser, 'Theorising Utility Regulation' (1999) 62 *MLR* 196.

[95] See now new Art. 16 of the EC Treaty inserted by the Amsterdam Treaty, and the Green and White Papers on Services of General Interest COM (2003) 270 final and COM(2004)374.

[96] See, T. Prosser, 'Public Service Law; Privatization's Unexpected Offspring' (2000) 63 *Law and Contemporary Problems*, 63–82.

FURTHER READING

Baldwin, R. and Cave, M. *Understanding Regulation* (1999).

Centre for the Study of Regulated Industries *Regulatory Review 2004/5* (2005, and published every two years).

Graham, C. *Regulating Utilities: A Constitutional Approach* (2000).

House of Lords Select Committee on the Constitution, 'The Regulatory State: Ensuring its Accountability' HL 68, 2003–4.

Morgan, B. and Yeung, D. *An Introduction to Law and Regulation* (2007).

Prosser, T. *Law and the Regulators* (1997).

USEFUL WEB SITES

Ofgem: **www.ofgem.gov.uk**

Ofwat: **www.ofwat.gov.uk**

ORR: **www.rail-reg.gov.uk**

Ofcom: **www.ofcom.org.uk**

Postcom: **www.psc.gov.uk**

Competition Commission: **www.competition-commission.org.uk**

Better Regulation Executive: **www.cabinetoffice.gov.uk/regulation/index.asp**

15

THE CONTROL OF PUBLIC EXPENDITURE

John McEldowney

SUMMARY

The modernization of the techniques to control public expenditure has resulted in improvements in the provision of financial information to Parliament and in the systems of audit and accountability. During the past decade there has been a noticeable shift towards increasing Treasury influence over public expenditure controls. Independence granted to the Bank of England since 1997 has enhanced its reputation in the setting of interest rates and managing the economy. It has also secured Treasury, rather than Prime Ministerial, influence over economic policy and relations with the Bank of England. Following implementation of the Government Resources and Accounts Act 2000, resource accounting and budgeting operate across all government departments. Since 1997 the introduction of the Chancellor's Pre-Budget Consultation Process in November allows some months of scrutiny before final budget decisions are taken and the budget is presented in April. Lord Sharman's Report, *Holding to Account: The Review of Audit and Accountability for Central Government* (2001) argued that public spending should receive greater scrutiny than private money and advocated a broader definition of 'public money'. Sharman defined 'public money' to include all money received by a public body from whatever sources and money raised by a private body where it is operating under a statutory authority. Sir Peter Gershon undertook a *Review of Public Sector Efficiency* in 2003 and considered how public resources might be better allocated. The Hampton Review, *Reducing Administrative Burdens* (Treasury, March 2005) identified the need to remove unnecessary and inefficient burdens on business because of public sector regulation. Financial information and procedures are regularly described in updating supplements to *Government Accounting 2000 (amendment 4/05)*. The Main Supply Estimates and Statistical Analysis are provided annually and *Supplementary Budget Information* (2002–3) provides the bulk of financial information. The *Fundamental Expenditure Review* introduced by the Treasury in 1993 continues to advise departments whether their spending trends over the long term are sustainable and appropriate. Controversy continues to surround the use of the Private Finance Initiative. Expenditure at local government and devolved levels also attracts attention. Control of public expenditure has developed sufficiently to improve the effectiveness of financial scrutiny so that overall

Parliament today has more opportunity to exercise financial scrutiny than in the past. The Scrutiny Unit established in 2002 provides specialist support for House of Commons Committees on expenditure matters. Doubts remain about the efficacy of managing taxation plans and the complexity of taxation. Strategic planning is central to the modernization agenda but this may be considered a means of increasing Treasury control. There is a noticeable increase in rules and procedures laid down by the Treasury to secure good financial control. This is undertaken with Parliamentary knowledge but may mark a further abdication of Commons control, and the willingness of individual MPs to develop a sustainable strategy to hold government to account rests with the political will and the determination of MPs.

INTRODUCTION

This chapter focuses on the management and control of central government funds available for the Government's own use or for that of other parts of the public sector. Controlling public expenditure involves: surveying public expenditure as a whole in relation to resources; improving management of the public sector through strict financial controls; and providing the opportunity for parliamentary control. Financial control[1] is best understood on the basis of the chronology of budgetary operations. This involves a planning phase before expenditure is undertaken and an accountability phase thereafter. The planning phase is undertaken by the Treasury's Annual Public Expenditure Survey and through Treasury-appointed Departmental Accounting Officers. In the case of trading funds the Treasury appoints the Chief Executive as the Accounting Officer. The accountability phase is carried out through the audit of public funds under the National Audit Office.

Local government is distinct from central government. Controls over local government expenditure include audit by the Audit Commission.

The chapter is structured as follows: First, the institutions relevant to the control of public expenditure and their roles in the process are considered. Secondly attention is given to the processes of planning public expenditure. Thirdly the accountability phase is assessed through the audit of public expenditure. Finally, some conclusions are offered as to the adequacy of financial control.

GOVERNMENTAL INSTITUTIONS

Central government is the amalgam of departments, ministers, and civil servants found at the heart of policy-making and the delivery of public services. Devolution to Scotland, Wales and when operational in Northern Ireland,[2] has financial implications briefly outlined separately below. The creation of various agencies falls under the responsibility of central government if they are in receipt of public funding which is authorized through a

[1] Alex Brazier and Vidya Ram, *Inside the Counting House: A Discussion Paper on Parliamentary Scrutiny of Government Finance* Hansard Society, London: December 2005; Alex Brazier and Vidya Ram, *The Fiscal Maze* (2006).

[2] See Chapters 9, 10 and 11.

government department. Generally public revenues are not hypothecated for specific purposes.[3]

ACCOUNTING OFFICERS

Each government department has an Accounting Officer appointed by the Treasury, responsible to the House of Commons for the authorization and control of departmental expenditure. If the permanent head of a department is appointed as an Accounting Officer, he is known as the Principal Accounting Officer and in large departments is supported by a Principal Finance Officer and the Principal Establishment Officer. Chief executives of agencies established under the Next Steps initiative may be designated Agency Accounting Officers. Accounting Officers are obliged to fulfill four functions: to ensure that resources in their department deliver departmental objectives 'in the most economic, efficient and effective way' taking account of regularity and propriety; to ensure that there is adequate internal audit conforming to the *Government Internal Audit Manual (GIAM)*; to maintain adequate and suitable financial records; and to manage and safeguard public funds. An Annex to *Government Accounting 2000* contains a detailed memorandum on the Responsibilities of an Accounting Officer.

Ministers may be held to account in matters of public expenditure by the departmental Accounting Officer acting on behalf of Parliament through various Committees of the House of Commons. Specifically Accounting Officers may be asked to defend before the Public Accounts Committee their performance of their wider responsibilities for the economy, efficiency, and effectiveness of departmental expenditure. The *Pergau Dam*[4] affair showed how Treasury procedures operated when the minister overruled the Permanent Secretary of the Overseas Development Administration acting as Accounting Officer, who had reservations about the economy and efficiency of the grant in aid to Malaysia for the construction of a dam. The Public Accounts Committee drew attention to the procedures in use. Following widespread criticism of the procedures an *Amendment No. 7* to *Government Accounting 1989* (now consolidated in a revised *Government Accounting 2000*) contained the requirement that on rare occasions in cases of ministerial overruling of the advice of the Accounting Officer, the Treasury and the Comptroller and Auditor General should be informed, 'without undue delay as in cases of propriety or regularity'.

As it is relatively rare for ministers to override the Accounting Officer, there is a presumption that the Accounting Officer will maintain, even in the face of any ministerial resistance, the standards of strict financial propriety and regularity as well as considerations of 'prudent and economical administration, efficiency and effectiveness'. In the context of the role of the Accounting Officer the constitutional wisdom that emphasizes ministerial responsibility in the relationship between civil servants and Parliament is thus too simplistic. Through the Accounting Officer structure (which includes the Principal Establishment Officer) a chain of command and control is exercised over public

[3] There are some an examples of hypothecation in the revenue from the licence fee paid to the BBC, and in the 1% increase in employers and employees National Insurance Payments for National Health Spending under the National Insurance Contributions Act 2002.

[4] See F. White, I. Harden, and K. Donnelly, 'Audit, Accounting Officers and Accountability: the Pergau Dam Affair' [1994] *Pub. L* 526–34. See *R.* v. *Secretary of State for Foreign Affairs, ex parte World Development Movement Ltd* [1995] 1 All ER 611. See further discussion below.

expenditure that is departmental, not ministerial, led. Annex 6.3 in the revised *Government Accounting 2000* contains explicit instructions to senior line-managers to ensure that standards of propriety and regularity are met.

THE TREASURY AND THE CHANCELLOR OF THE EXCHEQUER

The Treasury, one of the smallest of all the Government departments, fulfils a dual function in being a government department and also holding government departments to account through a system of internal controls over public expenditure. These functions are combined through the requirement of Treasury authority for lawful expenditure, and Treasury supervision of expenditure undertaken by departments.[5] The Treasury has become more powerful and influential under Gordon Brown, the longest continuously serving Chancellor of the Exchequer. Recently the Treasury has engaged departments with targets and value for money assessments. It is undertaking a short review of the effectiveness of the Comprehensive Spending Review and the outcome is expected shortly.[6]

The development of resource accounting and resource budgeting under the Government Resources and Accounts Act 2000, fully operational since 2003–4, is intended to gauge public expenditure more accurately. The Government is set to produce the first set of Whole Government Accounts for the year 2006–07 which treat government as a single consolidated whole and exclude transactions between departments. Whole Government Accounts include accounts of bodies within central government, also local authorities, trading funds and public corporations including NHS Trusts and Foundation Trusts.

The Government in its White Paper, *Modernising Government*,[7] has reflected on the fragmented approach to the tightening of financial control. According to this analysis, economic techniques such as departmental performance targets, budgetary constraints, and strategies for performance management have inhibited the achievement of common goals while admittedly improving efficiency and increasing productivity.

In local–central relations tight financial controls have been developed over capital and revenue spending, including over total expenditure of individual local authorities. The Community Charge was originally introduced for that purpose. The new Labour government inherited these controls in 1997, and has made some efforts to relax controls over the aggregate spending of some local authorities. The Local Government Act 1999 introduces the concept of 'best value' for local government activities and provides more autonomy to local authorities than hitherto.

The Chancellor of the Exchequer presents the annual budget, containing a financial statement and review of taxation levels, to the House of Commons in the spring of each year. For a brief period from 1993 to 1996, the Government adopted a 'unified budget' covering both the Government's tax plans[8] for the coming year *and* the Government's spending plans for the next three years. In July 1997 the Labour Government reverted to spring budgets with a Pre-Budget Report announced in the autumn of each year. The timetable for

5 See 'The Treasury Committee, Evidence on the Role of the Treasury' HC 73 I–II, 2000–1. Lucinda Maer and Mark Sandford, *The development of scrutiny in the UK: A review of procedures and practice* (2004).

6 See HM Treasury, *Releasing the resources to meet the challenges ahead: value for money in the 2007 Comprehensive Spending Review* Cm 6889.

7 Cm 4310, Mar.1999.

8 Tax Law Review Committee, *Making Tax Law* March, 2003, Institute for Fiscal Studies TLRC, Discussion Paper No.3 advocating simplification of the tax system and reviewing parliamentary scrutiny of tax legislation.

the financial year from April to March coincides with the announcements of taxation and spending plans. In addition to the oral Budget statement to the House of Commons there is the Financial Statement and Budget Report containing an analysis of financial strategy and proposed plans and developments. Treasury control of the purse will be at its most intense with the implementation of Whole Government Accounts; it remains to be seen how effective this will be in avoiding poor spending decisions and preventing waste.

THE BANK OF ENGLAND

The Bank of England is the United Kingdom's central bank, acts as a banker to the Government, and with the other major banks is a member of the clearing system. Only a few days after the General Election on 6 May 1997, the Chancellor of the Exchequer announced[9] that the Bank of England would be given operational responsibility for the setting of interest rates to meet the Government's inflation target. The Bank of England Act 1998 provides a statutory framework for the Bank's role, There is a requirement under section 4 of annual reports to the Chancellor of the Exchequer which must be laid before Parliament. There is a Monetary Policy Committee of the Bank that meets on a monthly basis and sets interest rates. The Chancellor of the Exchequer provides broad policy parameters for the Bank. Accountability for the new arrangements is through a report to the Treasury Committee and to the House of Commons. Senior officials from the Bank make regular appearances before the Treasury Committee, particularly on the work of the Monetary Policy Committee. The Treasury Committee holds hearings to confirm nominations to the Monetary Policy Committee and may question the proposed appointee.[10] The Bank issues a Quarterly Inflation Report, a Quarterly Bulletin containing research and analysis, an Annual Report and Accounts of its activities. The Bank also publishes the Financial Stability Report containing informed debate about financial stability . In extreme economic circumstances the Government retains the right to override the Bank, but subject to ratification by the House of Commons.

The Bank of England's *Framework for Monetary Policy*[11] has twin objectives, to deliver price stability through the Government's inflation target and to support the Government's economic policy. The Bank's performance over the past years has been well regarded[12] since the introduction of the Euro throughout most of Europe, but not in the United Kingdom.[13]

[9] HC Deb., 20 May 1997, col. 508.

[10] HC Deb. 520 (1999–2000) The Treasury Committee's views are not binding on the Treasury, and only in one instance was the nominee challenged by the committee.

[11] The accounts held in the Bank of England on the Government's behalf are the Consolidated Fund and the National Loans Fund. Also held are the accounts of the Inland Revenue and Customs and Excise (the Revenue Departments), the National Debt Commissioners, and the Paymaster General. There are detailed internal rules for the various financial transactions carried out by central government departments including the use of credit cards, debit cards, and the handling of receipts and payments. The Monetary Policy Committee comprises four external members appointed by the Government, the Governor of the Bank of England, two Deputy Governors, and two other senior officials of the Bank. Meetings are attended by a non-voting Treasury representative. The decision is frequently made by majority vote: see part II of the Bank of England Act 1998. See Bank of England, *Framework for Monetary Policy* (21 Oct. 1999).

[12] HM Treasury, *Reforming Britain's Economic and Financial Policy: Towards Greater Economic Stability* (eds E. Balls and G.O'Donnell) Palgrave, Basingstoke, 2002.

[13] R. Ware, *EMU: The Constitutional Implications*, House of Commons Research Paper 98/78, 27 July 1998.

Interest rates set by the Bank and removed from overt political manipulation by the Government of the day, have resulted in economic stability and low inflation.[14] The United Kingdom economy is scrutinized by external sources such as the International Monetary Fund (IMF) and the Organisation for Economic Cooperation and Development (OECD)[15] providing the Bank with comparative analysis in making decisions about the United Kingdom economy.[16] The Bank's performance is regularly monitored by the former House of Lords Select Committee on the Monetary Policy Committee of the Bank of England, now the House of Lords Economic Affairs Committee.

PARLIAMENT

'Parliamentary control of the purse' is a basic principle of the constitution that has evolved since before the Bill of Rights 1689. *Government Accounting 2000* stipulates the protection afforded by the constitutional principle of the requirement of statutory authorization for the expenditure of public funds and for the raising of finance through taxation.[17] The nature of the protection rests on three principles, namely that propriety and regularity require parliamentary approval for departmental activities and services; that the Treasury may be delegated approval for departmental expenditure subject to ultimate parliamentary authority; and finally, that parliamentary authority, while at times dependent on Treasury support for much of its control mechanisms, is nevertheless paramount.

The requirement of statutory authority instituted by Gladstone in the mid-nineteenth century created a 'circle of control' based on an annual cycle of revenue and expenditure. The management of public revenue is carried out by the Crown, but for practical purposes Cabinet decisions rest on the support of the House of Commons. Strong party controls over the members of the House of Commons and the general influence of ministers where the Government has a majority in the House of Commons reduce the House of Commons' powers of control in practice to the right to criticize. In reality both political power and economic control over public expenditure actually reside in the Government of the day.

An example of how both parliamentary authority and government control may operate is provided in the introduction to *The Code for Fiscal Stability* of March 1998. The Code is inspired by the Government's desire to bring 'openness, transparency and accountability' over monetary policy, especially with the Bank of England's new role in monitoring and adjusting interest rates. The Code was laid before Parliament and was approved by resolution of the House of Commons. It received statutory authority through the Finance Act 1998 which permits amending Codes to be introduced in the future to ensure 'transparency, stability, responsibility, fairness and efficiency' in the formulation and implementation of fiscal and debt management. The effect is to improve government information to

[14] Members of the Euro zone are subject to the Resolution of the European Council on the Stability and Growth Pact OJ c 236, 2.8 1997.

[15] OECD Economic Surveys: United Kingdom volume 2005/6. There are also IMF country reports.

[16] The Bank has a useful working paper series that provides authoritative analysis of the economy. See for example: Andrew Benito, 'How does the down-payment constraint affect the UK housing market?' Working Paper No. 294. In April 2007, the Bank of England wrote to the Chancellor of the Exchequer explaining why the Bank failed to meet inflation targets set by the Chancellor.

[17] The Bill of Rights 1689 Art. 4 requires parliamentary authority for the raising of taxation. See G. Reid, *The Politics of Financial Control* (1966); M. Wright, *Treasury Control of the Civil Service 1854–1874* (1969); Erskine May, *Parliamentary Practice* (1997) 732.

Parliament on economic and fiscal assumptions and to emphasize the importance of resource accounting as part of the Government's treatment of capital assets. More fundamental is the adoption of a 'golden rule' over the economic cycle where 'the Government will only borrow to invest and not to fund current expenditure'. A second rule is the Sustainable Investment Rule, requiring that over the economic cycle, the public sector national debt is to be held at 'a stable and prudent' level.[18]

The primacy of government control is evidenced in standing Orders of the House of Commons numbers 46 and 47, which provide the Crown with the initiative and sole responsibility for expenditure. Private members, including the Opposition, are unable to propose increased charges on public funds or initiate legislation involving expenditure out of public funds without a financial resolution. An Appropriation Act satisfies the requirement of statutory authority through the supply procedure of the House of Commons on an annual basis by means of the Consolidated Fund Acts and by an Appropriation Act. The revenue side is largely undertaken though the Inland Revenue, Customs and Excise, and as part of the Budget and Public Finance Directorate of the Treasury.

SUPPLY PROCEDURE AND THE CONSOLIDATED FUND

The supply procedures required to enable the House of Commons to vote supply and provide the Government with funds from the Consolidated Fund, are technical and formal. Little substantial scrutiny is involved in such procedures. The policy objectives on which the money is spent are not determined by the Commons but by the Government of the day. Policy objectives, however, underline the constitutional authority of Parliament and the internal controls exercised by the Treasury. It must be emphasized that presentation of the main estimates to Parliament does not provide sufficient authority for expenditure. Statutory authority from the Appropriation Act is required. The system is complicated by the fact that in any one Parliamentary session Parliament is asked to authorize estimates for the current year together with Votes on Account for future years and any excesses from the previous year.

Supply estimates provide the House of Commons with the information needed to provide the Government with funds from the Consolidated Fund. Votes on Account and the Consolidated Fund Act must be approved by the date of the budget. Estimates of departmental expenditure are drawn up and must be approved by resolutions of the Commons for the necessary release of funds from the Consolidated Fund. The Treasury publishes a single volume entitled *Central Government Main Estimates* containing one estimate for each department. The estimates provide the major part – over 70 per cent – of annual public expenditure. The Treasury persuaded Parliament in 2001 to replace cash based Appropriation Accounts with Simplified Estimates and Departmental Resource Accounts.[19]

There is an annual Appropriation Act, which is normally not subject to any debate, enacted by July/August each year authorizing the Bank of England to make payments from

[18] Since 1997 this is subject to the National Audit Office auditing the forecasts to ensure that Treasury assumptions are made transparent, though the system of making forecasts is not open to such scrutiny. See: Fabrizio Balassone and Daniele Franco, 'Public investment, the stability Pact and the "golden rule" *Fiscal Studies*' (2000) vol. 21, no. 2, pp. 207–9.

[19] HM Treasury, *Central Government Supply Estimates 2002–3 for the year ending 31st March 2003: Main Supply Estimates* (HC Paper 795), 2001–2.

the Consolidated Fund. The Appropriation Act gives statutory authority for the distribution of money between votes, but this often follows the spending of some of the money, which needs only the Consolidated Fund Act (giving a total figure) for approval. The estimates must conform to Treasury format and approval and must not be altered unless Treasury authority has been granted.[20] In 2004, the Government introduced a reform aimed to strengthen parliamentary and select committee scrutiny of the estimates. There are two Appropriation Acts in a Parliamentary session, one in March for the previous financial year, the other in July for the current main estimates.[21]

The audit carried out by the Comptroller and Auditor General discussed below is focused on the estimates which, when divided into heads of expenditure, appear as 'votes'.

Departments work on the supply estimates in the summer or early autumn of each financial year. On or about the time of the budget each year, the estimates are published. If a department's needs exceed the estimates, then a 'supplementary' may be passed subject to Treasury and parliamentary approval. The Standing Orders of the Commons provide the Government with three opportunities to introduce supplementary estimates, with the benefit of a guillotine procedure ensuring their speedy passage. Supplementaries for summer are presented in June, for winter in November, and for spring in February. At other times of the year estimates may be submitted but without the benefit of the guillotine procedure. In 2004 the Government introduced a change that provides select committees up to 14 days to consider supplementary estimates to allow more time for discussion.

The Treasury regards seriously the requirement for statutory authority for authorization of public expenditure which 'must be and can only be given year by year by means of votes and the Appropriation Act'.[22] A minister 'when exercising functions which may involve the expenditure of money may only do what he does if Parliament votes him the money'.[23] Since 1982, there have been three specific days to consider the Estimates. The Commons may only reduce the estimates, but even this is unlikely if the Government of the day has an overall majority. Parliament is unable to initiate its own expenditure on its own behalf rather than the Government's. In modern times the Commons has not rejected an estimate and the scrutiny function appears a limited one.

20 See HM Treasury, *Managing Resources – Full Implementation of Resources Accounting and Budgeting* London: April, 2001.

21 The reform was the result of the work of the Liaison Committee, the Public Accounts Committee, The Treasury Committee and the Procedure Committee. See Procedure Committee (2003–4) Estimates and Appropriation Procedure HC 393.

22 Details of the rules relating to supply may be found in Supply Procedure, *Government Accounting 2000* revised The Appropriation Act begins life as the Consolidated Fund (Appropriation) Bill. Estimate day debates may take place in July and at the time of the Appropriation Act; in Nov.–Dec. for the winter supplementary estimates followed by any debates and a Consolidated Fund Act; and in Feb.–Mar. for the spring supplementary estimates, followed by any debates on the Consolidated Fund Act. HM Treasury, *Supply and other Financial Procedure of the House of Commons* (1977), paras 47–49, now largely updated by *Government Accounting 2000*. The Public Accounts Committee considered in 1932 the question whether the Appropriation Act is sufficient authority for the expenditure, whether there is or is not specific statutory authority for the service concerned. The Treasury accepted that provided the Government of the day undertakes to ask Parliament for authorization, services under the Appropriation Act would come within the PAC Concordat. However, in the first instance, it is preferable to seek specific statutory authority. The Estimates indicate where proposed expenditure is to be met by the Appropriation Act as the sole authority.

23 HM Treasury, *Supply and other Financial Procedures of the House of Common*s (1977) paras 47–9.

Over the years the presentation of the Estimates has become more attractive and readable and today they contain economic information and are cross-referenced to the Departmental Report. Since agreement in March 1995 between the Public Accounts Committee, the Government, and the Treasury Committee to introduce a simplified format of the Estimates with effect from 1996–7, the estimates are published in a single volume divided into three parts and linked to overall government planning. There is a new requirement on departments to produce an Estimate Memorandum to their parliamentary select committee at the same time as Main or Supplementary Estimates are presented.

THE CONTINGENCIES FUND

An example of a lacuna in Commons control over expenditure is the Contingencies Fund which may be used to finance urgent expenditure. The fund is a reserve fund intended to meet unforeseen items of expenditure and where advances that are made are regarded as 'exceptional'. In technical terms it is used 'to meet payments for urgent services in anticipation of parliamentary provisions for those services becoming available'. Total advances outstanding from the fund should not exceed two per cent of the previous year's total estimates provision. Money withdrawn from the Fund must be repaid. The Treasury may authorize payment out of the Fund subject to the limit of two per cent set under the Contingencies Fund Act 1974. The use of the Fund is regarded as 'exceptional', particularly if the Fund is used for a new service. The instructions contained in *Government Accounting 2000* provide that the criterion is not convenience, but urgency in the public interest. If the amount of money involved, or the potentially contentious nature of the proposal is such as to create special difficulty in justifying anticipation of specific parliamentary approval, it may be necessary to consider the alternative of immediate presentation of a Supplementary Estimate, outside the normal time-table, to be followed by a special Consolidated Fund Bill.

The Contingencies Fund offers an unusual example in that the main scrutiny of the Government's use of the Fund largely depends on effective Treasury control. Legislation giving authority for the expenditure involved must be introduced at the earliest possible time and ought never to be postponed. Guidance issued in 1992 makes clear that the Government of the day must be prepared 'to take the responsibility of assuming that legislation being considered by parliament will pass into law'. In 1974 the then Financial Secretary to the Treasury explained that '[t]he Contingences Fund cannot be drawn upon for any purpose for which the statutory authority of Parliament is required until legislation seeking that authority has been given a Second Reading.' Underlying this point since 1997 are improvements in the format and detailed rules on how Parliament should be informed of any advances from the fund.[24]

The Contingencies Fund has been used for a variety of purposes. These include relief of national disasters, the manufacture of the first Atomic Bomb, victory celebrations, and in time of war for financing urgent supplies. Recently it has been used to fund the Pergau Dam project following the decision of the divisional court declaring the aid to be *ultra vires*.[25] Concern about the use of the Contingencies Fund is focused on the question of parliamentary accountability. The total expenditure from the Fund is considerable. There are no clear

[24] See J. McEldowney 'The Contingencies Fund and the Parliamentary Scrutiny of Public Finance' [1988] *Pub. L* 232–45.

[25] See discussion below.

statutory conditions for expenditure being advanced from the Fund. Reliance is placed on the system of internal Treasury control and audit[26] by the Comptroller and Auditor General. No select committee directly monitors the use of the Fund. In the area of policy there are no satisfactory means to inquire into the policy behind the Government's use of the Fund prior to the Fund being used. Any *ex post facto* inquiry faces a corresponding difficulty as the money has already been used. The fact that the money is to be repaid seems hardly an adequate safeguard when questions arise about the purpose for which the Fund has been used.

Doubts about the legality of the existence of the Fund were raised by MPs and members of the Treasury and Civil Service Select Committee in 1983, but have been seemingly resolved, and the Fund is assumed by the Treasury to be legal. The Contingencies Fund is an example of where Parliament has, through inactivity, allowed an exception to the principle that Parliament should vote money before expenditure is incurred. There is also tacit acceptance that Treasury control may be more effective in this instance than parliamentary scrutiny.

THE COURTS

The courts have, since the sixteenth century, accepted Parliament's role in the matter of financial control. However, some judicial involvement in public expenditure remains. While major issues about public finance arise on the supply side involving issues of taxation. there is limited opportunity for judicial oversight in matters of expenditure. In the case of central government, in *Auckland Harbour Board* v. *The King*,[27] Viscount Haldane noted that payments out of the Consolidated Fund without parliamentary authority were illegal. In *Woolwich Building Society* v. *Inland Revenue Commissioner (No. 2)*[28] the House of Lords considered the general principle that money paid to a public body pursuant to an *ultra vires* demand for tax should be repayable as of right. The *Woolwich* case arose out of an Inland Revenue demand for tax from the Woolwich Building Society. The demand was later declared by the courts to have no legal basis. It was accepted that the money paid to the Revenue was not paid under any mistake of law on the part of the taxpayer; but the Woolwich Building Society had no express statutory right to repayment of the money. The House of Lords held that money paid pursuant to an *ultra vires* demand was *prima facie* repayable as a common-law right of the subject. In the *Woolwich* case the payment of tax amounted to almost £57 million with interest and dividends, an illustration of the role of the courts in revenue matters with an indirect effect on expenditure totals. The government has estimated that the total cost of repaying composite rate tax to all Building Societies

26 See Contingencies Fund 2004–5 HC 755, 3 March 2006.

27 [1925] AC 318, 326.

28 [1992] 3 All ER 737 at 764 D–E (also see Lord Slynn at 783E–G). J. Beatson, 'Restitution of Taxes, Levies and Other Imposts: Defining the Extent of the *Woolwich* Principle' [1993] 109 *Law Quarterly Review* 401. *Pepper* v. *Hart* [1993] 1 All ER 86 on the taxation of benefits in kind which may lead to £30 million in refundable taxes.

In *Metzger and others* v. *Department of Health and Social Security* [1977] 3 All ER 444 the duty of the Secretary of State for Social Services to carry out reviews of the rates of pension payable under the Social Security Act 1975 was considered and the cost of uprating pension benefits ascertained. The impact on public expenditure would have been large if the court had decided to grant a declaration. In the event it refused to do so.

which had overpaid amounted to £250 million. There is also the prospect for challenges due to the Human Rights Act 1998.[29] A challenge from 'tax-paying pacifists'[30] seeking to adopt the jurisprudence of the European Court of Human Rights on Article 9 (freedom of thought and conscience) to challenge the use of taxation for military purposes was rejected by the Court of Appeal. This does not rule out the use of Article 9 arguments in the future, depending on how far the Strasbourg court is willing to develop its jurisprudence on human rights into this area.[31]

THE PERGAU DAM CASE

Although the role of the courts generally in decisions on taxation and public expenditure[32] has been slight, there is considerable scope for future development. This is highlighted when apparently technical issues of the legality of expenditure raise broader questions of policy involving concepts such as propriety and regularity which also raise questions about the economy and efficiency of expenditure. In *R* v. *Secretary of State for Foreign Affairs, ex parte World Development Movement Ltd*,[33] the Pergau Dam case, already mentioned in this chapter, the applicant, an international pressure group, challenged the legality of aid granted by the Secretary of State for Foreign Affairs to fund the construction of the Pergau Dam in Malaysia. The pressure group relied on information obtained through a National Audit Office Report and information gleaned from debates and evidence taken by the Public Accounts Committee and the Foreign Affairs Committee. The National Audit Office and the Public Accounts Committee assumed the legality of the aid but criticized aspects of its value for money. The National Audit Office regarded the allocation of money as falling under policy matters that fell within the remit of ministers. This excluded from its consideration the merits of the policy. However it appeared that the Accounting Officer had serious reservations about the project.

Despite such reservations written ministerial instructions were given to proceed with the financial aid. The Pergau project was funded, purportedly under section 1 of the Overseas Development and Co-operation Act 1980. The Divisional Court held that the provision of

[29] *R(Wilkinson) v IRC* [2005] UKHL 30 and *R (Morgan Grenfell) v Special Commissioner* [2002] STC 786.

[30] *The Peace Tax Seven Case*, High Court. See [2005] EWRC 1914(Admin) CO/1698/2005 and in the Court of Appeal, [2006] EWCA Civ 504.

[31] See *R (Wilkinson)* v. *IRC* [2005] UKHL 30.

[32] In 1975, in *Congreve* v. *Home Office* [1976] QB 629, the Court of Appeal held that it was unlawful for the Home Office to make use of its revocation powers under the Wireless Telegraphy Act 1949, to revoke TV licences to prevent licence holders benefiting from an overlapping licence purchased to avoid an increase in the licence fee. Congreve and about 20,000 other licence holders had purchased a second licence, while their existing licence was still valid in anticipation of an increase in the licence fee. Lord Denning claimed that the Bill of Rights 1689 had been infringed as a levying of money without grant of Parliament. There is some doubt on this interpretation as Congreve had sought avoidance of a tax through the purchase of a second licence, clearly not intended by the Wireless Telegraphy Act. However the case illustrates how the judges will use statutory interpretation to uphold the principle of authorization. In *Bowles* v. *Bank of England* [1913] 1 Ch. 57 Bowles was successful in suing the Bank of England for declarations that income tax could not be deducted by virtue of a budget resolution alone, and until such tax had been imposed by Act of Parliament he was not required to pay it. The case provided the background for what is now the Provisional Collection of Taxes Act 1968 which gives statutory force for a limited time to resolutions of the House of Commons varying taxation levels pending the enactment in the Finance Act.

[33] [1995] 1 All ER 617. See I. Harden, F. White, and K. Hollingsworth, 'Value for Money and Administrative Law' [1996] *Pub. L* 661 at 674.

aid was *ultra vires* the 1980 Act. As a result of this decision, the Comptroller and Auditor General qualified his opinion of the aid on the basis of irregularity. Despite this finding and the decision of the Divisional Court, the Government found the necessary additional aid required to finance the dam from a repayable charge on the Contingency Fund. Eventually the money was found from the Reserve Fund. The significance of the case for our purposes is that issues of the legality of public expenditure may involve questions of value for money.

PUBLIC EXPENDITURE BY LOCAL AUTHORITIES

The courts have been more active in the control of public expenditure by local authorities. The opportunity for the courts to exercise control may arise through the audit of local authorities as seen in such cases as *Roberts* v. *Hopwood.*[34] This case led to the imposition of surcharges on the local authority councilors. The House of Lords upheld the use of the surcharge power in the case of *Porter v Magill*[35] involving allegations of local authority-owned homes being allocated on the basis of likely voting preferences. Local government surcharge power is being abolished. Additional powers granted to local government auditors under the Local Government Act 1988 include powers to seek judicial review or apply for prohibition orders to take pre-emptive action to restrain a local authority from unlawful action. Such powers are intended to prevent the local authority from spending illegally or incurring unlawful losses.

There is a long history of courts becoming involved in disputes between central and local government, especially during a period in the 1980s when central government had determined to control high-spending local authorities.[36] Local authorities engaged in innovative schemes or forms of 'creative accounting' to increase expenditure. The courts upheld action by auditors to challenge the legality of such schemes.

In a landmark decision of the House of Lords in *Hazell* v. *Hammersmith*[37] the investment powers of local authorities in loan swap markets was considered. Hammersmith invested substantial sums in the swaps market in order to finance its expenditure when tightly controlled by central government. The swaps market operated on the principle that a borrower at a fixed interest rate contracts with a third party to pay or receive the difference between his interest liability and what it would have been at a variable rate. Many local

34 [1925] AC 318, 326. 35 [2002] 2WLR 37.

36 See M. Loughlin, *Legality and Locality* (1996) 277–90. In *Bromley* v. *Greater London Council* [1982] 1 AC 768 the concept of fiduciary duty was developed and extended to apply to the duty owed by a local authority to its ratepayers. The case involved the now defunct Greater London Council and its policy of providing cheap fares on London Transport. Having regard to the term 'economic' in ss. 1 and 5 of the Transport (London) Act 1969, the House of Lords held that the GLC was not empowered to adopt a fares policy unduly beneficial to transport users at a cost to ratepayers in London. The interpretation of 'economic' involved judicial consideration of the benefits and costs involved. See *R.* v. *Secretary of State for Education, ex parte Avon CC* [1991] 1 QB 558; see also *North Tyneside Metropolitan Borough Council* v. *Allsop* [1991] RVR 104. Also see The Widdicombe Committee, *The Conduct of Local Authority Business*, June 1986 Cmnd 9797; M. Loughlin, *Local Government in the Modern State* (1986), and *Hammersmith and Fulham London Borough Council* v. *Secretary of State for the Environment* [1990] 3 All ER 589, upholding the Secretary of State's charge-capping powers in a draft order approved by resolution of the House of Commons.

37 [1991] 1 All ER 545. But see *Bromley LBC* v. *GLC* [1983] 1 AC 768 on the meaning of 'economic'; see M. Loughlin, 'Innovative Financing in Local Government: The Limits of Legal Instrumentalism – Part I' [1990] *Pub. L* 372–405; S. 111(1) of the Local Government Act 1972. See also the analysis offered by Sir Robert Carnwath, 'The Reasonable Limits of Local Authority Powers' [1996] *Pub. L* 244.

authorities participated in the swap market and at times of growth large returns were received. The auditor questioned the legality of Hammersmith entering the market when doubts were raised about the scale of debt incurred in the market. The House of Lords held that all interest rates swaps and similar schemes were *ultra vires* and void as speculative activities that fell outside the powers of the local authority. The effect of the decision was far-reaching in setting controls over many local authority strategies to find revenue to meet expenditure needs.

In *Crédit Suisse*[38] the District Auditor queried the legality of Allerdale local authority's joint venture companies set up and run by the local authority to support a leisure complex. Crédit Suisse, a leading international banking group, provided the finance for the complex. The Auditor's concerns arose when it was feared that Allerdale might not be able to repay its loans to Crédit Suisse. The Court of Appeal held that such joint venture companies were beyond the powers of the local authority, thus exposing Crédit Suisse to potential liability for any debts. The case underlines a longstanding limitation of creative financing by local authorities .

Central government controls over local authority activities include controls over expenditure and over the amount of central government expenditure allocated to local authorities. Such expenditure controls involve complex economic instruments of wide ranging application and often directly enforced by the courts.

PLANNING AND CONTROLLING PUBLIC EXPENDITURE

We now turn to processes, planning, and control.

THE TREASURY'S ANNUAL PUBLIC EXPENDITURE SURVEY (PES)

It is over 40 years since the Plowden Report recommended that decisions on public expenditure should be taken 'in the light of surveys of public expenditure as a whole over a period of years, and in relation to prospective resources'. The Treasury's annual Public Expenditure Survey (PES) is the central factor in planning and controlling public expenditure.

Inside the Treasury the Budget and Public Finances Directorate sets the agenda between differing departmental demands for money. The Central Expenditure Policy group referees the bids between spending departments and reports through the Chief Secretary to the Treasury to the Cabinet in July on the likely outcome in expenditure totals. Between the end of the PES round in October and the autumn statement in November, winners and losers in the expenditure debate have to be settled. The new Labour government in 1998 introduced

[38] *Crédit Suisse* v. *Borough Council of Allerdale* [1996] 4 All ER 129. See P. A. Watt and J. Fender, 'Feasible Changes in the UK Controls on Local Government Expenditure' (1999) *Public Money and Management* July–Sept. 17–21; DETR, *Modernizing Local Government. Improving Local Financial Accountability* (1998), DETR, *Modernizing Local Government. Capital Finance* (1998), DETR, *Modern Local Government: In Touch with the People* (1998). For a comparative evaluation in this area see D. King and Y. Ma, 'Central Government Control over Local Authority Expenditure: The Overseas Experience', *Public Money and Management*, July–Sept. 1999, 23–8.

the *Code for Fiscal Stability* (referred to earlier), with an emphasis on principles of fiscal management such as transparency, stability, responsibility, fairness, and efficiency.

In September 1992, after the UK's withdrawal from the Exchange Rate Mechanism, the Government's Autumn Statement introduced changes to the system of public expenditure control through the introduction of a New Control Total. This replaced the planning total and excludes the main elements of cyclical social security expenditure and privatization proceeds. It includes local authority self-financed expenditure. Totals for the control of public expenditure include both local and central government expenditure. Refinements have been made, such as, in 1998, the introduction of Total Managed Expenditure (TME) comprising the total of public sector current expenditure and public sector net investment. All expenditure under TME facilitates better management under Treasury scrutiny. In 1998 the introduction of a Comprehensive Spending Review (CSR) allowed departments to take a more radical look at across-the-board expenditure and resist the temptation to see expenditure planning only in terms of an annual review. It also allowed comparison between Departmental Expenditure Limits (DEL) which set firm three-year spending limits (the limits for departmental spending within the public expenditure total) and Actually Managed Expenditure (AME) which covers items which are reviewed and set on annual basis (the actual expenditure undertaken by the department).

PES continues to provide a politically expedient outcome which achieves consensus from ministers, even those with different policy perspectives and even when there may be losers in the rounds of expenditure battles. PES underlines the Treasury's pre-eminence and the role of the Chief Secretary in the development of ministerial policy. PES supported by the Comprehensive Spending Review, and the *Code of Fiscal Stability* has the potential to transform the setting of public expenditure totals through greater transparency and openness in the planning process.

THE TREASURY AND DEPARTMENTAL CONTROLS OVER PUBLIC EXPENDITURE

The Bank of England's role in respect of interest rates marked a shift from prime ministerial influence to Treasury control. This shift is most marked in recent years and is well documented in accounts on the role of the Chancellor of the Exchequer.[39] The various rules that set out apparent controls on the discretion of the Treasury and Chancellor, such as fiscal rules that determine the amount of borrowing relative to the size of the economy, are Treasury made rules. The Treasury is effectively empowered to self-regulate. The perception of increasing Treasury influence is apparent from the reconstruction of the old building into a newly designed set of offices for the 1,050 staff. The offices were designed by Norman Foster and opened in 2002. The Treasury has undoubtedly gained from its newly-found self-esteem[40] and improvements in the economic instruments to manage the economy.

39 Robert Preston, *Brown's Britain*, London: Short Books (2004) pp. 76–7. The importance of removing unnecessary burdens is highlighted in the Hampton Review, *Reducing Administrative Burdens* (2005).

40 There is also the quality of the civil service and a list of distinguished outsiders including Shriti Vadera from UBS, Nick Stern from the World Bank and John Kingman from BP.

The pre-eminence afforded to the Treasury through PES is complementary to the overall role of the Treasury in managing and controlling public expenditure.[41] It exercises internal and less visible systems of control as well as external and more visible techniques. Treasury control is much improved through the adoption of a variety of *a priori* techniques. It prepares, monitors, audits, and authorizes under parliamentary scrutiny according to set rules and procedures. It produces a large loose-leaf guide to *Government Accounting 2000* which is regularly up-dated with amendments, currently No4/05. Conventions, practices, and statutory arrangements are noted and described. In addition, and dating back to 1934, with a revision in 1977, there is a *Treasury Handbook: Supply and other Financial Procedures of the House of Commons*. The *Code of Fiscal Stability* provides an important foundation for future developments that contains affirmation by the House of Commons. In addition the Treasury has a *Handbook on Regularity and Propriety*. There is also a *Financial Reporting Manual 2006–07* that sets out all the technical accounting and disclosure requirements for the annual report and accounts.

In preparing legislation, departments are required to keep the Treasury informed of any proposal with a financial implication. Consultation is expected at an early stage and the amendments to Bills should be included if they affect the financial arrangements. This represents a major influence over how departments consider spending public money. Since the late 1990s the Treasury has adopted a more strategic role with re-organization and regular contact with spending departments through regular spending reviews and targets setting inputs and outputs.

Treasury control may be exercised within government departments through the Accounting Officer appointed by the Treasury, whose responsibilities are contained in detailed Memoranda. Accounting Officers are in effect expected to combine their task of ensuring a high standard of financial management in their departments with their duty to serve their ministers. The Accounting Officer is given responsibility for signing accounts and appearing as the principal witness on behalf of the department before the Committee of Public Accounts (PAC). The Accounting Officer has the crucial role in ensuring that Treasury sanction is obtained for expenditure and that funds are applied to the extent and for the purposes authorized by Parliament. The internal network of Treasury control over expenditure depends on his exercise of authority. He is a powerful ally to government, Treasury, and the PAC in controlling expenditure and ensuring propriety. He provides the link between internal control and the external audit carried out by the Comptroller and Auditor General (C & AG) and the Public Accounts Committee while maintaining his independent status. It can be appreciated that in practical terms the effectiveness of the C & AG depends on his obtaining the cooperation of Accounting Officers and government departments which is of crucial importance to the Treasury system of internal audit.

There is a specialized manual for Government Internal Audit. This contains the basic standards for the Treasury's internal audit representing good practice. An internal audit is an independent appraisal within a department as a service to management in measuring and evaluating standards within the department. Through the system of internal audit the Accounting Officer may be assisted in his task. Internal audit is not however seen as a

[41] See House of Commons Research Paper 05/92 *The Centre of Government – No. 10, The Cabinet and HM Treasury* 21 Dec. 2005, C. Thain 'Treasury Rules OK? The Further Evolution of a British Institution' British Journal of Politics and International Relations Vol. 6 No. 1 Feb. 2004.

substitute for line management; it is a means to ensure that appraisal within a department is properly carried out. It is usual practice to carry out such appraisal by the appointment of a unit charged with responsibility to the Accounting Officer. As the Accounting Officer is usually the permanent head of the department this 'reflects the view that finance and policy cannot be considered separately'. Thus good management is the key to his function. He must ensure compliance with parliamentary requirements in the control of public expenditure. In his role he is to avoid waste and extravagance and to seek economy, efficiency, and effectiveness in the use of all the resources made available to the department. It appears that the Accounting Officer carries out internally, as part of his management function, a similar function to the external examinations carried out by the C & AG. Achieving internal audit in these terms means having a clear view of objectives and the use of resources, assigning well defined responsibilities and processing the correct information, particularly about costs in the training and expertise required. However the Accounting Officer is also expressly concerned with *policy*. He has responsibility to advise ministers on all 'matters of financial propriety and regularity' and to ensure that departmental expenditure is justified to the PAC. In matters where a minister may disagree he is free to set out his own advice and the overruling of it by the minister. He is free to point out to ministers the possibility of potential criticism by the PAC of ministerial decisions. This in effect was the procedure followed in the Pergau Dam affair discussed above.

Procedures exist for an Accounting Officer to notify the Comptroller and Auditor General should his advice be overruled. There are important responsibilities to ensure that appropriate advice is tendered to ministers 'on all matters of financial propriety and regularity', and more broadly as to all 'considerations of prudent and economical administration, efficiency and effectiveness'. Thus where the Accounting Officer is unhappy with a course of action he is free to draw the attention of the minister to his advice. If overruled then 'both the advice and the minister's instructions are recorded in writing immediately afterwards'.[42]

RESOURCE ACCOUNTING

Consistent with a more managerial approach to budgeting than in the past is the development of resource accounting based on an accruals accounting system intended to match more closely resources used to meet departmental objectives. The Government Resources and Accounts Act 2000 provides for the adoption of resource accounting and budgeting [43] and eventually the introduction of *Whole of Government Accounts* consistent with the United Kingdom Generally Accepted Practice regime,[44] providing a more complete financial analysis than at present.

42 *Government Accounting 2000* and amendment 4/05 s. 4.1.2 para. 15.

43 The Government Resources and Accounts Act 2000 amends the 1866 and 1921 Exchequer and Audit Departments Act.

44 D. A. Heald and G. Georgiou, 'Consolidation principles and practices for the UK government sector' (2000) 30 *Accounting and Business Research* 153. HM Treasury, Whole of Government Accounts progress to December 2000, *Memorandum to the Committee of Public Accounts and the Treasury Select Committee* (unpublished).

Broadly defined, an accruals accounting system adopts 'a balance sheet' approach to public sector accounts intended to provide an accurate and detailed account of public expenditure by considering the true costs to departments. The main benefits of accruals accounting are that: it records expenditure and income in the accounting period to which they relate; spreads the cost of capital items across their useful lives; provides a detailed snapshot of the assets, liabilities, and net worth of an organization at a given moment of time; and through a balance sheet provides a better picture of the true cost of departments' activities. Finally, accruals accounting is intended to increase information and detailed inventories of departmental holdings, deployment, and stewardship of assets.

Resource accounting is intended to match more closely resources used to departmental objectives. The publication of Whole of Government Accounts provides transparency and helps delineate the line between public and private sector more clearly.

DEVOLUTION AND FUNDING THE SCOTTISH PARLIAMENT, NATIONAL ASSEMBLY FOR WALES AND THE NORTHERN IRELAND ASSEMBLY

The creation of the Scottish Parliament, National Assembly for Wales, and Northern Ireland Assembly requires consideration of the financial relationship between the United Kingdom's financial system of control and the new devolved administrations. The general principles are contained in *A Statement of Funding Policy* issued by the Treasury. These are: that responsibility for overall fiscal policy, and in the drawing up of budgets and public expenditure allocation is retained within the UK's Treasury; that the UK government funding of devolution will normally be determined through departmental spending reviews; and that devolved administrations will make decisions for programmes within the overall totals.

The UK Parliament will vote the relevant provision for the devolved administration by means of a grant. At the devolved level additional elements of the budget will come from locally financed expenditure, funds from the European Commission, and borrowing undertaken by local authorities. In the case of Scotland, additional funds may arise from tax raising powers under devolution through the Scottish Variable Rate of Income Tax and also through non-domestic rates. These arrangements have given the Scottish Parliament and committees an opportunity to scrutinize the spending plans and priorities of the Scottish Executive. There is a three-stage process from April to June (Year 1) and September to December (Year 1) and January to February (Year 2). There are some striking innovations such as the Finance Committee that overseas the consultation process within Parliament and an annual evaluation report allowing strategic planning throughout each year of the spending review period. The Executive submits a provisional expenditure plan (an annual evaluation report) and this is considered by Parliament, along with a report of the Finance Committee. The Executive prepares a draft budget in September including spending plans for the following financial year. Based on comments made and information received that it is possible for the Finance Committee to make out an alternative budget, but within spending limits set by the Executive. In December, the Finance Committee prepares a report which is debated in plenary session and this allows amendments to be made to the Executive's spending plans. There is an annual Budget and accompanying Bill presented in

January by the Executive. This provides parliamentary authority for spending in the coming financial year. Once the Bill is introduced it is given a speedy passage as only members of the Executive are able to move amendments. The advantages of this system are that there is more transparency than is the case with the UK Parliament and an opportunity for fuller debate and reflection on spending plans; counter-proposals may be made through the Finance Committee.

It is clear that in respect of devolution, the UK government retains a number of techniques of overall financial control.[45] These include the right to make adjustments to the budgets to devolved administrations, and the assumption that devolved administrations will carry the burden of any additional or unforeseen financial burdens. The UK government retains responsibilities for the receipt and disbursement of funds from the European Community.

It is generally assumed that any changes in the budgets for devolved administrations funded from the UK's tax revenues or by borrowing will depend on the spending plans of the comparable departments of the UK. The requirement of apparent 'parity' will be achieved in general through an ingenious formula known as the Barnett formula.[46]

The Barnett Formula determines changes to expenditure within the assigned budgets of the devolved administrations. Under the Formula, Scotland, Wales and Northern Ireland receive a population-based proportion of changes in planned spending on comparable UK Government services in England, England and Wales or Great Britain as appropriate.

The formula works on the principle that changes to the planned spending of departments of the UK government are calculated and applied against a comparability percentage and against each country's population as a proportion of the UK's population.

There is an Auditor General for Scotland, and his office scrutinizes the departments that fall under the Scottish Executive, NHS trusts and health boards, further education colleges, Scottish Water and various government agencies.[47] This amounts to nearly 200 public bodies in Scotland with expenditure in excess of £26 million. There is a separate Accounts Commission with the remit of scrutinizing the accounts of 32 local councils and 34 joint boards and reports with recommendation to the Scottish Executive.

45 See Iain McLean and Alistair McMillan, 'The distribution of public expenditure across UK regions' *Fiscal Studies* (2003) vol. 24, no. 1 pp. 45–71.

46 The Barnett formula was first adopted in the 1978 Public Expenditure Survey under Joel Barnett, then Chief Secretary to the Treasury. *Scotland's Parliament*, Cm 3658; Scotland Act 1998; 'Serving Scotland's Needs: Department of the Secretary of State for Scotland and the Forestry Commission: The Government's Expenditure Plans for 1999–2002' Cm 4215 (Mar. 1999). *A Voice for Wales*, Cm 3718; Government of Wales Act 1998; The Government's Expenditure Plans 1999–2002, Departmental Report by the Welsh Office, Cm 4216 (Mar. 1999). *Belfast Agreement*, 10 Apr. 1998; Northern Ireland Act 1998; Northern Ireland Expenditure Plans and Priorities – The Government's Expenditure Plans 1999–2002 Cm 4217 (Mar. 1999). HM Treasury, *Funding the Scottish Parliament, National Assembly for Wales and Northern Ireland Assembly*, 31 Mar. 1999. In Scotland, Northern Ireland, and Wales local authorities may borrow within set limits to fund their capital expenditure. There are some exceptions to the Barnett formula, as where various categories of expenditure are the sole responsibility of the devolved administration. HM Treasury, *Funding the Scottish Parliament, National Assembly for Wales and Northern Ireland's Assembly*, 31 Mar. 1999, para. 3.3. See further Chapters 9, 10 and 11.

47 This amounts to about 200 public accounts. There are 25 Scottish Executive departments, 23 NHS boards and trusts, 32 councils, 40 police, fire and other bodies, 39 further education colleges, and 37 non-departmental public bodies.

In Wales there is an Auditor General for Wales with a Wales Audit Office, established in 2005 and replacing the Audit Commission and the National Audit Office in Wales. This has resulted in a unified system of audit for public services with a staff of around 230. Reports are laid before the Welsh Assembly, specifically the National Assembly's Audit Committee and this provides an opportunity for issues to be raised and discussed. In the cases of Scotland and Wales, both Auditor Generals exercise similar functions to their English equivalent considered in more detail below. However, unlike England, both Auditor Generals are able to scrutinize local and central government. This encourages an interconnected approach to auditing the public sector.

Taken together accountability falls on the devolved administration, with the UK Treasury operating under the system of financial control.

PRIVATE FINANCE AND PUBLIC PROJECTS

Private financing[48] for public projects provides an important opportunity to shift the burden that falls on the public purse onto the private sector.[49] The principle underlying encouraging private finance is that it may lead to better executed projects, provide close cooperation between private and public sectors, avoid government deficits, and bridge the gap between public spending and revenue income. The Private Finance Initiative was launched in 1992 and was intended to achieve closer cooperation between the public and private sectors. A variety of projects for PFI were identified in the National Health Service, roads, prisons, tunnels, light railway systems, major equipment, and office accommodation.[50] PFI developed the twin objectives of encouraging value for money in any public sector expenditure and placing the financial risks on the private sector. Arising out of PFI arrangements is the Public Private Partnerships Programme, introduced by the Labour Government and intended to encourage rationalization and upgrading of local authority property, to improve value for money, to encourage the use of joint ventures, and to remove unnecessary obstacles to partnership.

PFI has grown in scale since 1992 and has particularly increased in the past few years. Taken as a whole it is estimated that 'investment in the private sector under the PFI is equivalent to 17 per cent of total public sector investment under the three-year period covered by the Comprehensive Spending Review'. According to the National Audit Office,[51] by

[48] See *Economic and Fiscal Strategy Report 1998: Stability and Investment for the Long-term*, Cm 3978 (June 1998).Until 1989 private capital could be advanced for the public sector only in strict accordance with the Ryrie rules, Treasury enforced restrictions on private-sector involvement in public projects. See Memorandum by Professor David Heald, 'Private Finance in the UK Public Sector: Escaping from the Dilemmas of the Ryrie Rules' *Treasury and Civil Service Select Committee* 1992–3 HC 508–1; M. Freedland, 'Public Law and Private Finance – Placing the Private Finance Initiative in a Public Law Frame' [1998] *Pub. L* 288. See *PFI: Strengthening long-term partnerships* (2006).

[49] See Grahame Allen, *The Private Finance Initiative(PFI)* Research Paper 03/79 21 Oct. 2003.

[50] For details see HC Debs, 12 Nov. 1992, col. 998; *Private Finance*, Treasury Release 20/93, 17 Feb. 1993. NAO, *PFI Contract for the New Dartford and Gravesham Hospital*, HC 423 (1998–9); NAO, *Examining the Value for Money of Deals under the Private Finance Initiative*, HC 739 (1998–9). NAO, *PFI: The First Four Design, Build, Finance and Operate Road Contracts*, HC 476 (1997–8); NAO, *PFI Contract to Complete and Operate A74(M) M74 Motorway in Scotland*, HC 356 (1998–9). NAO, *PFI Contracts for Bridgend and Fazakerley Prisons*, HC 253 (1997–8). See NAO, *Examining the Value for Money of Deals under the Private Finance Initiative*, HC 739 (1998–9).

[51] National Audit Office, *Managing the relationship to secure a successful partnership in PFI projects*, HC 375 (2001–2). See National Audit Office Annual Report 2006.

2001/2 there were over 400 PFI contracts with departmental expenditure of around £100 billion. This was increased by 1 April 2003 to 570 PFI contracts with a total capital value of £36 billion with departmental expenditure of over £110 billion. Currently, there are at least 700 PFI projects with a total value of £46 billion that cover over 20 different sectors. The significance of PFI is likely to increase following the 2006 budget. These further increases bring PFI to 10–15 per cent of total investment in public services. This figure relates to England only as PFI is a devolved matter. This means that the operation of PFI is one of the largest programmes in the world. Assessing the value of PFI projects is controversial.[52] Criticism of PFI is long standing and the lack of transparency over complex and technical details has added to the suspicion and controversy that surround many schemes. A further concern is that parliamentary scrutiny of PF is ad hoc, and is too narrowly focused on issues of impropriety. Departmental select committees might become more involved in monitoring PFI schemes, and public unease might be allayed by the increase in parliamentary scrutiny. The NAO have undertaken more than 50 studies of individual PFIs and claims substantial savings of £750 million over six years. Risk management has improved as public sector experience has grown. Improvements to PFI have included better controls and monitoring, shortening procurement times and overruns, and strengthening payment systems and avoiding fraud. Refinancing of some projects has come about because of poor central government controls.[53]

AUDIT TECHNIQUES IN THE CONTROL OF PUBLIC EXPENDITURE

The adoption of audit strategies for the public sector infiltrates almost every form of decision-making in a wide variety of institutions.

PARLIAMENT'S ROLE: THE COMMITTEE OF PUBLIC ACCOUNTS (PAC), THE NEW SELECT COMMITTEES AND THE COMPTROLLER AND AUDITOR GENERAL (C&AG)

Once expenditure is settled the question of scrutiny and audit arises. Since 1861 the Committee of Public Accounts (PAC) acts on behalf of Parliament to examine and report on accounts and the regularity and propriety of expenditure, which are matters usually covered by the Comptroller and Auditor General's (C & AG) certification audit. In more recent times value for money audit (VFM) examinations have become a major part of the work of the PAC. In that regard the PAC works with the assistance of the C & AG. The constitutional importance of the PAC is beyond question, but any assessment of its role needs to consider how it has impacted on efficiency in government expenditure. There is a case for a systematic rather than a random follow up by the PAC of how its recommendations have been treated by the Government. Is this possible within its resources and workload? Currently the PAC produces about 50 reports a year and there may be little possibility for an extended role. The specialist and technical nature of the work of the PAC makes it difficult to devolve its powers to other bodies. Indeed, the PAC may become more effective by linking its work

52 HM Treasury, *PFI: Strengthening Long-Term Partnerships* (March 2006).

53 Ibid.

into the work of other committees in a more joined up and coordinated way than is possible at present.[54]

Select committees generally may exercise *ex post facto* control over public expenditure. The Select Committee on Procedure and the Treasury and Civil Service Committee have been particularly active in assisting in developing strategies for obtaining more information on public expenditure and its more effective control. The PAC's authority and remit[55] differ from those of other select committees in two ways. First is the non-party political approach it adopts to its task and the fact that it is chaired by a senior opposition MP and has no more than 15 members. Secondly, its inquiries are almost all audit-based and it receives expert assistance from the C & AG through the work of the National Audit Office. In the case of VFM examinations its reports to Parliament carry considerable weight.

A significant innovation is the Scrutiny Unit established in November 2002 in the Committee Office of the House of Commons. Its role is to provide select committees of the House of Commons and joint committees of the two Houses, with advice on expenditure matters but also on the impact of draft Bills. The work carried out by the Scrutiny Unit has a research as well as policy impact. It also publishes a Review of Departmental Annual Reports. In 2005 for the first time it analyzed all 21 reports to identify good and bad practice. This provides a detailed and in depth overview of how departments are performing in terms of Treasury guidance and output measurements.

The primary function of the C & AG since the Exchequer and Audit Act 1866 has been the requirement to examine accounts on behalf of the House of Commons. The 1983 National Audit Act recognized the constitutional implications of this requirement and made the C & AG an Officer of the House of Commons and provided for his appointment. As head of the National Audit Office (NAO), which was created under the 1983 Act and replaced the Exchequer and Audit Department, the C & AG is independent from both politics and political influence of the Government of the day. This independence allows the C & AG to qualify financial accounts when he is not satisfied with the financial arrangements. In November 2002 this occurred over the Strategic Rail Authority sponsored by the Department of Transport[56] until it was agreed that Network Rail should be consolidated.

The NAO's activities[57] cover benchmarking, quality control, developing efficient and effective monitoring systems, and engaging in annual reporting functions over departmental spending involving the audit of more than 600 accounts covering over £800 billion of public expenditure.[58] The remit of the NAO was established under the 1983 Act, which has been criticized for failing to give the C & AG the right to trace 'all public money'. The NAO has also undertaken a significant monitoring of the Financial Management of the European

[54] See Public Accounts Committee Reports HC 1530, 2006, *63rd Report on Delivering high quality services for all.*

[55] See Public Accounts Committee Reports HC 283, 2000–1 on the poor quality of higher education and on the C & AG's Report on the Millenium Dome HC 936, 1999–2000, HC 989-I, 2000–1.

[56] *Eleventh Report of the Public Accounts Commission* HC Paper 1251, 2001–2, London, Stationery Office, 2002.

[57] There is a Public Audit Forum providing a discussion for the audit agencies; the NAO, the Northern Ireland Audit Office, the Audit Commission for Local Authorities and the National Health Service in England and Wales and Audit Scotland.

[58] NAO, *Corporate Plan 2003–4 to 2005–6* National Audit Office, London, 2005 contains details of the bodies audited.

Union[59] Excluded from the jurisdiction of the NAO in Schedule 4 to the 1983 Act is the audit of the nationalized industries and other public authorities. Local authorities are separately audited by the Audit Commission which is itself subject to audit by the NAO. After privatization the remaining nationalized industries fall under the system of private sector audit since the nationalization legislation setting up each industry, required that the industry should follow 'best accounting practice'.

CERTIFICATION AUDIT

The NAO[60] undertakes two forms of auditing, Certification Audit and Value For Money Audit. In the case of certification audit, the C & AG carries out on behalf of the House of Commons the audit and certification of all government departments and a wide range of public-sector bodies. These include appropriation accounts of departments. The C & AG provides an audit certificate which states his opinion as to whether either (a) the 'account properly presents' the expenditure and receipts of the vote and payments of the organization or (b) the account presents a 'true and fair view' where accounts are prepared on an income and expenditure basis.

This form of audit is 'departmental led', that is, focused on departments. Increasingly the style of the audit is to ensure 'regularity and propriety' with the addition that the custodians of public money have stewardship responsibilities. The link between the Treasury and the NAO is through the Departmental Accounting Officer and is one of partnership but based on independent actors with specific responsibilities. The C & AG may seek an explanation from the department concerned if he is dissatisfied with any aspect of the accounts and may qualify his certificate with his reservations. The primary focus of such an audit is to assess whether accounts are accurate or whether they may mislead someone relying on them. They must present a 'true and fair view', must be 'properly presented', and in the case of Agencies must follow the format of Treasury accounts. In particular, if there is expenditure which requires Treasury authority which has not been given, the matter is reported through a draft report in the first instance to the Accounting Officer and then to the PAC and Parliament.

Normally the audit work involved in certification audit is confined to the proper presentation of receipts and expenditure. In common with most of the auditing work of the NAO it is scrutiny *ex post facto* with the implication that any past errors may provide lessons for the future. This is open to the criticism that an *a priori* examination might offer a means of avoiding mistakes and therefore save public money.[61] The NAO has claimed that in 2005–06, its work resulted in £555 million in savings as a result of auditing over 500 accounts covering £800 billion in expenditure.

VALUE FOR MONEY EXAMINATIONS

Value For Money (VFM) examinations are potentially more far-reaching as a means of audit. Section 6 of the 1983 Act provides a statutory basis for VFM examinations at the

[59] See Report by the Comptroller and Auditor General, *Financial Management of the European Union: A Progress Report* HC 529 (2003–4).

[60] Tom Ling, *The NAO and Parliamentary Scrutiny, a new audit for new times* (CfPs Policy Paper Series, 2005).

[61] Public Accounts Committee (2004–05) *Managing Risks to Improve Public Services* HC 444.

discretion of the C & AG. Included within this jurisdiction are government departments and other public bodies where the C & AG has statutory rights of inspection or where he is the statutory auditor. VFM audit is not extended to the nationalized industries.[62] The 1983 Act placed VFM examinations on a statutory basis and over 60 reports are produced on an annual basis. However the Act makes an important proviso that VFM examination shall not be construed as entitling the C & AG to question the merits of the policy objectives of the department or body concerned.[63]

Evaluating efficiency and effectiveness has been a common theme in recent years in the development of government policy objectives.[64] The NAO is ambitious in developing VFM examinations and claims that at least £500 million is saved annually through their efforts to identify and prevent waste. It has become commonplace that government borrows techniques, methods, and objectives from business or commerce. How to measure efficiency and effectiveness is the key issue, and evaluation may be as difficult as setting the objectives in the first place.

In 1981 the Treasury and Civil Service Committee in its *Report on Efficiency and Effectiveness*[65] set out some criteria for evaluating efficiency and effectiveness. The criteria include clarifying the intention of the programme, setting *objectives* which are quantified as targets. Objectives may be assessed in terms of *output*. An *efficient* programme is one where the target is achieved with the least use of resources and instruments for change. An *effective* programme is one where the intention of the programme is being achieved. This means that the intention is contained in operational objectives that are set as defined targets. Thus the output of the programme is equal to the target set. In this way an effective and efficient programme may be evaluated.

The NAO has developed VFM strategies[66] that emphasize the avoidance of waste, the setting of clearly defined policy objectives, and obtaining good value for the tax-payer. There is a duty on government departments to consider the NAO's reports and the PAC recommendations, and to provide replies to the House of Commons on matters raised in the reports. There is a strong parliamentary link with the PAC following up the recommendations made by the NAO.[67] This is consistent with the Gershon report that argued strongly for making efficiency savings to redistribute funds for better use. The Government's claim is that £4.7 billion savings might be so identified[68] but there is a considerable risk that a reduction in the quality of services might result if over-ambitious targets have to be met. There is

[62] *Government Accounting 1989* para. 7.1.20 revised in 2003.

[63] See C. Beauchamp, 'National Audit Office: Its Role in Privatization' *Public Money and Management*, Summer 1990, 55–8 at 57. For examples see: National Audit Office, HC 645, Session 1995–6; *The Work of the Directors of Telecommunications, Gas Supply, Water Service and Electricity Supply*. Compare the approach to the early comments made to the *Fourth Report of the Public Accounts Committee*, HC (1988), 4 Nov. 1988.

[64] See a critical analysis by the NAO over selling the National Air Traffic Control System HC 1096, 2001–2.

[65] Treasury and Civil Service Committee, *Efficiency and Effectiveness in the Civil Service*, 236 HC. Also see *Helping Managers Manage Cabinet Office Efficiency Unit* (1984).

[66] NAO, *Helping the Nation Spend Wisely Annual Report* (1999) 13. See *A Framework for Value for Money Audits* (National Audit Office) Cmnd 9755; Treasury Minute on the First Four Reports from the Committee of Public Accounts Session 1985/86 paras 21–3; Cmd 8413 para. 87; A. Hopwood, 'Accounting and the Pursuit of Efficiency' in A. Hopwood and C. Tomkins, *Issues in Public Sector Accounting* (1984); J. Sizer, *An Insight into Management Accounting* (1989).

[67] PAC (2005–6) *Achieving Value for Money in the Delivery of Public Services* HC 742.

[68] NAO (2005–6) *Progress in Improving Government Efficiency* HC 802.

the need for a cost benefit analysis to be used to assess the amount of savings as against the quality of services.

VFM examinations seem to be a blend of conventional auditing skills with management consulting techniques. In the former they benefit from a degree of independence and objectivity and the ascertaining of facts through the skills of an auditor. The latter draws on the analytical skills of the management consultant. In comparison with ordinary certification auditing VFM takes the opportunity to understand the effects of policy and whether those effects relate to the intention behind the policy. The NAO's experience has increased given the large number of VFM studies since 1983.[69] In 2005–6 the NAO provided Parliament with 61 major reports on VFM, representing a substantial part of the NAO's work.[70]

Particularly difficult to categorize is the distinction to be drawn between the implementation of policy, a legitimate concern of VFM, and the merits of policy which is outside the jurisdiction of the NAO. A criticism levelled at all public-sector VFM examinations is that the emphasis on economic criteria may not take account of political choices and policy-making or whether the merits of the policy, outside the remit of the NAO, impacted on the efficiency of the decision-making. Given its present remit it is clearly impossible for the NAO to move so broadly in the direction of assessing the merits of policy even where this may be indicated by their examination. The *ex post facto* nature of this examination has the benefit of hindsight but this may make it difficult to evaluate all the pressures experienced by a sponsoring department.[71]

Perversely the very transparency encouraged by audit systems may also inhibit initiative and risk-taking of a creative kind in favour of a cautious approach over-reliant on audit advice. Placing trust in the audit process itself may be a worthy goal in terms of achieving better control over expenditure but it may encourage too heavy reliance on monitoring techniques instead of a more fundamental assessment of priorities. The political agenda may also become heavily dependent on the audit trail to gain legitimacy and public confidence for policies. This may obscure the setting of priorities and lead to short-term as opposed to long-term goals.

In conclusion the independent status of the C & AG means that heavy reliance is placed on cooperation between the departments, their Accounting Officers, and the NAO. This is indicative of the delicate balance between gaining access to information through cooperation and maintaining an independence in review. In the past three years, the NAO claims that it saves the taxpayer an average of £512 million per annum.[72] The NAO has achieved international status as a public sector audit office of high reputation and quality.

LOCAL GOVERNMENT AND THE AUDIT COMMISSION

The inclusion of various heads of local authority expenditure within the PES made it inevitable that central government would seek real savings in local government

69 See J. McEldowney, 'Audit Cultures and Risk Aversion in Public Authorities: An Agenda for Public Lawyers' in R. Baldwin (ed.), *Law and Uncertainty Risks and Legal Processes* (1997) 185–210.

70 NAO, Annual Report 2006.

71 F. White and K. Hollingsworth, *Audit, Accountability and Government*, Oxford: Clarendon Press, 1999.

72 NAO, Corporate Plan op. cit. para. 1.2.

expenditure. It is estimated[73] that local government spends about 25 per cent of all state spending amounting to nearly 10 per cent of the National Income (GNP). There is a long history of central government financial controls over local government. The replacement of the community charge by the council tax and the introduction of a central government determined Standard Spending Assessment with universal capping over local government budgets introduced in 1992 effectively set strict controls over local government expenditure totals.

Accompanying tight financial controls are changes in the actual role of local authorities. Traditionally being *providers* of services, local authorities are increasingly used as *enablers* by setting standards specifying how work is to be performed and monitoring performance. Market testing and the requirement in some cases to contract out services are designed to provide best services at least cost.

An additional means of securing local authority compliance with financial controls came from the establishment of the Audit Commission under the Local Government Finance Act 1982. The Audit Commission covers the traditional financial audit of local authorities and it is the only statutory body apart from the NAO required to carry out VFM examinations.[74] Regularity audit requires a review of accounts, auditing the financial statements, evaluating financial systems, considering steps to prevent fraud or irregularity, and providing an analysis of the financial standing of the local authority. The Audit Commission occasionally provides evidence to various select committees, but lacks a formal role linked to the PAC equivalent to central government audit by the NAO. The absence of an equivalent select committee to the PAC to oversee local government expenditure is a weakness of the existing arrangements considering that central government provides £128 billion to be spent by local government.[75]

Section 15 of the 1982 Act requires the Commission to carry out VFM Audit. Section 14 requires the Commission to keep under review at five-yearly intervals a code of audit practice. More recently the Local Government Act 1999 further strengthens this role by empowering the Secretary of State to stipulate that certain local authorities must conform to 'a best value authority' set of standards. This covers annual reviews, performance plans, and the Commission under section 7 of the Local Government Act 1999 has powers to oversee best value authorities and carry out audit duties.

The Audit Commission may take legal action against a local authority under section 19 of the Local Government Act 1982 to avoid loss through wasteful expenditure identified in an audit report. Expenditure is unlawful if it lacks statutory authority or is so unreasonable in the *Wednesbury*[76] sense as to amount to an abuse of discretion. While poor value for money is not of itself unlawful it is possible under section 15(3) for a public interest report to be made stating that unsatisfactory progress has been made in meeting the standards expected of the local authority. There are additional powers to seek judicial review. The Audit Commission had a major impact on the management culture of local authorities. There are

[73] T. Byrne, *Local Government in Britain* 7th ed., Penguin, 2000, p. 334.

[74] Audit Commission, Auditor Briefing 26/2004: Planning Local Government Audits 2005/06.

[75] House of Commons, 15 Feb. 2006, col. 667.

[76] *Associated Provincial Picture Houses Ltd* v. *Wednesbury Corporation* [1948] 1 KB 223. See M. Sunkin, L. Bridges, and G. Meszaros, *Judicial Review in Perspective*, The Public Law Project 1993 (revised and updated 1999). B. McSweeney, 'Accounting for the Audit Commission' (1988) 59 *Political Quarterly* 28–43, at 42; M. Radford, 'Auditing for Change: Local Government and the Audit Commission' (1991) 54 *Modern Law Review* 912.

however doubts about the weight given to the different criteria included in VFM studies since more weight is given to economy and efficiency than to effectiveness. The Audit Commission is said to have succeeded in changing the culture of local government.[77] This has come about through audit techniques that have become the catalyst for change and have reinvigorated local government. It is noteworthy that this success has been achieved by adopting a similar stance to that of central government in the strategy of setting tightly enforced legal controls over local government. The *Code of Audit Practice* supported by legal powers has enabled the Audit Commission to achieve many of its goals. The increasing use of local authority owned companies that are outside of the Audit Commission's remit should be addressed. There is a need for formal oversight of the Audit Commission from a parliamentary committee. This would encourage debate and transparency.

CONCLUSION

Improvements in the systems and techniques for the control of public expenditure have resulted in better provision of financial information and the strengthening of the systems of accounting and auditing.[78] The government's expenditure objectives are more visible and transparent than before. The *Code of Fiscal Stability* creates a new relationship between government policy and Treasury controls through the system of PES. Government strategy has also included setting departmental targets to achieve planned efficiencies of over £20 billion, with each department publishing Efficiency Technical Notes scrutinized by the NAO and the Audit Commission.

However, it remains the case that the systems that manage and control expenditure, nominally subject to parliamentary accountability, are in practice directly under the influence of government ministers. While Parliament retains theoretical 'control of the purse', this conceals the fact that power lies in the hands of ministers and the Treasury. The latter intends to reduce civil servant numbers by 84,000 and deliver savings in posts in London. Despite the many improvements in the procedures of financial control through improved transparency it remains uncertain whether the House of Commons in general or individual MPs regard financial control as relevant in its overall role in the scrutiny of government. Historically, governments with large majorities appear relatively immune from opposition counter measures on targets and spending plans. There is some evidence that departmental select committees have begun to adopt public expenditure as a means of scrutiny[79] aided by the establishment in 2002 of the Scrutiny Unit[80] which also aids select committees in pre-legislative scrutiny. The Scrutiny Unit has found financial controls a useful mechanism for

[77] M. Radford, 'Auditing for Change: Local Government and the Audit Commission' in J. Fredman and M. Power (eds), *Law and Accountancy – Conflict and Co-operation in the 1990s* (1992) 64. Audit Commission, *Changing Picture Sharper Focus Strategy 1999–2002* (1999). Audit Commission, *The Impact on Local Authorities' Economy, Efficiency and Effectiveness of the Block Grant Distribution System* (1984).

[78] Mark Sandford, *External Scrutiny: The Voice in the Crowded Room* (CfPs Policy Paper Series 2002).

[79] See Education and Skills Committee, *Public Expenditure on Education and Skills* HC 2004–5 HC 168, The Home Affairs Committee HC 2004–5 HC 280, the Northern Ireland Affairs Committee 2004–5 Northern Ireland Departments' 2002–3 Resource Accounts HC 173.

[80] Scrutiny Unit set up under the late Robin Cook, then Leader of the House of Commons.

aiding the effectiveness of select committees, and its own contribution looking across departmental annual reports is a welcome development.

However, audit systems have a remarkable tendency to centralize control. This is clear from the example of local authority financing and the work of the Audit Commission. It is equally clear when devolution to Scotland, Wales, and Northern Ireland is considered. Outside only limited exceptions financial controls remain broadly centralized in contrast to the devolution of political and administrative decision-making. Centralization is a recurrent theme in setting targets, determining efficiency gains and strategies.

Constitutional lawyers have accepted that controls over public expenditure lie at the heart of Parliament's control over government. The plethora of controls such as internal Treasury rules and procedures, audit systems, parliamentary reports, and management systems are fashioned to serve the dual purpose of the economic needs of the Government of the day, and the interests of Parliament. It is a noticeable feature of the current improvements in managing the economy that they have benefited the Treasury and enhanced the reputation of the Chancellor of the Exchequer. Inside the system of financial control may be detected the internal workings of government, often less visible and transparent than the workings of the external systems of parliamentary accountability in select committees and in the role of the courts. Financial control systems share many characteristics familiar in the development of the common law – continuity and certainty in developing rules with the potential for incremental change. But, equally incrementally, financial controls appear to have developed many of the qualities of a codified system – written manuals containing fundamental principles that have been improved, up-dated, and strengthened containing many years' experience. It is possible to see financial controls as a model of what can be achieved with systemic change over 40 years through the appropriate combination of external expertise in the form of the NAO and the internal scrutiny performed by select committees. Treasury dominance in its influence over public expenditure is most marked. Significantly *Government Accounting 2000 Amendment 4/05* explains that Treasury administrative controls '. . . are rules and practice that have been laid down by the Treasury rather than Parliament.' They relate to the 'need for Treasury approval for certain spending decisions and . . . requirements that the Treasury rather than Parliament has laid down'. All this is undertaken with Parliamentary knowledge and justified on the basis that Parliament assumes 'that controls of this nature are in place'. This is a systemic weakness at the heart of public expenditure control, namely that gaps left by Parliamentary inertia are readily filled by executive controls driven by Treasury influence. Greater emphasis must be given in Parliamentary debate to the policies and decisions that inform, manage, and control public expenditure. At a time when audit systems are strengthened, Parliament's relevance faces further decline. The weaknesses and inertia in parliamentary control appear to reflect a decline in the standard and quality of our democracy today.[81]

[81] O. Gay and B. Winetrobe, *Parliamentary Audit: the Audit committee in Comparative Context* (2003).

FURTHER READING

Balls E. and O'Donnell G. (eds) *Reforming Britain's Economic and Financial Policy: Towards Greater Economic Stability* (2002).

Blackburn R. and Kennon A., with Wheeler-Booth M. *Griffith and Ryle on* (2003).

Brazier A. and Ram V. *The Fiscal Maze* (2006).

Daintith T. and Page A. *The Executive in the Constitution: Structure, Autonomy and Internal Control* (1999).

Gay O. and Winetrobe B. *Parliamentary Audit: The Audit Committee in Comparative Context, Report to the Audit Committee of the Scottish Parliament* (2003).

Hansard Society, Commission on Parliamentary Scrutiny, *The Challenge for Parliament: Making Government Accountable*, 2001.

Heald D. and McLeod A. *Public Expenditure, The Laws of Scotland: Stair Memorial Encyclopaedia* (2002).

Limon D.W. and McKay W.R. *Erskine May Parliamentary Practice* (22nd edn, 1997).

Sharman of Redlynch, Lord *Holding to Account: The Review of Audit and Accountability for Central Government* (2001).

Thain C. and Wright M. *The Treasury and Whitehall: The Planning and Control of Public Expenditure 1976–1993* (1995).

White F. and Hollingsworth K. *Audit, Accountability and Government* (1999).

USEFUL WEB SITES

www.parliament.uk

www.hm-treasury.gov.uk

www.parliament.uk/commons/lib

www.nao.gov.uk

www.audit-commission.gov.uk

www.statistics.gov.uk

www.public-audit-forum.gov.uk

16

THE FREEDOM OF INFORMATION ACT 2000 – A SHEEP IN WOLF'S CLOTHING?

Rodney Austin

SUMMARY

The principle of freedom of information was accepted by the Labour Party when in opposition, and has now been embodied in legislation, the Freedom of Information Act 2000. However, that legislation falls far short of the ideal in numerous ways. The range of exemptions from access to government information is unduly wide; the right of access is not to records themselves but to information held by public authorities; the system of publication schemes, while mandatory, leaves wide discretionary powers in the hands of public officials to decide what to publish; there is no duty to provide reasons for administrative decisions; there is a wide discretionary power vested in ministers and other public authorities to decide whether or not to disclose exempt documents in the public interest; above all, ministers are given an absolute override power to prevent disclosure of some information. The Act has now been fully in force since 1 January 2005. This chapter will examine the first two years of operation of the Act with the aim of determining whether the Act contributes to the achievement of a genuinely open democracy in the UK.

INTRODUCTION

In the first four editions of this volume, this chapter was devoted to an analysis of the arguments for and against freedom of information, that is, a statutory, legally enforceable right of access to all governmental information subject only to limited, specific and justifiable exceptions. The history of the peculiar British culture of, even obsession with, governmental secrecy for most of the twentieth century was explored, as were the more recent attempts to open up British government to greater public scrutiny. The principal thesis of the chapter was twofold: first, that British government would only become truly democratic and accountable, that its decisions would only become fully informed, efficient and effective, and that its citizens would only have a meaningful right of participation in the making of decisions which affect them, if there was full access to governmental information, and secondly, that the only way to prise open the clam-like files of British government and public authorities was to enact legislation creating a legally enforceable right of access to governmental records.

It is no longer necessary to make those arguments, since the UK Government has not only publicly accepted the case for freedom of information but has legislated to that end. The aim of this chapter in the fifth edition was to examine the Freedom of Information Act 2000 and to measure it against the criteria put forward in those previous chapters as the desiderata for an ideal system of truly open and transparent government. Those criteria are that there should be a legally enforceable right of access; that there should be access to all government records, at all levels of government and public authority, whether national, regional, or local; that the only exceptions to that right should be records relating to certain specific interests, such as national security, defence, foreign relations, the efficient conduct of government policy-making, criminal law enforcement, commercial secrecy, and privacy; that such exceptions should be justified only where the provable likely harm to such interests outweighed the public interest in disclosure; that the right of access be open to all without the need for reasons justifying access; that access should be provided promptly and free of charge or at no more than a reasonable charge for copying; and that there should be an independent appellate authority to adjudicate upon refusals by government or public authorities to grant access requests, with the power to enforce disclosure of the records requested.

When measured against these criteria, it was argued that the Freedom of Information Act 2000 fell far short of the ideal. The question then to be considered was whether the Act fell so far short of the ideal, whether it was such a pretence by government to hold itself out as open and transparent, that it would have been better not to have legislated. While one conclusion could have been that the Act is a sheep in wolf's clothing, a masquerade by government with no real intention of opening up Whitehall to public scrutiny, and worse, a legislative fixing in stone of the existing system of ministerial discretion, another could have been that the practice and habits of statutory freedom of information would in time so alter the culture of government and public administration that the Act would ultimately bring about something approximating true freedom of information. It would be wholly appropriate to the traditional British constitutional culture of reform by evolution, not revolution, that an apparently radical reform should eventually achieve its purpose by gradual change of the habits of behaviour of government ministers, civil servants, and other public officials. This chapter will endeavour to examine the practice of freedom of information under the Act thus far and determine which of these two conclusions can be drawn.

THE LAW AND PRACTICE BEFORE THE FREEDOM OF INFORMATION ACT 2000

In the two decades prior to the enactment of the Freedom of Information Act 2000, significant steps had been taken to make both central and local government more open, and to break down and change the official culture that all governmental information was secret unless its disclosure was authorized. Legislation had been passed providing rights of access to local government documents,[1] personal files,[2] environmental information,[3] the Land Registry,[4] and health and safety information.[5] The Official Secrets Act 1911 had been reformed so as to remove the sanction of the criminal law from the unauthorized disclosure of all but a limited range of sensitive information, with *mens rea* and harm requirements providing defences to the accused.[6] The Citizen's Charter, now Service First, had sought to make public service providers more accountable to their consumers by requiring the measuring of performance and the publication of such performance measures. Punctuality of trains, school examination results, waiting lists and morbidity rates of hospitals, all these and much else became public information.[7] The reform of public audit in the 1980s equally had a dramatic impact on the provision of information on government spending at all levels.[8] The creation in 1979 of a coherent system of parliamentary scrutiny of central government by the reformed Select Committees opened up government departments with the publication of vast quantities of hitherto unavailable material.[9] Yet in a crisis, ministers could refuse to provide information or instruct their officials not to disclose information, and the Select Committees were powerless to overrule the ministers.[10]

THE CODE OF PRACTICE ON GOVERNMENT INFORMATION

But the single most important reform was the Code of Practice on Government Information, brought about by the White Paper on Open Government[11] in 1993. Under this Code,[12] a non-statutory right of access to government information was created, together with a duty upon government departments and other public authorities to provide reasons for decisions affecting individuals. Equally, government departments were placed under a duty to publish the facts and research on which policy decisions were based, though not the advice of civil servants to ministers in relation to policy decisions. If access was refused, an individual could complain to the Parliamentary Commissioner for Administration (PCA), who could decide that the refusal was unjustified.

Although in some ways a radical reform, a recognition and acceptance, albeit belated and grudging, of the principle of open government and transparency by the UK Government, the White Paper and the Code were subjected to much criticism. The right of access was unenforceable, since the PCA had no power to order or enforce disclosure. The exceptions to the right of access were numerous and broad, including every statutory or statute-based prohibition on disclosure, of which there were over 200. There were no tests of harm or of overriding public interest in disclosure applicable to the exceptions to the right of access.

1 Local Government (Access to Information) Act 1985.

2 Access to Personal Files Act 1987.

3 Environmental Protection Act 1990, Environmental Information Regulations 1992 (SI 1992/3240), *inter alia*.

4 Land Registration Act 1988.

5 Health and Safety at Work Act 1974, as amended.

6 Official Secrets Act 1989.

7 For detailed description of the Citizen's Charter and its effects, see R. Austin, 'Administrative Law's Reaction to the Changing Concepts of Public Service', in P. Leyland and T. Woods (eds), *Administrative Law Facing the Future: Old Constraints and New Horizons* (1997).

8 National Audit Act 1983.

9 See generally G. Drewry, *The New Select Committees* (2nd edn, 1989).

10 This occurred in the Westland Affair, see R. Austin and D. Oliver, 'The Westland Affair' (1987) 40 *Parliamentary Affairs* 20; in the Salmonella in Eggs affair, see HC 108 (1988–9); and in the Arms to Iraq affair, see Trade and Industry Select Committee, Exports to Iraq: Project Babylon and Long Range Guns, HC 86 (1991–2).

11 Cm 2290 (1993) HMSO. For draft code of practice, see Annex A to the White Paper.

12 Code of Practice on Access to Government Information, 1994, revised 1997.

The right of access was to information, not to records, so that government and public authorities could prepare the information to release from their records, raising fears of selective editing. The person requesting access could be charged not only for the cost of copying but also for the time spent finding and preparing the information, thereby creating prohibitive obstacles for all but the wealthiest of applicants. Despite these criticisms, the Code of Practice contributed significantly for more than a decade to the process of making UK Government more transparent and to a changed culture of openness in central government.[13] Nonetheless, the fact remained that if a government minister decided to keep secret an embarrassing piece of information, even if the information revealed unlawful actions by government officials or ministers, there was no means by which Parliament, (other than by an adverse vote against a minister of a government holding a majority in the House of Commons), or an individual citizen, could force the minister to disclose that information.

THE ARMS TO IRAQ AFFAIR

The extent to which it remained possible, despite all these reforms, for government to keep its secrets, was brought to public notice in the 1990s by one of the biggest scandals in recent British history, the Arms to Iraq affair, and the massive public inquiry which ensued, the Scott Inquiry into the Export of Defence Equipment and Dual-Use Goods to Iraq,[14] which reported in 1996.[15]

What became evident from the report of that inquiry was that a small number of government ministers, acting covertly and without the knowledge of their respective Secretaries of State, had changed the guidelines on the ban on exports of arms and defence equipment to Iraq and Iran during the war between those states, following the cessation of hostilities. The effect of the change was to make it possible to export to Iraq certain dual-use equipment which could be used for military purposes. Ministers had then actively encouraged British manufacturing companies to describe such equipment in a misleading way when applying for export licences. Despite numerous parliamentary questions, any change to the ban on exports was denied in Parliament, denials which were subsequently proved to be false.

Later, when Customs and Excise prosecuted the directors of Matrix Churchill, one of the companies involved in the export of embargoed equipment, for obtaining export licences by deceit, government ministers sought to prevent disclosure in court of much government information concerning the affair, by claiming public interest immunity, even though this could have led to the conviction of the Matrix Churchill defendants. The Attorney-General had advised the ministers that they were under a duty to claim immunity from disclosure of information. Fortunately, the trial judge overruled the claims, a government minister was forced to admit that he had been 'economical with the actualités', the prosecution offered no further evidence, and the defendants were acquitted. The Matrix Churchill directors had in fact been acting for British intelligence, obtaining information about Iraq, and the government ministers responsible for export licences and defence sales had actively collaborated to ensure that Matrix Churchill was granted export licences for the dual-use equipment so that the directors would be able to visit defence installations in Iraq.[16]

13 See A. Tomkins, *The Constitution after Scott: Government Unwrapped* (1998), 123.

14 Report ordered to be printed by the House of Commons, 15 Feb. 1996, HC 115, 1995–96, London, HMSO.

15 See Tomkins, n. 13 above, for a detailed history of the affair and its outcome.

16 See P. R. Henderson, *The Unlikely Spy* (1993).

Even when the Scott Report was delivered to the Government, the press, the public, and the official Opposition were denied access for a week until the morning of the Parliamentary debate. The shadow Foreign Secretary, Robin Cook MP, was given three hours in which to digest the contents of a five-volume report of approximately 2,300 pages with appendices. The Government issued a summary of the report which could at best be described as selective, at worst deliberately misleading. Despite the report's findings that various government ministers had covertly altered the guidelines on exports to Iraq, had condoned or even induced civilians into falsifying applications for export licences, had lied to the House of Commons, had improperly claimed public interest immunity in a criminal trial where the liberty of subjects was at stake, and had failed to inform the prosecution of the doubts of one senior minister about the public interest immunity claims, the Government won the vote on the report by one vote and no ministers resigned over the affair.[17] The lack of parliamentary accountability revealed by the report, and by the earlier Trade and Industry Select Committee report on the Iraqi Supergun affair, demonstrated beyond contradiction that British government secrecy could not be reformed without legislative action. The opposition Labour Party included in its manifesto for the election in 1997 a commitment to the enactment of a Freedom of Information Act if elected.

THE LEGISLATIVE HISTORY OF THE FREEDOM OF INFORMATION ACT 2000: YOUR RIGHT TO KNOW

Following the election of the Labour government in May, 1997, David Clarke MP, the Chancellor of the Duchy of Lancaster, a Cabinet minister without portfolio, was entrusted with the task of researching and formulating detailed policy proposals for Freedom of Information legislation. Within six months he had published a White Paper[18] containing the Government's detailed policy proposals. *Your Right to Know* proposed a statutory right of access on request to all government records, subject only to a limited range of exemptions, where disclosure would cause substantial harm to identified governmental interests, and even then only where the public interest in keeping the information secret outweighed the public interest in disclosure.

There were to be administrative 'gateways' to exclude repetitious, excessively voluminous, or vexatious requests for records.[19] There were to be publication schemes[20] under which government departments and a wide range of other public bodies subject to the Act would be required to make available to the public a wide range of information in their possession, including the facts and analysis important in the framing of major policy proposals and decisions, explanatory material on dealings with the public, reasons for administrative decisions to those affected by them, and lastly operational information about how public services are run, how much they cost, performance targets, expected standards and results, and complaints procedures, this last group mirroring the Citizen's Charter requirements. There was also to be a statutory right of access for individuals to personal information held by public bodies about them,[21] to supplement existing and future rights of access under the

[17] See Tomkins, n. 13 above.

[18] *Your Right to Know: The Government's Proposals for a Freedom of Information Act*, Cm. 3818 (1997).

[19] Ibid., paras 2.23–2.27. [20] Ibid., paras 2.17–2.18. [21] Ibid., paras 4.1–4.5.

data protection legislation. The two access regimes were not, however, to be merged under the Government's proposals, but the Information Commissioner and the Data Protection Registrar would be required to work closely together where cases involved both jurisdictions, so as to avoid conflicts.[22]

To enforce the individual right of access, there was to be an obligatory internal review. There was also to be an Information Commissioner to whom individuals could appeal against a refusal of access to records, but with no further right of appeal, though the decisions of the Information Commissioner would be subject to judicial review.[23] Most importantly, the decisions of the Information Commissioner would be final and binding on the Government or public body. There would be no ministerial certification that information was to fall outside the right of access, nor any ministerial veto or override of the finding or decision of the Information Commissioner. The government had considered the possibility of such a power, but decided against it, 'believing that a government veto would undermine the authority of the Information Commissioner and erode public confidence in the Act'.[24] Any individual, company, or body would be entitled to seek access under the Act without having to demonstrate or state any purpose for making a request for information.[25] There would be a basic flat fee of £10 for all access requests, except for large requests by corporate or commercial bodies, though the detail of charging schemes was not finalized.[26] The rights of third parties who had supplied information to the Government or other public bodies, to which access was being sought, to object to disclosure or to participate in the proceedings, were raised but left open.[27]

The range of public bodies intended to be covered by the legislation was extensive, and included not only central government departments and their executive agencies, but also local authorities, public corporations and all 1,200 Quangos, the National Health Service, administrative functions of Courts, Tribunals, the Police and Police Authorities, the Armed Services, schools, colleges and universities, public service broadcasters, the privatized public utilities, and private organizations insofar as they carry out statutory functions.[28] This unprecedented list of those included in the scope of the proposed legislation was marred only by the complete institutional exclusion of the Security Service, the Secret Intelligence Service, the Government Communications Headquarters (GCHQ), and the Special Forces (the SAS and the SBS). Also excluded were all law enforcement functions of the police, prosecutors, and other bodies carrying out law enforcement such as the Department of Social Security or the Immigration Service.[29]

The range of exemptions from the proposed legislation was relatively narrow, certainly narrower than in the then existing Code of Practice on Access to Government Information. Furthermore, the Government proposed that the legislation should not contain exempt categories at all, but rather that disclosure should be assessed on a 'contents basis', echoing the former Attorney-General's policy statement following the publication of the Scott Report. In place of the Code's 15 exempt categories, the White Paper identified seven specified interests which would be the basis for claims to exemption from disclosure. These were: national security, defence, and international relations; law enforcement; personal privacy; commercial confidentiality; the safety of the individual, the public, and the environment;

[22] Ibid., paras 4.6–4.13. [23] Ibid., ch. 5, 'Review and Appeals'. [24] Ibid., para. 5.18.
[25] Ibid., paras 2.6–2.7. [26] Ibid., paras 2.28–2.34. [27] Ibid., para. 5.19.
[28] Ibid., paras 2.1–2.2. [29] Ibid., paras 2.3–2.4, para. 2.21.

information supplied in confidence; and lastly, the integrity of the decision-making and policy advice processes in government.[30] Actually, since some of these categories contain multiple interests, the real figure is 10 exemption interests. In each of these interests, exemption could only be justified if disclosure would cause damage, harm, or substantial harm, or pose a significant threat, to the identified interest.[31] Furthermore, exemption should be claimed only in respect of that part of a record whose disclosure would cause such harm. Records should be disclosed in partial form with the exempt material deleted.

Lastly, and most importantly, the White Paper proposed a public interest disclosure override for exempt material, so that even if information fell within the exemption interests and satisfied the harm or substantial harm tests, there could still be an overriding public interest in disclosure.[32] Equally, the proposed legislation was intended to repeal or amend many of the several hundred statutory bars to disclosure identified in the 1993 White Paper on Open Government, so as to bring them into line with the harm and public interests tests proposed in *Your Right to Know*.[33]

The White Paper was welcomed by proponents of freedom of information, despite the substantial institutional exemptions, as a sound set of proposals which would bring about a freedom of information regime at least matching and in some cases improving upon those in other common law and parliamentary jurisdictions. The White Paper was personally supported by the Prime Minister who, in the preface, stated:

> 'The traditional culture of secrecy will only be broken down by giving people in the UK the legal right to know. This fundamental and vital change in the relationship between government and the governed is at the heart of this White Paper.'

THE DRAFT FREEDOM OF INFORMATION BILL

In the White Paper, the Government promised that the White Paper proposals would 'form the basis for a thorough and informed public debate. As an open Government our next step will be to conduct a careful consultation exercise on the basis of a draft Bill.' But it was to be a year and a half before the draft Bill emerged, not from the Cabinet Office Freedom of Information Unit which had published the White Paper, but from the Home Office. In the meantime, the White Paper's ministerial author, David Clarke MP, had lost ministerial office in an early government reshuffle. Responsibility for the Government's proposed legislation on Freedom of Information had been transferred to the Home Office, to which the Freedom of Information Unit had been transferred, from the Cabinet Office. The Home Office is responsible for the Security Service, for the police and police authorities, for the public prosecution authorities, the prison service, and the immigration service. Thus a large proportion of the interests identified by the White Paper as justifying exemption from the proposed legislation fall within its jurisdiction. The Home Office is not a disinterested or neutral party, and was therefore hardly the appropriate department to sponsor freedom of information legislation.

This was reflected in the draft Freedom of Information Bill, published in May 1999, two years after the election of the Labour Government. Although the Bill followed the basic

[30] Ibid., paras 3.11–3.12. [31] Ibid., paras 3.6–3.7. [32] Ibid., paras 3.15–3.21.
[33] Ibid., para. 3.20.

structure set out in the White Paper, its contents were remarkably different. The range of exemptions had expanded dramatically from the White Paper's seven to 24. These exemptions included not only the usual suspects, such as defence, security, intelligence, international relations, law enforcement, personal privacy, and commercial confidentiality, but an extraordinary catalogue of information, much of which might be thought to be precisely the sort of information which ought to be disclosed rather than withheld. Thus, information already accessible to the public; information that will in future be published; information likely to prejudice relations between devolved administrations in the UK; information likely to prejudice the economic interests of the UK or of any devolved administration in the UK; information likely to prejudice the efficient functioning of Cabinet government and the public service; information in court proceedings; information relating to public audit functions; information which would cause an infringement of the privileges of either House of Parliament; information relating to communications with the Queen, other members of the Royal Family, the Royal Household, or the conferment of honours by the Crown; health and safety information; environmental information; information the disclosure of which is prohibited by or under any enactment: all of these areas were proposed to be exempt from the right of access.[34]

It was not only the broad range of the exemptions which gave cause for concern, but also the broad scope of particular exemptions and the watering down of the substantial harm test of exemption. For example, the law enforcement exemption provisions provided exemption not only for the investigation of crimes by the police and other prosecutorial bodies, but also for public inquiries investigating the cause of an accident, or the health, safety, and welfare of persons at work, or whether statutory regulatory action is justified, or the fitness or competence of any person in relation to corporate management or any profession.[35] Thus rail and air accident investigations could be withheld, as could reports on accidents at work, or investigations by the Department of Trade and Industry into the fitness of company directors, or by the Bar Council into the fitness of barristers. Many of the exemptions no longer carried any harm test at all, but were absolute exemptions, and others carried a diluted test of prejudice to the identified interest. No proposed exemption in the Bill carried a substantial harm or significant threat test.

The Bill also provided for public bodies to set up their own charging regimes permitting them to charge for the cost of providing the information to which access is requested.[36] The White Paper's proposed £10 standard fee was omitted. The duty to establish publication schemes under the Bill no longer required publication of specific types of information but was diluted to a duty to have regard to the public interest in allowing public access to information held by, and in the publication of reasons for decisions taken by, public authorities.[37]

The Bill provided for the merging of the Information Commissioner and the Data Protection Registrar into one office to administer both jurisdictions.[38] It also provided for a further right of appeal, to an Information Tribunal.[39] But the most controversial of all the Bill's provisions was the introduction of an absolute ministerial veto on disclosure,[40] in respect of which no appeal was provided, in a complete reversal of the White Paper's explicit rejection of such a veto power.[41] Equally worrying was that the Bill no longer referred to records, but to a right of access to information,[42] echoing the Code of Practice.

34 Draft FoI Bill, Part II, cll. 21–44.
35 Ibid., cl. 31.
36 Ibid., cll. 12–13.
37 Ibid., cl. 19.
38 Ibid., cl. 18.
39 Ibid., Part V.
40 Ibid., cl. 53.
41 See n. 24 above.
42 Draft Bill, cl. 1.

The Bill was subjected to pre-legislative scrutiny by the Commons' Select Committee on Public Administration and the House of Lords Select Committee specially appointed to consider the Draft Freedom of Information Bill, during the summer of 1999, but despite highly critical reports[43] from the Committees, the Government's official response was to reject almost all of the criticisms and to introduce the Freedom of Information Bill, in the 1999/2000 Parliamentary session, with no significant changes of substance. The Bill became the Freedom of Information Act 2000, with no significant amendments. Despite its enactment in 2000, the Act did not come fully into force until 1 January 2005, under a rolling programme of implementation. Publication schemes were introduced in central government first followed by local government and other public authorities, with the individual right of access coming into effect last, in January, 2005. Publication schemes commenced operation formally in 2004, though many pilot publication schemes had already been implemented and the Information Commissioner had given his approval to many full publication schemes submitted to him for approval, well before that deadline.[44]

THE FREEDOM OF INFORMATION ACT 2000

Part I of the Act creates a statutory right of access to information held by a wide range of public authorities.[45] It then provides exemption from that right of access if the information falls under an absolute exemption or, if not an absolute exemption, if the public interest in maintaining the exemption, i.e. keeping the information secret, outweighs the public interest in disclosure.[46] The range of public authorities, already wide, to which the right of access applies,[47] can be extended by ministerial order.[48] Part I also sets out the requirements with which a request for information must comply, such as being in writing, identifying the applicant, providing the applicant's address, and specifying the information sought.[49] The fees regime for charging is to be established by regulations under Part I, including a power to charge no fee at all. Fee notices may be issued to an applicant, specifying a fee and requiring it to be paid in advance of providing access.[50]

Time limits for compliance with requests for access are established,[51] as are the means by which access should be granted.[52] The Act does not grant a right of access to government records, but to information, and this may be satisfied by providing a copy of the information, by permitting inspection of the record, or by providing a digest or summary of the information.[53] The public authority should, so far as reasonably practicable, comply with the applicant's wishes as to the form in which the information is provided, but there is no specific, enforceable duty to provide the applicant with a copy of the Government record containing the information sought.[54]

Part I also establishes the administrative gateways by providing exemption from complying with a request where the cost of compliance is excessive,[55] or where requests are

[43] Select Committee on Public Administration, Third Report, HC 1998–9; Report from the Select Committee appointed to consider the Draft Freedom of Information Bill, HL 1998–9.

[44] See the Annual Report of the Lord Chancellor's Department (www.lcd.gov.uk/foi/imprep/annrep02) for a full progress report on the implementation of the Act.

[45] Freedom of Information Act 2000, ss. 1–7.

[46] Ibid., s. 2.

[47] Ibid., s. 3.

[48] Ibid., ss. 4 and 5.

[49] Ibid., s. 8.

[50] Ibid., s. 9.

[51] Ibid., s. 10.

[52] Ibid., s. 11.

[53] Ibid., s. 11(1).

[54] Ibid., s. 11(2)–(4).

[55] Ibid., s. 12.

vexatious or repeated.[56] In the case of excessive requests, the public authority, rather than claim exemption, may charge a fee reflecting the excessive cost of compliance with the request.[57] Where a public authority proposes to refuse a request for access, because it claims an exemption from disclosure, it must inform the applicant of its claim for exemption and the reasons therefor.[58] Part I also establishes the Information Commissioner and the Information Tribunal,[59] and creates the duty to establish publication schemes,[60] subject to approval by the Information Commissioner.[61]

Part II of the Act creates the numerous exemptions, contained in sections 21 to 44 inclusive. These exemptions are identical to those in the Bill, set out above, and far exceed both the existing exemptions in the Code of Practice on Access to Government Information, and those recommended in the White Paper. Part III establishes general duties and functions under the Act for the Lord Chancellor, the Secretary of State, and the Information Commissioner, concerning codes of practice and recommendations as to good practice.

Part IV of the Act sets out the enforcement powers of the Information Commissioner, which are extensive. Where an applicant applies to the Commissioner for a decision as to whether a public authority has, in relation to a request for information, complied with the duties of the public authority under Part I of the Act, the Commissioner may issue a decision notice.[62] Where a public authority refuses to provide information as to whether it has in its possession the information sought by the applicant, i.e. refuses to comply with the duty to confirm or deny, or to provide access to the information requested, the Information Commissioner may issue either an information notice[63] or an enforcement notice.[64] The former requires the public authority to provide the Information Commissioner with sufficient information to determine whether the public authority has failed to comply with any of its duties under Part I of the Act, while the latter requires the public authority to comply with a specified duty under Part I of the Act. Failure to comply with any notice issued by the Commissioner, unless the public authority is appealing against the notice, may be certified to the High Court by the Commissioner, and the Court may deal with the failure as if it were a contempt of court.[65]

The ministerial veto power is contained in section 53, which provides that the responsible minister may give to the Commissioner a certificate stating that he has on reasonable grounds formed the opinion that there has been no failure by the government department or designated public authority, against whom a decision notice or enforcement notice has been issued by the Commissioner, to comply with the duty under section 1(1)(b), i.e. the duty to give access to the information requested by the applicant, in respect of exempt information. Such a certificate overrides the Commissioner's notice, which ceases to have effect. The minister must lay any such certificate before each House of Parliament. There is no right of appeal against such a certificate. This appears therefore to be an absolute ministerial veto power, in semi-subjective terms which arguably exclude judicial review. Careful reading of section 53, however, reveals that the veto is limited to non-absolute exempt information only, i.e. that the ministerial veto operates only on the issue of whether the public interest in disclosure of exempt information outweighs the public interest in keeping the information secret. The veto cannot therefore be used to prevent disclosure of information

56 Ibid., s. 14. 57 Ibid., s. 13. 58 Ibid., s. 17. 59 Ibid., s. 18. 60 Ibid., s. 19.
61 Ibid., s. 20. 62 Ibid., s. 50. 63 Ibid., s. 51. 64 Ibid., s. 52. 65 Ibid., s. 54.

which is not exempt. Any attempt by a minister to do so would be *ultra vires* and illegal and could be prevented by a prohibiting order or struck down by a quashing order, under judicial review. The minister concerned must be a Cabinet minister, the UK or Scottish Attorneys-General, the Advocate-General of Scotland, the First Minister in Northern Ireland, or the Welsh Assembly First Secretary.[66] Failure to comply with any duty imposed on a public authority under the Act does not give rise to any right of action in civil proceedings, so there is no possibility of obtaining damages for breach of statutory duty or even for negligence in the performance of a statutory duty.[67] Thus there is a high level of political accountability attached to the exercise of the veto power, but relatively weak legal accountability.

Rights of appeal to the Information Tribunal from the Information Commissioner's decision, information, and enforcement notices are conferred by Part V. The applicant and the public authority may appeal against a decision notice, but only the public authority may appeal against an information or enforcement notice.[68] There does not appear to be any provision enabling an applicant to appeal against a decision by the Information Commissioner not to issue a decision notice, information notice, or enforcement notice. The Tribunal may uphold the appeal where it considers that the notice was not in accordance with law, or, if it involved an exercise of discretion by the Commissioner, that he should have exercised his discretion differently.[69] The Tribunal may also review any finding of fact on which the notice was based.[70] The Tribunal may also entertain appeals against ministerial national security certificates given under Part II of the Act.[71] But there is no provision for appeal against a veto certificate issued by a minister under section 53. There is a further right of appeal from the Tribunal, on a point of law only, to the High Court.[72]

Parts VI and VII of the Act concern respectively the application of the Act to historical and public records held in the Public Record Office and to the amendments necessary to the Data Protection Act 1998. Part VIII contains miscellaneous and supplemental provisions, and there are numerous Schedules to the Act, containing, for instance, lists of the public authorities to which the Act applies, or partially applies.

CRITIQUE OF THE FREEDOM OF INFORMATION ACT 2000

In this author's view, the Act is a brilliant piece of *trompe l'oeil*, a sheep in wolf's clothing. It purports to provide a legally enforceable individual right of access to governmental information subject only to specified and justifiable exemptions. It purports also to provide general publication duties in respect of governmental information. But in reality it does neither of these.

First, the range of exemptions is far wider and more extensive than in any other statutory freedom of information regime in any comparable democratic state. Many of the exemptions are absolute, requiring no proof, other than wide, conclusive, discretionary ministerial certification, of identifiable harm to national or public interests, and even the qualified exemptions are subject to a test of simple prejudice which is relatively easy to

66 Ibid., s. 53. 67 Ibid., s. 56. 68 Ibid., s. 57. 69 Ibid., s. 58(1). 70 Ibid., s. 58(2).
71 Ibid., s. 60. 72 Ibid., s. 59.

satisfy. The range and scope of exemptions is wider than even that contained in the existing Code of Practice on Access to Government Information. Contrary to the White Paper, the majority of the enormous number of existing statutory prohibitions on disclosure has been retained under the Act, with no obligation on government to repeal or amend any of them, as promised in *Your Right to Know*. However, the Government has repealed 13 such provisions,[73] and under a recent review,[74] has undertaken to repeal a further 40 and impose time limits on a further 19. Nonetheless, even after the review, the repeals and the 'sunset' clauses, 140 such provisions will remain in force. Under this new statutory regime, the citizen will be entitled to less than s/he is already able to obtain under the non-statutory regime. The exemptions far exceed those specified in *Your Right to Know*, which was perceived by most commentators as striking a fair balance between governmental interests and the legitimate right of the public to know what its government does in its name.

Second, there is no right of access to government records, but to information, and the duty to comply with the applicant's preferences is a qualified one. Hence the Act is subject to the same criticism as the Code of Practice, that it confers editorial control on the Government or public authority over what it actually discloses to the applicant. Only if there is a specific legal right to government records, as in the USA, and various other freedom of information regimes, will there be genuine freedom of information.

Third, the fee-charging regime[75] does not set a standard nominal fee for FoI requests, but provides for charging for specified tasks in relation to complying with requests,[76] in accordance with a specified hourly rate,[77] currently £25 per hour, with upper limits for total charges.[78] Depending on the type of public authority, the maximum fee is either £450 or £600,[79] but under aggregation provisions, the fee for complying with a number of related requests can be charged for each related request.[80] These provisions raise the same fears as applied to the fee-charging practices under the previous Code of Practice, namely that applicants other than large commercial corporations will not be able to afford the cost of access. It was precisely this problem that the White Paper sought to address by proposing an affordable standard fee of £10, subject to special provision for particularly voluminous or burdensome requests. The right to know what our government does in our name should not have set upon it a price which the average individual citizen cannot afford.

Fourth, the obligations to establish publication schemes have been so diluted that there is no duty to publish information of any specified type. Since the Croham Directive of 1978,[81] government has published the facts and research underlying its policy decisions, and this was required by the 1993 Code of Practice. The duty to give reasons for administrative decisions to those affected by them was clearly laid down in the Code of Practice. Now, under the Act, there is merely an unenforceable general duty to have regard to the public interest in the

[73] The Freedom of Information (Removal and Relaxation of Statutory Prohibitions on Disclosure of Information) Order 2004 (SI 2004/3363).

[74] *Department for Constitutional Affairs Review of Statutory Prohibitions on Disclosure 2004.*

[75] The Freedom of Information and Data Protection (Appropriate Limit and Fees) Regulations 2004 (SI 2004/3244).

[76] Ibid., regs 4, 6 and 7.

[77] Ibid., reg. 4(4). [78] Ibid., reg. 3. [79] Ibid., reg. 3. [80] Ibid., reg. 5.

[81] The Civil Service Department Directive on Disclosure of Official Information, 6 July 1977, issued by Sir Douglas Allan (later Lord Croham), which required all central government departments to publish the factual information and research on which policy decisions were based. Policy advice was to be separated from the factual material and not to be published.

public having access to government information and in the giving of reasons for administrative decisions. This is such a weak provision that its value must be questionable. In effect, public authorities may decide for themselves what to publish in their publication schemes. Although the Information Commissioner may appear to have enforcement powers by virtue of the approval provisions, the withholding of approval does not have any sanction. Section 19 appears to provide an unenforceable statutory duty, other than by judicial review. Since there is no particular specified content to a publication scheme, it would be very difficult to establish that the Commissioner was justified in withholding his approval. *Wednesbury*[82] unreasonableness is a high threshold to surmount, but it would probably be necessary to show that the public authority had acted irrationally in the super-*Wednesbury*[83] sense in order to uphold the Commissioner's refusal to approve its publication scheme.

Fifthly, the right of ministerial veto undermines any credibility to the claim that the Act creates a legally enforceable individual right of access. The scope of the discretionary power is extraordinary: the minister need only certify that on reasonable grounds he has formed the opinion that there has been no failure to comply with the duty to grant access to information requested.[84] There is no obligation to give reasons for his opinion, nor to provide the information or grounds upon which he formed his opinion. Given the highly subjective formulation of the veto power, the sensitive nature of the information likely to be involved, and the very high level of government at which the decision has to be taken, it is extremely unlikely that a veto could be successfully reviewed, or that a court would require the giving of reasons.

FREEDOM OF INFORMATION IN PRACTICE: THE FIRST TWO YEARS

The first two years' operation of the Freedom of Information Act 2000 has been a mixed success. Departments and public authorities have frequently failed to comply with the time limits provided under the Act. Time extensions are routinely sought by some public authorities. Long delays occur when public authorities carry out internal reviews or need to consider the public interest in disclosing exempt information. Exemptions are frequently claimed with little justification. A number of errors have been made in the interpretation of the Act. Appeals to the Commissioner have been so numerous that a substantial backlog of cases has developed that is only slowly being reduced. Substantial fees have been charged by some departments and public authorities. Records management by many public authorities is of poor quality, and, in particular, the storage and preservation of information held in changing electronic media is a matter of major concern.

On the positive side, a very large number of requests for information has been made, a majority from members of the public, the remainder from journalists, pressure groups and other organizations. Much valuable information has been released into the public domain that would not have been disclosed without the Freedom of Information Act. There has

82 *Associated Provincial Picture Houses* v. *Wednesbury Corporation* [1948] 1 KB 223.

83 See *R. (Daly)* v. *Secretary of State for the Home Department* [2001] 2 WLR 1622, for discussion of the different levels of irrationality developed in recent judicial decisions.

84 Freedom of Information Act 2000, s. 53.

been a significant number of high profile disclosures, in response to requests made under the Act, of information that was highly sensitive, politically embarrassing and of major public interest. Much of the information is being used in a constructive and positive way. Although there have been reservations about the Information Commissioner's resolution of complaints, the Information Tribunal has taken a strong, positive, pro-disclosure approach in appeals from the decisions of the Information Commissioner.

The number of FoI requests across all government departments was approximately 38,000 in 2005, according to statistics published by the Department for Constitutional Affairs (DCA).[85] Local authorities reported having received around 70,000 requests and the police service around 21,000, giving a total of approximately 130,000 in the first year of operation.[86] The Information Commissioner estimated that 100–130,000 FoI requests had been made in the Act's first year of operation.[87] Although the number of requests in the first quarter of 2005 (when the access rights first came into effect) was greater than in subsequent quarters, the number of requests per quarter has steadied at approximately two-thirds of the first quarter's figure. Not all bodies are monitored by the DCA, but those monitored are currently receiving 8–9,000 per quarter.[88] It is clear then that the Act is being used extensively to obtain information from both central government and other public authorities.

Evidence given to the Constitutional Affairs Select Committee indicates that the majority of FoI requests come from ordinary members of the public, not principally from the media and pressure groups as predicted,[89] and the Select Committee cited several examples of the type of information disclosed and the valuable uses to which released information had been put.[90] Not only were individuals able to obtain information 'of real value to people's daily lives, public service and the environment'[91] but the media had succeeded in obtaining information that had 'led to a wide range of investigative reports.'[92] Information released included: subsidy payments to individual farmers under the Common Agricultural Policy; historical information relating to the Falklands war, the Exchange Rate Mechanism and nuclear waste storage; information relating to Porton Down, the Government's chemical and biological weapons research facility; Home Office information relating to arranged marriages, gambling law reviews and the classification of cannabis; hygiene reports for restaurants, hotels and school kitchens; information about faulty TB vaccines given to nearly one million children; information about doctors' incomes under the new NHS settlement for general practitioners; the heart surgery survival rates for different hospitals; public authorities' spending on consultants' fees; percentages required for school and university examination pass grades; the best and worst performing schools in each county; and the safety of Britain's nuclear energy plants.[93] The overall thrust of evidence given to, and the conclusion reached by, the Select Committee was that the first year's operation of the Act was 'a significant success.'[94]

85 Department for Constitutional Affairs FoI Statistics; www.dca.gov.uk/foi/reference/statsandreports.

86 House of Commons Select Committee on Constitutional Affairs, 7th Report 2005–06, para. 5.

87 Ibid.

88 Department for Constitutional Affairs FoI Statistics for January to March and April to June 2006; www.dca.gov.uk/foi/reference/statsandreports.

89 House of Commons Select Committee on Constitutional Affairs, 7th Report 2005–06, para. 7.

90 Ibid., paras 10–12.

91 Ibid., para. 8.

92 Ibid., para. 10.

93 Ibid., paras 6, 11 and 12. See also Government Response to the Constitutional Affairs Select Committee Report, 'Freedom of Information – one year on' Cm 6937 (2006), para. 8.

94 Ibid., para. 13.

Unfortunately, however, this success was not unqualified. The Select Committee received overwhelming evidence of serious problems with the operation of the Act. Delays in responding to requests were widespread, with some departments and public authorities failing to meet the 20 working days deadline in a significant proportion of cases. The Home Office, for example, achieved only 30 per cent success in meeting the deadline in the first quarter of 2005, and by the end of 2005 this had risen that to 64 per cent; i.e. in over a third of all requests, the Home Office failed to meet the deadline, in some cases by several months. Many, but not all, other departments and public authorities achieved much higher compliance with the deadline, some in excess of 90 per cent.[95]

Much more significant was the absence of deadlines when departments or public authorities are permitted such extra time as is reasonable to consider and decide whether the public interest in disclosure of exempt information outweighs the public interest in maintaining the exemption. DCA statistics indicate that these permitted extensions were used by central government departments in approximately 10 per cent of all requests in 2005, but do not record the length of such extensions. Requestors experienced delays of several months in some cases. The Information Commissioner considered that the maximum period necessary to consider and decide the public interest question was two months, but this was frequently exceeded.[96]

A further cause of significant delay in responding to requests was the time taken to conduct internal reviews, sometimes several months. Again, there is no statutory deadline for the conduct of internal reviews; although DCA guidance sets a deadline of six weeks, the DCA acknowledges that internal reviews often take several months. As exhaustion of administrative redress is a mandatory prerequisite before a requestor can complain to the Information Commissioner about the failure of a department or public authority to respond to a request,[97] delay in carrying out internal reviews is a way of stalling requests indefinitely, unless the Information Commissioner is willing to consider a complaint where there has been excessive delay in conducting the internal review. The Commissioner gave evidence to the Select Committee that he intended to use his formal powers to consider complaints when he considers that the internal complaints procedure has effectively been exhausted, thereby putting pressure on public authorities to complete internal reviews more quickly.[98] Given the substantial backlog of cases to be considered by the Information Commissioner's Office (ICO), it is suggested that this may be easier said than done.

The delays in complaints resolution by the ICO is a major source of dissatisfaction on the part of requestors. By the end of the first year of operation of the FoI Act, the ICO had received 2,385 cases, and had resolved only 1,060 of these, leaving a backlog of 1,325. Although additional resources were allocated to the ICO for the 2006–07 financial year, a backlog of 700 cases remained in October, 2006.[99] The ICO is now receiving approximately 225 new cases per month, and is resolving around 240 per month. On this basis it would take almost four more years to clear the backlog, and the Commissioner has sought and obtained additional resources to clear it,[100] but the Select Committee was not convinced that adequate resources had been allocated to resolve this problem, or that they had been allocated sufficiently early.[101] Complaints about the length of time taken by the ICO to

95 Ibid., paras 16–17, 33–5. 96 Ibid., paras 18–21.

97 Freedom of Information Act 2000, s. 50(2).

98 Select Committee on Constitutional Affairs, 2005–06, 7th Report, paras 22–4.

99 Ibid, paras 51–5. 100 Ibid., paras 60 and 61. 101 Ibid., para. 62.

resolve cases have also been widespread, some cases taking several months to complete.[102] Here again there is no statutory deadline set for the resolution of complaints. Not only does this mean that by the time the complaint is resolved the information may no longer be current or of use but, as was pointed out in evidence to the Select Committee,[103] in the early stages of the Act's operation it is essential to have authoritative rulings through decision and enforcement notices clarifying interpretation of the Act's substantive provisions. Without speedy resolution of these early cases, many requestors and many government departments and public authorities will have no clear guidance or certainty as to the operation of the Act.

One of the problems faced by the Commissioner was in seeking information from public authorities, including government departments, which would enable him properly to conduct his investigations into requestors' complaints, in particular the requested information, without which he cannot 'form a judgment about the applicability of exemptions or public interest factors.'[104] In some cases where public authorities had been reluctant or slow to disclose the information to the Commissioner, he had recently issued enforcement notices requiring the disclosure to him of the information.[105] The Commissioner also noted that there had been 'pockets of resistance' and 'some evidence of more entrenched attitudes regarding openness and even resistance to constructive dialogue with the ICO.'[106] This was not in accordance with the Memorandum of Understanding (MoU) between the DCA and the Commissioner to promote good standards of cooperation between government departments and the ICO.[107] Although the ministerial veto under section 53 has not been invoked, the Speaker of the House of Commons has used his power under section 36 to issue a certificate that information relating to MPs' salaries and expenses is personal data the disclosure of which would prejudice the effective conduct of public affairs. It is understood that the Information Commissioner intends to issue an enforcement notice against this certificate.[108]

There was also criticism that there was a lack of guidance from the Commissioner on decisions taken by the ICO, which would enable public authorities to consider whether to amend their policies, practices and staff instructions on disclosure.[109] The DCA has already established a clearing house to enable government departments to share experience and best practice of FoI, and ACPO have made similar arrangements for the police service. The DCA clearing house provides guidance, including case-specific advice, for the wider public sector as well as government departments.[110]

Further criticisms were that many public authorities had interpreted the exemptions 'in an excessively broad manner'[111] and that some authorities failed properly to distinguish between requests under the FoI Act and the parallel but different regime under the Environmental Information Regulations (EIR), which apply to a wider range of organizations, impose stricter time limits and have fewer exemptions from disclosure. It was feared

[102] Ibid., paras 25–6, 51–62. [103] Ibid., para. 26. [104] Ibid., para. 65.

[105] Ibid., para. 65. [106] Ibid., para. 65.

[107] Memorandum of Understanding signed by the Secretary of State for Constitutional Affairs, on behalf of all government departments, in February 2005, agreeing to cooperate with the Commissioner in respect of his investigations into complaints against departments under the FoI Act.

[108] Information obtained on an unattributable basis from a Constitution Unit FoI seminar, 10 October 2006. [109] Select Committee on Constitutional Affairs, 2005–06, 7th Report, para. 36.

[110] Ibid., para. 37. [111] Ibid., para. 27.

that this could lead to erroneous decisions to deny information under the FoI regime, which should be disclosed under the EIR regime. The Select Committee recommended that a shared code of practice be developed between DCA and DEFRA in order to resolve any confusion over the operation and application of the two regimes.[112]

Further, serious concern was expressed by the National Archive that many public authorities had poor records management and specifically in relation to the keeping of electronic records in different media that would become obsolete.[113] Given the speed of developments in the electronic storage of information and the likelihood of deterioration of electronically-stored information or the media on which it is stored, records of only 10 years ago would become irretrievable. Professionals in the field of records management concurred with that view and indicated that there would be major problems unless the issue was addressed as a matter of urgency.[114] Although the DCA minister denied that there was such a problem,[115] the Select Committee thought it would be complacent for the Government to ignore this issue.[116]

Lastly, both the Commissioner and the Select Committee took the view that the Commissioner's relationship with the DCA gave rise to concern. The DCA is the Government department responsible for implementation, compliance and promotion of FoI. For this department to be responsible for funding the independent regulator creates potential conflicts of interest, and potentially undermines the Commissioner's independence. Some problems had already arisen in the provision of adequate resources. The Select Committee recommended that the Commissioner become directly responsible to and funded by Parliament.[117]

The Government Response to the Constitutional Affairs Select Committee Report[118] accepted many of the Select Committee's findings and recommendations, but rejected some of the more contentious ones, including those concerning records management and preservation, fees, the arrangements for securing the independence of the Information Commissioner, and the role of the DCA Clearing House. Of particular concern is the Government's proposal,[119] based on an independent economic report[120] commissioned by the Government, to make substantial charges to the calculation of fees. The report calculated that the annual cost of operating the FoI Act was £24.4 million. In order to reduce both the volume of requests and their cost, the Government proposes to:

> include reading time, consideration time and consultation time in the calculation of the appropriate limit (£600) above which requests could be refused on cost grounds, and [to] aggregate requests made by any legal person (or persons apparently acting in concert) to each public authority, (e.g. Government Department) for the purpose of calculating the appropriate limit.[121]

This proposal, if carried out, would seriously undermine the ability of requestors to obtain information and calls into question the Government's commitment to freedom of information. Admittedly it applies to legal persons only, i.e. companies, but it also

112 Ibid., para. 30. 113 Ibid., para. 44. 114 Ibid., para. 46. 115 Ibid., para. 45.
116 Ibid., para. 46. 117 Ibid., paras 50, 105–8.
118 Freedom of Information – one year on, Cm 6937, October 2006, TSO, www.foi.gov.uk.
119 Ibid, para. 50.
120 Frontier Economics, Independent Review of the Impact of the Freedom of Information Act, a Report prepared for the Department for Constitutional Affairs, October 2006, www.foi.gov.uk.
121 Supra, Cm 6937, para. 50.

includes natural persons who may be acting together to make a number of requests to obtain information from the same public authority, thus preventing the employees of companies from making numerous different requests. This could seriously affect some of the main users of the Act, the press and media, and is a highly retrograde step in the process of making the UK Government more transparent.[122]

The Information Tribunal has already established itself as a strongly pro-disclosure, independent adjudicator, despite the relatively small number of cases decided thus far.[123] Nearly one-third of the appeals to the Tribunal resulted in reversals of the Information Commissioner's decision. The Tribunal has interpreted its jurisdiction under section 58, to consider whether notices issued by the Commissioner are in accordance with law, and whether any discretion exercised by the Commissioner ought to have been exercised differently, as conferring upon the Tribunal a full *de novo* power of appeal on merits.[124] Further, if the Commissioner has based his decision on a mistake of fact, that will be regarded as not in accordance with law; accordingly the Tribunal may review any finding of fact upon which a decision notice is based.[125] The Tribunal may and will substitute its own decision for that of the Commissioner if it thinks the Commissioner's decision is wrong. The public interest balancing test on qualified exemptions is not a matter of discretion but a mixed question of fact and law.[126] There is a presumption in favour of disclosure of exempt information unless the public interest in maintaining the exemption **outweighs** the public interest in disclosure, so that if the issue is evenly balanced, the information must be disclosed.[127] There must be a real likelihood, a real and significant risk, of prejudice to particular interests to justify an exemption.[128] A report originally made for journalistic purposes may subsequently be held by a public authority for managerial and personnel purposes and thus fall outside the exclusion of material held for the purpose of journalism.[129] A transcript of criminal proceedings made by a third party is not a document created by a court for the purpose of proceedings, and is therefore not exempt from disclosure.[130] Travel expenses claimed by Members of Parliament are not exempt from disclosure on the grounds of personal privacy.[131] In addition to these substantive rulings, the Tribunal has been very pro-active in advising the Information Commissioner as to how to proceed with investigations and his use of enforcement powers. Tribunal decisions are fully reasoned with detailed analysis of the relevant statutory provisions and strong reliance on judicial decisions. It is perhaps a cause for concern that the Commissioner has been reversed in quite a high proportion of appeals, but it is also laudable that the Tribunal has taken such a strongly pro-active and pro-disclosure approach to its jurisdiction.

122 In March, 2007, the Government announced that it was deferring the proposed change pending full consultation and research.

123 www.informationtribunal.gov.uk/our_decisions. The Tribunal website carried 23 decisions as of 30 October, 2006, but in two cases there were two separate decisions, thus reducing the number of completed cases to 21.

124 *Bellamy* v. *Information Commissioner*, Appeal no. EA/2005/23.

125 *Barber* v. *Information Commissioner*, Appeal no. EA/2005/0004; *Bowbrick* v. *Information Commissioner*, Appeal no. EA/2005/0006.

126 *Hemsley* v. *Information Commissioner*, Appeal no. EA/2005/26.

127 *Hogan & Oxford City Council* v. *Information Commissioner*, Appeals nos. EA/2005/26 EA/2005/30.

128 *Hogan & Oxford City Council* v. *Information Commissioner*, Appeals nos. EA/2005/26 EA/2005/30; *John Connor Press Associates* v. *Information Commissioner*, Appeal no. EA/2005/0005.

129 *Sugar* v. *Information Commissioner*, Appeal no. EA/2005/32.

130 *Mitchell* v. *Information Commissioner*, Appeal no. EA/2005/0002.

131 *The Corporate Officer of the House of Commons v The Information Commissioner and Norman Baker MP*, Appeal no. EA/2006/0015 & 0016.

CONCLUSIONS

Many commentators have argued that it is better to have the principle of freedom of information enshrined in statute, in a full legislative scheme, because once thus firmly established, it will be impossible for government to turn back the clock, to reverse the process of reform, and that a statutory freedom of information regime, however weak, will change the culture of secrecy to one of openness, by establishing a clear presumption in favour of disclosure rather than withholding. With respect, that argument only succeeds where the statutory regime creates a legally enforceable right of access to all governmental records subject only to specific, limited, and justifiable exceptions. Where, as in the case of the Freedom of Information Act 2000, the right of access is so drastically limited by such an extensive range of broad exemptions, where it does not grant a right of access to records but to information, where there is an absolute right of ministerial veto, and where the general publication duties are so weak as to be virtually unenforceable, it might have been better not to have legislated.

Only if the Act is shown to operate in a manner that does force government to disclose significant levels of official information that would not have been disclosed without the Act, could the new Freedom of Information regime be deemed a success. The Select Committee's conclusion that the Act had been a significant success in its first year of operation must be tempered by the serious difficulties and problems experienced by many requestors when seeking information under the Act, and documented in the Select Committee's report. In addition, evidence given to the Committee indicated that a change in bureaucratic culture was unlikely.[132] The Committee took the view that culture change was a long-term aim, and that what was needed as an immediate priority under the new FoI regime was 'a more effective and assertive enforcement of the law.'[133] In the light of the first two years' experience of the operation of the FoI Act, it must be concluded that the new FoI regime still falls far short of the ideal, and that unless the legislation is significantly improved by amendments, it will continue to do so. The Government's response to the Select Committee Report, in particular its proposals concerning fees, give little cause for optimism.

This conclusion has been reached because ultimately, in reality, what the Government has enshrined in this Act is a discretionary power to choose what information to disclose, subject only to the weak constraint of ministerial accountability to Parliament. We have returned under this Act to the state of affairs prior to the Croham Directive, to an all-pervasive culture of secrecy and of seeking to find a reason for not disclosing, rather than a culture of openness. Of course, for most routine, non-sensitive information, the right of access under the Act will work, and no government department or public authority is likely to have a publication scheme which publishes no useful information at all. But the true test of a freedom of information regime is when it is tested in the crucible of major, politically sensitive crises such as the Arms to Iraq scandal. If the Freedom of Information Act had been in force at that time, it would have given us even less information than was extracted from government during that crisis. Every sensitive piece of information would have been justifiably exempt, or the responsible cabinet minister would have exercised the veto under section 53. Governments are naturally secretive and never more so than when under attack

132 Select Committee on Constitutional Affairs, 2005–06, 7th Report, para. 112.

133 Ibid., para. 113.

for actions or decisions which may threaten loss of office. The White Paper rightly acknowledged that the existence of a ministerial veto power would in effect undermine the legitimacy of the Act. The Freedom of Information Act 2000 remains a sheep in wolf's clothing but its operation may, despite its limitations, save it from becoming a fraud on democratic accountability.

FURTHER READING

Birkinshaw, P. *Freedom of Information, The Law, the Practice and the Ideal* (3rd edn, 2001)

McDonald, A. and Terrill, G. (eds) *Open Government* (1998).

USEFUL WEB SITES

Department for Constitutional Affairs web site on freedom of information: **www.dca.gov.uk/foi**

The Information Commissioner's website: **www.informationcommissioner.gov.uk**

The Information Tribunal's website: **www.informationtribunal.gov.uk**

17

STANDARDS OF CONDUCT IN PUBLIC LIFE

Patricia Leopold

SUMMARY

Since 1995 there have been a variety of reforms aimed at encouraging ethical behaviour by those in public life. This has resulted in new legislation, the introduction of soft-law codes, the creation of new regulators and the establishment of new procedures. The aim is to provide systems that are sufficiently robust to satisfy an increasingly distrustful public. The challenge has been to provide clear, transparent, and fair schemes that retain self-regulation but include an independent or external element or both. The Westminster Parliament and Government have often been the most reluctant of all the public bodies to take adequate account of these requirements. This can be compared with the very different approach, partly imposed by Westminster, that applies to local authorities and the devolved institutions. Reforms since 2003 to the scheme regulating conduct at Westminster appear to have reassured MPs. However despite the widespread growth in ethical regulators there does not appear to have an improvement in public confidence in the honesty of public office holders.[1] This may not be because the reforms since 1995 have been inadequate. Rather it may be a reflection of how public concerns have changed: the debate has moved from 'sleaze' to 'spin', from the activities of individual MPs to the actions of political parties and government ministers, from buying and selling influence to buying and selling political honours. However, it may also be a reflection on how some of the reforms have worked.

INTRODUCTION

Allegations that standards of conduct in public life have declined are not new. Several financial scandals featured in the period 1860 to 1930, the most notable of which were the Marconi affair, which involved allegations of corrupt financial speculation by members of the Government, and where the subsequent select committee inquiry split along party lines,[2] and the sale of political honours by the Lloyd George Coalition Government.[3]

[1] See the two national surveys on public attitudes towards conduct in public life prepared for the Committee on Standards in Public Life in 2004, and 2006.

[2] See (1913) HC 152 and 217.

[3] See the report of the Royal Commission on Honours, Cmd 1789 (1922), and the Honours (Prevention of Abuses) Act 1925.

Reforms consequent upon those scandals, such as the establishment of a statutory power to set up an inquiry[4] and the requirement that candidates for political honours should be vetted, are still in operation.[5] The scandals of the late 1950s and 1960s were mainly of a sexual nature. It was not until the 1970s that cases of major financial impropriety arose again, in particular with respect to the architect John Poulson bribing civil servants, local councillors, and MPs to assist him to secure official contracts. Two inquiries followed this affair, one of which[6] resulted in the establishment of new rules for the conduct of local government.[7] Another consequence of the Poulson affair was the introduction in 1974 of a register of members' interests for the Commons. However it was another 20 years before a series of scandals resulted in more widespread reforms regulating standards of conduct in public life. Although many of the allegations of misconduct in the mid-1990s were of sexual misbehaviour, it was the allegations of financial impropriety and abuse of governmental power that caused most concern. These included: the taking by MPs of cash for asking parliamentary questions; the relationship of MPs with lobbying companies and multi-client consultants – 'MPs for hire'; the acceptance by MPs, ministers, and civil servants of gifts, favours, or hospitality from businessmen; wrongdoing in local councils. It was not surprising that opinion polls at that time showed that the public standing of politicians had declined over a 10-year period. The range of reforms since 1995 appear to have resulted in a reduction in complaints concerning in particular financial scandals in Parliament. However, the public standing of politicians as a body continue to decline. Concerns now are with respect to the funding of political parties, ministerial conflicts of interest and the resurrection of allegations of 'cash for honours'.

THE COMMITTEE ON STANDARDS IN PUBLIC LIFE

The response of the Government to the scandals in the 1990s was to establish the independent advisory Committee on Standards in Public Life (CSPL). It was asked to:

> Examine current concerns about standards of conduct of all holders of public office, including arrangements relating to financial and commercial activities, and make recommendations as to any change in the present arrangements which might be required to ensure the highest standards of propriety in public life.[8]

4 The Tribunal of Inquiry Evidence Act 1921 which was repealed and replaced by the Inquiries Act 2005.

5 The Political Honours Scrutiny Committee (PHSC) was established in 1923 by Order in Council. It was charged with making inquiries into the background of those put forward for political honours and with deciding whether the nominees were 'fit and proper' persons. In 2000 a non-statutory body, the Appointments Commission, took over the functions of the PHSC.

6 The Committee on Local Government Rules of Conduct (the Redcliffe–Maud Report), Cmnd 5636 (1974). The other was the Royal Commission on Standards of Conduct in Public Life (Salmon Report), Cmnd 6524 (1977), see text at n. 27 below.

7 The Local Government Act 1972 required councillors to disclose the existence of any direct or indirect financial interest in council business. As a consequence of the Redcliffe–Maud Report, a nationally agreed code of practice, DoE Circular 94/75, supplemented the existing rules. The Local Government and Housing Act 1989 implemented some of the recommendations of the Widdicombe Committee, Cmnd 9797 (1986) including the establishment of a statutory register of members' interests and a statutory code of conduct.

8 HC Debs, 25 Oct. 1994, col. 758.

'Public life' and 'holders of public office' included ministers, civil servants and advisers, MPs and MEPs, non-ministerial office holders, members and senior officers of various other bodies discharging public-funded functions, and elected members and senior officers of local authorities.

The work of the CSPL has been central to the post-1995 approach to the regulation of standards of conduct. Its First Report[9] provided the basis for much of the initial reforms, and identified seven generally applicable principles of public life (the Nolan principles). These were: selflessness, integrity, objectivity, accountability, openness, honesty,[10] and leadership. To further implement and apply these principles it made three broad recommendations: the establishment of codes of conduct reiterating the Nolan principles throughout the public sector; that the internal systems of scrutinizing and monitoring the behaviour of those in public life should be supported by independent scrutiny; education and training should be used to inculcate high ethical standards. As will be seen, the relevant public bodies responded positively to most of these recommendations. As a consequence there has been a process of lucidification of much political activity,[11] that is the codification in writing of standards which had been assumed (wrongly in many cases) to be commonly understood.

The CSPL is free to choose its subjects of inquiry (after consultation with the Cabinet Secretary) and since 1994 it has examined arrangements in most areas of the public sector, both local and national, and issued 11 reports.[12] 70 per cent of its recommendations have been accepted and implemented by government.[13] It has also conducted reviews of the implementation of its recommendations (Sixth[14] and Eighth[15] Reports), and commissioned and published two quantative studies of public attitudes to public office holders.[16]

The way in which the First CSPL report was implemented varied. At Westminster, in order to preserve the privilege of 'self-regulation', both Houses devised new rules and procedures to be administered internally. Although the rules and procedures in the House of Commons have been revised several times since 1996, self-regulation remains the norm at Westminster. In contrast, Westminster was not prepared to allow the devolved institutions the same degree of self-regulation. The 1998 devolution legislation that granted powers to the Scottish Parliament and the Welsh and Northern Ireland Assemblies, also imposed certain minimum requirements and enforcement procedures, involving in places the criminal law. Since 1998, both Scotland and Wales, acting within the devolution legislation framework, have reformed the rules and procedures concerned with the regulation of conduct. Criminal sanctions to regulate conduct is also found with respect to local authorities. The Local Government Act 2000[17] introduced a new ethical framework to replace the piecemeal system introduced in 1972. A highly centralized Standards Board for England[18] was established to enforce this framework and to supervise arrangements for the

[9] Cm 2850 (1995).

[10] The CSPL may consider recommending a broader definition of honesty to reflect the value the public attaches to the principle of 'telling the truth'. *Survey of public attitudes towards conduct in public life*: Summary of key findings (2004), p. 15.

[11] Dawn Oliver, *Constitution Reform in the UK* (2003).

[12] A full list of its reports can be found in the back of each report.

[13] Annual Report from CSPL (2005).

[14] Cm 4557 (2000).

[15] Cm 5663 (2002).

[16] Nn. 1 and 10 above.

[17] Following in part recommendations from the CSPL in its Third Report Cm 4057 (1998).

[18] In Wales it is the Commission for Local Administration; Scotland regulates standards in local authorities under the Ethical Standards in Public Life (Scotland) Act 2000. As yet Northern Ireland does not have a statutory framework for local councils.

investigation of complaints. This framework proved unsatisfactory and, following the Tenth report from the CSPL,[19] the Government accepted the need to amend the 2000 Act, particularly with respect to enforcement. The discussion of the regulation of standards of conduct in this chapter will be primarily with respect to both Houses of Parliament, ministers, and the devolved bodies.

Two aspects of the regulation of standards in public life will be considered: codes of conduct and enforcement procedures. The values and rules on the disclosure of interests are set out in each code of conduct. These may prohibit holders of public office from undertaking certain activities or from holding certain interests. They may also require other interests to be publicly registered and declared before certain activities are undertaken. There are two main reasons why outside interests have to be disclosed: first, to provide information about those in public life that might be thought by others to influence their actions or conduct, and to demonstrate an individual's particular expertise in a matter; second, to promote a culture among those active in public life which supports and sustains ethical behaviour. Although there are common values in the various codes, the promotion of ethical behaviour is encouraged by the assumption that each public body will produce its own code of conduct.

The second aspect of regulation, the enforcement procedures and sanctions, should be evaluated in the light of the minimum requirements of fairness.[20] There are variations between how different bodies enforce these rules. At Westminster the rules can be described as 'soft law', that is their breach does not lead to legally enforceable sanctions such as prosecution. However, in the devolved institutions (and in local government) some of the rules can be legally enforced.

THE HOUSE OF COMMONS

The rules on standards of conduct in Parliament have to be seen in the context of a number of ancient and undoubted rights and privileges regarded as essential for parliamentary independence. The most important parliamentary privilege is freedom of speech. Article 9 of the Bill of Rights 1689 provides that 'the freedom of speech and debates or proceedings in Parliament ought not be impeached or questioned in any court or place out of Parliament'. Parliamentary privilege does not give members of either House general immunity from the civil or criminal law. However no liability will lie if the alleged activity, or the evidence with respect to it, was done or said in the course of 'proceedings in Parliament'. One aspect of parliamentary privilege is that members should be free from undue influence from financial and other interests outside Parliament and they should not use the position of MP as a means to gain personal financial advantage. Another is 'exclusive cognisance', which means that Parliament has exclusive jurisdiction over its own affairs, the concept of self-regulation. This allows each House to decide its own procedures and to regulate the conduct of its members, usually by passing resolutions. Allegations of breaches of these resolutions are for Parliament to investigate and enforce. Parliament's reluctance to regulate its affairs by

[19] Cm 6407 (2005).

[20] See the Joint Committee on Parliamentary Privilege Report (1998–9), HL 43, HC 214 (the Nicholls Report), which suggested six minimum requirements for fairness in enforcement procedures, para. 281.

statute or to introduce an external element into its proceedings is based on a fear that to do so would enable the courts to intervene in its procedures and activities.[21]

It would be inaccurate to suggest that until 1995 Parliament had neither rules on conduct nor a code of conduct. The resolutions discussed below, reports from committees and decisions of each House, together with the standing orders, provided rules and a type of code of conduct. Although the various rules and resolutions could be found in *Erskine May*,[22] updated editions of *Erskine May* are relatively infrequent, and it is a weighty tome and not user-friendly. There was no accessible and comprehensive account of the ethical standards expected of members. Prior to 1995, resolutions passed by the Commons to regulate standards of conduct were reactions to events, rather than proactive, principled decisions to improve behaviour.

The earliest attempt to regulate the conduct of members of the House of Commons was in 1695 when it was resolved that the acceptance of a bribe by a member of either House to influence him in his conduct as a member was a contempt of Parliament. In 1976 the view of the Salmon Commission,[23] was that neither the statute law[24] nor the common law[25] on corruption applied to MPs,[26] since for the purpose of the legislation Parliament was not a 'public body' and nor was a MP an 'agent' – the terms used to define subjection to the statutory requirements.[27] Only Parliament's own law of contempt applied, something the Salmon Commission recommended should be rectified. Although there is no suggestion that the bribery of members of either House in their capacity as such is, or ever has been, a major concern it was clearly unsatisfactory that there was uncertainty in the application of the law. Draft legislation to reform the law on corruption generally, including provisions to bring members of both Houses of Parliament within the reformed law on bribery and to remove the protection of Article 9 of the Bill of Rights 1689 from MPs and peers in corruption prosecutions, was put before Parliament only in 2003.[28] However, no further progress has been made, a matter of some concern.

To understand the other resolutions of the House of Commons on standards of conduct it should be remembered that it is only since 1911 that MPs who are not ministers have received a salary.[29] It had always been accepted that they could take paid employment outside the House, practise in their professions, own land and property. However, as the resolutions attempt to make clear, payments for such activities should not be connected with the parliamentary actions of MPs. Members should not place themselves under any financial or other obligation to those outside Parliament that could interfere with or inhibit the exercise of their right to freedom of speech. A resolution passed in 1858 against professional advocacy was interpreted as aimed specifically at prohibiting MPs who were

21 This would not necessarily be the case, see *Hamilton* v. *Al Fayed* [2001] 1 AC 395.

22 W. R. MacKay and R. Wilson (eds), *Erskine May, Parliamentary Practice (The Law, Privileges, Proceedings and Usage of Parliament)* (23rd edn, 2004).

23 N. 6 above.

24 The Prevention of Corruption Acts 1889 to 1916.

25 For an alternative view on the application of the common law offence to MPs see the judgment of Buckley J in *R.* v. *Greenway* reported in [1998] *Public Law* 356–63 with commentary by A. W. Bradley.

26 The corruption legislation applies to local authorities, the Scottish Parliament, and the Welsh National Assembly.

27 The Salmon Report (n. 6 above), para. 307.

28 The Corruption Reform Bill 2003; a Joint Committee reported on the draft Bill: (2002–3), HL 157, HC 705; see also the Home Office consultation paper, *Clarification of the Law Relating to the Bribery of Members of Parliament*, Cm 2931 (1995).

29 A consequence of the decision of the House of Lords in *Amalgamated Society of Railway Servants* v. *Osborne* [1910] AC 87 which prevented trade unions from paying salaries to Labour MPs.

barristers from practising as counsel in the House upon private Bills and from advocating or promoting matters with which they had been professionally concerned. In 1947, in response to a concern that an outside body was attempting to instruct a member, a resolution was passed prohibiting members from entering into contractual agreements with any body that would control or limit a member's complete independence and freedom of action in Parliament. It was the ambiguity of this resolution, which was interpreted as allowing members to enter into contracts with organizations which would pay them for certain parliamentary activities so long as the agreement did not *require* them to act in particular ways (which would fetter their freedom of action and thus be contrary to their duties to the public interest and their constituents), that allowed the growth of 'parliamentary consultancies', one of the main concerns of the First CSPL Report.

It had long been the case that members were prohibited from voting upon a matter in which he or she had a direct pecuniary interest of an immediate or personal character. It was also the practice that MPs were expected to declare direct pecuniary interests with respect to certain parliamentary proceedings. However this was not formally the subject of a House of Commons resolution until 1974 which also expanded the scope of the requirements for the declaration of interests to include direct or indirect benefits, of whatever nature, existing at the time, or expected. A non-mandatory register of members' interests was established in which members were expected to register, under several specified categories, pecuniary or other material benefits that might reasonably be thought by others to influence their parliamentary activities. A committee of MPs assisted by a senior clerk as registrar supervised the register. This was a paper recording exercise: there was no attempt by the Commons to establish or codify the ethical standards expected of members in their outside activities.

In its First Report[30] the CSPL identified several shortcomings with the regulation of standards of conduct in the House of Commons. These included: defects in the description of the nature and scope of the registration requirements leading to a laxity in registration; the belief by many MPs that if an interest was registered it was legitimated; the inadequacy of the procedures and mechanisms for investigating complaints about misconduct. The nub of the problem of MPs' outside interests identified by the CSPL was not the activities of members who continued to practise in the careers or occupations they had followed before their election to Parliament, for example as lawyers or journalists. Rather it was the growth in the outside employment of members which arose directly from their membership of the House of Commons, such as consultancy agreements with lobbying firms for whom members did work which was closely related to their activities in Parliament. This had given rise to public anxiety that influence, whether real or imagined, could be bought and sold through members.[31] However, rather than prohibit agreements for 'paid advocacy', the CSPL proposed tighter controls on the types of agreements MPs could make. The CSPL made four main recommendations: a new code of conduct for MPs; an improved register of members' interests; the establishment of an independent Parliamentary Commissioner for Standards; and a strengthened Committee on Standards and Privileges.

These recommendations were broadly implemented and a new regime governing the registration and declaration of interests and the investigation of complaints took effect in

[30] N. 9 above.

[31] See also the Second Report of the Select Committee on Standards in Public Life (1994–5), HC 816.

1995–6. In some respects the Commons went beyond the CSPL recommendations. In particular it decided that all paid advocacy agreements should be banned, and in consequence MPs could not accept payment for speaking in the House, asking a parliamentary question, tabling a motion, voting, or moving amendments to motions or Bills. However, the rules allowed MPs to continue as remunerated advisers to companies, pressure groups, etc., provided the agreement to do so was registered and declared. In this role an MP could speak out in support of a campaign that was of particular interest to the organization, but could not advocate any measure that would be for the exclusive benefit of that organization. The rules also provided that members should disclose the payments received for the provision of parliamentary services. The rules acknowledged that one of the roles of an MP is to represent constituency interests, and that this could conflict with the advocacy ban. MPs could pursue any constituency interests in proceedings in the House except where the member had a financial relationship with a company in the constituency. MPs were also required to avoid using a constituency interest as a means to raise a matter that could not otherwise be pursued.

THE CODE OF CONDUCT AND THE REGISTER OF MEMBERS' INTERESTS

The first House of Commons code of conduct and a *Guide to the Rules relating to the Conduct of MPs* was approved in July 1996. The arrangements were an important departure for the Commons, and over the next 10 years they have been subject to revision and refinement. The original code was a short document based on the Nolan Principles. It set out both broad principles of conduct – such as the obligation of members to the monarch, the law, and Parliament – and more specific obligations such as those to avoid conflicts of interests, not to accept bribes, to register interests, not to act as paid advocates. In 2003 the Commons agreed that the Parliamentary Commissioner for Standards (PCS) should review the code in the life of each Parliament, and in July 2005 it approved a revised code.[32] The changes were described by the PCS as 'a substantial re-casting and re-presentation of the Code intended to make it more useful to both the public and Members.'[33] In addition to expanding the explanation of the purpose and scope of the code, the 2005 revision added a duty on MPs to cooperate with all stages of an investigation into their conduct, and to refrain from lobbying members of the Committee on Standards and Privileges. Several significant substantive additions included bringing complaints about the use of expenses, allowances and facilities within the code, and a specific requirement to uphold the law against discrimination.

The *Guide* was more detailed than the code, with sections on the registration and declaration of interests, paid advocacy, and complaints procedure. The rules on the registration of interests require a variety of categories of interests to be registered including: directorships, remunerated employment and profession, gifts and hospitality, financial sponsorship, overseas visits, land and property, shareholdings, related undertakings, sponsorship, gifts, heritable property, interests in shares. However, unlike the position before 1996, the *Guide* provides guidance for MPs as to what is or is not acceptable. By way of example, although employment agreements involving the provision of services in a member's

[32] The PCS proposals for revision of the code were reviewed and approved (in all major respects) by the Committee on Standards and Privileges (2004–05) HC 472.

[33] Parliamentary Commissioner for Standards, Annual Report (2004–05) HC 264 para. 1.4.

capacity as an MP must be registered, if the employment is for a newspaper column or a radio programme wholly unrelated to parliamentary or public affairs, it does not have to be registered. Gifts and material benefits that do not relate to membership of the House do not have to be registered, but before deciding not to register the member should consider both the possible motive of the giver and the use to which the gift will be put. The register is compiled by the Registrar afresh at the start of every Parliament, and regularly updated. In debates or other proceedings, members are required to declare not only interests currently on the register, but also interests held in the recent past or expected in the future. The early version of the *Guide* caused more controversies than the code. Revisions in 2002 addressed some of these, for example the operation of the advocacy rule in such as way that it prevented the most knowledgeable MPs from contributing to the work of the House, and in particular prevented opposition frontbench spokesmen who had visited a country at the expense of that country's government from taking part in parliamentary procedures directly connected with the country in question. Other changes included: a renaming of the 'advocacy rule' as 'lobbying for reward or consideration', and a narrowing of the rule;[34] a simplification and clarification of the rules relating to the registration and declaration of interests, in particular with respect to the thresholds for the registering of gifts, benefits, and services; and the inclusion of partners as well as spouses in a number of categories. One particular change, an alignment with the Electoral Commission rules on the thresholds for political donations,[35] continued to cause problems with members having to comply with dual reporting requirements. An amendment included in the Electoral Administration Act 2006 will enable a 'one-stop shop' for donations and sponsorships to be established following discussions between the PCS and the Electoral Commission. Following his review of the Code, the PCS is now reviewing the *Guide* with the aim of simplifying and clarifying the expectations of MPs.[36]

ENFORCEMENT AND SANCTIONS

The procedures established are internal to the House, and are implemented by the PCS, the Committee on Standards and Privileges (the Committee), and the House itself. These are in effect disciplinary powers. The Commons is unusual in regulating such matters almost completely internally. By contrast, in the devolved institutions[37] and local government, statute provides that a failure to register interests or provide information necessary for investigations could be prosecuted as criminal offences, and alleged breaches are independently investigated. The system for enforcing standards of conduct in the House of Commons proved more controversial than either the code or the *Guide*. Perceived problems with the actual procedures originally established were addressed in 2003.[38] A lack of accessible information and guidance for either MPs or the public as to how the rules and procedures worked was addressed by a series of guidance notes written by the PCS.[39]

34 See (2001–2), HC 478 and HC 763 for details.

35 As provided by the Political Parties, Elections and Referendums Act 2000.

36 Parliamentary Commissioner for Standards, Annual Report (2005–06) HC 1480, para. 1.8.

37 See text at n. 85 below.

38 For the background see the Nicholls Report, n. 20 above; CSPL Sixth Report, n. 14 above. CSPL Eighth Report, n. 15 above; Second Report from the Committee on Standards and Privileges (2002–3), HC 403.

39 All of which are available from the Westminster Parliament web site.

The PCS has said of the current arrangements that they provide, 'a robust and impartial means of investigating complaints and seeking to prevent wrong-doing'.[40]

THE PARLIAMENTARY COMMISSIONER FOR STANDARDS

The PCS, the independent element in the scheme for regulating standards in the Commons, was established by standing order. It is likely that any suggestion to put it on a statutory basis[41] would be met by resistance in the Commons, not least because of the risk that this could expose the PCS's activities and decisions to judicial review.[42] Unsurprisingly perhaps, aspects of the status and tenure of this new post proved to be unclear,[43] and reforms were made in June 2003. As a consequence the PSC is appointed for a five-year non-renewable period, he can only be dismissed by the House after receipt of a reasoned adverse report from the Standards and Privileges Committee, and he must present an annual report to the Commons.[44] The roles of the PSC include the maintenance of the register of interests,[45] advising MPs on registration requirements and receiving and investigating specific complaints about the conduct of MPs.

In carrying out the first two of these roles the PCS has the assistance of the Registrar who is the first port of call for members who require advice. In this way the PCS avoids conflicts between these roles and his investigatory role. The present PCS has taken the view that the accuracy of the Register is best ensured by a proactive preventative approach. This approach was most in evidence after the 2005 general election when a programme of briefings was organized by his office. To ensure that the Register was complete and accurate there was 'vigorous follow-up' by his staff.[46]

It was the third of the roles that attracted most attention and caused the greatest controversy in the early days of the PCS. The PSC receives complaints and conducts an investigation into those that fall within his terms of reference. At the conclusion of the investigation the PCS reports to the Committee with his finding of fact and an opinion on whether there has been a breach of the code. The Committee does not have to accept the conclusion of the PCS that the facts as found by him amount to a breach of the code, but can conduct its own investigation, reach its own conclusion, and issue a report to the House. One issue was the procedure in the rare cases where there was a disagreement with the PCS or a dispute as to the facts, or where the consequences of an adverse decision and the subsequent imposition of a substantial penalty, and this could have a detrimental effect on the career of the MP concerned.[47] The Commons rejected the proposal from the CSPL that for this type of case there should be some form of independent tribunal or panel, composed not only of MPs.[48] Instead in 2003 the Commons agreed that the PCS, on his own initiative or on the

40 N. 36 above.

41 The Council of Europe's Group of States against Corruption (GRECO) in its first report on the UK had recommended this, but its later compliance reports accepted the status quo.

42 N. 21 above.

43 See the Eighth Report from the CSPL (n. 15 above), ch. 8.

44 HC Debs, 26 June 2003, cols 1239–58.

45 There are several other registers of interests: members' staff, journalists and All Party Groups. The maintenance of these registers is also the responsibility of the PCS. In 2005–06 for the first time complaints about two of these Registers were investigated. See text at n. 113 below.

46 See n. 36 above, section 2.

47 See for example the investigations into the activities of Neil Hamilton, (1997–8) HC 30 and HC 261, and Keith Vaz (2000–1), HC 314 and 605 .

48 See Sixth Report (n. 14 above) and the Eighth Report (n. 15 above).

recommendation of the Committee, could appoint an investigatory panel to assist him to establish the facts relevant to an investigation.[49] Since its establishment this procedure has not been required. Unlike the Scottish Commissioner, the PCS has no independent powers to summon persons or to require the production of papers or records. Only the Committee can do so on his behalf and a proposal by the CSPL to give the PCS such powers was rejected.[50] The absence of such powers does not in fact appear to have caused any problems. Another concern was where the PCS found a minor or inadvertent failing by a member. In 2003 this was dealt with by the introduction of a rectification procedure.[51] In 2005, following the inclusion in the code of misuse of allowances, facilities or services, a similar procedure was introduced to cover those who make a reimbursement to the relevant Officer of the House within a reasonable time.

The proactive approach by the PCS designed to ensure that MPs comply with the registration requirements, and the strengthening of the machinery for maintaining high standards of conduct, would appear to have been successful. Figures released by the PCS in his annual reports show that not only are the majority of complaints outside his terms of reference, but also the majority of those he does investigate result in no further action. Relatively few investigations have been into financial matters. Many of the problems of the early years of the PCS, such as frivolous or vexatious complaints,[52] seem to have either been resolved or disappeared.

COMMITTEE ON STANDARDS AND PRIVILEGES

The Commons Select Committee on Standards and Privileges oversees the work of the PCS and is at the heart of the self-regulatory process acting as a quasi-judicial body. The CSPL in its Eighth Report[53] questioned whether the Committee was sufficiently independent and impartial.[54] This was in part based on a perception that the Committee was more willing to overturn PCS decisions involving ministers than those involving backbench MPs.[55] The Commons accepted the CSPL recommendation that the Committee should have equal numbers of government and opposition members, and that Parliamentary Private Secretaries would not be appointed to it. It also accepted that the Committee should be able to appoint legal advisers. The Committee, not the PCS, recommends what punishment, if any, should be imposed on an MP. These range from a reprimand, suspension from the House with loss of salary, to expulsion and imprisonment.[56] An additional punishment of loss of salary without suspension was agreed in 2003. The final decision is for the House, which (being made up of politicians who may be influenced by consideration of whether the MP in question is a member of their party and of the political consequences of a

49 See SO 150 (4)–(9).

50 Eighth Report (n. 15 above), and response by the Committee on Standards and Privileges (2002–3) HC 403.

51 See SO 150 (3). A distinctive style is used to identify entries made under this procedure.

52 In 2003 the Committee issued a guidance note indicating how it would in future deal with such complaints.

53 N. 15 above, ch. 7.

54 As required by Art. 6 ECHR. Although the Human Rights Act 1998, s. 6 expressly excludes both Houses of Parliament from the duty to act compatibly with ECHR rights, this would not prevent an aggrieved individual taking a case to the ECtHR. In *Demicoli* v. *Malta* (1991) 14 EHRR 47, the ECtHR decided that parliaments were not exempt from Art. 6 requirements.

55 See reports in (2000–1) on: Mr John Maxton and Dr John Reid, HC 89; Mr Keith Vaz, HC 314, HC 605; Mr Nigel Griffith, HC 625.

56 The threat of imprisonment is more theoretical than real.

decision) is not of course an impartial body. It may decide to reject the Committee's report, or not to accept the recommended punishment. It is questionable whether this final decision by the House can be properly regarded as providing an appeal mechanism for MPs dissatisfied with the Committee's recommendation. The Commons has consistently rejected any suggestion of an appellate tribunal, as it would break the principle of self-regulation.

The reforms agreed in 2003 with respect to the investigations of complaints strengthened the arrangements for the regulation of standards of conduct in the Commons, but they did not really address what was seen as arguably the main problem: the suitability of the Commons as the body responsible for deciding on the acceptability of the conduct of its own members. The absence of controversial cases since 2003 has meant that there has not been the need to address this issue again.

THE HOUSE OF LORDS

The House of Lords was slower than the Commons to regulate the standards of conduct of its members. There were several reasons for this: until the House of Lords Act 1999 the majority of its members were there by virtue of heredity rather than voluntary acceptance of appointment to a peerage and it could be argued that it would be unfair to require them to register outside interests; its members are answerable to no one for their actions in Parliament; almost all its members are unsalaried and by necessity have an outside income; there was no evidence of public lack of confidence in the Lords or wrongdoing by its members.

It was a long-established practice that a member of the House of Lords should not advocate, promote, or oppose any legislation in the House if he was, or had been, acting in connection with it for any fee or reward. If a peer had a direct pecuniary interest in a subject being debated, he could take part in the debate but was expected first to declare the interest. Codification and elaboration of this practice and the possibility of establishing a register of interests was considered in 1974, but no action was taken. In 1990 the Lords amended its rules to expand the types of interest which should be declared, and in 1995 a review by the Lords[57] postponed an investigation by the CSPL. Later that year the House amended its rules on the declaration of interests on the ground that they were imprecise and allowed abuses. It also agreed, somewhat reluctantly, that a register of interests should be established. Three categories of interest were covered. Interests that fell within the first two categories had to be registered, whereas it was at the discretion of the peer whether or not to register interests that fell into the third category. These reforms were introduced in the context of two guiding principles included in the subsequent resolution passed by the Lords. The first is that members should always act on their personal honour, from which followed the second: Lords should never accept any financial inducement as an incentive or reward for exercising parliamentary influence. Guidance on the registration of interests was provided by an official, the Lords' Registrar, and a sub-committee of the Lords Committee on Privileges which could also investigate any allegations of a failure to register. The requirements were both vague and undemanding. From 1995 until 2000 there were no allegations of failures to register or declare interests.

The Seventh Report of the CSPL[58] recommended that all members of the House of Lords in receipt of a writ of summons and not on leave of absence should be required to register

[57] (1994–5), HL 90. [58] Cm 4903 (2001).

all 'relevant interests'. It suggested these should cover both financial and non-financial interests. It also recommended that the Lords should adopt a code of conduct. These recommendations were examined by the Williams Committee in the Lords, and the House agreed with the recommendation of the Committee[59] to accept the majority of the CSPL proposals. However it did so only by a majority of three.[60] Several peers doubted the need for a code of conduct, arguing that the expectation that Lords should always act on their personal honour was sufficient.

The Lords' code of conduct came into effect in April 2002. It includes the Seven Nolan Principles,[61] detailed rules on the registration and declaration of both financial and other interests, and provisions on enforcement of the rules. Only two of the Seven Principles – openness and accountability – were in any sense a new departure for the Lords. The mandatory requirements to register a wide range of interests reflects the requirement of openness. Clearly, as an unelected body, the Lords can not be accountable in the same way as the Commons. However, by making public fuller details of their interests, peers can be said to be acting in accordance with a concept of accountability appropriate to their position.

COMPLIANCE AND SANCTIONS

The House of Lords has few formal rules or sanctions and is said to thrive on self-discipline. The Registrar advises members on the registration of interests and maintains the register. A sub-committee on Lords' interests advises the Registrar on the declaration and registration of interests and also investigates complaints. There is no equivalent to the PCS in the Lords. The CSPL did not consider such a position was necessary 'at this stage'. The Lords sought to avoid the type of politically motivated 'tit for tat' allegations of a failure to register interests which had plagued the Commons; building on its culture of personal honour, the code of conduct provides that where a member wishes to raise another member's non-compliance with the rules of the House, he or she should first do so in a private communication with the member concerned.

For several reasons the investigatory machinery in the Lords is more in accordance with the requirements of procedural fairness than is the case in the Commons. Its rules provide that,

> In (all) investigations and adjudication of complaints against them, Members of the House have the right to safeguards as rigorous as those applied in the courts and professional disciplinary bodies.

The investigation will be by the sub-committee on Lords' interests, which is chaired by a Lord of Appeal. If it decides that an allegation is particularly complex or sensitive it can appoint an *ad hoc* independent investigator. This is likely to be a member of the House, possibly a retired Law Lord, and not an outsider. Finally, a member who receives an adverse ruling from the sub-committee may appeal to the full Committee for Privileges (excluding any members who were also on the original sub-committee). The conclusions of the sub-committee and the Committee for Privileges are reported to the House. One objection to the imposition of a mandatory register of interests was that the Lords had no real sanction to deal with those found in breach of the rules. In theory it has a power to imprison and to

59 (2000–1), HL 68. 60 HL Debs, 2 July 2001, cols 631–85. 61 See text at n. 9 above.

fine, but neither has been used for over a hundred years. It is uncertain whether or not the Lords could temporarily suspend a member, and virtually certain that it could not expel a member.[62] The only sanction available is that of 'naming and shaming', which the CSPL accepted was a real and effective sanction.

As a concession to concerns expressed by many peers, it was agreed that the code would be reviewed after 18 months. The Lords accepted the conclusion of the sub-committee of the Committee of Privileges that conducted this review, that a detailed review was premature as there had been almost no complaints about non-compliance, and that the code should be allowed to settle for a period of years before changes were considered.[63] However, the plan to remove the Law Lords from the Chamber (and thus remove non-political members with the necessary expertise, who can comprise or chair independent and impartial investigative panels) could cause some problems for the investigatory machinery established in 2001.

GOVERNMENT MINISTERS

Ministers, as members of one or other House, are bound by the relevant code of conduct. They are also required to comply with the ministerial code. This Code, now sub-titled *A Code of Ethics and Procedural Guidance For Ministers*,[64] is the responsibility of the Prime Minister and is revised by him from time to time. Only in 1992 was the predecessor of this code publicly published, and in 1997 for the first time it included a foreword by the Prime Minister. The significance of this was said by the CSPL in its Sixth Report to underline the status of the code not only as guidance for ministers, but also as a pledge to the public, a benchmark document that sets out standards for ministerial conduct.[65] Two changes in 2005 reflect how the regulation of ethical standards has continued to develop. The first is the change of sub-title to include the word 'ethics', the second is the splitting of the code into two parts: the code of ethics and the procedural guidance.[66] The separate identification of the ethical principles governing ministerial conduct is an acknowledgement of their importance. The first section of the code, entitled 'Ministers of the Crown', reinforces the Nolan Principles and also sets out specific principles of ministerial conduct, several of which reiterate a 1997 resolution of the House of Commons which attempted to reassert the accountability of ministers to Parliament.[67]

The ministerial code also provides rules regulating ministers' private interests. These rules are more detailed and demanding than the rules on members' interests that apply by virtue of Parliament's codes of conduct. The rules provide guidance on, for example, the use by ministers of 'blind trusts' that enable them to retain certain financial interests that would otherwise be prohibited. However, the information that ministers are expected to provide (to their permanent secretary) remains confidential. The CSPL has indicated that one of the matters it will pursue as part of a constructive dialogue with the Government

62 Except by Act of Parliament, as was proposed in September 2003 for peers who have been imprisoned for more that a year.

63 HL Paper 69 (2003–4).

64 The text of the 2005 code can be found at www.cabinet-office.gov.uk.

65 N. 14 above, paras 4.8, 4.77.

66 As recommended by the CSPL Ninth Report Cm 5775 (2003) ch. 5.

67 HC Debs, 19 Mar. 1997, cols 1046–7.

will be the revisions needed to resolve potential conflicts of interest in relation to the ministerial code.[68]

There remain various areas of controversy and concern with the ministerial code. The distinction between the conduct of ministers in their capacity as ministers and their conduct in their capacity as MPs has been a continuing source of confusion. Although the investigation of allegations of breaches of the ministerial code are the responsibility of the Prime Minister, in its first section it recognizes that 'Ministers must also comply at all times with the requirements which Parliament itself has laid down'. A challenge to this provision was presented in 2000 by the refusal of Mr Keith Vaz – then minister for Europe – to cooperate with an investigation by the PCS into his alleged failure to register payments and other benefits in the register of members' interests.[69] Despite his clear breach of the ministerial code, Mr Vaz did not resign. The ministerial code was amended specifically to require ministers to comply with Parliament's codes of conduct.[70] A continuing controversy has been how to investigate alleged breaches of the ministerial code.[71] Governments have repeatedly refused to contemplate establishing a system whereby there could be an independent investigation into allegations of ministerial misconduct. The preferred method is to ask a permanent secretary to hold an *ad hoc* inquiry to establish the facts. Any other scheme is said to risk fettering the freedom of the Prime Minister to decide how to handle individual cases, and to undermine ministerial accountability to Parliament. In March 2006 it was announced that Sir John Bourn[72] was to become the adviser on ministerial interests. His roles include providing private advice to the Prime Minister and, if so requested, establishing the facts for the Prime Minister when a matter of possible breach of the code is alleged. This development falls short of proposals by either the CSPL[73] or the Public Administration select committee.[74] However it was welcomed by the PCS,[75] and the select committee described it as, 'a small step towards adequate investigations of breaches of the Ministerial Code.'[76]

THE AWARD OF HONOURS

Concerns about the propriety of the honours system and allegations that it is open to abuse are not new.[77] A Commons committee report in 2005 raised the lack of transparency in the system and its use to reward those who were party donors or in some other way provided a service to a political party.[78] The matter came to a head in late 2005 with

68 Annual Report of the Committee on Standards in Public Life (2005), App. 2.

69 N. 47 above.

70 The Commons code of conduct now requires all MPs to cooperate with any investigation into their conduct, see text at n. 33 above.

71 For e.g. the Budd Report into the actions of the then Home Secretary, the Rt. Hon David Blunkett, *An Inquiry into an Application for Indefinite Leave to Remain* (2004–05) HC 175.

72 Who, in his position as Comptroller and Auditor General, is an officer of the House of Commons; he will continue in this post.

73 CSPL Ninth Report (n. 66 above).

74 *Government by Inquiry* (2004–05) HC 51; *The Ministerial Code: the case for independent investigation* (2005–06) HC 1457.

75 Annual Report n. 36 above, para. 1.16.

76 N. 74 above, para. 41.

77 N. 3 above.

78 Report from the Public Administration Select Committee (2003–04) HC 22 and Government response Cm 6479 (2005).

allegations in the media concerning the sale of honours.[79] There were two main allegations: first, that the House of Lords Appointments Commission (HLAC) had advised against several nominations for new 'working peers'; and, secondly, that being willing for example to sponsor a city academy could result in an honour on a sliding scale from OBE to peerage. About the same time the Electoral Commission reported that there was evidence that political parties were asking supporters for loans rather than donations, in order to avoid the Political Parties Elections and Referendums Act 2000 (PPERA).[80] This added to the general unease. A further series of press revelations suggested that all the major parties were involved in this breach of the spirit of the PPERA and this resulted in a late amendment of the Electoral Administration Bill[81] requiring parties to declare loans. What started as a regulatory, political and parliamentary matter being investigated by the Electoral Commission and the Public Administration Select Committee[82] took a further twist with the announcement that the police and the CPS were to investigate whether there had been breaches of either the Honours (Prevention of Abuses) Act of 1925 or the PPERA and even the possibility of offences of corruption. The 1925 Act makes it an offence to take money as an 'inducement or reward' for procuring an honour for someone else. As the Public Administration select committee said when announcing an enforced pause in its enquiry, the allegations 'go to the heart of the political and parliamentary process'.[83] Interviews, including some under caution, have been held with senior members of all political parties. The eventual decision as to prosecutions is awaited. A further twist is whether it would be appropriate for the CPS in making the decision whether to prosecute, to seek the advice of Attorney-General.

The controversy over political honours spills over into other areas of constitutional concern: the funding of political parties; the system of appointment to the House of Lords, particularly after the next stage in reform; the scrutiny of nominations for higher honours. With respect to the final point, recent events highlighted the inadequacy of relying on the register of donations (and now loans) kept by the Electoral Commission, as a means to assess the appropriateness of financial connections between candidates and political parties. It could be argued that since it was the independent HLSC which identified the connection between nominations for a peerage and the giving of loans to political parties, the system of vetting nominations for their propriety is working. However it cannot be overlooked that it was the media who drew attention to the possibility of links between honours and the funding of or support for a political party. It also raises the questions as to how the suitability (as opposed to propriety) of political nominations to part of the legislature should be determined.

[79] It is perhaps not surprising that the 2006 national survey found that the public had greater confidence in the media than the authorities to uncover wrongdoing (n. 1 above).

[80] Election 2005: *Campaign Spendings: The UK Parliamentary Election* March 2006 Electoral Commission para. 2.27.

[81] See ss 61–63 and Sched. 1 of the Electoral Administration Act 2006.

[82] Which had decided, as part of its inquiry into the role and independence of ethics and standards watchdogs, to look at the propriety of the honours system.

[83] (2005–6) HC 1020, para. 3. It eventually published an Interim Report which it considered did not pose risks to the police investigation or any subsequent trials (2005–6) HC 1119.

SCOTLAND, WALES, AND NORTHERN IRELAND

A study of the regulation of standards of conduct in Scotland, Wales, and Northern Ireland demonstrates how standards of conduct can be regulated by legislation, enforced by the criminal law and supervised by the courts.[84] The lack of an historical context and the experience at Westminster meant that certain requirements as to standards of conduct and their enforcement could be imposed from the outset by the devolution legislation. The extensive freedom possessed by Westminster to regulate its own affairs, derived from parliamentary privilege, does not apply to the devolved institutions, as they derive what rights and privileges they have from the devolution legislation. However it was not just Westminster politicians who desired to ensure that the new devolved bodies would aspire to high ethical standards; this was also the desire of politicians in each of the countries concerned.[85]

The devolved institutions were each required by the devolution legislation to: establish and publish a register of members' interests; provide rules on the declaration of interests; and prohibit paid advocacy by members, either directly or through another member.[86] A breach of these rules may be a criminal offence.[87] The application of the criminal law to aspects of standards of conduct is one of the most striking differences between Westminster and the devolved institutions. In addition the devolution legislation provides that the corruption legislation applies to devolved bodies in Scotland and Wales.[88] As at Westminster, there have been changes and reforms, both actual and proposed, to the standards of conduct regime in all three countries. There are certain similarities in the procedural and institutional provisions in each of the three institutions. All have standards committees to supervise standards of conduct, and all have appointed standards commissioners (SC). It is the standards committee in each institution that has taken the lead in investigating, and proposing reforms to, the regulation of standards of conduct.

CODES OF CONDUCT, REGISTERS OF MEMBERS' INTERESTS

All three institutions have adopted codes of conduct. Only the Scottish Parliament was enabled to lay down its own code. The Welsh and Northern Ireland Assemblies had codes – virtually identical to that found at Westminster – imposed on them that were then approved by resolution. In all three jurisdictions there have been reviews by the relevant Standards Committee[89] of the codes and the registration requirements with a view to replacing them

84 See *Whaley* v. *Lord Watson of Invergowrie* 2000 SLT 475.

85 See the Consultative Steering Group on the Scottish Parliament, *Shaping Scotland's Parliament* (Scottish Office, 1998); on Wales see the *National Assembly Advisory Report to the Secretary of State for Wales* (Welsh Office, 1998); sentiments of openness, inclusiveness, and integrity are also implicit in the new form of governance found in the Good Friday Agreement for Northern Ireland.

86 For details of the original provisions see Oonagh Gay, *The Regulation of Parliamentary Standards – A comparative Perspective*, Annex to the CSPL Eighth Report (n. 14 above); Diana Woodhouse, 'Delivering Public Confidence: Codes of Conduct, A Step in the Right Direction' (2003) *Public Law* 511.

87 Punishable with a fine up to level 5 on the standard scale, currently £5,000.

88 N. 26 above. That there is no equivalent provision in the Northern Ireland Act 1998 is thought to be an oversight. The Corruption Reform Bill that was published for scrutiny in 2003 would have applied to the devolved institutions.

89 See *Review of the Standards of Conduct Regime of the National Assembly for Wales*, STD 04–02(03) (the Woodhouse Report) and response from the Standards Committee; Second Report from the Northern Ireland

with something more tailored to their respective circumstances, for example the proposal in Northern Ireland that members of the Legislative Assembly should be required to 'uphold the law . . . and act in the interests of the electorate and the community as a whole'. In addition they should be required to promote equality, and to act in a way that was conducive to promoting good community relationships.[90] An interesting provision in the code in Scotland is the requirement that members should be accessible to constituents and should conscientiously serve and represent their constituents' interests.[91] A substantial proportion of complaints are on the level and quality of service given by a MSP, and there has been an adverse report on a member. There has caused disquiet,[92] and this provision is likely to be removed in the current review of the code on the ground that the scheme was set up to prevent corruption and encourage openness and not to police the quality of service offered by members.

The three codes are broadly similar and based on the Nolan Principles. In all three institutions the rules on members' interests require the registration and declaration of various types of financial or remunerated interests, and this is enforced by criminal sanctions. Only in Scotland are these rules found in legislation with the passing of the Interests of Members of the Scottish Parliament Act 2006.[93] A notable provision in the 2006 Act is the requirement that any financial interest a member had before his election that 'is reasonably considered to prejudice, or give the appearance of prejudicing, the ability of the member to participate in a disinterested manner' should be registered. The categories for registerable financial interests in all three institutions are similar to those at Westminster[94] but, unlike in the early days at Westminster, these rules have caused few problems. This may be because members of the devolved institutions are less likely than Westminster MPs to have either additional sources of income or directorships. In Wales and Northern Ireland the Assemblies were required to make provision for the registration and declaration of a range of non-financial interests also enforced by criminal sanctions. In Northern Ireland, before suspension of the Assembly, an additional discretionary section was used by some members to register membership of the 'Loyal Orders', various charities, interest groups, professional bodies, and school boards of governors. Mandatory registration of a wide range of societies and bodies has been proposed in Northern Ireland. In Wales the categories of interests required to be registered include contracts with the Assembly and 'paid or unpaid membership or chairmanship' of any public body funded in whole or in part by the Assembly. This is a reflection of the type of devolution arrangements found in Wales. A controversial requirement in Wales, whereby Assembly members were required to register membership of the Freemasons (but not of other societies), was removed in 2005. Rules on the interests of members' families introduced in 2002 gives Wales the most stringent registration requirements on 'indirect interests' of all the devolved institutions. The registration rules for the Welsh Assembly are closer to those that apply to members of local

Committee on Standards and Privileges, *Consultation on Proposed Amendments to the Northern Ireland Assembly 'Code of Conduct and the Guide to the Rules Relating to the Conduct of Members'*, Report 02/01R, 2001/2002. The Scottish Standards and Appointments Committee (as it became in 2005) is conducting a review.

[90] However, due to the suspension of devolution, no further progress has been made on this, or other proposals for the Assembly.

[91] Section 2.4 of the code.

[92] See the SC Annual Report (2004–05), SPSC/2005/1.

[93] Which will replace the Members' Interest Order in May 2007.

[94] See text at n. 34 above.

authorities than is the case in the other devolved bodies. This can be explained in the context of the executive functions of the Welsh Assembly, which are similar to some of the functions possessed by local authorities, for example with respect to planning appeals. The Scottish Parliament decided not to include non-financial interest in its statutory registration scheme, partly to preserve the privacy of members, although members may chose to register membership of charities, trade unions etc. Scotland continues to have the least onerous requirements with respect both to non-financial interests and to the interests of partners and dependent children.

An important distinction between both Scotland and Northern Ireland and Westminster is that the Standards Commissioner in each devolved body is not involved in compiling the register of members' interests or giving advice to members. Instead it is the Clerk to each of the Standards Committees, acting under the authority of the relevant Committee, who is responsible. The rationale for this is to keep separate the giving of advice and the receipt and initial investigation of complaints.

STANDARDS COMMISSIONERS AND THE INVESTIGATION OF COMPLAINTS

At an early stage all three devolved institutions decided that the provision of an 'independent element' in investigations was essential to ensure public confidence in the robustness of the investigative procedures and, in the case of Northern Ireland, to avoid the risk of the Committee splitting on party lines every time it investigated a complaint. In Wales the original Independent Advisor was replaced by a more robust Standards Commissioner in 2005, who is expected to work closely with the Assembly members and officers to build a standards culture in the Assembly. In all cases the Commissioner undertakes an initial investigation similar to that undertaken by the PCS, and passes his report to the Committee, which may accept it or conduct its own investigation. The initial decision on sanctions is for the Committee. It is for the Parliament/Assembly to decide whether to approve the Committee's report and its recommendations. In this way the devolved institutions have an element of self-regulation. In Scotland, as in the Commons, the final decision by the Parliament is seen as constituting an appeal by a member dissatisfied with the Committee's decision. In 2005 the Welsh Assembly introduced an arrangement whereby the Presiding Officer could, in certain circumstances, set up a panel to hear an appeal before the matter was considered by the Assembly.

In enacting the Scottish Parliamentary Standards Commissioner Act 2002, Scotland was the first Parliament/Assembly in the UK to make such a position statutory.[95] Although the 2002 Act sought to make Commissioner independent[96] and accountable in a variety of ways that were unique at the time,[97] it has not stopped controversy on these issues.[98] In his

95 The Welsh Assembly will have power to do this under Schedule 5 of the Government of Wales Act 2006.

96 For example a statutory power to call for witnesses and documents, the only SC to have such a power.

97 Many of these requirements, such as the publication of an annual report, a fixed term appointment, an open recruitment process were introduced in 2003 for the non-statutory Westminster PCS.

98 In his 2004–05 Annual Report (n. 92 above) the SC referred to a case where there was a disagreement between the SC and the committee and warned that if this should happen more regularly it would be a matter of serious concern.

first annual report the Commissioner complained that he had not, as promised, been given formal notice of the grounds upon which he could be dismissed.[99] In 2005 the Scottish Parliamentary Corporate Body, which is responsible for appointments, announced that the appointment of the new Standards Commissioner would be by an 'administrative process' without a full recruitment competition. When, as required by the 2002 Act, the re-appointment of the existing Commissioner came up for Parliamentary approval quite considerable disquiet was expressed about the office, the process and the individual.

A potentially interesting suggestion made before the suspension of the Northern Ireland Assembly was that legislation should be introduced to enable the existing Northern Ireland Assembly Ombudsman to undertake the role of independent investigator.[100] There are several advantages in this arrangement: the working methods of an Ombudsman and a Commissioner are similar; the Assembly Ombudsman is already appointed through the public appointments process, promoting transparency and removing the appointment and tenure from the political arena; the office of Assembly Ombudsman has a standing in Northern Ireland which commands widespread support. It would also be an example of 'joined up governance' as to have in the one office different roles and functions provides the potential to: 'judge elected officials, elected representatives, public officials in terms of their work as public servants . . . applying a single standard to all aspects of our public life'.[101]

SANCTIONS

Unlike the Commons, none of the devolved institutions has the power to expel a member. Members may have their rights and privileges withdrawn or may be excluded from the Parliament or Assembly for a period with or without salary. The police may investigate several types of breaches of the codes of conduct, including a failure to attend as a witness or answer questions, with the possibility of prosecution in the courts. In these circumstances members of the devolved institutions will have access to fairer procedures than is the case for those accused of similar breaches at Westminster. They will also be subject to more severe penalties.

Each devolved institution in addressing issues of standards of conduct appears keen to 'own' its rules and procedures on standards, and is not slavishly following Westminster. There is a greater willingness in these institutions to provide for a more independent outside figure to adjudicate on standards of conduct. However there is some indication in Scotland of disillusionment in independent figures overseeing aspects of public affairs, not least because of the cost involved.

CONCLUSION

It is perhaps not surprising that more 10 years after the first report from the CSPL and the subsequent establishment of a variety of bodies and offices concerned with the regulation of standards of conduct, some stocktaking is happening. This is part of the process of

99 This was reported as having been rectified in his next report.

100 See the Assembly Ombudsman for Northern Ireland (Assembly Standards) Bill 2002.

101 Oral evidence from the Assembly Ombudsman cited in the CSPL Eighth Report, n. 15 above.

accountability – the various committees and commissioners must face an audit. What is perhaps surprising is a sense that some of the systems of regulation are falling out of favour. In Scotland there is concern at the cost and value for money of the various bodies that regulate, audit, inspect and hear complaints across Scotland, which includes the Standards Commissioner.[102] At Westminster the Public Administration Select Committee has commenced a wide ranging inquiry into ethics and standards in public life. Meanwhile the CSPL has instituted an investigation into the Electoral Commission, which was established as a consequence of a CSPL recommendation.[103] A further inquiry[104] on funding of political parities was set up in 2006 by the Prime Minister to be carried out by Sir Hayden Phillips.

The flurry of investigations and inquiries should not be allowed to detract from the significant changes there have been to the ethical landscape of public life in the UK since 1995. Unfortunately this change has not resulted in the increased public confidence in standards of conduct that might have been expected.[105] It is possible that some of the inquiries taking place will be able to suggest how public confidence might be enhanced.

A starting point may be the CSPL itself. There is no doubt that this body has been at the forefront of embedding ethical standards of conduct into public life. One of the reasons in the past for poor ethical standards on the part of some of those in public life was a lack of interest in such matters, by both institutions and their members. The CSPL has ensured that this should no longer be possible. Codes of conduct for those in public life are becoming the norm, not just in the UK but also more generally in other liberal-democratic systems. They are a response to the demand that those in public life should be accountable. Their existence also acknowledges the importance of a collective standards culture for each institution. It is only recently that there has been both public debate and debate in the Westminster Parliament and elsewhere as to what this culture should be, and the CSPL has contributed to this. As a standing body[106] the CSPL has been able to conduct investigations and make follow-up reports. As such it has provided not just a mechanism to initiate investigations into specific aspects of public life, but also a means whereby the bodies concerned can be publicly monitored with respect to their implementation of its recommendations. However, it may be asked, could this be part of the problem? Reports from bodies like the CSPL that draw attention to ethical shortcomings and failures by governments to implement its recommendations can give rise to further disillusionment on the part of the public. The balance between reassuring the public by the very existence of bodies like the CSPL, and making them work in such a way that progress in improving standards is reflected in increased public confidence, has yet to be achieved. The CSPL was established as a body to establish general principles, and the time may have come to accept that it has done this and it should no longer exist as a permanent body. This view could be said to be reinforced by recent comments by its chairman on particular cases.[107] These interventions may suggest a desire by the committee to go beyond the establishment of general principles

[102] Reviews are being carried out by the Parliament's Finance Committee and by an Independent Review established by the Scottish Executive in June 2006.

[103] Fifth Report, Cm 4057 (1998).

[104] The CSPL had reported on this in 1998 (n. 103 above).

[105] N. 1 above.

[106] In this way it has been able to be more successful than the Royal Commission on Standards in Public Life (n. 6 above), whose proposals were allowed to gather dust.

[107] In May 2006 Sir Alistair Graham suggested that the Prime Minister saw standards as a peripheral matter, and later that year he attempted to intervene in the row over Tessa Jowell's knowledge of her husband's financial activities. The committee is thought to have wanted to investigate the cash for honours affair.

and investigate individual cases of alleged wrongdoing or situations where the principles it has laid down have been repeatedly ignored. This was not the purpose of the CSPL.

One of the matters that the various reviews should consider is whether the ethical landscape is too cluttered with rules. A concentration on rules and improving and refining rules will not necessarily result in an improved ethical culture. Where there are rules people will inevitable attempt to circumvent them, as was seen with the rules on the registration of political donations under the PPRA 2002.[108] At Westminster there has been an attempt to rationalize the position so that MPs are not subject to a plethora of potentially overlapping rules laid down in the code and *Guide*, by the Speaker and other House authorities, and by electoral law on the registration of political donations.[109]

Effective regulation of standards appears to have greatest effect where the concentration has been on education and training and the establishment of a culture where standards are applied and expected. This has been the approach by the present PCS at Westminster. However the success of this depends on the willingness of members to respond to such opportunities, and it is not encouraging that the PCS noted in his annual report in 2003 that turnout at seminars to explain the 2002 revision to the rules was lower than hoped for.[110] Again in 2005 he reported that attendance at briefings for returning MPs was low. However the participation of the PCS in the political party inductions for new members after the election was a successful innovation, not least because it required the cooperation of the party whips. It is not only in the interests of members to reduce the number of complaints and improve compliance with the rules on conduct; it could also raise public confidence in those who are active in public life. Revisions to codes of conduct are a further important opportunity to inform and educate those to whom they apply. The CSPL in its Tenth Report returned to the theme of guidance and education and the importance of personal standards of conduct.[111]

The requirement that those in public life should reveal information about their financial affairs and other outside interests has implications other than the establishment of an ethical framework. One is whether legislatures should be full or part-time. Historically membership of both Houses of Parliament was part-time for all but a few politicians and the parliamentary day was designed to allow members to work in the morning and attend Parliament later in the day. Changes in the working day of the Commons have reduced the opportunity for MPs to undertake outside employment, and the rules on outside interests have curtailed some of the more recent income-generating activities of members. In consequence the pressure on MPs to be full-time has increased, which may result in a different type of politician at Westminster – something already seen in the devolved institutions where most members are full-time.

In its Sixth Report the CSPL concluded that:

> There has been a shift from allegations of direct financial reward for dubious ethical practices to allegations of **privileged access**, the exercise of undue influence through political, social or business contacts or the donation of money or any other means of gaining preferential treatment. As before, a key feature is the impression of secrecy.[112]

[108] See text at n. 80 above. [109] See text at n. 35 above. [110] HC (2002–03) 905, para. 3.7.
[111] Cm 6407 (2005). [112] N. 14 above, para. 2.20 (emphasis in original).

In the six years since that report these concerns remain, brought to the forefront by the allegations on the award of honours and controversies about the ministerial code. The recent investigation by the PCS into suggestions that some All Party Groups were failing to include on the Register the name of the ultimate client of the public affairs group that was providing administrative support for the relevant group is a further illustration that these concerns remain.[113] It is clear that issues with respect to the regulation of standards of conduct will continue to evolve. Exactly how this will occur may be determined by the outcome of the current reviews.

FURTHER READING

Ten Years After Nolan A special edition of Parliamentary Affairs Vol. 59 No. 3 (2006).

Gay, O. and Leopold, P. (eds) *Conduct Unbecoming* (2004).

Leopold, P. 'The application of the civil and criminal law to members of Parliament and parliamentary proceedings', in D. Oliver and G. Drewry (eds), *The Law and Parliament* (1998) ch. V.

Oliver, D. 'Regulating the Conduct of MPs. The British Experience of Combating Corruption' in P. Heywood (ed.), *Political Corruptions* (1997).

Ridley, F. F., and Doig, A. (eds) '"Sleaze": Politics, Private Interests and Public Reaction' (1995) 48 *Parliamentary Affairs* 551–749 (special edition).

Ryle, M. 'The law relating to members' conduct', in D. Oliver and G. Drewry (eds), *The Law and Parliament* (1998) ch. VII.

USEFUL WEB SITES

Parliamentary Commissioner for Standards: **www.parliament.uk/about_commons/pcfs.cfm**
Committee on Standards in Public Life: **www.public.standards.gov.uk/**

[113] (2005–06), HC 1145.

INDEX